Manchester Medie

series advisers Rosemary Horrox and Janet L. Nelson

This series aims to meet a growing need among students and teachers of medieval history for translations of key sources that are directly usable in students' own work. It provides texts central to medieval studies courses and focuses upon the diverse cultural and social as well as political conditions that affected the functioning of all levels of medieval society. The basic premise of the series is that translations must be accompanied by sufficient introductory and explanatory material, and each volume, therefore, includes a comprehensive guide to the sources' interpretation, including discussion of critical linguistic problems and an assessment of the most recent research on the topics being covered.

also available in the series

Mark Bailey *The English Manor c. 1200–c. 1500*

Malcom Barber and Keith Bate *The Templars*

Simon Barton and Richard Fletcher *The world of El Cid: Chronicles of the Spanish Reconquest*

Trevor Dean *The towns of Italy in the later Middle Ages*

P. J. P. Goldberg *Women in England, c. 1275–1525*

Samuel K. Cohn, Jr. *Popular protest in late-medieval Europe: Italy, France and Flanders*

Rosemary Horrox *The Black Death*

I. S. Robinson *The papal reform of the eleventh century: Lives of Pope Leo IX and Pope Gregory VII*

Michael Staunton *The lives of Thomas Becket*

Craig Taylor *Joan of Arc: La Pucelle*

Elisabeth van Houts *The Normans in Europe*

David Warner *Ottonian Germany*

Diana Webb *Saints and cities in medieval Italy*

Andrew Brown and Graeme Small *Court and civic society in the Burgundian Low Countries c. 1420–1520*

ELEVENTH-CENTURY GERMANY

MANCHESTER
1824

Manchester University Press

MedievalSources*online*

Complementing the printed editions of the Medieval Sources series, Manchester University Press has developed a web-based learning resource which is now available on a yearly subscription basis.

MedievalSources*online* brings quality history source material to the desktops of students and teachers and allows them open and unrestricted access throughout the entire college or university campus. Designed to be fully integrated with academic courses, this is a one-stop answer for many medieval history students, academics and researchers keeping thousands of pages of source material 'in print' over the Internet for research and teaching.

Visit the site at *www.medievalsources.co.uk* for further information and subscription prices.

ELEVENTH-CENTURY GERMANY
The Swabian chronicles

selected sources translated and annotated with an introduction
by I. S. Robinson

Manchester University Press
Manchester and New York

distributed exclusively in the USA by Palgrave

Published by Manchester University Press
Oxford Road, Manchester M13 9NR, UK
and Room 400, 175 Fifth Avenue, New York, NY 10010, USA
www.manchesteruniversitypress.co.uk

Distributed exclusively in the USA by
Palgrave, 175 Fifth Avenue, New York, NY 10010, USA

Distributed exclusively in Canada by
UBC Press, University of British Columbia, 2029 West Mall,
Vancouver, BC, Canada V6T 1Z2

British Library Cataloguing-in-Publication Data
A catalogue record for this book is available from the British Library

Library of Congress Cataloging-in-Publication Data applied for

ISBN   978 0 7190 7733 3 *hardback*
       978 0 7190 7734 0 *paperback*

First published 2008

17 16 15 14 13 12 11 10 09 08   10 9 8 7 6 5 4 3 2 1

Typeset in Monotype Bell
by Koinonia Ltd, Manchester
Printed in Great Britain
by Antony Rowe Ltd, Chippenham, Wiltshire

CONTENTS

SERIES EDITOR'S FOREWORD

In the mid-eleventh century, as currents of Church reform swirled into the politics of the southern parts of the kingdom of Germany, a new wave of chroniclers was among the signs of turbulence. Three of the most important are translated into English for the first time in the present volume. The first two authors were monks at the island monastery of Reichenau on Lake Constance. The older man was the severely disabled yet intellectually dynamic Herman, the younger his former student Berthold. In their hands, a world chronicle which began as an account of imperial doings was refocused on the papacy, and became a vivid contemporary history of the struggle for righteousness which Pope Gregory VII inspired and briefly directed. The third author, Bernold, was a member of the cathedral clergy at Constance, where reforming struggles raged in the 1070s. Bernold's trajectory drew him too into pro-papal writing, increasingly so when he became a monk, first at St Blasien in the Black Forest, then nearer home at Schaffhausen. All these chronicles, then, were written by intellectuals for whom history and ideology were inseparable. Ian Robinson has done more than any living scholar to highlight the exceptional interest of writers who traced the implementation, before their eyes, of radical reform, and articulated new political ideas to justify the reformers' agenda. As in his previous volume in this series, Robinson has put his outstanding scholarship at the service of a wide readership. His translations, introduced and annotated in engaging and clear fashion, give access to challenging and richly rewarding texts, and through them, to a crucial dimension and epicentre of what R.I. Moore has called 'the first European revolution'.

Janet L. Nelson
King's College London

PREFACE

The Swabian chroniclers of the eleventh century worked in a historiographical tradition of which the source was the fourth-century chronicle of Eusebius of Caesarea, which they knew through the Latin translation of Jerome. The model of the chronicle was disseminated in the west by the historical writings of Jerome, Isidore of Seville and Bede. One function of *chronica* was to establish an accurate chronology of historical events, dating them according to the era of Christ's Incarnation and sometimes according to the regnal years of kings. Our three Swabian chroniclers – Herman of Reichenau, Berthold of Reichenau and Bernold of St Blasien – were keenly aware of the importance of chronology. A second function is emphasised in this definition of the word *chronica* from *ca.* 1200: 'a temporal narrative from the beginning of the world concerning times and persons and their deeds – not all of them but those that it now seems to us expedient to remember and to set down in writing as an example (*exemplum*) and a warning'. Our Swabian chroniclers clearly understood the exemplary character of historical events and of the fates of individuals. All three were monks and they wrote chronicles suited to the monastic exercise of *lectio divina*, the edifying reading required by the *Rule* of Benedict. They provided *exempla* of righteous conduct, to be imitated, and of wicked conduct, to be avoided.

The Swabian chroniclers were heirs also to a historical tradition quite distinct from that of the *chronica*, namely *annales*. Annals were originally disparate historical observations that were casual, literally marginal additions to manuscripts that had a non-historical, usually liturgical function. Sometimes these notes were liberated from their liturgical context, transcribed on to blank pieces of parchment, becoming a recognisable historical work, *annales minores*. This simple historical genre was transformed in the eighth century, when it began to be used in the courts of the Carolingian rulers for the purposes of political propaganda. The *annales minores* evolved into the much more expansive *annales maiores*, recounting the military and political successes of kings. From the tenth century onwards the two distinct historical genres of *chronica* and *annales* began to coalesce. This is apparent, for example, in the chronicle of Regino, abbot of Prüm, which he entitled 'The book concerning the times of the Lord's Incarnation' and which was well known to our three Swabian chroniclers. The work begins as 'world history', a compilation surveying the history of the ancient Roman empire and its enemies and subsequently the successor states of the Roman empire in the west. On nearing his own times, however, Regino narrowed the scope of his work, abandoning world history for an annalistic treatment of the deeds of the rulers of East *Francia*.

The eleventh-century Swabian chronicles have the same hybrid character as Regino's work, half *chronica*, half *annales*. As he reached his own times and became independent of the sources that he had used for the period 1-1000,

Herman of Reichenau focused on the kingdom of Germany, especially on his own Swabian homeland, with occasional excursions to the emperor's other kingdoms of Italy and Burgundy. The two scholars who continued Herman's chronicle after his death in 1054, Berthold of Reichenau and Bernold of St Blasien, similarly concentrated mainly on events in Germany, particularly in the later pages of their works, when their annals become a contemporary record of events. These translations offer a view of events in eleventh-century Germany and the western empire from the perspective of the three Swabian chroniclers: the chronicle of Herman from 1000 to 1054, the first version of the chronicle of Berthold from 1054 to 1066, Berthold's revision of his chronicle, extending to 1080, and Bernold's chronicle from 1054 to 1100.

This book is based on a study of the Swabian chronicles undertaken for the Monumenta Germaniae Historica in Munich. My visits to Germany were made possible by a fellowship from the Alexander von Humboldt Foundation, for which I record my grateful thanks. I am also deeply grateful to the Monumenta Germaniae Historica for permission to work in that renowned institute and to consult the unpublished writings of Dr Georgine Tangl, who devoted many years to the study of the Swabian chronicles. The President of MGH, Professor Dr Horst Fuhrmann, and his successor, Professor Rudolf Schieffer, were unfailing in their support and valuable advice. The *Geschäftsführer* of MGH, Dr Wolfram Setz, was the most generous and hospitable of friends and the most patient of scholarly advisers. I must also record my particular indebtedness to Dr Detlev Jasper of MGH, to whose remarkable erudition so many scholars are indebted, for his indispensable help and advice.

My thanks are also due to the staff of the Library of Trinity College, Dublin, especially Ms Anne Walsh and Ms Mary Higgins, the History Librarians; to Dr Thomas McCarthy of Trinity College, Dublin, who advised me on the music of Herman of Reichenau and William of Hirsau; to Dr Patrick Healy, Dr Conor Kostick, Dr Margaret Norton, Jeremy Quartermain and Dr Jochen Schenk, who generously supplied me with material from distant libraries. Ms Jane Finucane and Mr Charles Larkin most kindly assisted me with my word-processing problems. Ms Monica Kendall copy-edited the text. Above all I record my thanks to my wife, Dr Helga Robinson-Hammerstein, without whose selfless support and encouragement my long struggle with the Swabian chronicles would never have come to an end.

ABBREVIATIONS

CC	*Corpus Christianorum, Series Latina*
CSEL	*Corpus scriptorum ecclesiasticorum Latinorum*
D.H.III	*Diploma Heinrici III*
D.H.IV	*Diploma Heinrici IV*
Die Salier	*Die Salier und das Reich* ed. S. Weinfurter, 3 volumes (Sigmaringen, 1991)
Investiturstreit	*Investiturstreit und Reichsverfassung* ed. J. Fleckenstein (Vorträge und Forschungen 17: Sigmaringen, 1973)
JE, JK, JL	P. Jaffé, *Regesta pontificum Romanorum* ed. W. Wattenbach, S. Loewenfeld, F. Kaltenbrunner, P. Ewald (second edition, Leipzig, 1885)
MGH	*Monumenta Germaniae Historica*
Briefe	*Briefe der deutschen Kaiserzeit*
Constitutiones	*Constitutiones et acta publica imperatorum et regum*
DD	*Diplomata*
Libelli	*Libelli de lite imperatorum et pontificum*
SS	*Scriptores* (in Folio)
SS rer. Germ.	*Scriptores rerum Germanicarum in usum scholarum separatim editi*
MPG	J.P. Migne (ed.), *Patrologiae cursus completus. Series Graeca*
MPL	J.P. Migne (ed.), *Patrologiae cursus completus. Series Latina*
Sacra Concilia	J.D. Mansi (ed.), *Sacrorum conciliorum nova et amplissima collectio* 1-31 (Venice–Florence, 1759-98)

INTRODUCTION

The chronicle of Herman of Reichenau

The first half of the eleventh century witnessed in the island monastery of Reichenau on Lake Constance a second flowering of literary activity that equalled in its quality and surpassed in its range of subjects the first flowering in the abbatiate of Walahfrid Strabo (838–49) during the 'Carolingian Renaissance'.[1] The two dominant figures in the intellectual life of early eleventh-century Germany were Bern, abbot of Reichenau (1008–48), and his pupil, the monk of Reichenau, Herman 'the Lame' (1013–54), 'one of the greatest scholars of the day'.[2] Bern's eminence 'in human and divine knowledge' was still recalled by twelfth-century scholars, notably his authorship of 'a most excellent work on music'.[3] Besides his influential works on musical theory, Bern's extant writings include treatises on the liturgy, a *Life* of St Udalric, bishop of Augsburg, sixteen sermons and a collection of thirty letters.[4] His pupil Herman was described at the end of the eleventh century as 'the miracle of our age'.[5] In the mid-twelfth century he was remembered as 'more subtle than almost all the moderns in music', 'a most subtle philosopher' in the *computus* and an author whose 'distinction shone forth clearly enough' in his historical writings.[6]

The abbatiate of Bern was characterised by dedication to monastic reform and loyalty to the German king and emperor, the patron and protector of the imperial abbey of Reichenau. Bern wrote to the distinguished reformer, Abbot Odilo of Cluny, acclaiming him as 'our sweet splendour and the crown of all monks' and describing himself as 'the insignificant follower of St Benedict'.[7] He wrote to Emperor Henry II,

1 Klüppel (1980) pp. 12, 141–2.

2 Bern, *Letters*, ed. Schmale: Introduction p. 4.

3 Sigebert of Gembloux, *Catalogus de illustribus viris* c. 157, p. 98; Anonymus Mellicensis (Wolfger of Prüfening?), *De scriptoribus ecclesiasticis* c. 81, p. 82.

4 Oesch (1961) pp. 43–83; Bern, *Letters* pp. 17–69.

5 *Annals of Augsburg* 1054, p. 126.

6 Anonymus Mellicensis, *De scriptoribus* c. 91, p. 85.

7 Bern, *Letter* 2, p. 19.

informing him that 'the Lord ... has caused the magnificence of [his]
office to excel that of all kingdoms' and describing himself as 'your
humble and insignificant follower'. The letter thanked the emperor
for appointing him abbot of Reichenau and promised that he and his
monks would pray day and night for Henry's prosperity in life and
eternal happiness in death.[8] Imperial patronage and monastic reform
were strongly linked in the history of Reichenau as in that of numerous
imperial abbeys in eleventh-century Germany. The model of monastic
reform with which Bern and Henry II were most familiar was that
of Lotharingia, notably that of the abbey of Gorze. Although Bern
wrote to Odilo of Cluny of his wish to model himself on that celebrated
reformer, his own antecedents and his closest ties were in the Lotharingian monastic reform movement.[9]

The Lotharingian reform had already been introduced to Reichenau a
generation before Bern's abbatiate when Emperor Otto I intervened to
appoint Abbot Ruodmann (972–85), who was revered at the imperial
court as a reformer.[10] In a second imperial intervention in 1006 Henry
II imposed Abbot Immo of Gorze on Reichenau. Gorze had been the
most important influence on Lotharingian monasticism since it was
reformed in 933. Immo had held office there since 984 'in a most saintly
and most kindly manner', according to a fellow Lotharingian abbot.
He had also been appointed to rule over the abbey of Prüm.[11] Henry II
had similarly intervened to impose reformers on other imperial abbeys
– on Hersfeld, Tegernsee, Fulda and Corvey – and in each case the
reforming abbot had met with resistance.[12]

The resistance in Reichenau is recorded in a striking passage of Herman's
chronicle. 'Against the will [of the brethren, Henry II] appointed to
rule them a certain Immo, abbot of Gorze, a harsh man ... Some of
the brethren, therefore, left that place of their own accord and some of
them were severely afflicted by him with fasts, scourges and exile. Thus
the noble monastery suffered for its sins a heavy loss in great men,
books and church treasures, as Rudpert, a noble and learnedly witty
monk and my mother's uncle, mournfully lamented in prose, rhythm
and metre.' Two years later, Herman recorded, Henry II, 'learning at

---

8 *Ibid.*, 4, pp. 23–4.

9 Cf. Bern, *Letter* 5, pp. 24–5, to Abbot Hildrad of Prüm, the friend of his youth.

10 Hallinger (1950–1) pp. 108, 187, 611–12.

11 Constantine, abbot of St Symphorian, Metz, *Vita Adalberonis* c. 26, p. 668. See
Hallinger (1950–1) pp. 613–14; Bulst (1973) pp. 86–7.

12 Holtzmann (1941) pp. 434–6; Hauck (1954) pp. 454–8.

last of the cruelty of Immo, removed him and appointed Bern, a learned and pious man and a monk of Prüm'.[13] In Herman's account, evidently coloured (as elsewhere in the chronicle) by family feeling, the reformer Immo is portrayed as the cruel persecutor of the monks of Reichenau.[14] His successor Bern, however, whom Herman greatly admired, was no less a representative of the Lotharingian monastic reform. He was a pupil of Immo in Prüm and may well have owed his appointment to Immo's recommendation.[15] During Bern's forty-year abbatiate there is no sign of opposition in Reichenau either to him or to the Lotharingian monastic 'customs' that, like Ruodmann and Immo, he must have perpetuated in the abbey.[16]

It was during Bern's abbatiate that Herman 'the Lame' entered Reichenau and at Bern's urging that 'he received holy orders … around his thirtieth year', ca. 1043.[17] According to his own autobiographical entries in his chronicle, Herman was born on 18 July 1013 as one of the fifteen children of Count Wolferad II of Altshausen (✝1065).[18] This Swabian prince built up a powerful lordship on the basis of his family lands in Altshausen, Isny and Veringen. How formidable he appeared to a neighbour can be seen in a letter of Abbot Bern, complaining of 'Wolferad, whose name seems to me rightly to be interpreted "wolf's counsel"'. The count 'bit [the abbot] with his wolfish teeth' by claiming to Reichenau's diocesan, the bishop of Constance, and to King Conrad II that Reichenau's estates of Bierlingen, Empfingen and Binsdorf had been promised to him.[19] That Wolferad II was not merely a persecutor of churches is clear from his foundation of the church of Isny in 1042.[20] This church was refounded as an abbey in 1096 by Wolferad's son, Count Manegold of Altshausen-Veringen (✝1104/9). Count Manegold – 'perfectly educated

13 Herman, *Chronicle* 1006, 1008, below pp. 59, 60.

14 In *Chronicon Suevicum universale* 1006, p. 69 – perhaps the work of Herman's pupil, Berthold of Reichenau (see below p. 12) – Immo is described as 'the destroyer of the monastery and the expeller of the brethren'. Monastic reform as 'persecution of the monks': Nightingale (2001) p. 19.

15 Hallinger (1950–1) pp. 613–14; Oesch (1961) pp. 33–5; Borst (1978) pp. 104–5.

16 But cf. Bern, *Letter 3*, p. 21, composed 1012/14, complaining to his friend Archbishop Gero of Magdeburg that the envious repeat to the king rumours 'about us and our [monks] … concerning our customs'.

17 Berthold of Reichenau, *Life of Herman* in his *Chronicle* 1054, below p. 109.

18 Herman, *Chronicle* 1009, 1013, below pp. 61, 62.

19 Bern, *Letter 14*, p. 47, to Bishop Werner of Strasbourg (between September 1024 and March 1027).

20 Kerkhoff (1964) p. 33.

in all the observances of the Christian religion by his very wise brother, Herman the Lame' – became a stalwart supporter of the papal party in the Investiture Contest.[21] The counts of Altshausen could indeed claim kinship with a saint whose cult was widespread in eleventh-century Swabia: they were 'born of the eminent and pious lineage of the blessed Udalric, bishop of Augsburg' (923–73). Through his mother Bertha (who was of the family of the counts of Dillingen), Wolferad II was the great-grandson of a sister of St Udalric.[22] Wolferad's wife, the pious Hiltrud, built a chapel dedicated to St Udalric in Altshausen, where she was buried in 1052.[23] Abbot Bern of Reichenau composed a biography of Udalric.[24] His pupil Herman recorded in his chronicle 'the wonderful piety and religion' of St Udalric, the divine protection that he enjoyed and the divine vengeance that pursued his enemies, concluding with the report that 'he is resplendent in miracles even to the present day'.[25]

According to his friend and biographer, Berthold of Reichenau, Herman 'was from his earliest years ... totally lame in all his limbs from a paralytic disease'. 'He could not without help move himself ... but he could sit with difficulty and in a crooked posture in a sedan chair, into which he was lifted by a servant.' 'With his feeble mouth, tongue and lips [he] produced only broken and scarcely intelligible sounds of words.'[26] It has been suggested that the medical condition described by the biographer corresponds to cerebral palsy.[27] Herman could never undertake the military training received by his brothers, the future counts Wolferad III and Manegold of Altshausen and perhaps others of the fifteen children of Wolferad II and Hiltrud,[28] nor could he hope to be admitted to the service of the secular Church. Noble families frequently brought such disabled members of their family to monasteries as oblates, that is, minors surrendered to the monastery by parents or guardians according to the prescribed ritual of the Benedictine *Rule*. Hence the monastic reformer Udalric of Zell would write *ca.* 1080 of an abbot's 'need to

---

21 Paul of Bernried, *Life of Pope Gregory VII* c. 91, p. 333. See Kerkhoff (1964) pp. 26, 30–4, 36, 39–41, 95–6, 108–13.

22 Paul, *Life of Pope Gregory VII* c. 91, pp. 332–3. See Oesch (1961) p. 122; Kerkhoff (1964) pp. 15–16; Borgolte (1979) pp. 3, 5–6.

23 Herman, *Chronicle* 1052, below p. 91. See Kerkhoff (1964) pp. 9, 28.

24 Bern, *Vita sancti Udalrici, MPL* 142, 1183B–1204B.

25 Herman, *Chronicon* 924, 953, 955, 972, 973, pp. 113–14, 116.

26 Berthold, *Life of Herman, Chronicle* 1054, below p. 108.

27 Oesch (1961) p. 127.

28 Herman, *Chronicle* 1009, below p. 61. By 1052 seven children survived: p. 90.

beware the cunning of certain secular men, not greatly caring for the other life but only for this temporal life, who have a house, so to speak, full of sons and daughters. If any of these is lame or infirm, somewhat deaf or blind, hunchbacked or leprous or anything else that makes him in any way less acceptable to the world, they offer him to God in a most solemn vow, although it is clearly done not for God's sake but solely for this reason, that they may free themselves from the necessity of rearing and feeding them.' On such occasions a noble family was expected to make a generous gift to the monastery.[29]

The date of Herman's entering the abbey of Reichenau is unknown. An autobiographical record in the annal of his chronicle for 1020 reads: 'I, Herman, began to be taught my letters on 15 September.'[30] This has been suggested as the date of his reception into Reichenau as an oblate.[31] An alternative account of his education is found in a twelfth-century collection of miracle stories. Here Herman's parents 'brought him to be instructed in liberal studies in the church of the most blessed Mother of God, Mary, ever virgin, which is in Augsburg'.[32] The claim that Herman was educated in Augsburg, although it has been accepted by some scholars,[33] seems improbable, since it is mentioned neither by Herman himself nor by his friend and biographer Berthold. Since the two churches shared a patron, perhaps the twelfth-century author (or a scribe copying his work) confused the church of St Mary in *Augia* (Reichenau) with the church of St Mary in *Augusta* (Augsburg).

Certainly from *ca.* 1043, when 'he received holy orders ... at the urging of Abbot Bern', until his death on 24 September 1054, Herman remained in the abbey of Reichenau and it was there that he composed the works that ensured his fame. His remarkable productivity in literary and musical composition must have been partly inspired by the example of Abbot Bern, whose erudition he celebrated in his chronicle.[34] Herman may also have been influenced by the monk Burchard, who perhaps

---

29 Udalric of Zell, *Consuetudines Cluniacenses*, col. 635A–636A (letter to Abbot William of Hirsau). Cf. *Rule of St Benedict* c. 59, CSEL 75, 138–9. See Hofmeister (1961) pp. 5–45. Noble oblates and benefactors: Southern (1970) pp. 223–4, 228–30.

30 Herman, *Chronicle* 1020, below p. 63.

31 Borst (1978) p. 107.

32 The legendary material concerning Herman: Cambridge, Corpus Christi College MS 111, fol. 47–8, quoted in Oesch (1961) p. 130 and Hörberg (1983) p. 217.

33 Most recently by Hörberg (1983) pp. 216–24. I owe this reference to Dr Thomas McCarthy.

34 Herman, *Chronicle* 1008, 1048, below pp. 61, 84. But Herman sometimes disagreed with Bern's musicological opinions: McCarthy (2004) pp. 80–9.

taught him as a boy in Reichenau. Burchard, who served as cantor in the abbey, is also identified as one of the teachers in the monastic school of Reichenau in the dedication of a treatise of Bern on musical theory written *ca.* 1008.[35] This same Burchard was the author of a metrical account of the late tenth-century abbatiate of Witigowo of Reichenau.[36] Herman noted in his chronicle Burchard's promotion as abbot of St Emmeram in Regensburg.[37] Herman himself, despite his difficulty in speaking, taught pupils in Reichenau. Berthold, who was one of them, wrote that 'to his students he proved an eloquent and diligent teacher' and was particularly effective in the scholarly exercise of disputation.[38] Herman's correspondent, Meinzo, master of the cathedral school of Constance, who discussed the method of measuring the diameter of the earth, was perhaps a former pupil.[39] Bishop Benno II of Osnabrück was identified by his biographer as a pupil of Herman.[40] A visitor to Reichenau who 'saw and heard' Herman was Henry, monk of Weissenburg, who at some date after 1061 made a compilation of Herman's works on the *computus* (the science of reckoning time). To this he added an account of the author in which Herman has already become a legendary figure. 'Virtually from his earliest years he was lame from his loins downwards and throughout his life he was deprived of the power of walking. Because he bore this punishment from God most patiently and moreover very frequently thanked Him for it, through the gift of God, without any human teaching he appeared in every one of the liberal studies a new philospher.'[41]

A century later the bibliographer of Prüfening, while saying nothing of the miraculous origin of Herman's erudition, had no doubt of his pre-eminence among scholars. 'Herman the Lame, a Swabian, was a most subtle philosopher in computation ... In music indeed he was

---

35 Bern, *Letter* 1, p. 17. Burchard as cantor: Beyerle (1925b) p. 1191. See Oesch (1961) pp. 41, 48; Hiley, introduction, *Hermannus Contractus, Historia sancti Wolfgangi* pp. xxii–xxiii.

36 Burchard of Reichenau, *Carmen de gestis Witigowonis, MGH Poetae latini medii aevi* 5, 260–79 (composed 994/6). See Hauck (1954) pp. 316–17; Klüppel (1980) pp. 15, 141.

37 Herman, *Chronicle* 1030, below p. 66.

38 Berthold, *Life of Herman*, below p. 108.

39 Dümmler (1879–80) pp. 202–6.

40 Norbert of Iburg (?), *Vita Bennonis* c. 3, p. 4.

41 Henry of Weissenburg, *Epilogue on the Life of lord Herman the Lame*, printed in Borst (1984) p. 395 n. 27. Henry was unaware of Berthold's *Life of Herman* and believed that Herman was still alive in 1061.

more subtle than almost all the moderns.'[42] Berthold of Reichenau's account of 'the studies of Herman' combines both these themes of the pre-eminence and the novelty of this 'new philosopher'. In his works on the *computus* Herman 'greatly surpassed all his predecessors'. 'No one in former times was gifted with so great a knowledge and penetration in [geometry].' 'No musician was more skilled than he.' 'No one was his equal in constructing clocks, musical instruments and mechanical devices.'[43] Modern studies have similarly emphasised the originality of Herman's writings, particularly on that part of the school curriculum of the seven liberal arts known as the *quadrivium*, the arts of arithmetic, geometry, astronomy and music. (Reichenau was evidently a principal centre for the study of the quadrivium in western Europe in the first half of the eleventh century. What Meinzo of Constance observed of Abbot Bern – he 'is reputed to be the greatest authority on the quadrivium in the present time' – was also true of Herman.)[44]

Recent analyses of Herman's work on the length of the lunar month and of his *Rules for the computus* have demonstrated that he refused to be bound by the conclusions of the ancients and insisted on the importance of observation and scientific experiment.[45] The method that Herman used to calculate the earth's diameter – which differed from the calculations of Eratosthenes and Macrobius and puzzled Herman's correspondent Meinzo of Constance – was characteristic of the novelty of Herman's approach.[46] Similarly in his works on musical theory Herman invented new signs for the notation of melodic intervals.[47] While Abbot Bern declared that his treatise on musical theory adhered to the traditions of the ancients, who possessed more wisdom than their successors, Herman wrote that he had 'laboured to clarify what was obscure in the statements of the ancients, to restore what they had omitted and to correct whatever was blameworthy'.[48] The extant writings of Herman on the subjects of the quadrivium include three treatises on arithmetic, four on astronomy, a treatise on the *computus*, a treatise on

42 Wolfger (?), *De scriptoribus* c. 91, p. 85.

43 Berthold, *Life of Herman*, below p. 110.

44 Meinzo, letter to Herman, ed. Dümmler (1879–80) p. 202 (between 1043 and 1048).

45 Borst (1984) pp. 407–59; Bergmann (1988) pp. 103–17.

46 Dümmler (1879–80) pp. 202–6. See Oesch (1961) pp. 171–2; Borst (1984) p. 396 and n. 31.

47 Herman, *Musica* pp. 9, 11. See Oesch (1961) pp. 136–7, 209–11, 242–8; McCarthy (2004) p. 33.

48 Bern, *Prologus in tonarium* c. 2, ed. Rausch p. 33; Herman, *Musica* p. 66. See Oesch (1961) pp. 249–51; Borst (1984) p. 397; McCarthy (2004) pp. 80–9.

the theory of music and three mnemonic verses for students of music. His 'work on geometry according to the natural method and order with figures and diagrams', described by his biographer, Berthold, has not survived. Berthold also attributed to Herman five *historiae*, that is, cycles of chants for the hours of the office on the feast-days of saints, of which two have survived. His other extant liturgical compositions are five sequences and two antiphons: his authorship of other liturgical works is disputed. A long poem *On the eight principal vices* remained unfinished at his death.[49]

All Herman's writings were composed solely to serve the needs of the monastic life. Arithmetic, astronomy and the *computus* were necessary for the exact calculation of the liturgical year and the monastic timetable, without which the daily services could not be celebrated correctly.[50] Music was the essential medium of monastic spirituality. 'The whole structure of our soul and body is joined together by music', wrote Abbot Bern.[51] In singing the liturgy, wrote Herman, echoing the *Rule* of Benedict, 'we raise our hearts from earthly to heavenly things; for he sings in vain, whose mind does not agree with his voice'.[52] Herman's chronicle belongs in the same devotional context as his works on the quadrivium, and both the selection of material and the interpretation of historical events were intended to be appropriate to monastic study. Bernold of St Blasien in his treatise *On the sources of ecclesiastical law* was to recommend Herman's work as an indispensable guide to the dates of the councils of the Church.[53] With equal care Herman worked out the chronology of the papal succession, from 'Linus, the first after blessed Peter' (in the annal for the year 69) to Leo IX, 'the 153rd pope' (in 1049).[54] The chronicle also served the monastic reader as a work of reference on the lives and works of the Church Fathers and the later ecclesiastical authors whom he might study during the *lectio divina* of the monastic timetable.

In addition the structure of Herman's chronicle reveals the theological dimension characteristic of a chronicle inspired by the Eusebian

---

49 Berthold, *Life of Herman* below pp. 109–10. See Oesch (1961) pp. 135–83; Dronke (1968) pp. 44–7; Borst (1984) pp. 392–477; Bergmann (1988) pp. 103–17; Hermannus Contractus, *Historia sancti Wolfgangi* pp. xxii–xxvi.

50 Schmale (1981) col. 1088–9. See also Southern (1953) pp. 185–7.

51 Bern, *Prologus in tonarium*, dedicatory letter, ed. Rausch pp. 31–2.

52 Herman, *Musica* p. 47. Cf. *Rule of St Benedict* c. 19.7, CSEL 75, 82.

53 Bernold, *De excommunicatis vitandis* pp. 153–4.

54 Herman, *Chronicon* 69, p. 75 and below p. 85.

model.[55] This is already apparent in the opening annal. 'In the forty-second year of Emperor Octavian Augustus, in the twenty-eighth year since Egypt was reduced to a province and Cleopatra was defeated, together with Antony, in the 752nd year from the founding of the City, in the third year of the 193rd Olympiad, our Lord Jesus Christ was born in Bethlehem in Judea, when 3,952 years had elapsed since the beginning of the world according to the Hebrew Bible, but 5,199 according to the Septuagint.'[56] The opening annal of Herman's chronicle records the most important event in world history, the Incarnation, dated with the greatest precision according to the chronologies of the ancient world, which were now superseded by the era of Christ's Incarnation. The foundation of the Christian religion is here juxtaposed to a key event in secular history, the foundation of the Roman empire, the fourth and last of the monarchies by which the world was destined to be ruled.[57] After three centuries of mutual hostility, in which the Roman empire persecuted the Christian Church, the two institutions were reconciled. Herman's annal for 305 records how Emperor Constantine I was converted 'and from this time the emperors began to be Christians'.[58]

In the subsequent annals, which primarily record the deeds of secular rulers, there is a particular emphasis on the services rendered by pious kings to the Church. Clovis, 'the great king of the Franks, after many victories possessing almost the whole of Gaul', owed his triumphs to his conversion, 'invoking the God of heaven and promising his fidelity to Christ'.[59] 'The most Christian Oswald', king of Northumbria, remarkable for his veneration for the holy Cross, 'reigned nobly, full of piety' and 'after his death became renowned for very many miracles'.[60] Pippin III, who became king of the Franks 'by the authority of Pope Zacharias and, not long afterwards, of Stephen [II]', intervened in Italy 'to restore the property of St Peter' to the pope.[61] Charlemagne was 'summoned by Pope Hadrian [I] in defence of the property of St Peter' and subsequently 'restored Pope Leo [III] to his see' after a rebellion in

55 See von den Brincken (1957) p. 154.

56 Herman, *Chronicon* 1, p. 74. See Buchner (1960b) p. 38; Borst (1975–6) pp. 13–14.

57 See Krüger (1976) pp. 24–5.

58 Herman, *Chronicon* 305, p. 79.

59 *Ibid.*, 494, 495, 509, p. 85.

60 *Ibid.*, 634, 642, pp. 93, 94. His source was Bede, *Ecclesiastical history* III.9 (Oxford, 1969) pp. 241, 243. Herman's account of Oswald was used by the south German polemicist Manegold of Lautenbach, *Liber ad Gebehardum* c. 49, p. 399.

61 Herman, *Chronicon* 752, 754, 756, p. 99.

Rome and 'was called august emperor by Pope Leo'.[62] Emperor Otto III was closely associated with two distinguished popes: firstly, Gregory V, 'the venerable pope striving to restore canonical discipline' in Rome;[63] secondly, Silvester II, who 'was extremely devoted to secular learning and for this reason very much loved by the emperor, who was himself eager for knowledge'.[64]

Herman portrayed a similarly close relationship between Emperor Henry III and Pope Leo IX. The pope, 'who had been elected by the emperor and sent to Rome', returned to Germany to visit the emperor on three occasions. In 1049 he held a reforming council in Mainz in Henry's presence; in 1051 he celebrated Candlemas with the emperor in Augsburg. On his visit of 1052–3 'he found [Henry] in all respects in agreement with him' on the matter of the war with Hungary and, after spending Christmas with him, 'he departed from the emperor in supreme charity'.[65] Herman himself must have seen the emperor in Reichenau on the occasion recorded in his annal for 1048. 'Coming back to Swabia, [Emperor Henry III] entered our own Reichenau. Here on 24 April he caused the new basilica of St Mark the Evangelist, our patron, built by the lord Abbot Bern, to be dedicated in his presence by Bishop Theoderic of Constance. He celebrated the feast of the same saint on the day of the greater litany [25 April] with us.'[66] The consecration of a church was always a particularly impressive and memorable occasion in the eleventh century.[67] The ceremony in Reichenau in the emperor's presence, six weeks before the death of Abbot Bern, must have seemed the remarkable culmination of a highly successful abbatiate. Bern's death is already foreshadowed in Herman's chronicle in the annal for 1008, which notes that Bern was appointed 'as the twenty-ninth abbot of this place and ... he ruled for forty years'. The annal for 1008 must therefore have been composed after 7 June 1048.[68] Perhaps indeed the death of Abbot Bern and the memorable ceremony that preceded it in April 1048 was the stimulus that prompted the composition of the chronicle.

---

62 *Ibid.*, 773, 800, 801, pp. 100, 101.

63 *Ibid.*, 997, p. 118.

64 Herman, *Chronicle* 1000, below p. 58.

65 *Ibid.*, 1049, 1051, 1052, 1053, below pp. 86, 88, 92, 94.

66 *Ibid.*, 1048, below p. 84.

67 Cf. Bloch (1986) pp. 41–2, 118–21, describing the consecration of the basilica of Monte Cassino by Pope Alexander II in 1071 as 'one of the most brilliant events in the history of the eleventh century'.

68 Herman, *Chronicle* 1008, below p. 61.

'With careful labour,' wrote Herman's biographer, 'searching every-where, he compiled this book of chronicles from the Incarnation of the Lord up to his own times.'[69] (The reference to 'this book' indicates that Berthold of Reichenau's biography of Herman was originally intended to be copied into a Reichenau manuscript of Herman's chronicle.) Bernold of St Blasien referred to Herman's work methods in similar terms, describing 'that chronicle that the lord Herman, the excellent calculator and most subtle researcher of chronologies, very diligently composed from various chronicles and histories, which faithfully continues up to the year 1054 of the Lord's Incarnation'.[70] Herman himself punctuated his chronicle with bibliographical references to his principal sources. At the end of the annal for 378 he noted: 'Jerome continued the chronicle of Eusebius thus far.'[71] After the annal for 395: 'Thus far Rufinus continued the Ecclesiastical History of Bishop Eusebius of Caesarea, translated by himself.' After the annal for 454: 'Prosper continued his chronicle thus far.' After that for 551: 'Thus far Bishop Jordanes continued his abridged chronicle of the deeds of the Romans.' After the annal for 616 Herman noted: 'Bishop Isidore of Seville ... continued his abridgement of the times thus far.' After the annal for 703: 'Bede ... continued the chronicle of his lesser book on the times.'[72]

Herman's chronicle was described by Wilhelm Wattenbach as 'compiled from many sources like a mosaic', 'a monument to his great industry, his extraordinarily wide reading and his careful accuracy'.[73] This judgement of 1858 was followed by more than a century of specula-tion concerning the *fons formalis* of Herman's chronicle. This debate centred on an anonymous Incarnation chronicle named by Harry Bresslau 'the Swabian universal chronicle' (*Chronicon Suevicum univer-sale*). Bresslau's explanation of the resemblances between this work and Herman's chronicle was that the anonymous chronicler and Herman both drew heavily on a lost work that he called 'the Swabian imperial

---

69 Berthold, *Life of Herman* in his *Chronicle* 1054, below p. 110.

70 Bernold, *De excommunicatis vitandis* p. 153. Cf. Bernold, *Chronicle* 1093, below p. 315.

71 Herman, *Chronicon* 378, p. 80 (Jerome, *Chronicon Eusebii Caesariensis*). The fullest extant manuscript of Herman's chronicle, Karlsruhe Augiensis CLXXV (see below p. 20) adds: 'Hereafter Herman.' Cf. Bernold of St Blasien, *Chronicon* 377, p. 408: 'Hereafter, however, up to the 1,054th year from the Lord's Incarnation the lord Herman continued his chronicle.'

72 Herman, *Chronicon* 395, p. 80 (Rufinus of Aquileia, *Historia ecclesiastica*); 454, p. 83 (Prosper of Aquitaine, *Epitoma Chronicon*); 551, p. 88 (Jordanes, *Historia Romana*); 616, p. 92 (Isidore of Seville, *Chronica minora*); 703, p. 97 (Bede, *Chronica minora*).

73 Wattenbach (1858) p. 35.

annals'.[74] Later studies have denied the existence of this last work and accounted for the resemblance between 'the Swabian universal chronicle' and Herman's chronicle by attributing both works to Herman. The anonymous chronicle was allegedly Herman's first attempt at a historical work, while the well-known chronicle was his later, longer, improved version of that work.[75] The most recent study of this question has returned to the opinion of Wilhelm Wattenbach and of G.H. Pertz, the editor of Herman's chronicle,[76] and identified 'the Swabian universal chronicle' as an abridged version of the chronicle of Herman. This study, on the basis of the manuscript evidence and to a lesser extent on stylistic evidence, attributes this abridgement to Herman's pupil, Berthold of Reichenau. For of the five surviving exemplars of 'the Swabian universal chronicle', one is found in a compilation of chronicles including the first version of Berthold's chronicle and three are found in association with the second version of Berthold's chronicle.[77] Both these solutions to this problem of identification – 'the Swabian universal chronicle' as an early version of Herman's chronicle or as a later abridgement of Herman's chronicle – confirm Herman's originality as a historian and restore 'the renown of having been the first German world chronicler'.[78] He was as much an innovator in his chronicle as in his writings on the quadrivium. It was he who took 'the enormous step' of using the year of the Incarnation as his method of dating throughout the chronicle. In particular for the years from the fifth century to the beginning of the eighth century, a period relatively poor in chronologically accurate materials, he produced the first consistent chronology dated according to the Incarnation years.[79]

'Herman very deliberately withholds his subjective judgement,' wrote Wilhelm von Giesebrecht, 'and allows his own personality to intrude very little: where his opinion appears, it is neither courtly nor monastic. In most cases he lets the facts speak for themselves and presents them

---

74 Bresslau (1877) pp. 566–76. For Bresslau's further contributions to this debate: Robinson (1980) p. 84. Bresslau produced a partial edition (the annals for 768–1043) in *MGH SS* 13, 61–72. Duch (1961) p. 187 renamed the work 'the Reichenau imperial chronicle' ('Reichenauer Kaiserchronik').

75 Dieterich (1925) pp. 787–8; Buchner (1960a) pp. 389–96; Schmale (1974) pp. 132–49.

76 *MGH SS* 5, 72–3, naming the text, like Wattenbach, *Epitome Sangallensis* and identifying it as an abridgement, like that of Bernold of St Blasien.

77 Robinson (1980) pp. 84–136.

78 Dieterich (1925) p. 785.

79 Buchner (1960a) pp. 390–1; Schmale (1974) p. 132.

in few words in what was for his time very pure Latin.'[80] There is one area, however, where Herman's personal sympathies are clear enough, namely the history of his own family, that of the counts of Altshausen. The ten annals identifying his parents, one of his brothers, his grandparents, his great-uncle and his father's great-uncle, reflect his keen concern for the *memoria* of his family.[81] Too complex and too precise in their chronology to be derived entirely from oral tradition, the information in these annals was perhaps drawn from entries in necrologies or even from a lost family history.[82] In particular he celebrated the virtues of his mother, Hiltrud, including in the annal for 1052, recording her death, his verses requesting the reader's prayers on her behalf.[83] Of his own generation Herman mentioned only one sibling, his brother Werner, who was also a monk of Reichenau. Herman recorded his birth in 1021 and his departure from Reichenau on a pilgrimage in 1053. The first version of the chronicle of Berthold of Reichenau supplies the information that Werner's destination was Jerusalem and that he died on the outward journey in 1054, in the same year as his brother.[84] Herman was, therefore, primarily concerned with the *memoria* of those children of Count Wolferad II who entered the religious life. Other evidence of Herman's family sympathies, more oblique in character, has been suggested by Rudolf Buchner. In the precisely detailed and well-informed reports of Henry III's campaigns in Hungary in 1044 and 1051 he detected the keen interest in war of a grandson, son and brother of counts of Altshausen. 'These are the words not of a monk detached from the world, of an ascetic, but a member of a noble family, who despite ill health observes the world from his monastery with open, appreciative and critical eyes.'[85]

The world that the chronicler observed was that traversed by the itinerary of the German king and Roman emperor or by the journeys of his envoys. The annals for 1000–54, which are translated here, range from eastern Saxony to Lotharingia, from Bohemia, Hungary, Poland and the territory of the Slav confederation of the Liutizi to Flanders and Champagne, from northern Italy to Rome and the principalities of the south.

---

80 Giesebrecht (1885) p. 562.

81 Herman, *Chronicon* 955, p. 115; also *Chronicle* 1006, 1009, 1010, 1013, 1020, 1021, 1032, 1052, 1053, below pp. 60, 61, 62, 63, 67, 90, 96.

82 Borgolte (1979) pp. 1–15.

83 Herman, *Chronicle* 1052, below p. 91.

84 *Ibid.*, 1053, p. 96; Berthold, *Chronicle* I, 1054, below p. 99.

85 Buchner, introduction to his edition of Herman, *Chronicon* p. 623.

Herman recorded the episcopal succession in Augsburg, Bamberg, Cologne, Constance, Liège, Mainz, Metz, Regensburg, Speyer, Strasbourg, Trier, Verdun and Würzburg. Besides continuing to record the papal succession, as he had done from the beginning of his chronicle, he now noted the episcopal succession for Aquileia, Milan and Ravenna. He recorded the ducal succession not only in his native Swabia but also in Bavaria, Carinthia and Lotharingia. The range of his information reflects the stream of news that flowed into an imperial abbey, whose abbot was an influential figure in the kingdom. The correspondence of Abbot Bern conveys the same impression of Reichenau as an institution in close touch with the power centres of the empire.[86]

Although Giesebrecht concluded that 'Herman very deliberately withholds his subjective judgement,' it is evident that Herman revealed his sympathies by his distinctive use of the first person plural.[87] A monk's *patria* was his monastery and hence Herman wrote of 'our own Reichenau'. In April 1048 Emperor Henry III visited 'our own Reichenau' and 'caused the new basilica of St Mark the Evangelist, our patron ... to be dedicated' and 'celebrated the feast of the same saint ... with us'.[88] Herman also used the first person plural to denote the Germans vis-à-vis their enemies. In his account of the battle of the Lech (955) he reported the many casualties 'on our side', including two Swabian counts who were his own kinsmen.[89] He recorded in 1035 a raid by the Slav confederation of the Liutizi, who 'killed or led away captive many of our men' and in 1040 the fate of 'our men' on an unsuccessful campaign against the Bohemians.[90] The annals of 1041 and 1051 reported the negotiations of the Hungarian king with 'our margrave', that is, Adalbert of Babenberg, margrave of Austria.[91] Herman's account of the battle of Civitate (18 June 1053) between the army of Pope Leo IX and the Normans of southern Italy distinguished between 'our men', the Germans in the papal army, and 'the Italians' who were the pope's allies, whose premature flight occasioned the defeat of the pope's army.[92]

Equally indicative of the chronicler's loyalties is the central role of

86 Schmale, introduction to Bern, *Letters* pp. 2–7; Erdmann (1951) pp. 112–19.

87 Buchner (1960b) pp. 54–7.

88 Herman, *Chronicle* 1048, below p. 84.

89 Herman, *Chronicon* 955, p. 115 (Count Theodpald, brother of Bishop Udalric of Augsburg, and their nephew, Count Reginbald).

90 Herman, *Chronicle* 1035, 1040, below pp. 69, 72.

91 *Ibid.*, 1041, 1051, pp. 73, 90.

92 *Ibid.*, 1053, p. 95.

the German monarchy in Herman's chronicle. The work is initially an 'imperial chronicle', in which the reigns of the Roman emperors determine the chronological structure of the work. At the beginning of each reign a marginal note announces the length of the reign: 'Tiberius, the stepson of Augustus, reigned for twenty-three years'; 'Gaius, a very wicked man, [ruled] for three years, ten months and eight days'; 'Claudius [ruled] for thirteen years, eight months, twenty-eight days'.[93] In 714 Herman began to substitute for the Roman emperors, the Frankish rulers of the Carolingian dynasty: 'Charles [Martel], mayor of the palace, [ruled] for twenty-seven years'; 'Pippin, mayor of the palace, [ruled] for ten years'; 'the same Pippin [ruled] as king for sixteen years'; 'Charles the Great, king and emperor, [ruled] for forty-six years'.[94] In his annal for 911 he noted that 'the royal line [of the Carolingians] failed in our territory', that is, in East Francia, as opposed to West Francia.[95] Thereafter, until 1002, he noted in the margin the length of the reigns of the rulers of the East Frankish, German kingdom. In the eleventh-century section of the chronicle the itinerary of the German monarch and especially his military expeditions usually provide the structure of each annal. Herman noted the monarch's celebration of Easter, Whitsun and Christmas sporadically from 1026 and regularly from 1046 onwards.

The annals for 1043–5 are remarkable for their enthusiastically positive attitude towards King Henry III, in marked contrast to the non-committal language with which he had described the deeds of kings in the previous, shorter annals. In the annal for 1043 Herman recorded, firstly, the synod of Constance, in which Henry III 'forgave every trespass on the part of all those who had committed offences against him' and called on all the nobles present to forgive their enemies. Henry 'was eager that the same thing should be done in the other provinces of his kingdom' and 'thus brought about a peace unheard of for many centuries'.[96] Herman's language echoed that of Abbot Bern of Reichenau in the letter of 1044/5, in which he congratulated the king on 'such great treaties of concord throughout your kingdom as are unheard of in all the centuries before'.[97] The same annal for 1043 reported the wedding of Henry III and Agnes of Poitou, when the king 'offered a useful

93 Herman, *Chronicon* 16, 38, 42, p. 75.

94 *Ibid.*, 714, 741, 752, 768, pp. 97, 98, 99. See Buchner (1960b) pp. 38–9.

95 Herman, *Chronicon* 911, p. 112. See Buchner (1960b) p. 42.

96 Herman, *Chronicle* 1043, below p. 74. See Ladner (1936) pp. 70–8.

97 Bern, *Letter* 27, p. 57.

example to everyone by treating as worthless the vain applause of the stage players and sending them away empty-handed and lamenting'.[98] The annal for 1044 records the opposition of Godfrey 'the Bearded' of Verdun, duke of Upper Lotharingia to Henry III in highly partisan terms: Godfrey 'disregarded his oath and his fealty and presumed to rebel against the pious king'. In his account of their troubled relationship Herman consistently portrayed Henry III as victim and Godfrey as tyrant.[99]

Later in the annal for 1044 Herman reported that Henry III 'invaded Hungary with a very small force' and, 'trusting in divine help', encountered a much larger Hungarian army at Menfö (5 July), where 'he himself fought bravely' and 'won a most glorious victory'. Henry, 'being in all things a most pious man', used his victory to restore the deposed King Peter to the Hungarian throne.[100] Again there is an echo here of Abbot Bern's letter of congratulations to Henry III. 'You recently fought courageously with the Hungarians and defeated them in battle'; 'with Christ's help you restored [Peter] to the kingship'.[101] The annal for 1045 records an incident during Henry's visit to Persenbeug, where he 'climbed up into a certain old balcony' and 'the building collapsed and he, with many others, fell to the ground'. Some members of his entourage died of their injuries but 'through the protection of God [Henry] himself was unhurt'.[102] In these passages the author clearly shared the admiration that Abbot Bern had expressed in his letters to 'the most unconquered of kings, Henry the peaceable, the most glorious disseminator of the orthodox faith', addressing him in the language of eleventh-century sacral kingship.[103]

After this annal there are no more references to Henry III's piety and

---

98 Herman, *Chronicle* 1043, below p. 75.

99 *Ibid.*, 1044, p. 75. Cf. 1047, p. 83 ('Godfrey, among the other deeds that he perpetrated against the king, captured the city of Verdun by guile'); 1054, p. 98 ('Duke Godfrey once more raised up a tyrannical power against the emperor'). In his revisionist account of the career of Godfrey, Boshof (1978) pp. 66–70 argued that Godfrey's father, Duke Gozelo I of Upper and Lower Lotharingia, had been promised by Henry III that Godfrey could inherit both his duchies. It was because the king broke his promise that Godfrey rebelled in 1044 and 1047. Herman's negative account of Godfrey's conduct perhaps reflected royal propaganda.

100 Herman, *Chronicle* 1044, below pp. 75–6.

101 Bern, *Letter* 27, pp. 58, 59.

102 Herman, *Chronicle* 1045, below p. 77.

103 Bern, *Letters* 26, 27, pp. 55–64. See Erdmann (1951) pp. 112–19.

courage.[104] There could hardly be a sharper contrast than that between the allusions to Henry III in the annals for 1043–5 and the description of the emperor in the annal for 1053. The context was the deposition of Duke Conrad of Bavaria. 'At this time both the foremost men and the lesser men of the kingdom began more and more to murmur against the emperor and complained that he had long since departed from his original conduct of justice, peace, piety, fear of God and the manifold virtues in which he ought to have made progress from day to day, that he was gradually turning towards acquisitiveness and a certain negligence and that he would become much worse than he was before.'[105] The framework of ideas is once more that of Abbot Bern's letters to Henry III. Drawing on the definition of Isidore of Seville, Bern had distinguished between those rulers who were 'called tyrants because of the cruel ferocity of their conduct' and Christian rulers, who 'were called kings [*reges*] from the fact that they ruled rightly [*a recte regendo*], because they repressed animal instincts and showed themselves through their vigorous discretion to be rational beings'. Bern had reminded Henry III that he was descended 'from a line of ancestors as religious as it was noble': he would be a Christian king 'as long as [he] continually represent[ed] such great ancestors in [his] morals and [his] life'.[106] In Herman's view Henry III had ceased to heed Bern's advice and no longer exhibited the qualities that distinguished the Christian king from the tyrant.

Herman continued his polemic against Henry III later in the annal for 1053 with a report on the election of his three-year-old son Henry IV as king. 'Emperor Henry held a great assembly in Tribur and caused his son of the same name to be elected king by all who were present and caused them to promise subjection to him after the emperor's death, if he was a just ruler.'[107] This is the only extant account of the election of 1053 and it has been variously interpreted. Herman's account implies that the princes made Henry IV's succession to his father conditional on his future conduct. The clause 'if he was a just ruler' amounted to a criticism of the regime of Henry III, who had ceased to be a just ruler. Since

---

104 Although the chronicler noted the 'great glory' of his imperial coronation (25 December 1046) and the honour in which he was held by the Romans, his veneration for the relics of the saintly Abbot Wido of Pomposa, which he transferred to the church of St John the Evangelist in Speyer, and his harmonious relationship with Pope Leo IX, who 'found [Henry] in all respects in agreement with him': Herman, *Chronicle* 1047, 1052, pp. 80, 81–2, 92.

105 *Ibid.*, 1053, p. 95.

106 Bern, *Letter* 26, pp. 55–6. Cf. Isidore of Seville, *Etymologiae* 9.3.19–20.

107 Herman, *Chronicle* 1053, below pp. 96–7.

such a conditional election of a king was without precedent,[108] some historians have doubted the accuracy of Herman's account, arguing that Herman was not reporting an actual condition imposed by the princes but simply stating his own view of the qualifications necessary for a Christian king.[109] If the formulation was indeed Herman's own, it was a significant contribution to political thought. For the idea that a king may be rejected by his subjects if he proves to be unjust anticipates the contractual theory of monarchy that would appear in the anti-imperial polemics of the Investiture Contest.[110]

As Herman's enthusiasm for Henry III waned in the early 1050s, so his interest in the papacy grew. Throughout his chronicle, as we have seen, he had carefully recorded the papal succession. In the annal for 1032 he first introduced a reference to the papacy independent of the chronology of the papal succession: a report of Pope John XIX's privilege of 28 October 1031 for Reichenau, which provoked the bitter opposition of Bishop Warmann of Constance.[111] Herman's more detailed reporting of papal history begins in the annals for 1033 and 1044, which reflect his knowledge of the proceedings of the synods of Sutri and Rome in December 1046. Recording the succession of Pope Benedict IX, Herman added that 'he was unworthy of so high a rank, both in his character and in his deeds' and in 1044 he noted that 'the Romans drove Pope Benedict, who was accused of many crimes, from his see and put a certain Silvester [III] in his place'. After his restoration to the papacy Benedict 'later deprived himself of office and appointed another [Gregory VI] in his place, prompted by avarice and contrary to canon law'.[112] Herman recorded the inauguration of the reform papacy without, however, mentioning the motive of reform and noting only that the German popes Clement II and Damasus II were 'elected by the emperor'.[113]

With the beginning of the pontificate of Leo IX (who, like Damasus II, was 'elected by the emperor and sent to Rome'), the treatment of papal history becomes much more expansive. The annals for 1049–54 show

108 Cf. Herman's account of the election of Henry III in Conrad II's lifetime (*Chronicle* 1028, below p. 65) and the promise of fidelity and subjection by 'many of the princes' to Henry IV, Christmas 1050 (*Chronicle* 1051, p. 88).

109 Gericke (1955) pp. 737–41; Haider (1968) pp. 31–3; Scheibelreiter (1973) p. 3; Reinhardt (1975) pp. 251–2; Reuter (1991b) p. 316 (trans. Reuter (2006) pp. 376–7); Robinson (1999) pp. 21–2.

110 See below p. 129 and n. 192.

111 Herman, *Chronicle* 1032, below p. 67.

112 *Ibid.*, 1033, 1044, pp. 68, 76–7.

113 *Ibid.*, 1046, 1048, pp. 80, 84.

a keen interest in the papal itinerary. Herman recorded that Leo IX consecrated Abbot Udalric of Reichenau on 26 March 1049 and visited the abbey the following 26 November.[114] The annal for 1049 records Leo IX's first synod in Rome, 'particularly against simoniacal heresy', his 'great synod in Rheims with the bishops of France' and his 'synod of nearly forty bishops in the presence of the emperor and the princes of our kingdom' in Mainz. Herman recorded in all eight of Leo IX's reforming councils.[115] The annal for 1052 reports Leo IX's mediation in the emperor's conflict with Hungary.[116] The pope's measures against the Normans in southern Italy fill more than half of the annal for 1053, which includes a polemic against the 'abominable and indescribable crimes' of the Normans. The report ends with an attempted explanation of the papal defeat by the Normans at the battle of Civitate (18 June 1053): 'perhaps ... spiritual battle was more appropriate to so great a priest than carnal battle in pursuit of transitory ends'. Herman's was the earliest attempt to provide an explanation of this defeat, which so troubled admirers of Leo IX throughout the eleventh century.[117] In 1054, the final annal of Herman's chronicle, the author reported Leo IX's 'glorious death', adding that 'it is recorded that he was distinguished by miracles'.[118] Herman's report, composed before 24 September 1054, is the earliest known assertion of the sanctity of Leo IX. This detailed interest in the events of Leo IX's pontificate, the polemical defence of his Norman policy, and ultimately the conviction that he was a saint, identify Herman as a supporter of the reform papacy. (It is noteworthy that in his allusion to Leo's campaign against simony, Herman used the characteristic reforming term 'simoniacal heresy'.) There is no reference in Herman's chronicle to the claims made during Leo IX's pontificate for the papal office, no allusion to the papal primacy with which Herman's continuators would be so familiar: Herman's concern was with the personal qualities of Leo, his 'exceeding compassion and accustomed mercy'.[119] Nevertheless Herman's annals for 1049–54 reveal the attraction that the papal reform movement was already beginning to exert in south-western Germany at the end of Leo IX's pontificate.

114 *Ibid.*, 1049, pp. 85–6.

115 *Ibid.*, 1049, p. 86 (Rome, Pavia, Rheims, Mainz); 1050, pp. 87, 88 (Rome, Vercelli); 1051, p. 89 (Rome); 1053, p. 95 (Rome).

116 *Ibid.*, 1052, pp. 92–3.

117 *Ibid.*, 1053, p. 96. See Robinson (2004a) pp. 8–9, 29, 52–3, 94.

118 Herman, *Chronicle* 1054, below p. 98.

119 *Ibid.*, 1053, p. 94.

The only complete modern edition of Herman's chronicle is that of G.H. Pertz in *Monumenta Germaniae Historica, Scriptores* 5, 74–133. Since no complete manuscript of the chronicle survives, Pertz's edition is necessarily a reconstruction, derived from a number of different partial versions of the text. The most important and the version closest to Herman's original text is that of the eleventh-century codex Karlsruhe, Badische Landesbibliothek, MS Augiensis perg. CLXXV, which, however, breaks off towards the end of the annal for 1051. For the end of this annal and half of the annal for 1052 Pertz's edition depends on Göttweig MS 110 and three of the manuscripts of Berthold of Reichenau's continuation of Herman's chronicle. For the rest of the work there is no reliable manuscript and Pertz was obliged to use a printed source, the compilation of chronicles printed by the Basel jurist Johannes Sichard in 1529 from an unknown manuscript.[120]

The two versions of the chronicle of Berthold of Reichenau

The chronicle of Berthold of Reichenau, whose authorship has been debated for two centuries, survives in two versions. One is a shorter and clearly earlier version, which begins in 1054 with a report of the death of Herman of Reichenau and breaks off in mid-sentence in the annal for 1066 ('Berthold I'). It is found only in the compilation of chronicles printed in 1529 by Johannes Sichard, the Basel jurist, and intended to provide the reader with a complete chronology of world history from the Creation to the year 1512.[1] The second version is obviously later and much more extensive ('Berthold II'). It also begins in 1054 and in the two Vienna manuscripts, Österreichische Nationalbibliothek MS 3399 and MS 7245, it extends to 1080, breaking off in mid-sentence. In the exemplars of Sarnen, Kollegiumsbibliothek MS 10 and Engelberg, Stiftsbibliothek MS 9 the scribes evidently chose to omit the fragmentary annal for 1080. This second version is preceded in all the manuscripts by a biography of Herman of Reichenau.[2]

---

120 Robinson (1980) pp. 88–95. The annals for 901–1054 were reprinted by Rudolf Buchner with a German translation and commentary in the collection *Quellen des 9. und 11. Jahrhunderts zur Geschichte der Hamburgischen Kirche und des Reiches* (Darmstadt, 1961) pp. 628–707.

1 [Johannes Sichard], *En damus Chronicon divinum plane opus eruditissimorum autorum, repetitum ab ipso mundi initio, ad annum usque salutis MDXII* … (Basel, 1529) pp. 175v–205v.

2 See the manuscript descriptions in Robinson, introduction, *Die Chroniken Bertholds und Bernolds* pp. 3–24.

In the first version of the chronicle (that of the Sichard printing) there is no indication of authorship. Three of the five manuscripts of the second version of the chronicle identify the author. The early sixteenth-century Vienna MS 3399, the most reliable and most complete exemplar of 'Berthold II', contains a marginal note marking the beginning of the continuation of Herman's chronicle: 'Henceforward after Herman *Bertolus* continues the chronicle' (fol. 109ᵛ). The twelfth-century Sarnen MS 10 (fol. 97ʳ) and Engelberg MS 9 (fol. 87ᵛ) marked the transition with the words: 'Up to this point the chronicle of Herman. Henceforward *Berctoldus (Berhtoldus)*.'[3] The late twelfth-century bibliographer of Prüfening made the same identification: 'Berthold, who was [Herman's] pupil, wrote a *Life* of his master and a chronicle.'[4] On the basis of this evidence G.H. Pertz published his edition of the chronicle in 1844 under the title *The Annals of Berthold*.[5] He did not, however, differentiate between the two versions of the chronicle, conflating the Sichard text and that of the Vienna, Sarnen and Engelberg manuscripts into a single work. The first edition of 'Berthold I' as an independent text was that of Georg Waitz in 1881, under the title *The Continuation of the Chronicle of Herman ... composed, it seems, by Berthold*.[6] Waitz believed that 'Berthold I', the Sichard text, was the authentic chronicle of Berthold of Reichenau, while 'Berthold II' was an anonymous compilation, most of which was not the work of Berthold. Gerold Meyer von Knonau (1894) called the compiler of this work 'the Swabian annalist' and 'the annalist of 1075'. He thus drew attention to the annal in which the work abandons its brevity and its relatively neutral tone (similar to that of 'Berthold I') and suddenly swells into a verbose and unrestrainedly polemical narrative, dedicated to the defence of the papal reform movement and its adherents.[7] When J.R. Dieterich summarised the state of scholarly opinion in 1925, he emphasised the contrast between the 'unadulterated' text of 'Berthold I', which he perceived as imperialist in sympathy, the characteristic product of the imperial abbey of Reichenau, and 'Berthold II', whose compiler was 'a zealous Gregorian'.[8]

---

3 *Ibid.*, pp. 9, 13, 19.

4 Wolfger (?), *De scriptoribus* c. 92, p. 85. It is possible that his information derived from an exemplar of Berthold's chronicle and was consequently not independent of the manuscript tradition of the chronicle.

5 *Bertholdi Annales*, MGH SS 5, 264–326.

6 *Chronici Herimanni Continuatio ... auctore, ut videtur, Bertholdo*, MGH SS 13, 730–2.

7 Meyer von Knonau (1894) pp. 905–7 (excursus 8).

8 Dieterich (1925) pp. 798–9.

It was Bernhard Schmeidler who in 1938 restored the disputed text to
Berthold of Reichenau, identifying it not as a compilation but as the
composition of a single writer, the pupil of Herman of Reichenau. He
used the method of 'stylistic criticism' (*Stilkritik*) to demonstrate the
stylistic unity of *The Life of Herman* – whose author identified himself as
the pupil and friend of Herman – and the *Chronicle*. They were the work
of the same author, that Berthold who, according to the bibliographer
of Prüfening, 'wrote a *Life* of his master and a chronicle'.[9] Schmeidler
turned upside-down the scholarly consensus of the previous generation by ascribing 'Berthold II' to Berthold of Reichenau, while identifying 'Berthold I' as an 'anonymous imperial chronicle' that provided
Berthold with material for his annals 1054–66. 'We need not so much
new material, as new methods and new ideas,' wrote Schmeidler, in
response to the opinion of Harry Bresslau (1902) that the problem of
the authorship of 'Berthold I' and 'Berthold II' could be resolved only if
new manuscript material was discovered.[10] Schmeidler's 'new method'
for the solution of the problem was 'stylistic criticism' but other 'new
methods and new ideas' were already being applied to the narrative
sources of the Central Middle Ages that had important implications for
the Berthold problem.

In the same year that Schmeidler published his study of Berthold's
chronicle, there appeared a study of the annals composed by Gerhoch of
Reichersberg, which noted that they survived in two different versions.[11]
Schmeidler himself in 1939 published a study of the relationship of the
Nienburg annals to the work of 'Annalista Saxo', apparently without
noticing that here was an analogy to the relationship of 'Berthold I' and
'Berthold II'.[12] The case of the *Chronographia* of Heimo of Bamberg is
also instructive. He completed a first version in 1135 but later published a
revised version, explaining in the preface that his purpose was to correct
a number of errors.[13] Where the autograph of a chronicle survives – as in
the case of Berthold's contemporaries, Bernold of St Blasien, Marianus
Scotus and Hugh of Flavigny – the chronicler's working methods are

---

9 Schmeidler (1938) pp. 159–234. He conceived this study as part of a large-scale investigation of the Latin literature of the Middle Ages, intended to demonstrate the value
   of *Stilkritik* (*ibid.*, p. 234).

10 Schmeidler (1938) p. 166; Bresslau (1902) p. 133.

11 Fichtenau (1938) pp. 43–56.

12 Schmeidler (1939) pp. 88–167.

13 Heimo of Bamberg, *Chronographia seu de decursu temporum, praefatio*, ed. P. Jaffé,
   Bibliotheca rerum germanicarum 5 (Berlin, 1869), 543. See von den Brincken (1957) p.
   176.

easier to discern: the erasures, rewriting and additions in the margins bear witness to a continual process of revision.[14] It was on the basis of such analogous cases that F.-J. Schmale in 1974 suggested that the brief and sober chronicle 'Berthold I' and the extensive and polemical 'Berthold II' were 'two works by one and the same author'.[15] The recent edition of the two versions of the chronicle for the Monumenta Germaniae Historica has confirmed this conclusion.[16]

There are only two references to the chronicler Berthold independent of the manuscripts of his work: that of the bibliographer of Prüfening and a single sentence in the chronicle of Bernold of St Blasien. In his annal for 1088 Bernold wrote: 'The excellent teacher Berthold, who was extremely learned in sacred literature, departed to the Lord in a good old age, full of years, on 12 March.'[17] The report is disappointingly meagre: Berthold is identified neither as a monk of Reichenau nor as a chronicler. The reference to 'a good old age' is, however, appropriate to one who had been the friend of Herman the Lame thirty-four years before. The description 'extremely learned in sacred literature' would also be appropriate to Berthold if he was indeed the author of 'the Swabian universal chronicle', since Christian history was regarded in the eleventh century as a continuation of the narrative of the New Testament and well suited to the monastic *lectio divina*.[18] (Berthold's inclusion of patristic and canon law texts in his chronicle might also qualify him for the compliment 'extremely learned in sacred literature'.) Since no other candidate has ever been suggested, we may assume that Bernold of St Blasien was indeed referring to Berthold of Reichenau, whose chronicle was his principal source for his own annals for 1054–75.[19]

Other than the date of his death, 12 March 1088, our sole source of biographical information for Berthold is his *Life of Herman*: this text alone identifies him as a monk of Reichenau. The *Life* contains an account of a conversation that Berthold had with Herman shortly before the latter's death on 24 September 1054 (the only recorded event

---

14 Bernold's autograph: below pp. 48, 50–1. Marianus Scotus: von den Brincken (1957) p. 167. Hugh of Flavigny: Healy (2005) pp. 34–7; Healy (2006) pp. 91–3.

15 Schmale (1974) p. 152.

16 Robinson, introduction, *Die Chroniken Bertholds und Bernolds* pp. 44–67.

17 Bernold, *Chronicle* 1088, below p. 291.

18 Robinson (1980) pp. 84–136. According to the Augustinian and Bedan chronology of the 'seven ages of the world', the sixth age began with Christ's Incarnation and continued to the present day: Krüger (1976) pp. 26–7.

19 See below p. 50.

in Berthold's career, independent of his literary activity). Herman fore-
told to Berthold, 'with whom he was on more friendly terms than the
others', his imminent death and described a vision that he had experienced the previous night. Herman then entrusted his pupil with the
correction of his poem on the eight principal vices, which existed only
as a rough draft on wax tablets and had yet to be committed to parchment: 'Take my writing tablets, I beg you, and firstly, correct carefully whatever still remains there to be copied out.'[20] Berthold was
clearly anxious to emphasise his role as the trusted friend of Herman,
the scholar whose genius 'wonderfully outdistanced all the men of his
age'.[21] This emphasis was intended to support the authenticity of his
account and to cast some reflected glory on himself: he was considered
by Herman worthy to correct the latter's text before a fair copy was
made. Berthold inserted this compliment to himself, which was irrel-
evant to his narrative, in order to establish his credentials as Herman's
intellectual heir and the worthy continuator of his chronicle.

Both versions of Berthold's chronicle, as we have already seen, are
preceded in all their exemplars by a revised abridgement of Herman's
chronicle, the so-called 'Swabian universal chronicle', which there is good
reason for supposing to be Berthold's work. This in turn is preceded
by two shorter texts, which were perhaps also part of Berthold's plan
for his chronicle. The first is a rapid sketch of world history entitled
'Concerning the principal kingdoms according to the chronicles of
Eusebius and Jerome'. The second is entitled 'Concerning the six ages
of the world' and is an extract from Bede, *De temporum ratione* c. 66.
In 'Berthold II' the abridgement of Herman's chronicle ('the Swabian
universal chronicle') is linked with this Bedan text by being given the
title 'The course and order of the sixth age of the world'. For according
to the chronology of Bede (as of Augustine) the sixth age of the world
began with the Incarnation.[22] The inclusion of these texts suggests that
Berthold intended to expand the scope of his master Herman's project
so as to produce a chronicle beginning not with the Incarnation but
with the creation of the world.

It is likely that Berthold began to compose the first version of his
chronicle soon after his master's death, since 'Berthold I' clearly reflects
the attitudes of the later annals of Herman's chronicle. J.R. Dieterich in

---

20 Berthold, *Life of Herman* below pp. 110–11.

21 *Ibid.*, p. 108.

22 Robinson, introduction, *Die Chroniken Bertholds und Bernolds* pp. 4–5, 8–9, 19. The six
    ages of the world: von den Brincken (1957) pp. 108–13; Krüger (1976) pp. 26–7.

1925 contrasted 'Berthold I', which he regarded as the authentic work of Berthold of Reichenau, with the supposedly inauthentic 'Berthold II' in the following terms. 'While Berthold, like his teacher, was an imperialist, the author of the compilation [‘Berthold II’] was a zealous Gregorian.'[23] In fact, as we have already seen, in the final annals of his chronicle Herman was critical of the emperor and it is this negative attitude towards Henry III that appears in 'Berthold I'. Berthold reported the emperor's treatment of Margravine Beatrice of Tuscany after she had angered him by her marriage to the rebel Godfrey 'the Bearded' of Verdun: 'Beatrice came to surrender to the emperor and, although she had sworn fidelity, she was held prisoner because of her husband.'[24] Berthold recorded the premature death of Welf III, duke of Carinthia in 1055 as 'a matter of great lamentation for his vassals and for all people'. At the time of his death Welf III had been the ringleader of a conspiracy to assassinate Henry III and replace him with Conrad, the duke of Bavaria whom he had deposed.[25] Similarly, when he reported that Bishop Herman of Bamberg obtained his bishopric 'by means of simony', Berthold was echoing his master's account of Pope Leo IX's campaign against 'simoniacal heresy'.[26] Certainly there is no trace in 'Berthold I' of the pro-papal polemic that characterises 'Berthold II' but the simple reason for this was that Berthold was composing the first version of his chronicle in the later 1050s and 1060s, before public opinion in the German kingdom had begun to be polarised by the claims and the actions of Pope Gregory VII.

The two most striking differences between the annals for 1054–66 in 'Berthold I' and the revised version of these annals in 'Berthold II' are found in the reports of the death of Henry III in 1056 and of the papal schism in 1061. The changes that Berthold made in these accounts help to explain the circumstances in which he abandoned the composition of 'Berthold I' and produced the revised text. The death of Henry III, firstly, was reported in 'Berthold I', probably very soon after the event, with brevity and in neutral language. 'While he was staying in Saxony, in Bodfeld, weakened by a constantly worsening illness, he died in the

---

23 Dieterich (1925) p. 799.

24 Berthold, *Chronicle* I, 1055, below p. 100.

25 *Ibid.*, 1055, p. 100. Berthold claimed that the conspiracy was the work of Welf's knights, without his knowledge. See Steindorff (1881) pp. 317–21; Robinson (1999) pp. 23–4. The deposition of Conrad of Bavaria had provoked Herman's denunciation of Henry III's 'acquisitiveness' and 'negligence': above p. 17 and below p. 95.

26 Berthold, *Chronicle* I, 1065, below p. 106. Cf. Herman, *Chronicle* 1049, below p. 86.

thirty-ninth year of his life, in the eighteenth year of his kingship and
the fifteenth year of his emperorship, in the tenth indiction.'[27] Berthold
was evidently more interested in the exact chronology than in the
memoria of the emperor. In 'Berthold II' the following passage is added.
'Fortified by a good conversion, by penitence and a most free confession, he wholeheartedly forgave his debtors and he restored everything
that he had not acquired fairly to those who were present. To those
who were absent, however, he arranged very carefully for the restoration of property by the empress [Agnes] and his son [Henry IV],
identifying the recipients by name. And, thus placing all his hope in
God, he died – happily, I trust! – on 5 October.'[28] Here Henry III is
restored to the status of 'the pious king' that he enjoyed in Herman's
annals for 1043–5. Berthold indeed hinted at the emperor's 'acquisitiveness', which Herman had denounced in his annal for 1053, but emphasised that Henry III had made full amends for his former offences: 'he
restored everything that he had not acquired fairly'.

Herman's attitude towards Henry III in his final annals and that of
'Berthold I' was coloured by the apprehension of the south German
nobility in the light of the deposition of Duke Conrad of Bavaria. The
rehabilitation of Henry III in 'Berthold II' reflects the high regard in
which 'Emperor Henry of pious memory' was held by the papal reform
movement in the decades following his death because of his opposition to simony.[29] The allegations of simony that were made against
the regime of Henry IV in the later 1060s and early 1070s served in
retrospect to enhance the reputation of Henry III, who had been more
correct in his ecclesiastical appointments. (A similar retrospective wave
of enthusiasm is apparent in the *Annals* of Lampert of Hersfeld. In the
light of the conduct of his successor, the reign of Henry III appeared
to Lampert to be a golden age of just kingship.)[30] A comparison of the
two reports of the death of Henry III, therefore, suggests that that
of 'Berthold I' was composed only a few years after Herman's death,
when the chronicler's attitude was still that of his master. The account
in 'Berthold II', however, belongs to the period of the investigations
of simony in the German kingdom between 1069 and 1075, with their

27 Berthold, *Chronicle* I, 1056, below p. 101.

28 Berthold, *Chronicle* II, 1056, below pp. 113–14.

29 Gregory VII, *Register* II.13, p. 145; cf. I.9, II.44, pp. 32, 180. Cf. Peter Damian, *Letter*
    40, pp. 501–2; Humbert of Silva Candida, *Adversus simoniacos* III.7, p. 206. The reha-
    bilitation of Henry III is also apparent in the work of Bernold of St Blasien, who
    included the emperor in his necrology: Bernold, *Calendar* p. 516.

30 Struve (1969) pp. 34–9.

deleterious effects on the relations of the imperial court, the imperial Church and the reform papacy, and with a resultant nostalgia for the reforming regime of Henry III.[31]

The greatest factual divergence between 'Berthold I' and 'Berthold II' is in the reporting of the papal schism of 1061. The earlier version of the chronicle records without comment the appointment of Bishop Cadalus of Parma as Pope 'Honorius II' at the council of Basel (26 October). Henry IV 'held a general assembly in Basel, where he ... was called patrician of the Romans. Then with the common consent of them all he elected the bishop of Parma as supreme pontiff of the Roman church.' On 1 October, however, Bishop Anselm I of Lucca had been elected Pope Alexander II by the cardinal bishops in Rome. 'Berthold I' reports this as follows. 'While this was happening, Bishop Anselm of Lucca usurped the apostolic see for himself with the support of certain Romans.'[32] When he wrote this annal, therefore, Berthold assumed that Cadalus of Parma was the lawful pope, Anselm of Lucca the usurper. At that time he knew nothing of the Papal Election Decree of 1059, reserving the election of the pope to the cardinals, and accepted the right of Henry IV as patrician of the Romans to preside over the election of the pope.[33] The annal for 1061 in 'Berthold I' represents the initial response to the papal schism of a chronicler accustomed to the usages of the 'German papacy' of 1046–57. It may be compared with the report of Lampert of Hersfeld, who mentioned only the candidature of Cadalus: on the death of Nicholas II 'the bishop of Parma was put in his place by the election of the king and of certain princes'.[34] Subsequently acknowledging that by 1064 Alexander II had emerged as the lawful pope, Lampert represented this turn of events as a graceful concession by the imperial court to Roman opinion.[35]

The annal for 1064 in 'Berthold I' refers to the synod of Mantua, without mentioning that it was in this assembly that the German government recognised Alexander II as pope and abandoned its support for Cadalus

---

31 Schieffer (1972) pp. 19–60.

32 Berthold, *Chronicle* I, 1061, below p. 104.

33 The schism of 1061: Meyer von Knonau (1890) pp. 216–17, 223–9; Schmidt (1977) pp. 104–14, 125–31; Robinson (1999) pp. 41–3, 48–51. The office of patrician (the title that Henry III acquired after his imperial coronation, by virtue of which he had appointed three popes): Vollrath (1974) pp. 11–44; Robinson (1999) p. 36; Robinson (2004a) pp. 5–6, 56–8.

34 Lampert, *Annales* 1063, p. 81.

35 *Ibid.*, 1064, pp. 91–2.

of Parma.[36] Nowhere in 'Berthold I' is Alexander identified as the legiti-mate pope. Berthold's annal for 1061 was indeed too outspoken to allow him to make a simple adjustment like that of Lampert of Hersfeld's annal for 1064. The revised version of Berthold's annal contains much infor-mation that had not been available to him at the time of his first attempt. 'On 26 October Bishop Cadalus of Parma was elected pope by an act of simony, since (it is said) many bribes were given to certain persons. He was called Honorius, but he was destined never to possess the papacy. Twenty-seven days before his appointment, however, the bishop of Lucca, named Anselm, was ordained as the 157th pope by the Normans and by certain Romans and was called Alexander. He reigned for twelve years.'[37] The date of the revision is indicated by this statement that Alex-ander was pope for twelve years. Later in the same annal Berthold gave a brief account of Alexander's reforming legislation, including his prohi-bition of laymen from hearing the masses of unchaste clergy, adding: 'The author of this regulation was principally Hildebrand, who was at that time archdeacon of the Roman church.' The phrase 'at that time' confirms that this annal of 'Berthold II' was written after Hildebrand had become Pope Gregory VII. By this time the account of the schism of 1061 in 'Berthold I' must have seemed inaccurate and insufficient to its author, not least because of the debt that his abbey now owed to that pope whom he had erroneously described as a usurper.

Between the composition of the annal for 1061 in 'Berthold I' (probably soon after the event) and that of the revised annal (some time after the accession of Gregory VII in 1073) Reichenau had suffered a prolonged crisis, in which it had sought the help of Pope Alexander II. This crisis is recorded in four short entries in 'Berthold II'. In 1069 'Abbot Udalric of Reichenau died. In his place a certain Meginward of Hildesheim was with difficulty appointed abbot by the king, for the appointment was simoniacal and the brethren rebelled against him.' In 1070 'Meginward, who was unwilling to tolerate the exactions and commands and services imposed on him by the king, voluntarily gave up the office of abbot of Reichenau.' In 1071 'a certain Rupert, an abbot in Bamberg, acquired the office of abbot of Reichenau by means of simony, having given the king much gold. He was afterwards excommunicated and expelled.' The crisis was eventually resolved in 1073. 'After Rupert, already excom-municated by the pope [Alexander II], had likewise been expelled by the king, as befitted a sacrilegious pupil of Simon, at length Ekkehard,

36 Berthold, *Chronicle* I, 1064, below p. 105.
37 Berthold, *Chronicle* II, 1061, below pp. 116–17.

one of the brethren of Reichenau and elected by them, was made abbot of Reichenau.'[38] It is only from the account of Lampert of Hersfeld that we learn more details of the resistance of the monks and of the advocate of Reichenau to Abbot Rupert and of the coercive measures taken by Henry IV against the monks.[39]

Berthold did not expressly denounce the king's conduct in the case of Reichenau until his annal for 1079, in which he wrote that Henry IV 'had previously twice sold [Reichenau] in acts of simony'.[40] The theme of these earlier annals was the prevalence of simony in the empire during the late 1060s and early 1070s and the role of the pope in combating this heresy. The annal for 1067 is devoted to the case of Bishop Peter Mezzabarba of Florence, who was deposed by Pope Alexander II when he was proved guilty of simony.[41] The annals for 1069–71 contain a detailed account of the case of Bishop Carloman (Charles) of Constance, who resigned his office after being confronted with the evidence of his simony at a council held in Mainz 'at the command of Pope Alexander'.[42] 'The heresy of simony', which Herman's chronicle had reported in the context of Pope Leo IX's reforming activity and which Berthold in the first version of his chronicle had mentioned in the case of Bishop Herman of Bamberg, had become the dominant theme of 'Berthold II'. Berthold's reforming stance reflected the experience of Reichenau in 1069–71 and especially the rapprochement of Reichenau with the reform papacy. It was this rapprochement above all that prompted Berthold to revise the first version of his chronicle, which meant essentially revising his account of Alexander II's accession.

The cases of the simoniac bishop of Florence deposed by an alliance of the monks of Vallombrosa and the papacy and the simoniacal bishop of Constance forced to resign by an alliance of his cathedral clergy with Alexander II had obvious parallels with the case of the two simoniac abbots of Reichenau whom the monks had denounced to the pope. 'Berthold II' is an important witness to the adoption by a prelate's subjects of this new reforming strategy of the appeal to Rome as a means of removing the unwanted prelate.[43] In Reichenau's case the

38 *Ibid.*, 1069, 1070, 1071, 1073, pp. 123, 125, 126, 130.

39 Lampert, *Annales* 1071, p. 128.

40 Berthold, *Chronicle* II, 1079, below p. 228.

41 *Ibid.*, 1067, pp. 120–2.

42 *Ibid.*, 1069, 1070, 1071, pp. 123, 124–5, 125–6.

43 Robinson (1999) p. 119.

strategy was vindicated by the deposition of the simoniac Abbot Rupert by Alexander II in 1072 and the papal consecration of his successor, Abbot Ekkehard II (1072–88). The event brought Reichenau simultaneously into closer contact with the papacy and the new monastic reform movement in southern Germany. For Abbot Ekkehard belonged to the family of the counts of Nellenburg, who were the founders of the reformed monastery of All Saints, Schaffhausen and who (despite their kinship with Henry IV) were among the supporters of Rudolf of Rheinfelden, duke of Swabia and later anti-king (1077–80).[44] It was perhaps Ekkehard who towards the end of his abbatiate concluded the agreement of confraternity between Reichenau and the reformed monastery of St Blasien.[45] A link between Reichenau and the south German monastic reform was also provided by the advocate of Reichenau, Hezelo. He was the founder of the reformed monastery of St Georgen in the Black Forest and a member of the Swabian nobility who supported Rudolf of Rheinfelden.[46] 'Berthold II', with its enthusiasm for the reformer Abbot William of Hirsau and for the anti-king Rudolf, patron of the reformed monastery of St Blasien, provides further evidence for this shift in loyalties from the imperial monasticism of the days of Abbot Bern to the south German monastic reform of the late eleventh century and the Swabian nobility who were its patrons.

Reichenau's rapprochement with the papacy in the late eleventh century was the culmination of the process that was already beginning in 1032, when Abbot Bern received from Pope John XIX the privilege that involved him in controversy with Bishop Warmann of Constance, and in 1049, when Abbot Udalric was consecrated by Pope Leo IX in Rome.[47] A letter of Pope Gregory VII of 6 May 1074 reveals the pope's attitude towards Reichenau at the time of the papal consecration of Abbot Ekkehard II. The letter demands the restoration of the property of the abbey currently held by supporters of the excommunicated former abbot Rupert. The pope was moved to act 'since the monastery of Reichenau is connected to this holy and apostolic see by

---

44 Cowdrey (1970) pp. 202, 206–9; Schmid (1973) pp. 299–300, 302; Robinson (1999) p. 127.

45 Jakobs (1968) p. 150. This was perhaps the reason for Bernold's grudging tribute to Ekkehard II, *Chronicle* 1088, below p. 294: 'although he was not very devout, [he] nevertheless in the end – so they say – underwent a praiseworthy conversion'.

46 Cf. Bernold, *Chronicle* 1088, below p. 292: he ended his life as a monk of St Georgen. See Jakobs (1968) pp. 228–30. He was perhaps the same advocate who had resisted the simoniac Abbot Rupert: Lampert, *Annales* 1071, p. 128.

47 Herman, *Chronicle* 1032, 1049, below pp. 67, 85–6.

a direct and indivisible line'.[48] A papal letter of 13 March 1075 reveals that Ekkehard was now involved in a conflict with Bishop Otto of Constance. The letter commands the bishop to bring the dispute to neutral arbitration or to accompany the abbot to Rome in time for the next autumn synod.[49] Neither the cause nor the result of the conflict is known. 'Berthold II' is, however, very well informed about events in Rome in late 1075 and early 1076, which suggests that a delegation from Reichenau attended the autumn synod.[50] Berthold's annal for 1075 contains a lengthy account of the visit of Abbot William of Hirsau to Rome that autumn, seeking papal protection for his monastery. His encounter with Gregory VII initiated his break with the traditional imperial monasticism in which he had been trained and the establishment of Hirsau as the most influential centre of monastic reform in southern Germany.[51]

Ekkehard II did not proceed so far, but while he never abandoned the monastic 'customs' of Reichenau, he certainly discarded the political outlook of imperial monasticism. Like William of Hirsau, Ekkehard became a supporter of the anti-king Rudolf, an alliance in keeping with the sympathies of his family, the counts of Nellenburg. 'Abbot Ekkehard of Reichenau stood steadfastly with the false king Rudolf,' wrote the hostile annalist of St Gallen.[52] In consequence Ekkehard was taken prisoner by adherents of Henry IV while en route for Rome in 1079 and the king installed in Reichenau the royalist Abbot Udalric III of St Gallen.[53] Gregory VII complained of his treatment: 'one who has been consecrated by me in the apostolic see ought not to be judged by any other person. It was certainly a grave presumption to lay hands on one who was protected by so great a privilege.'[54] Ekkehard evidently fulfilled his obligations to the Roman church. Early in 1079 he was employed as a papal legate in company with the loyal Gregorian bishops Altman of Passau and Herman of Metz.[55] Ekkehard's willingness to accept the protection of the apostolic see and its attendant obligations

48 Gregory VII, *Register* I.82, p. 117.

49 *Ibid.*, II.60, pp. 214–15.

50 Berthold, *Chronicle* II, 1075, 1076, below pp. 138–46.

51 Büttner (1966) pp. 321–38; Cowdrey (1970) pp. 197–209. Tangl (1967) p. 516 suggested that Berthold himself accompanied William to Rome in autumn 1075.

52 *Casuum sancti Galli continuatio* II.7, p. 156.

53 Berthold, *Chronicle* II, 1079, below p. 224.

54 Gregory VII, *Epistolae Vagantes* 31, p. 82 (to the papal legates in Germany).

55 *Ibid.*, 26, p. 68 and n. 6.

must be explained by the attitude of his diocesan, Otto of Constance, who was assertive, confident of the king's support, and hostile towards the Gregorian reform programme and towards Reichenau.[56] Gregory VII's way of dealing with recalcitrant bishops was to build up centres of reform and resistance within their dioceses[57] and this was presumably the role that he intended Reichenau to play in the diocese of Constance. ('Berthold II' accordingly presents a hostile view of Otto of Constance: he was afflicted by lameness as a punishment for his opposition to the pope, 'which we note down as a miracle of fitting divine vengeance'.)[58]

The alliance between Reichenau and the papacy was mutually advantageous as long as there was an anti-Gregorian bishop of Constance. The situation changed radically, however, with the election of the Gregorian Gebhard III as bishop of Constance in 1084. It now became clear that the abbot of Reichenau had used the opportunity of the papal excommunication and deposition of Otto of Constance to lay claim to episcopal authority on the island of Reichenau. This claim was now contested by a bishop of Constance who, soon to become a permanent papal legate and the leader of the Gregorian party in southern Germany, enjoyed the complete confidence of the pope.[59] The chronicle of Bernold of St Blasien (in which Gebhard III of Constance is portrayed as a hero of the papal party's resistance to Henry IV) records the victory of the bishop in this conflict. In the council of Piacenza (March 1095) Pope Urban II decided the dispute in favour of Gebhard against Ekkehard's successor, Udalric II (1088–1122).[60]

This deterioration of the relationship of Reichenau and the papacy occurred, however, only after Berthold had composed his chronicles and 'Berthold I' and 'Berthold II' reveal the same growing enthusiasm for the reform papacy that is already visible in Herman's annals for 1049–54. 'Berthold I' remembers Pope Leo IX as 'blessed' and records the reforming synod of Pope Victor II in Florence (June 1055), in which 'many errors were corrected'. It contains precise accounts of the election of Pope Stephen IX, of the election of Benedict X 'contrary to the canons' and of the substitution of Pope Nicholas II.[61] 'Berthold II'

---

56 Maurer (1991) pp. 170–3.
57 Robinson (2004b) pp. 328–33.
58 Berthold, *Chronicle* II, 1077, below p. 169.
59 Maurer (1991) pp. 183–4; Robinson (1999) pp. 245, 275, 284, 286, 292–3, 299–300.
60 Bernold, *Chronicle* 1095, below p. 326.
61 Berthold, *Chronicle* I, 1057, 1055, 1057, 1058, pp. 102, 99, 102.

is dominated by papal history. Berthold's detailed knowledge of the reforming synods of Gregory VII suggests the frequent presence of Reichenau monks in Rome, while Berthold's extensive quotations from papal letters and synodal decrees indicates that Reichenau was a centre for the copying and dissemination of papal propaganda.

Gregory VII's reforms and especially his handling of relations with King Henry IV and the opposition faction of princes in Germany constitute the largest single topic in 'Berthold II'.[62] Berthold's report of the Roman synod of Lent 1075 derives from Gregory VII's letter of that year to Bishop Otto of Constance, the widely circulated letter that Bernold of St Blasien also quoted in his pro-papal polemic, the *Apologeticus*.[63] Berthold's account of the relations of king and pope from late 1075 to Gregory's excommunication of Henry IV in February 1076 is taken often verbatim from the papal letter of summer 1076 justifying the excommunication to the faithful in the German kingdom.[64] Berthold's lengthy account of the absolution of Henry IV by Gregory VII at Canossa in January 1077 quotes extracts from 'the oath of Henry, king of the Germans' sworn at Canossa and appended by Gregory VII to his letter reporting the absolution to the German princes (late January 1077).[65] Berthold's annal for 1078 consists almost exclusively of descriptions of the Lenten and autumn synods in Rome, that of the autumn synod including the synodal protocols in full. Berthold's text of the protocols is of particular interest because it appears in a version earlier than that found in the papal register of Gregory VII. Berthold's version does not include the corrections added above the line by the scribe who copied this text into the Register. Berthold's chronicle, therefore, offers important evidence for the study of the transmission of the synodal protocols. It is possible that Berthold obtained the text (and his other Gregorian materials) through visits to Rome made by his abbot or by monks of Reichenau.[66] The availability of this material to the chronicler is clear evidence of the rapprochement of Reichenau and the papacy during Ekkehard II's abbatiate, as are the passages in defence of papal

---

62 The 'deposition faction' of German princes: Robinson (1999) pp. 153–7.

63 Berthold, *Chronicle* II, 1075, below pp. 132–3. Cf. Gregory VII, *Epistolae Vagantes* 8, pp. 16–18; Bernold, *Apologeticus* c. 1, pp. 60–1. See below pp. 45, 254.

64 Berthold, *Chronicle* II, 1075, pp. 138–40; 1076, pp. 143, 145. Cf. Gregory VII, *Epistolae Vagantes* 14, pp. 32–41.

65 Berthold, *Chronicle* II, 1077, below p. 161. Cf. Gregory VII, *Register* IV.12a, pp. 314–15.

66 Berthold, *Chronicle* II, 1078, below pp. 217–19. Cf. *Register* VI.5b, pp. 402–6. See E. Caspar's variant apparatus, *ibid.*, pp. 403–6 nn. o–y; Hoffmann (1976) p. 115.

authority that Berthold interpolated in the second version of his chronicle.

The canonical 'authorities' quoted in these digressions are closely related to the *Collection in 74 titles*, a canon law collection compiled to defend the aspirations of the reform papacy at some date before 1076. Berthold had access to a copy of this collection that also contained 'the Swabian appendix' of canons, attributed to Bernold of St Blasien.[67] Bernold's earliest polemic, his *Apologeticus*, probably composed in mid-1075, provided Berthold with the material for the digression in his annal for 1076 on the impossibility of reversing the judgements of the apostolic see.[68] It is possible that all the source materials for the polemical digressions in 'Berthold II' derive from the contemporary research in the cathedral library of Constance, which Johanne Autenrieth has particularly linked with the writings of Bernold of St Blasien.[69] This conclusion is strongly suggested by the longest of Berthold's digressions, the historical justification of the papal deposition of Henry IV in the annal for 1077, consisting of seven case-studies (*exempla*) of depositions of kings ranging from the fourth to the ninth century.[70] All seven of the *exempla* recur in the works of 'the south German Gregorian circle', that is, the group of polemicists who drew on the research in the library of Constance in the later eleventh century and used it in support of the Gregorian papacy.[71] Berthold's source for this digression was presumably a catalogue of excommunicated and deposed kings, no longer extant, compiled in the cathedral library of Constance (perhaps by Bernold) and disseminated by the various 'south German Gregorian' authors who wrote in defence of Gregory VII's sentence on Henry IV. The chronicler Berthold was clearly a member of 'the south German Gregorian circle', with access to their canonical and historical 'authorities'.

Pope Gregory VII himself is presented in 'Berthold II' in the hagiographical manner universally used in Gregorian sources, in particular

---

67 Berthold, *Chronicle* II, 1076, pp. 145, 149; 1077, p. 169. The 'Swabian appendix' see below p. 49.

68 Berthold, *Chronicle* II, 1076, p. 149. Cf. Bernold, *Apologeticus* c. 22–3, pp. 86–7. See below p. 45.

69 Autenrieth (1956) pp. 122–34. See below p. 49.

70 Berthold, *Chronicle* II, 1077, below pp. 176–7 and nn. 416–23.

71 The 'south German Gregorian circle', i.e. Bernold of St Blasien, his former master, Bernard of Hildesheim, Manegold of Lautenbach, Archbishop Gebhard of Salzburg, the anonymous polemicist of Hirsau and the anonymous compiler of the sentence collection of Göttweig MS 56: Robinson (1978b) pp. 101–22.

as the patient victim of the deceptions of Henry IV and the violence
of Cencius, son of the Roman prefect Stephen.[72] Berthold provided
a fictionalised account of Hildebrand's election to the papacy, which
applies to the papal election of April 1073 the miraculous events of the
election of Pope Gregory I in 590. The account was later borrowed by
Bernold of St Blasien in his chronicle and by the polemicist Manegold
of Lautenbach.[73] Berthold reported a series of miraculous punishments
visited on the enemies of Gregory VII, as evidence of the efficacy of
papal excommunications. The simoniac Bishop Henry of Speyer was
struck down by a fatal illness 'on the same day and at the same hour'
as he was excommunicated and deposed by the Roman synod of Lent
1075, 'so that through this miracle the strength and truth of the words
of God were proved: *whatsoever you will bind on earth, shall be bound in
heaven* (Matthew 16:19)'. Bernold of St Blasien also used this anecdote in
his chronicle and in one of his early polemics.[74] A similar fate overtook
Bishop William of Utrecht, a loyal supporter of Henry IV, soon after
the church of St Peter in Utrecht, 'suffering the contempt of God and
St Peter, was miraculously consumed by an avenging fire'.[75] Patriarch
Sigehard of Aquileia, because of his sycophantic devotion to the king,
went mad, 'an object of fear to all and a lesson to liars and renegades',
prompting Berthold's exclamation, 'O how much to be feared is the Lord
God of vengeance!'[76] When in July 1077 Bishop Embriko of Augsburg
wished to prove the legitimacy of Henry IV's royal title by submitting
to the ordeal of the holy wafer, he was immediately 'seized by a deadly
affliction and … wretchedly tormented by the just judgement of God'.
On this occasion Gregory VII, 'who was no false prophet', was vouch-
safed advance information of the bishop's fate.[77]

With equal partisanship Berthold recorded the evidence of the sanctity
of the pope's allies. It is to Berthold's annal for 1077 that we owe the

---

72 See, for example, the similar presentation by Gregory VII's biographers, Bonizo
   of Sutri and Paul of Bernried (whose principal source was 'Berthold II'): Robinson
   (2004a) pp. 60–3, 79–81.

73 Berthold, *Chronicle* II, 1073, below p. 128. Cf. John the Deacon, *Vita Gregorii Magni*
   I.44, *MPL* 75, col. 81B. The same account appears in Bernold, *Chronicle* 1073, below
   p. 253 and Manegold, *Ad Gebehardum* c. 14, pp. 336–7. See Robinson (1978a) pp. 31–9;
   Cowdrey (1998) p. 73.

74 Berthold, *Chronicle* II, 1075, below pp. 133–4. Cf. Bernold, *Chronicle* 1075, below p. 254
   and *De incontinentia sacerdotum* V, p. 26.

75 Berthold, *Chronicle* II, 1076, below p. 147. Cf. Bernold, *Chronicle* 1076, below p. 256.

76 Berthold, *Chronicle* II, 1077, below p. 174.

77 *Ibid.*, 1077, p. 175. Cf. Bernold, *Chronicle* 1077, below p. 261.

information that Gregory VII performed the canonisation of the Gregorian heroes Herlembald, leader of the Milanese Patarini and the Roman prefect Cencius, son of John Tiniosus. Berthold portrayed Cencius, 'a perfect zealot', concerned 'to practise Christian knighthood', and Herlembald, 'a most skilful athlete of God following the secular way of life', as martyrs for the catholic faith. The miracles at their tombs demonstrated divine approval for their military struggle for reform.[78] Cardinal bishop Peter of Albano, hero of the campaign against simony and papal legate in Germany, was 'full of faith and truth'. Abbot Bernard of St Victor in Marseilles, another papal legate in Germany, 'a man of great sanctity, wisdom, piety and charity', suffered 'numerous injuries through persecution for righteousness's sake' at the hands of Henry IV's followers.[79] The chronicler's attitude was accurately summed up by Georgine Tangl: 'as a rigid Gregorian, fanatically one-sided in his judgement, he loved sharp contrasts in black and white'.[80]

In his reporting of secular politics Berthold was best informed about events in southern Germany. He was unable, for example, to provide place-names or dates for the important battles of Homburg (1075), Mellrichstadt (1078) and Flarchheim (1080). The assembly of princes in Tribur in October 1076 was placed by Berthold in Magdeburg.[81] His local patriotism is revealed in his use of the expression 'our men', 'our compatriots' or simply of the first person plural to denote the Swabians, 'our land' or 'our territory' for Swabia. 'Our cathedral' denotes Constance.[82] Berthold was even prepared to concede that the battle of Homburg (9 June 1075) was a victory for the hated Henry IV ('although a bloody victory') because it was won for him by 'our compatriots'. The crucial first attack was made by the duke of Swabia and his knights, 'as the Swabian law requires'.[83] Rudolf of Rheinfelden, duke of Swabia is a focus of interest in 'Berthold II' even before his elevation as anti-king makes him the principal secular figure in the chronicle. His allies, Duke Welf IV of Bavaria and Berthold I of Zähringen, duke of Carinthia are also given great prominence. (Duke Berthold gains added lustre in the annal

78 Berthold, *Chronicle* II, 1077, p. 196.

79 *Ibid.*, 1079, pp. 237, 239.

80 Tangl (1967) p. 518.

81 Berthold, *Chronicle* II, 1076, below p. 152. Meyer von Knonau (1894) p. 727 n. 178: Berthold meant to refer to Madenburg on the Rhine near Speyer, perhaps the site of a preliminary meeting before the main assembly.

82 See Robinson (1980) p. 129 and n. 61.

83 Berthold, *Chronicle* II, 1075, below p. 135 and n. 224.

for 1073 from the monastic profession of his son, Margrave Herman I of Baden, 'who already as a young man strove for the perfection of the Gospels' and died as a monk of Cluny.)[84] The annal for 1069, recording the death of Godfrey 'the Bearded' of Verdun, duke in Lotharingia and margrave of Tuscany, is the occasion for a celebration of his virtues as a prince 'entirely outstanding among secular men'. Mindful of the negative judgement of Godfrey in Herman's chronicle, Berthold wrote that 'he became a new man by means of penitence so perfect … that there is no reason to doubt that he happily departed from here to citizenship of the court of highest heaven'.[85] The longest and most elaborate obituary in the chronicle is that, in the annal for 1077, of Empress Agnes. In a eulogy strongly influenced by the writings of Jerome on holy widowhood Agnes is presented as a model of Christian conduct.[86]

'Berthold II' ranges furthest from the horizon of 'our territory', the diocese of Constance and the duchy of Swabia, in its reporting of ecclesiastical history. Like its model, Herman's chronicle, 'Berthold II' records wherever possible the episcopal succession in the German kingdom. The author obtained accurate information about the succession in the archbishoprics of Mainz (1060), Cologne (1056, 1075, 1078), Trier (1066), Magdeburg (1063, 1079), Hamburg-Bremen (1072) and Besançon (1066), in the bishoprics of Augsburg (1063, 1077), Bamberg (1065, 1075), Chur (1070, 1078/9), Hildesheim (1079), Constance (1069, 1071), Liège (1075), Paderborn (1076), Passau (1065), Regensburg (1061), Speyer (1055, 1060, 1067, 1075) and Utrecht (1076). Vaguer is his information about Naumburg (1079) and outside the kingdom, Aquileia (1077) and Milan (1072). His interest in religious houses is narrower: Fulda (1059) and St Gallen (1077) are each mentioned only once but particular attention is paid to the reform of Hirsau.[87] Of the churchmen of the German kingdom, Archbishop Siegfried of Mainz is the most frequently mentioned, culminating in his role in the election and consecration of the anti-king Rudolf (1077).[88] Next in prominence is Bishop Altman of Passau, notably as papal legate and as a member of the entourage of the anti-king. The bishops Adalbero of Würzburg and Adalbert of Worms are commended for their opposition to Henry IV. In the annal for 1075 Archbishop Anno of Cologne is given an elaborate obituary as a 'faithful and wise servant

---

84 *Ibid.*, 1073, p. 128.

85 *Ibid.*, 1069, pp. 123–4. See above p. 16.

86 Berthold, *Chronicle* II, 1077, below pp. 191–4.

87 *Ibid.*, 1075, pp. 141–2.

88 *Ibid.*, 1077, p. 167.

of Jesus Christ', who 'became renowned as a most saintly man through the many miracles' that occurred at his grave in Siegburg.[89]

The second version of Berthold's work retains the chronicle format adopted in the later annals of Herman's chronicle. Each annal begins with the formula 'the king celebrated Christmas ...'. The royal itinerary provides the framework of each annal and the narrative of the king's proceedings is a principal topic in most of the annals. The Christmas festivities of Henry IV comprise the first entry in each of the annals 1056–77. From 1076, however, the statement of the place where Henry celebrated Christmas is made the occasion for polemic. 'King Henry spent Christmas in Goslar, although the Saxons were greatly enraged against him and not entirely faithful to him, because in subduing them to his royal authority he had shown such savage and unjust rage.'[90] In the annal for 1077: 'The king celebrated Christmas as best he could in Besançon in Burgundy, remaining there scarcely one day.'[91] In 1078 the Christmas celebrations of the anti-king Rudolf comprise the first entry: 'King Rudolf celebrated Christmas with the greatest splendour in Goslar in Saxony with very many multitudes of the Saxon people.' This is followed by a contrasting account of his enemy's celebrations: 'King Henry, however, after spending only two days somehow or other in Regensburg with little festivity ...'.[92] Inconsistently, in 1079 the order is reversed. The first entry begins: 'King Henry celebrated Christmas in Mainz with little appearance of splendour' and then follows Henry IV's itinerary into Lent. Turning then to Rudolf, the chronicle records that he 'most joyfully celebrated Christmas in ...'.[93] Characteristically in this entry Berthold showed himself less well informed about the movements of the anti-king whom he regarded as the lawful ruler than he was about the Salian king who was the object of his bitterest polemic. In 1080 the first entry is: 'King Rudolf most solemnly celebrated Christmas with all the splendour and magnificence of a king in ...'. This is followed by a reference to Henry IV: 'He remained during these days in Mainz, not with the dignity of a king but living as best he could.'[94] Similarly the Easter and Whitsun festivities of the king (from 1077, of the two

89 *Ibid.*, 1075, p. 138.

90 *Ibid.*, 1076, p. 142. In Berthold's chronicles, as in Herman's, the year begins on Christmas day. The Christmas mentioned here was 25 December 1075.

91 Berthold, *Chronicle* II, 1077, below p. 157.

92 *Ibid.*, 1078, p. 198.

93 *Ibid.*, 1079, pp. 219, 221.

94 *Ibid.*, 1080, pp. 239–40.

kings) are recorded and sometimes also the celebration of the feast of the Purification and the lesser festivals. The chronicle of the 'zealous Gregorian' Berthold is in fact a true 'imperial chronicle', adhering even more rigidly than Herman's chronicle to a structure based on the royal itinerary. In the interstices of these liturgical processions through the kingdom appear the king's military adventures, reported in increasing detail: interventions in the Arpad dynastic struggles in Hungary (1059, 1060, 1063, 1074), campaigns against the rebel Saxons (1071, 1073–5), the civil war between the two kings (1077–80).

This thoroughly conservative format serves as a framework for Berthold's political ideas. From the annal for 1072 onwards Berthold used the conflicts of king and princes, and from 1077 of the two kings, to exemplify his theories of righteous kingship and tyranny. The reader is already made aware of Berthold's opinion of Henry IV at the end of the annal for 1056, where appears the subtitle: 'Henry IV, son of Henry, reigned for twenty years.'[95] Berthold considered, therefore, that Henry IV's reign ended in 1076, when he was deposed and excommunicated by Pope Gregory VII in the Lenten synod in Rome. The criticism of Henry IV begins in the annal for 1068 with an apparent reference to the king's attempt to dissolve his marriage with Bertha of Turin in that year. 'Led astray by the folly of his youth, he was so forgetful of his lawful wife and was widely rumoured to be implicated in such abominable offences that his princes even attempted to deprive him of the kingship.'[96] The criticism is resumed in the annals for 1072–3 in the context of the king's policy of recovering royal property. 'The king ... unjustly seized for himself very many fortifications and thus aroused the minds of many men against himself.' 'The whole of Thuringia and Saxony rebelled against King Henry because of the fortifications ... and many other things that the king had done insolently and unadvisedly in their territory against the will of that people.'[97] From the moment of the papal rebuke for his conduct towards the Church, issued in December 1075, Henry IV is consistently depicted as an 'insane and treacherous' tyrant, characterised by 'savage and unjust rage', arbitrary in his conduct towards his vassals and falsehearted in his relations with the pope before and after the reconciliation at Canossa.[98] The tyrant unleashed against his kingdom the 'heathen madness' of his Bohemian vassals and

95 *Ibid.*, 1056, p. 114.
96 *Ibid.*, 1068, p. 122.
97 *Ibid.*, 1072, 1073, pp. 127, 129.
98 *Ibid.*, 1076, pp. 139, 140, 143, 156–7, 163.

allowed it to be destroyed by an army drawn from 'the worst and most inhuman robbers'.[99] Henry himself showed cowardice in battle, being the first to leave the field ('without delay the king was the first to flee in a shameful manner').[100] In this case Berthold's polemical falsification of events is made clear by the parallel sources.[101]

By contrast the anti-king Rudolf is represented as a 'just king'. He was elected king at Forchheim in March 1077 against his will ('unwilling and compelled to accept' the kingship) – a singular mark of merit in a king as in a bishop – and accepted by princes and people as 'the just king, ruler and defender of the whole kingdom'.[102] Rudolf's conduct in 'his land of Saxony' – Berthold thought of him as ruling an independent kingdom of Saxony[103] – is contrasted with the earlier proceedings of Henry IV. 'Their former ruler always treated them with savagery according to his will and raged against them with plundering, pillage and all manner of oppression, while this ruler judged justly and with the severity of justice restored what was crooked and made it straight.'[104] Obedient to the instructions of the pope in all things, Rudolf strove to negotiate the peace in Germany earnestly desired by Gregory VII and his legates, only to be treacherously deceived again and again by Henry. He desired to encounter his rival 'with the Lord God deciding between them, either in single combat or ... in a full-scale battle'.[105]

Characteristic of the 'royal theology' that governed his interpretation of political events is Berthold's conception of the weather as an indicator of 'divine judgement' on the claims of the rival kings. The unprecedentedly harsh winter ('a forecast and a sign of future evils') beginning in November 1076 began to recede only with the election of the anti-king at Forchheim.[106] A similar instance was the snowstorm during the battle of Flarchheim in January 1080, which 'is believed to have happened as a divine judgement', ensuring the defeat of Henry IV.[107] The political narrative in the chronicle is moulded, therefore, by

99 *Ibid.*, 1077, p. 173; 1078, p. 214.

100 *Ibid.*, 1078, p. 212 (Mellrichstadt). Cf. 1080, p. 242 (Flarchheim).

101 Robinson (1999) pp. 348–9.

102 Berthold, *Chronicle* II, 1077, below p. 167.

103 *Ibid.*, 1079, p. 237 and n. 651.

104 *Ibid.*, 1077, p. 181.

105 *Ibid.*, 1077, p. 185.

106 *Ibid.*, 1076, p. 155.

107 *Ibid.*, 1080, p. 242.

thoroughly traditional ideas of kingship, the principal source of which Berthold made clear in the longest of the polemical digressions that he included in his text. This is Isidore of Seville's definition of kingship and tyranny (the same text that Abbot Bern had quoted to Henry III in his letter of 1043/4). Berthold's quotations from Isidore's definitions of kingship and tyranny summarise the reasons why the royal title should be denied to Henry IV and given to Rudolf. 'The title of king is, therefore, retained by doing right and is otherwise lost: hence derives this old maxim: "You will be a king if you do right; if you do not do so, you will not be [a king]."'[108] Berthold, therefore, wrote the second version of his chronicle as a Gregorian polemicist, dedicated to the cause of the papal anti-king, in a bombastic and exaggerated style (which is particularly difficult to translate).[109]

The first critical edition of Berthold's chronicle was that in 1844 of G.H. Pertz in *Monumenta Germaniae Historica, Scriptores* 5, 264–326, in which 'Berthold I' and 'Berthold II' are conflated into a single text. In 1881 Georg Waitz published a separate edition of 'Berthold I' in *Monumenta Germaniae Historica, Scriptores* 13, 730–2. The two versions of the chronicle have recently been edited by I.S. Robinson in *Monumenta Germaniae Historica, Scriptores rerum germanicarum, nova series* 14 (Hanover, 2003).

The chronicle of Bernold of St Blasien

The manuscript Munich, Bayerische Staatsbibliothek Clm 432 contains a continuation of Herman's chronicle that presents none of the problems of authorship presented by the two versions of Berthold's continuation. For this is the autograph of Bernold, successively a member of the cathedral clergy of Constance, a monk of St Blasien and finally a monk of All Saints, Schaffhausen. Bernold's highly individual and recognisable hand has been described definitively by Johanne Autenrieth.[1] Clm 432 alone contains the full text of the chronicle. On folio 12^v appears the title (in a hand later than that of Bernold): 'These are the chronicles of Bernold, which he composed in the monastery of the Lord Saviour,' that is, in All Saints, Schaffhausen, where Bernold spent the last decade of his life. Five other manuscripts present the chronicle with varying

---

108 *Ibid.*, 1077, p. 178. Cf. Isidore, *Etymologiae* 9.3.4–18. See above p. 17.
109 Berthold's Latin: Prinz (1974) pp. 488–504.
 1 Autenrieth (1956) pp. 24–6; Robinson, introduction, *Die Chroniken Bertholds und Bernolds* pp. 84–5.

degrees of completeness. Additionally the printed edition of the Basel mathematician Christian Wurstisen (Urstisius) preserves the text of the manuscript of Bernold's chronicle from St Georgen in the Black Forest, lost in a fire in St Blasien in 1768.[2]

Bernold of St Blasius – also known as Bernold of Constance – chronicler, canonist, liturgist, polemicist and one of the most important writers of the eleventh century, has long been the subject of systematic study by historians.[3] A single biographical reference to Bernold survives independently of his own writings. The record of benefactions of the abbey of All Saints, Schaffhausen (which survives in a thirteenth-century German translation) notes the arrival in the abbey of 'an outstandingly good monk of the monastery of St Blasien, who was called Bernold', adding that 'he had there [St Blasien] been informed by God that he should end his days here in Schaffhausen'.[4] It is to Schaffhausen tradition that we owe the information that Bernold died on 16 September (1100).[5] This date fits in with our only other indication of the date of his death: the last datable entry in the final annal of Bernold's chronicle is the death of Bishop Otto of Strasbourg on 3 August 1100.[6] The twelfth-century bibliographer of Prüfening included Bernold in his catalogue of authors – identifying him simply as 'Bernold, the priest, a learned and catholic man' – with an almost complete list of his writings. The author, however, must have compiled this entry from the Bernoldine manuscripts available to him and possessed no independent information.[7]

It is generally assumed that Bernold was Swabian, although there is no certain corroboration of this assumption.[8] The suggestion that he was

2 Christianus Urstisius, *Germaniae historicorum illustrium, quorum plerique ab Heinrico IIII Imperatore usque ad annum Christi M.CCCC* (Frankfurt, 1585) p. 229 (St Georgen manuscript), pp. 341–78 (Bernold's chronicle). See Robinson, introduction, *Die Chroniken Bertholds und Bernolds* pp. 120–3.

3 For a survey of Bernoldine studies, beginning with the first monograph on Bernold by Abbot Martin Gerbert of St Blasien (1792), see Robinson (1989) pp. 155–70.

4 Cited by Robinson, introduction, *Die Chroniken Bertholds und Bernolds* p. 102.

5 D. Stöckly and D. Jasper, introduction to Bernold, *De excommunicatis vitandis* p. 2 n. 6.

6 Bernold, *Chronicle* 1100, below p. 337. Bernold's chronicle does not record the death of the antipope 'Clement III' on 8 September 1100.

7 Wolfger (?), *De scriptoribus* c. 101, pp. 89–90. Honorius Augustodunensis, *De scriptoribus ecclesiasticis* IV.13, *MPL* 172, col. 231A, knew him only as the author of the liturgical treatise *Micrologus*: 'Bernold, priest of the church of Constance, composed a Roman *ordo* under Henry IV.'

8 The single appearance of his mother tongue in his writings (Bernold, *De incontinentia sacerdotum* V, p. 26) is insufficient to identify the particular region of his origin.

born *ca.* 1050 is based principally on a reference in Bernold's polemic, the *Apologeticus*, to Pope Leo IX, who died in 1054, as 'almost bordering on our own time'.[9] In his correspondence of 1075 with the priest Alboin on the subject of clerical marriage, the latter called Bernold 'a beginner' (*tyro*) and referred to his 'youth, too elevated before its time'; while in a letter of 1076 his former master, Bernard of Hildesheim, addressed him as 'Bernold, blooming little flower of longed-for genius'.[10] Alboin's hostile response to Bernold's condemnation of clerical marriage in their correspondence of 1075 contains a further piece of biographical evidence: 'it is certain that you were born of this same sin, to use the language of your own sect'.[11] That is, Bernold was the child of a clerical marriage. This riposte recalls the claim of Bernard of Hildesheim in 1076 that clerical marriage was so strongly entrenched in the diocese of Constance that in the previous year a diocesan synod had rejected the synodal decree of Pope Gregory VII against clerical unchastity.[12]

Bernold was taught in the cathedral school of Constance by the masters Adalbert and Bernard. 'The priest Adalbert' appears as the co-author of Bernold's correspondence with Bernard (*On the condemnation of schismatics*) and he may also be 'the teacher Adalbert, skilful in deeds and words', subsequently a monk, whose death is recorded in the annal for 1079 in Bernold's chronicle.[13] Bernard, at first a master in the cathedral school in Constance, from *ca.* 1072 a master in the cathedral school in Hildesheim and finally a monk in Saxony, canonist and pro-papal polemicist, remained in correspondence with his former pupil.[14] In a letter to Bernard composed between 1084 and 1088 Bernold addressed him as 'most wise teacher' and referred to himself as 'we who in former times very often drew our hands away from your rod in the schools'.[15] 'Bernard, master of the schools in Constance, a most learned man, most ardent in the cause of St Peter' is recorded in the annal for 1088 in Bernold's chronicle. The annal for 1091 contains a lengthy résumé of

---

9 Bernold, *Apologeticus* c. 7, p. 67. See Strelau (1889) p. 3, dating his birth 'perhaps in 1054 or at least around this time'.

10 Alboin in: Bernold, *De incontinentia sacerdotum* II, pp. 11, 12; Bernard, *De damnatione scismaticorum* II, p. 47.

11 Alboin in: Bernold, *De incontinentia sacerdotum* II, p. 12.

12 Bernard, *De damnatione scismaticorum* II, p. 45.

13 Bernold, *De damnatione scismaticorum* I, p. 27; II, p. 29; III, p. 47; Bernold, *Chronicle* 1079, below p. 265. Cf. Bernold, *Calendar* p. 520: 'Adalbert, a priest and truly a monk'.

14 Erdmann (1938) pp. 203–10.

15 Bernold, *De sacramentis excommunicatorum* p. 89.

Bernard's arguments 'on the sacraments of schismatics' in his contribution to the correspondence *On the condemnation of schismatics* and in his
Book of canons against Henry IV.[16]

In his earliest writings Bernold appears as a member of the cathedral clergy in Constance, who defended papal reforming decrees and
attacked clerical marriage in defiance of his bishop Otto (1071–86). These
polemics were prompted by the letters that Pope Gregory VII sent to
the diocese of Constance in 1075, at first announcing the decrees of
the recent Roman Lenten synod and subsequently announcing Bishop
Otto's excommunication for failing to implement the reforms.[17] The
first of these papal letters is used in Bernold's chronicle as the basis of
the account of the Roman synod of 1075.[18] Bernold's relationship with
the papacy became closer in 1079, when he was present in the Lenten
synod on 11 February, an experience that has left its traces in a number
of his writings. It was here that he met the distinguished Gregorian
bishop Anselm II of Lucca, whom he later cited in his works.[19] It was
here also that he heard the condemnation of 'the writing concerning
the marriage of priests that is said to have been addressed by St Udalric
to Pope Nicholas and the chapter of Paphnutius on the same subject',
the target of his own polemical attacks in the correspondence with
Alboin on clerical marriage.[20] Bernold's chronicle alone records the
papal condemnation of these false 'authorities'. Above all, it was in the
Lenten synod of 1079 that Bernold heard the definitive condemnation of
the eucharistic doctrine of Berengar of Tours. 'In the last general synod
under Pope Gregory VII in the year of the Lord's Incarnation 1079
we ourselves were present and saw that Berengar stood in the midst
of the synod and … rejected his heresy concerning the Lord's body
in the presence of them all with an oath taken by his own hand.'[21] The
principal result of his visit to Rome was Bernold's anti-Berengarian
treatise *Concerning the truth of the Lord's body and blood*, but the experience of the Lenten synod of 1079 also prompted his preoccupation with

16 Bernold, *Chronicle* 1088, below p. 293; 1091, pp. 302–4 and nn. 423–4.
17 Gregory VII, *Epistolae Vagantes* 8–10, pp. 16–26. It is to Bernold that we owe the
   survival of these papal letters since he compiled and circulated the Gregorian letter
   collection in which they were transmitted: Robinson (1978b) pp. 65–82.
18 Bernold, *Chronicle* 1075, below p. 254.
19 Bernold, *Micrologus* c. 16, col. 988B; *Fragmentum libelli deperditi, MGH Libelli* 2, 150.
20 Bernold, *Chronicle* 1079, below p. 264. Cf. Bernold, *De incontinentia sacerdotum* I, p. 13;
   III, p. 17; V, pp. 20, 21.
21 Bernold, *De veritate corporis et sanguinis Domini* p. 380. Cf. Bernold, *Chronicle* 1079,
   below pp. 263–4 and n. 171.

Berengar's career in his chronicle. It was perhaps soon after 1079 that Bernold undertook the revision of the earlier annals of his chronicle. The earlier versions of the annals 1056 and 1060 have been erased in the autograph, Clm 432, to make way for reports of the earlier papal condemnations of Berengar's teaching, while the account of Berengar's condemnation in the Roman autumn synod of 1078 has been partially erased and rewritten.[22]

A crucial stage in the development of Bernold's relationship with the reform papacy is described in the annal for 1084. In the course of his legatine journey to Germany Cardinal bishop Odo I of Ostia (later Pope Urban II) came to Constance to appoint there as bishop, in place of the excommunicated and deposed Otto, the monk of Hirsau Gebhard of Zähringen. On the day before Gebhard's episcopal consecration, 21 December, the legate raised him to the priesthood, together with a number of other clerks, 'among whom in the same ceremony he promoted the writer of these chronicles to the priesthood and granted him by apostolic authority the power to reconcile the penitent'.[23] The moment of the elevation of Bishop Gebhard III of Constance (1084–1110), soon to be the leader of the Gregorian party in Germany,[24] was also the moment of Bernold's emergence as an important agent of the reform papacy in the kingdom, as papal penitentiary with full authority to absolve excommunicates. Bernold was to give a definition of this authority in his treatise *On priests*.[25] He was to refer to it again in his chronicle in the annal for 1094, describing how the same power was conferred by Pope Urban II on the reformer and polemicist Manegold of Lautenbach.[26] It is from Manegold's polemic addressed to Archbishop Gebhard of Salzburg *ca*. 1085 that we can gain an impression of Bernold's standing among the German papal party at this time. Bernold's *Apologeticus* was the principal source for this polemic and Manegold identified the author as 'a man of our time, whose name we do not mention but the virtuousness and gravity of whose words we regard as an index and a witness of his wisdom'.[27]

It is reasonable to suppose that from 1084 onwards Bernold was a close associate of Bishop Gebhard III of Constance. Not only did he compose

22 Bernold, *Chronicle* 1056, 1060, below pp. 246, 247; 1078, p. 263.

23 *Ibid.*, 1084, p. 278.

24 See Becker (1964) pp. 148–51; Wollasch (1987) pp. 27–53; Robinson (1999) p. 275.

25 Bernold, *De presbyteris* pp. 142–6.

26 Bernold, *Chronicle* 1094, below p. 322.

27 Manegold, *Ad Gebehardum* c. 70, p. 423.

a polemic in defence of the validity of the ordination of Gebhard in the lifetime of the deposed Bishop Otto[28] but his chronicle is also the fullest extant source of information for the activities of 'the venerable Gebhard, bishop of Constance and legate of the apostolic see' during the first sixteen years of his episcopate.[29] The first clear evidence of an association occurs in the annal for 1085 in an account of the synod held by the cardinal legate Odo of Ostia in Quedlinburg on 20 April. Bernold's extensive account is a slightly interpolated version of the synodal protocol of Quedlinburg found in the Vatican codex Reg. lat. 979. The information in the synodal protocol that Bishop Gebhard of Constance was represented at Quedlinburg by 'a legation', combined with the fact that Bernold clearly had access to the official *acta* of the synod, has prompted the suggestion that Bernold himself was Gebhard's representative in Quedlinburg.[30] Bernold's statement in the annal for 1086 that he was present at the battle of Pleichfeld between Henry IV and his enemies on 11 August prompted the suggestion that he had 'come to the camp before Würzburg with his bishop, Gebhard', a leader of the opposition to Henry IV.[31] The most convincing evidence of a close association between the chronicler and his bishop, however, is the knowledge that Bernold shows of papal letters addressed to Gebhard of Constance. The annals for 1089 and 1092 contain quotations from letters of Pope Urban II and that of 1100 shows knowledge of the letter, no longer extant, in which Paschal II confirmed Gebhard's legatine office in Germany.[32]

Bernold first identified himself as a monk of St Blasien in a treatise of *ca.* 1086: 'Bernold, last of the brethren of St Blasien'.[33] Ernst Strelau in

---

28 Bernold, *Pro Gebhardo episcopo Constantiensi epistola apologetica* pp. 108–11.

29 Bernold, *Chronicle* 1099, below p. 335. Strelau (1889) p. 9 suggested that Gebhard, while still a monk of Hirsau, was already aware of Bernold's abilities and on becoming bishop, 'drew him into a close association'. Bernold's attitude towards Hirsau: *Chronicle* 1083, below p. 272 (the Hirsau reform and especially the recruitment of 'a wonderful host of noble and prudent men'). Bernold's own contacts with Hirsau: Robinson (1978b) pp. 94, 116.

30 Bernold, *Chronicle* 1085, below pp. 279–82 and n. 276. See Strelau (1889) pp. 9, 90–1.

31 Bernold, *Chronicle* 1086, below p. 287: 'I myself ... have contrived to proclaim ... what I myself saw and heard.' See Meyer von Knonau (1903) p. 126.

32 Bernold, *Chronicle* 1089, 1092, 1100, below pp. 295–6 and n. 373, 307–8 and n. 452, 336 and n. 628.

33 Bernold, *Apologeticae rationes* p. 95. Strelau (1889) pp. 10–11 noted that the adjective 'last' is not used in a chronological sense, i.e. 'the most recent of the brethren to enter St Blasien', but in a self-deprecatory rhetorical sense, analogous to Bernold's descriptions of himself as 'priest only in name, not in his conduct' (*MGH Libelli* 2, 89, 104, 107, 109, 112, 142, 150) and 'an unworthy priest' (*ibid.*, pp. 105, 146). See Wollasch, introduction to Bernold, *Calendar* p. 33.

1889 suggested that 'Bernold resided in the Black Forest monastery [already] in the 1070s', since, firstly, events in Constance in the 1070s are not recorded in Bernold's chronicle. Secondly, the Gregorian attitudes displayed in Bernold's early polemics would have been unacceptable to Bishop Otto and therefore incompatible with the polemicist's remaining in Constance.[34] This is perhaps to exaggerate the degree of control that Otto of Constance exercised over his episcopal city. In 1077 he fled from Constance at the approach of the anti-king Rudolf of Rheinfelden and in his absence papal legates met in his episcopal city to undertake disciplinary proceedings against him.[35] The rival who was installed in his see in 1084, Gebhard III, was the only Gregorian bishop in southern Germany who was in secure possession of his see at this period of the nadir of Gregorian fortunes.[36] It is not necessary, therefore, to imagine Bernold as being driven out of Constance in the 1070s because of his Gregorian ideas.[37] In fact neither the chronicle nor any other source identifies Bernold's whereabouts in the years preceding his visit to Rome in 1079 or in the subsequent period until his ordination in Constance in December 1084.

The south German reformed monasteries first appear prominently in Bernold's chronicle in the annal for 1083, in the famous description of St Blasien, Hirsau and All Saints, Schaffhausen. 'At that time, however, three monasteries, together with their dependencies, excellently founded on the basis of the discipline of the *Rule*, were held in high esteem in the kingdom of the Germans.'[38] This may indicate that Bernold had recently entered St Blasien. Thereafter monastic reform in southern Germany is not mentioned again until the annal for 1091 in the extensive obituary of Abbot William of Hirsau.[39] It is only in the last ten annals of Bernold's chronicle that there is a consistent interest in the south German monastic reform and the related canonical reform 'according to the *Rule* of St Augustine'.[40] This growing preoccupation with monastic history coincided with Bernold's migration from St

34 Strelau (1889) pp. 7, 37–8.

35 Berthold, *Chronicle* 1077, below p. 169. See Maurer (1991) p. 170.

36 See Becker (1964) p. 139; Maurer (1991) p. 180.

37 Autenrieth (1956) p. 133: a considerable number of clergy in the cathedral of Constance remained on the papal side even during the most serious conflict. 'Whether they had to leave the city at times and take refuge in reformed monasteries loyal to the pope remains undecided.'

38 Bernold, *Chronicle* 1083, below p. 272.

39 *Ibid.*, 1091, pp. 301–2.

40 *Ibid.*, p. 304.

Blasien to All Saints, Schaffhausen. That migration can be dated to the latter part of the year 1091 by the evidence of the codex Sarnen, Kollegiumsbibliothek MS 10.

The manuscript contains the annals of Bernold's chronicle from 1080 to 1091 but the text breaks off after recording events in August 1091. The final sentence of this text reads: 'For this reason excommunication was so prevalent in Swabia that many religious men and women chose rather to be exiled forever than to perish through communion with excommunicates.' This passage does not appear in Bernold's autograph, Clm 432, where instead is written over an erasure: 'The duke [Welf IV of Bavaria], however, once more incited many of his supporters against Henry, urging them to make the decision to elect a new king, if the indolence and malice of certain persons did not hinder them.'[41] The likelihood is that the Sarnen manuscript preserves Bernold's original version of the text, which was subsequently erased in Clm 432 and rewritten in the light of new information that subsequently became available to him. There is a number of smaller discrepancies between the two manuscripts in the annals for 1088–91, in which more precise information in Bernold's autograph replaces the vaguer formulations of the Sarnen manuscript.[42] The original manuscript from which the Sarnen Bernold-text was copied must have been an exemplar of Bernold's chronicle left behind in St Blasien when the chronicler took his autograph with him to Schaffhausen. Bernold must therefore have departed from St Blasien in autumn 1091.

From 1092 until the end of the chronicle the affairs of the abbey of All Saints, Schaffhausen appear in every annal except 1095 and 1097. These reports reveal an abbey involved in a protracted quarrel with a former benefactor, Tuto of Wagenhausen;[43] it was torn apart by factions and deprived of leadership by the abdication of Abbot Gerard (1096–8), attacked and plundered by its advocate, Count Adalbert of Mörsburg and abandoned by many of the brethren.[44] While Bernold's removal from Constance to St Blasien seems to have been accompanied by an extension of the range of subject-matter and of the length of the annals of his chronicle, the migration to Schaffhausen was accompanied by the narrowing of the chronicler's horizons. The work never dwindles into

---

41 *Ibid.*, p. 305 and n. 438.
42 Robinson, introduction, *Die Chroniken Bertholds und Bernolds* pp. 96–7.
43 Bernold, *Chronicle* 1092, below pp. 307–8; 1094, p. 319.
44 *Ibid.*, 1098, p. 333.

an exclusively monastic chronicle but there is a noticeable lack of detail in the reports of events beyond the ambience of the south German monastic reform movement. An important exception, however, is the annal for 1095, which is enriched by Bernold's extensive use of two curial documents, the synodal protocols of the council of Piacenza (1 March) and 'The meeting of Urban II and King Conrad'.[45]

Bernold is the eleventh-century scholar whose research and work methods can be most fully studied. This has been shown above all by the pioneering work of Johanne Autenrieth on the manuscripts formerly held by the cathedral school of Constance.[46] Professor Autenrieth traced fifty of these manuscripts (now scattered in libraries throughout Germany), principally codices of canon law and patristic works, many of them heavily glossed. Among the glossators she identified the hand of Bernold, apparently at work in the library between 1074 and 1076, the period in which he composed his earliest polemics. There are clear links between the glosses in these manuscripts and a number of the German polemical writings of the Investiture Contest. The glossed passages and sometimes the actual wording of the glosses themselves recur not only in Bernold's own polemics but also in the polemical treatises and letters of Bernold's teacher, Bernard of Hildesheim, and of Manegold of Lautenbach, in the polemic issued in the name of Archbishop Gebhard of Salzburg and in the fragmentary work of the anonymous polemicist of Hirsau.[47] Indeed all the most important German pro-papal polemics of the last quarter of the eleventh century drew on the glossed manuscripts of the cathedral library of Constance.

There is good reason to ascribe to Bernold a central role in the dissemination of the glossed material used by other authors. He undoubtedly compiled handbooks of canons and patristic sentences in which he used his glosses.[48] The most widely distributed of these is 'the Swabian appendix', a collection of canons on the subject of excommunication, which circulated as a supplement to the canon law *Collection in 74 titles*.[49] Bernold's research in the library of Constance was above all exploited in his seventeen polemical treatises, written mainly in the form of letters

---

45 *Ibid.*, 1095, pp. 323, 325, 326 and n. 558.

46 Autenrieth (1956) pp. 24–6, 41–50, 68–75, 81–2, 88–9, 94–6, 99–102, 106–14, 118–42; Autenrieth (1975) pp. 5–21.

47 Robinson (1978b) pp. 93–122.

48 Robinson (1989) pp. 169–70.

49 Identified as the work of Bernold by Autenrieth (1958) pp. 375–94. Cf. Gilchrist, introduction to *Collection in 74 titles* pp. xxvii–xxxi, 180–96.

to individual members of the pro-papal party in Germany who had sought his advice on reforming issues. The themes are the validity of the sacraments of unworthy priests, the effects of simony, the problem of contact with excommunicates, the reconciliation of excommunicates and especially the necessity of obedience to the pope.[50] Of the other writings in which Bernold used his research, his treatise on the liturgy, *Micrologus*, must count as the most influential, surviving as it does in more than sixty manuscripts. The theme of the work is essentially that of all Bernold's writings: the binding nature of papal decrees for the universal Church.[51]

Bernold's most extensive work, his chronicle, also shows the results of his research in the cathedral library of Constance. For the earlier pages of the chronicle he was dependent on the compilation of Berthold of Reichenau. Bernold included the texts 'Concerning the principal kingdoms' and 'Concerning the six ages of the world' that Berthold had introduced to extend the original scope of Herman's chronicle. He also used the 'Swabian universal chronicle', that abridgement of Herman's chronicle that seems to have been the work of Berthold. Numerous interpolations, however, sometimes in the margins and sometimes written over erasures, bear witness to Bernold's own research, in canon law and patristic as well as historical sources.[52] Bernold also added to the preliminary materials of his chronicle a 'Catalogue of the holy Roman pontiffs', ending with the accession of Paschal II in 1099.[53] The annals for 1054–75 often depend on the second version of Berthold's chronicle. It is clear from Bernold's autograph that he revised and extended these annals, erasing Berthold's original text and introducing new material of his own: for example, the attempted poisoning of Pope Victor II and papal interventions in the career of Berengar of Tours.[54] From the beginning of the annal for 1076 Bernold's text is completely independent of that of 'Berthold II', and from 1083 onwards – to judge from

---

50 D. Stöckly and D. Jasper, introduction to Bernold, *De excommunicatis vitandis* pp. 7–10, discussing the chronology of Bernold's polemics, identified three distinct periods of activity: firstly, his youthful writings, principally of 1075–6; secondly, works from the aftermath of Pope Gregory VII's death (1085), written in St Blasien; thirdly, works from the pontificate of Urban II (1088–99), written in Schaffhausen.

51 Bernold, *Micrologus*, col. 978–1022 (previously attributed to Ivo of Chartres). See Taylor (1998) pp. 162–91.

52 In G.H. Pertz's edition, *MGH SS* 5, 400–26. Bernold's personal contributions are indicated in italics.

53 *MGH SS* 5, 395–400. See Robinson (1978b) pp. 82–92.

54 Bernold, *Chronicle* 1054, 1056, 1060, below pp. 245, 246, 247.

the appearance of the entries in Bernold's autograph – it is a strictly contemporary source.[55]

Bernold's chronicle, like 'Berthold II', is a thoroughly Gregorian work, sharing the pro-papal sympathies of Bernold's polemical and theological writings. Just as 'Berthold II' reflects the situation of Reichenau during the abbatiate of Ekkehard II, so Bernold's chronicle is shaped by the attitudes of the pro-papal clergy of Constance and the monks of the south German reform movement. There are numerous cross-references between the chronicle and Bernold's other writings. For example, the reports in the chronicle concerning Berengar of Tours are closely linked with Bernold's treatise against Berengar's eucharistic doctrine. That treatise is indeed as much a historical as a theological work, basing its repudiation of Berengar's doctrine on the evidence, also provided by the chronicle, that this doctrine had been condemned in a number of papal and legatine councils.[56] Bernold's polemic in defence of Gebhard III's claim to be the lawful bishop of Constance is likewise closely connected with the presentation of Gebhard in the chronicle. The polemic defends the validity of Gebhard's claim by citing, in terms similar to those in the chronicle, the papal condemnations of his rival, Otto of Constance, and the papal confirmation of his own authority.[57] Two of Bernold's earlier polemics, *On the unchastity of priests*, letter 5 (1075) and *On the condemnation of schismatics*, letter 3 (1076), contain historical narratives – of the death of Bishop Henry of Speyer (26 February 1075) and the conflict between the king and the pope at the beginning of 1076[58] – which are much more extensive than the equivalent reports in Bernold's chronicle. In these two cases the accounts in the polemics seem to predate those in the chronicle, which may indeed be a précis of the earlier writings.

Unlike 'Berthold II', Bernold's chronicle does not interrupt its narrative with lengthy polemical digressions. Only one interpolation is found in Bernold's chronicle, in the annal for 1091, where the chronicler refutes the opinions of his former master, Bernard of Hildesheim, on the subject of reordination. 'In [his] writings he was in some passages led by excessive zeal to overstep the bounds of moderation: namely,

55 Robinson, introduction, *Die Chroniken Bertholds und Bernolds* pp. 86–7.

56 Bernold, *De veritate corporis et sanguinis Domini* pp. 355–403. See Montclos (1971) pp. 234–40.

57 Bernold, *Pro Gebhardo episcopo Constantiensi epistola apologetica* pp. 108–11.

58 Bernold, *De incontinentia sacerdotum* V, p. 26; Bernold, *De damnatione scismaticorum* III, p. 49.

where he deals with the sacraments of the schismatics.'[59] In this annal Bernold concluded the debate with his master that had begun in the correspondence *On the condemnation of schismatics* and had continued in the polemic of about a decade later, *On the sacraments of excommunicates.* The plain, businesslike Latin prose style of Bernold's chronicle in no way resembles the polemical exuberance of 'Berthold II'. In his vocabulary and sentence structure Bernold more closely resembles Herman of Reichenau than he does the mature Berthold. The single reflection that Bernold permits himself in the course of his chronicle on the historian's duty seems to be modelled on Isidore of Seville's empirical conception: 'Among the ancients no one wrote history except him who was present and saw the events that were to be recorded.' Bernold's own reflection occurs at the end of his account of the battle of Pleichfeld (11 August 1086): 'I myself, who have compiled this chronicle from the 1,054th year of the Lord's Incarnation up to this point, have contrived to proclaim to the faithful, to the praise and glory of God, not so much what others reported about the aforementioned battle, but rather what I myself saw and heard.'[60]

Although the language of Bernold's chronicle is more moderate than that of 'Berthold II', the Gregorian bias is no less evident. The annal for 1082, for example, contains a miracle performed by Gregory VII: the extinguishing, by means of the sign of the cross, of a fire that threatened St Peter's basilica.[61] The chronicler was above all concerned with the deeds of the Gregorian heroes, secular and ecclesiastical. Three of these heroes were also celebrated in 'Berthold II': Cardinal bishop Peter of Albano, Abbot William of Hirsau and the anti-king Rudolf of Rheinfelden. Bernold, like Berthold, included (in two separate annals) the story of Peter, as a monk of Vallombrosa, undergoing the ordeal by fire in order to secure the condemnation of the simoniac bishop of Florence.[62] William of Hirsau — 'most ardent in the cause of St Peter and most zealous in monastic piety, for he was the father of many monasteries' — received the most extensive obituary in the chronicle.[63] Given the role of Rudolf of Rheinfelden as patron of the abbey of St Blasien,[64] it

---

59 Bernold, *Chronicle* 1091, below p. 303.

60 *Ibid.*, 1086, p. 287. Cf. Isidore, *Etymologiae* 1.14.1.

61 Bernold, *Chronicle* 1082, below p. 268. This miracle story was later used by Paul, *Life of Pope Gregory VII* c. 8, pp. 265–6 ('as we read in the chronicles of venerable men').

62 Bernold, *Chronicle* 1079, 1089, pp. 264, 297–8.

63 *Ibid.*, 1091, pp. 301–2.

64 See Jakobs (1973) pp. 105–7; Robinson (1999) pp. 126, 127, 356.

is not surprising that the anti-king is accorded particular honour in the chronicle. The obituary of Rudolf contains the only biblical *exemplum* in the chronicle: 'he, I say, another Maccabeus when in the front ranks he fell upon the enemy'.[65] In the annals for 1077–80 Bernold attributed the royal title to Rudolf while denying it to Henry IV: the term 'king' here always means Rudolf. The chronicler's description of Henry IV holding court at Whitsun 1077 is characteristic. 'At that time Henry crowned himself in Ulm and usurped the kingship that had been forbidden to him.'[66] (Bernold was more consistent in this respect than Berthold, who did not deny Henry the royal title.) Bernold's friendship with Bishop Anselm II of Lucca naturally prompted his inclusion in the chronicle with particular emphasis on the miracles that followed his death, which strengthened the resolve of the Gregorian party.[67] In the later annals of the chronicle heroic status is similarly conferred on Bishop Gebhard III of Constance, 'noble by birth but more noble by virtue of the monastic way of life'.[68] The papal penitentiary and polemicist Manegold of Lautenbach is similarly presented as a Gregorian hero.[69]

Conversely the enemies of the Gregorian cause are consigned to hell, although in less bloodthirsty language than in 'Berthold II'. The antipope 'Clement III' (Archbishop Wibert of Ravenna) never appears in the chronicle without an opprobrious epithet: 'the oath-breaker and excommunicated heresiarch Wibert of Ravenna'.[70] Like Berthold, Bernold recorded the vengeful miracle that caused the death of Bishop Embriko of Augsburg in 1077 and the equally miraculous death of Patriarch Sigehard of Aquileia in the same year.[71] In similar vein the annal for 1087 contains a report of the deathbed vision experienced by the imperial anti-bishop Herman of Passau, in which his pro-papal rival Altman appeared 'so that he would know more clearly the fault that he must expiate in hell'.[72] The ambiguous career of Margrave Ekbert II of Meissen prompts a series of reports that demonstrate Bernold's

---

65 Bernold, *Chronicle* 1080, below p. 266.

66 *Ibid.*, 1077, below p. 260 and n. 145.

67 *Ibid.*, 1086, pp. 285, 287.

68 *Ibid.*, 1084, p. 278.

69 *Ibid.*, 1094, 1098, pp. 320, 322, 333.

70 *Ibid.*, 1087, p. 288. Bernold's account of Wibert's papal consecration, duplicated in the annals for 1083 and 1084, is based on Archbishop Gebhard of Salzburg's letter to Bishop Herman of Metz: *ibid.*, 1083, p. 269 and n. 212; 1084, p. 275 and n. 251.

71 *Ibid.*, 1077, pp. 260–1.

72 *Ibid.*, 1087, p. 290.

polemical instincts at work. In the annal for 1088 Ekbert is rebuked
for plotting to replace the anti-king Herman of Salm. In the following
annal, however, his rebellion against Henry IV prompts a reaction in
his favour on the part of the chronicler. After Ekbert 'courageously
attacked Henry' and put him to flight, 'he did not cease to offer thanks
to God and to St Peter and resolved that he would cling to them thereafter with a more spotless fidelity'.[73] In the annal recording his death
in 1090 (which Bernold attributed to the treachery of Henry IV's sister,
Abbess Adelaide of Quedlinburg and Gandersheim) Ekbert is awarded
the chronicler's greatest accolade: he 'was most active in the cause of St
Peter'.[74] Bernold's black-and-white categories could not accommodate
the political tergiversations of the Saxon maverick Ekbert II of Meissen.[75]

The central theme of the chronicle, as of all Bernold's writings, is reverence for the authority of the pope. Reverence for the holy see is demonstrated by the particular attention paid to Roman reforming synods. Of
the few additions made by Bernold to the material that he borrowed
from 'Berthold II' for his annals of the 1050s and 1060s, two were
reports of synods held by Pope Stephen IX and Pope Nicholas II. (The
other two record a miracle of Pope Victor II and Hildebrand's legatine
synod in Tours.)[76] The annal for 1079 is devoted almost exclusively to
the Roman Lenten synod of 1079, which Bernold himself attended, and
the annal for 1083 contains a lengthy account of the Roman autumn
synod of that year.[77] The reforming councils of Pope Urban II are also
given prominence, notably that of Piacenza (1 March 1095), Bernold's
account of which is based on the synodal protocol.[78] Bernold could also
quote the text of four letters of Urban II to south German recipients,
in one of these cases offering the sole surviving text of Urban II's letter
in praise of 'the common life' in southern Germany.[79] Equally indicative of respect for papal authority in Bernold's narrative are the visits
of papal legates to Germany and their legatine councils. The chron-

---

73 *Ibid.*, 1088, 1089, pp. 294, 295.

74 *Ibid.*, 1090, p. 299.

75 Meyer von Knonau (1903) pp. 171–2, 206–7, 258, 291–2; Fenske (1977) pp. 113–14;
    Robinson (1999) pp. 264–72.

76 Bernold, *Chronicle* 1054, 1056, 1057, 1060, below pp. 245, 246–7.

77 *Ibid.*, 1079, 1083, pp. 263–4, 270–1.

78 *Ibid.*, 1095, pp. 323–6.

79 Ibid., 1088, p. 292 and n. 352; 1089, p. 295–6 and n. 373; 1091, p. 306 and n. 443; 1092,
    p. 308 and n. 452.

icle traces the vicissitudes of Gregory VII's legates of 1077, Cardinal deacon Bernard and Abbot Bernard of St Victor in Marseilles,[80] and the Gregorian legates of 1079–80, Cardinal bishop Peter of Albano and Bishop Udalric of Padua.[81] The most extensive report is devoted to the legation of Cardinal bishop Odo of Ostia, whom Bernold encountered in Constance in December 1084. The report culminates in the account of the legatine synod of Quedlinburg on 20 April 1085.[82] Bernold's report of this synod is an almost verbatim copy of the synodal protocol of Quedlinburg, which, in the light of the conjecture that Bernold was the representative of Bishop Gebhard III of Constance at the synod, prompts the theory that Bernold himself was the author of the synodal protocol.[83] The role of Gebhard of Constance as papal legate was naturally of great importance to Bernold. It is to his chronicle that we owe our knowledge of Gebhard's legatine synods in Ulm in late autumn 1093 and in Constance in April 1094.[84]

A final aspect of the reverence for papal authority in Bernold's chronicle is the author's preoccupation with the cult of St Peter.[85] It was Carl Erdmann who drew attention to Bernold's elaboration of Gregory VII's expression 'knighthood of St Peter'. 'He saw in this designation an honorific title that he bestows in his obituaries on a series of counts and knights who distinguished themselves in the struggle against the supporters of Henry IV ... He meant by this term "champion of the cause of St Peter".'[86] This honorific title is bestowed in the chronicle on the Roman prefect Cencius, son of John Tiniosus ('a tireless knight of St Peter fighting against the schismatics'), on a Swabian or Bavarian Count *Berthaldus* ('a most faithful knight of St Peter'), on Hezelo, the advocate of Reichenau (also a 'most faithful knight of St Peter'), on Count Hugh of Egisheim ('a tireless knight of St Peter'), on Count Cuno of Wülflingen ('a most energetic knight of St Peter'), on Margrave

---

80 *Ibid.*, 1077, 1079, pp. 259, 260, 261, 265.

81 *Ibid.*, 1079, pp. 264–5.

82 *Ibid.*, 1084, 1085, pp. 278, 279–82.

83 See Robinson (1989) pp. 182–4. See above p. 46. There is a parallel here with Bernold's teacher, Bernard of Hildesheim, evidently the author of a similar record of the council of Gerstungen-Berka (21 January 1085): Erdmann (1938) p. 204 and n. 7.

84 Bernold, *Chronicle* 1093, 1094, pp. 315–16, 318–19.

85 The scribe of the copy of Bernold's chronicle in Würzburg, University Library MS M.p.h.f.1 (from the monastery of Gengenbach) sought to excise the references to St Peter from Bernold's text, although his censorship was unsystematic: Robinson, introduction, *Die Chroniken Bertholds und Bernolds* pp. 93–4.

86 Erdmann (1935) p. 189.

Leopold of Austria ('most faithful in the cause of St Peter against the schismatics'), on Count Udalric X of Bregenz ('a most fervent defender of the cause of St Peter against the schismatics') and on Count Liutold of Achalm ('a tireless defender of the cause of St Peter against the wickedness of the schismatics').[87] The same theme occurs in the obituary of the anti-king Rudolf: he 'deserved to fall in the service of St Peter'. A more elaborate version of the honorific title is found in the obituary of Count Frederick of Montbéliard, who attracted the particular attention of the chronicler by dying on the feast-day of St Peter. 'This count, however, was a most energetic knight of Christ in the secular sphere, according to the model of St Sebastian: that is, a most fervent lover of ecclesiastical piety and a tireless defender of catholic peace ... He struggled most zealously against the schismatics even unto death in his fidelity towards St Peter.'[88] Count Frederick's kinswoman Margravine Matilda of Tuscany is described as 'the most wise duchess and most faithful knight of St Peter' and 'the most devoted daughter of St Peter'.[89] Bernold formulated his conception – the Gregorian conception – of the role of the laity in Christian society very clearly in the annal for 1089, in which he reported the marriage of Matilda and Welf V of Bavaria. This took place 'not indeed because of unchastity but rather because of obedience towards the Roman pontiff: namely so that she might the more effectively come to the aid of the holy Roman church against the excommunicates'.[90] The theme of 'obedience towards the Roman pontiff' is, as in Bernold's other writings, central to the chronicle.

This didactic theme of the duty of obedience of laity and clergy towards St Peter and his vicar increasingly dominates the structure of Bernold's chronicle. The format of the chronicle initially resembles that of the later annals of Herman's chronicle and of 'Berthold II'. The early annals usually begin with the ruler's Christmas festivities. This framework is gradually affected, however, by Bernold's growing consciousness of 'obedience towards the Roman pontiff'. In the annals for 1075 and 1076 the Christmas celebrations of Henry IV appear in the characteristic manner of an 'imperial chronicle' in which the secular ruler stands at the centre of the narrative. This format is abandoned in the annals for 1077–81 but restored for the annals for 1082–8. In these annals the

87 Bernold, *Chronicle* 1077, below p. 260; 1087, p. 288; 1088, p. 292; 1089, p. 296; 1092, p. 310; 1095, p. 328; 1097, p. 332; 1099, p. 335.

88 *Ibid.*, 1080, p. 266; 1092, pp. 308–9. See Erdmann (1935) p. 254.

89 Bernold, *Chronicle* 1085, below p. 283; 1097, pp. 331–2.

90 *Ibid.*, 1089, p. 297.

chronicle records the Christmas celebrations and the itinerary of the anti-king Herman of Salm, who now assumes the role in the chronicle that the Salian emperor occupies in Herman of Reichenau's chronicle. Finally the annals for 1092–1100 record the Christmas celebrations of the popes Urban II and Paschal II. The reorientation of the chronicle was now complete. In the annals of the 1090s the itinerary of Urban II is traced with the same care as that of Emperor Henry III in Herman's chronicle and the itinerary first of Henry IV and subsequently of the anti-king Rudolf in 'Berthold II'. The Swabian chronicle tradition, which begins in the chronicle of Herman of Reichenau as a record mainly of the military and political activities of the Salian emperor, ends in Bernold's continuation of Herman's chronicle as a defence of the Gregorian conception of papal authority.

The chronicle of Bernold was edited in its entirety (with all its preliminary material) from Bernold's autograph, Munich, Clm 432, by G.H. Pertz in 1844 in *Monumenta Germaniae Historica, Scriptores* 5, 385–467. A new edition of Bernold's annals 1054–1100 (the continuation of the chronicle of Herman) has been published by I.S. Robinson in *Monumenta Germaniae Historica, Scriptores rerum germanicarum, nova series* 14 (Hanover, 2003).

HERMAN OF REICHENAU
CHRONICLE

1000. After Widerold, bishop of the church of Strasbourg, died in Italy,[1] Abbot Alawich of Reichenau[2] was raised to his place by the emperor[3] and Werner was established in Reichenau as the twenty-seventh abbot and he ruled for six years.[4] In Rome on the death of Pope Gregory,[5] Silvester II, who was also called Gerbert,[6] was ordained as the 143rd in the series of the popes and reigned for five years. He was archbishop first in Rheims and afterwards in Ravenna and was extremely devoted to secular learning and for this reason very much loved by the emperor, who was himself eager for knowledge.

1001. Emperor Otto travelled through Italy, which was everywhere subject to him.[7] In St Gallen Abbot Burchard ruled for twenty-three years.[8]

1002. Emperor Otto died a premature death on 23 January in Italy in the castle of Paterno[9] in the nineteenth year of his reign. He was brought away from there and, after his entrails had been interred in Augsburg, he was buried in Aachen. And Duke Henry of Bavaria received the insignia of the kingship and was made king in his place and reigned for twenty-three years.[10]

1003. King Henry attacked Margrave Henry,[11] who was rebelling

---

1 Widerold (991–9) died in Benevento.

2 Alawich II, abbot (997–1000), bishop of Strasbourg (1000–1).

3 Otto III, king (983–1002), emperor (996).

4 Werner (1000–6).

5 Gregory V (996–9).

6 Gerbert of Aurillac, archbishop of Rheims (991–8), Ravenna (998–9), Pope Silvester II (999–1003).

7 Returning to Italy (July 1000) Otto put down a rising in Tivoli early in 1001, whereupon the Romans compelled him to leave the city.

8 Burchard II (1001–22).

9 Paterno at Mount Soracte near Città Castellana. He died on 24 January 1002 according to Thietmar of Merseburg, *Chronicon* IV.49, p. 188.

10 Henry (IV), duke of Bavaria (995–1004), King Henry II (1002–24), emperor (1014).

11 Henry of Schweinfurt, margrave of the Bavarian Nordgau (980–1017).

against him, and destroyed very many of his fortresses. Ernest[12] was taken prisoner, while Bruno, the king's brother,[13] and Henry escaped with difficulty and fled. Strasbourg was plundered by Duke Herman of Swabia,[14] who was in rebellion against the king, and was grievously avenged through divine intervention against the perpetrators of the crime. Reparation was made to the holy place by the duke himself.

1004. King Henry went by way of Verona into the region of Italy on this side of the Po and subjected to himself all the cities in that region. On the very day on which he was crowned, he broke into Pavia and subdued it by fire and sword.[15] After taking hostages, he returned from there into Saxony and after a few days he turned his arms against the Slavs. He forced the Bohemians to accept their former duties of service and payment of tribute;[16] he also brought Boleslav, the duke of the Polish Slavs,[17] into subjection, together with all his people, and returned to Saxony victorious. Duke Herman of Swabia died[18] and he was succeeded in the duchy by his son, Herman,[19] who was a boy and acceptable to all the people.

1005. There was a great famine. In Rome, after Gerbert, John XVI, the 144th pope, reigned for one year.[20]

1006. In Reichenau on the death of Abbot Werner the brethren elected the monk Henry. King Henry, however, loathed his arrogance – although he had received money from him – and was hostile towards the brethren, who had been the subject of accusations in his presence. Against their will he appointed to rule them a certain Immo, abbot of Gorze, a harsh man who at that time also held Prüm.[21] Some of the

---

12 Ernest I, duke of Swabia (1012–15), Henry of Schweinfurt's cousin (Babenberg family).

13 Bruno, bishop of Augsburg (1006–29).

14 Herman II (997–1003), Henry II's rival for the throne, plundered Strasbourg in June 1002. Cf. Thietmar V.12, p. 234.

15 14 May 1004. Fighting broke out between Pavians and Germans on the evening of Henry's coronation as king of Italy: Thietmar VI.6–7, pp. 281–2.

16 In autumn 1004 Henry restored the exiled Duke Jaromir of Bohemia: Thietmar VI.10–12, pp. 286–90.

17 Boleslav Chrobry, duke (992–1025), king (1025). On this expedition (August–September 1005): Thietmar VI.22, 26–7, pp. 300–1, 305–6.

18 4 May 1003.

19 Herman III (1003–12), probably three years old on his succession.

20 John XVII (June–December 1003).

21 Immo, abbot of Gorze (984–1012/17), Prüm and Reichenau (1006–8). He was described in the *Chronicon Suevicum universale* 1006, p. 69 (perhaps the work of Berthold of

brethren, therefore, left that place of their own accord and some of
them were severely afflicted by him with fasts, scourges and exile. Thus
the noble monastery suffered for its sins a heavy loss in great men,
books and church treasures, as Rudpert, a noble and learnedly witty
monk and my mother's uncle, mournfully lamented in prose, rhythm
and metre.[22]

In Rome John XVII, who was also called Fasanus, was ordained as the
145th pope.[23]

1007. King Henry with the greatest zeal established a noble and rich
bishopric in his fortress called Bamberg and Eberhard was promoted as
the first bishop there in this year.[24]

1008. When the learned man Archbishop Liudolf of Trier died,[25]
Megingaud[26] was promoted by the king as archbishop in his place. The
clerk Adalbero,[27] a brother of Queen Cunigunde,[28] however, strove with
the support of certain persons to obtain the archbishopric, alleging that
it was due to him by royal promise. He stationed a garrison in the palace
of Trier and, together with his brothers, Bishop Theoderic of Metz
and Duke Henry of Bavaria and Count Frederick,[29] rebelled against the
king, supported also by Count Gerard[30] and many others. Nevertheless after some time they were all defeated by the king and Henry was
deprived of the duchy of Bavaria.[31]

In the same year King Henry, after two years learning at last of the
cruelty of Immo, removed him and appointed Bern, a learned and pious
man and a monk of Prüm, as abbot in Reichenau.[32] He was joyfully

---

Reichenau, above p. 12) as 'the destroyer of the monastery and the expeller of the
brethren'. The conduct of Henry II and the imputation of simony: Vollrath (1991) pp.
290–2; Hoffmann (1993) pp. 32–3, 38 n. 65.

22 Not extant: Klüppel (1980) p. 141.

23 John XVIII (1004–9).

24 Eberhard (1007–40). The foundation of Bamberg: Arnold (1997) pp. 140–1.

25 Liudolf (994–1008).

26 Megingaud (Megingoz) (1008–15).

27 Adalbero, provost of St Paulinus, archbishop elect of Trier (1008–16, † after 1037).

28 Cunigunde (Luxemburg family), queen and empress, consort of Henry II (†1033).

29 Theoderic II, bishop of Metz (1006–47); Henry V, duke of Bavaria (1004–9, 1018–26);
    Frederick, count of the Ardennes.

30 Gerard I, count of Alsace, count of Metz (ca. 1000–20), brother-in-law of Cuni-
    gunde.

31 April 1009. Cf. Thietmar VI.35, 41, pp. 317–18, 324.

32 Bern (Berno) (1008–48). See above p. 3.

received and gathered the scattered brethren together again. He was consecrated by Bishop Lambert of Constance[33] as the twenty-ninth abbot of this place and, distinguished by his great learning and piety, he ruled for forty years.

1009. Count Wolferad[34] took as his wife Hiltrud,[35] the daughter of Pilgrim and Bertrada, from whom he afterwards had fifteen children, including me, Herman.

1010. The elder Count Wolferad,[36] my paternal grandfather, a merciful man, steadfast for justice and eminent among his own people, died as an old man on 4 March.

1011. Archbishop Willigis of Mainz died[37] and Erchenbald[38] succeeded him. Theoderic, duke of part of Lotharingia,[39] was captured and taken away by Henry, formerly duke of Bavaria, and certain Lotharingians virtually in the presence of the king. Nevertheless he was afterwards released and Henry himself recovered the king's grace and his duchy.[40]

1012. Duke Conrad of Carinthia,[41] son of Duke Otto and brother of Bruno, the former pope, died. His son, the boy Conrad,[42] was deprived of the duchy and Adalbero[43] received it. When Herman the younger, duke of Swabia, also died, his successor was Ernest, the husband of his sister Gisela.[44]

1013. In Rome after the death of Pope Sergius, Benedict VIII ruled for

33 Lambert (995–1018).

34 Wolferad II, count of Altshausen (†1065). Herman's family: above pp. 3–4.

35 The ancestry of Hiltrud (†1052) is unknown. Herman's verses on her death (below p. 91) emphasise her 'distinguished lineage'.

36 Wolferad I, count of Altshausen, perhaps the 'Count Wolferad' named in documents concerning a donation of 972 to the church in Chur: Kerkhoff (1964) pp. 14–16.

37 Willigis (975–1011).

38 Erchenbald (1011–21).

39 Theoderic I, duke of Upper Lotharingia (978–1026/7), the king's principal Lotharingian supporter, was ambushed by Henry of Luxemburg (n. 29) in Odernheim, while returning from a royal assembly in Mainz: cf. Thietmar VI.52, p. 339.

40 In 1017: cf. Thietmar VII.66, p. 480.

41 Conrad I (1004–11), son of Duke Otto of Carinthia (978–85, 1002–4), brother of Pope Gregory V (Salian dynasty).

42 Conrad II ('the younger'), duke of Carinthia (1036–9).

43 Adalbero (of Eppenstein), duke of Carinthia (1012–35, †1039).

44 Gisela, daughter of Duke Herman II of Swabia married (1) Count Bruno of Brunswick, (2) Duke Ernest I of Swabia, (3) Conrad II (n. 49); queen, empress (†1043).

almost twelve years as the 147th pope.[45] I, Herman, was born on 18 July.
King Henry went to Italy with an army.

1014. King Henry was crowned and received the imperial consecration
from Pope Benedict in Rome.[46]

1015. Duke Ernest of Swabia was wounded while hunting, by an arrow
aimed at a wild beast by Count Adalbero,[47] and he died. His son of
the same name[48] obtained his duchy, while his widow Gisela married
Conrad,[49] son of Henry, son of Duke Otto, who afterwards became
emperor. Archbishop Megengaud of Trier died and the venerable man
Poppo,[50] the brother of Duke Ernest, succeeded him.

1017. Godfrey, duke of part of Lotharingia,[51] did battle with Count
Gerard, the uncle of Conrad, the future emperor, and defeated him.

1018. In Constance, after the death of Bishop Lambert, Rudhard
received the bishopric and ruled for almost five years.[52]

1019. The youth Conrad, son of Conrad, the former duke of Carinthia, with the help of his paternal cousin Conrad, the future emperor,
defeated Adalbero, then duke of Carinthia, in a battle at Ulm and forced
him to flee.[53]

1020. Pope Benedict came at the emperor's invitation to Bamberg
and there dedicated the church of St Stephen.[54] Bishop Werner of
Strasbourg[55] with the aid of certain Swabians attacked the Burgundians
and defeated them in battle.

45 Sergius IV (1009–12); Benedict VIII (1012–24).

46 14 February. Cf. Thietmar VII.1, pp. 396–7.

47 Unknown. According to Thietmar VII.14, p. 414, the perpetrator was 'one of his
vassals'.

48 Ernest II, duke of Swabia (1015–30).

49 Conrad II, king (1024–39), emperor (1027); son of Henry 'of Worms' (+990/1), grandson of Duke Otto of Carinthia (n. 41).

50 Poppo (1015–47), brother of Ernest I of Swabia.

51 Godfrey II, duke of Lower Lotharingia (1012–23). During his campaigns against the
emperor's enemies in Lotharingia he defeated (27 August) Count Gerard I of Alsace
(n. 30), brother of Adelaide of Metz, mother of Conrad II. Cf. Thietmar VII.62, pp.
475–6.

52 Rudhard (1018–22).

53 Conrad 'the younger' (n. 42) and Conrad 'the elder' (n. 49) drove Adalbero (n. 43)
from the Swabian lands inherited by his wife, a daughter of Duke Herman II of
Swabia.

54 24 April. Henry II's foundation of Bamberg was placed under papal protection.

55 Werner (1001–28). This expedition was in response to the rescinding by King Rudolf
III of Burgundy of his promise of the Burgundian succession to Henry II.

I, Herman, began to be taught my letters on 15 September.

1021. There was a great earthquake on Friday, 12 May. Archbishop Heribert of Cologne,[56] a man of great sanctity, departing this life, became renowned through many miracles and Pilgrim succeeded him.[57] When Archbishop Erchenbald of Mainz also died, Aribo was made archbishop.[58] After Wolbodo of Liège, Durand was appointed bishop.[59] Irmendrud, the venerable abbess of Buchau, also died on 20 February and Abbess Abarhild succeeded her. Thenceforward that place began increasingly to deteriorate.[60] Emperor Henry undertook an expedition to Italy.[61]

My brother Werner was born on 1 November.[62]

1022. Emperor Henry went to Campania, entered Benevento, besieged and captured Troia and received the surrender of Naples, Capua, Salerno and all the other cities of that region. It is said that he granted a certain territory in that region to Normans who had flocked there in his time.[63] Thus, passing through the city of Rome, he returned victorious to Germany. A plague broke out in the army and killed many: among them Bishop Rudhard of Constance and Abbot Burchard of the monastery of St Gallen died. In their places Bishop Heimo ruled for almost four years and Abbot Theobald for eleven years.[64] Master Notker[65] and other eminent brethren of St Gallen also died.

1023. In Regensburg after the departure from this world of Bishop Gebhard, a chaste man, renowned for his distinctive manners, his unusual love of cleanliness and splendid apparel and most zealous

---

56 Heribert (999–1021). The miracle tradition: Rupert of Deutz, *Vita sancti Hereberti* c. 35, col. 424B–428A.

57 Pilgrim (1021–36).

58 Aribo (1021–31).

59 Wolbodo (1018–21); Durand (1021–5).

60 The links between Herman's family and the convent of Buchau (on the Federsee): Dieterich (1925) pp. 793–4.

61 November 1021.

62 Werner, monk of Reichenau (†1054). See Borgolte (1979) pp. 3–5, 7, 9.

63 On these developments, including the capture of Prince Pandulf IV of Capua and the successful siege of Troia (June 1022): Holtzmann (1941) pp. 477–8; Deér (1972) pp. 26–7; Bloch (1986) pp. 14–18.

64 Heimo, bishop of Constance (1022–6); Theobald, abbot of St Gallen (1021–34).

65 Notker Labeo ('the German'), monk of St Gallen († 29 June 1022), author of works on the liberal arts, translator of classical, scriptural and patristic works into Old High German.

in the performance of the divine office, another Gebhard, a canon of Augsburg, succeeded.[66]

1024. In Rome on the death of Benedict, his brother John XVIII, a layman, was ordained the 148th pope and reigned for almost nine years.[67] Emperor Henry also died on 13 July without children and was buried in the basilica of St Peter in the bishopric of Bamberg, which he himself had constructed and which he had left as the heir of all his estates and treasures. Then since in particular Conrad the elder, the son of Henry and Adelaide,[68] and his paternal cousin Conrad, the son of Duke Conrad by Matilda,[69] strove for the kingship, an assembly of princes was held in the village of Kamba.[70] Conrad the elder was raised to be king and was anointed by Archbishop Aribo in Mainz on 8 September.[71] Not long afterwards his wife Gisela was nevertheless[72] consecrated queen by Archbishop Pilgrim in Cologne on 21 September.

1025. There was rebellion and great dissension against King Conrad on the part of his paternal cousin Conrad and Duke Ernest of Swabia, his stepson, and also Welf, a Swabian count,[73] and very many others.

1026. When the rebels had in part been subdued, around the season of Lent, King Conrad went to Italy with an army.[74] He celebrated Easter [10 April] in Vercelli and subjected to himself all Italy on this side of Rome except for Lucca, a city in Tuscany. Duke Ernest of Swabia made peace with him in this year at the insistence of his mother.[75] He received the abbey of Kempten as a benefice and distributed it among his vassals.

---

66 Gebhard I (994–1023); Gebhard II (1023–36).

67 Romanus, count of Tusculum, Pope John XIX (1024–32).

68 Conrad (n. 49), son of Henry of Worms and Adelaide of Metz, daughter of Count Eberhard of Alsace.

69 Matilda, daughter of Duke Herman II of Swabia, sister of Gisela (n. 44), married Duke Conrad I of Carinthia (n. 41).

70 Kamba is identified as the place of the election only by Herman and Bern of Reichenau, *Letter* 10, p. 37: 'there is to be a public assembly of all of us on 4 September in the place that is called Kamba' (to Bishop Alberic of Como). See Bresslau (1879) pp. 17–18.

71 Cf. Wipo, *Deeds of Conrad* c. 2, 3, pp. 14–22. See Bresslau (1879) pp. 18–24, 26–7.

72 Herman's 'nevertheless' perhaps alludes to Aribo of Mainz's refusal to crown Gisela because he considered her marriage unlawful: Bresslau (1879) pp. 28–9, 36–7.

73 Welf II, count in Swabia (†1030). On this 'dissension': Wipo, *Deeds* c. 10, p. 32. See Bresslau (1879) pp. 57–8, 92–4.

74 Lent began on 23 February. Cf. Wipo, *Deeds* c. 11, 12, 13, pp. 32–5. See Bresslau (1879) pp. 121–31.

75 Queen Gisela. Cf. Wipo, *Deeds* c. 10, 11, pp. 32–3.

Not long afterwards, diverted by bad advice, he rebelled again.[76] In the same year in Constance Bishop Heimo was struck down by pleurisy and died a sudden death and Warmann succeeded him, ruling for almost eight years.[77] Abbot Burchard of Kempten and Rheinau died[78] and Abbot Pirchtilo replaced him in Rheinau. Bishop Bruno of Augsburg and Count Welf raged wildly against each other with mutual pillage and arson.[79]

1027. King Conrad celebrated Christmas [25 December 1026] in Ivrea and advanced into the territories beyond. He received the surrender of Lucca, together with Margrave Rainer,[80] and, arriving in Rome, he was crowned emperor by Pope John [XIX] on Easter day [26 March]. After he had conquered the whole of Italy, he returned and held a court in Ulm in Swabia. There he received his stepson, Duke Ernest, Count Welf, together with others who came to surrender, and condemned them to a period of exile.[81] Kyburg, a fortress of Count Werner[82] that continued to resist, and some other rebel fortresses were captured. His paternal cousin Conrad also surrendered to the emperor[83] and was likewise sent into exile. Bishop Werner of Strasbourg was sent by the emperor as an envoy to Constantinople[84] and when he died there the following year, he was succeeded by William.[85] Hildegard became abbess of Buchau.

1028. Henry, the son of the emperor,[86] was elected king by all the princes, while he was still a boy, in Aachen on the holy day of Easter [14 April] and he was anointed by Archbishop Pilgrim of Cologne.

---

76 During Conrad's absence in Italy. Cf. Wipo, *Deeds* c. 19, p. 39: 'on the advice of certain of his vassals'.

77 Warmann (1026–34).

78 It was after Burchard's death (15 September 1026) that Conrad granted Kempten to his stepson Ernest. See Bresslau (1879) p. 199; Seibert (1991) pp. 521–3.

79 Cf. Wipo, *Deeds* c. 19, p. 38. See Bresslau (1879) pp. 197–8.

80 Rainer, margrave of Tuscany (1016–30). Cf. Wipo, *Deeds* c. 15, p. 36. See Bresslau (1879) pp. 137–8.

81 July 1027. Ernest was imprisoned in the Saxon fortress of Giebichenstein: Wipo, *Deeds* c. 20, p. 40.

82 Werner (Wezilo), count of Kyburg and Thurgau (✝1030), vassal of Ernest II of Swabia: Wipo, *Deeds* c. 25, p. 43.

83 September, probably in Worms: Bresslau (1879) p. 223.

84 His purpose was probably to obtain a Byzantine princess as a bride for the emperor's son, Henry: Bresslau (1879) pp. 234–5; Steindorff (1874) p. 13 n. 1.

85 William (1029–46), uncle of Conrad II.

86 Henry III, king (1039–56), emperor (1046). He was eleven years old in 1028: Wipo, *Deeds* c. 23, p. 42.

1029. When the emperor was celebrating the festival of Easter [6 April] in Regensburg, Bishop Bruno of Augsburg, his most important adviser,[87] died there and was buried in Augsburg in the newly begun basilica of St Maurice. Eberhard was his successor.[88]

1030. After Duke Ernest had been released from his exile and had recovered his duchy, he heeded the advice of wicked men, opposed the emperor once more and was deprived of his duchy.[89] His younger brother Herman was made duke of the Swabians.[90] Hostilities had flared up long before with Stephen, king of the Hungarians[91] and Emperor Conrad went to Hungary and, as much as he could, wherever rivers and marshes did not hinder him, he laid it waste as far as the Raab. Meanwhile in Swabia Ernest the former duke and his supporters, who with small forces were assailing the emperor, molested and plundered the peasants in the region of the Black Forest. They were observed by Count Manegold, who belonged to the vassals of Reichenau, and on 17 August they were defeated in battle.[92] Manegold himself was killed there and Ernest the former duke and Count Werner, the head of the rebellion, also the noble knights Adalbert and Werin,[93] together with other men, died there. Ernest was buried in Constance, while Manegold was buried in Reichenau. Burchard, a monk of Reichenau, was promoted to be abbot of St Emmeram in Regensburg.[94]

1031. Peace was restored with Stephen, king of the Hungarians.[95]

---

87 'The genius of Bishop Bruno of Augsburg' influenced the management of affairs at the royal court (Wipo, *Deeds* c. 4, p. 24) and Conrad entrusted the young Henry III to Bruno's 'guardianship' in 1026 (c. 11, p. 32).

88 Eberhard (1029–47).

89 According to Wipo (*Deeds* c. 25, pp. 43–4), Ernest recovered his duchy (in 1028) on condition that he proceed against his outlawed vassal Werner (n. 82). When he refused, 'he was judged to be a public enemy of the emperor'.

90 Herman IV (1030–8).

91 Stephen I (1001–38). Cf. Wipo, *Deeds* c. 26, p. 44: 'many conflicts arose between the Hungarian people and the Bavarians, through the Bavarians' fault, and therefore King Stephen of the Hungarians made many incursions and plundered the kingdom of … the Bavarians'. Conrad's expedition was unsuccessful: Bresslau (1879) pp. 298–300.

92 Count Manegold, 'a vassal of the emperor, holding a great benefice from the abbey of Reichenau' (Wipo, c. 28, p. 46), 'probably belonged to the house of the counts of Nellenburg' (Bresslau [1879] p. 302). Wipo gave the date 18 August, but all other annals and necrologies agree with Herman: Bresslau (1879) p. 303 n. 1.

93 'Adalbert and Werin, noble men': Wipo, *Deeds* c. 28, p. 46.

94 Burchard (1030–7).

95 Cf. Wipo, *Deeds* c. 26, pp. 44–5. See Bresslau (1879) pp. 312–13.

Aribo, archbishop of the see of Mainz, departed this life while jour-
neying to Rome for the sake of prayer.[96] Bardo, worthy of veneration for
his monastic life and habit, succeeded to him in the archbishopric.[97]

1032. Rudolf, the indolent petty king of Burgundy, died[98] and his crown
and the insignia of the kingship were brought to Emperor Conrad by
Seliger.[99] In these days, while the emperor was leading an army against
Miesco, the king of those Slavs who are called Poles,[100] Odo, the son
of the sister of the same Rudolf, a prince of Champagne in France,[101]
invaded the kingdom of Burgundy, captured the fortresses of Neuen-
burg and Murten and placed his own garrisons in them.

Abbot Bern of Reichenau sent the privileges of his monastery to Rome
and received from Pope John the additional privilege of celebrating
mass in episcopal garments, together with the gift of sandals. Thereupon Bishop Warmann of Constance was moved to anger and accused
him to the emperor as an invader of his office and his honour, so that
he was hard pressed by both parties until he surrendered that privilege together with the sandals to the bishop himself publicly in his
synod to be burned, namely on Holy Thursday of the following year
[30 March].[102] In the same year the convent of Buchau burned down
on 12 January.

Bertha, my grandmother,[103] a very devout woman, died in the twenty-
third year of her widowhood on 22 December.

---

96 He died in Como on the return journey (6 April): Bresslau (1879) pp. 306, 317.

97 Bardo, monk of Fulda, abbot of Hersfeld, archbishop of Mainz (1031–51).

98 Rudolf III (993–1032) † 6 September.

99 Seliger, known only from this reference by Herman, 'a Burgundian magnate …,
who must have belonged to the German party at Rudolf's court': Bresslau (1884)
p. 10. The *Chronicon Suevicum universale* 1032, p. 71 (perhaps the work of Berthold of
Reichenau) clarifies this report: 'When Rudolf, king of Burgundy died, he sent his
crown to Emperor Conrad.'

100 Mieszko II (1025–34). The emperor's unsuccessful expedition was in September:
Bresslau (1884) p. 9.

101 Odo II, count of Blois-Champagne (995–1037), son of Bertha, sister of King Rudolf
III, claimed Burgundy as the grandson of King Conrad of Burgundy. Cf. Wipo,
Deeds c. 29, p. 47. See Bresslau (1884) pp. 13–17.

102 John XIX's privilege of 28 October 1031: *JL* 4093, confirming the privilege of Gregory V, *JL* 3880, for Abbot Alawich II: Zimmermann (1969) no. 825. See Bresslau
(1884) pp. 124–5; Brandi (1890) pp. 19–20; Herrmann (1973) p. 41.

103 According to Oesch (1961) p. 122 and Kerkhoff (1964) p. 8 with n. 9, Bertha was
the daughter of Count Manegold of Sulmetingen, nephew of St Udalric, bishop of
Augsburg (923–73). But see Borgolte (1979) p. 6.

1033. After Christmas [25 December 1032] the emperor went to Burgundy and laid siege to Murten but the coldness of the winter hindered him from achieving there anything worthy of himself.[104] In the summer, therefore, he again attacked Odo's own province of Champagne in France and laid it waste with fire and pillage until Odo himself came to him as a suppliant. He was received mercifully and he promised to make reparation, although in a dissembling fashion.[105]

In Rome on the death of John, Benedict IX, also called Theophylact, was ordained as the 149th pope, although he was unworthy of so high a rank, both in his character and in his deeds, and he reigned for more than twelve years.[106] There was an eclipse of the sun on 29 June about the seventh hour of the day.

1034. The emperor again went to Burgundy with many troops, subjected all the fortresses on this side of the Rhone, destroyed Murten and entered the city of Geneva. He received the surrender of Archbishop Burchard of Lyons (a vigorous man of noble origin but thoroughly wicked and sacrilegious),[107] together with many other princes. When the kingdom of Burgundy had been subjected, he returned.[108] In the same year on the death of Bishop Warmann of Constance, his brother Eberhard succeeded and ruled for more than twelve years.[109] Bishop Meginhard of Würzburg[110] also died and Bruno, a paternal cousin of the emperor (namely the son of Duke Conrad by Matilda),[111] received the bishopric on Easter day [14 April]. In St Gallen Abbot Theobald also died and Norbert succeeded.[112] The pagan Slavs known as the Liutizi[113] attacked the frontiers of Saxony.

---

104 February 1033: cf. Wipo, *Deeds* c. 30, p. 49. See Bresslau (1884) pp. 70–1.

105 September 1033: cf. Wipo, *Deeds* c. 31, p. 50. See Bresslau (1884) pp. 87–9.

106 Benedict IX (elected December 1032, resigned 1 May 1045, deposed 20 December 1046). His reputation: Poole (1934) pp. 199–200, 202–6; Herrmann (1973) pp. 166–9.

107 Burchard III, bishop of Aosta, archbishop of Lyons (1031–4). His character: Ralph Glaber, *Historiae* V.21, p. 246.

108 The formal surrender was on 1 August 1034: cf. Wipo, *Deeds* c. 32, p. 51. See Bresslau (1884) pp. 111–12.

109 Eberhard (1034–46).

110 Meginhard (1019–34).

111 Bruno, son of Duke Conrad I of Carinthia (n. 41) and Matilda (n. 69), bishop of Würzburg (1034–45).

112 Norbert (1034–72).

113 A confederation of the Slav tribes of the Zirzipani, Tollensi, Kessini and Redarii living between the Rivers Elbe and Oder. See Reuter (1991a) pp. 178–9, 213, 256–7, 260, 262.

1035. In Italy the lesser vassals[114] rose against their lords and formed a powerful conspiracy, wishing to oppress them and to live by their own laws. The magnates united together to restrain them and there was a battle and many were killed on both sides, among whom was the bishop of Asti,[115] who died of his wounds. Duke Adalbero of Carinthia and Istria lost the emperor's favour and was also deprived of his duchy.[116] The Liutizi captured the fortress of Werben, which was secretly betrayed to them, and killed or led away captive many of our men. The emperor forced a crossing of the River Elbe, entered their province and laid it waste far and wide.[117] A great synod was assembled by the emperor in Tribur.[118]

1036. Archbishop Pilgrim of Cologne died and Herman, the grandson of Emperor Otto II by his daughter,[119] succeeded him. Bishop Gebhard II of Regensburg died on 15 February. In his place Gebhard III, the brother of Emperor Conrad by his mother Adelaide,[120] was ordained bishop. King Henry, the emperor's son, was joined in matrimony to Gunhild, the daughter of Cnut, king of the Danes and the English,[121] in a royal wedding in Nimwegen. Conrad, the emperor's paternal cousin, received from the emperor his father's duchy in Carinthia and Istria, which Adalbero had held.[122] Duke Herman of Swabia also received from the emperor the march of his father-in-law Manfred in Italy.[123] The

---

114 The *valvassores* of Lombardy, i.e. the sub-vassals holding a rank between the *capitanei* and the *plebs*: see Niermeyer and van de Kieft (2002) p. 1390. Cf. Wipo, *Deeds* c. 34, p. 54: 'saying that if their emperor would not come, they would make their own law for themselves'.

115 Adelrich (1008–35) died in battle at Campo Malo (between Milan and Lodi). See Bresslau (1884) pp. 210–13; Schwartz (1913) pp. 93–4; Cowdrey (1966) p. 9.

116 At an assembly in Bamberg, 18 May 1035: Bresslau (1884) pp. 133–40.

117 Cf. Wipo, *Deeds* c. 33, p. 53. See Bresslau (1884) pp. 132, 150–2.

118 May 1036: Bresslau (1884) pp. 161–2.

119 Herman II (1036–56), son of Otto II's daughter Matilda (†1025) and the Lotharingian count palatine Ezzo.

120 Gebhard III (1036–60), half-brother of Conrad II, son of Adelaide (n. 68) by her second husband (unknown). See Bresslau (1879) pp. 340–2.

121 Gunhild (Cunigunde in Germany), queen (†1038), daughter of Cnut II 'the Great', king of Denmark (1017/18–35), England (1016–35), Norway (1028–35). The wedding was in June 1036: Bresslau (1884) p. 169.

122 2 February in Augsburg: Bresslau (1884) p. 158. See above n. 42.

123 Olderich-Manfred II, margrave of Turin (†1034/5), whose daughter Adelaide married Herman IV of Swabia. See Bresslau (1884) p. 189.

Liutizi Slavs were obliged to pay tribute to the emperor.[124] Burchard [III], the archbishop or rather the tyrant of Lyons, a sacrilegious plunderer of churches and incestuous adulterer, made war on Udalric, the son of Seliger, and was defeated and captured by him and brought to the emperor. He was put into fetters and thrown into prison and for many years he was held in chains.[125] In the winter the emperor set out for Italy.[126] Nuns were brought to Altdorf by the lady Irmgard, widow of Count Welf [II],[127] in place of the secular clergy.

1037. The emperor celebrated Christmas [25 December 1036] in Verona and came by way of Brescia and Cremona to Milan. Going from there to Pavia, he ordered the arrest of Archbishop Aribert of Milan,[128] who was accused of disloyalty, and placed him in the custody of Patriarch Poppo of Aquileia.[129] He escaped and strove with all his might to mount a rebellion against the emperor. After celebrating Easter [10 April] in Ravenna, the emperor returned to Milanese territory, besieged the city and laid waste castles, villages and everything in the surrounding area that belonged to the rebels. He easily suppressed the forces of the conspirators and confirmed for them in writing the law that they had had in earlier times.[130] Pope Benedict [IX] came to the emperor in Cremona.[131] The bishops of Piacenza, Cremona and Vercelli were accused by the emperor, taken prisoner and sent into exile.[132] In the same year a battle was fought between Odo, the prince of Champagne in France, and Gozelo, duke of the Lotharingians.[133] Odo was

---

124 Cf. Wipo, *Deeds* c. 33, p. 53: 'afterwards they paid to Emperor Conrad the tribute imposed by the emperors of old, which was now increased'.

125 See above nn. 99, 107. He was at liberty again in 1039/40: Bresslau (1884) p. 421 n. 2.

126 December: Bresslau (1884) p. 227.

127 Irmgard (Imiza, + after 1037), widow of Welf II (n. 73). Altdorf (near Ravensburg) was the Welf family monastery: see Hauck (1954) p. 1020.

128 Aribert (1018–45). The events took place in March 1037. Cf. Wipo, *Deeds* c. 35, pp. 54–5. See Bresslau (1884) pp. 228–36; Cowdrey (1966) pp. 8–10.

129 Poppo (1019–42).

130 Cf. Wipo, *Deeds* c. 35, p. 55: 'he eliminated the lawless conspiracies of Italy after restoring just law', an allusion to the *Constitutio de feudis* of 28 May (*MGH Constitutiones* 1, 89–91, no. 45). See Bresslau (1884) pp. 244–7; Cowdrey (1966) pp. 10–11.

131 Cf. Wipo, *Deeds* c. 36, p. 56. See Bresslau (1884) p. 253; Herrmann (1973) pp. 106, 148.

132 Peter of Piacenza (1031–8); Hubald of Cremona (1031–67); Arderic of Vercelli (1027–?44). Cf. Wipo, *Deeds* c. 35, p. 55. See Bresslau (1884) pp. 256, 265–7.

133 Gozelo I, duke of Lower Lotharingia (1023–44), duke of Upper Lotharingia (1033–44) defeated Odo (n. 101) at the battle of Bar (15 November). Cf. Wipo, *Deeds* c. 35, p. 55. See Bresslau (1884) pp. 269–72.

defeated and fled with his men and during that flight he was struck down and died.

1038. While the emperor was celebrating Christmas [25 December 1037] in Parma, a fight broke out between his army and the citizens of Parma in which many were killed. After very many of the citizens had been slaughtered, the city was consumed by fire.[134] The pope excommunicated the archbishop of Milan, who was still rebelling against the emperor.[135] After the emperor had travelled through the regions beyond Rome and returned from there along the coast of the Adriatic Sea, in the month of July a great plague attacked the army and indiscriminately destroyed very many people. Among them was Queen Gunhild, the wife of King Henry, who died on 16 July[136] and was brought to the fortress of Limburg[137] and buried there. Duke Herman of Swabia also succumbed to death, greatly lamented by his followers, on 28 July and was buried in Trento. When the emperor returned from Italy, he held an assembly in Solothurn and caused very many of the Burgundian magnates to confirm on oath their subjection both to himself and to his son.[138]

In the same year died Stephen, king of the Hungarians,[139] very many years after he had converted, together with all his people, to the faith of Christ, after he had built many churches and bishoprics and had bestowed great pains on the government of his kingdom, being most gentle towards the virtuous. He installed Peter, his sister's son, born in Venice, as king in his place.[140]

1039. While Emperor Conrad was celebrating Whitsun in Utrecht, a city of Frisia, he died suddenly and unexpectedly on 3 June[141] and was brought to Speyer and buried there. His son, King Henry, took up the government of the kingdom. Bishop Reginbald of Speyer, a man reverend both in his life and in his monastic habit, also died, on 13

134 Cf. Wipo, *Deeds* c. 37, p. 57. See Bresslau (1884) pp. 274–7.

135 Benedict IX visited the imperial camp at Spello (near Foligno) in March: Bresslau (1884) pp. 285–6.

136 18 July, according to Wipo, *Deeds* c. 37, p. 57. See Bresslau (1884) p. 318 n. 1.

137 Limburg on the Hardt, the Salian family monastery. See Hauck (1954) p. 1023.

138 'In the autumn'; Wipo, *Deeds* c. 38, p. 58. See Bresslau (1884) pp. 322–5.

139 15 August.

140 Peter (king, 1038–41, 1044–6, †1059), son of Otto Orseolo, duke of Venice and a sister of Stephen I (name unknown).

141 4 June (Whit Monday), according to Wipo, *Deeds* c. 39, p. 59 and to other evidence in Bresslau (1884) p. 335 n. 2.

October. Sibicho, a man of very different reputation, succeeded him.[142] Duke Conrad of Carinthia and his rival Adalbero, who had held the same duchy before him, also died in the same year.[143]

King Henry undertook an expedition to Bohemia, but when Bretislav, the duke of that people, had sent him his son as a hostage[144] and had promised – although it was a feigned promise – that he himself would come and perform what was commanded of him, he at once returned. During the winter Peter, king of the Hungarians invaded the frontiers of his kingdom and laid it waste, plundering, burning and taking captives.[145]

1040. King Henry attacked the duke of the Bohemians, who was once again in rebellion. In order to storm the forest obstruction or rampart[146] on both sides, he sent the lightly armed part of the army through a lonely mountain pass into the province. When, however, the knights entered the difficult and heavily wooded terrain, on 22 August on this side and on the following day on the other side, and while with futile labour, already wearied, they sought in vain to attack a particular earthwork, the Bohemians poured in on all sides and they were slaughtered, taken prisoner or put to flight. Those of our men who still remained in the province were brought out through the intervention of the hermit Gunther[147] and returned safely. Meanwhile the king departed with the loss of very many knights and princes and with his purpose unfulfilled.[148]

Eberhard, the first bishop of the church of Bamberg, died in the thirty-third year after his promotion. Suidger, a Saxon by birth and a praiseworthy man, succeeded him.[149]

---

142 Reginbald (?1032–9); Sibicho (Sigebod) (1039–54). The latter's evil reputation: *Life of Pope Leo IX* II.12, p. 139. See Friedmann (1994) pp. 113–20.

143 Conrad on 20 July, Adalbero on 28/29 November.

144 Bretislav I (1034–55) had intervened in Poland and plundered Cracow. His sons were Spitignev, Vratislav, Conrad and Otto: Cosmas of Prague, *Chronica Boemorum* I.41, II.15, pp. 77, 105. Steindorff (1874) pp. 69–70 suggested that Spitignev was the hostage.

145 Probably early 1040, in support of Bretislav: Steindorff (1874) pp. 76–7.

146 Mentioned also by the *Annalista Saxo* 1040, p. 684 and Cosmas, *Chronica* II.3, p. 84, it was perhaps a permanent frontier rampart, such as was later recorded in Bohemia: Steindorff (1874) p. 94 n. 3.

147 Gunther (✝1045), from the Thuringian comital family of Schwarzburg and Käfernburg, monk of Niederaltaich, founded a settlement of hermits at Rinchnach.

148 The completeness of the defeat: *Annalista Saxo* 1040, p. 684. See Steindorff (1874) pp. 94–7.

149 Suidger (1040–7); Pope Clement II (1046–7).

1041. King Henry restored to the Bohemian duke his son, who had been held as a hostage, and ransomed the prisoners who had been captured in the forest. The following summer he collected a great army, entered that province by an unfrequented route and laid everything waste with pillage and burning until the duke was compelled by hardship to sue for peace.[150] He summoned the king's vassals to him and promised them his own surrender and subjection together with all his people and also promised that he would come to the king in Regensburg and perform what was commanded him. He soon fulfilled this promise through his actions after the king had departed.[151]

In the same year the treacherous Hungarians set up a certain Aba as their king[152] and strove to kill their king Peter. He barely escaped and came as a fugitive at first to our Margrave Adalbert, his sister's husband.[153] From there he came to King Henry and, throwing himself at his feet, he begged for and obtained pardon and favour.[154]

1042. King Henry entered Burgundy during the winter and received many of the princes who submitted to him and judged some cases according to the laws.[155]

Because our king acknowledged Peter, Aba, the tyrant of the Hungarians, divided his army into two and pillaged, burned and laid waste the territory of Bavaria on both sides of the Danube. One part of his army, however, in the northern region of the Danube, was slaughtered to the last man by Margrave Adalbert and his son Liutpald.[156] In the autumn King Henry also invaded Hungary, destroyed Hainburg and Pressburg and either laid waste or received the surrender of the northern region of the Danube as far as the River Gran, because rivers and marshes

150 Henry entered Bohemia on 15 August and campaigned until 29 September: Steindorff (1874) pp. 107–10.

151 He appeared in Regensburg in October, paid tribute, took an oath of fidelity and promised service to Henry and received from him Bohemia and two Polish provinces: Steindorff (1874) pp. 111–13.

152 Aba-Samuel, king of Hungary (1041–4).

153 Adalbert (of Babenberg), margrave of Austria (1018–55). His wife's name is unknown.

154 Cf. Bern, *Letter* 26 (to Henry III), p. 59: 'you opened the bosom of piety to King Peter when he humbly sought refuge with you'.

155 January–February 1042. An assembly of the Burgundian princes was held in Besançon in February. Cf. Ralph Glaber, *Historiae* V.22, p. 246. See Steindorff (1874) pp. 136–40; Müller (1901) p. 36.

156 Liutpald (of Babenberg), margrave (†1043): see n. 153. Aba's expedition began 13 February: *Annals of Niederaltaich* 1041, p. 28. See Steindorff (1874) pp. 149–51.

protected the southern region. Part of the army twice encountered attacking Hungarians and wrought great slaughter. After the subjection of the Hungarians of that territory, since they refused to accept Peter, he installed for them as duke one of their number who was at that time in exile among the Bohemians.[157] Immediately after the king's departure, however, Aba drove the duke back into Bohemia and the latter was unable to put up any resistance.

Patriarch Poppo of Aquileia died and Eberhard, canon of Augsburg, was appointed by the king as his successor.[158]

1043. Empress Gisela died in Goslar on 14 February[159] of the disease of dysentery, although she believed – having been deceived by soothsayers who had sometimes made true predictions for her – that she would outlive her son, the king. She was buried in Speyer next to her husband, the emperor.[160] A rainy summer caused a scarcity of crops and wine.

King Henry again went to Hungary. From Aba, who with great difficulty obtained a treaty with him, he received reparation, hostages, gifts and the part of the kingdom extending to the River Leitha,[161] and then departed. From there he came into Swabia and in a synod in Constance he first forgave every trespass on the part of all those who had committed offences against him. Then through prayers and exhortations he achieved a mutual reconciliation of all the Swabians present, when they had forgiven trespasses and enmities, and he was eager that the same thing should be done in the other provinces of his kingdom. He thus brought about a peace unheard of for many centuries and confirmed it by an edict.[162] Next he received as his bride Agnes, daughter of William of Poitou,[163] and caused her to be anointed as queen

---

157 Name unknown: Steindorff (1874) p. 161.

158 Eberhard (1042–8).

159 15 February, according to the necrologies: Steindorff (1874) p. 173 n. 1.

160 11 March. Bern, *Letter* 24 (to Henry III), p. 54 describes Henry's public penitence at the funeral.

161 Confirmed by Henry III's diploma *D.H.III* 277 (25 October 1051) recording donations of land near the Leitha. See Steindorff (1874) pp. 180–1.

162 Cf. Bern, *Letter* 27 (to Henry III), p. 57: '[justice and peace] have framed such great treaties of concord throughout your kingdom as are unheard of in all the centuries before'. Henry's 'peace council': Steindorff (1874) pp. 185–7; Ladner (1936) pp. 70–8; Hoffmann (1964) pp. 88–9; Wadle (1973) pp. 159–62.

163 Agnes of Poitou (?1025–77), queen (1043), empress (1046), daughter of William V, duke of Aquitaine-Poitou (995–1029).

in Mainz. He celebrated the royal nuptials in Ingelheim[164] and he offered a useful example to everyone by treating as worthless the vain applause of the stage players and sending them away empty-handed and lamenting.[165] There also Liutpald, son of Margrave Adalbert, a youth of great valour and piety, was promoted by the king to be a margrave. A few days later, however, he died[166] and was buried in Trier by his paternal uncle, Archbishop Poppo.

1044. A very great pestilence of cattle and a rather harsh and snowy winter destroyed a large part of the vineyards through cold and the failure of the crops caused a great famine.

At his death Gozelo, duke of the Lotharingians determined to bequeath his duchy to his son Gozelo,[167] although he was incapable, and this was promised by King Henry. His other son, Godfrey, however, who had long been a duke,[168] tried unlawfully to obtain for himself from the king the duchy that was rightfully his brother's. When he proved unable to do so, he disregarded his oath and his fealty and presumed to rebel against the pious king.

When King Aba had broken his oath and his treaty, King Henry invaded Hungary with a very small force. Aba, who had equipped a very large army, held him in such contempt that he allowed him to enter the province, as though it would be easy to kill or to capture him. Henry, however, trusting in divine help, rapidly crossed the River Raab

---

164 The coronation in Mainz probably in mid-November, the wedding in Ingelheim late November: cf. *DD.H.III* 112–18 (Ingelheim, 20 November–1 December). See Steindorff (1874) pp. 192–3.

165 Cf. the description of the wedding of Margrave Boniface of Tuscany and Beatrice (1037?) by Donizo of Canossa, *Vita Mathildis* I.10, p. 368: 'Drums resounded here, together with citharas and lutes and the renowned duke gave very great rewards to the actors.'

166 9 December: Steindorff (1874) p. 195.

167 Gozelo II, duke of Lower Lotharingia (1044–6). Cf. *Annals of Niederaltaich* 1044, p. 34: 'Duke Gozelo of the Lotharingians died and a struggle arose between his sons concerning his property. For he had possessed two duchies and the same number of sons and he had permitted his own duchy to be granted to one of them, Godfrey, during his lifetime, while retaining the other for himself until the end of his life and this the king wished, on the father's death, to give to the other son, Gozelo.' See Steindorff (1874) p. 201; Boshof (1978) pp. 65–6.

168 Godfrey III ('the Bearded'), duke of Upper Lotharingia (1044–7), duke of Lower Lotharingia (1065–9), margrave of Tuscany (1054–69). The royal diploma *D.H.III* 52 (5 June 1040) identifies 'Dukes Gozelo [I] and Godfrey'. Boshof (1978) pp. 66–70 argued that Gozelo I had received a promise from the king that both his duchies would be inherited by Godfrey and that the latter rebelled because the king broke this promise.

with part of his force and began the battle, while all the knights rushed
hither and thither. In the first attack he defeated and put to flight the
innumerable army of the Hungarians, losing very few of his own men.
He himself fought very bravely and he won a most glorious victory on 5
July.[169] King Aba narrowly escaped by fleeing, while all the Hungarians
rushed in crowds to surrender to King Henry and promised subjection
and service. He, however, being in all things a most pious man, restored
King Peter, who had been expelled long before, to his kingdom.[170] He
endowed the Hungarians at their own request with the Bavarian law[171]
and returned in triumph to his own kingdom. Not long afterwards Aba
was taken prisoner by King Peter and paid the penalty of his crimes
with his head.[172]

In the same year, while Prince Reginold, the maternal uncle of Queen
Agnes,[173] but hostile to King Henry, was preparing with a large force
to storm a certain castle of Count Louis,[174] which is called Montbéliard,
the count began the battle with a small force of his knights and defeated
him. Many were killed and he put the rest to flight.

The Romans drove Pope Benedict, who was accused of many crimes,
from his see and put a certain Silvester[175] in his place. Benedict, however,
subsequently excommunicated and expelled him with the support of
certain persons. Once restored to his see, he later deprived himself of

---

169 Battle of Menfö. Cf. Bern, *Letter* 27 (to Henry III), p. 58: 'You recently fought courageously with the Hungarians and defeated them in battle, so that a very great multitude of the enemy were both cut down by the sword and drowned in the waters.'
See Steindorff (1874) pp. 205–9. Otto of Freising, *Chronica* VI.32, p. 298 mentions
'that poem composed by Herman the Lame on the subject of that victory' and quotes
the opening words: 'This voice declaims a song.' The poem is otherwise unknown.
Oesch (1961) pp. 181–2 suggested that Otto ascribed to Herman in error a poem by
the imperial chaplain Wipo.

170 In a ceremony in the church of St Mary in Székesfehervar (Stuhlweissenburg):
Annals of Niederaltaich 1044, p. 37. See Steindorff (1874) p. 210.

171 Cf. *Annals of Niederaltaich* 1044, p. 37: 'At [the Hungarians'] request the king granted
them the German laws.' The significance of this grant is unknown: Steindorff (1874)
p. 211.

172 Cf. the revised version of this annal by Bernold of St Blasien, *Chronicon* 1044, p. 425:
'Peter ... caught Aba, together with his wife and children, and beheaded him.'

173 Reginold, count in Upper Burgundy, son of Count Otto-William of Burgundy,
whose daughter Agnes was the queen's mother.

174 Louis, count of Montbéliard. Cf. Bernold, *Chronicle* 1092, below p. 309.

175 John, cardinal bishop of Sabina; Pope Silvester III (elected 10 January 1045, deposed
10 March 1045). See Hüls (1977) p. 125. The rebellion against Benedict IX (September 1044): Poole (1934) pp. 150–1, 197–8; Herrmann (1973) pp. 150–4.

office and appointed another[176] in his place, prompted by avarice and contrary to canon law.[177]

Archbishop Aribert of Milan died.[178] Godfrey's fortress of *Beggelinheim*[179] was captured by the king and destroyed. Archbishop Gebhard of Ravenna died[180] and Widger was appointed in his place.[181]

1045. The Burgundians Reginold and Gerold[182] came to surrender to the king in Solothurn.[183] During Easter week [7–13 April] the count palatine Otto was appointed duke of Swabia[184] by the king in Goslar.

King Peter issued an invitation to King Henry and received him with great magnificence at the feast of Whitsun [26 May] and presented him with very great gifts. He resigned to him the kingdom of the Hungarians, while the princes of the Hungarians confirmed their fealty to him and his successors by an oath. Peter, however, received the kingdom back from him to possess during his lifetime.[185] During this journey the king climbed up into a certain old balcony;[186] the building collapsed and he, with many others, fell to the ground. Through the protection of God he himself was unhurt but Bishop Bruno of Würzburg, together with others,[187] was mortally injured by the fall. He died a week later, on 26

---

176 John Gratian, archpriest of St John at the Latin Gate; Pope Gregory VI (elected 1 May 1045, deposed 20 December 1046). See Poole (1934) pp. 206–13; Herrmann (1973) pp. 155–6, 158–60; Cowdrey (1998) pp. 22–6.

177 Cf. Bernold's revised version of this annal, *Chronicon* 1044, p. 425: '[Benedict] voluntarily departed from the papacy and permitted Gratian to be ordained as the 151st pope in his place under the name Gregory VI.'

178 16 January 1045.

179 Possibly Böckelheim near Kreuznach on the River Nahe: Steindorff (1874) p. 219.

180 Gebhard (1028–44).

181 Widger (1044–6).

182 Perhaps Gerold, count of Geneva (Egisheim family).

183 Henry III was in Solothurn on 23 January 1045: *D.H.III* 129. See Steindorff (1874) p. 219.

184 Otto II, Lotharingian count palatine (1035–45), duke of Swabia (1045–7), son of the count palatine Ezzo and Matilda (daughter of Otto II).

185 Cf. *Annals of Niederaltaich* 1045, p. 40: 'King Peter delivered up the kingdom of Hungary to the emperor with a golden lance'; Wipo, *Deeds* c. 1, pp. 12–13: 'after his victory [Henry] confirmed [Hungary] for himself and his successors by means of the wisest counsels'. See Steindorff (1874) pp. 233–5; Boshof (1986) p. 183.

186 In the residence of Richlind, widow of Count Adalbero II of Ebersberg, in Persenbeug: Steindorff (1874) pp. 229–31.

187 Including Richlind herself and Abbot Altman of Ebersberg and Tegernsee.

May,[188] and was brought back to his see. His successor was Adalbero.[189]

Duke Godfrey, despairing of the success of his rebellion, came to surrender to the king and was sent to prison.[190] Wido was appointed archbishop in Milan.[191] The Slavs who are called the Liutizi were troubling the borders of Saxony; but when the king came there with a force of vassals, they surrendered and promised the customary tribute.[192]

In the autumn the hermit Gunther departed to Christ[193] and was laid to rest in Prague, a city of Bohemia. At the same time the king was seriously ill, which prevented the meeting of a royal assembly intended to be held in Tribur.[194] At this time also Queen Agnes bore the king a daughter.[195]

1046. The king celebrated Christmas [25 December 1045] in Saxony at Goslar. A great sickness destroyed many people on all sides. The very wealthy Margrave Ekkehard[196] died suddenly and left the king as the heir of his estates.

The king celebrated Easter [30 March] in Utrecht, a city of Frisia, and in the following days he crossed with a fleet to the sound of Vlaardingen and seized from Margrave Theoderic[197] a certain property that he had usurped[198] and the latter subsequently made this the grounds for a rebellion. The king celebrated the holy day of Whitsun [18 May] in Aachen and Duke Godfrey, released from prison, appeared before him and prostrated himself at full length on the earth. The king had compassion

---

188 27 May, according to other sources: Steindorff (1874) p. 231 n. 2.

189 Adalbero (1045–90).

190 July. He was imprisoned in Giebichenstein (near Halle): Lampert of Hersfeld, *Annales* 1045, p. 59. See Steindorff (1874) p. 237; Boshof (1978) pp. 84–5.

191 Wido (1045–71).

192 August: see Steindorff (1874) pp. 285–6; Müller (1901) p. 55. On the Liutizi see above n. 113.

193 9 October: Steindorff (1874) p. 289 n. 1.

194 According to *Annals of Niederaltaich* 1045, p. 40, the king's illness was so severe that some princes and bishops began to debate the succession, deciding on the Lotharingian count palatine Henry I. See Steindorff (1874) p. 287.

195 Adelaide II, abbess of Quedlinburg and Gandersheim († ?1096). See Black-Veldtrup (1995) p. 11.

196 Ekkehard II, margrave of Meissen (1032–46), last of the Ekkehardiner dynasty.

197 Theoderic IV, count of Holland (1039–49).

198 Perhaps the Frisian county of Drenthe (formerly held by the Lotharingian duke Gozelo I), which Henry III granted to the church of Utrecht (22 May): *D.H.III* 152. See Steindorff (1874) pp. 293–4; Boshof (1978) p. 88.

on him and restored his duchy.[199] In these days he summoned to him Widger, who for the past two years had held episcopal office in Ravenna in an improper and cruel manner and who had not yet been consecrated, and deprived him of the bishopric.[200] Subsequently the king prepared an expedition to Italy. Frederick, brother of Duke Henry of Bavaria,[201] was made duke of the Lotharingians in place of the incapable Gozelo, brother of Godfrey.

The following autumn the Hungarians remembered their former treachery and set up a certain Andreas as their king.[202] They killed the many foreigners who had fought for King Peter; they inflicted various injuries on him and his wife and finally they deprived Peter of his eyes and sent him, together with his wife, to be kept in a certain place. At the same time many foreigners in that country were despoiled, exiled and killed. When he learned of this, King Henry had gathered a powerful army and had already begun the expedition to Italy. He was sorely troubled; nevertheless he did not abandon the expedition that he had begun. He therefore assembled his army and held a synod in Pavia.[203] From there he came to Piacenza and gave an honourable reception to Gratian [Gregory VI],[204] who came to him there. The Romans had set up this Gratian as pope after driving out his predecessors. All things thus turning out well, towards Christmas the king again held a synod in Sutri, not far from the city of Rome, and when the case of the false popes had been investigated more carefully, Pope Gratian was convicted and the king deprived him of the pastoral staff.[205] Then with the consent

---

199 Cf. *Annals of Niederaltaich* 1046, p. 41: Henry 'gave to Duke Godfrey the grace of his reconciliation and the one duchy over which he ruled in his father's lifetime', i.e. Upper Lotharingia. See Steindorff (1874) p. 295; Boshof (1978) pp. 85–6.

200 Cf. Peter Damian, *Letter* 20 (to Henry III), p. 200: 'In the expulsion of Widger ... the church is snatched away from the hands of a furious plunderer.' See Steindorff (1874) pp. 295–7; Schwartz (1913) p. 156.

201 Frederick (of Luxemburg), duke of Lower Lotharingia (1046–65), brother of Henry VII, duke of Bavaria (1042–7). On the probable fate of Gozelo II: Boshof (1978) pp. 85–6.

202 Andreas I (1046–60), son of Vaszoly, nephew of King Stephen I. See Steindorff (1874) pp. 305–6; Boshof (1986) p. 183.

203 25 October. Cf. synodal *acta* of Pavia, *MGH Constitutiones* 1, 94–5. See Boye (1929) p. 272.

204 See above n. 176. Cf. Bonizo, *To a friend* V, p. 184. See Schmale (1979) pp. 88–90; Schmid (1975) pp. 79–97.

205 20 December. Cf. the revised version of this annal by Bernold, *Chronicon* 1046, p. 425: 'Pope Gratian, Gregory VI by name, ... at Sutri in a synod laid down the pastoral office not unwillingly.' See Steindorff (1874) pp. 313–14, 456–510; Poole (1934) pp. 185–222; Zimmermann (1968) pp. 119–39; Schmale (1979) pp. 55–103.

of all, both Romans and others, he elected as supreme pontiff of the Roman church Bishop Suidger, who after Eberhard, the first bishop, as the second bishop of Bamberg was now in his sixth year as ruler of that church and who strongly resisted his election.²⁰⁶ Thus on Christmas Eve they entered the city. On that same night Eberhard of good memory, bishop of the church of Constance, died in the thirteenth year of his episcopate and was buried there in the portico of St Peter's.

1047. On Christmas day [25 December 1046] the aforementioned Suidger, a Saxon by birth, was consecrated to the apostolic see in the customary manner as the 151st pope and was dignified with the name Clement II. Immediately on the same day he exalted King Henry and his wife Agnes with the imperial consecration. When the solemnities of the mass had been completed, the lord pope and the emperor, crowned as he was, together with the empress, set out with great glory for the Lateran palace, to the wonder of all the Roman citizens, each of whom according to his ability showed him honour as he passed by.²⁰⁷ After spending some days in Rome in the utmost peace, the emperor permitted a great part of the army to return to the fatherland, while he himself advanced to the more distant regions with the rest.²⁰⁸

About this time the emperor appointed some prelates. Among these he promoted as bishops: in the church of Ravenna, Hunfried, his chancellor in Italy; in the church of Constance, Theoderic, his chancellor for the other provinces and archchaplain and provost in Aachen;²⁰⁹ in the church of Strasbourg, Herrand, provost in Speyer, in place of William, who had died during the autumn;²¹⁰ in the church of Verdun, Theoderic, provost in Basel and his chaplain.²¹¹ Departing from Rome, the

---

206 Clement II (n. 149) was elected on 24 December. Bernold, *Chronicon* 1046, p. 425 added here: 'In the time of this pope there were innumerable earthquakes, especially in Italy, and this was perhaps because this pope was substituted for his predecessor, who had not been canonically deposed; for it was not a fault that deposed him but simple humility persuaded him to give up his office.'

207 See Steindorff (1874) pp. 315–17; Schramm (1929) pp. 228–38. The imperial coronation ceremony: *Die Ordines für die Weihe und Krönung des Kaisers* pp. 34–5 (no. XIII); Robinson (1999) pp. 230–1.

208 Cf. *DD.H.III* 178 (1 January 1047 in Colonna near Frascati), 179–81 (3 January in Rome), 183 (7 January in Colonna). He travelled by way of the abbey of Monte Cassino (*Chronicle of Monte Cassino* II.78, pp. 322–3) to Capua (*D.H.III* 184, 3 February).

209 Hunfried, archbishop of Ravenna (1047–51); Theoderic, bishop of Constance (1047–51).

210 Herrand (1046–65); William (1029–46) † 7 November.

211 Theoderic, bishop of Verdun (1046–89).

emperor captured some fortresses that were rebelling against him;[212] he ordered those provinces as seemed to him fit and appointed dukes over the Normans who were living in those regions and over other cities in that territory.[213] When the emperor's mother-in-law[214] returned from Monte Gargano to Benevento, however, there was a riot and the citizens of Benevento inflicted injuries on her. Fearing a harsh punishment from the emperor on that account and not daring to submit themselves to him, they began a rebellion. The emperor, however, had already sent back a great part of his army (as was reported above); his mind was preoccupied with other matters and he was already bending his course towards the fatherland. He deferred an attack at that time on so great a city with a view to its capture and decided meanwhile to return home.[215] That business remained unfinished, although elsewhere the whole of Italy was obedient and peaceful.

Meanwhile Empress Agnes, who had departed from the emperor in Rome, gave birth to a daughter[216] in the territory of Ravenna. The emperor, however, during his return journey celebrated the festival of Easter [19 April] in Mantua and, falling very seriously ill, remained there.[217] When he subsequently recovered, he brought back with him from Italy with great honour the body of the blessed Wido, abbot of the monastery of Pomposa, who had died in great sanctity less than a year before and had been glorified with very many miracles,[218] to be translated from the city of Parma, where he was buried, to the city of Speyer. During this journey he came to Augsburg in the Rogation Days before the Ascension of the Lord [25–27 May] and, since Eberhard, the

212 Steindorff (1874) p. 323 n. 7, linking this passage with Henry's presence in Colonna (*D.H.III* 178), suggested that the counts of Tusculum (kindred of Benedict IX) were the rebels.

213 Cf. Benzo of Alba, *Ad Heinricum IV* I.13, p. 139: Henry III 'subjected [the Normans] under the feet of the princes'. See Steindorff (1874) p. 327; Deér (1972) pp. 44, 46–7.

214 Agnes, widow of Duke William V of Aquitaine, wife of Count Geoffrey II of Anjou (n. 173).

215 Cf. *Annals of Benevento* 1047 (codex 3) p. 179: 'King Henry … came to Benevento, together with Pope Clement, excommunicated the city and set fire to the suburbs'; *Chronicle of Monte Cassino* II.78, p. 323. Henry's siege of Benevento was unsuccessful: Steindorff (1874) pp. 328–9.

216 Gisela, who predeceased her father, probably in 1053: Black-Veldtrup (1995) pp. 19, 109–10. According to *Annals of Niederaltaich* 1047, p. 43, she was born in Mantua.

217 Until 1 May: *DD.H.III* 198–9.

218 Wido, abbot of Pomposa (✝ 31 March 1046). Cf. *D.H.III* 193, Henry III's privilege of 9 April 1047 for the abbey of Pomposa.

bishop of that city, died on his arrival,[219] he appointed his chaplain Henry as his successor.[220] After celebrating that feast there, he celebrated the festival of Whitsun [7 June] in Speyer and there held an assembly with the princes of the kingdom and caused the body of the aforesaid abbot to be entombed in the basilica that was being built outside the city.[221]

At that time he promoted the Swabian count Welf, son of the former count Welf, to be duke of Carinthia.[222] He also appointed the latter's maternal uncle Adalbero, the brother of the dukes Henry and Frederick, as bishop of the church of Metz[223] in succession to the recently deceased Theoderic.[224] Also, when Archbishop Poppo died in these days,[225] he set Eberhard, provost of Worms, over the city of Trier as archbishop.[226]

At the same time, while he was planning an expedition to Hungary to avenge Peter, he was informed that Duke Godfrey, together with Baldwin of Flanders[227] and some others, had renewed the rebellion, had gathered troops and had prepared for war and also that Margrave Theoderic of Vlaardingen had rebelled and had laid waste the neighbouring bishoprics in order to affront the emperor. Moreover Andreas, who obtained Peter's kingdom, had already sent frequent envoys with humble entreaties, confirming that he had been compelled by the Hungarians to accept the kingship, exculpating himself from the injuries inflicted on Peter and announcing that, of those men who had conspired against the latter, he himself had killed some and others were to be surrendered to the emperor. He declared his subjection to the emperor, an annual tribute and faithful service, if the emperor permitted him to hold the kingship.[228] For these reasons that expedition was deferred and, since Duke Godfrey very cunningly used his envoys to conceal his

---

219 26 May: Steindorff (1881) p. 7 n. 7.

220 Henry II (1047–63).

221 The church of St John the Evangelist, north of the city.

222 Welf III, duke (1047–55), son of Count Welf II (n. 73).

223 Adalbero III (1047–72), brother of Duke Henry VII of Bavaria and Duke Frederick of Lower Lotharingia (Luxemburg family) and Irmgard (Imiza), mother of Welf III.

224 Theoderic II (1006–47) † 2 May.

225 16 June.

226 Eberhard (1047–66).

227 Baldwin V, count of Flanders (1035–67). Cf. *Annals of Niederaltaich* 1047, p. 44: Godfrey 'took up with Theoderic, Baldwin and all those whom he could seduce to be companions of his iniquity'. See Steindorff (1881) p. 19. Boshof (1978) p. 94 dated Godfrey's renewal of the rebellion after Henry's failure in Holland (below n. 233).

228 See Steindorff (1881) pp. 12–14; Boshof (1986) pp. 183–4.

rebellion, in the autumn[229] the emperor assembled a fleet and turned his arms against Theoderic in Vlaardingen.

Meanwhile Otto, duke of the Swabians, who had now for three years piously and vigorously ruled the province that had been entrusted to him, died prematurely.[230] In these days also Henry, duke of Bavaria died[231] and was buried in Trier. Pope Clement, who was also called Suidger, likewise died in the region of Rome in the ninth month after his appointment.[232] He was brought back to his bishopric of Bamberg and buried there.

When the expedition had crossed to Vlaardingen, the emperor could make little progress because the waterlogged terrain hindered him. When he turned back, he suffered no small damage to his army because the enemy gave chase by sea in light boats, in the manner of pirates, and attacked and killed those in the rear.[233] At that same time Godfrey, among the other deeds that he perpetrated against the king, captured the city of Verdun by guile and burned and destroyed it.[234] The emperor conferred his duchy on a certain Adalbert.[235]

1048. The emperor remained in Saxony at Christmas [25 December 1047],[236] then immediately came by way of Würzburg into Swabia. He held an assembly in Ulm and placed Margrave Otto of Schweinfurt over the Swabians as their duke.[237] From there he came to Bavaria, where he spent Lent and Eastertide. During that same Lent [16 February–2 April] it is believed that the Lord's blood was found in the city of Mantua by a certain blind man through a divine revelation and was made

---

229 On 7–8 September Henry was in Xanten: Steindorff (1881) p. 17. According to Boshof (1978) p. 93, 'the emperor was slow to react; at first the danger seems to have been underestimated'.

230 7 September.

231 14 October.

232 9 October. See Hauck (1959b) pp. 265–74.

233 Cf. *Annals of Niederaltaich* 1047, p. 47: 'nevertheless, alas! he achieved nothing that could confer praise or honour on the kingdom'.

234 25 October: Hugh of Flavigny, *Chronicon* II, p. 406. Cf. the description of 'the cruel destruction' of Verdun, attacked by 'the savagery of tyrants' in Leo IX's letter, *JL* 4192, col. 628C (1049).

235 Adalbert (of Châtenois), duke of Upper Lotharingia (1047–8). See Steindorff (1881) p. 24; Boshof (1978) p. 96.

236 In Pöhlde.

237 Otto III (1048–57), Babenberg family. The assembly was in late January: cf. *D.H.III* 209 (25 January).

manifest by very many miracles.[238] The emperor left Regensburg, where he celebrated Easter [3 April] with Duke Otto and Duke Bretislav[239] and many princes, and, coming back to Swabia, he entered our own Reichenau. Here on 24 April he caused the new basilica of St Mark the Evangelist, our patron, built by the lord Abbot Bern, to be dedicated in his presence by Bishop Theoderic of Constance. He celebrated the feast of the same saint on the day of the greater litany [25 April] with us, but celebrated the Lord's Ascension [12 May] in Zürich and Whitsun [22 May] in Solothurn. After he had held an assembly there with the Burgundians, he returned to Saxony through eastern Franconia.[240]

At the same time the lord Abbot Bern of Reichenau, a man distinguished both for his learning and for his character, in the fortieth year since his appointment and of a good old age, worn out by sickness, breathed his last on 7 June and lies buried in the basilica of St Mark. In his place the dean Udalric was elected by the brethren and appointed abbot by the emperor.[241] The learned man Wazo, bishop of Liège also died and Dietwin succeeded him.[242]

The following July Bishop Poppo of Brixen, who had been elected by the emperor, was sent to Rome. He was received with honour and ordained to the apostolic see as the 152nd pope; his name was changed and he was called Damasus II.[243] After a few days had passed, however, he died[244] and was buried in S. Lorenzo outside the city.

During the autumn Emperor Henry and King Henry of France[245] met in the territory of Metz and confirmed on oath peace and a treaty between them. In these days a great earthquake occurred during the night of 13 October.[246] In these days also Empress Agnes bore the

238 Cf. *Annals of Augsburg* 1048, p. 126: 'The Lord's blood, it is said, was found in Mantua.'

239 Duke Bretislav I of Bohemia, whose wife Judith (Jutta) of Schweinfurt was Duke Otto's sister.

240 He had reached Minden by 20 July: cf. *D.H.III* 221.

241 Udalric I (1048–69).

242 Wazo (1042–8) ✝ 8 July; Dietwin (1048–75).

243 Poppo, bishop (?1039–48); Damasus II (1047–8), appointed by the emperor in Pöhlde in December 1047, consecrated in Rome on 17 July 1048: Steindorff (1881) pp. 29, 37.

244 9 August 1048: Steindorff (1881) pp. 52–3.

245 Henry I, king of France (1031–60). The conference was in Ivois in mid-October: Steindorff (1881) p. 43; Boshof (1978) pp. 96–7.

246 12 October: *Annals of Niederaltaich* 1048, p. 45; other annals agree with Herman: see Steindorff (1881) p. 43 n. 3.

emperor a daughter.[247] At the same time Godfrey went in pursuit of Duke Adalbert, who had plundered his property, and found him after he had dismissed the majority of his men and had only a few with him and he killed him, together with others who tried to resist.[248] Gerard was appointed duke by the emperor after him.[249] In these days the emperor came to Strasbourg and from there to Ulm towards Christmas and thus he set out for Bavaria.

1049. The emperor celebrated Christmas [25 December 1048] in Freising and the Purification of St Mary [2 February] in Regensburg and he appointed Conrad duke of Bavaria.[250] Around the time of Lent [8 February – 25 March] he departed from there and entered Saxony. Gotebald, provost of Speyer, was promoted by the emperor patriarch of Aquileia,[251] after Eberhard died in these days. Meanwhile in the midst of an icy winter some knights and princes from the coastal regions joined with the bishops [Dietwin] of Liège, [Bernulf of] Utrecht[252] and [Adalbero III of] Metz and prepared an ambush for Theoderic in Vlaardingen. In the ensuing battle they defeated and killed him[253] and subjected that province to the emperor. Nevertheless not long afterwards Godfrey took possession of it; but he was assailed by the same opponents in a battle and was defeated and barely escaped.[254]

At the same time Bruno, bishop of Toul, who had been elected by the emperor and sent to Rome, was received with the highest honour and ordained during Lent as the 153rd pope. He took the name Leo IX.[255] The following Easter, when Udalric, the guardian of the monastery of Reichenau, came to Rome, he consecrated him as abbot and on 26 March, in the second indiction, he confirmed and renewed by his authority the privileges of that same monastery that had been conferred in ancient

---

247 Matilda (✝1060), wife of Rudolf, duke of Swabia: Black-Veldtrup (1995) p. 11. See below p. 102.

248 At Thuin on the Sambre: Steindorff (1881) p. 46.

249 Gerard (of Châtenois), duke of Upper Lotharingia (1048–70), brother of Adalbert.

250 Conrad I (1049–53), of the Ezzonid family.

251 Gotebald (1048–63), appointed at Christmas 1048.

252 Bernulf (1026/7–54).

253 14 January in Dordrecht: Steindorff (1881) p. 66.

254 'It seems that the deposed duke had the plan of operating out of the former Frisian stronghold of his dynasty': Boshof (1978) p. 97.

255 Bruno, bishop (1026–51); Leo IX (1048/9–54), elected at an assembly in Worms in December 1048, consecrated on 12 February 1049. On the different versions of his papal election: Robinson (2004a) pp. 33–5, 57.

times by the apostolic see.[256] In the week after White Week [2–8 April] the same pope celebrated a synod in Rome with the bishops of Italy, particularly against simoniacal heresy.[257] In the week of Whitsun [14–20 May] he assembled another synod in Pavia.[258] From there he came with very many Romans through the Great St Bernard Pass into the territory on this side of the Alps. Odilo, the venerable father of the abbey of Cluny and of many monasteries, ended his days and departed to the Lord on 2 January.[259]

The following summer, when the emperor was preparing an expedition against Godfrey and Baldwin, who had been excommunicated by the lord pope, Godfrey – fearing both the emperor's power and the pope's excommunication – came to Aachen to surrender and with the pope's help he obtained the grace of the emperor.[260] Baldwin, however, held them both in contempt but after his province was in large part laid waste by an army, he at last gave hostages and made a treaty with the emperor.[261] In the autumn the lord pope held a great synod in Rheims with the bishops of France.[262] From there he came to Mainz and celebrated another synod of nearly forty bishops in the presence of the emperor and the princes of our kingdom.[263] Afterwards he entered Swabia and celebrated the feast of St Clement [23 November] and the Sunday before the Advent of the Lord on 26 November in Reichenau and, passing through Augsburg and Bavaria, he kept Christmas in Verona.

256 The privilege Leo IX, *JL* *4155 (the first issued by the new pope to a German recipient) survives only in a falsified version: Steindorff (1881) p. 81 n. 1; Bloch (1930) p. 215.

257 Bernold, *Chronicon* 1049, p. 426 added to this annal: 'In a full meeting of the synod he decreed that the concubines of Roman priests should henceforward be assigned to the Lateran palace as servants. He forbade the buying and selling of altars under anathema.' The *acta* of this first Roman synod have not survived: *Sacra Concilia* 19, col. 721–6; Steindorff (1881) pp. 78–80; Capitani (1966) p. 144; Petrucci (1977) pp. 31–2; Munier (2002) pp. 116–19.

258 The *acta* have not survived: Steindorff (1881) p. 82.

259 Odilo, abbot since 996, died on the night of 31 December 1048–1 January 1049. Bernold's revised version of this annal (p. 426) reads '1 January'.

260 In July: Steindorff (1881) p. 83. Cf. *Annals of Niederaltaich* 1049, p. 45: Leo 'obtained life and safety for [Godfrey and Baldwin] on this condition, that they submitted to imperial lordship'.

261 In Aachen: Sigebert of Gembloux, *Chronica* 1049, p. 359.

262 3–5 October. See *Sacra Concilia* 19, col. 727–46; Steindorff (1881) pp. 87–92; Capitani (1966) pp. 149–81; Munier (2002) pp. 125–30.

263 19–26 October. See *MGH Constitutiones* 1, 97 (no. 51); Steindorff (1881) pp. 93–9; Munier (2002) pp. 130–1.

1050. The emperor, however, remained in Saxony during that festival [25 December 1049].[264] That winter, while Bishop Gebhard of Regensburg, who had recently received the abbey of Kempten from the emperor as a benefice,[265] was lingering on the frontier of Hungary, the Hungarians withdrew and he invaded their lands and brought back plunder. When he had departed, however, a very great army of Hungarians invaded our territory, taking prisoners, burning and causing devastation over a large area.[266] The emperor spent Eastertide [15 April] in Maastricht.[267]

After Easter the lord pope again assembled a synod in Rome[268] and, subsequently advancing beyond Rome, he subjected some of the princes and cities in that region both to himself and to the emperor by means of an oath[269] and excommunicated the Beneventans, who were still in rebellion.[270] Some princes of the foreign nations also sent envoys to him as pope and promised him subjection.[271] The emperor prepared an expedition against Casimir, duke of the Poles, who was planning a rebellion. He was, however, held back by a serious illness and received him when he requested peace and a treaty and departed.[272]

264 In Pöhlde.

265 Cf. above, 1026, p. 64. See Seibert (1991) pp. 526, 554.

266 'The frontier conflict of the year 1050, evidently again provoked by Bavarians, behind whom Bishop Gebhard III of Regensburg was the driving force ...': Boshof (1986) p. 184.

267 'Maastricht' is the translation of Steindorff (1881) p. 106 for Herman's *Traiectum*, which is usually translated 'Utrecht'; but, argues Steindorff (p. 106 n. 1), when Herman referred to Utrecht, he customarily added the gloss 'a city of Frisia'. Cf. above 1039, 1046, pp. 71, 78.

268 29 April. See *Sacra Concilia* 19, col. 769–71; Steindorff (1881) pp. 119–20; Munier (2002) p. 134. In his version of this annal Bernold, *Chronicon* 1050, p. 426, added: 'a synod ... in which he condemned the Berengarian heresy, which had recently been denounced to the apostolic see'. See above pp. 44–5.

269 Deér (1972) p. 88 saw this as evidence of 'an imperial–papal condominium in southern Italy'.

270 Prince Pandulf III of Benevento had refused to submit to Henry III in 1047 (above p. 81) and had been excommunicated by Clement II. In August 1050 the Beneventans expelled Pandulf and invited the pope to assume the lordship of the principality. See Vehse (1930–1) pp. 92–3.

271 According to Steindorff (1881) p. 130, an allusion to King Andreas of Hungary (cf. below 1052, p. 92) and to King Swein Estrithson of Denmark (cf. *Life of Pope Leo IX* II.9, p. 135); according to Deér (1972) p. 88, an allusion to the Normans of southern Italy.

272 Casimir I (1034–58). Cf. *Annals of Niederaltaich* 1050, p. 47: 'Casimir, duke of the Poles was accused of having usurped by force a province given by the emperor to the duke of the Bohemians. He came to the emperor on the royal estate of Goslar

Bishop Gebhard of Regensburg, together with Duke Conrad of Bavaria and Margrave Adalbert [of Austria] and certain other bishops and princes of Bavaria, rebuilt Hainburg and defeated a great force of Hungarians who attacked them and pursued them as they fled until they came into the presence of their innumerable army. Since, however, all the forces of the Hungarians were affected by a panic, which was sent from heaven, and fled, they returned to their camp, giving thanks to God.[273]

That same autumn the lord pope held a synod in Vercelli and suspended Archbishop Hunfried from his office because of a dispute between Ravenna and the Roman church.[274] From there he came again to Lotharingia and to his bishopric of Toul.[275] At that time also Empress Agnes at last bore the emperor a son.[276]

1051. The emperor celebrated Christmas [25 December 1050] in Saxony at Goslar and caused many of the princes to promise on oath fidelity and subjection to his son.[277] Not long afterwards he and the lord pope, together with many bishops and princes, met in Augsburg and celebrated the Purification of the Mother of God [2 February]. There the archbishop of Ravenna was reconciled with the pope[278] and, when they had taken an affectionate leave of one another, the pope returned to Rome. The emperor spent part of Lent in Speyer[279] but celebrated the festival of Easter [31 March] in Cologne and there his son Henry was baptised by Archbishop Herman.

---

and defended himself against the accusation by means of an oath and those matters in which he was guilty he corrected according to the emperor's judgement.' See Steindorff (1881) pp. 112–14.

273 22 September: cf. *Annals of Niederaltaich* 1050, p. 47. See Steindorff (1881) pp. 111–12.

274 Early September: Steindorff (1881) pp. 131–3. The case of Hunfried of Ravenna: Schwartz (1913) p. 157. Bernold, *Chronicon* 1050, p. 426 gives a revised version of this annal: 'In the autumn he assembled a synod in Vercelli, in which he excommunicated that same [Berengarian] heresy.'

275 He had reached Toul on 20 October: cf. Widrich, *Vita et miracula Gerardi* c. 9, p. 509; Leo IX, *JL* 4239–41, col. 654C–659A. See Steindorff (1881) pp. 133–5.

276 Henry IV, king (1056–1106), emperor (1084), born 11 November. On the significance of Herman's 'at last': Steindorff (1881) p. 117; Robinson (1999) p. 19. Cf. *Annals of Niederaltaich* 1050, p. 47: 'In the autumn the empress bore a son, thanks be to God!'

277 In Pöhlde, according to *Annals of Niederaltaich* 1051, p. 47. The significance of the oath-taking: Gericke (1955) pp. 735–7; Robinson (1999) pp. 20–1.

278 Cf. *Life of Pope Leo IX* II.15, pp. 142–3. See Steindorff (1881) p. 138; Schwartz (1913) p. 157; Munier (2002) p. 136.

279 Lent 1051: 13 February–30 March. Henry III in Speyer: *DD.H.III.* 264 (4 March), 266 (15 March), 267 (19 March). See Steindorff (1881) pp. 139–40.

After Easter the lord Pope Leo again assembled a synod in Rome,[280] in which among other matters he excommunicated Bishop Gregory of Vercelli,[281] in his absence and without his knowledge, because of the adultery that he had committed with a certain widow, the bride of his uncle, and because of the perjuries that he had perpetrated. When, however, not long afterwards, he came to Rome and promised to make amends, he restored him to his previous office.

At the same time the emperor forced the surrender of Count Lambert, who was planning to rebel.[282] In this same summer the venerable Bardo of the see of Mainz, who had been a monk before he became an arch-bishop and was remarkable for his thorough piety and sanctity, was taken from the light of this world on 11 June.[283] After his death he was distinguished by many miracles. In his place the emperor appointed Luitpold, provost of Bamberg.[284] Likewise in place of Bishop Theoderic of Constance, who died on 22 June in the fifth year of his episcopate after a long illness, he appointed Rumold.[285] Archbishop Hunfried of Ravenna also died suddenly, so it is said, from poison.[286]

The following autumn the emperor, disdaining to accept the pact that King Andreas offered through his envoys, invaded Hungary with a great army. While Bishop Gebhard of Regensburg, Duke Welf and Duke Bretislav were sent to lay waste to the northern Danube region, he himself marched through the territory of Carinthia. He made a long detour because of the overflowing of the rivers, while supplies were brought from the ships, as far as possible on horses. He invaded the treacherous kingdom and laid waste all the surrounding territory, as long as supplies were available for the army, since the Hungarian army fled rapidly hither and thither like a band of robbers, nowhere daring to give battle on equal terms. When, however, the army began to suffer from scarcities and hunger, the Hungarians prepared to cut off their retreat, having stationed their forces on the riverbanks that they had

---

280 The *acta* of this synod have not survived and it is recorded only by Herman. See Steindorff (1881) p. 139; Munier (2002) pp. 136–7.

281 Gregory (1044–77). See Schwartz (1913) p. 138.

282 Lambert II, count of Louvain (1041–62). See Steindorff (1881) p. 150.

283 10/11 June. The necrologies give both dates: see Steindorff (1881) p. 144 n. 6.

284 Luitpold (1051–9).

285 Rumold (1051–69).

286 23/24 August: see Steindorff (1881) p. 138 n. 6. Herman alone recorded this rumour. The *Life of Pope Leo IX* II.15, pp. 142–3 represented Hunfried's death as a divine punishment for his resistance to the pope.

previously fortified and in shallow marshes, and threatened either to force them all to surrender or to starve them to death. The knights were undismayed and unhesitatingly waded over and put to flight the enemies who opposed them on the rivers. Certain Burgundian, Saxon and Polish knights crossed the river, not without danger to themselves, and in a short time stormed and captured a very strong fortress built at the bridge over the River Repcze, in which the enemy had the greatest trust. They cut down and scattered the Hungarians and opened the way for the rest of the army. After almost all had passed through, the fortress was set on fire, which cut off some of the hindmost, placing them in great danger because the enemy was pursuing them.[287] The emperor thus returning and those whom he had sent beyond the Danube having long since come back after achieving success in their enterprises, King Andreas sent a request for peace to our Margrave Adalbert and promised peace on his own part.[288]

In these days the abbesses of Lindau and Buchau died almost at the same time and Touta, a noble, prudent and religious widow, was set over both places by the emperor in order to reform them.[289]

1052. The emperor celebrated Christmas [25 December 1051] in Goslar. There, lest the disease of heresy should gradually spread more widely and infect more people, he commanded, with the consent of all, that certain heretics were to be hanged on a gibbet, who among other wicked and erroneous doctrines detested the eating of all animal flesh, like the Manichean sect.[290]

At that same time on 9 January my mother Hiltrud, wife of Count Wolferad, an extremely pious, mild, generous and religious woman, survived by her husband and seven children, ended her days with a pious and, as far as could be seen by human eyes, a happy death, about the sixty-first year of her life and the forty-fourth year of marriage with her husband. She was buried in the village of Altshausen under the chapel

---

287 Cf. *Annals of Niederaltaich* 1051, p. 47: 'An unfortunate and very difficult expedition was made against the Hungarians.' According to Steindorff (1881) p. 158, 'the over-all outcome of this expedition hardly differed from a defeat'.

288 This remained only a treaty between Andreas and Adalbert of Austria, in which the emperor was not involved: Steindorff (1881) p. 158; Boshof (1986) p. 184.

289 Herman is our sole source for this reform.

290 According to Lampert, *Annales* 1053 [for 1052], p. 63, 'heretics were apprehended by Duke Godfrey ['the Bearded'] and hanged [in Goslar]'. This suggests that these heretics may have been Lotharingians, as does the interest of Anselm of Liège, *Gesta episcoporum Leodiensium* c. 64, p. 228. See Steindorff (1881) pp. 165–6; Moore (1977) pp. 39, 244, 252.

of St Udalric, which she had built,[291] in the tomb that she had prepared
for herself. It is pleasant to write down these verses as her epitaph.[292]

> Hiltrud, mother of the poor, the hope and help of her own people,
> in this tomb gives back what is due to the earth.
> She rendered more noble her eminent parents, of distinguished lineage,
> and exalted them by the renown of her devotions.
> She reverently cherished her chaste monogamy
> and her life was dedicated to the divine service.
> She *occupied herself* with sharing the good *portion* of *Martha*[293]
> and in her active life she strove to follow what she taught.
> She showed herself bountiful and pious towards the wretched,
> giving clothing and food, striving in word and deed with all her might.
> She loved above all pious and religious friends
> and she appeared compliant and gentle in all things.
> Remaining mild and patient, knowing nothing of strife,
> she pleased the world; I trust that she also pleased the Lord!
> Mortifying the flesh, frequently visiting holy places to pray there,
> full of zeal, her custom was to seek the help of heaven.
> Believe that I am not inventing these things, uttering empty eulogies,
> nor am I exalting my mother with lying words.
> Seek out the opinion of the people wherever you will:
> a very few words will convince you of the facts.
> Finally, after pure confession had frequently purified her,
> dedicated to the Lord, with a pure heart,
> strengthened by faith, protected by hope, vigorous in her piety,
> she happily abandoned this wretched life.
> When the ninth day of the month of January rolled by,
> she inspired very many tears by her death.
> Reader, I ask, I pray, I entreat, I request, I demand
> that you urge the Lord with humble prayers on her behalf
> so that He may have mercy on her because of her piety towards Him
> and may graciously cleanse her from all her faults
> and generously grant her everlasting rest
> in the happy ranks of His blessed ones.

The following Lent [4 March–18 April] the emperor appointed Archbishop Henry of Ravenna.[294] Bishop Nizo of Freising, who had previ-

---

291 See Kerkhoff (1964) pp. 9, 28. On the kinship of Herman's family with St Udalric,
   bishop of Augsburg: above n. 103.

292 For the commemoration of Hiltrud in the abbey of Reichenau: Kerkhoff (1964) p. 9;
   Borgolte (1979) p. 11. Herman's authorship of these verses (which have not survived
   independently of the chronicle) and their 'genuinely childlike simplicity': Oesch
   (1961) p. 179.

293 Luke 10:40.

294 Henry (1052–72).

ously converted from a very haughty disposition to the appearance of humility and religion but had once more returned to the insolence of his former manners, after he had brought [Henry] to Ravenna at the emperor's command, suddenly died there.[295] The emperor celebrated the festival of Easter [19 April] in Speyer and from that time onwards, so they say, he valued that place less and less, although it possessed the tombs of his father [Conrad II] and mother [Gisela]. He departed in anger and at odds with the bishop of that place [Sibicho].[296]

In these days Boniface, the very wealthy margrave, or rather tyrant, of Italy[297] was ambushed by two knights and wounded by arrows. He died and was buried in Mantua.

When the emperor held an assembly in Solothurn in Rogationtide [25–27 May], certain of the Burgundians departed from there in anger but not long afterwards some of them were restored to his favour.[298] After he had celebrated Whitsun [7 June] in Zürich,[299] he set out from there on another expedition to Hungary. Because Andreas, the king of the Hungarians was less and less inclined to send envoys and to make promises concerning a peace treaty, [the emperor] laid siege to the fortress of Pressburg and for a long time attacked it with various machines of war. Since, however, God aided the besieged, who anxiously called on Him, his efforts were always frustrated and he could by no means capture it.[300] Meanwhile the lord Pope Leo had intervened at the request of Andreas to make peace and he called on the emperor to end the siege. Since he found him in all respects in agreement with him, while discovering that Andreas on the contrary was less obedient to his advice, he was angry and threatened the latter with excommunica-

---

295 Nizo (Nithard, Nitker) (1039–52) ✝ 6 April. Cf. *Life of Pope Leo IX* II.15, p. 142: 'the divine power saw fit to visit a terrible vengeance on [Nizo]'.

296 See above n. 142. Cf. Adam of Bremen, *Gesta Hammaburgensis ecclesiae pontificum* III.30, p. 172: in 1049 he was 'accused of the offence of adultery'; *Life of Pope Leo IX* II.12, p. 139: when he wished to prove his innocence by an 'oath on the body of the Lord' (the communion wafer), 'his jaw was seized by paralysis and so it remained as long as he lived'. In 1052 Henry III's generous series of donations to Speyer ceased: Steindorff (1881) p. 168.

297 Boniface II (of Canossa), margrave of Tuscany (1030–52) ✝ 6 May. See Steindorff (1881) pp. 172–3; Goez (1995) p. 20.

298 See Steindorff (1881) pp. 169–70.

299 He was still in Zürich on 17 June: *D.H.III* 293.

300 Cf. *Annals of Niederaltaich* 1052, p. 48: 'Again an expedition against the Hungarians but nothing of honour or utility achieved for the kingdom.' See Steindorff (1881) pp. 179–82.

tion for mocking the apostolic see. He departed with the emperor and remained with him for some time.[301]

In these days the empress bore the emperor another son, whom they afterwards called Conrad.[302] A dispute broke out between Bishop Gebhard of Regensburg and Duke Conrad of Bavaria and the discord grew worse.[303] The relics of the blessed confessor Zeno were brought by Bishop Walter of Verona[304] to Ulm in Swabia and were renowned at this time for very many miracles. In Constance the church of St Mary fell to the ground.[305]

1053. The emperor spent Christmas [25 December 1052] in Worms with the lord pope and many bishops and princes. There the pope (as he had previously begun to do) demanded and claimed from the emperor the abbey of Fulda and some other places and monasteries that were said to have been given to St Peter in ancient times. Finally the emperor made over to him almost everything that belonged to his jurisdiction in the territory beyond Rome in exchange for the pope's possessions on this side of the Alps.[306] After the pope had made many complaints about the acts of violence and the injuries perpetrated by the Normans, who held the property of St Peter by force against his will, the emperor assigned a military force to help him to expel them from there.[307] That people had since the time of the previous emperor Henry [II][308] gradu-

---

301 They were in Regensburg on 7 October and in Bamberg on 18 October (Leo IX, *JL* 4283, col. 697D). See Steindorff (1881) pp. 183, 186.

302 Conrad II, duke of Bavaria (1054–5).

303 Cf. *Annals of Niederaltaich* 1053, p. 48: 'The Bavarian duke Conrad [I: above n. 250] and the prelate Gebhard of Regensburg [above n. 120] conducted the most serious hostilities against each other at that time,' i.e. 25 December 1052. See Steindorff (1881) p. 218.

304 Walter (1037–55), perhaps of Swabian origin: Schwartz (1913) p. 65.

305 See Hillenbrand (1989) pp. 85–6.

306 The emperor granted the pope Benevento and his other rights in southern Italy, while the pope surrendered the rights of the Roman church over various German churches, notably the bishopric of Bamberg and the abbey of Fulda. Cf. *Chronicle of Monte Cassino* II.46, p. 254 (which speaks of a papal 'vicariate' over Benevento) and *ibid.*, II.81, p. 329 (which refers to 'the exchange of Benevento and the bishopric of Bamberg'). See Steindorff (1881) pp. 214–16; Vehse (1930–1) pp. 95–7; Deér (1972) p. 89; Partner (1972) p. 113; Munier (2002) pp. 138–9.

307 Cf. *Chronicle of Monte Cassino* II.81, pp. 328–9, 'after a very great army had been handed over to the pope and had already completed a considerable part of the journey', Henry's adviser, Bishop Gebhard of Eichstätt, 'approached the emperor, warmly opposing him in this matter, and he cunningly brought it about that his whole army turned back'. See Steindorff (1881) pp. 216–18.

308 See above p. 63 and n. 63.

ally moved as immigrants from the shores of the Gallic Ocean into the territories of Calabria, Samnia and Campania and because they seemed more warlike than the Italian peoples, they were at first gladly received and they helped the natives by frequently fighting boldly against the attacks of the Greeks and the Saracens. Subsequently, however, after very many of them hastened to the fertile land and their strength increased, they made war on the natives themselves and oppressed them; they usurped for themselves an unjust dominion; they snatched by force from the lawful heirs their castles, estates, villages, houses, even their wives, according to their will; they plundered the property of churches; finally they threw into confusion, as far as their strength enabled them, all the divine and human laws and indeed they submitted neither to the pope nor to the emperor, merely paying lip-service to them. The lord pope, therefore, turned his attention to removing their abominable and indescribable crimes from that territory and to freeing the natives from them and he departed from the emperor in supreme charity in order to return to Rome.

Very many Germans followed him, however, drawn partly by the commands of their lords, partly by the hope of gain, together with many shameless rogues, driven from the fatherland because of their various offences. He received them all mercifully and joyfully, both because of his exceeding compassion and his accustomed mercy and because he seemed to need their help for the impending campaign. Passing through Swabia, therefore, he celebrated the Purification of St Mary [2 February] in Augsburg. He spent Quinquagesima Sunday [21 February] in Mantua, where some of his men were killed when a riot broke out,[309] and he arrived in Rome during Lent [24 February–10 April].

In these days in Italy certain lakes, which are said to have been blocked up with squared stones in former times by Julius Caesar and expected to remain so forever, burst out as a result of an excessive deluge. This caused the River Nera and the Tiber to overflow their banks and in the sudden flood many buildings were destroyed, including the bridge of Narni, which was demolished, and many human beings were lost.

While the emperor was staying in Saxony at Merseburg, he celebrated Easter [11 April] with the king of the Danes.[310] In these days an

---

309 During the papal council in Mantua (*Sacra Concilia* 19, col. 799–800): *Life of Pope Leo IX* II.17, p. 145.

310 Swein Estrithson (1047–74). Cf. Adam, *Gesta* III.18, p. 161: 'each swore to the other perpetual friendship'. See Steindorff (1881) p. 222.

accusation was made against Conrad, duke of Bavaria, towards whom the emperor had for some time been hostile, and he deprived him of his duchy according to the judgement of certain princes.[311] At this time both the foremost men and the lesser men of the kingdom began more and more to murmur against the emperor and complained that he had long since departed from his original conduct of justice, peace, piety, fear of God and the manifold virtues in which he ought to have made progress from day to day, that he was gradually turning towards acquisitiveness and a certain negligence and that he would become much worse than he was before.[312]

The monastery of Altdorf was destroyed by fire.[313]

The lord pope held a synod in Rome after Easter[314] and then led an army against the Normans, as he had planned. They sought peace, promised him subjection and service and said that they wished to hold according to his goodwill and favour whatever they had previously invaded and unjustly seized for themselves.[315] The pope, however, rejected this, demanded the return of the property of St Peter that had been taken forcibly and injuriously and ordered them to withdraw from the place that they had unlawfully invaded. They, however, because they were far superior in numbers, rejected this proposal as impossible and declared that they would rather go to war and defend with their arms the fatherland that they had obtained by their arms or die. Thus they came to blows in a mighty battle on 18 June[316] and in the first onset they were almost defeated by the Germans. By means of an ambush, however, they surrounded our men with their reinforcements. The Italians turned tail

---

311 Herman's reference to 'certain princes' is presumably intended as a criticism (especially in the light of the following sentence). Contrast this account with *Annals of Niederaltaich* 1053, p. 48: the emperor 'summoned both [Conrad and Bishop Gebhard of Regensburg] to a general conference and likewise very many of the princes of the whole kingdom, according to whose judgement the aforementioned duke was deposed from his duchy'. See Steindorff (1881) p. 223.

312 Herman's criticism of Henry III: Reuter (1991b) pp. 315–16.

313 The Welf family monastery: see above p. 70 and n. 127.

314 The *acta* are not extant but the synod is mentioned in Leo IX, *JL* 4295, col. 727B. See Steindorff (1881) pp. 235–6; Munier (2002) p. 143.

315 Cf. Leo IX, *JL* 4333, col. 779A: the Normans 'feignedly' promised the pope 'total subjection'. See Steindorff (1881) p. 244; Deér (1972) p. 100.

316 The battle of Civitate, fought against Count Humphrey of Apulia, Robert Guiscard and Richard of Aversa. See Steindorff (1881) pp. 245–50; Taviani-Carozzi (1996) pp. 181–211; Munier (2002) pp. 212–15.

all too quickly;[317] the greatest part of the Germans fell, although not without being avenged, and by the secret judgement of God the enemy obtained the victory, although an excessively *bloody victory*[318] – perhaps because spiritual battle was more appropriate to so great a priest than carnal battle in pursuit of transitory ends;[319] or because he brought with him so many criminals who flocked to him only to obtain impunity for their offences[320] or because they were greedy for gain, to attack men who were equally wicked; or because divine justice punished our men for other offences of which it alone had knowledge. The lord pope was besieged by them in a certain castle. When, just as the fortress was about to be stormed, he was compelled by necessity to restore to them the communion of which they had previously been deprived, he was received by them and brought back to Benevento, although in an honourable fashion. He was detained there for some time and was not permitted to return.[321]

Both in this year and in the previous year there was a considerable scarcity of crops. My brother Werner, a monk of Reichenau, an extremely learned young man, truly dedicated to religion, together with another monk named Liuthar, burning with zeal for a life of greater perfection, secretly undertook a pilgrimage for Christ's sake,[322] after seeking and obtaining the abbot's permission, which was granted in a letter. Subsequently Abbot Richard of Rheinau[323] and Henry, also a monk of Reichenau, followed this example, left everything behind them and undertook the same enterprise.

Emperor Henry held a great assembly in Tribur and caused his son of the same name to be elected king by all who were present and caused

---

317 Leo's German recruits were reinforced by those of Italian princes, including the duke of Gaeta and the counts of Aquino, Teano and Teate: Steindorff (1881) pp. 216, 240–1. Herman's identification with the Germans ('our men') in this battle: Buchner (1960b) p. 53.

318 Sallust, *Catilina* 58.21.

319 The eleventh-century reaction to Leo IX's defeat: Erdmann (1935) pp. 112–13, 131; Robinson (2004a) pp. 8–9, 51, 52, 94.

320 This phrase, together with a more explicit passage in Amatus of Monte Cassino, *Ystoire de li Normant* III.23, p. 138 ('[Leo] promised to give them absolution from their sins') prompted Erdmann (1935) p. 111 to the conclusion that Leo 'announced a crusading indulgence'. A different interpretation of Herman's phrase: Paulus (1922) pp. 69–70.

321 He arrived in Benevento on 23 June and remained there until 12 March 1054. See Steindorff (1881) pp. 251, 266; Munier (2002) pp. 247–56.

322 Werner (n. 62) undertook a pilgrimage to Jerusalem: see below p. 99.

323 Cf. *D.H.III* 240.

them to promise subjection to him after the emperor's death, if he was a just ruler.[324] Conrad, the former duke of Bavaria, refused to come to this assembly and with lightly armed forces set in motion a rebellion against the king. After he had attempted to make an alliance with the Hungarians and had invaded the territory of Carinthia, he was deprived of certain possessions that he had previously held there by the emperor, who acquired them under the appearance of legality.[325] Envoys of Andreas, king of the Hungarians were also sent there to seek peace and a treaty. Supported by the bishop of Regensburg, they promised an immense sum of money and part of their province and also the participation of their men in all the emperor's expeditions, except the Italian expedition, and they promised on oath that their king would perform all this. The emperor promised faithfully that he would accept this and sent them back.

The venerable Abbess Hadamut of Neuburg, who had restored her place both internally and externally in a praiseworthy manner – it having previously fallen almost into ruins – and who had brought it back into an excellent condition, departed – happily, I trust – on 29 October, after designating a successor and with pious exhortations saying a last farewell to the sisters. The infamous Bishop Hazilin of Bamberg also died and left his office vacant.[326]

At this same time Conrad the former duke was joyfully received by Andreas, king of the Hungarians and he dissuaded him from carrying out the aforementioned treaty with the emperor. He invaded and occupied part of Carinthia with the help of the king and through the machinations of certain princes who held that territory and who had expelled other magnates.[327] The emperor, however, came to Bavaria and gave the

---

324 The election of Henry IV (perhaps in November) is reported only by Herman, who seems to describe a conditional election of a kind unprecedented in German history. The suggestion that, rather than recording an actual condition imposed by the electors, Herman was expressing his personal reservations about Henry III's regime (cf. above p. 95 and n. 312), inspired by Old Testament ideas of kingship and the Augustinian ideal of 'the just king': Steindorff (1881) pp. 227–8; Gericke (1955) pp. 737–41; Haider (1968) pp. 31–3; Scheibelreiter (1973) p. 3; Reinhardt (1975) pp. 251–2; Robinson (1999) pp. 21–2.

325 Herman showed the same doubts about the legality of these proceedings that he expressed in the case of Conrad's deposition: cf. above p. 95 and n. 311. See Steindorff (1881) pp. 228–9 and n. 1.

326 Hartwig (Hazilin) (1047–53). No other source refers to his 'infamy'.

327 Cf. *Annals of Niederaltaich* 1053, p. 49: 'Joining with the Hungarians, [Conrad] invaded Carinthia and, laying waste to very many areas, he seized a certain fortress named Hengstburg and, placing a garrison there, he returned to Hungary.'

duchy of that province to his son of the same name.[328]

1054. Remaining in that province, he celebrated Christmas [25 December 1053] on the estate of Ötting and there conferred the office of bishop of the church of Bamberg òn his cousin, Adalbero.[329] Then after holding an assembly in Regensburg, he passed through Swabia and, angered by the presence of robbers, he ordered some of their hiding-places to be set on fire. He began Lent in Zürich[330] and slowly moving downstream through the cities on the banks of the Rhine, he celebrated the festival of Easter [3 April] in Mainz. There Theobald, son of Odo,[331] came to him from France and became his vassal and promised him his aid.

After the lord pope had remained for a long time in Benevento, dedicated to the service of God, finally at the approach of Eastertide he returned to Rome, a sick man. His weakness increased from day to day and on 16 April he died a glorious death,[332] after first blessing everyone, exhorting them and bidding them farewell and after confessing his sins to St Peter and devoutly commending himself to him. He was buried in the basilica of St Peter, next to the tomb of the holy Pope Gregory, and it is recorded that he was distinguished by miracles.[333]

Duke Godfrey once more raised up a tyrannical power against the emperor. He went secretly to Italy and took as his wife Beatrice,[334] the widow of Boniface, the former margrave. Baldwin [V of Flanders] rebelled against the emperor.[335]

---

328 Cf. *Annals of Niederaltaich* 1054, p. 49: 'The emperor celebrated Christmas in Ötting, a royal manor, and there he conferred the Bavarian duchy on his elder son.' That the emperor did not respect the Bavarians' right to elect a duke: Steindorff (1881) p. 230; Boshof (1986) p. 184.

329 Adalbero (of Eppenstein) (1053–7), son of Duke Adalbero of Carinthia (n. 43) and Beatrix, sister of Gisela, Henry III's mother.

330 He was in Zürich from 12 to 19 February: *D.H.III* 315–17. Lent began on 16 February.

331 Probably Theobald III, count of Blois, Chartres and Champagne (1037–47, +1089), son of Count Odo II (n. 101). See Steindorff (1881) pp. 274–5.

332 19 April: Steindorff (1881) p. 267 n. 5.

333 I.e. the tomb of Pope Gregory I (590–604). The miracle tradition of Leo IX: see Tritz (1952) pp. 310–11, 321–53.

334 Beatrice of Lotharingia, margravine of Tuscany (+1076), daughter of Duke Frederick II of Upper Lotharingia, married (1) Boniface of Tuscany (n. 297); (2) Godfrey 'the Bearded' (n. 168).

335 See Steindorff (1881) pp. 276–7.

BERTHOLD OF REICHENAU
CHRONICLE: THE FIRST VERSION

[1054] Herman,[1] son of Count Wolferad,[2] who from his infancy had been lame in all his limbs[3] but who surpassed all the men of that time in wisdom and virtues, died and was buried on his estate of Altshausen.[4] Werner and Liuthar died on the journey to Jerusalem.[5]

An assembly was held by the emperor[6] in Mainz, in which Bishop Gebhard of Eichstätt[7] was elected by the bishops and sent to Rome. He was honourably received there and during the following Lent on Maundy Thursday [13 April 1055] he was consecrated as the 154th pope and took the name Victor II.

1055. The emperor celebrated Christmas [25 December 1054] in Goslar and then prepared an expedition to Italy.[8] He celebrated the holy day of Easter [16 April] in Mantua,[9] but that of Whitsun [4 June] in Florence.[10] A general synod was held there in his presence by the lord pope and many errors were corrected.[11] At the intercession of the

---

1 Herman 'the Lame', monk of Reichenau (1013–54). See Oesch (1961) pp. 117–203; Borst (1978) pp. 102–18, 545–6; Borst (1984) pp. 379–477. See above pp. 3–8.

2 Wolferad II of Altshausen (+1065). See Kerkhoff (1964) pp. 8–9, 16–17.

3 On Herman's illness see below p. 108 n. 3.

4 The place-name Altshausen (in the Saulgau region): Oesch (1961) p. 121 n. 2; Kerkhoff (1964) p. 27.

5 Werner, brother of Herman of Reichenau (above p. 63 n. 62) and Liuthar, monks of Reichnenau, began their pilgrimage in 1053: above p. 96.

6 Henry III, king (1039–56), emperor (1046). He was in Mainz on 17 November 1054: *DD.H.III* 327–9.

7 Gebhard I (1042–57); Pope Victor II (1055–7). According to the Anonymous of Hasenried (c. 38, p. 265), he declined the papacy in Mainz but subsequently accepted it at an assembly in Regensburg. See Steindorff (1881) pp. 285, 292–3.

8 By 22 March 1055 he was in Brixen, by 27 March in Trient (*DD.H.III* 335–6).

9 He was still in Mantua on 18 April (*D.H.III* 338).

10 *DD.H.III* 341–3 show him in Florence 27 May–9 June.

11 The pope forbade the alienation of ecclesiastical property (Peter Damian, *Letter* 74, p. 370), condemned simony and clerical marriage and deposed 'many bishops' for these offences (*Annals of Niederaltaich* 1055, p. 51; Bonizo, *To a friend* V, p. 195). See Steindorff (1881) pp. 305–6.

bishops the emperor pardoned Adalbert,[12] who had been condemned to death. At the same time fifty or more armed knights secretly crossed the sea from Normandy, desiring to aid the Normans against the emperor. They were captured by citizens of Pisa and dispatched to the emperor.[13] The emperor sent Bishop Oddo of Novara[14] to Constantinople, where in place of Michael, who had recently died,[15] he found a certain woman[16] in sole control of the whole kingdom. The following year she sent him back to the emperor, together with her own envoys, in order to confirm their friendship and a treaty.

Beatrice[17] came to surrender to the emperor and, although she had sworn fidelity, she was held prisoner because of her husband.[18] For this reason her son, the boy Boniface,[19] feared to come. Not many days later, however, while the emperor still lingered in the same place, that boy died. Bishop Gebhard of Regensburg[20] and Duke Welf[21] had obtained permission to return home from Italy and their vassals – without their knowledge, it is said - formed a conspiracy against the emperor.[22] At this time Duke Welf was overtaken by death,[23] a matter of great lamentation for his vassals and for all people, and he was buried in the monastery of Altdorf.[24] Bishop Arnold of Speyer died.[25]

---

12 Perhaps the 'Margrave Adalbert' mentioned by Arnulf of Milan, *Liber gestorum recentium* III.4, p. 171. See Steindorff (1881) p. 307.

13 Cf. Lampert, *Annales* 1055, p. 67: 'the Normans troubling Italy'. No other source offers an exact parallel to Berthold's report.

14 Oddo II (1053/4–78/9).

15 The recently deceased Byzantine emperor was Constantine IX Monomachus (1042–55).

16 Empress Theodora (1055–6).

17 Beatrice, margravine of Tuscany (✝1076): see above p. 98 and n. 334.

18 Godfrey III ('the Bearded'), duke of Upper Lotharingia (1044–7), duke of Lower Lotharingia (1065–9), margrave of Tuscany (1054–69).

19 Boniface, son of Margrave Boniface of Tuscany, Beatrice's first husband. He is named Frederick by Donizo of Canossa, *Vita Mathildis* I.10, p. 368. See Goez (1995) pp. 16, 21, 203–4.

20 Gebhard III (1036–60).

21 Welf III, duke of Carinthia (1047–55), margrave of Verona.

22 *Annals of Niederaltaich* 1055, p. 51 ascribe full responsibility for the conspiracy to Gebhard and Welf. Gebhard was still with the emperor on 27 May 1055 in Florence (*D.H.III* 341). See Steindorff (1881) pp. 318–19.

23 13 November: Steindorff (1881) p. 320 n. 4.

24 Altdorf (near Ravensburg in Swabia), the Welf family monastery: see above p. 70 and n. 127.

25 Arnold I (1054–5) ✝ 2 October.

1056. The emperor, returning from Italy through Bavaria,[26] celebrated Christmas in the fortress of Zürich and there he betrothed the daughter[27] of Margrave Odo[28] to his son, who bore his own name.[29] Bishop Gebhard of Regensburg was found guilty by the emperor of having conspired against him and was kept for some time in prison, at first in the fortress of Wülflingen and afterwards in Stoffeln.[30] In Speyer Conrad[31] was appointed by the emperor in the place of Bishop Arnold. Herman, archbishop of the city of Cologne died.[32] In his place Anno, formerly provost in Goslar, succeeded to the office of archbishop.[33] The emperor celebrated the holy day of Easter [7 April] ...[34] In the same year the Slavs who are called Liutizi attacked the territory of the Saxons and killed very many of their princes, including Margrave William.[35]

During the autumn Emperor Henry summoned the lord pope to him.[36] While he was staying in Saxony, in Bodfeld, weakened by a constantly worsening illness, he died in the thirty-ninth year of his life, in the eighteenth year of his kingship and the fifteenth of his emperorship, in the tenth indiction.[37] He was brought from there to Speyer and buried next to his father and mother in the church of St Mary, which he himself had built and which was still unfinished. His son Henry, who was seven years old, received authority over the kingdom in his place. He was entrusted by the princes to his mother, the empress,[38] to be brought up.

26 Cf. *DD.H.III* 359 (Brixen, 20 November 1055), 360 (Neuburg, 10 December), 361 (Ulm, 14 December).

27 Bertha of Turin (1051–87), queen (1066). See Steindorff (1881) p. 324; Meyer von Knonau (1890) pp. 9–10; Previté-Orton (1912) pp. 32–7, 66, 207, 231; Robinson (1999) p. 25.

28 Odo, count of Savoy (✝1057/60).

29 Henry IV, king (1056–1106), emperor (1084).

30 Cf. *Annals of Augsburg* 1055, p. 127: 'Bishop Gebhard of Regensburg was declared to be guilty of treason.' See Steindorff (1881) p. 323; Boshof (1991) p. 125.

31 Conrad (1056–60).

32 Herman II (1036–56) ✝ 11 February.

33 Anno II (1056–75).

34 In Paderborn (*Annals of Niederaltaich* 1056, p. 52; Lampert, *Annales* 1056, p. 68).

35 William, count of 'Haldensleben', margrave of the Saxon Nordmark. See Fenske (1977) p. 23; Robinson (1999) pp. 24, 63. For the Liutizi: above p. 68 and n. 113.

36 The meeting with Victor II was in September in Goslar: Steindorff (1881) p. 350.

37 Born 28 October 1017, acceded 4 June 1039, crowned emperor 25 December 1046, died 5 October 1056 and buried in Speyer 28 October. The indiction as a means of reckoning time: Cheney (1961) pp. 2–3.

38 Agnes of Poitou (?1025–77), queen (1043), empress (1046). See above p. 74 and n. 163.

1057. King Henry celebrated Christmas [25 December 1056] in Regensburg. On 25 April the great abundance of snow and hoar-frost destroyed a great part of the vines. In Rome Victor II died.[39] In his place Frederick, brother of Duke Godfrey, formerly archdeacon of the blessed Pope Leo but at that time abbot of the monastery of St Benedict, was consecrated as the 155th pope and named Stephen IX.[40] Otto, duke of the Swabians died and Rudolf received his duchy.[41] In this year stones of remarkable size, mixed with hail, fell from heaven and some men were killed by lightning.

1058. In Rome Pope Stephen died.[42] The Romans, however, took bribes and elected, contrary to canon law, a certain John, who held the see for some days without consecration.[43] He was expelled by Duke Godfrey and the bishop of the city of Florence was substituted as the 156th pope and called Nicholas II.[44] At the same time Bishop Henry of Augsburg[45] had the role of chief adviser of the empress, which greatly displeased some of the princes of the kingdom, who would not tolerate his arrogance.

1059. In this year there were many deaths among men and a sickness among cattle. War broke out between the Milanese and the Pavians and many died on both sides.[46] Rudolf, duke of the Swabians married Matilda, the sister of King Henry.[47] In Fulda Abbot Eberhard died[48] and

---

39 28 July in Arezzo.

40 Frederick of Lotharingia, brother of Godfrey 'the Bearded' (n. 18), chancellor of the Roman church (1051), abbot of Monte Cassino (1057), Pope Stephen IX (1057–8).

41 Otto III (of Schweinfurt) (above p. 83 n. 237) † 28 September. Rudolf of Rheinfelden, duke of Swabia (1057–79), anti-king (1077–80). See Meyer von Knonau (1890) pp. 48–50; Robinson (1999) pp. 33–4.

42 29 March in Florence.

43 John II Mincius, cardinal bishop of Velletri († ca. 1073), Pope Benedict X (1058–9), expelled from Rome in mid-January 1059 by Godfrey 'the Bearded': Hüls (1977) p. 144; Schmidt (1977) pp. 78–80.

44 Gerard, bishop of Florence (1045–61), Pope Nicholas II (1058–61).

45 Henry II (1047–63). Hostility towards him: *Annals of Niederaltaich* 1060, p. 56; Lampert, *Annales* 1061, 1064, pp. 79, 92. See Black-Veldtrup (1995) pp. 356–60; Robinson (1999) pp. 30–1.

46 Hostilities culminating in the battle of Campo Morto (23 May 1061): Arnulf, *Liber gestorum recentium* III.6, pp. 172–3.

47 Matilda (1048–59), daughter of Henry III and Agnes: see above p. 85 n. 247. See Black-Veldtrup (1995) pp. 78, 108–9; Robinson (1999) p. 33 and n. 48.

48 Ekbert, abbot of Fulda (1047–58).

Siegfried succeeded him.[49] After King Andreas of Hungary[50] had first confirmed peace and a treaty with King Henry by means of envoys, he obtained the latter's younger sister[51] as a bride for his son, who was still a boy.[52]

1060. King Henry of France[53] died and his son,[54] who was still a boy, received the kingdom to govern it with his mother.[55] Archbishop Luitpold of Mainz[56] died and Abbot Siegfried of Fulda succeeded him. Bishop Conrad of Speyer died and Einhard was appointed in his place.[57] Matilda, the sister of the king, died.[58] The count palatine Henry went mad after apparently abandoning the world under the pretext of a religious vocation and entering the monastery of Echternach.[59] He withdrew from there and killed his wife.[60] And in this year, as in the previous one, many perished from disease. The winter, which was hard, snowy and longer than usual, caused very great damage to the wheat and to the vines. Andreas, king of the Hungarians, after suffering many injuries from his brother,[61] who had laid waste the length and breadth of his kingdom, was at last struck down by fever. He sent all his treasure to the castle of Melk and sent his son to King Henry through the agency of Count Dietpald.[62]

49 Siegfried of Eppenstein, abbot (1058–60), archbishop of Mainz (1060–84).

50 Andreas I (1046–60). The treaty was concluded in September 1058: Meyer von Knonau (1890) pp. 95–6; Boshof (1986) p. 185; Robinson (1999) p. 35.

51 Judith (?1054–92/6), known in Hungary as Sophia, married (1) Salomon, (2) Duke Vladislav-Herman of Poland.

52 Salomon, king of Hungary (1063–74, †1087).

53 Henry I (1031–60).

54 Philip I (1060–1108).

55 Anne of Kiev († before 1090).

56 Luitpold (1051–9) † 7 December 1059.

57 Einhard II (1060–7). Conrad died 12 December 1060.

58 12 May 1059.

59 Henry, count palatine of Lotharingia (1047–60) was briefly a monk in Gorze. Echternach was the place of his subsequent imprisonment. See Meyer von Knonau (1890) pp. 162–4, 199–200.

60 Matilda, daughter of Duke Gozelo II of Lower Lotharingia (above p. 75 and n. 167), niece of Godfrey 'the Bearded'.

61 Bela I, king of Hungary (1061–3). See Meyer von Knonau (1890) pp. 192–8; Boshof (1986) p. 185.

62 The ancestor of the margraves of Cham-Vohburg.

1061. A great famine killed many men. Bishop Gebhard of Regensburg died[63] and Otto succeeded him.[64] Conrad, who was duke of the Carinthians in name only, died[65] and vacated his office and the Swabian Berthold received his duchy.[66] In Rome after the death of Pope Nicholas[67] the Romans sent a crown and other gifts to King Henry and appealed to him about the election of the supreme pontiff. He summoned all the bishops of Italy to him and held a general assembly in Basel, where he put on that crown and was called patrician of the Romans. Then with the common assent of them all he elected the bishop of Parma as supreme pontiff of the Roman church.[68] While this was happening, Bishop Anselm of Lucca usurped the apostolic see for himself with the support of certain Romans.[69] Burchard and Wezil of Zollern were killed.[70] The church of Speyer was dedicated.[71] After setting aside her royal garments, Empress Agnes was adorned with the holy veil.[72]

1062. On 8 February there was an earthquake, lightning and thunder. The subsequent plague and sickness wiped out many men. King Henry celebrated Easter day [31 March] with his mother, the empress, in Utrecht, a city of Frisia. In these days[73] Archbishop Anno of Cologne, with the support of certain princes of the kingdom, seized King Henry by force from his mother, the empress, together with the lance and the other insignia of the empire, and brought him with him to Cologne. The bishop of Parma, who had been elected a short time before, went to

---

63 2 December 1060.

64 Otto (1060/1–89)

65 Conrad III (1056–61), duke 'in name only' because he was unable to gain control of the duchy: Meyer von Knonau (1890) pp. 208–9.

66 Berthold I ('the Bearded' of Zähringen) (1061–78).

67 Probably 20 July.

68 Cadalus, bishop of Parma (?1046–?71), antipope Honorius II, elected in Basel 28 October 1061. See Meyer von Knonau (1890) pp. 224–7; Schmidt (1977) pp. 108–10, 126–7. Henry IV as patrician: Vollrath (1974) pp. 14–25; Martin (1994) pp. 257–95.

69 Anselm I, bishop of Lucca (1057–73), Pope Alexander II (1061–73), elected during the night of 30 September–1 October. See Meyer von Knonau (1890) pp. 220–2; Schmidt (1977) pp. 80–8.

70 Swabian counts who died at the end of August in a conflict, causes unknown: Meyer von Knonau (1890) p. 214; Reuter (1991b) p. 305.

71 4 October. The cathedral had been rebuilt after collapsing in 1052: see above p. 92 and Gugumus (1961) pp. 175–87.

72 22 November in Speyer, according to Black-Veldtrup (1995) pp. 91, 364, 367–72.

73 Berthold alone, by linking these events with Eastertide, gives an approximate date for the abduction of Henry IV at Kaiserswerth: Meyer von Knonau (1890) pp. 274–9; Jenal (1974) pp. 175–6, 183–5; Robinson (1999) pp. 43–4.

Rome to be consecrated. When the Romans opposed him with weapons and prevented him from entering, a host of them were killed by his knights or drowned in the Tiber, while the rest fled.[74]

1063. In springtime, in the middle of April, severe windy and snowy winter weather lasting for four days killed the birds and the cattle by cold and destroyed the greater part of the trees and the vines.[75] Bishop Engelhard of Magdeburg died[76] and the brother of the archbishop of Cologne succeeded him.[77] Bishop Henry of Augsburg died[78] and Embriko succeeded him.[79] In the same year near Constance a certain woman gave birth to a child with two heads and also the other limbs double as far as the haunches.

1064. King Henry celebrated Christmas [25 December 1063] in Cologne,[80] but celebrated Easter day [11 April] in Liège. A synod in Mantua.[81]

1065. King Henry celebrated Christmas [25 December 1064] in Goslar,[82] but celebrated Easter day [27 March] in Worms. The royal palace in Goslar was burned down. This happened on 27 March in the third indiction.[83] And in the same place he was girded with the sword in the ninth year of his reign but in the fourteenth year of his life and Duke Godfrey was chosen as his shieldbearer.[84] The bishop of Passau died[85]

---

74 His army reached Sutri 25 March; he defeated the army of Alexander II's supporters in a battle on the Field of Nero (14 April) and seized the Leonine city: Meyer von Knonau (1890) pp. 250–2, 254–9; Schmidt (1977) pp. 111–14.

75 Cf. *Annals of Augsburg* 1063, p. 127. See Curschmann (1900) p. 120.

76 Engelhard (1051–63) † 30/31 August.

77 Werner (Wezilo, 1063–78), brother of Anno II of Cologne.

78 3 September.

79 Embriko (1063–77).

80 In Worms, according to the *Annals of Niederaltaich* 1064, p. 64. Meyer von Knonau (1890) p. 360 concluded that Berthold's account was correct and that the celebration had originally been scheduled for Worms.

81 The synod of 31 May, which recognised Alexander II's claim to the papacy.

82 In Cologne, according to *Annals of Niederaltaich* 1065, p. 66; but Lampert, *Annales* 1065, p. 92 agreed with Berthold.

83 This is mentioned only by Berthold and Bernold: Meyer von Knonau (1890) p. 400 n. 11. The report is clearly a later interpolation (perhaps originally a marginal gloss) since 'in the same place' in the following sentence refers to Worms rather than Goslar.

84 29 March. The ceremony declared Henry to be of age: Meyer von Knonau (1890) pp. 400–2; Robinson (1999) pp. 51–2. His shieldbearer was Godfrey 'the Bearded', who later that year was invested with the duchy of Lower Lotharingia.

85 Egilbert (1045–65) † 17 May.

and Altman, the chaplain of the empress, succeeded him.[86] At this time Archbishop Siegfried of Mainz, Bishop William of Utrecht,[87] Bishop Gunther of Bamberg[88] and Bishop Otto of Regensburg with great pomp and an extensive entourage set out for Jerusalem. During that journey they suffered much from the pagans, for they were even compelled to do battle with them.[89] Gunther died on that same journey and Ricimann succeeded him by means of simony.[90]

1066. Many noblemen died in a civil war.[91] King Henry celebrated Christmas [25 December 1065] ...,[92] but he celebrated Easter [16 April] in Utrecht.

Archbishop Eberhard of Trier[93] departed in peace on 15 April, the Saturday before the holy day of Easter, after he had himself completed the offices of that day and while he was still clad in his priestly vestments. Conrad, the provost of Cologne,[94] was elected by the king and ought to have succeeded him, but he was opposed by the clergy and citizens of Trier. A certain count among the vassals of Trier named Theoderic,[95] therefore, seized the same Conrad, as he travelled to Trier. After tormenting him for a long time in prison, he entrusted him to four knights to be killed. When they had thrown him three times down a precipice and had been able to do no more than bruise his arm, one of

---

86 Altman (1065–91).

87 William (?1054–76).

88 Gunther (1057–65) † 23 July.

89 This pilgrimage, including 'a multitude of counts and princes, rich and poor' (*Annals of Niederaltaich* 1065, p. 66) began November 1064 and ended summer 1065. See Meyer von Knonau (1890) pp. 390–4, 445–50; Joranson (1928) pp. 3–43.

90 Herman I, bishop of Bamberg (1065–75). Allegations of simony against him: Schieffer (1972) pp. 22–46; Schieffer (1975) pp. 55–76; Cowdrey (1998) pp. 110–14, 124–7.

91 The reference is unclear. Lampert, *Annales* 1066, p. 101 reported an 'atrocious battle' in Ingelheim, in which the Hessian count Werner III was killed, but this could not be described as 'a civil war'. The conspiracy of the princes that brought about the fall from power of Archbishop Adalbert of Bremen (Meyer von Knonau [1890] pp. 487–9) was bloodless. Perhaps Berthold referred to the unrest in Saxony following Adalbert's fall: Meyer von Knonau (1890) pp. 514–17.

92 In Goslar, according to Lampert (*Annales* 1066, p. 100); in Mainz, according to *Annals of Niederaltaich* 1066, p. 71, which Meyer von Knonau (1890) p. 483 considered more likely.

93 Eberhard (1047–66).

94 Conrad of Pfullingen, archbishop elect of Trier, nephew of Anno II of Cologne.

95 Theoderic, burgrave of Trier, advocate of the church of Trier (†1073) captured Conrad 18 May. See Meyer von Knonau (1890) pp. 498–500, 503–9; Robinson (1999) pp. 116–17.

them was led by penitence to seek pardon from him. Another, however, wishing to behead him, only cut off his jaw. And thus that martyr worthy of God departed to the Lord on 1 June. He was buried in a certain abbey named Tholey. A fitting vengeance, however, afterwards pursued the three knights who were the perpetrators of that death. For one of them was unable to swallow the food that he received; the other two mutilated their hands ...[96]

---

96 The text ends in mid-sentence (see below p. 119). In Sichard's text follows the *explicit* 'The Chronicle of Herman the Lame ends.' See above p. 20.

BERTHOLD OF REICHENAU
CHRONICLE: THE SECOND VERSION

The life of Herman Herman[1] (which means 'great hero'), the son of the pious Count Wolferad,[2] was from his earliest years in his outward person totally lame in all his limbs from a paralytic disease.[3] As for his inner genius,[4] however, he wonderfully outdistanced all the men of his age and by his own efforts and through his own understanding he had a virtually complete grasp of the difficulties of all the arts and the subtleties of poetic metre. From his earliest years he always devoted himself entirely and unceasingly to such studies and to literary composition and he became so highly esteemed for the completeness of his knowledge of divine and secular literature that he was regarded with astonishment and admiration by all those who came from every direction to experience his teaching and his erudition.[5] That bodily frame was indeed so cruelly weakened in all its limbs that he could not without help move himself one way or another from the spot in which he had been placed nor could he even turn on his other side, but he could sit with difficulty and in a crooked posture in a sedan chair, into which he was lifted by his servant to carry out some activity. Although this useful and miraculous pupil of holy charity with his feeble mouth, tongue and lips produced only broken and scarcely intelligible sounds of words, slowly and as best he could, nevertheless to his students[6] he proved an eloquent and diligent teacher, very lively and humorous, with the greatest facility in disputation and never lacking in a ready reply to their questions. When he was not writing something new, a great effort for his weakened fingers, or reading either to himself or to others, he always most eagerly occupied himself with useful or necessary exercises. He was

---

1 Herman 'the Lame', monk of Reichenau (1013–54). See Oesch (1961) pp. 117–203; Borst (1978) pp. 102–18, 545–6; Borst (1984) pp. 379–477 and above pp. 3–8.

2 Wolferad II, count of Altshausen (✝1065). See Kerkhoff (1964) pp. 8–9, 16–17.

3 This description of the illness is consistent with cerebral palsy, according to A. Hottinger, cited in Oesch (1961) p. 127.

4 Cf. Horace, *Ars poetica* 409–10, *Carmina* 2.18.9–10; Quintilian, *Institutiones oratoriae* 6.2.3.

5 Herman's fame: Oesch (1961) pp. 133–4.

6 His students included, besides Berthold, Bishop Benno II of Osnabrück and Meinzo, canon of Constance: Oesch (1961) p. 133.

indeed a man who never made complaints and who *thought that nothing human was foreign to*[7] him. For he assiduously practised the most humble charity and charitable humility; he showed remarkable patience; he was a servant most prompt in his obedience; he was a lover of chastity, a preserver of uncorrupted virginity; he most joyfully cultivated mercy; he was a truly catholic spokesman of the faith in all its purity, a most invincible advocate and defender of the truth, a most experienced teacher of the Christian religion. He was a man of no little modesty, sobriety and temperance, to such a degree that from his early childhood he had never eaten meat. Like a faithful servant he was utterly devoted to psalmody, prayer and hymn singing. Both before and after he received holy orders, which he undertook to do around his thirtieth year at the urging of Abbot Bern of Reichenau,[8] a holy and wise man, he discharged his duties as an orthodox man throughout his holy and honourable life. In all his endeavours he showed extraordinary kindness, courtesy, cheerfulness and humanity, conducting himself towards all men in a pleasing and suitable manner, so that being *made all things to all men*,[9] he was loved by all men. Until the end of his life, however, he happily remained a tireless enemy and attacker[10] of iniquity, injustice and every kind of evil and malice and whatever is opposed to God.

The studies of Herman[11] He collected together, therefore, and set in order very lucidly the method and the rules of the *computus*, including some proofs, in which he greatly surpassed all his predecessors.[12] Above all he discovered the most reliable rules concerning the natural illumination of the moon, by means of which it may very clearly be known at what hour of the day or night the moon is illuminated by the sun. He also worked out the most reliable rules for calculating the eclipse of the moon.[13] He also wrote a work on geometry according to the natural method and order with figures and diagrams, which was certainly very useful in studying that art, since no one in former times was gifted with so great a knowledge and penetration in this field.[14] Moreover he wrote

---

7 Terence, *Heautontimorumenos* 1.1.25.

8 Bern (Berno), (1008–48). See above pp. 1–6.

9 I Corinthians 9:22.

10 Cf. Deuteronomy 25:16.

11 Berthold's account of Herman's works is incomplete: Oesch (1961) pp. 135–203; Borst (1984) pp. 443–4.

12 Oesch (1961) pp. 174–5; Bergmann (1988) pp. 103–17.

13 *De defectu solis et lunae*: Oesch (1961) pp. 173–4.

14 This treatise seems not to have survived: Oesch (1961) pp. 161–2. His extant works on mathematics: *ibid.*, pp. 157–60.

and provided musical notation for full-length liturgical chants about St George, SS. Gordian and Epimachus, the martyr St Afra, the confessor St Magnus and the holy Bishop Wolfgang, besides very many others of the same character, of admirable sweetness, graceful and pleasing to the ear;[15] for no musician was more skilled than he. With careful labour, searching everywhere, he compiled this book of chronicles from the Incarnation of the Lord up to his own times.[16] He also very beautifully described the deeds of the emperors Conrad and Henry.[17] In addition he devised with the greatest poetical skill a delightful little work on the eight principal vices, using a variety of verse metres.[18] No one was his equal in constructing clocks, musical instruments and mechanical devices.[19] He had always totally preoccupied himself, as far as his weakness permitted, in these activities and in very many of the same kind, which it would take a long time to recount.

Finally, however, when God's mercy saw fit to release his holy soul from the loathsome prison of this world, he succumbed to an attack of pleurisy. For ten days he gradually wasted away, suffering terribly and almost uninterruptedly from this deadly attack. Then one day, early in the morning, after the morning service[20] had been celebrated, I (with whom he was on more friendly terms than the others) approached his sickbed in order to ask him whether he felt somewhat better. He replied, 'Do not, I say, do not ask me about this, but rather listen carefully to what I tell you, in whom I have great trust. I shall doubtless die shortly: I shall not survive and shall not recover. I therefore urgently commend my sinful soul to you and to all my brethren. Throughout the whole of this night I was held in a kind of trance and it seemed to me that from memory and from my own knowledge – just as we are accustomed to recite the Lord's Prayer[21] – I was reading and re-reading and

---

15 Two of these *historiae* or *officia* have survived: *Historia sancti Wolfgangi* (ed. Hiley), *Historia sanctae Afrae martyris Augustensis* (ed. Hiley and Berschin).

16 Herman's *Chronicle*: see above pp. 8–19.

17 Not extant and mentioned nowhere else, except in the work of the Prüfening bibliographer *ca.* 1130, who probably derived his information from Berthold's *Life of Herman* ([Wolfger?] *De scriptoribus* c. 91, p. 85). But see above p. 76 n. 169.

18 Herman, *De octo vitiis principalibus*, ed. Dümmler pp. 385–431. See Oesch (1961) pp. 177–9.

19 Herman's writings on the astrolabe and the sundial and a possible work on the measurements of organ pipes: Oesch (1961) pp. 162–73, 139–40.

20 Cf. *Rule of St Benedict* c. 17.

21 Matthew 6:9–13.

carefully examining the *Hortensius* of Tullius Cicero[22] and similarly I was reading that part that was yet to be composed of the work that I planned concerning vices,[23] just as if I had already written it down, and I experienced many other things of this kind. As a result of the inspiration and encouragement that I derived from this reading, this present world, together with all that belongs to it, and this mortal life itself became contemptible and wearisome to me. By contrast that future imperishable world and that eternal and immortal life filled me with such unspeakable desire and love that I regard and value all these transitory things as worthless and empty.[24] I am indeed weary of living.'[25]

I, however, was greatly astounded by the communication of this vision and by this speech and, as was inevitable at the departure of so great a friend and such a master, I utterly dissolved in tears and was moved to lamentation and I could scarcely contain myself in a seemly manner. He at once rebuked me almost with severity; looking at me askance, astonished and trembling, he said: 'Do not, my friend, do not weep for me, but rather wish me joy and be glad. Take my writing tablets, I beg you, and firstly, correct carefully whatever still remains there to be copied out;[26] afterwards entrust the writings to those who consider them worthwhile. As for yourself, however, every day remember that you will die, prepare yourself always in all your labours and all your meditations for that same journey, because you *know neither the day nor the hour*[27] when you will follow me, your greatest friend.' And with these words he fell silent. Thereafter from day to day, as is usual, his weakness increased and, alas! his life came to an end and at that very moment he was raised up to heaven. After most freely and wholeheartedly confessing his sins and most devoutly receiving the eucharist of Christ and amidst the psalm singing, prayers and lamentations of the brethren, friends and intimate acquaintances who flocked to visit him, that fortunate and incomparable man of God happily breathed his last on 24 September, the blessed death that was his sole wish before all else. Leaving all who

22 Only fragments of Cicero's *Hortensius* survive.

23 Herman, *De octo vitiis* (n. 18) lines 1707–22 announce a continuation of the work.

24 Cf. Terence, *Eunuchus* 3.1.21.

25 Cf. Genesis 27:46; Job 10:1; II Corinthians 1:8.

26 The first draft was written on wax tablets and, after being corrected, was transcribed on parchment. Schmeidler (1938) p. 189 used this as evidence that Berthold revised the last annal of Herman's chronicle but the context suggests that what was to be revised was the poem *De octo vitiis*.

27 Matthew 25:13.

knew him in the deepest grief, he was buried in a solemn and sorrowful funeral on his estate of Altshausen[28] and he rests in peace.

[1054] An assembly was held by the emperor in Mainz,[29] in which Bishop Gebhard of Eichstätt was elected by the bishops and sent to Rome. He was honourably received there and during the following Lent on Maundy Thursday [13 April 1055] he was consecrated as the 154th pope and took the name Victor II.[30]

1055. The emperor celebrated Christmas [25 December 1054] in Goslar and then prepared an expedition to Italy.[31] He celebrated Easter [16 April] in Mantua; Whitsun [4 June], however, he celebrated in Florence.[32] A general synod was held there in his presence by the lord pope and many errors were corrected.[33] At the intercession of the bishops the emperor pardoned Adalbert,[34] who had been condemned to death. The emperor sent Bishop Oddo of Novara[35] to Constantinople, where in place of Michael, who had recently died,[36] he found a certain woman[37] in sole control of the whole kingdom. The following year she sent him back to the emperor, together with her own envoys, in order to confirm their friendship and a treaty.

Beatrice[38] came to surrender to the emperor and, although she had sworn fidelity, she was taken captive and held prisoner because of her husband.[39] For this reason her son, the boy Boniface,[40] feared to come. Not many days later, however, while the emperor still lingered in the

---

28 The place-name Altshausen: Oesch (1961) p. 121 n. 2; Kerkhoff (1964) p. 27.

29 Henry III, king (1039–56), emperor (1046), was in Mainz on 17 November 1054: *D.H.III* 327–9.

30 Gebhard (1042–57), Pope Victor II (1055–7). See above p. 99 and n. 7.

31 By 22 March 1055 he was in Brixen and by 27 March in Trient.

32 He was still in Mantua on 18 April and in Florence 27 May–9 June.

33 See above p. 99 n. 11.

34 Perhaps the 'Margrave Adalbert' mentioned by Arnulf, *Liber gestorum recentium* III.4, p. 171.

35 Oddo II (1053/4–78/9).

36 The recently deceased Byzantine emperor was Constantine IX Monomachus (1042–55).

37 Empress Theodora (1055–6).

38 Beatrice, margravine of Tuscany (✝1076): see above p. 98 and n. 334.

39 Godfrey III ('the Bearded'), duke of Upper Lotharingia (1044–7), duke of Lower Lotharingia (1065–9), margrave of Tuscany (1054–69).

40 Boniface, son of Margrave Boniface of Tuscany, Beatrice's first husband. See above p. 100 n. 19.

same place, that boy died. Bishop Gebhard of Regensburg[41] and Duke Welf[42] had obtained permission to return home from Italy and their vassals – without their knowledge, it is said – formed a conspiracy against the emperor.[43] At this time Duke Welf was overtaken by death,[44] a matter of great lamentation for his vassals and for all people. He truly dedicated himself to God by undertaking the vow of the holy monastic life and he was buried in the monastery of Altdorf.[45] Bishop Arnold of Speyer died and Conrad succeeded him.[46]

1056. The emperor, returning from Italy,[47] celebrated Christmas [25 December 1055] in Zürich and there he betrothed the daughter[48] of Margrave Odo[49] to his [son], who bore his own name.[50] Gebhard of Regensburg was found guilty of having conspired against him and was kept for some time in prison.[51] Duke Godfrey ['the Bearded'] came to surrender to the emperor.[52] Archbishop Herman of Cologne died[53] and Anno, provost of Goslar succeeded him.[54] The emperor celebrated the holy day of Easter [7 April] …[55]

The emperor summoned the lord pope [Victor II] to him in Germany.[56] While he was staying in Saxony, in Bodfeld, he was weakened by a constantly worsening illness. Fortified by a good conversion, by penitence and a most free confession, he wholeheartedly *forgave* his *debtors*[57] and he restored everything that he had not acquired fairly to those who

---

41 Gebhard III (1036–60).

42 Welf III, duke of Carinthia (1047–55) and margrave of Verona.

43 See above p. 100 n. 22.

44 13 November.

45 The Welf family monastery: see above p. 70 and n. 127.

46 Arnold I (1054–5) ✝ 2 October; Conrad (1056–60).

47 He was in Brixen on 20 November, in Neuburg on 10 December and in Ulm on 14 December.

48 Bertha of Turin (1051–87), queen (1066).

49 Odo, count of Savoy (✝1057/60).

50 Henry IV (1050–1106), king (1056), emperor (1084).

51 See above p. 101 and n. 30.

52 Probably in May/June, when the emperor was in Lotharingia (*D.H.III* 372). See Steindorff (1881) pp. 353–4.

53 Herman II (1036–56) ✝ 11 February.

54 Anno II (1056–75).

55 In Paderborn.

56 In September in Goslar.

57 Matthew 6:12.

were present. To those who were absent, however, he arranged very carefully for the restoration of property by the empress[58] and his son, identifying the recipients by name. And thus placing all his hope in God, he died – happily, I trust – on 5 October, in the thirty-ninth year of his life, in the eighteenth year of his kingship, in the tenth year of his emperorship, in the tenth indiction.[59] He was brought from there to Speyer and was buried by the lord pope next to his father and mother in the church of St Mary,[60] which he himself had built and which was still unfinished. His son, Henry IV, however, who had already been made king by his father[61] and who was then seven years old, was entrusted by the princes to his mother, the empress, to be brought up and he began to reign with his mother.

Famine afflicted many provinces.

Henry IV, son of Henry, reigned for twenty years,[62] as the ninetieth [emperor] after Augustus.

1057. King Henry celebrated Christmas [25 December 1056] in Regensburg. In Rome Victor II, the 154th [pope], died.[63] After him Frederick, brother of Duke Godfrey ['the Bearded'], formerly archchaplain of Pope Leo of blessed memory, who, having been a clerk, became a monk and was afterwards promoted to be abbot in Monte Cassino, took the name Stephen IX and, as the 155th pope, reigned for nine months.[64] Otto, duke of the Swabians died[65] and Rudolf received his duchy.[66] In this year stones of remarkable size, mixed with hail, fell from heaven.

1058. In Rome after Stephen a certain Benedict was elected contrary to canon law and through the personal favour of certain men and presided over the church without consecration for seven months.[67] He was expelled

58 Agnes of Poitou (✝1077), queen, empress. See above p. 74 and n. 163.

59 Born 28 October 1017, acceded 4 June 1039, crowned emperor 25 December 1046.

60 He was buried on 28 October next to his parents, Emperor Conrad II and Empress Gisela.

61 For his designation (1051) and election (1053) see above pp. 88, 96–7.

62 Berthold considered that Henry IV's reign ended with his excommunication and deposition by Pope Gregory VII: see below p. 145.

63 28 July in Arezzo.

64 Frederick of Lotharingia, chancellor of the Roman church (1051), abbot of Monte Cassino (1057), Pope Stephen IX (1057–8).

65 Otto III (of Schweinfurt)) ✝ 28 September (see above p. 83 n. 237).

66 Rudolf of Rheinfelden, duke of Swabia (1057–79), anti-king (1077–80).

67 John II Mincius, cardinal bishop of Velletri; Benedict X (1058–9). See above p. 102 and n. 43.

by Duke Godfrey, and Bishop Gerard of Florence, called Nicholas II, ruled as the 156th pope for almost three years.[68] He decreed that those who at that time had been promoted by simoniacs should be permitted to exercise their office. Thereafter, however, whoever might be ordained by them should obtain no advantage from such a promotion.[69] Peter Damian, the bishop of Ostia[70] of pious memory also incited this pope to correct the unchastity of the clergy according to canon law.[71]

1059. In this year there were many deaths among men. Strife arose between the Milanese and the Pavians and very many died there in battle.[72] Duke Rudolf married Matilda, the king's sister.[73] In Fulda Abbot Eberhard died[74] and Siegfried succeeded him.[75] After King Andreas of Hungary[76] had first confirmed peace and a treaty with King Henry by means of envoys, he obtained the latter's younger sister Judith[77] as a bride for his son Salomon, who was still a boy.[78] Frederick of Gleiberg and his brothers rebelled against King Henry and afterwards came to surrender to him.[79]

1060. King Henry of France[80] died and his son Philip,[81] who was still a boy, received the kingdom to govern it with his mother.[82] Archbishop Luitpold of Mainz died[83] and Abbot Siegfried of Fulda succeeded him. Bishop Conrad of Speyer died and Einhard, provost of Augsburg was appointed in his place.[84]

---

68 Gerard, bishop of Florence (1045–61); Nicholas II (1058–61).

69 Cf. Nicholas II, *Decretum contra simoniacos* (*JL* 4431a, *MGH Constitutiones* 1, 549, no. 386). See Schieffer (1981) pp. 61–2.

70 Peter Damian, cardinal bishop of Ostia (1057–72).

71 Peter Damian, *Letter* 61, pp. 206–18 (January–July 1059).

72 See above p. 102 n. 46.

73 Matilda, daughter of Henry III and Agnes: see above p. 85 n. 247.

74 Ekbert (1047–58).

75 Siegfried of Eppenstein, abbot of Fulda (1058–60), archbishop of Mainz (1060–84).

76 Andreas I (1046–60). See above p. 103 n. 50.

77 Judith, known in Hungary as Sophia. See above p. 103 n. 51.

78 Salomon, king of Hungary (1063–74, †1087).

79 The rebellion of these brothers, kinsmen of Duke Frederick II of Lower Lotharingia (Luxemburg family), happened in 1057: Meyer von Knonau (1890) p. 43.

80 Henry I (1031–60).

81 Philip I (1060–1108).

82 Anne of Kiev († before 1090).

83 Luitpold (1051–9) † 7 December 1059.

84 Einhard II (1060–7). Conrad died on 12 December 1060.

Matilda, the wife of Duke Rudolf, died.[85] And in this year, as in the previous one, many perished from disease. The count palatine Henry[86] went mad after apparently abandoning the world under the pretext of a religious vocation and entering the monastery of Echternach. He withdrew from there and killed his wife.[87] In Hungary a certain Bela[88] expelled his brother, King Andreas, who was already an old man, from the kingship and brought him to the point of death. After suffering extreme injuries from his brother, this Andreas was at last struck down by fever. He sent all his treasure to the castle of Melk and sent his son to King Henry through the agency of Count Dietpold.[89]

1061. A great famine killed many men. Bishop Gebhard of Regensburg died[90] and Otto succeeded him.[91] Conrad, who was duke of the Carinthians in name only, died[92] and the Swabian Count Berthold received his duchy.[93]

In Rome after the death of Pope Nicholas on 27 July,[94] the Romans sent a crown and other gifts to King Henry and appealed to him about the election of the supreme pontiff. He held a general council in Basel, put on the crown sent by the Romans and was called patrician of the Romans. Then with the common consent of them all and according to the election of the envoys of the Romans on 26 October Bishop Cadalus of Parma was elected pope[95] by an act of simony, since (it is said) many bribes were given to certain persons. He was called Honorius, but he was destined never to possess the papacy. Twenty-seven days before his appointment, however, the bishop of Lucca, named Anselm, was ordained as the 157th pope[96] by the Normans[97] and by certain Romans

---

85 12 May 1059.

86 Henry, count palatine of Lotharingia (1047–60). See above p. 103 n. 59.

87 Matilda, daughter of Duke Gozelo II of Lower Lotharingia. See above p. 103 n. 60.

88 Bela I, king of Hungary (1061–3).

89 The ancestor of the margraves of Cham-Vohburg.

90 2 December 1060.

91 Otto (1060/1–89).

92 Conrad III (1056–61). See above p. 104 n. 65.

93 Berthold I ('the Bearded', of Zähringen), duke of Carinthia (1061–78).

94 Probably 20 July: Schmidt (1977) p. 81.

95 Cadalus, bishop of Parma (?1046–?71), antipope Honorius II (1061–4). See above p. 104 n. 68. On Berthold's revision of this annal see above pp. 27–8.

96 Anselm I, bishop of Lucca (1057–72); Alexander II (1061–73). See above p. 104 n. 69.

97 The Norman prince and papal vassal, Richard I of Capua. See Meyer von Knonau (1890) pp. 219–22; Schmidt (1977) p. 88.

and was called Alexander. He reigned for twelve years. The man of Parma in fact collected a great army from wherever he could and decided to take possession of the see by force and when he thus arrived before the city of Rome, he was not permitted by the Romans to enter. Consequently a great slaughter occurred there.[98] It was not, therefore, without *a bloody victory*[99] – for many Romans were killed – that the unhappy man returned to his city of Parma, where with only the title of pope, which he had usurped, he remained unhappily until the end of his life. This Alexander, as a catholic doctor, with great vigour destroyed simoniacal heresy and forbade the ministers of the altar to cohabit with their wives on pain of excommunication, according to the decrees of canon law. He forbade laymen, using the sanction of anathema, to attend the services of clergy who were openly unchaste and thus he very prudently restrained their unchastity.[100] The author of this regulation was principally Hildebrand, who was at that time archdeacon of the Roman church[101] and who was extremely hostile towards heretics.

At this time, after setting aside her royal garments and wearing the holy veil, Empress Agnes dedicated herself to Christ. She went to the town of Fruttuaria.[102]

1062. On 8 February there was an earthquake, lightning and thunder. The subsequent plague and sickness wiped out many men and a great famine occurred. King Henry celebrated Easter [31 March] together with his mother, the empress, in Utrecht, a city of Frisia. In these days Archbishop Anno of Cologne, with the support of certain princes of the kingdom, seized King Henry by force from his mother, the empress, together with the lance and the other insignia of the empire, and brought him with him to Cologne.[103] A great quarrel broke out between the empress and Bishop Gunther of Bamberg.[104]

---

98 A battle on the Field of Nero, 14 April 1062. See above p. 105 n. 74.

99 Sallust, *Catilina* 58.21. Cf. Herman, *Chronicle* 1053, above p. 96.

100 Alexander II, *JL* 4501, c. 3, ed. Schieffer (1981) p. 219. See *ibid.*, pp. 84–95.

101 Hildebrand, archdeacon of the Roman church, Pope Gregory VII (1073–85).

102 Agnes took the veil on 22 November in Speyer: Black-Veldtrup (1995) pp. 91, 364, 367–72. Her letter of late 1061 to the abbey of Fruttuaria, announcing a visit: *ibid.*, p. 351. She visited Fruttuaria in October 1066; perhaps also in 1070 and 1072: *ibid.*, pp. 95–6.

103 See above p. 104 n. 73.

104 Gunther I (1057–65). On this quarrel: Meyer von Knonau (1890) pp. 270–4; Black-Veldtrup (1995) pp. 365–6.

1063. King Henry led an army into Hungary and restored Salomon, the son of King Andreas, to his father's kingdom.[105] An extremely harsh winter killed the birds and the cattle with cold and caused a great dearth of crops and wine.[106] Archbishop Engelhard of Magdeburg died and Werner, brother of the bishop of Cologne, succeeded him.[107] Bishop Henry of Augsburg died and Embriko, canon of Mainz, succeeded him.[108] In the church in Goslar there was great bloodshed in the presence of the king.[109] In the same year near Constance a certain woman gave birth to a child with two heads and the other limbs double as far as the haunches.

1064. King Henry celebrated Christmas [25 December 1063] in Cologne, but celebrated Easter [11 April] in Liège. A great conflict took place between Archbishop Adalbert of Hamburg and the princes of the kingdom.[110] A synod in Mantua.[111]

1065. King Henry spent Christmas [25 December 1064] in Goslar, but spent Easter [27 March] in Worms. The royal palace in Goslar was burned down. This happened on 27 March in the third indiction.[112] And in the same place he was girded with the sword in the ninth year of his reign but in the fourteenth year of his life and Duke Godfrey ['the Bearded'] was chosen as his shieldbearer.[113] The bishop of Passau died and Altman, the chaplain of the empress, succeeded him.[114] At this time

105 See Meyer von Knonau (1890) pp. 345–8; Boshof (1986) p. 185.

106 See above p. 105 n. 75.

107 Engelhard (1051–63) † 30/31 August; Werner (Wezilo, 1063–78).

108 Henry II (1047–63) † 3 September; Embriko (1063–77).

109 A dispute over precedence between Abbot Widerad of Fulda and Bishop Hezilo of Hildesheim caused this armed struggle on 7 June: Meyer von Knonau (1890) pp. 328–31, 664–8; Robinson (1999) pp. 61–2.

110 Adalbert, archbishop of Bremen (1043–72) was in conflict in 1064 with Duke Ordulf Billung of Saxony. Berthold may, however, have been referring to the successful conspiracy of the princes against Adalbert in January 1066. See Meyer von Knonau (1890) pp. 386–7, 487–9.

111 This synod of 31 May recognised Alexander II's claim to the papacy against Cadalus of Parma.

112 This event is mentioned only by Berthold and Bernold: Meyer von Knonau (1890) p. 400 n. 11. The report is a later interpolation (perhaps originally a marginal gloss) since 'in the same place' in the following sentence refers to Worms rather than Goslar.

113 29 March. The ceremony declared Henry to be of age: see above p. 105 n. 84.

114 Egilbert (1045–65) † 17 May; Altman (1065–91).

Archbishop Siegfried of Mainz and Bishop Gunther of Bamberg, Bishop Otto of Regensburg, Bishop William of Utrecht,[115] with great pomp and an extensive entourage, set out for Jerusalem. During that journey they suffered much from the pagans, for they were even compelled to do battle with them.[116] Gunther died on that same journey[117] and Ricimann succeeded him by means of simony.[118]

1066. Many noblemen died in a civil war.[119] King Henry celebrated Christmas [25 December 1065] ...,[120] but he celebrated Easter [16 April] in Utrecht.

Archbishop Eberhard of Trier[121] departed in peace on 15 April, the Saturday before the holy day of Easter, after he had himself completed the offices of that day and while he was still clad in his priestly vestments. Conrad, the provost of Cologne,[122] was elected by the king and ought to have succeeded him, but he was opposed by the clergy and citizens of Trier. A certain count among the vassals of Trier named Theoderic,[123] therefore, seized that same Conrad, as he travelled to Trier. After tormenting him for a long time in prison, he entrusted him to four knights to be killed. When they had thrown him three times down a precipice and had been able to do no more than bruise his arm, one of them was led by penitence to seek pardon from him. Another, however, wishing to behead him, only cut off his jaw and thus that martyr worthy of God departed to the Lord on 1 June. He was buried in a certain abbey named Tholey. A fitting vengeance, however, afterwards pursued the three knights who were the perpetrators of that death. For one of them was unable to swallow the food that he received; the other two mutilated their hands and thus breathed their last. In addition very many miracles took place at his tomb, by which his martyrdom was proved to be worthy of veneration. After his murder Udo, canon of Trier was elected by the clergy and appointed archbishop.[124]

115 William (?1054–76).

116 See above p. 106 n. 89.

117 23 July 1065.

118 Herman I (1065–75). See above p. 106 n. 90.

119 Perhaps the unrest in Saxony following the fall of Archbishop Adalbert of Bremen. See above p. 106 n. 91.

120 Probably in Mainz. See above p. 106 n. 92.

121 Eberhard (1047–66).

122 Conrad of Pfullingen, nephew of Archbishop Anno II of Cologne.

123 Theoderic, burgrave of Trier: see above p. 106 n. 95.

124 Udo of Nellenburg (1066–78).

Comets were seen on the octave of Easter, that is on 23 April, and they remained for thirty days.[125] The wedding of King Henry in Tribur.[126] Again a comet was seen.

At this time the venerable Peter Damian, who was originally a hermit and became a cardinal bishop, wrote many works and attacked the unchastity of priests in his writings with very many arguments. They say, however, that he treated those ordained by simoniacs with too much indulgence.[127]

Archbishop Hugh of Besançon,[128] a pious man and a *faithful* and prudent *servant* of the Lord, happily *entered into the joy of* his *Lord*, to be *made ruler over many things*.[129] His successor, who was canonically elected by the brethren, was a canon of the same church.[130]

1067. King Henry celebrated Christmas [25 December 1066] in Speyer,[131] but Easter [8 April] …[132] Saxony was afflicted by civil strife.[133] Bishop Burchard of Halberstadt[134] courageously wrought destruction among the people of the Liutizi. Bishop Einhard of Speyer died on a journey to Rome[135] and was buried in Siena and a certain Henry succeeded him.[136]

At this time certain monks from the valley that is called Vallombrosa[137]

---

125 Halley's Comet. Sightings reported in German and Italian narrative sources: Meyer von Knonau (1890) p. 523 n. 55.

126 Lampert, *Annales* 1066, pp. 103–4 also placed the wedding of Henry IV and Bertha of Turin (above n. 48) in Tribur, while the *Annals of Niederaltaich* 1066, p. 72 placed it in Ingelheim. See Meyer von Knonau (1890) p. 526 ('probably in Tribur').

127 Peter Damian, *Letter* 40 (*Liber Gratissimus*), pp. 384–509. His views on simoniacal ordinations: Dressler (1954) pp. 103–4.

128 Hugh I (1031–66).

129 Matthew 25:21.

130 Hugh II (1066–85).

131 In Bamberg: Meyer von Knonau (1890) p. 533, on the authority of *Triumphus sancti Remacli Stabulensis* c. 18, p. 446. *Annals of Niederaltaich* 1067, p. 72 name Regensburg.

132 In Goslar: Meyer von Knonau (1890) p. 564.

133 Perhaps the conflict between Adalbert of Bremen and the Saxon nobility: Meyer von Knonau (1890) pp. 513–16.

134 Burchard II (1059–88). His expedition against the Liutizi (above p. 68 n. 113) took place in 1068: see Meyer von Knonau (1890) p. 585; Robinson (1999) p. 78.

135 23 March 1067.

136 Henry I (1067–75).

137 The reforming monastery of Vallombrosa and Abbot John Gualbert: Goez (1973) pp. 229–39.

in the diocese of Florence refused to receive their bishop[138] because of simoniacal heresy and turned the clergy and people against him to such an extent that they would in no way deign to receive his offices. They also declared publicly in certain writings that the sacraments that were celebrated by him and by all simoniacs and married priests were utterly invalid and must be treated with contempt. Hence there arose dissensions and divisions, not only in this place but also in neighbouring places. When he heard of this case and this accusation, however, Pope Alexander [II] summoned both the bishop and the monks to his presence in Rome so that a binding judgement on these matters might be decided in a catholic manner in a Roman synod. In that place, therefore, this decision was reached at their urgent request: that the truth should be investigated and made known to holy Church through a trial by fire. While both parties were expressing their approval of this, one of the monks[139] declared that he would submit to that ordeal with God as the witness and the judge of his righteousness. After this decision had been promulgated by the pope, they returned to Florence so that the matter might be brought to a conclusion there in the presence of the clergy and people. Finally a great council was gathered there and in the churchyard a pyre, standing higher than a man, twelve feet long and containing a space of two feet, built of very dry wood, was very eagerly ignited. Since Bishop Peter of Florence dared not enter the fire in order to prove himself and his colleagues innocent of the criminal accusation made against them, that aforementioned monk, who had received Christ's eucharist and who was clad as though he was to read mass there, with bare feet and holding a cross in his hands, in the hearing of the whole church, for the sake of God's justice and in the interests of proving the truth, having taken an oath, he thus declared in Christ's name that that Peter who was called bishop of Florence obtained his bishopric by simony and that the sacraments that were conferred by him and by other simoniacs and married priests were by no means to be accepted by catholics. And according to the terms of that declaration he moved step by step into the midst of the flames and walked through them confidently in the name of the Lord without any injury from heat or fire. As they saw this judgement, all the people unanimously

138 Peter Mezzabarba (?1061–8).

139 Peter 'Igneus', monk of Vallombrosa, cardinal bishop of Albano (?1072–89). See Hüls (1977) p. 90. His trial by fire in Settimo (13 February 1068): Meyer von Knonau (1890) pp. 600–1; Miccoli (1960) pp. 147–57; Cowdrey (1998) pp. 66–7. Cf. Berthold's account below, 1078, p. 199 and the accounts of Bernold in his *Chronicle* 1079, 1089, below pp. 264, 297–8, and his polemic *De emtione ecclesiarum* p. 108.

gave thanks to God and praised the just judge of heaven. Finally Peter was summoned to Rome by the lord pope and on the evidence of this judgement he was convicted of the offence of the aforesaid heresy.[140] Confounded, he resigned the episcopal staff and ring to the pope and, having been thus justly deprived of the office to which he had been unjustly promoted, he departed. Nevertheless he took possession of the property of that church for a while with the help of Duke Godfrey ['the Bearded'],[141] hoping that he could somehow or other be restored to his see. Finally, however, when he was disappointed of this hope, he gave up everything that he seemed to possess, underwent a conversion and now became a monk in the monastery of Pomposa.

The Normans wished to make an attack on Rome but when Duke Godfrey threatened them, they gave up their plan.[142]

1068. King Henry celebrated Christmas [25 December 1067] in Cologne,[143] but Easter [23 March] …[144] Led astray by the folly of his youth, he was so forgetful of his lawful wife [Bertha] and was widely rumoured to be implicated in such abominable offences that his princes even attempted to deprive him of the kingship.[145] All that year was rainy.[146]

1069. Peace and reconciliation were confirmed among the people on oath by royal edict at Christmas [25 December 1068] in Goslar.[147] King Henry brought destruction to the people of the Liutizi.[148] The Saxon

---

140 In the Roman synod of 30 March 1068: Meyer von Knonau (1890) pp. 600–1.

141 Godfrey's support for Peter Mezzabarba: Goez (1973) pp. 234–5.

142 In 1066 Prince Richard I of Capua captured Ceprano and plundered the Campagna but Godfrey's campaign of spring 1067 forced him back over the River Garigliano. See Meyer von Knonau (1890) pp. 543–7, 551–6; Goez (1995) pp. 161, 209.

143 In Goslar: Lampert, *Annales* 1068, p. 105; *Annals of Niederaltaich* 1068, p. 74.

144 Probably in Goslar, where the king suffered a serious illness: Meyer von Knonau (1890) p. 585.

145 A polemical allusion to the king's unsuccessful attempt to obtain a divorce from Bertha, announced in an assembly in Worms in June 1069: Meyer von Knonau (1890) pp. 612–17, 624–7; Robinson (1999) pp. 109–13.

146 The Vienna manuscripts add: 'Werner, the second abbot of St Blasien, died,' i.e. Werner I (?1045–68). See above p. 20 and n. 2.

147 Henry IV spent Christmas in Goslar (not, as reported by *Annals of Niederaltaich* 1069, p. 76, in Mainz): cf. *D.H.IV* 214 (3 January, Goslar). On this event as an instance of 'the peace of God' movement: Wadle (1973) p. 159. Cf. Herman, *Chronicle* 1043, above p. 74.

148 Cf. *Annals of Niederaltaich* 1069, p. 76: 'The king … immediately [after Christmas] ordered an expedition to be prepared against the Liutizi even though it was wintertime.' See Meyer von Knonau (1890) pp. 610–11.

margrave Dedi[149] rebelled against the king but was subsequently forced to come to surrender.

Abbot Udalric of Reichenau died.[150] In his place a certain Meginward of Hildesheim[151] was with difficulty appointed abbot by the king, for the appointment was simoniacal and the brethren rebelled against him.

Bishop Rumold of Constance, an extremely pious and humane man, who was the most sagacious restorer of the cathedral, which fell down in his time,[152] and the most careful enlarger and steward of the church's treasure, left behind the shadowy vanities of this world and happily ended his life on 4 November. He was solemnly buried in the same cathedral, which he had already begun to build. At that time simoniacal heresy in all its savagery ruled over our compatriots everywhere, not as in former times in secret, but openly, with shameless power and with *no respect of persons*,[153] and lamentably defiled the dovelike beauty of holy mother Church with its contagious corruption. Finally it compelled a certain Carloman,[154] a canon of Magdeburg but also provost at the Harzburg, to enter – *not by the door but by some other way*,[155] namely, over the wall – the sheepfold of the cathedral church of Constance, after he had given and promised to the king and his advisers a large sum of sacrilegious money as well as church benefices. That most wretched purchaser of the miseries of hell tried most diligently and with the greatest longing to be enthroned in our cathedral, contrary to the law. He also strove by every possible means to render invalid the canonical election by all the clergy and people of Siegfried,[156] one of their brethren and also a royal chaplain, whom they sought to have as their bishop.

Duke Godfrey ['the Bearded'], who was entirely outstanding among secular men, very easily moved to tears by the memory of his sins and

---

149 Dedi, margrave of Lower Lusatia (1046–75). His rebellion: Meyer von Knonau (1890) pp. 617–23; Fenske (1977) pp. 34–6; Robinson (1999) pp. 64–5.

150 Udalric I (1048–69) † 7 November.

151 Meginward, prior of the abbey of St Michael, Hildesheim; abbot of Reichenau (1070). His simony: Lampert, *Annales* 1070, p. 111; *Annals of Niederaltaich* 1071, p. 83. See Meyer von Knonau (1894) pp. 2–3 and above p. 28.

152 Rumold (1051–69). Cf. Herman, *Chronicle* 1052, above p. 93.

153 II Chronicles 19:7; Romans 2:11; Ephesians 6:9; Colossians 3:25; James 2:1; I Peter 1:17.

154 Charles (Carloman, 1070–1). His simony: Lampert, *Annales* 1069, p. 111; *Annals of Niederaltaich* 1071, p. 82. See Meyer von Knonau (1894) pp. 1–3, 5; Schieffer (1972) pp. 46–50; Robinson (1999) p. 118.

155 John 10:1.

156 Siegfried, canon of Constance: Schieffer (1972) p. 50.

most generous in the distribution of alms, gave away all his property and his treasure to the poor and the churches so that he was left virtually as a naked bearer of the naked cross. He became a new man by means of penitence so perfect and so very tearful that there is no reason to doubt that he happily departed from here to citizenship of the court of highest heaven. The most devout man, commending his spirit into the hands of Him by whose grace he drew breath, was caught up to heaven and died a joyful death. He was finally buried with appropriate funeral solemnities in Verdun, where he had also died, on 24 December:[157] there may he rest in peace.

1070. The king spent Christmas [25 December 1069] in Freising and, passing through that region, he arrived in Augsburg at the Purification of St Mary [2 February].[158]

The brethren of Constance, therefore, came there in order to secure the acceptance of the candidate whom they had elected by obtaining the king's agreement, since that aforementioned simoniac [Carloman] had been imposed on them whether they wanted him or not. Since, however, the king with many threats commanded them to receive him, they sadly returned home. Thus that obstinate intruder, worthy of anathema – unluckily for himself – usurped the cathedral church. Without delay he applied himself at once most eagerly to the task for which he came, namely that what he had obtained by evil means, he might sell by even more evil means and that he might *steal and kill and destroy*[159] the sheep of another man. He secretly divided up the sacred vessels, the ceremonial vestments and the altar-fronts, worked with silver; he scattered gold, jewels and all the treasure of the church among his followers and for their use, like a sacrilegious thief.[160] When Pope Alexander [II] was fully informed of this by the brethren in a letter of complaint, he forbade them by his apostolic authority ever to communicate with him and at the same time he sent a letter to the archbishop [Siegfried] of Mainz,[161] with the command that he should by no means consecrate him as bishop unless he cleared himself of the aforesaid heresy according to

---

157 † 30 December: G. Despy in *Lexikon des Mittelalters* 4 (1989) col. 1601. See also Meyer von Knonau (1890) pp. 634–7.

158 He was still in Freising on 29 December: *D.H.IV* 229. Cf. *Annals of Augsburg* 1070, p. 128.

159 John 10:10.

160 The same charges appear in the *acta* of the synod of Mainz, 1071 (*Codex Udalrici* 37, p. 72).

161 Neither the canons' letter to Alexander II nor that of the pope to Siegfried of Mainz is extant.

canon law. He, however, somehow or other defended himself according to the promises and the authority of the king and his fellow traffickers and protracted his case into the second year.

Franconia was afflicted by civil strife.[162] Duke Otto of Bavaria[163] was accused by certain men of treachery against the king and an opportunity was given to him by the king to clear himself in a judicial duel. Since he did not wish to do so, he seized on this as a pretext for rebellion and Magnus, son of Duke Otto of northern Saxony,[164] joined with him. When the aforesaid Otto, after being lawfully summoned to make amends for his conduct, refused to come, the king deprived him of his duchy and of his other benefices.

Bishop Thietmar of Chur died and Henry, a monk of Reichenau, succeeded him.[165] Meginward, who was unwilling to tolerate the exactions and commands and services imposed on him by the king, voluntarily gave up the office of abbot of Reichenau. The winter was windy and rainy.

1071. The king spent Christmas [25 December 1070] ...[166] Welf was made duke of Bavaria.[167] Otto, the former duke of Bavaria, together with his allies, came to the king at Whitsuntide to surrender.[168] King Henry was subjected to many plots by the Saxons but he manfully withstood them all.[169]

At a council held in Mainz[170] at the command of Pope Alexander [II], Carloman, that man who had been appointed to Constance, was proved guilty of the aforesaid heresy and of the many sacrileges that he had

162 Perhaps in connection with the growing unrest in Thuringia: Meyer von Knonau (1894) p. 28.

163 Otto I, count of Northeim, duke of Bavaria (1061–70; † 1083) was accused by 'Egeno, a knight', of having suborned him to murder the king. His trial (1 August 1070 in Goslar), deposition (2 August) and rebellion: Meyer von Knonau (1894) pp. 9–23; Lange (1961) pp. 25–31; Fenske (1977) pp. 62, 64, 92–4; Robinson (1999) pp. 65–70.

164 Magnus Billung, duke of Saxony (1073–1106), son of Ordulf (Otto, 1059–72).

165 Thietmar (1040–70) † 29 January; Henry I (1070–8).

166 In Goslar: Meyer von Knonau (1894) p. 41.

167 Welf IV (1070–1101) was invested with the duchy at Christmastide 1070: Meyer von Knonau (1894) p. 24.

168 14 June (Tuesday in Whitsun week): Bernold, *Chronicle* 1071, below p. 251. Otto and Magnus Billung surrendered in Halberstadt: Meyer von Knonau (1894) p. 70.

169 Perhaps an allusion to Otto's failure to force the king to do battle at Hasungen, January/February 1071: Meyer von Knonau (1894) pp. 42–3.

170 15–18 August: *Codex Udalrici* 36–8, pp. 68–81. See Meyer von Knonau (1894) pp. 78–85; Schieffer (1972) pp. 46–50; Robinson (1999) pp. 118–19.

committed, according to synodal procedure by the canons of Constance unanimously in a letter of accusation that was presented to him. Since he could not deny that he had acted contrary to the rules of church discipline, namely by obtaining a church by means of payment, he was cast out in confusion from the see into which he had intruded by simony – although not, as would have been appropriate, by an act of public deposition. The king indeed protected him as much as he possibly could and [Carloman] resigned the episcopal staff not in the synod but in the king's chamber, still with a hardened heart,[171] rebellious and unwilling. And if such a judgement awaits one who is condemned while not yet consecrated, what awaits those who have been consecrated? And if this is the case of the bishops, what of the priests? Here you have grounds for deposition derived from a greater case and applied to a lesser one. And since, according to the precepts of the holy Fathers, it is not permissible for any of the clergy to be ignorant of canon law,[172] it is not superfluous to recommend that they remember, of the many texts, this one short chapter from the decrees of the holy Pope Nicholas. *Any priest who has obtained a church for payment is by all means to be deposed, since he is perceived to have acted contrary to the rule of church discipline. If, however, anyone by means of money drives out another priest who has lawfully been appointed to a church and in such a manner claims it for himself, this unhappily widespread vice is to be corrected with the utmost zeal.*[173]

Otto, a canon of Goslar, was put in Carloman's place by the king.[174] A certain Rupert, an abbot in Bamberg,[175] acquired the office of abbot of Reichenau by means of simony, having given the king much gold. He was afterwards excommunicated and expelled.

1072. The king spent Christmas [25 December 1071] ...[176] and over-came those who were rebelling against him virtually without the trouble of fighting a battle.

---

171 Cf. Exodus 7:13.

172 Cf. Celestine I, *JK* 371: *Epistola* 5.1 (*MPL* 50, col. 36A).

173 There are similar expressions in Nicholas II, *JL* 4405 c. 6, 9 (Schieffer [1981] pp. 222–3) and *JL* 4431a (*MGH Constitutiones* 1, 547–8, no. 384) but the direct source is council of Tours (813) c. 15 (*MGH Concilia* 2, 288), most widely circulated (abbreviated) in Burchard of Worms, *Decretum* III.10, col. 695.

174 Otto I, bishop of Constance (1071–86).

175 Rupert, abbot of Michelsberg, Bamberg (1066–71), abbot of Reichenau (1071–2), abbot of Gengenbach (1074–5). He was deposed by Alexander II in the Easter synod of 1072: Meyer von Knonau (1894) pp. 45, 165–6; Schieffer (1972) p. 47.

176 In Worms: Meyer von Knonau (1894) p. 88.

Cardinal bishop Peter Damian of pious memory, who had long been crucified by the world, departed to the Lord on 23 February.[177] The lord Gerald, a monk of Cluny, who was distinguished for his knowledge of the Scriptures and whose character was similar to that of his predecessor, succeeded him in the bishopric.[178] Archbishop Adalbert of Bremen died and Liemar succeeded him.[179]

The king built for himself many very strongly fortified castles in the regions of Saxony and Thuringia and also unjustly seized for himself very many fortifications and thus aroused the minds of many men against himself.[180]

In these days also the church of Milan remained vacant for some time after the death of its bishop.[181] His successor was a certain man[182] who had given a very large sum of money to the king and his advisers. The pope excommunicated him but the king ordered that he should be consecrated. The clergy, however, had elected another,[183] whom they considered suitable but who was compelled to swear an oath and was then driven out by that man.

1073. The king celebrated Christmas [25 December 1072] ...[184] Duke Rudolf of Swabia, Duke Berthold [I] of Carinthia and Duke Welf [IV] of Bavaria dissociated themselves from the king because they perceived that their advice carried no weight with him, other men having insinuated themselves into his counsels.[185]

---

177 Peter Damian + 22 February: Lucchesi (1972) 2, pp. 146–7; Hüls (1977) p. 100. Bernold, *Chronicle* 1072, below p. 252 gives the date 22 February, but 21 February in his *Calendar* p. 498.

178 Gerald, cardinal bishop of Ostia (1072/3–77).

179 Adalbert (n. 110) + 16 March; Liemar (1072–1101).

180 See Meyer von Knonau (1894) pp. 857–69; Fenske (1977) pp. 28–32; Robinson (1999) pp. 82–7.

181 Wido, archbishop of Milan (1045–71).

182 Godfrey, invested by the king 1071, consecrated 1072 but unable to establish himself in Milan: Meyer von Knonau (1894) pp. 101–7, 196–7; Schwartz (1913) pp. 80–1; Cowdrey (1968a) p. 36.

183 Atto, archbishop of Milan (1072), cardinal priest of S. Marco (+ before 1086), elected 6 January 1072 but forced 7 January to renounce the archbishopric: Meyer von Knonau (1894) pp. 174–6; Schwartz (1913) pp. 81–2; Hüls (1977) p. 185.

184 In Bamberg: Meyer von Knonau (1894) p. 174.

185 Cf. *Annals of Niederaltaich* 1072, p. 84: 'the bishops, dukes and other princes withdrew from royal affairs. Among them, the dukes Rudolf and Berthold were often summoned to the king but refused to come, so that the king even began to suspect that they were preparing to rebel against him.' See Meyer von Knonau (1894) pp. 155–6; Robinson (1999) pp. 125–8.

Count Theoderic was moved to penitence for the crime that he committed against the blessed Conrad, who had been assigned to the people of Trier as their archbishop.[186] Although many dangers stood in his way, he nevertheless began the journey to Jerusalem with eager faith, in the company of many others. After they had gone on board a ship at Laodicea, they were beset by a sudden storm; the day immediately darkened and they were uncertain where they were going. After four days during which the gale continually shook their ship with the same ferocity, one night they were repeatedly cheered by a heavenly light that descended to them. Thereafter they no longer feared death in the midst of their dangers but fixed their thoughts on the eternal life that was to come. Cleansed of their filthy sins by the waves of the sea, they were shipwrecked and departed to the Lord on 17 February. They were Count Theoderic, Widerold, Marchwald, together with 113 men.

Margrave Herman,[187] the son of Duke Berthold [of Carinthia], who already as a young man strove for the perfection of the Gospels, abandoned everything that he had possessed; together with his wife and his only son,[188] as a true follower of Christ and a naked bearer of the naked cross, he became indeed a monk in Cluny. After living there entirely according to the *Rule* for little more than one year, he happily departed to the Lord on 25 April,[189] but still admonishes the brethren about their secret and careless actions by means of frequent visions.

In Rome Pope Alexander [II] died.[190] It was the universal opinion that Hildebrand, archdeacon of the Roman church, a prudent, sober and chaste man, should be appointed pope in his place. When he heard of this, regarding himself as unequal to so great an honour, or rather so great a burden, he obtained from them with great difficulty a delay before giving his answer and then fled and remained hidden for some days in St Peter ad Vincula. At length he was with difficulty discovered and brought to the apostolic see by force, ordained as the 158th pope and called Gregory VII.[191] It was through his wisdom that the

---

186 See above p. 119 and n. 123.

187 Herman I, margrave of Baden (†1074), son of Berthold I of Carinthia.

188 Judith, daughter of Count Adalbert of Calw (†1091); Herman II, margrave of Baden (†1130).

189 26 April 1074: Wollasch (1987) p. 29.

190 21 April 1073.

191 Gregory VII was elected on 22 April. This fictitious version is based on the account of Pope Gregory I's election (590) by John the Deacon, *Vita Gregorii Magni* I.44, *MPL* 75, col. 81B. The use of John's account by pro-Gregorian authors: Robinson (1978a) pp. 31–9; Cowdrey (1998) p. 73.

unchastity of priests was held in check not only in Italy but also in the German territories, so that what his predecessors had forbidden in Italy, he himself zealously attempted to forbid in the other lands of the catholic Church.

The whole of Thuringia and Saxony rebelled against King Henry because of the fortifications mentioned above and because of many other things that the king had done insolently and unadvisedly in their territory against the will of that people,[192] which they could no longer suffer and support with equanimity. They formed a conspiracy and decided to take him by surprise with a large army and to compel him to do as they were inclined. He, however, learned their plan and, hastily gathering up his treasure, as far as the limited time permitted, he escaped from them with difficulty and came with a few followers to Worms, where he remained for some time in ill health.[193] When subsequently the king arranged an expedition into Saxony, the Saxons forestalled him and unanimously promised him satisfaction, if he would grant them the rights of their ancestors. A conference was held concerning this agreement in Würzburg,[194] where, after many complaints about the intolerable injustices that they had suffered, nothing was done except that they disdainfully promised the king once more that at Christmas they would give him satisfaction (although it was a false promise). This they did according to the advice of certain bishops and of the aforementioned dukes. When this was accomplished, one of the king's advisers[195] parted company with him and publicly accused him in the presence of the aforementioned dukes [Rudolf of Swabia and Berthold of Carinthia] of having made a plan with him and with his other close advisers to kill them all somehow or other. He openly declared that he himself had been intended and induced by very large bribes to commit this crime. Consequently such great strife arose between the king and the

---

192 Cf. the political theory of Manegold, *Ad Gebehardum* c. 47, pp. 491–2. The term 'the will of the people' seems to derive from Pseudo-Chrysostom, *Opus imperfectum in Matthaeum, Homilia* 37 c. 21, *MPG* 56, col. 835. See Fuhrmann (1975) p. 25; Robinson (1978a) pp. 124–31.

193 After binding themselves by an oath at Hoetensleben (July), the rebels marched on the Harzburg. Henry fled from the Harzburg on the night of 9/10 August. He fell ill in Ladenburg (near Worms) in December (Lampert, *Annales* 1073) and after his recovery entered Worms (cf. *D.H.IV* 267). See Meyer von Knonau (1894) pp. 242–55, 294–7; Robinson (1999) pp. 73–4, 93–4.

194 The conference between rebels and royal representatives took place at Gerstungen (20 October), while the king was in Würzburg: Meyer von Knonau (1894) pp. 287–9.

195 Regenger, identified by Lampert, *Annales* 1073, pp. 166–8. See Meyer von Knonau (1894) pp. 291–3; Robinson (1999) pp. 92–3, 359–60.

princes that it was only with difficulty that he escaped the ambush that
they planned and entered Worms with the help of the citizens.[196] There
he gathered auxiliary forces from all sides and waited for the day on
which he could clear himself by judicial combat of the accusation of
the aforementioned crime. When at last the appointed day arrived, on
which he was either to clear himself in the presence of the princes of the
kingdom or be driven out of the kingdom, that man who had betrayed
him and who had come forward as his enemy, died a sudden death.[197]
And thus, since [the princes] rejected the oath by means of which the
king wished to clear himself, the case arising from that same accusation
was deferred. He himself again gathered from every quarter contingents of his knights and vassals, whomsoever he could, and began from
day to day to care less and less for the stratagems of his opponents.

After Rupert [abbot of Reichenau], already excommunicated by the
pope, had likewise been expelled by the king, as befitted a sacrilegious
pupil of Simon,[198] at length Ekkehard, one of the brethren of Reichenau
and elected by them, was made abbot of Reichenau.[199] According to their
privileges he was consecrated by the aforementioned pope in Rome after
Easter.[200] Rupert, however, became abbot in Gengenbach, where he was
killed by a certain servant of the church because of a benefice that [the
abbot] wished to take away from the man.[201]

1074. King Henry celebrated Christmas [25 December 1073] in
Worms, although he was beset by the greatest dangers and difficulties.
He next assembled help from wherever and from whomsoever he could
and at the Purification of St Mary [2 February] he suddenly attacked
the Saxons. Fearing the shock of war, they came to surrender with this
stipulation, that the fortifications about which the quarrel had arisen
should be destroyed; and this was subsequently carried out.[202] Thus

---

196 See above n. 193.

197 The judicial duel was to have taken place soon after 13 January 1074: Meyer von
   Knonau (1894) pp. 297, 308–9.

198 Simon Magus (Acts 8:9–24), regarded by reformers as the first heresiarch, founder
   of the heresy of simony. See above p. 126 and n. 175.

199 Ekkehard II (1072–88).

200 After Easter 1073 or 1074: Gregory VII, *Register* I.82, pp. 117–18.

201 Rupert, successor of Acelin (✝1074) as abbot of Gengenbach, died soon after being
   severely wounded on 12 November 1075. Lampert, *Annales* 1076, p. 259: he was the
   victim of his zeal in recovering the alienated property of the abbey. See Meyer von
   Knonau (1894) pp. 409–10.

202 Peace of Gerstungen, 2 February 1074: Meyer von Knonau (1894) pp. 318–27; Robinson (1999) pp. 95–6.

in the absence of the aforesaid dukes and the other magnates of the kingdom the king feigned a reconciliation with the Saxons and he came with them as far as Goslar, but he did not greatly trust them. Duke Rudolf and the other rebels were reconciled to the king.[203]

During this Lent [5 March–19 April] the empress, together with two bishops, legates of the apostolic see, came from Rome to the king in Pforzen in Swabia with the purpose of correcting the king's morals.[204] The king celebrated Easter [20 April] in Bamberg. From there he came to Nuremberg[205] to his mother and the other legates of the apostolic see and, in the presence of the bishops [Siegfried] of Mainz and [Liemar of] Bremen and many others, he committed himself into their hands with a promise of amendment and most firmly promised his help to the lord pope in deposing simoniacs. The king's advisers also promised on oath in the presence of those same legates that they would restore all the church property that they had unjustly acquired. They had indeed bought it from simoniacs when helping those unworthy men to ecclesiastical office by their advice. After these matters had been settled, the empress and the legates of the apostolic see returned.

That summer the king undertook an expedition into Hungary to help King Salomon, who also because of his insolent and shameful crimes had been deposed from his office by his father's brother[206] and the other magnates of the kingdom, for whose counsels he cared little. The king, however, was able to achieve nothing of what he wished there, namely to restore Salomon. Finally, bringing back his sister, Queen Judith, the wife of Salomon, he returned home to Worms,[207] no longer under the favourable auspices with which he had set out.

A son was born to the king.[208] During the autumn he went again to Bavaria and remained in that region for some time.[209] From there by way of Augsburg and Reichenau he reached the city of Strasbourg.

203 Through the mediation of Empress Agnes: Meyer von Knonau (1894) p. 383.

204 Agnes was escorted to Nuremberg by cardinal bishops Gerald of Ostia and Hubert of Palestrina. See Meyer von Knonau (1894) pp. 377–81; Black-Veldtrup (1995) p. 97; Robinson (1999) pp. 132–3. Henry IV's advisers: below n. 215.

205 26–27 April.

206 Salomon (n. 78) was deposed by his cousin, Duke Geisa (king of Hungary, 1074–7), son of King Bela I (n. 88). The Hungarian expedition of August 1074: Meyer von Knonau (1894) pp. 384–8, 402–4; Boshof (1986) p. 186; Robinson (1999) p. 99.

207 After 29 September: Lampert, *Annales* 1074, p. 198. Judith see above n. 77.

208 Conrad (1074–1101), duke of Lower Lotharingia (1076–87), king (1087–98).

209 Cf. *D.H.IV* 276 (26 November, Regensburg). See Meyer von Knonau (1894) p. 407.

1075. The king celebrated Christmas [25 December 1074] ceremoniously in Strasbourg, glorying in the great numbers of his magnates who were present. There he busily devised with his vassals an artful plan: that while publicly announcing another Hungarian expedition immediately after Easter [5 April], he would use the army for a surprise attack on Saxony.[210] Thus he carefully assembled from all sides a large force of knights and concentrated his mind entirely on avenging his injuries, which he would be able to do all the more easily since it was not at all expected by his enemies.

A synod was assembled in Rome during the days of Lent [24–28 February] by Pope Gregory [VII][211] in a supreme effort to put an end somehow to the many, nay the innumerable, monstrous and audacious scandals in holy mother Church and to some extent to issue a reminder of the need to observe the canonical regulations of the holy Fathers, which our modern times have almost completely contradicted and annihilated. He indeed, *hoping against hope*[212] and placing great trust in the supreme Farmer and strong Helper, strove to clear the field of the Lord properly with the authentic axes of catholic and apostolic discipline, despite the fact that for a long time now, because of the negligent idleness of his predecessors, it had become overgrown by the thorn bushes of abuses and misappropriations and was turning into a rank wilderness as a result of a lethargic and lamentable neglect of the fruits of the Church. The thorns, the thistles and the tares that it would have been very easy for his predecessors to cut down gradually in their day with the scythe of discipline, he strove to tear up by the roots with the hoe of doctrine.[213] According to the judgement and with the agreement of all the holy council, therefore, he most firmly decreed by apostolic authority that the authentic rules of the holy Fathers, as they were lawfully established in the separate councils up to the present, should be regarded as possessing perpetual authority and that anyone who obstinately presumed to oppose them, should be entirely excluded from the members of the Church. Next, besides other matters *in*[214] *that synod,*

---

210 Cf. Lampert, *Annales* 1075, p. 202.

211 Cf. Gregory VII, *Register* II.52a, pp. 196–7. See Meyer von Knonau (1894) pp. 451–5; Schieffer (1981) pp. 118–19; Cowdrey (1998) pp. 100–8; Robinson (1999) pp. 134–8.

212 Romans 4:18.

213 Cf. Genesis 3:8; Matthew 13:7; Mark 4:7; Luke 8:7; Hebrews 6:8.

214/214 Gregory VII, *JL* 4933 (*Epistolae Vagantes* 8, pp. 16–18) to Bishop Otto of Constance, quoted by Bernold, *Apologeticus* c. 1, pp. 60–1; Manegold, *Ad Gebehardum* c. 17, p. 340.

following the authority of the holy Fathers, he *judged that those who have been promoted to any rank or office of holy orders by means of simoniacal heresy, that is, through the intervention of money, are no longer to have any opportunity of serving in holy Church.* Those also who acquire or will acquire *churches by means of the gift of money are to* forego *them entirely. No one hereafter is to* presume *to sell or buy* them nor to make use of tithes except according to the rule of canon law. *Those who commit the crime of fornication must not celebrate mass nor serve at the altar in the lesser orders.* He *also decided that, if* the aforesaid men *show contempt for* his *decrees, or rather those of the holy Fathers, the people are by no means to accept their* ministry, because they are separated from the members of the Church; *so that those who* refuse to be *corrected from* the fear *of God and the dignity of their office,* may be *brought to their senses by the shame of the world and the rebuke of the people.*[214] The obedient and those who truly repented of their error, however, he absolved from their sins with apostolic gentleness and authority and he mercifully pardoned them. Thus he must undoubtedly be regarded as one who justly judged and condemned the stubborn, while piously pardoning and absolving the truly penitent in the catholic faith. There also he excommunicated the king's advisers[215] again because of simoniacal heresy, caring little for what they had promised his legates on oath.[216] The king, who was angered by this, in no way avoided their company.

In that same synod a sentence of deposition and also of excommunication, according to the rules of the canons, was pronounced on Bishop Henry of Speyer.[217] He had long before been accused canonically of simoniacal heresy before the Roman see and, when he was summoned to come there for the examination of his case, he obstinately refused to do so. In a miraculous manner, however, on the same day and at the same hour at which he was judicially deposed from the priesthood and from the office of bishop and excommunicated in Rome, he himself being in Speyer and rising from the table after a delicious meal (as was his custom), his throat was suffocated by a stab of pain so very sharp and lethal that afterwards he could very rarely utter a word and it was with difficulty that he survived until the morning of the next day. After

215 Five advisers (including Udalric of Godesheim, Count Eberhard and Hartmann) first excommunicated by Alexander II in the Lenten synod of 1073 (Bonizo, *To a friend* VI, p. 218). See Meyer von Knonau (1894) pp. 198–9; Schieffer (1981) pp. 109–10; Cowdrey (1998) pp. 92, 99, 101; Robinson (1999) pp. 125, 133, 135, 360–1.

216 In Nuremberg, 26–27 April: above p. 131 and n. 204.

217 Cf. Gregory VII, *Register* II.52a, p. 196. The fate of Henry (n. 136): Bernold, *Chronicle* 1075, below p. 254 and his polemic *De incontinentia sacerdotum* V, p. 26.

midday he suffered the doom of a most bitter death and was deposed at the same time from episcopal office and from life, so that through this miracle the strength and truth of the words of God were proved: *whatsoever you will bind on earth, shall be bound in heaven.*[218] Behold! the sword of Peter, the all-knowing judge of fraud and a most powerful zealot against his enemies has now been drawn from its sheath: the sword by means of which he himself struck dead Ananias and Sapphira when they fraudulently concealed the price of their field and lied to the Holy Spirit[219] and by means of which he also cast down to earth the heresiarch Simon, when he flew up into heaven, so that he was cut into four pieces and thereafter condemned to hell forever.[220] It is now and always to be feared by all simoniacs, the more intensely as there is no defensive shield by means of which so long, piercing and inescapable an avenger is ever to be avoided except complete penitence.

After the aforementioned decisions and almost all the other decrees of the apostolic see had been made known throughout the various churches either by letters or by commands, however, they almost all met with resistance. Very great hatred was thereby kindled against the lord pope and against the very few who were in agreement with him, chiefly by the clergy, and very great schisms were created on all sides. And because the issues were of universal concern, the lord pope commanded that a general council should be held in Mainz in order that they might be settled according to canon law. The archbishop [Siegfried] immediately informed his suffragans that this command would be complied with on 17 August. They were already planning disobedience and they showed contempt for the pope's command and did nothing to carry it out.[221]

After Henry died a wretched death, Huzmann, a canon of Speyer, became his successor.[222]

King Henry celebrated Easter [5 April] in Worms. And after Whitsun [24 May] he suddenly advanced into Saxony with the numerous army that had previously been announced as intended for Hungary. The Saxons and Thuringians, however, had long before learned of this plan for a crafty attack and, as far as they could in the limited time available,

---

218 Matthew 16:19.

219 Acts 5:1–5.

220 Cf. Ps.-Marcellus, *Passio Petri et Pauli* c. 56, *Acta Apostolorum Apocrypha*, ed. R.A. Lipsius and M. Bonnet 1 (Leipzig, 1891), 167.

221 This council did not take place: Siegfried of Mainz's letter of explanation to Gregory VII, *Codex Udalrici* 45, pp. 97–100.

222 Huzmann (1075–90).

they formed a conspiracy and decided to encounter the king. Their agreed intention nevertheless was that they would humble themselves and surrender to the king if they could by any effort on their part make reparation to him with a guarantee of their physical safety and freedom and retaining their claim to the laws and rights of their ancestors. If not, however, they would rather perish as innocent victims fighting for their lives, for their fatherland and for all their countrymen against this unlawful coercion by the king rather than unwisely deliver themselves up to the king and to his vassals in order, as was previously the custom, to suffer intolerable tortures, together with all their adherents, although they were guiltless, and to be plundered and enslaved. The haughty king, however, had come with quite a different purpose: he would not receive their promise of reparation unless they unconditionally gave themselves up into his hands, admitting their guilt, as his honour required. If not, he would rather do battle with them until he defeated them and subjected them to his will as men guilty of treachery towards him. They rejected his terms in a public statement of their grievances, because they thought that the yoke of subjection was too heavy, nay altogether too harsh, and since it had already proved an unjust and intolerable burden, they could no longer, as free men, allow it to rest on their necks.

Finally the king took counsel with his vassals and with the magnates of the kingdom, although it was not wholesome advice that was given. He had skilfully drawn up the battle lines so that the troops from his camp, who were suitably equipped with weapons, should make the first surprise attack.[223] He took care to send in advance of himself the dukes of the Swabians [Rudolf] and the Bavarians [Welf IV] with their valiant forces to make the first charge, as the Swabian law requires,[224] while he very prudently decided to remain at the rear with his elite warriors to serve as his protection and support. When the Saxons saw the sudden assault of the enemy warriors, however, they were astonished and rightly terrified, since neither time nor opportunity remained for them to arm themselves with care and to draw up their troops for battle according to custom. Nevertheless, although in disorder and with only moments in which to prepare themselves, snatching up their weapons as the tumult circled around them, they stood ready for their warlike

---

223 Battle of Homburg on the River Unstrut, 9 June 1075. Cf. Lampert, *Annales* 1075, pp. 217–22; Bruno of Merseburg, *Saxon War* c. 46, pp. 44–5. See Meyer von Knonau (1894) pp. 496–506, 874–84; Giese (1979) pp. 159–61; Robinson (1999) pp. 100–2.

224 Cf. Lampert, *Annales* 1075, p. 218 ('the special privilege of the Swabians'); *Carmen de bello Saxonico* III.56–60, 140–2, pp. 16, 18. See Meyer von Knonau (1894) p. 875 n. 6.

enemies. And thus the battle that was boldly begun by our compatriots, was most vigorously fought by both armies, threw both sides into confusion and lasted some considerable time. At last indeed the Saxons were no longer able to bear the powerful attack of the warriors, who were in every respect equipped for battle, and they turned to flee. They cruelly pursued the fugitives for nearly two miles, receiving help on both flanks from Duke Godfrey[225] and the duke of the Bohemians,[226] and almost 8,000 of them perished. Very many who had been wounded, however, with difficulty made their escape. At length our compatriots obtained a victory, although a *bloody victory*,[227] since more than 1,500 of them were killed. After they had ranged through that land and laid waste a large part of it with fire and plunder, they returned home with their purpose not accomplished and the king somewhat displeased. After their flight, however, Otto [of Northeim] the former duke and Duke Magnus [Billung] and the other Saxon magnates remained obstinately rebellious and combative and still in the same treacherous state of mind as before.

During the following autumn, therefore, the king once more assembled from here, there and everywhere a large contingent of knights, offering them rewards,[228] and set out, very clever and harsh as he was, to conquer the remaining territories of the Saxons and subject them to his will, making speeches that were full both of threats and of promises. He promised that henceforward and in future he would certainly be pious, mild, conciliatory and generous and towards all those who obeyed him he would be a most just judge and ruler, according to their ancestral laws and rights, and, so some say, he made many flattering declarations on oath. If, however, on the contrary they remained hostile and would not assent to his demands, he became menacing and grim and obdurately threatened that, as long as he lived, they would discover, and suffer much from the discovery, that he was their hard, cunning, utterly tireless enemy and their most troublesome plunderer, even to their total destruction. These and similar menaces and promises were spread abroad on all sides in a very cunning manner to each individual by sweetly spoken, seductive and misleading mediators. Finally [the Saxons] became all too credulous and too trusting towards the king, who feigned grief and penitence for the many injuries that had been

---

225 Godfrey IV ('the Hunchback'), duke of Lower Lotharingia (1069–76).

226 Vratislav II, duke of Bohemia (1061–85), king (1085–92).

227 Sallust, *Catilina* 58.21. Cf. above p. 117 and n. 99.

228 22 October in Gerstungen: Lampert, *Annales* 1075, p. 234.

inflicted on them, especially since (so it is said) besides these other promises, they were secretly assured on his behalf, and this was sworn on the most sacred oaths, that they should have, firstly, the requested guarantee of their lives, an inviolable treaty of peace and unfeigned trust and the full and free enjoyment of their ancestral rights and laws, provided that they did not hesitate to come to surrender to him without making any public conditions and thus show him honour. After very many promises and declarations of this kind, which seemed so very much akin to faith and truth, they expected nothing less than tricks and treachery. Finally, following the reckless persuasions of the bishops, especially [Siegfried] of Mainz and [Embriko of] Augsburg, and also of Duke Godfrey [IV of Lower Lotharingia] and others,[229] who stated their refusal to go to war against them unless they were compelled by the greatest necessity, they came altogether at the same time to surrender to the king according to the terms of the published promises.[230] He, treacherously falling in with the seductive whisperings of his advisers, alas! at once in obdurate vein commanded that they should be brought to various fortresses and prisons and should be held captive there. He entirely disregarded his faithful promises, so earnestly did he desire to inflict a harsh revenge for the injuries inflicted by their treason. He then seized the possessions of certain of them, claiming to do so by royal authority and, like an overbearing ruler, he reoccupied all the castles that he had previously usurped for himself in the manner of a plunderer throughout Saxony; he placed his garrisons there and no one even said a word against him.[231]

Herman, the so-called bishop of Bamberg, was deposed from the priesthood and from his bishopric and excommunicated by Pope Gregory [VII] for the offence of simoniacal heresy.[232] After a pretended

---

229 Lampert, *Annales* 1075, p. 235 identified Archbishop Gebhard of Salzburg and Bishop Adalbero of Würzburg. Cf. Embriko of Augsburg, letter to Burchard of Halberstadt: *Briefsammlungen der Zeit Heinrichs IV.*, pp. 100–1. These negotiations: Meyer von Knonau (1894) pp. 531–3.

230 26/27 October in Spier: Meyer von Knonau (1894) pp. 533–4; Giese (1979) pp. 161–2; Robinson (1999) p. 102.

231 Cf. Lampert, *Annales* 1075, p. 239: 'He commended the castles ... to his followers and ordered them to implement tyranny throughout the region.' See Meyer von Knonau (1894) pp. 538–40.

232 The Roman synod of Lent 1075 suspended Herman I from his office (*Register* II.52a, p. 196); on 12 April Gregory VII announced his excommunication to the clergy and people of Bamberg (*Register* II.76, pp. 239–40); on 20 July he exhorted the king to secure a new bishop for Bamberg (*Register* III.3, p. 247). See Schieffer (1972) pp. 22–46; Schieffer (1975) pp. 55–76.

conversion he was soon reconciled by the pope and entered the monastery of Schwarzach,[233] where he made his profession as a monk. The
king replaced him by a certain Rupert,[234] who possessed the provostship
of Goslar and very many other offices and who was his chosen confidential adviser, but who was unacceptable to almost all the clergy and
people. He was immediately consecrated by the bishop [Siegfried] of
Mainz on the nativity of St Andrew [30 November] at the command
of the king.[235]

At the same time Archbishop Anno of Cologne, the *faithful and wise*[236]
servant of Jesus Christ, joyful and most generous in distributing the
goods entrusted to him among the poor of Christ and the diligent
and lavish builder and provider of five new churches, after gathering
all the temporal property that he seemed to possess and *laying it up
for himself* in the heavenly *treasury*,[237] he followed it there through the
happy completion of his life.[238] He *entered* – most blessedly, I trust – *into
the joy of* his *Lord*, to be *made ruler over many things*[239] and to be repaid
with never failing rewards. He was buried in the monastery of Siegburg
and became renowned as a most saintly man through the many miracles
that truly happened there.[240] He was replaced by a certain Hildulf,[241] a
canon of Goslar and a royal servant, who was with difficulty appointed
by royal authority, against the protests of the clergy and people and
ordained in a simoniacal manner, only to be deposed for this reason and
for disobedience in the next following Roman synod.[242]

During that same summer, *after*[243] the king *had shown contempt* for so
many of his promises and undertakings, the lord pope, *still* attempting

233 Münsterschwarzach on the Main (diocese of Würzburg).

234 Rupert (1075–1102).

235 See Meyer von Knonau (1894) pp. 541–2.

236 Luke 12:42.

237 Matthew 6:20.

238 † 4 December.

239 Matthew 25:21, 23.

240 11 December. Siegburg was Anno's own foundation (1070). His reputation for sanctity: Lampert, *Annales* 1075, pp. 242–50. See Meyer von Knonau (1894) pp. 606–10.

241 Hildulf (1076–8). See Schieffer (1991) pp. 15–17.

242 Cf. *Chronicle* 1078, below p. 216. There is no other reference to this deposition, which
is not mentioned in Gregory VII's letter to Hildulf, *JL* 5043 (*Epistolae Vagantes* 20,
pp. 54–6), dated January–June 1077.

243/243 Extracts from Gregory VII, *JL* 4999 (*Epistolae Vagantes* 14, pp. 34–8), to the
German princes, dated summer 1076.

to use *apostolic gentleness*, sent him a *warning* letter[244] so that he might consider and *remember what he promised and to whom he promised it* and might not, like a false and insolent man, boldly set himself up to *scorn* and injure *God and the apostolic* dignity and might not stubbornly and incorrigibly give the lie to God, who raised him to such an honourable position before the rest of mankind. He should rather concentrate all the ingenuity of his mind always on this thought: that He *resists the proud but gives grace to the humble.*[245] He, however, did not, as he ought, give the most grateful *thanks to God*, who allowed him to conquer and triumph, *for the victory* [Homburg] that he so magnificently achieved, but his thoughts were always and entirely fixed on his own delight and enjoyment. He received with pretended expressions of the utmost gratitude the gentle advice of the pope, who had many times before urged him, *'convincing, rebuking, exhorting',*[246] *to amend his life, but he nevertheless trampled* it entirely *underfoot through his deeds, as he increased* his error. At other times, on the contrary, he sent him *devout greetings and letters* excusing himself, confessing and complaining *both because his time of life was unreliable and weak and because on many occasions he had been wrongly advised and persuaded by those who* had *controlled the court.* On other occasions he sent him *suppliant* letters, *full of all humility, in which* he declared himself *most guilty* and sinful *towards God* and *St Peter*, moreover offering *prayers that whatever* harm had been done *through his own fault in ecclesiastical matters against the justice of canon law and* the decretals *of the holy Fathers*, should be *corrected by* his *apostolic foresight and authority* and in this he would find in effect that [the king] would not fail him with *his obedience, counsel and aid.*[247] Now, however, the obstinate man thought nothing at all of the very many promises of correction both of himself and of the churches that he had made so often and in so many ways through his envoys and in his letters to the lord pope and he recklessly communicated with his advisers and familiars who had been excommunicated in the last Roman synod[248] and he ceaselessly despoiled and brought to confusion the churches of God, as he had been accustomed to do in the past.

When he learned this, the pope, perceiving that he was openly held in contempt, decided to make yet one more trial of the shameless man. He

244 Gregory VII, *Register* III.10, pp. 263–7 (8 December 1075).
245 I Peter 5:5.
246 II Timothy 4:2.
247 Henry IV, *Letter* 5, pp. 8–9.
248 See above p. 133 and n. 215.

sent back in all haste as his legates *three religious men*, that man's *own faithful followers*,[249] two of whom, closer to him than all the others, he had already sent to [the pope] in Rome, and they were to address him on confidential terms and to win him over to the teaching of the Gospel. By means of their persuasive suggestions and secret inducements, with their fairspoken words of friendship and simple freedom they were – as befits friends – to arouse and to recall him to a worthy *repentance for his offences* and to point these out to him, offering a partial commentary on them, although, *dreadful to relate*, they were well known on all sides, and thus *in the mouth of* these *three witnesses* should *every word be established*.[250] Through these men [the pope] also caused [the king] to be informed in no uncertain terms that if he did not listen to them when they spoke to him in confidence, he would formally and publicly make his shameful acts known to the Church. If, however, he did not listen to the Church, [the pope] himself would separate him completely from its members, as *a heathen man and a publican*.[251]

They reached the king in Goslar around Christmastide[252] and carried out the task that had been imposed on them[253] according to the duty of obedience in an extremely circumspect manner but not without the greatest danger to their lives. He did not receive them with patience and moderation but was immediately inflamed with no small degree of anger and indignation. He assembled his advisers and, full of complaints, allowed everything that had been spoken secretly into his ear to be expounded publicly, with the intention, it is said, that they would attempt to defend not only his cause but even more their own causes. Immediately afterwards he communicated intentionally and obstinately with the excommunicates, which the lord pope among other things particularly forbade him to do. He did not reflect on the forbearance, the fatherly *charity* and patience with which [the pope] *most faithfully promised* him through these men that he would *embrace his salvation and his honour in the bosom of the holy Church*,[243] if he came to his senses. Nor, on the other hand, did he fear the threatening sword of his severity, which at the same time he irresistibly stretched out towards him if he persisted obstinately and disobediently in his accustomed error.

249 Radbod, Adelpreth and Gottschalk, identified in Gregory VII, *Register* III.10, p. 267. See Meyer von Knonau (1894) p. 580.

250 II Corinthians 13:1.

251 Matthew 18:17.

252 1 January 1076: Bernold, *Chronicle* 1076, below p. 255.

253 Cf. Bernold, p. 255: to tell the king 'that he would be excommunicated in the next Roman synod if he did not come to his senses'.

During that same autumn the monastery of Hirsau (which had been founded according to the *Rule* long ago by Erlefred, a certain noble and religious senator, in the reign of King Pippin,[254] so they say, but which through the incursions of the latter's successors had been for a long time ruined and plundered) was given, having now been restored for some time, to the Lord God, St Peter, St Aurelius and St Benedict by Count Adalbert,[255] with the consent of his wife Wiltrud and their children,[256] in a testamentary document lawfully issued by royal authority and conferring the fullest freedom. And thus releasing it entirely from their own proprietorship and lordship, they made it completely free and independent of themselves by means of a statement of renunciation according to Swabian law enacted in the presence of many witnesses at that same place and on the very day of the feast of St Aurelius [14 September]. They confirmed entirely lawfully that it was dedicated to the service of God and given to Abbot William[257] and to his successors with full power to direct it and to the brethren who were to live there under the monastic *Rule* with the necessary maintenance. In order to confirm the ordinances that decreed the complete freedom of this foundation with a privilege issued by apostolic authority, William, the abbot of this place, went immediately to Rome and in the presence of Pope Gregory [VII] he successfully accomplished the purpose of his journey according to his desire.[258] While he was endeavouring to return home, he was attacked there by that very severe illness that the Greeks call 'atrophy',[259] that is, the cessation of nourishment, which takes the form of a lessening and thinning of the flesh through some hidden natural causes that gradually take a stronger hold. In addition he wasted away with wandering fevers, dysentery and haemorrhoids (that is, discharge of blood) and at the same time he was swelled to a great size by an abdominal tumour. He was thus miserably tortured for

254 By Count Erlefred of Calw, not in the reign of Pippin III (751–68) but in 830.

255 Adalbert II of Calw (✝1099) restored the monastery in 1065 in fulfilment of a promise to his uncle, Pope Leo IX, and established monks of Einsiedeln there under Abbot Frederick. See Cowdrey (1970) pp. 197–201; Seibert (1991) pp. 552–4.

256 Wiltrud (✝1093, daughter of Godfrey 'the Bearded'); Bruno, Adalbert, Godfrey, Ota and Irmingard (identified in the 'testamentary document', *D.H.IV* ✝280, the 'Hirsau Charter' of 1075): Hallinger (1950–1) pp. 564, 840–3; Cowdrey (1970) pp. 198–9.

257 William, abbot of Hirsau (1069–91). See Büttner (1966) pp. 321–38; Cowdrey (1970) pp. 197–209.

258 Gregory VII, *JL* 5279, ed. Santifaller pp. 71–3 (no. 88). See Büttner (1966) pp. 330–8; Cowdrey (1970) pp. 199–203.

259 Cf. Isidore, *Etymologiae* 4.7.27: '*Atrophy* takes its name from the diminution of the body.'

about five months, given up for dead even by his doctors but not alone among his own followers. Finally, however, when through the compassion of God, the almighty Physician, the merciful time arrived, he was anointed with holy oil by the brethren and released from his sins and the prayer of faith saved the sick man. Thus, soon recovering his health, he went home with difficulty to his monastery with the privileges and blessings that he had acquired through apostolic generosity.

Bishop Dietwin of Liège died and Henry, the provost of Verdun, succeeded him.[260]

1076. King Henry spent Christmas [25 December 1075] in Goslar, although the Saxons were greatly enraged against him and not entirely faithful to him, because in subduing them to his royal authority he had shown such savage and unjust rage.[261]

Pope Gregory, as was necessary for a good shepherd, most shrewdly and like one whose eyes were everywhere, protected Christ's sheepfold from the fury of the wolves and not only elsewhere but even in the city of Rome itself he suffered *for righteousness's sake*[262] at the hands of anti-Christian enemies and plotters. One of these, named Quintius,[263] a sacrilegious robber and a vicious plunderer, after carrying out many plots, like a savage and sacrilegious mocker of everything that is sacred to God, rose up against him on the most holy night of the Lord's Nativity, when he was celebrating mass at S. Maria Maggiore. Like a fury he burst into the church with a savage band of armed men and before the celebrant finished the prayer after the communion, he seized him from the altar, wounded him, took him captive, dragged him with the utmost derision, wretchedly constrained as he was, and, like a sacrilegious thief, imprisoned him in his tower.[264] There for a long time like a madman he placed his sword on [the pope's] neck and, grim, threatening and in every way terrifying, he never ceased to demand from him the treasure

---

260 Dietwin (1048–75) † 23 June; Henry (1075–91).

261 Lampert, *Annales* 1076, p. 250; Bruno, *Saxon War* c. 57, p. 52: the court was far from festive and not well attended. This was the occasion, however, when Henry IV secured from the princes an oath to elect his son to the kingship and was reconciled with Otto of Northeim: Meyer von Knonau (1894) pp. 583–5.

262 Matthew 5:10.

263 Cencius Stephani (de Praefecto), whom Berthold also called Crescentius (†1077), son of the Roman prefect Stephen. See Borino (1952) pp. 373–440; Cowdrey (1998) pp. 326–8.

264 Cencius abducted the pope during the midnight mass of Christmas Eve 1075: Borino (1952) pp. 431–6; Cowdrey (1998) p. 327. His tower was in the district of Parione, in the south-western part of the Campus Martius: *Liber pontificalis* 2, 262.

and the strongest castles of St Peter as benefices for himself; but he was totally unable to achieve this. It was not long before the whole city was moved to great distress by this sacrilege so deeply lamentable for the whole Church. Fired by supreme divine zeal, they attacked that tower and destroyed it, after bringing out the pope, whom they believed to have been killed. In a short time they scattered abroad everything that belonged to Crescentius and expelled him, sparing his life only because of the intervention of the pope, to whom he had surrendered himself as a prisoner. One man only was killed there, however, because he had sacrilegiously wounded the pope on the head. Thus the pope thankfully returned to the altar and completed the celebration of mass.

Quintius had with his customary folly deceived the pope. For when from his tower he saw the uproar among his fellow citizens and their most ardent divine zeal directed against him, he feared for his own life and the lives of his followers and confessed his sin to [the pope] and promised him obedience and appropriate penitence and reparation, although with simulated piety. Caring nothing for this, however, he fled from the city by night. The pope then, granting him a delay, summoned him back to perform the penance that he had imposed on him. He, however, not only became an apostate on this account but also seized a very strong fortress in the neighbourhood and there he lived by robbery, plunder and bloodshed. The pope thereupon caused him to be excommunicated by the bishop of Palestrina.[265] He, however, continued with his thievish designs for two years,[266] obedient in all respects to the king but a hardened despiser of God.

At length, however, the king, greatly angered after the departure of the aforementioned men [Radbod, Adelpreth and Gottschalk] and *taking*[267] *it ill that he should be held in check or rebuked by anyone, not only* did not come to his senses: rather with *even greater* twisting and turning he rashly continued his senseless and dangerous course, contrary to law. For after taking ill-omened counsel with his followers, he summoned to Worms[268] very many of the bishops and princes of the kingdom and especially those whom he knew to be amenable to his will. He *forced* almost all of them *to deny the obedience due to blessed Peter and to the apostolic see*[267] and to join together in a conspiracy whereby each one of

265 Hubert, cardinal bishop of Palestrina (?1073–?82).

266 See below pp. 163–4.

267/267 Further extracts from Gregory VII, *JL* 4999 (*Epistolae Vagantes* 14, p. 38).

268 Council of Worms, 24 January 1076: Meyer von Knonau (1894) pp. 613–28; Schneider (1972) pp. 146–53; Cowdrey (1998) pp. 135–8; Robinson (1999) pp. 143–6.

them renounced [the pope] publicly in a document especially written in his name, with his own name set at the beginning.[269] From there he sent the letter of renunciation by means of two bishops, those of Speyer [Huzmann] and Basel,[270] at first to Italy, in order to win over the princes and bishops of that land as parties to this conspiracy, then to Rome. After holding a great assembly in Piacenza,[271] they all immediately decided unanimously not to show the obedience due to the lord pope, not only by their words and in a letter but also confirming it by means of an oath, since they were very much afraid that they would be condemned by him for simoniacal heresy. Finally they hastily sent to the Roman synod a letter containing this declaration of disobedience by means of envoys, a certain canon of Parma[272] and a certain servant of the king. There the letter and the orders were read out publicly in the hearing of the whole assembly;[273] there was a proclamation of the disobedience to the lord pope that had been decided upon; and on behalf of the king he was commanded with many threats to step down from the see over which he was unworthy to preside. Only those who were present know what a tumult, what an outcry, what a disordered attack on the envoys occurred there.[274] One thing we ought to say about it: that the lord pope, not without great danger to his own person, *snatched*[275] them *away with difficulty* half-dead *from the hands of the Romans*.

When at last *there was silence*[275] the lord pope caused to be investigated and read out the synodal decrees concerning those who virtually in the presence of the whole Church obstinately and rashly denied on oath the supreme bishop after God and their ruler and who were not ashamed to declare their disobedience publicly in documents containing their own names, not understanding nor fearing what pertains to him and to the other masters of the Church, concerning which Paul says, 'always ready

269 The bishops' letter withdrawing obedience from the pope: Henry IV, *Letters* appendix A, pp. 65–8.

270 Burchard (1072–1107). They were escorted by Count Eberhard III of Nellenburg: Meyer von Knonau (1894) p. 629.

271 Synod of Piacenza: Meyer von Knonau (1894) pp. 629–30; Robinson (1999) p. 147.

272 Roland, canon of Parma, bishop of Treviso (?1078–?89). See Schwartz (1913) p. 61.

273 Roman synod of Lent 1076: Gregory VII, *Register* III.10a, pp. 268–71. See Meyer von Knonau (1894) pp. 632–45; Schneider (1972) pp. 154–7; Cowdrey (1998) pp. 140–2.

274 Cf. Empress Agnes, letter to Bishop Altman of Passau (in Hugh, *Chronicon* II, p. 435): 'The envoys of my son the king came into the synod and … told the pope, on my son's behalf, that he should rise and renounce the apostolic see … They were at once seized by the Romans.'

275/275 Extracts from Bernold, *De damnatione scismaticorum* III, p. 51.

to avenge all disobedience.[276] For they ought to have considered more carefully what the holy Pope Silvester has already decreed inviolably in a Roman synod: '*No one will judge the first see because all sees desire to be regulated by the justice of the first see and the judge will be judged neither by the whole clergy nor by the whole people*'[277] and that decree of the blessed Pope Gregory: '*We decree that kings shall lose their offices and shall not be partakers of the body and blood of our Lord Jesus Christ if they presume to show contempt for the commands of the apostolic see*';[278] and many statements of this kind. This synodal judgement, therefore, *confirmed*[279] *by the authority of divine and human laws*, was delivered there: that King Henry *must not only be excommunicated but also be deposed from the office of the kingship without hope of recovery* so that *he might be in the company of the excommunicates, with whom* he chose to *associate rather than with Christ. Firstly, because he* obstinately *refused to abstain from the company of those who were excommunicated for the sacrilege and the offence of simoniacal heresy; then* because, as an open despiser of God, *not only would he not undertake penance for* his *guilty actions* but he would not even *promise* to do so, in no way keeping the *promises that he had* already *made* to the papal *legates; also because* the wilful man *was not afraid* with open disobedience stubbornly to resist the apostolic see and thus *to rend asunder the body of Christ, that is, the unity of holy Church* and shamelessly to cause scandal. *Finally for these offences* the lord pope *according to the judgement of the synod* excommunicated him and all who through their own efforts and of their own will stubbornly remained in that state of disobedience and all, both the greater and the lesser men, who actively supported him in this affair, and separated them forever from the members of the Church until they made fitting reparation, so that, *having failed to recall him to the way of salvation by mildness*, he *might through* God's mercy *do so by means of severity*.[279] Empress Agnes, the king's mother, was present

---

276 II Corinthians 10:6.

277 *Constitutum Silvestri* c. 27 (ed. P. Coustant, *Epistolae Romanorum Pontificum* 1 [Paris, 1721] appendix col. 52A), a version resembling that in Bernold, *De damnatione scismaticorum* III, pp. 50–1 and Bernard of Hildesheim, *Liber canonum* c. 27, p. 498.

278 Spurious version of Gregory I, *Registrum* XIII.11, *MGH Epistolae* 2, 376, originally formulated in Gregory VII, *Register* IV.2, p. 294 (and *Register* VIII.21, pp. 550–1) and disseminated in *Collection in 74 titles*, 'Swabian appendix' c. 330, p. 196. Cf. Manegold, *Ad Gebehardum* c. 45, p. 389; Bernard, *Liber canonum* c. 25, p. 495; Bernold, *Apologeticae rationes* p. 97.

279/279 Further extracts from Gregory VII, *JL* 4999, pp. 38–9. With polemical intention Berthold misrepresented the papal threat conveyed by Radbod, Adelpreth and Gottschalk (above p. 140 and n. 249) as the sentence of the Lenten synod of 1076 and thus suggested that Henry had been deposed 'without hope of recovery'. The actual sentence: Gregory VII, *Register* III.10a, pp. 270–1.

at all these proceedings[280] and the sword that condemned him deeply
wounded her soul.

During these days of the synod, as Duke Godfrey [IV of Lower Lotha-
ringia] was returning from that conspiracy in Worms, of which he had
been a great supporter and instigator, he was wounded from below by
a certain knight while he was sitting in a privy, relieving nature, and
he unhappily died as an excommunicate.[281] The son of his sister, who
bore his name,[282] came into possession of his march, purchasing it from
the king with difficulty for forty pounds of gold, but he was unjustly
deprived of his duchy, although his uncle had already granted it to him
and he had obtained it from [the king]. The king caused his own son
[Conrad], who was barely two years old, to rule over it.

After they learned about the papal anathema, the king and his followers
almost all spoke out against it, declaring that it was utterly unjust and
not according to canon law, that whatever was done in the Roman
synod by so sacrilegious a man was erroneous and that they regarded
it as absolutely worthless. This was done only by the king's accomplices
and supporters, not by those who were of sounder mind. Among the
latter were certain bishops – the patriarch of Aquileia,[283] the bishops
of Salzburg,[284] Passau [Altman], Worms (who had been expelled from
his see by the king)[285] and Würzburg[286] – and almost all the Saxons
and the dukes Rudolf [of Swabia], Berthold [I of Carinthia] and Welf
[IV of Bavaria] and a considerable number of the other princes of the
kingdom, who unwaveringly agreed with the pope and who refused to
participate in the aforesaid conspiracy. From this time forward, therefore, when they were summoned by the king, they avoided him both
because of the anathema and because they did not greatly trust him.[287]

280 Cf. Empress Agnes, letter (n. 274). See Meyer von Knonau (1894) p. 641; Black-
    Veldtrup (1995) p. 98.

281 26 February in Utrecht: Meyer von Knonau (1894) pp. 650–2. Berthold falsely
    assumed that the excommunication pronounced on the bishops at the council of
    Worms (*Register* III.10a, pp. 268–9) also applied to Godfrey IV.

282 Godfrey V (of Bouillon), duke of Lower Lotharingia (1087–96, †1100), son of Ida
    (daughter of Godfrey 'the Bearded'), obtained the march of Antwerp. See Meyer von
    Knonau (1894) pp. 658–9; Robinson (1999) p. 148.

283 Sigehard (1068–77).

284 Gebhard, archbishop of Salzburg (1060–88).

285 Adalbert (1070–1107) was expelled from Worms in 1073: Meyer von Knonau (1894)
    pp. 294–5.

286 Adalbero (1045–90).

287 Lampert, *Annales* 1076, p. 257 dated the alienation of the south German dukes from
    Eastertide.

The bishop of Paderborn died and Poppo, the provost of Bamberg, succeeded him,[288] although not strictly according to canon law, since he received the bishopric from a king who was now an excommunicate and he actually communicated with him. The bishop [William] of Utrecht, however, had previously received this [bishopric] from the king to be given as a gift to a certain kinsman of his, on condition that he would not oppose the consecration of the bishop of Cologne, who *entered* simoniacally and *not by the door*,[289] but that he himself would consecrate him.[290] After he was deceived in this fashion, he no longer stood wholeheartedly by the king as he had done before.

The king spent Easter [27 March] in Utrecht,[291] after assembling there from all sides large numbers of accomplices in his rebellion and disobedience.[292] At that time the church there, which had been built long before at the greatest expense and with the greatest effort, suffering the contempt of God and St Peter, was miraculously consumed by an avenging fire.[293] From there he returned through Lotharingia[294] to Worms in order to hold a conference there at Whitsun [15 May] with his fellows. Bishop William of Utrecht angrily parted company with the king and, coming home, he most eagerly had himself served with a banquet of the greatest magnificence. Thus, withdrawing from the table at which he feasted three times on one day and shamelessly became drunk, he was overtaken by a sudden and unexpected death, undoubtedly condemned by the sting of anathema, and he perished very miserably.[295] He was succeeded by Conrad, the chamberlain of Mainz,[296] who assiduously communicated with the king and was conciliated by him with the gift of the bishopric, but not according to canon law.

The conference that the king appointed to be held in Worms was

---

288 Imad (1051–76) † 3 February; Poppo (1076–83). See Meyer von Knonau (1894) pp. 649–50; Schieffer (1981) p. 154 n. 212.

289 John 10:1.

290 Lampert, *Annales* 1076, p. 257 tells the same story and adds that William consecrated Archbishop Hildulf of Cologne (n. 241).

291 This was the occasion of a 'crown-wearing': Klewitz (1939) pp. 93–6; Schneider (1972) p. 166; Robinson (1999) p. 149.

292 Synod of Utrecht, 26 March: Erdmann (1936) p. 499; Kieft (1955) pp. 70–9.

293 The church of St Peter was struck by lightning. Cf. *D.H.IV* 284 (donation to St Peter, Utrecht): 'we grieve that [the church] was consumed by fire, ascribing this to our sins'. See Meyer von Knonau (1894) pp. 662, 677; Robinson (1999) p. 151.

294 He was in Aachen on 21 April: *D.H.IV* 283.

295 27 April. See Meyer von Knonau (1894) pp. 669–70.

296 Conrad (1076–99).

undertaken (so they say) for this purpose: that the pope should be submitted to an unjust judgement there, ostensibly according to canon law, by the three bishops who seemed to be senior to the rest, and should be condemned for the offences of which he had been accused and should somehow or other be deposed from the apostolic see, and thus another man, whom they found compliant and obsequious towards them according to their wishes, might be set up immediately in his place. The three who had already been nominated for this conspiracy, however, were by God's predestination prevented from reaching there. Of these men, the bishop [William] of Utrecht (as has already been told) died suddenly;[297] the bishop of Brixen[298] was captured during his journey by Count Hartmann[299] and, since he had already been excommunicated by the pope, he was sent to prison; only the third, the bishop of Naumburg,[300] arrived. But according to the precept of the law, no one may be condemned if only one person testifies against him.[301] Moreover Duke Godfrey [IV], who had boldly promised the king that he would conduct to the Roman see the pope who was to be appointed there [in Worms], himself died as an excommunicate, as is known to everyone. After God thus broke up this conference, they met once again in Mainz on the feast-day of the apostles Peter and Paul [29 June] and, in order to avenge themselves in an even more lawless manner and, with the apostles as their judges, to condemn themselves even more than they had already been condemned, they made as if to judge the pope according to false evidence, motivated by sacrilegious daring, and they very rashly excommunicated him.[302] They declared, as if it was a judicial decision, that the anathema pronounced by the pope according to a synodal judgement against the king and against the other members of his alliance was unconsidered, unjust and of no weight, to be treated with utter contempt and to be regarded as of no account.[303]

---

297 He was with the king in Aachen on 21 April (*D.H.IV* 283), six days before his death, at which point the court was already en route for Worms for the conference of 15 May.

298 Altwin (1049–97).

299 Hartmann I, count of Dillingen-Kyburg (†1121). See Meyer von Knonau (1894) p. 671.

300 Eberhard (Eppo), bishop of Naumburg (Zeitz) (1045–79) was with the king in Aachen on 21 April (*D.H.IV* 283).

301 Perhaps an allusion to Ps.-Eleutherius, *Epistola* 1.3 (*JK* †68), *Decretales Pseudo-Isidorianae* p. 126 (*Collection in 74 titles* c. 47, pp. 45–6).

302 Council of Mainz: Meyer von Knonau (1894) pp. 681–3.

303 Cf. Terence, *Eunuchus* 3.1.21.

For they did not pay careful attention to the fact that, according to what is inviolably ordained by the decrees of the holy Fathers, whoever presume to alter or revise a judgement of the apostolic see on the grounds that it should be rejected, are guilty of a crime against the papal majesty and that it is never permitted to anyone to reject [the pope's] judgement and to make his own. The holy Pope Silvester therefore decreed in a Roman synod, in which 284 bishops with forty priests and very many deacons subscribed [the decrees] in the presence of Emperor Constantine and his mother, St Helena, as follows: '*No one will judge the first see*' etc., as is written above.[304] And the blessed Pope Gelasius in the second chapter of his decree says: '*The whole Church throughout the world knows that the most sacred Roman church has the right to judge every church and that no one is permitted to judge her judgement. In fact appeals are to be made to her from any part of the world, but no one is permitted to appeal from her.*'[305] *Nor*[306] shall we pass over the fact that the apostolic see possesses the power* without *a preceding synod* of absolving *those whom an unjust synod had condemned, and when no synod is in existence, of condemning* those who ought to be condemned, which *is* certainly *stipulated by the most holy pontiffs Calixtus, Fabian, Xistus, Julius and others* without number, *who so cherished the truth that they were determined to die rather than to tell a lie. And this they* did *doubtless because of their pre-eminent position which, according to* the word *of the Lord, the blessed apostle Peter held* and *always*[306] will hold. The most blessed Pope Hadrian follows them in the eighteenth chapter of his decrees, saying: 'We have laid down in a general decree that any king, prince or bishop who hereafter believes that the ordinances of the Roman pontiffs are to be violated in any way or who permits them to be violated, is to be accursed and anathematised and is always to be guilty before the Lord as an apostate from the catholic faith.'[307] No less to be feared is this dreadful statement that St Leo issued in his decrees. He said: 'Everyone who strives to weaken our decisions by disobedience is to be struck by anathema and he who stubbornly opposes our

304 See above p. 145 and n. 277.

305 Extracts from Gelasius I, *Epistola* 26 (*JK* 664), in the version of *Collection in 74 titles* c. 10, p. 24. Cf. Bernold, *Apologeticus* c. 23, p. 87; Bernold, *De damnatione scismaticorum* III, p. 48; Manegold, *Ad Gebehardum* c. 7, p. 323.

306/306 Bernold, *Apologeticus* c. 23, p. 87 (order of the second and third sentences reversed). Cf. Bernold, *De damnatione scismaticorum* III, pp. 48–9; Manegold, *Ad Gebehardum* c. 7, p. 323 (where Bernold's opening sentence appears as part of the quotation from Gelasius I).

307 Paraphrase of *Capitula Angilramni* ser. 2, c. 20 (*Decretales Pseudo-Isidorianae* p. 769). Berthold's attribution resembles that of *Collection in 74 titles*, 'Swabian appendix' c. 329, p. 195.

most wholesome ordinances is to be separated from the members of the Church for all time.'[308] Whoever, therefore, comes to doubt the judgement of the apostolic see, must debate the matter not with other men but only with the pope himself, without whom the judgement that he made can by no means be revised or altered. For it is our duty to obey papal ordinances without any hesitation and to avoid foolish and undisciplined questions, which generate strife and contribute greatly to the destruction of those who hear them. It is the business of the lord pope, however, to corroborate his judgements with explanations, if anyone seems to detect anything doubtful in them.

Different opinions indeed circulated endlessly throughout the whole kingdom among the clergy in their synods concerning this same excommunication of the king and whether it was justly or unjustly enacted. This, however, was especially the case among the contentious, who tried to serve the cause not of the truth but of controversy. For either they were ignorant of the fact or else they deliberately pretended not to know that two judicial procedures are set down in the holy Scriptures: one in doubtful cases, in which a delay is necessary in order to obtain witnesses and defenders (the refusal of which, as they themselves declare and testify, is their principal cause of dispute); the other is the case of public crimes in which we read that no delay is to be granted since the judicial punishment is to be imposed without delay on the stubborn and the disobedient without an accuser or a witness.[309] For *in*[310] *doubtful* cases – which, *although true, have not yet been made public* or voluntarily confessed or clearly proven – *a delay* must *necessarily* be granted in order to investigate them and provide proof, *so that, according to the ordinances of the apostolic men Pope Felix and Julius and the rest, the accused can prepare himself fully against the accusers so as to remove the charges* that have been brought. *Hence also the blessed Eleutherius, the twelfth* pope *after the blessed Peter, bears witness in the first chapter of his decrees,* saying: *'A considerable delay is to be granted for the purposes of investigation so that nothing seems to be done over-hastily by any party, because many consequences flow from deception.'*[310] St Ambrose, therefore, also bears witness in his exposition of the letter to the Corinthians, saying: *'A judge must not condemn without an accuser because the Lord did not reject Judas,* since, *although he was a thief, he was*

308 Paraphrase of Leo I, *Epistola I.4* (*JK* 398, *MPL* 54, col. 596A).

309 Cf. Bernard of Hildesheim in the correspondence with Bernold, *De damnatione scismaticorum* II, p. 30.

310/310 Bernold, *Apologeticus* c. 22, p. 86, including Ps.-Eleutherius, *Epistola* c. 3, p. 126.

not accused';[311] and thus all doubtful cases must be treated. For this reason the Lord Himself also gave us an example so that we should not readily believe without proof and examination what we hear at random, when He went to Sodom in the shape of angels and said to Abraham, *'I will go down and see whether they have done altogether according to the outcry that has come to me and if not, I will know.'*[312] But after He proved that the outcry that He heard was true, immediately without delay, like a most effective avenger from heaven, fire and storms of sulphur rained down from the Lord. They, however, who do not deny their fault, which has long ago been specifically condemned by the holy Fathers, but who somehow or other attempt to defend themselves from their public and stubborn contempt for the apostolic ordinances, are most justly condemned without a delay. In a case that is self-evident and well known to very many men, therefore, it is not necessary to seek witnesses. Hence the apostle commanded that that fornicator among the Corinthians should be driven out of *the*[313] *assembly of the brotherhood* because *the deed* that he had done *was known* to them all, saying: *'You are arrogant and should rather have mourned, so that he who has done this would have been removed from among you.'*[314] *All men* certainly *knew of his offence and did not rebuke him.* For *he publicly kept his stepmother in the place of a wife and in this case there was no need of witnesses* or an investigation *nor could the offence be concealed by any subterfuge.* For this reason the apostle did not delay the judgement against him, saying, *'though absent in body, I am present in spirit'* — whose *authority* is *nowhere*[313] lacking — *'and as if present I have already pronounced judgement on him who* has done *this* deed.'*[315]

The whole body of the Scriptures, therefore, supports the judgements of the lord pope. Hence those who contradict or undermine them can very easily be refuted. For he has in no way strayed from the tracks of the holy Fathers.[316] It was in vain, therefore, that certain disputatious men grumbled that no delay was granted to the king and to his accomplices and that [the pope] excommunicated them immediately, after they had so insolently made their offences public and considered them a trifling matter and defended them so stubbornly and after they had most wretchedly defiled holy Church and with extreme temerity

311 Ambrosiaster, *Commentaria in Epistolam ad Corinthios* I.5, *MPL* 17, col. 208A.

312 Genesis 18:21.

313/313 Ambrosiaster, *Commentaria in Epistolam ad Corinthios* I.5, col. 208A (with altered word order). Cf. Bernard (as n. 309) p. 33.

314 I Corinthians 5:2.

315 I Corinthians 5:3.

316 Cf. Gregory VII, *Register* IV.24, p. 338.

and obstinacy declared their disobedience in so many widely known instances in no less a place than the Roman synod and published it in documents in their own names.

In the anathema itself the lord pope, *on behalf of* and in the name of *the almighty Father and of the Son and of the Holy Spirit* and *through the authority* of St Peter, commanded all Christians henceforward not to obey the excommunicated king as a king in any respect or *serve* him or keep the oath that they had sworn or would swear to him.[317] The greater part of the princes of the kingdom paid heed to this and, although they were very often summoned by the king, they refused to come to him, endeavouring most diligently to *have* a zeal *for God* that is *enlightened*.[318] Even if they had known him to have been excommunicated unjustly and not according to canon law, nevertheless, according to the decrees of the council of Sardica,[319] they must in no way communicate with him unless they knew beforehand that he had been reconciled. They therefore feared to communicate with the king, whose attitude remained unalterable, because they could not censure him, punish him or correct him and since they shrank from reaching any agreement with him, they rightly strove to avoid him. For this reason, in the autumn the magnates of the kingdom decided that they should hold a conference with him in Magdeburg[320] to deal with this situation, in which they could by common counsel settle what ought to be done about so important an affair and in which it would become lawful for them to serve their king and lord after he had been admonished and converted to penitence and reconciled. After they had assembled there with a considerable military force, the king, threatening and proud in his exhortations and persuasions, together with his flatterers, set up camp beside the Rhine in the village of Oppenheim with a large crowd of his sworn followers. The magnates of the kingdom, however, remained on this side of the Rhine

---

317 *Register* III.10a, p. 270: 'Excommunication of Henry, king of the Germans'. The dissemination of this sentence in southern Germany: Manegold, *Ad Gebehardum* c. 14, p. 337; Paul, *Life of Pope Gregory VII* c. 76, pp. 317–18.

318 Romans 10:2.

319 Council of Sardica c. 17 (*MPL* 67, col. 181C). Cf. *Collection in 74 titles*, 'Swabian appendix' c. 322, p. 183; Bernard (as n. 309) p. 33; Bernard, *Liber canonum* c. 11, pp. 484–5; Gebhard of Salzburg, *Epistola* c. 13, p. 269.

320 The assembly of princes met in Tribur on 16 October. Meyer von Knonau (1894) p. 727 n. 178 suggested that Berthold intended to refer to Madenburg near Speyer, where there was a preliminary meeting before the main assembly. See Meyer von Knonau (1894) pp. 729–35, 885–93; Erdmann (1940) pp. 486–95; Schneider (1972) pp. 171–87; Beumann (1973) pp. 33–44; Hlawitschka (1974) pp. 25–45; Robinson (1999) pp. 155–8.

and earnestly enquired among themselves and, each one showing the degree of close attention that God granted him, they discussed together what they ought to decide in so grave a case. Legates of the apostolic see[321] had arrived there, bringing a letter pertaining to this case, in which the pope now charged the bishop of Passau, to whom he had long before granted the office of papal representative, with the responsibility of reconciling according to canon law all – except only the king – who came in a fitting manner to perform reparation and worthy penitence, those, that is, who wished henceforth to stand in the party of St Peter. Among these were the archbishop [Siegfried] of Mainz with his vassals, the bishops [Udo] of Trier,[322] Strasbourg,[323] Verdun,[324] [Henry of] Liège, Münster,[325] the bishop elect [Conrad] of Utrecht, the bishops [Huzmann] of Speyer and [Burchard of] Basel[326] – the bishop of Constance, however, in Ulm[327] – and very many abbots and also a large crowd of greater and lesser men. Guilty of communicating with the king or excommunicated for their disobedience or for receiving the masses and offices of priests condemned for unchastity or simoniacal heresy, they were reconciled there and received into communion.

Finally, when ten days[328] had been devoted to these concerns and when the king saw and heard that so many men of such distinction had humbly submitted to the apostolic dignity and that they had resolved to set up another king in his place, he himself, although reluctant, unwilling and virtually enfeebled by grief, pretended with difficulty that he also had submitted not only to the pope but also to the princes of the kingdom in all those matters to which they had wished him to pay attention. It then seemed to them among other things that, first and foremost, in the case of the bishop [Adalbert] of Worms, his see and his city should freely be restored to him, that the queen [Bertha] should depart from there with her entourage, that the hostages of the Saxons should be returned

321 Patriarch Sigehard of Aquileia and Bishop Altman of Passau.

322 Archbishop Udo must already have been reconciled: Gregory VII, *Register* III.12, pp. 273–4 (April 1076).

323 Werner II (1065–77).

324 Theoderic (1046–89) must already have been reconciled: Gregory VII's letter of April 1076, above n. 322.

325 Frederick I (1064–84).

326 According to Lampert, *Annales* 1076, pp. 282–3, they remained with the king in Oppenheim until the end of the negotiations.

327 Otto appeared in Ulm 'in the autumn' (perhaps September): Bernold, *Pro Gebhardo episcopo* p. 110.

328 'Seven days': Lampert, *Annales* 1076, p. 277: i.e. 16–22 October.

to them and that the king should separate himself entirely from his excommunicated followers and also that without delay he should send a letter to Pope Gregory [VII], announcing that he would faithfully observe due obedience, reparation and a fitting penitence and that in the meantime he would abide by their advice and await the pope's reply and a reconciliation with him.[329] The king performed this and everything else immediately, although not with complete honesty. Hence he sent to Rome through the agency of the bishop [Udo] of Trier a letter to be presented to the pope, which had been composed along the lines that they had agreed and sealed in the presence of [the princes], but which he himself had afterwards secretly altered and changed according to his will.[330] The magnates of the kingdom, however, were afraid of the deceptions and the accustomed folly of the king's advisers, which they had so often experienced, and, so that the pope should not be deceived by their guile, they likewise sent in great haste to Rome envoys whose testimony could be relied on and who had been present at all the negotiations there and they entreated [the pope] and humbly implored him by God's mercy that he might deign to come to this region to settle this discord.[331] Moreover, before they parted from one another, in order to constrain the king more effectively to show obedience to the apostolic see, they swore an oath that if through his own fault he remained excommunicate for more than a year, they would no longer have him as king.[332] Then, because they feared the revenge and the injuries that the king would inflict on them in the future – for very many of them had abandoned him without seeing him and greeting him and had aroused his anger against them – they each faithfully promised aid one to another, whatever opposition they might meet as a result of this affair, and thus each of them returned home, rejoicing.

Immediately after this conference came to an end, around 1 November, a snowfall of extraordinary magnitude began, which covered the earth everywhere. As a forecast and a sign of future evils, this phenomenon, unusual in its scale, greatly astounded not only the regions on this side

329 The princes' demands: Meyer von Knonau (1894) p. 732; Robinson (1999) p. 156.

330 The 'Promise of Oppenheim': Henry IV, *Letters*, appendix B, p. 69. No other source claims that it was falsified. See Erdmann (1937) pp. 365–70; Schneider (1972) pp. 172–86; Cowdrey (1983) pp. 237–8; Robinson (1999) pp. 157–8.

331 In an assembly in Augsburg, 2 February 1077: Meyer von Knonau (1894) p. 734; Schneider (1972) pp. 176–7; Beumann (1973) pp. 42, 45; Hlawitschka (1974) p. 44.

332 Bruno, *Saxon War* c. 88, p. 83: this additional condition was imposed after the agreement had been reached with the king. Lampert, *Annales* 1076, p. 281: this was part of the original agreement.

of the Alps but also, which seemed even more remarkable, the whole of Lombardy. Because of the extreme cold and frost indeed the Rhine and likewise the Po, to say nothing of other rivers, were frozen so hard that for a long time they presented all travellers with an icy road that was like solid land. Thus the harsh and snowy winter and uninterrupted cold weather lasted until 15 March, that is, from the previously mentioned conference until the conference that was held by the magnates of the kingdom in Forchheim. Finally on that day the snow began gradually to decrease throughout all parts of our land, melting at different rates according to the nature of the places.[333]

After the conference in Oppenheim had ended, the king remained for some time in Speyer, living in the customary manner of the penitent, together with the guardians and stewards who had been allotted to him by the magnates of the kingdom.[334] Then because of the sworn association formed by the princes, he suspected that they would turn their treachery against him and develop stratagems to overthrow him. He reassembled his advisers from all sides, rashly disregarded the views of his magnates and most assiduously and carefully considered all the investigations and the counsels of his followers and thus very diligently fortified himself against an attempt to deprive him of the kingship.

The bishop of Toul,[335] however, together with the bishop [Huzmann] of Speyer and many others, on whom the bishop [Altman] of Passau imposed this, according to their duty of obedience, arrived in Rome and surrendered themselves to the pope, acknowledging their guilt, making reparation and showing due obedience. After he had reconciled them according to canon law, he tested their obedience for some time by causing them to be kept in solitary confinement in certain monasteries suitable for their detention until, through the intervention of the empress, they were with difficulty released and were permitted − without the restoration of their office and with permission only to receive communion − to return home.

Following immediately on their heels came the archbishop of Trier in great haste, as the king's envoy and bearing his letter. He greeted the

---

333 The severity of the winter of 1076–7: Meyer von Knonau (1894) p. 750 and n. 7. Berthold's idea that the election at Forchheim ended the winter (more emphatic in Bernold, *Chronicle* 1077, below p. 258): Hauck (1959a) pp. 180–1; Schneider (1972) p. 177.

334 Lampert, *Annales* 1076, p. 282: 'with only the bishop of Verdun and a few servants'.

335 Pibo (1069–1107) bringing the first news of Tribur to Rome: Meyer von Knonau (1894) p. 736. The role of Empress Agnes: Black-Veldtrup (1995) p. 55.

pope and presented the falsified letter to him. The latter refused to have it read out to him except in the presence of the envoys of the magnates of the kingdom, so that those who had been present and knew the circumstances of its composition and its sending, might themselves be witnesses when it was read out. After the letter was read, therefore, the envoys recognised that the contents were quite different from what had been set down and sealed in the presence of the magnates of the kingdom and they most freely declared by the Lord God that it was not the same but had been changed and in places falsified. Although the archbishop of Trier had at first begun to defend the letter, he was finally convinced by them and, remembering [the original version], he publicly acknowledged the forgery in the letter, saying that it was not his work but that of another, he knew not whom. Thus the lord pope in his vigilant way, together with the empress, realised that everything that the mendacious letter said about the king's obedience was not the truth of the heart but a dissembling invention, full of deceit. For this reason the pope would in no way agree to the king's most urgent request, that he might be permitted to come to the pope in Rome to be reconciled.[336] He had commanded by apostolic authority that [the king] should meet him in the presence of the magnates of the kingdom in Augsburg to be heard by him and to be reconciled and he sent back word to them through the envoys of both parties that he would most certainly come to them there at the feast of the Purification [2 February], if the Lord wished it.[337] After they had received the letter of the blessed pope, in which, as was fitting, he had carefully given them much advice concerning his escort and other necessary matters and concerning the peace, they joyfully returned to their homeland, proclaiming the arrival of so great a guest.

All the magnates immediately accepted with joy what was said in the letter and, preparing most earnestly to concentrate their minds on paying heed to it in every way, they rejoiced greatly in the real hope of restoring the Church's piety and worship. When the king, who was of a totally different opinion, had learned of the pope's intention, he strove with the utmost ingenuity and energy and after many consultations to meet him before he entered our region. For he decided to force [the pope] to his own way of thinking either by terrifying him and forcing

336 Cf. Gregory VII, *JL* 5013 (*Epistolae Vagantes* 17, p. 48): the pope's 'debates with the king's envoys' about the king's wish to come to Rome; *Register* IV.12, p. 312: the king's 'suppliant envoys to us'.

337 Cf. Gregory VII, *JL* 5013–14 (*Epistolae Vagantes* 17, 18, pp. 46–50), December 1076, announcing his arrival but mentioning neither Augsburg nor 2 February.

him to flee with a huge military force of his followers, who might somehow or other be enlisted by means of money, or with the help of the Romans and [the pope's] other advisers, who might be corrupted by large bribes and thus made [the king's] inseparable supporters. If this failed, however, they would fight against [the pope] with such hostility and ferocity that they would at once drive him, insulted and reviled, from his see and put another in his place according to the king's wish, so that he might be elected by him as emperor and consecrated, together with his wife [Bertha], and so return in glory to his homeland. If, however, the king could make the pope in all respects compliant towards him, by overwhelming him through fear and threats and the flattery of the Romans, he considered (in his great folly) that thereafter he would be dutiful towards him, but would be most severe towards his enemies.

Encouraged and urged on by these and many other mad counsels from his advisers (so the rumour went), he stubbornly resisted the correction and the restoration of Christian piety already proposed by the magnates of the kingdom and he did not cease by whatever means he could to overthrow their control and to free himself entirely from them, just as he pleased. A certain margrave named Opert,[338] who arrived at that time from Lombardy, greatly strengthened him, more than the rest, in this endeavour. After he had been magnificently rewarded and honoured by [the king] for this reason, as he returned home he was overtaken by sudden death near Augsburg. He fell from his horse and died, wretched and worthy of condemnation, at one moment regarding the papal anathema as meaning nothing and the next moment learning in fact how heavy a burden it was.

1077. The king celebrated Christmas [25 December 1076] as best he could in Besançon in Burgundy, remaining there scarcely one day. From there he took his wife and son [Conrad] and also his magnificent retinue of followers[339] and, as had already been decided, he crossed the Rhone at Geneva and, undertaking a most desperate journey, with difficulty he climbed and crawled up the Alps and hastily entered Lombardy by way of the bishopric of Turin. Gathering men wherever he could, he came from there to Pavia, where he also drew to himself from all sides

338 Probably a member of the Otbertine family and kinsman of Margrave Albert Azzo II of Este, a mediator at Canossa: Meyer von Knonau (1894) p. 741 n. 199.

339 Cf. Lampert, *Annales* 1076, p. 283: 'among all the Germans no native-born man accompanied him except for one and he was remarkable neither for his birth nor for his riches'. Bruno, *Saxon War* c. 88, p. 83: he was accompanied by 'a great army'. The king's route: Meyer von Knonau (1894) pp. 741–3, 748–52.

a crowd of excommunicated bishops. As if he was about to defend their cause somehow or other with his royal authority, he announced to them with great rhetorical skill that he would exhort the pope to examine not only his own case but also the sentence of excommunication wrongfully imposed on them. They, however, strongly urged him on the contrary not even to recognise him as pope, since at [the king's] command they had so solemnly sworn an oath to expel him and had separated him forever from the body of the Church, as one lawfully condemned with the judgement of anathema.[340] Nevertheless, since an unavoidable crisis held him in check, they considered it fitting that he should yield and be accommodating for the time being and that he should not be so completely rash as to annul the decision of the magnates of the kingdom of the Germans, like a pseudo-king, and thereby most justly incur their enmity. Afterwards, however – that is, after this meeting that would bring him a dispensation and that was so necessary for him – he should endeavour with all his might and with their help actively and most earnestly to free himself and the whole kingdom once and for all from such a sacrilegious man. If he failed to do this, however, he should be aware that he would doubtless be deprived of his kingdom, his honour and even of life itself through the most cunning madness and arrogance of him who had heretically usurped the benign title of pope. He should also be in no doubt that all those who were always invincibly prepared to go with him to death and destruction, must likewise perish and be doomed.

After the envoys of the king and those of the magnates of the kingdom had been dismissed by the pope and began their homeward journey, the pope immediately, being very ready to *lay down his life for his sheep*,[341] hastened to the place at the time that they had mutually agreed on and there waited most eagerly for those who were to escort him on his journey. But it was in vain.[342] For after the German princes had learned that the king had fled so unexpectedly and so secretly over the Alps, they greatly feared that he would make every effort to ambush and to attack them and, although it was much against their will, they failed to meet him and to provide the promised escort. So the pope waited for them

---

340 Cf. Gregory VII, *JL* 5019 (*Epistolae Vagantes* 19, p. 52): 'the Lombard bishops ... rose up against us'; cf. *Register* VIII.5, p. 522.

341 John 10:11.

342 Cf. Gregory VII, *JL* 5019 (*Epistolae Vagantes* 19, p. 52): 'We could indeed have arrived [in Germany] if we had obtained an escort from you at the time and in the place that was appointed.' Cf. *Register* IV.2, p. 312.

at the castle of Canossa[343] for some considerable time. While, hindered by so many dangers, they could scarcely send word to him that there was no way in which they could come to him, he was greatly annoyed that he had come there in vain but he did not despair of being able at a later date somehow or other to reach German territory for the sake of the needs of holy Church and he decided to wait there some time for such an opportunity. Then he considered that the journey undertaken by the king and his advisers would be of little profit to him and to holy Church, since indeed [the king] had found the Lombards in rebellion against God and [the pope] and had made them even more rebellious[344] and since he had to an extraordinary degree exasperated and distressed the German peoples, who were divided among themselves and totally at odds about what they should do in the case of such a madman, and since he had caused the greatest disturbance throughout the whole kingdom. [The pope] therefore *cast* all his *burden on the Lord*,[345] as a truly apostolic man ought to do, and addressed his tearful prayers to Him day and night that He might send heavenly inspiration so that he might settle so important a business lawfully, according to synodal procedure.

The king finally took the salutary advice of his followers and gave up entirely the previous wicked plan that he had insanely and hatefully devised against the pope. He resolved, primarily through the mediation and help of Margravine Matilda,[346] of his mother-in-law Adelaide, likewise a margravine,[347] and of the abbot of Cluny[348] (who had arrived with the pope, by whom he had recently been reconciled in Rome after communicating with the king) and also of all those, whoever they were, whom he could attract to his side,[349] to meet the pope and to subject

---

343 The fortress of Matilda of Tuscany, south-west of Reggio. The absolution of the king: Meyer von Knonau (1894) pp. 755–62, 894–903; Morrison (1962) pp. 121–48; Schneider (1972) pp. 201–13; Beumann (1973) pp. 48–55; Cowdrey (1998) pp. 156–66; Robinson (1999) pp. 160–4.

344 Cf. Gregory VII, *JL* 5019 (*Epistolae Vagantes* 19, p. 52): 'because of [the king's] presence certain very wicked men show boldness rather than fear towards us and the apostolic see'.

345 Psalm 54:23.

346 Matilda, margravine of Tuscany (1046–1115), daughter of Margrave Boniface of Tuscany (above p. 92 n. 297) and Beatrice of Lotharingia (above p. 98 n. 334).

347 Adelaide of Susa, margravine of Turin (?1015–91), mother of Queen Bertha.

348 Hugh I ('the Great'), abbot of Cluny (1049–1109), godfather of Henry IV. His contact with the king in Speyer, autumn 1076: Meyer von Knonau (1894) p. 740; Cowdrey (1970) p. 160; Cowdrey (1998) p. 156; Robinson (1999) pp. 158–9.

349 Lampert, *Annales* 1077, p. 290 identified Margrave Albert Azzo II of Este, Count Amadeus II of Savoy 'and some others from the leading princes of Italy'.

himself to him in all respects, to comply with his wishes, to obey him and
to reach an agreement with him. With that intention, which, however,
he concealed from the Lombards as best he could, he sent envoys in
advance to bring to him the aforementioned mediators and slowly
followed them to the castle mentioned above. [The envoys] hastened
to meet the king at the agreed place and for a long time they discussed
among themselves with many words the case concerning which they
had gathered together, weighing the arguments with him from every
point of view and with mature deliberation. But I do not know what
deceitful circumlocutions and feigning promises they detected in [his
case] after diligent and distrustful investigation, which they were afraid
to bring, instead of the simple truth and that alone, to the pope, who
had indeed long been most experienced in cases of this kind from daily
practice. Nevertheless they returned at once, since necessity demanded
it, and gave the pope a full account, truthful and coherent, of whatever
they considered to be false and treacherous. Without delay the king
followed close on their heels and unexpectedly rushed up to the gate
of the castle, sorrowful and in great haste, together with his excommunicated followers, although he had received no answer and no word
of invitation from the pope and, knocking loudly, he begged with all
his might for permission to enter. There he waited, clad in wool, bare-
foot, freezing, in the open air outside the castle for three days with his
followers.[350] In this he was most severely tested by many trials and
temptations and found to be obedient, as far as human judgement could
discern, and he tearfully waited for the grace of Christian communion
and papal reconciliation, as is the custom of the penitent.

The lord pope, however, who with great circumspection refused either
to be deceived himself or to deceive others and who had so very often
been deluded by so many promises from the king, did not very readily
believe his words. After many consultations and mature reflections
he was with difficulty induced to make this concession: that he would
not refuse to receive him into the Christian communion (but only into
communion)[351] if he would come without delay to confirm on oath –

---

350 25–27 January 1077. Cf. Gregory VII, *Register* IV.12, p. 313: 'He remained for three
    days before the castle-gate; having cast aside all the splendour of a king, in a
    wretched condition, barefoot and clad in wool, he did not cease to weep and beg for
    the aid and consolation of apostolic compassion.'

351 Cf. *Register* VII.14a, p. 484: 'I restored to [Henry] communion alone, but I did not
    install him in the kingship, from which I had deposed him in a Roman synod.' See
    Morrison (1962) pp. 121–48; Miccoli (1966) pp. 203–23; Beumann (1973) pp. 49–55;
    Cowdrey (1998) pp. 162–4.

either personally or through those witnesses whom he would appoint for himself – those conditions of obedience and reparation that [the pope] would now impose on him for the benefit and the well-being of holy Church and moreover if he would solemnise this oath, which was to be observed most faithfully in the future, in the hands of those mediators who were present and also of the empress,[352] who was not yet present, and thus conclude this agreement. When the king received such an answer from the pope, however, he and all his followers judged this proposal to be very harsh. Nevertheless, since otherwise he could by no means be reconciled, willy nilly he consented very sorrowfully. In fact representations were finally made with difficulty to the pope that [the king] should not himself swear the oath. Two bishops, however – the bishops of Naumburg [Eberhard] and Vercelli[353] – were chosen to take the oath on his behalf, besides the other members of his entourage, who were to swear afterwards. They swore as follows (to bring to mind the substance of the oath): that *within*[354] a year, whenever *Pope Gregory should determine* this for him, their lord Henry should reach an *agreement* and make peace with the princes of the kingdom either *according to his judgement* or according to his mercy. And neither he nor any of his followers were to inflict any *harm* on the lord pope or his legates, neither *taking them captive* nor *mutilating* their limbs, when they came to any *region* of the kingdom on the business of the government of the Church. And if they were injured by anyone else, [the king] would *help* them *in good faith* as soon as he could; and if *any obstacle*[354] impeded him, so that he could by no means adhere to the time of the appointment that the lord pope fixed for him, he should subsequently hasten to keep the appointment without any delay, as soon as he could.

By means of this agreement (as was mentioned above) permission to enter and to approach the pope was granted to the king, who uttered lamentations amidst floods of tears, and to the other excommunicates, who likewise loudly lamented. How many tears were shed there on both sides is not easy to relate. The lord pope was pitifully shaken by his weeping for the *sheep* that had been *lost*[355] and must be won back for

352 Empress Agnes's role in the negotiations leading to her son's reconciliation: *Register* IV.3, p. 299. See Bulst-Thiele (1933) pp. 102–3; Berges (1947) pp. 189–209; Black-Veldtrup (1995) pp. 99, 378–80.

353 Gregory (1044–77), Henry IV's Italian chancellor. See Meyer von Knonau (1894) pp. 761, 896; Cowdrey (1998) p. 157; Robinson (1999) p. 161.

354/354 Extracts from 'The oath of Henry, king of the Germans': Gregory VII, *Register* IV.12a, pp. 314–15.

355 Matthew 10:6.

God and, after they had humbly thrown themselves on the ground, as
was proper, and confessed their presumption and their stubbornness,
he offered them suitable expressions of canonical reconciliation and
apostolic consolation and thus he brought them back into the Church,
reconciled by the papal pardon and blessing and restored to the Christian communion. Then the customary prayer was said for them and
the king and the five bishops [Werner II] of Strasbourg, [Liemar of]
Bremen, Lausanne,[356] [Burchard of] Basel and [Eberhard of] Naumburg and the other magnates were given the fitting salutation of the
holy kiss. The pope himself celebrated mass and at the moment of the
communion he called the king to him and offered him the eucharist that
he previously denied him. The king declared that he was unworthy to
share it and he went away without receiving communion.[357] Through
the revelations of the Spirit the pope at once wisely concluded that this
was a sign of impurity and evidence of a certain latent hypocrisy in him
and thereafter he did not dare to believe fully in the good faith of his
words. Finally a meal was suitably prepared and they sat together at the
same table and they partook honourably of the modest dishes. With the
thanksgiving they rose and exchanged few words except for necessary
reminders about the promise of obedience, the pledge of fidelity, the
oath that must not be broken, the completion of the penance and the
need to beware of the anathema imposed on the Lombards. The king
received the pope's leave and blessing and departed with his followers,
except for the bishops, whom the pope ordered to be imprisoned there
according to his pleasure. Moreover the taking of an oath to the pope
was demanded from the members of the king's entourage, who had
hitherto resisted this demand. Amidst controversy and strife they tried
to have it set aside, contrary to what had been agreed, and because they
feared that they would quickly be imprisoned by the pope on a charge of
perjury, they scornfully fled in all directions so as not to swear the oath
at all. One of them, the bishop of Augsburg,[358] secretly fled by night
and made his escape without permission and without being reconciled.
Thus after the first agreement that they had concluded together they
departed like liars, cunningly mocking and deceiving the pope.

356 Burchard (1056–88). See Meyer von Knonau (1894) pp. 761–2.

357 Cf. Lampert, *Annales* 1077, pp. 296–7: the pope ascribed to the communion the character of a trial by ordeal and Henry, therefore, avoided receiving communion.

358 Probably Werner II of Strasbourg rather than Embriko of Augsburg. Berthold
   perhaps confused the fate of the imprisoned bishops with that of the bishops of Toul
   and Speyer, above p. 155.

Furthermore, when the pope sent the two bishops of Ostia and Palestrina[359] to Milan, Pavia and the other cities of that region and when, after achieving some success, they set out for Piacenza, they were captured by the perjured and excommunicated anti-bishop of Piacenza.[360] The bishop of Palestrina was shortly afterwards released, but the bishop of Ostia was sent to a certain castle and imprisoned. He was held there in chains for some considerable time and the king, entirely forgetting the oath that he had taken to aid the papal legates, showed no compassion for him and did not even utter a single word that would help him. Instead, together with his followers he strove with skill and cunning to pursue the profits of avarice, although the pope reluctantly gave him permission during his expedition through Lombardy to receive service from [the Lombards], but only what was necessary and on condition that he avoided any communication with them, as required by canon law. When, however, he wished to be crowned in Pavia according to the custom of the king of the Lombards[361] and sent mediators to the pope to obtain permission for this, they were given the reply that as long as Peter remained in chains, he would not receive the permission of papal authority in this matter. But [the pope] could not thus extort help from [the king]. At length, however, with the help of the empress and the lady Matilda [the bishop of Ostia] was released from prison after undergoing a period of trial.

At the same time that Roman Quintius,[362] who in order to ensure his own damnation had also held captive the bishop of Como[363] next to the church of St Peter in Rome, strove to go to see the king in Pavia,[364] together with the bishop, and to make him most generous towards him. Indeed he had no doubt at all that he had deserved to receive no small thanks and many gifts from him not only for capturing the bishop but also for sacrilegiously capturing the lord pope. After he had arrived at the court, the king did not dare to kiss and, as is customary with friends, to greet a man who had carefully to be avoided because of his

359 The fellow legate of Gerald of Ostia was not Hubert of Palestrina but Bishop Anselm II of Lucca: Bernold, *Chronicle* 1077, below p. 258. See Meyer von Knonau (1894) pp. 768–9; Vogel (1983) pp. 12–13, 18–20.

360 Denis (?1049–?82). See Schwartz (1913) pp. 191–2.

361 Cf. the version in Paul, *Life of Pope Gregory VII* c. 86, p. 329. See Meyer von Knonau (1894) pp. 769–71; Vogel (1983) pp. 29–32.

362 Cencius Stephani: see above n. 263.

363 Rainald (1061–84).

364 Henry IV in Pavia: *D.H.IV* 291 (3 April). Cf. the version of Bonizo, *To a friend* VIII, p. 242.

excommunication. He pretended that he could not yet receive him as was fitting and as he had so very much deserved because of the important business that preoccupied him and so he put off and delayed his welcome guest from day to day. The latter, however, was somewhat angered and declared that he was held in contempt and made sport of until at last he stubbornly obtained a fixed date at which he was to receive a suitable greeting and thanks from the king. On the very night before the appointed day, however, he was suddenly choked by a lethal swelling in his throat and at that moment he rapidly descended into hell, to be condemned to eternal death, without seeing and greeting the king.

After scouring that region during the whole of Lent [1 March–15 April] and most eagerly gathering together copious quantities of gold, silver and precious garments and then, without seeking permission from the pope to assume the kingship that had been forbidden him, the king celebrated Palm Sunday [9 April] in Verona with great rancour and perturbation of spirit. His closest follower, the anti-bishop [Gregory] of Vercelli, departed from there, only to be overtaken by sudden death on the road on which he had joyfully set out: he immediately fell from the horse on which he was riding and miserably perished at the same instant.[365]

After the princes of the kingdom had learned of the treachery of the king and the breach of the agreement that had been reached in Oppenheim, of his flight and his pretended reconciliation and of all his cunning undertakings throughout Lombardy, they assembled in Ulm after Christmas[366] to hold a consultation about so important a matter. And because few met there, the others being hindered by the excessive snow and the bitter cold of the winter, they sent letters and their envoys to the princes and bishops of the Lotharingians and the Saxons and also of the Bavarians and shrewdly admonished them by the fidelity that they had sworn among themselves and implored them especially by God's mercy; they eagerly asked them and strongly urged them to meet at least on 13 March in Forchheim, where, after holding a conference and offering wise advice, they might settle decisively what seemed to them best to do in the case of the kingdom, the

365 1 May. See Schwartz (1913) p. 138.

366 In mid-February. According to Lampert, *Annales* 1077, p. 301, they were Siegfried of Mainz, Adalbert of Würzburg, Herman of Metz, the dukes Rudolf, Berthold and Welf IV 'and very many others of the German princes'. See Meyer von Knonau (1894) pp. 775–6; Vogel (1983) pp. 40–6; Robinson (1999) p. 166.

Church and the need to preserve their own lives. Then, because they were very uneasy and sought to protect themselves on all sides, they sent a suppliant letter, full of their pressing cares, to the lord pope, who still remained in Canossa,[367] informing him of the conference on which they had agreed and of their wishes and intentions and they eagerly and most humbly asked for his advice, his authority and his help in this case, as was necessary in all their concerns, and also asked that he should send a letter indicating his views, together with his envoys, as soon as possible.

The lord pope, however, as he is a man of great compassion and kindness, with great care and sagacity fittingly carried out what they so much wished for and sent to that same conference a cardinal deacon of the holy Roman church[368] and the abbot of Marseilles[369] as his legates with a letter of advice.[370] But he himself remained in that castle until the month of August,[371] although he was greatly saddened by so many scandals and so much resistance on the part of the heretics and the schismatics. Because the road was not open to him to enter German territory to settle so many conflicts, he went from there to return with great glory to Rome, where he was received with the utmost respect by the Roman citizens, who came to meet him and greeted him[372] reverently.

After they had heard that the king had actually been reconciled, Duke Rudolf, on the advice of the other princes of the kingdom, sent a messenger[373] to him, entreating him most urgently and courteously not to come to German territory before he sent there in advance either the pope or the empress, who might carefully prepare a fitting and peaceful reception. The pope, who was approached and invited by this same envoy, had shown himself indeed most ready to do this, but only if he received

---

367 Their envoy was 'our son, Rapoto': Gregory VII, *JL* 5019 (*Epistolae Vagantes* 19, p. 52). Cowdrey (*ibid.*, p. 52 n. 1) suggests that he was the same envoy as above p. 140 n. 249.

368 Cardinal deacon Bernard, who had been with the pope in Canossa: Gregory VII, *Register* IV.12a, p. 315 n. See Hüls (1977) pp. 245–6.

369 Bernard, abbot of St Victor in Marseilles (1064–79). Their legation: Meyer von Knonau (1894) p. 778; Schumann (1912) pp. 36–44; Cowdrey (1998) pp. 169–75.

370 Gregory VII, *JL* 5019 (*Epistolae Vagantes* 19, pp. 50–4). Cf. below p. 166 and n. 377. See Vogel (1983) pp. 42–3; Cowdrey (1998) p. 169.

371 He stayed in a number of fortresses in the neighbourhood of Canossa, Carpi, Bianello, Ficarolo, Carpineto, 1 March–28 June (Gregory VII, *Register* IV.13–28, pp. 316–47) and returned to Rome by 16 September (*Register* V.3, pp. 350–1).

372 Cf. Mark 9:14.

373 According to Meyer von Knonau (1894) pp. 176–7, Rapoto (n. 367).

from the king himself a guarantee of peace and fidelity, confirmed to him on oath.[374] The king, however, in his obstinacy scorned the envoy's message and deigned neither to provide the pope with the guarantee nor to fulfil the request for a suitable advance mission.

Finally on the previously mentioned 15 [March][375] a large number of the magnates of the kingdom[376] assembled, as had been decided, and in the conference held there they made accusations against the king with extraordinarily numerous appeals and most unhappy complaints about the injustices and injuries that he had inflicted on them and on the foremost men of the whole kingdom and on the churches. And because the pope so clearly forbade them to obey or serve the king, they deprived him of the office of the kingship and judged him unworthy even of the name of king because of his myriad unheard-of shameful deeds, resolving unanimously to elect and appoint for themselves another man in his place. When, however, the legates of the apostolic see heard there that he was such a sacrilegious man, they were amazed that [the princes] had borne with his ruling over them for so long. Nevertheless they did not remain silent about the duty with which they had been charged, but published the instructions for their legation in the hearing of all: that since they had somehow or other endured this man for some time, they should refrain from appointing another king for themselves, if this could be done with ingenuity and caution. Otherwise, because they knew best from their experience how dangerous their situation was, they should do whatever they judged was best for them and the pope would not oppose them. In addition the papal letter[377] was read out in their presence. This contained, besides an account in the proper sequence of the granting of Christian communion to the king, the statement that there was little reason for his subjects to rejoice, as far as hopes for his penitence and his progress were concerned, since indeed he made the Lombards, whom he had found disobedient enough already, even more disobedient and had made bad men into the worst of men.

---

374 Cf. Gregory VII, *JL* 5019 (*Epistolae Vagantes* 19, p. 52): 'with the advice and help of the king'.

375 13 March: see above p. 155. The assembly of Forchheim: Meyer von Knonau (1900) pp. 3–8, 627–38; Schlesinger (1973) pp. 61–85; Giese (1979) pp. 37–49; Robinson (1979) pp. 721–33; Vogel (1983) pp. 41–6; Cowdrey (1998) pp. 167–71; Robinson (1999) pp. 167–70.

376 The assembly seems to have been attended only by the small 'deposition faction' of princes: Robinson (1979) p. 721; Cowdrey (1998) p. 170; Robinson (1999) p. 167.

377 Probably Gregory VII, *JL* 5019 (*Epistolae Vagantes* 19, pp. 50–4), of which Berthold gives a polemical paraphrase. Cf. Paul, *Life of Pope Gregory VII* c. 93, pp. 334–5.

All who were previously under the power of his sceptre were, therefore, exhorted and advised with much wisdom and apostolic vigilance to commend themselves solely to the Lord God so that they might happily overcome such distressing circumstances: they should walk every day with more care and more progress in the path of the love of righteousness[378] and by so walking they should earn a heavenly crown.

Hence, greatly trusting in God's grace and strengthened by it, the bishops and the senatorial order,[379] meeting separately, held long and deep consultations about the appointing of a king. Finally, while the whole assembly of the senators and of *the people, desirous of novelties*,[380] eagerly awaited first the divine and spiritual decision of the bishops, as spiritual men, in the nomination and election of the king, Duke Rudolf of Swabia was nominated and elected as king firstly by the bishop of Mainz,[381] then by the other [bishops]. The whole senate and the people followed them without delay and all subjected themselves to him lawfully with the customary oath of fidelity. This election was in truth not heretical[382] since it was lawfully carried out according to the general agreement and with the approval of all the people, electing a man who did not desire the office, but was unwilling and compelled to accept it.[383] He immediately set out from there and came, by way of Bamberg and Würzburg, to Mainz, arriving in the middle of Lent. There he was approved, anointed and ordained as the just king, ruler and defender[384] of the whole kingdom of the Franks by those same bishops and by an assembly of all the people.[385]

---

378 Cf. Psalm 118:26, 32.

379 A Ciceronian term also used by Berthold's contemporaries Adam, *Gesta* III.48, p. 191, Cosmas, *Chronica* II.31, p. 126. See Schlesinger (1973) p. 72.

380 Caesar, *Bellum Gallicum* I.18.3; V.6.1.

381 Archbishop Siegfried thus asserted the claim of Mainz to precedence in royal elections: Thomas (1970) pp. 368–99.

382 Cf. Bruno, *Saxon War* c. 91, p. 85: the papal legate declared 'that if [Rudolf] was elected … after making promises to individuals, the election would not appear authentic, but instead polluted by the poison of simoniacal heresy'. See Schlesinger (1973) pp. 73–4; Jakobs (1973) p. 89: Robinson (1999) p. 168.

383 Cf. Gregory VII, *Register* VII.14a, c. 7, pp. 484–5 ('compelled to assume the government of the kingdom'); Paul, *Life of Pope Gregory VII* c. 95, p. 336. The topos of the reluctant office-holder: Gregory I, *Regula pastoralis* I.6, 10, *MPL* 77, col. 19D–20A, 23AC. See Weiler (2000) pp. 1–42.

384 Cf. *Register* IX.3, p. 575: 'defender and ruler'.

385 26 March: Bernold, *Chronicle* 1077, below p. 258. See Meyer von Knonau (1900) p. 9. In crowning Rudolf, Siegfried of Mainz asserted a right of his church last exercised in 1024: Thomas (1970) pp. 394–9; Robinson (1999) pp. 22–3, 167.

On the same day the citizens of Mainz at once deliberately rose up against him and more than a hundred of them were killed, but only two of the king's party died: the rest [of the citizens] with difficulty escaped death by fleeing and taking advantage of nightfall.[386] Thus the knights of the king miraculously obtained the victory and instilled so great a fear into the citizens that immediately at daybreak they surrendered themselves as guilty men to their bishop and lord and, after obtaining his favour, through his intervention and that of all those whomsoever they could assemble, they also obtained with difficulty the favour of the king. The citizens of Worms also conspired in a rebellion against the king and their bishop [Adalbert],[387] recruiting considerable military forces from all sides. The king, therefore, passed by that city and changed direction to Tribur and thus, setting off by way of Lorsch and Esslingen and spending Palm Sunday [9 April] in Ulm, he pushed forward as far as Augsburg, in order to celebrate Easter [16 April] there. For during Easter week he intended to discuss and settle there with his princes very many matters of importance to the kingdom and to holy Church. They, however, at once began one by one – I do not know what misfortune caused it – to withdraw from him. Not only the new vassals indeed but also the veterans who had already long before confirmed their fidelity on oath thought nothing of committing perjury and broke their oaths. He had already sent a letter of invitation to the pope[388] from the city of Würzburg so that he might deign to come to our region in the interests of the government of the Church and he had decided to send escorts to him, but then he was utterly unable to perform this because of his lack of knights. He assembled about him only three bishops, [Adalbero] of Würzburg, [Adalbert of] Worms and [Altman of] Passau. A fourth, the bishop [Embriko] of Augsburg, very craftily using all the ingenuity of which he was capable and with a heart as hard as adamant, for two days so stubbornly resisted the legates of the apostolic see and their canonical judgements that he could by no means be compelled to obey the pope or the king. At last he was with difficulty persuaded by them all to confess, albeit insincerely, that he had sinned by communicating with his lord and king, Henry, and for this reason he was deprived of his priesthood by the papal legates [Cardinal deacon Bernard and Abbot Bernard of St Victor] and was subjected to

---

386 Bernold, *Chronicle* 1077, below p. 258. See Meyer von Knonau (1900) pp. 10–12, 632–3.

387 See above pp. 146 and n. 285, 153 and Büttner (1973) pp. 355–6.

388 Cf. Rudolf's letter described by Gregory VII, *JL* VII.14a, pp. 484–5; Paul, *Life of Pope Gregory VII* c. 98, p. 339.

an appropriate penance. Nevertheless, before they departed, they reluctantly conceded to him the exercise of his office, although only for the time being, because the king humbly implored them by all the means in his power.[389]

There indeed on the holy day of Easter [16 April], when the king and all the clergy and people were present in a great and solemn procession at the church of St John,[390] the papal legates issued and confirmed the precept, based on canon law, that this unlawful practice, which was rashly and presumptuously followed by the simpler brethren, contrary to the decrees of Pope Clement,[391] was no longer to exist in the Church. For they are accustomed on the Saturday before Easter, before the chrism is poured into the water for baptism, to sprinkle all the bystanders with it and to receive it in their vessels and thus throughout the whole fifty-day period to misuse it for this unlawful and irregular sprinkling, paying no heed to the reasonable and inviolable decision of the holy Pope Alexander, who commanded that every Sunday the exorcism of salt and water is to be performed by the priests and that the people, their workplaces and dwellings are to be sprinkled in this way.[392] And there Lutold, a venerable brother of the monastery, was elected according to the *Rule* by the brethren of the house of St Gallen and appointed abbot.[393]

After the king had celebrated Easter there in a festive manner, he returned by way of Ulm, entered Reichenau[394] and from there arrived in Constance. The bishop of that city [Otto] very carefully avoided an audience with the legates of the apostolic see and the presence of the royal majesty and withdrew to a certain castle of Count Otto,[395] where he remained for the whole of that year. Although the previous year he had been utterly forbidden by the pope to exercise his office, he had nevertheless not given it up. For immediately after he had put his

389 See Meyer von Knonau (1900) p. 23; Vogel (1983) pp. 56, 59.

390 This detail suggests a crown-wearing: Vogel (1983) p. 55.

391 Ps.-Clement I, *JL* ✝5340, *Briefsammlungen* pp. 257–8. See Schumann (1912) pp. 129–30 and n. 41.

392 Ps.-Alexander I, *Epistola* (*JK* ✝24) c. 9, *Decretales Pseudo-Isidorianae* p. 99 (*Collection in 74 titles* c. 211, p. 134).

393 Lutold was expelled soon after his election and took refuge in Reichenau: *Casuum sancti Galli continuatio* II.7, p. 156.

394 Cf. *ibid.*, describing Abbot Ekkehard of Reichenau as 'standing staunchly with the false king Rudolf'. Bernold, *Chronicle* 1077, below p. 260 gives a different itinerary for Rudolf.

395 Otto I, count of Buchhorn (Udalriching family). The castle was probably Burg Markdorf. See Meyer von Knonau (1900) p. 25.

name to the conspiracy of disobedience in Worms,[396] he began to limp and thenceforward he was crippled and lame, which we note down as a miracle of fitting divine vengeance. Nevertheless before the conference at Oppenheim he had already received communion, but not his office, from [Altman,] the bishop of Passau. From that time this enemy in his stubborn opposition to the law would not cease to ordain clergy, consecrate churches and exercise the other rights of a bishop, although for two whole years previously it had been impossible to compel him to do so. The papal legates, however, assembled the chapter of the brethren there and held a meeting with them concerning the flight and the disobedience of their bishop and also concerning his other rash actions, his negligence and his audacity. They set a date there, summoned the bishop to them and most vigorously commanded by papal authority that no one should receive his offices. They utterly condemned, according to the decision made in the Roman synod, the simoniacal and nicholaite heresies, which exceeded the bounds of moderation in that bishopric, to which an infinite number of people was subject.[397] And they repeated there above all the particular precept that no Christian was ever to receive the offices of clergy condemned for being unchaste. And there also, when they learned that that bishop was accustomed to accept the judgements of certain priests and the testimony of seven of his colleagues in connection with the possession of his churches, which were proved on the most trustworthy evidence of many laymen to have been acquired by simony, they confirmed irrefutably on the basis of canon law that it was not at all permissible to accept these judgements and testimonies. They did not, however, reject judgements and testimony of this kind in the case of accusations of any offence, except for heresies. They declared with good reason that in cases of heresy, if an accusation was made against a clerk, the testimony of all Christians holding to the catholic faith, whether clergy, laymen, men and women, must be accepted. Likewise they commanded by apostolic decree and compulsion that whatever they had proved by the canonical authority of the Scriptures was to be done, must in cases of this kind be entirely complied with.

Finally the king went from there to Zürich and remained in that place for some time. At that time the greatest part of the unchaste and simoniac clergy, showing contempt for the papal judgement, obstinately

---

396 Council of Worms, 24 January 1076: above p. 143–4.

397 Cf. the description of the diocese in Gregory VII, *JL* 4970 (*Epistolae Vagantes* 9, p. 20).

returned to its vomit,[398] encouraged by the hope of help and protection from King Henry and his anti-bishops. Because they greatly feared to be corrected by King Rudolf, they condemned him, anathematised him and cursed him in every way, never ceasing to oppose him and to misrepresent him by whatever means they could. On Henry they now on the contrary lavished the most immoderate praises and exalted him above the heavens – although almost the whole kingdom had formerly despised him as a man notorious for his widely reported crimes and shameful acts and as one who ought to be considered unholy and excluded from the Church – and they declared with great lamentations that he had been most unjustly condemned. The heretical and incorrigible persons, the anti-Christian bishops and those like them among the clergy, the canons, the monks, the village priests and the whole crowd of the synagogues (I say it with all due consideration) did not rest from uttering and spreading everywhere their sycophantic praises of one man and their hostile censures of the other and from bearing witness to them with unheard-of falsehoods. The throngs of the common people, who were misled by such persons, believed nothing, did nothing and knew nothing except what they constantly heard in their harangues and their false testimony. Obviously, therefore, great schisms and divisions broke out throughout the whole kingdom. No natural family ties, none of the trust of friendship, none of the obedience appropriate to a subject, no reverential fear or love of God, no contract of fidelity, no obligation of justice, no honour or respect for persons, virtually nothing of divine law and right survived in their statutes or had any place in their law, in their management of affairs or even in their observance of customs or in their imaginations, but all of them, from the least to the greatest among them, paying no heed to divine or human considerations, devoted themselves assiduously and indiscriminately to avarice. Discipline was nowhere to be found, a sense of shame was a thing of great price, truth was extremely rare; thousands upon thousands of falsehoods reigned everywhere. Thus a huge mass of deceits, a calamitous quantity of scandals and an infinite number of evils of all kinds ceaselessly and unrestrictedly manifested themselves.

King Henry remained in the bishopric of Aquileia at Eastertide after he had drawn the Lombards to his side by all possible means and, very skilfully binding them by an unaccustomed oath of fidelity and subjection, he employed them as adherents and helpers inseparable from his will. He had commended his son [Conrad] to the care of the simoniacal anti-

398 Proverbs 26:11; II Peter 2:22.

bishops of Milan,[399] [Denis of] Piacenza and the other excommunicates throughout Italy. Taking his wife and a large sum of money that he had somehow raked together in that region, he traversed the precipitous passes of Carinthia and with difficulty entered Bavaria, accompanied by a few followers, secretly and unexpectedly, like a thief. He soon held in Regensburg a conference concerning all that had happened, with the princes of the Bavarians, the Bohemians and also the Carinthians and with the patriarch [Sigehard] of Aquileia,[400] a not particularly honourable man, whom he had brought there with him. He tearfully presented to them, as he had recently presented to the Lombards, lengthy appeals and complaints about his deposition and in order to be able to avenge himself for these wrongs as he wished with the help of their wealth, he promised them, as his most faithful followers, whom he had raised up from poverty and elevated into such great lords, that he would gladly reward them and honour them for his own part with offices and benefices. In addition they were soon indiscriminately bribed with magnificent gifts and, by whatever ingenious means he could devise, they were drawn with might and main from all directions to help him, so that in a short time he assembled a considerable force of auxiliary troops, to the number of almost 12,000 men, with whom he tried to do battle with the new king and advanced with his warlike host to encounter him. Besides these, the following adhered to King Henry in all things: almost all the might of the Burgundians, the anti-bishops [Burchard] of Basel and [Werner II of] Strasbourg (who were recently reconciled by the pope and who declared that henceforward they would remain in the party of righteousness),[401] a considerable part of the Franconians, the count palatine Herman (who was to be the son-in-law of King Rudolf)[402] and the majority of the knights of the king, of whose supreme fidelity he had never doubted, since they had long ago sworn an oath to him, and also almost all his blood relations and his next of kin, to whom he himself had always been most loyal. From the other

399 Tedald, archbishop of Milan (1075–85): see Schwartz (1913) pp. 82–3. On Conrad (n. 208): Goez (1996) pp. 7–8; Robinson (1999) p. 166.

400 Sigehard's church was the beneficiary of the privileges *DD.H.IV* 293, 295–6 (11 June 1077). The princes presumably included the Bavarian count palatine Cuno, Margrave Diepold II of the Nordgau, Duke Vratislav II of Bohemia and the newly invested Duke Liutold of Carinthia, all of whom were interveners in *DD.H.IV* 293, 295 or 296.

401 Strasbourg was the recipient of *D.H.IV* 298 (1 July 1077). See Meyer von Knonau (1900) p. 44.

402 Herman II, Lotharingian count palatine (1064–85), of the family of the Ezzones, perhaps betrothed to Rudolf's daughter Adelaide, who later married King Ladislaus I of Hungary.

[king], however, they withdrew one by one, thinking nothing of their fidelity and their oath. And this occurred for three reasons, which we have particularly noted before all the rest: because (as has already been mentioned) they greatly feared to be corrected by [Rudolf] according to the rule of justice and because it is almost natural for bad citizens always to envy virtuous citizens[403] and because it is characteristic of them to serve idols.[404] For they all asked and demanded that he fill up the insatiable gulf of their avarice with extraordinary waste and unheard-of extravagance: that is to say, after he had, under compulsion, obtained a kingdom that had been wretchedly plundered, so that he might restore it, he should instead allow it to be divided up among them and thus totally plundered. And because he wisely did not consent to their demands, they all, except for a very few persons of sound mind, miraculously returned to their ancient plunderer, as though *flowing into a* contaminated *drain*.[405]

From there King Henry, strengthened by so great a force of auxiliary troops, invaded Swabia in order to lay it waste by plundering, pillaging and burning. There was no distinction *between the holy and the profane*.[406] The Bohemians indeed publicly ravished women in the churches, led them away as captives according to their custom and treated church and stable with the same degree of respect. And thus they all, confusing right and wrong together, swept through a large part of that land in an extremely hostile manner, indeed like mad heathens: that is to say, from the territory of eastern Franconia and the River Main and by way of the River Neckar and the town of Esslingen they somehow reached as far as Ulm and the Danube, although not without the greatest trepidation. For they knew that King Rudolf had laid siege to a certain castle on the Danube[407] with a considerable force and there he awaited the assembling of those of his knights whom he was able to gather together from all directions in so short a period of time.

King Henry, however, held a conference in Ulm with whomsoever he could and caused King Rudolf, together with his dukes, Berthold [I of Carinthia] and Welf [IV of Bavaria], and the other Swabian magnates who were his adherents, to be condemned by a judicial sentence

---

403 Cf. Gregory I, *Dialogi* II.8.1, *MPL* 66, col. 148A.

404 Cf. Ephesians 5:5.

405 Sallust, *Catilina* 37.5.

406 Ezekiel 22:26.

407 Sigmaringen, identified by *Casuum sancti Galli continuatio* II.7, p. 156; *Casus monasterii Petrishusensis* II.33, p. 646. See Meyer von Knonau (1900) pp. 35–6.

according to Swabian law as deserving death.[408] At the same time he
caused them to be deprived of their offices and benefices, which he
immediately conferred on some of his vassals and thus with a great
effort he brought the latter, and all those whom he could find, to his aid,
after he had received an oath from them according to his custom.[409]

There the above-mentioned patriarch [Sigehard of Aquileia] appeared
with a falsified letter allegedly sent by the lord pope to this region
through his agency, which was read out in the presence of the people.
Defending his king in every possible way and recommending him to
everyone by means of this supposedly authentic authority [of the papal
letter] he declared in a sycophantic manner that [Henry] was most
worthy of the high office of the kingship.[410] When at length after uttering
such mendacious flattery he hurried to his home and made lavish preparations, most assiduously pondering in what manner he would support
and serve the king, he suddenly went mad and raved like one possessed.
And after being tortured for some time like a demoniac by this affliction
of madness, an object of fear to all and a lesson to liars and renegades,
he perished utterly insane and worthy of damnation.[411] And thus he was
brought back to his see for burial, together with some of his followers,
who were similarly snatched away by sudden death. Oh how much to be
feared is *the Lord God of vengeance* and how *terrible in His counsels among
the sons of men!*[412] In former times that man had been fired with zeal for
God and the year before he had come with the most honourable men of
God, the archbishop [Gebhard] of Salzburg and the bishop [Altman]
of Passau and with other soldiers of Christ to the conference in Oppenheim. There he most sagaciously preoccupied himself – more indeed
than the other magnates of the kingdom – with the amendment of the
Church and with discipline and the need to improve Christian devotion and like *the angel of the Lord of hosts*[413] and in keeping with his title,

408 They were judged according to Swabian customary law because Rudolf was duke of
     Swabia, Berthold I of Carinthia was Swabian by birth and Welf IV of Bavaria had
     a Swabian mother. See Meyer von Knonau (1900) pp. 36–7; Vogel (1983) pp. 72–4;
     Robinson (1999) p. 173. The 'Swabian law': Krause (1965) p. 8.

409 Cf. Bernold, *Chronicle* 1077, below p. 260: Count Udalrich II of Lenzburg was one of
     the beneficiaries. Liutold of Eppenstein had already been invested as duke of Carin-
     thia.

410 He evidently participated in the crown-wearing in Ulm on 4 June: Bernold, *Chronicle*
     1077, below p. 260. See Vogel (1983) pp. 77–81; Robinson (1999) p. 174.

411 12 August. See Schwartz (1913) pp. 33–4.

412 Psalm 93:1; Psalm 65:5.

413 Malachi 2:7.

prince of fathers,[414] he had in every way manfully opposed King Henry and all those who disobeyed and resisted God and St Peter, threatening them and inspiring great terror with the two-headed sword of the Spirit. Now, however, this most inconstant renegade and prince of error unhappily turned away from the zeal and righteousness of God and was corrupted by the great temptations of mammon. According to the judgement of God, therefore, the most watchful Guardian of justice, and as an example to all who wish to take notice of it, he tasted in advance for a moment a drop from his chalice that the thirsty man would not cease to drink for all eternity and yet never drain it.

The bishop [Embriko] of Augsburg followed him in no less wretched a manner. The previous Easter he had allied himself most firmly, although unwillingly, with King Rudolf by means of homage and an unfeigned pact of fidelity. When, however, King Henry returned to that place, he hastened to meet and to congratulate him; he flattered him in every way and was present in his entourage as far as Ulm and eagerly served him and showed him honour. There he also celebrated mass and when he reached the moment of the communion, he turned to the king and to the others who were present and made a short announcement in obsequious language about the current circumstances. He then declared voluntarily in the presence of them all that he would receive the holy eucharist as a trial and as a judgement of the fact that the cause of his lord King Henry was just, while that of Rudolf was utterly unjust. And thus, as is customary in judgements, the presumptuous man, as if he was a judge recommending justice to the peoples, first took an oath in these terms, that the sacrament of the Lord's body and blood would prove conducive to the salvation of his body and soul if his lord King Henry's claim to possess the kingdom was just and valid, and with these words he received communion. Then he was actually seized by a deadly affliction and he wasted away from day to day, his sufferings constantly increasing until, wretchedly tormented by the just judgement of God, he confessed that this punishment had fallen upon him because of his aforementioned presumption. A few days afterwards he was overtaken by a most bitter death and breathed his last.[415] Duke Welf [IV] immediately took care to have this judgement reported to the lord pope. The latter, who was no false prophet, at once and without hesitation sent back word that he had in fact known in advance that

---

414 Isidore, *Etymologiae* 7.7.1.

415 30 July. He is identified as intervener, 'our familiar' and 'our vassal', in *DD.H.IV* 295–6 (11 June). See Meyer von Knonau (1900) p. 62.

this bishop would never taste the first fruits of that year and a little later the outcome proved to be just as the apostolic man had foreseen. Nevertheless, although the people had more than adequate confirmation through signs and wonders like these that the entirely just and desirable election of King Rudolf had been carried out for the sake of the Church's needs and for its improvement, hardly anyone was capable of persuading them of this: instead they earnestly desired with all their might to attach themselves indivisibly and forever to King Henry, who had burned and destroyed all their property and was the author and defender of so many heresies and schisms.

Then certain obstinate persons declared far and wide (which was a seedbed of heresy among the clergy) that neither the pope himself nor any other person in authority is to pass judgement or to impose sentence on kings, even though they are heretical and have long been involved in every kind of shameful and wicked act, guilty of the most abominable acts of bloodshed and in every way impious and sacrilegious.[416] For they had not borne in mind that Emperor Constantine, the adherent of the heretical Bishop Paul of Constantinople, was excommunicated in a Roman synod by the holy Pope Martin in the year 650 of the Lord's Incarnation.[417] They ought also to consider that Constantius was excommunicated by Pope Felix because of the Arian heresy.[418] They should not be unaware that Charibert, king of the Franks was excommunicated by the holy Bishop Germanus of Paris for the offence of lasciviousness and thus was damned and went down to hell.[419] They should learn that Childeric, king of the Franks was deposed from the kingship on the authority of Pope Stephen, was tonsured and sent into a monastery and thus Pippin was elected as king of the Franks and

416 The following catalogue of excommunicated and deposed rulers corresponds in many of its *exempla* with the *Sentences* of Göttweig MS 56, ed. Sdralek (1890) appendix III and with the polemics of the south German pro-Gregorian circle: Robinson (1978b) pp. 101–22.

417 Not Constantine but Constans II (641–68). The excommunication by the Lateran synod in 649 was directed against bishops, not the emperor, as correctly recorded in Herman, *Chronicon* 650, p. 94; Bernold, *Chronicon* 650, p. 451. Cf. Göttweig *Sentences* p. 174.

418 Felix II (355–8); Constantius II (337–61): Bernold, *Chronicon* 358, p. 408. Cf. Göttweig *Sentences* p. 174; Manegold, *Ad Gebehardum* c. 29, p. 362; Bernard, *Liber canonum* c. 3, p. 504.

419 The Merovingian Charibert I (561–7); Germanus (†576): Herman, *Chronicon* 563, p. 88; Bernold, *Chronicon* 563, p. 413. Cf. Göttweig *Sentences* p. 173; Manegold, *Ad Gebehardum* c. 29, p. 363; Bernold, *Apologeticae rationes* p. 97.

consecrated to the kingship by the holy Bishop Boniface of Mainz.[420] Pope Nicholas excommunicated Lothar, king of the Franks because after he had repudiated his lawful wife, he presumed to take Waldrada as his concubine. When he wished to clear himself in Rome of the crimes of which he was accused, this judgement was imposed on him: that if he was innocent, he should confidently draw near for communion. He rashly approached and received the judgement from the hand of the lord pope: for not long afterwards he and all his supporters died a sudden death.[421] Emperor Louis laid down his arms and was imprisoned by the judgement of the bishops in order to perform penance.[422] Emperor Theodosius was prevented by St Ambrose from entering a church and because of his crimes he was sent to prison for eight months to perform penance.[423]

Why should it be necessary to remind wise men of these and very many instances of the same kind unless it is to give answers to the very troublesome and mendacious chatter of certain fools? In their false synagogues indeed they produced very many ludicrous privileges full of trifling absurdity hitherto unknown among kings,[424] being ignorant of common law and not knowing enough about the decrees of the people, although they derive their name from the word 'knowing'.[425] For according to their whims they indiscriminately uttered praise and blame against each party. And just as already long ago things had lost their names, so among them still it is not the things but only the names that are praised and honoured and without their content and the offices

420 The Merovingian Childeric III (743–51); the Carolingian Pippin III (751–68); Boniface (†754). The pope was Zacharias (741–52): Herman, *Chronicon* 752, p. 99; Bernold, *Chronicon* 752, p. 418. This *exemplum* was first used by Gregory VII, *Register* IV.2, p. 294 (cf. *Register* VIII.21, p. 554). Cf. Göttweig *Sentences* p. 174; Manegold, *Ad Gebehardum* c. 29, p. 362; Bernard, *Liber canonum* c. 25, p. 496.

421 Nicholas I (858–67); the Carolingian Lothar II (855–69): Herman, *Chronicon* 867, p. 106; Bernold, *Chronicon* 867, p. 420. Cf. Göttweig *Sentences* p. 174; Manegold, *Ad Gebehardum* c. 29, p. 362; Bernard, *Liber canonum* c. 25, p. 497; Bernold, *Apologeticae rationes* p. 97.

422 Louis the Pious (814–40): Herman, *Chronicon* 834, p. 103; Bernold, *Chronicon* 834, p. 420. Cf. Göttweig *Sentences* pp. 174–5; Manegold, *Ad Gebehardum* c. 29, p. 362.

423 Theodosius I (379–95); Bishop Ambrose of Milan (374–97). This *exemplum* was first used by Gregory VII, *Register* IV.2, p. 294 (cf. *Register* VIII.21, p. 554). Cf. Göttweig *Sentences* p. 175; Bernard, *Liber canonum* c. 25, p. 497; Bernold, *Apologeticae rationes* p. 97.

424 Jordan (1938) pp. 122–3: this was a reference to the forged 'investiture privileges' in the names of popes Hadrian I and Leo VIII (*Hadrianum, Privilegium Maius, Privilegium Minus, Cessio donationum*). See Robinson (1978a) pp. 160–3.

425 Cf. Isidore, *Etymologiae* 5.11.

that belong to them they have an utterly empty sound.⁴²⁶ For just as [the term] *'law'*⁴²⁷ [derives] *from regulating,* 'priest' from sacred, 'duke' from command, *'consul' from consultation,* 'counts' from gravity of demeanour or because the more anyone is weighed down by the weight of their labours, the more he is placed in authority over the rest, so it is proved that *a king* is properly so called and designated *from the fact of his ruling.* It is known indeed that a rule is so named either because it leads in the right direction and does not sometimes draw one in another direction or because it goes straight or because it offers a model of right living or because it corrects what is distorted and perverse. *The title of king is, therefore, retained by doing right and is* otherwise *lost; hence* derives this *old* maxim: *'You will be a king if you do right; if you do not do so, you will not be [a king].'* There are, therefore, *two principal royal virtues, justice and piety; but piety in kings is praised more, for justice is* very strict. If, however, they neither judge justly nor piously humble themselves and do not conform in the slightest degree to the rule of their office or do so only for the sake of appearances, but instead, like men who are in every respect wicked and unnatural, they lead a life of excess and of criminal and *lascivious* freedom, outdoing the madness of the heathen; if they oppress *the people* with *a most cruel* power and *domination* and swallow up those whom they have most wretchedly oppressed and bring about their utter destruction, why are they not to be properly called the most powerful kind of tyrants rather than use the name of kings, which is misapplied and without any element of truth? The Greek word *'tyrant'* is *in fact* translated into Latin as 'strong'; *for among the ancients strong kings* were *called 'tyrants'. Among the Greeks,* however, *they are called 'basilei', because they support the people like the bases* [of columns]: *hence bases* show *crowns* encircled around themselves. Moreover Christian kings who greatly long to exercise dominion over the people rather than rule them in a manner in keeping with their name [of king], should note what is written in Roman history about Octavian. After he *was called Augustus and Caesar and emperor because he enlarged the State, while* he was present *at the games* and *the public shows* of the Romans *and the people called out* to him *that he should be called* god *and lord,* he at once opposed the unseemly *flatteries with* [a gesture of] *his hand and turned his face away and, as a human being, shunned the title of lord* and *on the following day he chided all the people in a very severe* speech *and afterwards he did not allow himself to*

---

426 Cf. Jerome, *Adversus Iovinianum* I.34, *MPL* 23, col. 270A (cited by Peter Damian, *Letter* 40, p. 411; Manegold, *Ad Gebehardum* c. 30, p. 365).

427/427 Extracts from Isidore, *Etymologiae* 9.3.4, 9.3.6, 9.3.22; 9.3.4–5, 9.3.16–20; cf. 2.10.1, 5.3.2, 7.12.17; 1.29.3, 6.16.1, 7.12.17.

be called lord even by his children.[427] And if then glass – that is, a heathen king – was of such worth, how much more valuable now is the noble pearl of the Christian dignity? But let these words against the chatterers suffice.

In these days after Easter letters were sent by papal authority to all the inhabitants – but to the bishops specifically by name – beyond the Rhine, throughout Alsace and Lotharingia and Franconia. These prohibited all conspiracies, disturbances of the peace and dissensions and forbade them to obey or serve King Henry as is customary in the case of a king.[428] The anti-bishops [Burchard] of Basel and [Werner II of] Strasbourg in particular treated [these letters] with contempt and regarded them as insignificant;[429] but others pretended, by whatever artifice and pretext they could, that they had never been sent to them; they did not make them public and they took care to obey them only when it was possible for them to do so.

At that same time the abbot [Bernard] of Marseilles and with him a very wise monk named Christian[430] were endeavouring to return to the lord pope, by whom they were sent into German territory to calm the dissensions among our compatriots, when they were captured by a certain Count Udalric,[431] plundered and imprisoned in the castle of Lenzburg. When King Henry learned that they had been taken captive, he did not order them to be released, according to the promise that he had formerly made on oath to the lord pope.[432] The abbot [Hugh I] of Cluny, however, soon afterwards sent him a warning letter, in which he offered more than adequate proof that he was guilty of perjury. For the whole case of the reconciliation and the agreement between the pope and the king was known to him because he was present on the occasion as the principal mediator.[433] Moreover, *with unveiled face*[434] he informed

---

428 No papal letter has been identified: Schumann (1912) p. 39 n. 25. 'Letters … by papal authority' might be letters issued by a papal legate. Cf. Abbot Bernard of St Victor, Marseilles, letter to Lotharingia (late 1077), *Briefsammlungen* pp. 69–72.

429 They were among Henry IV's most zealous supporters: Meyer von Knonau (1900) p. 39.

430 Christian-Guitmund, monk of La Croix-St-Leufroi (near Évreux), later bishop of Aversa (1088–before 1095). The identification is made by Paul, *Life of Pope Gregory VII* c. 90, p. 332.

431 Udalric II, count of Lenzburg (Aargau). Cf. Abbot Bernard's letter (n. 428) p. 70. See Schumann (1912) pp. 39–40.

432 See above p. 161. Cf. Gregory VII, *Register* V.7, p. 357, referring to the case of the legates Gerald of Ostia and Abbot Bernard.

433 The letter is not extant. See above p. 159 and n. 348.

434 II Corinthians 3:18.

him in the frankest terms that it would be a most certain sign that he
was a lost soul if, in his churlish contempt for the apostolic see, he did
not liberate such great and most holy men of God, who had been imprisoned *for righteousness' sake*,[435] but rather commanded them to be even
more closely guarded. After receiving that warning and that remarkably
frank denunciation, he was reluctantly brought to submit, not for God's
sake but because of the discomfort that so powerful an instructor caused
him. He agreed that God's prisoners should be released and should go
free, although they were despoiled of all their possessions. They waited
for some time, according to the king's command, to be compensated for
their plundered property, but at long last, disappointed and deceived,
destitute and almost naked, they made their way to the monastery of St
Aurelius [Hirsau]. There they were received with zealous humanity by
Abbot William[436] and for almost a whole year they were treated most
charitably, while they waited in most agreeable conditions for a time of
peace and calm and the possibility of a return journey.

King Rudolf, however, assembled his forces of knights from all directions and courageously decided to encounter King Henry and, with
God as his judge, to engage him with military might. When at last he
received the entirely unanimous advice of his dukes and counts and of
all his knights (who barely reached the number of 5,000 warriors), it
was that the plan for an attack of this kind seemed to them unsound.
They advised with wise caution that it should be delayed for a while
until he might by his great exertions bring together countless numbers
of warriors from every side, who would be sufficient for him to seize
the opportunity to defeat his enemies without the loss of his vassals
and, once victorious, to compel them by his royal authority to serve
him in every way. He acquiesced in their advice, although reluctantly
and unwillingly, and courteously dismissed the troops whom he had
assembled, while warning his close friends in the strongest terms
to defend the kingdom and to secure themselves against the horrors
of the imminent war. Because he was most insistently invited by the
princes of the Saxons, he hastened his journey into Saxony, taking with
him the three bishops [Altman] of Passau, [Adalbert of] Worms and
[Adalbero of] Würzburg and also the cardinal of the apostolic see
[Bernard], together with some of the closest advisers from among his

---

435 Matthew 5:10.

436 Cf. William of Hirsau, Prologue, *Constitutiones Hirsaugienses* col. 927–8: 'Abbot
   Bernard of Marseilles, performing a legation for the apostolic see, came to us and
   ... spent almost a year with us.' Cf. Abbot Bernard's letter (above n. 428) p. 71.

followers.[437] They greeted and exalted him most gloriously with all the marks of distinction and the praises with which royalty is honoured, as was fitting towards their king and lord, and they extolled and venerated the most welcome arrival with expressions of joy and with every exertion of subjection, reverence and esteem.[438] There as a most just arbiter, according to equity and the ancestral laws of that people, he attempted without *respect of persons*[439] to make a most painstaking investigation of all appeals, complaints and accusations and to settle them judicially in their presence. Therefore, since their former ruler always treated them with savagery according to his will and raged against them with plundering, pillage and all manner of oppression, while this ruler judged justly and with the severity of justice restored what was *crooked* and *made it straight*,[440] he was deservedly loved by all alike.

The king's wife,[441] however, leaving Zürich for the territory of Burgundy, stayed for longer than half a year in one of her castles, where she was to suffer very many injuries at the hands of the Burgundians. For the anti-bishops [Burchard] of Basel, Lausanne[442] and [Werner II of] Strasbourg, together with all those whose support they could attract, soon most eagerly destroyed everything that belonged to the king by plundering and burning and with every kind of pressure of persuasion and assault until they subjected almost all that land to themselves and to their own king. But this was not done without evil and harm to themselves. For when the troops of the Burgundians arrogantly invaded Swabian territory to attack and plunder it, they were twice defeated, slaughtered and put to flight by the knights of King Rudolf.

King Henry, however, hastened from Ulm into Bavaria. He divided up among his followers the benefices of Duke Welf [IV] and the others who rebelled against him and also the property of the churches, but especially of Passau, and everywhere he drew to himself all men, whomsoever and however he could, according to his custom, that is, by means of oaths.[443]

---

437 Rudolf was in Merseburg on 29 June: Bruno, *Saxon War* c. 93, p. 87. See Meyer von Knonau (1900) p. 45.

438 According to Scheibelreiter (1973) p. 21 and Giese (1979) p. 50, the 'electoral homage' of the Saxons, i.e. the formal recognition of Rudolf's kingship by Saxons not present at Forchheim.

439 Cf. Romans 2:11. See above n. 153.

440 Isaiah 40:4; Luke 3:5.

441 Rudolf's second wife, Adelaide of Turin (Susa, †1079), sister of Queen Bertha: Jakobs (1968) pp. 160, 264. Her role in Burgundy: Meyer von Knonau (1900) p. 39.

442 Cf. *Gesta episcoporum Lausannensium* c. 10, *MGH SS* 24, 799–800.

443 Cf. *DD.H.IV* 295–7 (Nuremberg, 11–13 June). Deposition of Welf IV and Berthold I

And thus he very carefully planned an expedition into Saxony against King Rudolf and into Swabia against Duke Berthold [I of Carinthia] and Duke Welf and their other supporters. And there was scarcely one of the Bavarians who did not willingly help him and take his part, except the archbishop [Gebhard] of Salzburg and a certain Count Ekbert.[444] At this time certain counts among the Swabians, who had previously been the foremost sworn vassals of King Rudolf, broke faith with him *for the sake of filthy lucre.*[445] After they had seized certain strongly fortified castles, they raged most savagely with all their strength and their skill throughout the whole province, as much as they could, plundering, burning and committing every kind of robbery and violence against their lord, against Duke Welf, against the property of the churches and against all those who were opposed to them. Everywhere conflicts of this kind, perpetrated by the supporters of both parties indiscriminately, as is usual in warfare, continued throughout all the provinces for the whole of that year. There was therefore a great famine throughout our region both because the earth had not yielded its produce and because, as a result of the violence already mentioned, thieves and pillagers had devoured everything and the famine caused many to waste away and to perish miserably. In these days there was no mention either of divine or of secular laws: instead each man existed, as far as he could, as his own judge and his own ruler. Hitherto unheard-of conflicts and schisms, disgraceful acts of deception and squalid love of gain reigned everywhere tyrannically and with deplorable arrogance, while innumerable sacrileges were perpetrated both secretly and openly by those who held God in contempt even in the churches, in which all men had accumulated their property to be kept there in the hope of peace and protection.

When the lord pope finally heard of this, he sent letters especially to his legates [Cardinal deacon Bernard and Abbot Bernard of St Victor][446] but also to all those, the greater and the lesser men, who were in German territory.[447] In truth he had an earnest longing and made every effort to come to this land, by whatever ingenious means he could and with

of Carinthia: above p. 174. *D.H.IV* 298 (1 July) confers on the church of Strasbourg the county in the Breisgau 'which was taken away from Berthold, now no longer a duke, by a just judgement'.

444 Ekbert I, count of Formbach and Neuburg. See Meyer von Knonau (1900) p. 40.

445 Titus 1:11; I Peter 5:2.

446 Gregory VII, *Register* IV.23, pp. 334–6 (31 May).

447 *Register* IV.24, pp. 336–8 (31 May) 'to the archbishops, bishops, dukes, counts and all the faithful of Christ, clergy and laymen, both the greater and the lesser, living in the kingdom of the Germans'.

our help, in order to make peace. In these letters, I say, he commanded his legates that they should most strictly admonish both kings to guarantee him access to this territory in peace and safety and also give him escorts in whom he could trust so that by God's favour he might settle such unprecedented strife. And they should condemn that man who in this matter refused to agree with and obey both them and the others, the wiser and more honourable men of the kingdom and should separate him utterly by public excommunication from the members of the Church. On him who was obedient, however, they should with papal authority confer the monarchy of the kingdom and all who were in the kingdom should, as was fitting, obey him as king, be subject to him, serve him and in every way honour him as one who had been elevated to that position in order to build up the Church.

In this matter King Rudolf was most ready to obey, together with all his followers. Since, however, King Henry controlled the passes through the Alps and they were everywhere closed and full of opportunities for an ambush, it was in vain that he wished for that which he could in no way achieve. But King Henry, fearing to face the judgement of papal authority, gave special commands to all his followers that no one holding the office of papal legate was to find access to him – as if this artifice was enough to defend him in a rational manner from an accusation that had been so widely published. For already his intention was something other than obedience: namely an expedition into Saxony, which all his followers had already sworn to undertake. He had therefore withdrawn in the month of July from Bavaria with all those whom he could bring to his own land of Franconia and there he assembled from all sides whatever troops he could to make a very large force.[448]

After King Rudolf finally learned that so great a body of knights had been gathered together and that it presented so great a threat to him and to his followers, he did not long delay. He did not cease in his constant and strenuous efforts to encounter and to engage him in battle. And thus he came as far as Würzburg and there he delayed for a while in laying siege to the city[449] and for this reason: that if he hastened towards the Rhine with such a numerous and mighty army, the fearful [Henry] would be terrified and would not dare to encounter him. While he also waited there for the dukes Berthold and Welf and the other auxiliary

---

448 He was in Mainz on 1 July (*D.H.IV* 298) and 13 August (*D.H.IV* 299).

449 'In the month of August': Bruno, *Saxon War* c. 94, p. 87. The siege of Würzburg: Meyer von Knonau (1900) pp. 46–8; Höss (1950) pp. 306–7; Robinson (1999) pp. 176–7.

troops of their Swabian knights, he most ingeniously endeavoured to destroy the walls of the city with certain machines and implements of war. They, however, were joyfully hastening to meet him with almost 5,000 men.

But King Henry had spied out their strength and for three days he occupied a certain point on their route, although with his limited number of troops he would not attempt to do battle with them. They, however, were most eager for that encounter and they hastened their march towards him. And when they had come so close that they were no more than two miles away from him and they all boldly intended to join battle with the king and were armed for this purpose, he fled from them with his followers that same night and before dawn he entered his city of Worms[450] before all the rest amidst the mockery and insults even of the peasantry. When they learned of his flight, [his opponents] proceeded with great haste and terrible force to pursue him even to his camp. And when they had discovered from their spies that he was so far distant from them and so very much afraid, they very sadly gave up their intended pursuit. Instead they gloriously continued their planned journey to their lord.

In these days, as he had been commanded, the Roman cardinal [Bernard] courteously sent to King Henry the letter of instructions concerning the aforementioned matter of the pope's coming to us and it was delivered by a certain monk of Würzburg.[451] Before he could reach him, however, certain of [Henry's] confidential advisers carefully spied out the reason for his journey, took him captive, treated him badly, also beating his servant, and imprisoned him. They took away the letter and treated it not as a papal letter but in every respect as if it were a diabolical letter. Soon afterwards the Roman cardinal again dispatched a letter to [Henry] on the same subject skilfully sending it by a certain knight who was his friend. It was brought to [Henry] as a communication from another person; he received it and caused it to be read out but he heard it with an ear that was at once closed to it. Angered, he held the letter that he had heard to be of no account and he commanded the bearer of it to be arrested and sent to prison. After a very short time [the bearer of the letter] fled from him, running away from his prison and barely escaping with his life.

450 On 'his city of Worms': Büttner (1973) pp. 355–6.

451 The letter responding to *Register* IV.23, p. 335 (above p. 182) is not extant. Cf. the Saxons' letter to Gregory VII in Bruno, *Saxon War* c. 112, p. 102. See Meyer von Knonau (1900) pp. 57–8.

Meanwhile [Henry] had busily assembled from all sides a great army, making every effort of which he was capable, and after he had crossed the Rhine again with all the men whom he had assembled, he pretended that he would encounter King Rudolf. They pitched camp between the Rhine and the River Neckar, after blocking the fords everywhere by some means or other, and waited for the help of the Bavarians. When King Rudolf finally heard that they had pitched camp, he left the siege of the city [of Würzburg], abandoning his machines, and boldly advanced towards him at a rapid pace, most eager to do battle with them. He soon arrived, therefore, on the bank of that river, intending with a coura-geous spirit to fight in defence of the kingdom that had been conferred on him and in defence of the Christian religion. The enemy, however, occupied the opposite bank with their forces for a stretch of almost three miles and he could find nowhere to make the crossing. For the opposite bank was so high that no one, not even a foot soldier, to say nothing of a knight on horseback, could find a way up there except for two very narrow fords.

Then King Rudolf called upon King Henry, together with the other commanders of the army, and repeatedly requested that if he was determined to claim the kingdom for himself so obstinately and with so strong a statement of his right, he should choose one of two courses. Either he should give him an opportunity of crossing or, failing that, he himself would leave the position that he had taken up and fall back two miles from the riverbank until [Henry] crossed over to him with all his troops and if [Henry] would not otherwise trust him, he would confirm this promise inviolably by means of an oath. Finally they should both most faithfully commend their cause to be judged according to the opinion of the most just Judge and they should strive without delay to prove their right, with the Lord God deciding between them, either in single combat or, if this seemed advisable to the more prudent and nobler men of the kingdom, in a full-scale battle. King Henry, however, was deaf and dumb and gave him no reply. In order to show that what he had so emphatically demanded of him was spoken in all honesty and in order to exasperate him by a cunning device and provoke him to this trial by battle, [Rudolf] withdrew with his men to a distance of two miles from his position and his camp, as though simulating flight.[452]

452 A familiar motif of Ottonian-Salian historiography, 'the challenge on the river': Cram (1955) pp. 68–70. Bruno, *Saxon War* c. 95, p. 88 offers a similar account with-out mentioning the idea of a judicial combat: the negotiations of the princes were begun without the king's knowledge and the truce was broken after the arrival of Henry's Bavarian and Bohemian auxiliary troops. See Meyer von Knonau (1900) pp. 51–4, 58–61.

On the following day, when he at last discovered that he had thereby achieved nothing, with a rapid and warlike advance he very boldly reoccupied his campsite of the previous day, so that, if he could accomplish it by any stratagem or act of valour, he would try somehow to engage him in battle.

Then certain of King Henry's magnates, who utterly refused to fight and wished to cover the disgrace of their cowardice and their consciousness of the manifest injustice of their cause with some appearance (although fabricated) of honour, strenuously sought from Duke Berthold [I of Carinthia] and Duke Welf [IV of Bavaria] a short period of peace and a guarantee of safety so as to permit them to hold a conference with the other side on friendly terms about the critical situation of the present time. When a peaceful conference had been granted to them, according to their request, those on each side who seemed to be suitable assembled there for that purpose. After various speeches had been made there by both sides at great length, this was finally established as the outcome of the conference: that firstly they should agree to a lasting peace among themselves and the imminent conflict should then be halted and entirely laid to rest on condition that all the magnates of the whole kingdom, with the exception of the two kings, should shortly afterwards meet at a conference on the Rhine.[453] There, together with the papal legates, they should consult together in a most equitable judicial investigation about what was the best and what was the most just decision to make in such an important case. They were to hold in contempt whichever of the kings did not agree with their decisions and were by common consent to oppose him but, finally, they were most obediently to serve the other king, who was in agreement with them, with total fidelity and subjection, as belongs to a king. At first, however, the bishops of Trier and Metz,[454] together with certain confidential advisers of King Henry, utterly refused to listen to the Roman cardinal [Bernard] in that conference because they had been able to obtain permission from the king to participate in that conference and that peace only after promising that they would by no means receive and hear the pope and his legate. Nevertheless they finally both

453 On 1 November: Marianus Scottus, *Chronicon* 1100 [=1077], p. 561. See Meyer von Knonau (1900) pp. 58–9 and n. 89.

454 Herman, bishop of Metz (?1073–90) and his metropolitan, Archbishop Udo of Trier, the recipients of *Register* V.7, pp. 356–8 and the letter of Abbot Bernard of St Victor (n. 428) pp. 69–72. Udo's role as negotiator: Vogel (1983) pp. 108–9, 111–13; Cowdrey (1998) pp. 179–81; Robinson (1999) pp. 178–9. Cardinal deacon Bernard accompanied Rudolf to the conference.

heard the legate and the papal letter and decrees, although it was under the greatest compulsion, and – as was fitting – they received them with every mark of reverence. Thus the promise of security was both given and received by both sides and likewise peace was made until all had returned to their homes so that the conference on which they had agreed might be carried out and no king or prince might hinder it by any act of cunning or any intrigue. King Rudolf and his followers then gloriously returned to Saxony.

King Henry, however, soon received in that same place his Bavarian followers, for whom he had been waiting for some days and who had escaped from the hands of King Rudolf, whom they had almost encountered, because of that peace that had been made. After consultation with them this man, resuming his great cruelty, laid waste Swabia with plundering and burning, and the Swabian princes, who had recently returned from the aforementioned campaign, found themselves thus unexpectedly and deceitfully attacked. They were thinking at that time principally of peace and therefore had already allowed their knights, who were wearied by the campaign, to go home in safety. Nevertheless it was not without very great losses among his followers that he marched through that land.

During his march over the plain he looked out over a region that was laid waste and was burning and smoking from the fires all around him and where, to say nothing of very many others, a church was destroyed by fire with more than a hundred people in it.[455] After Bishop Embriko of Augsburg had died miserably (as has already been mentioned), he rejected the candidate[456] whom the brethren had already elected according to canon law and somehow or other put in his place his chaplain Siegfried,[457] not that he might rule the church but in order that he might support him in the imminent struggle with all his wealth. The outcome subsequently proved this to be the case. On the same day, in the same place and with the same intention, after similarly rejecting the man who was elected by the brethren according to the *Rule* and appointed abbot there by King Rudolf, he appointed to the office of abbot of St Gallen a certain kinsman of his, who was not a monk of that

---

455 In Wiesloch: Bernold, *Chronicle* 1077, below p. 261. Henry's campaign: Meyer von Knonau (1900) p. 61.

456 Wigold, provost of the church of St Maurice, Augsburg; Gregorian anti-bishop of Augsburg (1077–88). See below p. 206.

457 Siegfried II (1077–96), invested in Augsburg, 8 September: *Annals of Augsburg* 1077, p. 129.

place.[458] Like the man imposed on Augsburg, he henceforward most expertly conducted an un-monklike war against King Rudolf, contrary to the *Rule* and always clad in a coat of mail. In Aquileia likewise he somehow or other imposed Henry, a canon of Augsburg and his chaplain, as patriarch, after rejecting the man who was elected by the clergy and people according to canon law.[459] He then continued the expedition that he had begun into Bavaria. After gathering auxiliary contingents of his knights from all directions, he returned from there again into Franconia. This was not, however, before he had summoned the archbishop [Gebhard] of Salzburg to him under a pretended promise of security and tried again and again by every kind of cunning device to make him his ally, but in vain.[460] The latter indeed, like a truly immovable pillar of holy Church,[461] most firmly established on the pedestal of the truth by the weight of heavenly love, tore himself away from there with all the exertion of which he was capable, once he had clearly perceived that he was ensnared by so much cunning and by such madness. Leaving all his followers behind, he fled with difficulty, virtually alone, by night and in secret, to Swabia and to the men of his own party and his communion.

Finally, therefore, when at the agreed time[462] the greater and nobler men of the kingdom who had been summoned and chosen for this purpose had already begun to assemble from all sides at the conference that had been planned, King Henry again gathered a considerable force of knights and treacherously broke the promise of security that had already been agreed by his princes. Like a savage, he showed utter contempt for the treaty of peace and he strove most strenuously everywhere and with all the ingenuity of which he was capable to hinder them from meeting. When they became aware, however, of his customary subterfuge and folly, each of them returned to his home, although they were moved to utter very loud complaints. Nothing came of their conference and their proposed future agreement about the conflicts and the

---

458 Udalric III of Eppenstein, abbot (1077–86), patriarch of Aquileia (1086–1121), brother of Duke Liutold of Carinthia, sharing with Henry IV a common great-grandfather in Duke Herman II of Swabia. See Meyer von Knonau (1900) p. 64; Schwartz (1913) pp. 35–6. The expelled abbot was Lutold: above p. 169 and n. 393.

459 Henry (1077–84). See Schwartz (1913) p. 34. The rejected candidate was the archdeacon of Aquileia, name unknown.

460 In Regensburg: *Vita Gebehardi* c. 3, p. 26. See Meyer von Knonau (1900) p. 67; Steinböck (1972) pp. 118–19.

461 Cf. Revelation 3:12; Ps.-Anacletus I, *Epistola* I.19, *Decretales Pseudo-Isidorianae* p. 76.

462 1 November: above p. 186 and n. 453. On 30 October Henry IV was in Worms: *D.H.IV* 301. The failure of these negotiations: Meyer von Knonau (1900) pp. 69–71.

divisions throughout the whole kingdom. [Henry], however, as he had already planned, vigorously applied himself to his usual burning and plundering and unyieldingly attacked those who rebelled against him everywhere with royal might.

One day, when [Werner II,] the bishop of Strasbourg (who was then his foremost instigator and helper in undertakings of this kind), clad in mail in warlike fashion like a knight and the commander-in-chief of so many evils and so many crimes, returned to the camp and to the king, to whom he was all too obedient in his cruelty, he was overtaken there by sudden death, the moment that he lay down on his bed.[463] His followers, to whom his shameful life had so often been a cause of scandal, were utterly terrified and much astounded by this. For contrary to the precepts of canon law, the shameless man openly and obstinately kept a certain widow as his concubine: he had taken her from one of his vassals, whom she had married, purchasing her from him with a large sum of money and with benefices. When an accusation was subsequently made against him to the pope because of this conduct, he denied her on oath but did not avoid her and despite the notorious suspicion of the most abominable incest, he never withdrew from his adulterous liaison. Thus the assiduous despiser of God – like Paul of Samosata, that *bishop*[464] of Antioch who delighted in *consorting with women* and *permitted* this *to his clergy so that* they *could not charge him with this offence* – caused the greatest scandal to all his canons and the clergy of his diocese and to the whole Church. He earned the wrath of God and deserved to be struck down by the punishment of eternal damnation: assuredly, *woe to the man by whom* such an *offence comes!*[465] For in holy Scripture 'woe' signifies eternal lamentation. *When* that heretic Paul, *having been condemned, refused to leave the church, he was – to add to his disgrace – expelled* from there *by the power of the State.*[464] This man had likewise already been condemned according to canon law by a papal decree for his heresies and shameful acts, when by a judgement of the supreme Judge, as a very clear example to all men, he was suddenly banished from this life and thus from the kingdom of

---

463 14 November: Meyer von Knonau (1900) p. 71. The accusations against him: Gregory VII, *Register* III.4, p. 249. He had been deposed by the Roman synod of Lent 1075: *Register* II.52a, p. 196.

464/464 Extracts from Bernold, *Chronicon* 270 (marginal note), p. 406. Cf. Bernold, *De incontinentia sacerdotum* III, V, pp. 14, 23, 35. Bernold's source was Rufinus's Latin version of Eusebius, *Ecclesiastical history* VII.30.12, 19.

465 Matthew 18:7.

God.[466] His followers received him and immediately took him on the sad journey back to his see for burial.

King Henry had decided to invade Swabia for the third time to lay it waste according to his custom but when he became certain that Duke Berthold [I of Carinthia] and Duke Welf [IV of Bavaria], together with the other forces of the Swabians, would meet him in battle, taking wise advice, he avoided an encounter with them and took the direct route into Bavaria with his followers, abandoning the battle. Then taking with him a force of knights of [Vratislav II,] the duke of the Bohemians, composed of his countrymen, this pertinacious destroyer made an attack on Ekbert [I of Formbach], a count of considerable strength and courage who had rebelled against him, plundering, burning and laying siege to his castles. This harshest of assailants spent the winter in this work of destruction, although he and his followers could scarcely endure the extremes of snow and cold. After besieging three castles of [the count] for some time, he finally captured and destroyed them with his siege machines. When at last [the count] was no longer able to resist him, [Henry] forced him to flee with his wife[467] and all his followers into exile with the king of the Hungarians.[468]

At that time King Rudolf – after returning to Saxony with his men at the end of the aforementioned expedition and after realising that the planned conference had been prevented by the intrigues and treachery of King Henry – had finally nothing else to do than to pacify the Saxon kingdom as a most impartial judge and to investigate and correct every wrongdoing most justly according to their laws. In addition he suppressed with royal authority certain of the Westphalians and Thuringians who rebelled against him.[469] Having already sent an envoy to Rome, he also informed the lord pope of the whole sequence of events and most urgently sought his advice and help about these matters. [The pope] sent nothing else back to him except the message that he awaited with great eagerness the consequences of the letter that he had recently sent both to his legates and to all the princes of the German territories.[470]

466 Cf. *Vita Willihelmi abbatis Hirsaugiensis* c. 26, p. 222: 'the most wicked and most dissolute of all the men whom the earth sustained … descended living into hell'.

467 Matilda of Lambach, niece of Bishop Adalbero of Würzburg. See above p. 182 and n. 444.

468 Ladislaus I (1077–95), son of Bela I, brother of Geisa I (canonised 1192).

469 Perhaps a reference to the Henrician bishops Eberhard of Naumburg and Benno II of Osnabrück.

470 See above p. 182 and nn. 446–7.

In response to the contents of the letter that Roman cardinal [Bernard], who was indeed much encouraged by it, assembled the whole body of the bishops and the other princes of the Saxon province in Goslar.[471] On 12 November according to the judgement of apostolic authority he issued a judicial condemnation of King Henry and excommunicated him from the communion of the Lord's body and blood and from the threshold of the holy catholic Church and entirely forbade him to govern the kingdom. For, becoming thoroughly disobedient to the supreme pontiff of the first apostolic see, without the latter's permission he so rashly took possession of the kingship, of which he had deprived him after he was condemned by a just judgement in a Roman synod, and after he had thus been deprived, he had anathematised him. Moreover the despiser of God and the apostolic see stubbornly refused to make any concession to [the pope], not even to grant him free passage and an escort to pacify so many conflicts, divisions and criminal and ruinous hostilities throughout the whole kingdom. [The legate], however, confirmed Rudolf in the kingship by apostolic authority and most strictly commanded all the magnates of the kingdom to support him as their king, as was fitting. Throughout Swabia also, but especially in the neighbourhood of the Danube, peace was utterly overthrown as the warlike hosts of the two factions raged against each other uncontrollably in various tumults on all sides, devoting themselves with all their might to plunder, destruction and burning and openly invading and seizing for themselves the property of others, especially church property.

At the same time Empress Agnes, who had long been making the greatest exertions to allay such discords, departed this life with a happy death on 14 December. For eighteen years[472] after she had been consecrated with the holy veil she eagerly followed the course of the religious life, rejecting royal glory and the alluring charms of a worldly existence in favour of the kingdom of God. She always tirelessly *continued in* psalm singing and *prayers night and day.*[473] As she was truly a follower of Christ, she most zealously *crucified* her *flesh with its vices and lusts*[474] and most truly denied herself. Indeed tears were given to her ceaselessly by

---

471 See Meyer von Knonau (1900) pp. 75–8; Schumann (1912) p. 43; Cowdrey (1998) p. 175; Robinson (1999) p. 172. The legate's judgement had no influence on the papal policy of neutrality: Gregory VII, *Register* V.14a, c. 6; V.15, pp. 370–1, 374–6. See Vogel (1983) p. 102; Robinson (1999) p. 179.

472 Sixteen years: above p. 117 and n. 102. Her death: Meyer von Knonau (1900) pp. 93–5; Bulst-Thiele (1933) pp. 110–11; Black-Veldtrup (1995) pp. 58–61, 100, 342.

473 Cf. I Timothy 5:5; Peter Damian, *Letter* 104, p. 150 (to Agnes).

474 Galatians 5:24.

heaven as her bread, together with remorse of the heart that is greatly to be desired, thus, like Hezekiah, always *reflecting all* her *years in the bitterness of* her *soul*.[475] For the greater she was in the great affairs of the world, the more she humbled herself in all things. The Holy Spirit, therefore, looked with favour on her who was humble and poor in spirit.[476] After she laid aside her royal ornaments and dispersed them among the poor of Christ and the churches, she wore ordinary garments, taking care especially, not only in this but in all things, that nothing should be excessive.[477] She was accustomed to be her own principal accuser and in her daily confessions to cleanse herself not only of her deeds but even of her irregular thoughts and dreams.[478] Indeed she was always to have with her as her inseparable companions spiritual directors to whom she owed obedience and whom she knew to be more devout and more prudent than the rest and she desired with the utmost discretion everywhere to be fortified by their daily reading, discourse, discipline and salutary meditation. For whatever burden they placed upon her, requiring her obedience, that willing subject of God would take upon herself in full and without delay. Her *fasting*[479] was *sincere* and *not superstitious*; her nourishment was moderate, very frugal and remarkably free from indulgence, and there was always a reading from the holy Scriptures at her table, which was also food and a delightful refreshment for the soul. There *Christ* was always courteously entertained *as a guest*[479] in the shape of the poor. For she *made friends* for herself *by the mammon of unrighteousness so that when* she *had used it all up, they might receive* her *into the eternal dwelling-places*.[480] Whatever was available to her from her hereditary estates, which in the case of so great a personage yielded a very handsome income, except for her obvious necessities, she had carefully given away in this manner every day. She entirely avoided *warm baths* and *the softness of feathers*. Her bed was very often the ground[481] or some other very hard surface, covered with a rush mat, a carpet or a very small quantity of straw,[482] and when, overcome by sleep, she had

475 Isaiah 38:15, perhaps confused with Ezekiel 27:31.

476 Isaiah 66:2; Luke 1:48.

477 Cf. Peter Damian, *Letters* 104, 124, pp. 149, 411.

478 Cf. Jerome, *Epistola* 23 c. 2, *CSEL* 54, 212.

479/479 Allusions to Jerome, *Epistola* 52 c. 5, 12, *CSEL* 54, 422, 435. Cf. *Epistolae* 125 c. 7, 130 c. 11, *CSEL* 56, 124, 191.

480 Luke 16:9 (a favourite quotation of Jerome).

481 Cf. Jerome, *Epistolae* 107 c. 11, 125 c. 7, *CSEL* 55, 124; *ibid.*, 56, 124; *Epistolae* 38 c. 4, 79 c. 7, 130 c. 4, *ibid.*, 54, 292, *ibid.*, 55, 96, *ibid.*, 56, 179.

482 Cf. Jerome, *Translatio latina Regulae s. Pachomii*, preface c. 4, *MPL* 23, col. 65; Caesarius of Arles, *Regula ad virgines* c. 41, *MPL* 67, col. 1116.

refreshed her frail body for a little while, she at once devoted herself again most diligently to her customary vigils and prayers. Christ was in her heart and His word or a psalm was always in her mouth. Of the hardships that she took upon herself, He alone with Whom she had so close a relationship *is a witness and has full knowledge.*[483] She impressed all her servants beyond measure by her long labours even during the night. The industrious woman served Christ by sewing clothes for the poor with her own hands, by very carefully bathing, cherishing, clothing and visiting the filthiest of the poor, especially those suffering from the scab, the leprous, the ulcerous, those who were wasting away through the issue of corrupted blood or stinking from some disease or other. Towards all the servants of God she showed herself humble in all things, most humane and generous in every way, as they themselves in their multitudes proclaimed without ceasing and as crowds of people throughout the lands also cried out together. She tried indeed to allow all persons who lived the religious life in churches and monasteries everywhere to share in some measure in the distribution of her bounty and thus that most zealous woman was remembered in both the private and the communal prayers of the brethren.[484]

She was violently opposed, however, to heretics and hypocrites, and especially nicholaites and simoniacs, and was authoritative and masterly in her refutation of their views, as she was very free with her invective against them all and very harsh *without respect of persons.*[485] For when at first she was urgently requested by some of the magnates of the kingdom to remain in the German territories in order to check or to moderate the childish and subsequently the juvenile errors of her son, as his adviser and corrector with maternal discipline and freedom, more skilful and on more confidential terms than the rest, for some time she agreed to the request.[486] Finally, however, after she had so often admonished her son and his closest advisers, *reproving*, chiding, *exhorting, in season* as well as *out of season*,[487] and they had not made the slightest improvement on that account but on the contrary were endeavouring to do worse, she came to seem totally detestable and wearisome. Refusing

483 Job 16:20.

484 Agnes's role in monastic reform: Jakobs (1968) pp. 266–8.

485 Romans 2:11. See above n. 153.

486 Agnes's relations with princes critical of Henry IV: Meyer von Knonau (1894) pp. 280–1, 383, 777; Jakobs (1968) pp. 269–71; Jakobs (1973) pp. 106–12; Robinson (1999) pp. 125–8. Her residence in Rome and later interventions at the German court: Black-Veldtrup (1995) pp. 37–61, 94–100.

487 II Timothy 4:2.

to endure any longer so many acts of insolence and robbery, of envy and hostility, their follies and their manifold acts of insanity, she removed herself once and for all with all her followers to Rome, to St Peter and the dwelling-places of so many saints. There every day she spent whatever she could of her property for the use of the poor and thus progressing from day to day in a holy and religious life, she always *reached forward to* what was to come and *forgot* what lay in the past. *Fighting* lawfully for *the prize of the high calling of God* and *finishing* her *race*,[488] she triumphantly and gloriously achieved her goal in that place.

When, however, the time was at hand when so very blessed a life was to be rewarded for its very many magnificent acts of piety, she was seized by a fever stronger than usual and indeed lethal, although she herself, being skilled in the art of medicine had been accustomed on many previous occasions to lessen such extreme attacks. For fourteen days she suffered greatly as she wasted and pined away, her body growing ever weaker from hour to hour, but her mind being strengthened and invigorated ever more graciously in Christ. Finally, when she had come to her end, after she had most wisely disposed of her property for the use of the poor and the churches, she summoned to her in the first place the lord pope and all the persons most dear to her among her faithful followers and friends and to them she said her last farewell and commended her soul. And after all her affairs had been settled according to her wishes and she had then most devoutly received the eucharist, while the others prayed and sang psalms and she herself joined them in psalm singing and thanksgiving, she joyfully commended her spirit into the hands of God and St Peter and St Paul. At last, after the funeral rites and masses and also almsgiving and vigils had been solemnly performed for some days for the sake of her soul, the lord pope gave honourable burial to the holy body of Empress Agnes, whom he had so often freed from her sins by his apostolic pardon and absolution, in a designated tomb in the church of St Petronella, which in ancient times was called the Vatican of Apollo, next to the altar of the Lord, namely at the side of St Petronella,[489] while the hymns and songs of praise of the whole Roman church harmonised with his action.

In the summer of the same year the prefect of the city of Rome[490] was

---

488 Cf. Philippians 3:13–14; II Timothy 4:7.

489 5 January 1078. Cf. Peter Damian, *Letter* 144, p. 526 (to Agnes, 1067): 'May it please you to have your burial [in Rome] together with St Petronella.' See Bulst-Thiele (1933) p. 111; Black-Veldtrup (1995) pp. 342–5.

490 Cencius, Roman prefect (?1071–7), son of the prefect John Tiniosus.

treacherously killed by certain kinsmen of Quintius.[491] He had already long before made a complete confession of his sins to the lord pope and, being converted to God, he most earnestly wished once and for all to leave the world with all its seductive delights and to enter the perfection of the monastic life. He was, however, utterly forbidden to do so by the pope, on his obedience, and commanded to remain in his office of prefect,[492] so that, armed with zeal for God, as *a judge* most devoted to equity and *justice*,[493] he might offer resistance to so many evildoers and joyfully fight for Christ in this obedience. And he obediently performed this with all his might, exerting himself in every way. He, therefore, very shrewdly opposed – *with perfect hatred*[494] and worthy persecution – Quintius, the chief of all the evildoers, because of his many acts of plundering and highway-robbery and because that wicked man in his contempt for God seized the lord pope while he was in the church, standing at the altar during the celebration of mass and dragged him off to his tower.[495] In this struggle, undertaken because of his obedience, this man of God was a perfect zealot, hostile towards heretics, a just judge, a generous distributor of alms, granted the gift of great remorse and of tears when he earnestly said his prayers, distinguished for his love of chastity and abstinence, for he was lawfully married in his youth and, becoming a widower soon afterwards, he *remained* in this condition thereafter, according to the advice of the apostle,[496] and manfully suppressed the youthful ardour within himself. He was charitable, humble, hospitable, pleasant, friendly, steadfast, modest, patient and long-suffering, an adherent of peace and truth, a diligent soldier and practitioner of remarkable piety. In his first attempt to lead a blessed life and to practise Christian knighthood[497] he *walked* wisely *in the flesh*, but *did not make war according to the flesh*,[498] and he ended his

491 Stephen, brother of Cencius Stephani (n. 263): Bonizo, *To a friend* VIII, p. 243. The date of the murder: Bernold, *Chronicle* 1077, below p. 260.

492 Cf. Paul, *Life of Pope Gregory VII* c. 47, p. 294 ('not like a layman but more like a faithful monk serving God'). See also Peter Damian, *Letters* 135, 145, pp. 456–62, 527–31; 155, pp. 71–3. Gregory VII and 'princes who fear God' wishing to renounce the world (cf. *Register* VI.17, pp. 423–4): Robinson (1973) pp. 190–1; Cowdrey (1998) pp. 674–6.

493 Psalm 9:5. 'Fighting for Christ' (*militare Christo*) in Gregorian thought: Erdmann (1935) pp. 185–211.

494 Psalm 138:22.

495 See above p. 142.

496 Cf. I Corinthians 7:39–40.

497 See Erdmann (1935) pp. 187, 189–94.

498 II Corinthians 10:3.

earthly life triumphant in a fortunate martyrdom for the sake of righteousness and faith and at once succeeded in exchanging for that life the ineffable immortality of eternal life and the loveliness of the ever verdant paradise that is to be desired before all things. He was indeed mourned by the Roman citizens, but especially by the magnates of the city, with great wailing and lamentation, as was fitting. After a funeral service of appropriate magnificence had been celebrated very dutifully and honourably in St Peter's according to the Roman rite, he was most devotedly placed in a marble tomb in the middle of the portico of [the church] with the necessary hymns of praise and thanksgiving and so by means of this most fitting burial he was most earnestly committed by all men to God and St Peter.

At last indeed because during his lifetime the young knight fought most zealously for the citizenship [of heaven] and because he truly *used the world as one who did not abuse it*,[499] it became clear to all men and as a result of so many miracles and wonders it was more and more obviously manifest not only to the Romans but also to all who flocked there from all sides how great he was before God. For God performed so many and such mighty works there because of his merits that it could be proved that they truly happened, except to certain persons, namely his enemies. In order, therefore, to refute publicly their envious refusal to believe, now in the following Roman synod[500] certain miracles were committed to writing as having happened beyond all doubt, according to the evidence of very many distinguished and trustworthy men of great authority, and were publicly read out and it is entirely unlawful for anyone to doubt the truth of their account. Something that is said actually to have happened to him during his lifetime, indeed in the very year of his murder, greatly astonished the Romans. For one day, when he entered a certain oratory in order to pray, before the end of his prayer two hairs measuring as long as a finger had grown on the thumb of his hand. When he saw this, both he and all those to whom he immediately showed it were amazed and both then and subsequently he used to ponder on it with wonder.

In that same synod certain miracles were also read out that happened in Milan at the tomb of the lord Herlembald,[501] who had *suffered for*

---

499 I Corinthians 7:31.

500 I.e. in the Roman synod of Lent 1078. Cf. Bonizo, *To a friend* VIII, p. 243; Paul, *Life of Pope Gregory VII* c. 92, p. 334. See Erdmann (1935) pp. 198, 231.

501 Herlembald Cotta, Milanese knight, leader of the Patarini (+1075). See Erdmann (1935) pp. 128–31; Cowdrey (1968a) pp. 31, 35.

righteousness' sake[502] three years before, and that were proved to be entirely true by trustworthy persons who were present there and by letters confirming them. He was a most eloquent orator and a most skilful athlete of God following the secular way of life, who restored canonical discipline and observance. In his zeal for God he offered such strong resistance to the nicholaites and simoniacal heretics that scarcely one of them remained in the whole bishopric of Milan who had not been corrected or converted. If anyone was found who was hostile and disobedient towards the rigour of canon law, however, [Herlembald] immediately took his troops of knights and compelled them to accept the judgement of the canons or put them to flight or captured and imprisoned them and plundered and squandered all their possessions. In revenge for his deeds certain of the Milanese, who were supporters and flatterers of their simoniac bishop [Godfrey] (whom he opposed with all the power at his disposal) and also of King Henry (who had set that same heretic over them), killed [Herlembald]. They craftily ambushed the champion of God, distinguished for his righteousness and faithfulness[503] and for the obedience that the lord Pope Alexander [II] imposed on him for this purpose,[504] and they pierced him with five lances at the same time. After they had killed him in a city street, for three days those most cruel men with swords in their hands forbade the burial of the lifeless corpse.[505] On the third night, however, a light came down from heaven in the dead of night that was so very bright that certain persons who were more than ten miles away from the city had no doubt at all that there was a fire in the city and it shone on the body for the space of three hours. And among the very many people who had flocked there because of that wondrous sign were certain brothers who had been forewarned of this by visions while they slept. Boldly approaching, they took up his body and buried him in the monastery of the holy martyr Celsus with the obligatory prayers and funeral service, giving thanks to God, as was fitting. Finally it was proved by heaven beyond all doubt on the evidence of many wonders and miracles that this man of God, who was so active an opponent of heretical wickedness, was truly a *friend of God*.[506] No one should regret the diligence and

502 Matthew 5:10.

503 Cf. I Maccabees 14:35.

504 See Erdmann (1935) pp. 127–30; Schmidt (1977) pp. 9–10.

505 15 April 1075. His assassin was Arnaldus, grandfather of Arnaldus de Raude, Milanese consul in 1136: Landulf Junior de sancto Paulo, *Historia Mediolanensis* c. 66, p. 48. See Meyer von Knonau (1894) pp. 474–6; Cowdrey (1968a) pp. 38–9.

506 Judith 8:22; James 2:23.

the energy with which any knight of the Supreme King and defender of the holy faith bravely and joyfully devotes himself to Christ, if after bringing his lawful struggle to an end, he earned the delight of being crowned forever with so excellent a triumph of heavenly glory.[507]

In this same year a certain woman in Swabia gave birth to a boy with very little life in him and with him a head like that of a human being but lacking any human limbs, although alive and with all its senses well fashioned in the manner of a human being. When that infant, being at the very point of death, was baptised, the midwives also took the other, although secretly because of a certain feeling of shame, and giving it a name, like a complete human being, they baptised it in the name of the holy Trinity. Shortly afterwards, however, it died.

1078. King Rudolf celebrated Christmas [25 December 1077] with the greatest splendour in Goslar in Saxony with very many multitudes of the Saxon people. King Henry, however, after spending only two days somehow or other in Regensburg[508] with very little festivity, hastily returned to the siege of a certain castle, from which he had come there. He wandered aimlessly from place to place in that region of eastern Bavaria until the middle of Lent and he attacked that land and laid it waste during his many comings and goings.[509] From there he also sent his envoys, the bishop of Osnabrück[510] and the bishop [Theoderic of] Verdun, to the lord pope in Rome and to the Roman synod to plead his cause there. In a very cunning subterfuge he made absolutely no mention of the papal legation and his contempt for, his trampling on and his disobedience towards the Roman cardinal [Bernard]'s letter of admonition to him[511] – about which he had strenuously made a public declaration to one and all – as if he had never heard of it or knew very little about it. He awaited their return from the synod to Regensburg[512] with no little anxiety, for he was in no doubt that some news would be

507 Cf. Wisdom 4:2; II Timothy 2:5.

508 Cf. the inauthentic *D.H.IV* 303, dated Regensburg, 30 December. See Meyer von Knonau (1900) p. 73.

509 Lent 1078: 21 February–7 April. On the basis of the undated *DD.H.IV* 304–5, Meyer von Knonau (1900) pp. 96–7 concluded that Henry was mainly in Passau in these weeks.

510 Benno II (1068–88). This mission: *Register* VII.14a, c. 7, p. 485 ('two bishops from among his supporters, namely of Verdun and Osnabrück, came to Rome and in the synod asked me on Henry's behalf to do justice to him'). See Meyer von Knonau (1900) pp. 98–9; Vogel (1983) pp. 104–5.

511 See above p. 184 and n. 451.

512 He was in Regensburg on 20 March: *D.H.IV* 306.

brought back to him from the apostolic see that would greatly displease him, as indeed he deserved (as his own conscience bore witness).

King Rudolf and likewise all his supporters had also sent envoys[513] to that same synod, although not the envoys whom they had wished but those whomsoever they had been able to send and then only by skilful and secret means. They promised the lord pope their true obedience in all things and unanimously and most sagaciously requested that he would deign to turn his attention with paternal solicitude to the tyrannical and so lamentable desolation of holy Church. But because the envoys of King Henry could openly travel and accomplish everything that they wished peaceably and according to their wishes, both in Lombardy and in the city of Rome itself, they never ceased, by means of gifts, lies, promises, flatteries, tearful complaints and all their skill and ingenuity (as they were most expert in such matters), to corrupt, deceive and seduce all men, from the least to the greatest, and bring them over to support their king and, on the other hand, to hate and to utter the most malicious falsehoods against King Rudolf.

The synod then began on the appointed date, that is 5 March, according to the regulations of canon law, and consisted of almost seventy bishops.[514] Among them was the bishop [Peter] of Albano, who was one of the brethren who dwell in the diocese of Florence, in the place that is called Vallombrosa. He passed through a fire twelve feet in length, untouched by the flames and unharmed, and thus proved through an obvious judgement that Peter, who was called the bishop of the church of Florence, was in truth a simoniacal heretic and that therefore neither he nor his heretical offices ought to be received.[515] Also present there, from the region of France, was the bishop of Die,[516] who became a bishop as a result not of human but of divine election. For when he was travelling from his home to Rome in order to pray there, he arrived in the city of Die to spend the night there. The legate of the apostolic see, Bishop Gerald of Ostia, however, was in that place at the same time, assembling a council for the sake of the welfare and the needs of

---

513 Names unknown: cf. Gregory VII, *Register* VII.14a, p. 485: 'Rudolf's envoys'.

514 *Register* V.13, p. 366: the synod was to take place 'in the first week of Lent', i.e. 27 February–3 March. *Register* V.14a, p. 368: it was attended by 'archbishops and bishops of various cities numbering almost 100'. See Meyer von Knonau (1900) p. 104; Cowdrey (1998) pp. 180–1.

515 See above pp. 120–2 and nn. 138–9.

516 Hugh, bishop of Die (1073–82/3), archbishop of Lyons (1082/3–1106). See Cowdrey (1998) pp. 356–66. His presence in Rome: *Register* V.22, p. 386. Cf. the account of Hugh's election in Hugh, *Chronicon* II, pp. 410–11.

the church,[517] and when he saw him, he rejoiced greatly at his arrival, for he was known to him and was his great friend. Kissing him, he at once said: 'You are welcome because this church has been bereaved and deprived of its bishop and, if God grants it, we shall have you as bishop and prelate in his place.' The other smiled very modestly, thinking that he had said this to him as a joke. Then, when he had realised the truth – that this was said to him not as a joke but in earnest – he obtained from him with difficulty a delay until the next day before he made his reply. That night he considered with all his might how he could possibly escape the burden of the pastoral office. Without his companions being aware of it, he secretly withdrew from their company and stole away alone to conceal himself in a hiding-place in a certain church in that place. When in the morning he could not be found despite long and extensive searches in all directions, the papal legate assembled the clergy and all the people and went with them from church to church in a great procession, with litanies and public prayers, most devoutly requesting him from the Lord. But when they arrived at the church where the runaway was hiding, a light sent from heaven shone down on him and disclosed God's elect.[518] After he had been discovered in this way, he submitted to the divine command and was compelled, although unwillingly, to undertake the high office from which he had fled with humble heart. The *faithful and wise steward*[519] of God's mysteries was accustomed always to have such men of great authority and reverence with him and he most sagaciously relied on their advice for the achievement of his concerns and his decrees.

In the same synod the envoys of King Henry – encouraged by so many supporters whom they had somehow or other acquired and putting their trust in them – had above all publicly promised the lord pope obedience in all things on the part of their lord and an obedience that might be tested in any way. Finally, presenting [Henry's] case, they complained about the injuries that he had suffered and did so very skilfully (for they were talkative and very well taught in all manner of rhetorical figures and in oratorical declamation), at first speaking particularly to [the pope] and afterwards to the whole assembly. All

---

517 Cf. Hugh, *Chronicon* II, p. 410: 'returning to Rome after holding a council in Chalon-sur-Saône and staying as a guest in the city of Die'.

518 This incident is not found in Hugh of Flavigny's account. Cf. the similar incident in Berthold's account of Gregory VII's election, above p. 128 and n. 191. The literary model for both passages is John the Deacon, *Vita Gregorii Magni* I.44, MPL 75, col. 81B. See Goggin (1995) pp. 6–9, 342–4.

519 Luke 12:42.

those who supported him murmured their unanimous support and very strongly recommended that the judgement of the pope and the synod should be that [his case] was most just. The main argument of his case was this: that Rudolf, a duke and vassal of King Henry, who had sworn oaths in confirmation of his promise to be faithful and to be his inseparable helper in all matters relating to the defence of his kingdom, had broken his oaths and committed treachery in that he had, together with his supporters, unjustly expelled him from his kingdom and that he had rashly seized the kingdom for himself.[520] They declared that their lord had not made this complaint out of desperation, that is, because he could not very easily overcome his enemies: he made it principally because it seemed to him just and fitting to appeal first and foremost to the apostolic see for a decision on this matter. Some judges, who were well disposed towards their plans, indiscriminately favoured the idea that King Rudolf deserved to be condemned without delay with the sentence of papal anathema because he was guilty of such palpable and sacrilegious wrongdoing and they requested very urgently that the judicial procedures should be followed and a decision reached according to canon law.

The lord pope, however, was fully aware of the confused circumstances of the present case and he could not easily be misled by anyone's flattering arguments into showing *partiality to certain persons*.[521] He declared publicly that he could make no decision about this before there had been a careful examination of both parties and while the truth about the excommunication pronounced by his cardinal [Bernard] was still in doubt.[522] He acknowledged that he had on many occasions heard promises of obedience, envoys' messages and declarations from each of the kings, both of whom indeed were followed and supported in different ways by a considerable party of the magnates, bishops and wise and religious men of the kingdom. He therefore announced that it was appropriate and necessary for him in such a matter to receive the advice of the great men and office-holders of the holy Roman see and of whomsoever he could, indeed of all wise men, and to take sufficient time

---

520 Cf. Henry IV, *Letter* 17, p. 25: 'our vassal, whom [the pope] himself appointed as a perjured king over us'; Wido of Ferrara, *De scismate Hildebrandi* I.7, p. 540. The Henrician argument: Wenrich of Trier, *Epistola* c. 6, p. 294; Theoderic of Verdun, letter in *Codex Udalrici* 62, p. 130; synodal decree of Brixen (1080) in Henry IV, *Letters* appendix C, p. 71; Wido of Ferrara, *De scismate* I.7, pp. 539–41. See the concern with oath-breaking in Wido of Osnabrück, *Liber de controversia* pp. 469–70, commissioned by Benno of Osnabrück, Henry 's envoy to the Lenten synod of 1078.

521 Romans 2:11. See above n. 153.

522 On 12 November 1077: above p. 191.

over this, so that the apostolic see should not make an unjust decision against either of [the kings]. For this reason he prudently requested and reminded them all most devoutly to pray together to God that He might deign to inspire them with the spirit of His heavenly counsel and that by His authority the holy mother Church, which was wretchedly torn apart by so many heresies, schisms and conflicts, might become worthy of being united and pacified in Christ.

In this way the decision was postponed until Saturday and other matters that were useful to the needs and the service of the Church were very carefully considered and settled with due regard to canon law. In the matter of King Henry's complaint the pope and all who consulted with him in Christ devised and decided on a wise and very just plan. Either the lord pope himself or suitable legates in his place would enter German territory[523] and there, in a place that was most appropriate for this purpose, should meet the magnates of the whole kingdom, the wise and every member of the nobility except for the two kings. A conference would be held there and every aspect of the cases of the two [kings] would be investigated and discussed most justly and *without respect of persons*[524] and would be either vindicated or condemned by them all. And thus according to the universal, wise and most just judgement and advice of all of them, they would decide irrevocably how a *kingdom* so wretchedly turned to schism and treachery *against itself* might at least not be *brought* entirely *to desolation*[525] but rather united and restored in Christ and strengthened in a reasonable manner.

On Saturday the lord pope, who had made his lawful and methodical preparations for this purpose, entered the synod together with his suffragans and publicly explained to them all the aforementioned plan. And when they had all given their approval, armed with confident eloquence and apostolic authority, he issued a general condemnation with the sanction of anathema, which is always greatly to be feared, of all men, whether kings or dukes, bishops, clergy or whoever else, greater or lesser men, who by means of cunning and subtlety, fraud, partisanship or any device whatsoever willingly exerted themselves somehow or other to undermine or hinder the planned conference so that it would not take place and those who in any way showed hostility towards the legates of the apostolic see so that they could not reach

---

523 Cf. Gregory VII, *Register* V.14a, c. 6, p. 370: 'suitable ... legates are to be sent from the side of the apostolic see to that territory'.

524 Romans 2:11. See above n. 153.

525 Luke 11:17.

that same conference and those who refused to accept and to observe inviolably the decisions concerning this matter and also concerning the conflict and the very great dissensions, decisions reached by the general agreement of the papal legates and the magnates of the kingdom, noble and wise men nominated and chosen to give their consent.[526] After this sentence of condemnation was decreed and after the pope and his suffragans had thrown burning candles on the ground and extinguished them, to complete that anathema according to canon law, [the pope] first, in order to test the obedience of King Henry, most urgently begged and implored him by the Lord God and with the feeling of an apostolic father admonished him through his envoys that, if he loved him, he should keep the peace with all his enemies until the end of the conference. Then [the pope], exerting himself to bring [Henry] to consent to the agreement and to honour it in all respects, wisely resolved to send to him his messengers together with [Henry's] own envoys so that he himself might decide the time and the place of the future conference according to his own pleasure. And when this had been announced and made known without prevarication to the magnates of the kingdom and all those who were to be summoned there, the papal messenger[527] was to return to Rome so that the legates of the apostolic see, appointed and chosen for this task, might reach the assembly dealing with this present case at the appropriate time and by a direct route, to act as suitable advisers, mediators and correctors. After the lord pope had dismissed the royal envoys, without, however, giving them the papal blessing that they were to have brought to the king – because a rumour current everywhere, although of dubious value, asserted that he had already been excommunicated by the papal legates – he preoccupied himself efficiently with the business that remained to be settled in the synod.

In the same synod sentence of excommunication was imposed on the bishops of Ravenna,[528] [Tedald of] Milan, Cremona[529] and Treviso[530] and on all simoniacal heretics and nicholaites who obstinately and disobediently persevered willingly and deliberately in their insane

---

526 Cf. Gregory VII, *Register* V.14a, c. 6; V.15, pp. 370–1, 375–6.

527 I.e. the unknown 'bearer' mentioned in *Register* V.15, p. 376.

528 Wibert of Parma, archbishop of Ravenna (1072–1100), antipope Clement III (1084–1100). See Schwartz (1913) p. 158. Cf. synodal protocol, *Register* V.14a, c. 1, p. 369.

529 Arnulf (1066–?91). See Schwartz (1913) p. 112. Cf. synodal protocol c. 2, p. 369.

530 Roland (n. 272). Cf. synodal protocol c. 3, p. 369. The following canons in Berthold's text do not appear in *Register* V.14a. Englberger (1997) pp. 100–1 argued that they were an invention of Berthold.

error and especially on those who, rashly, obstinately and intemperately had within two years received back ecclesiastical orders that they had acquired through payment and had then abandoned and who with the presumption of apostates had taken back concubines who had been forbidden to them. There was indeed a considerable number of such men in our region who in open tyranny raged most insanely against the authentic decrees of the holy canons. Those who presumed to have themselves ordained, or rather unordained, by bishops who had been deprived by apostolic decree of their office and of the priestly dignity – and who had not yet been restored to their orders either by [the pope] himself or by an approved legate, wherever they had dared to usurp their office – were deprived by judicial sentence irrevocably, without hope of restoration, of all orders and consecrations, except only for baptism. It was there decided and decreed that any churches that such men had consecrated, since they had never been dedicated to God according to canon law, ought to be consecrated afresh.[531]

The sentence of excommunication was imposed also on laymen, whatsoever their rank, on clergy and on all persons, whoever they might be, who, contrary to the decrees of the holy canons, presumed to give bishoprics, abbacies, provostships, any churches of whatever kind, tithes or any ecclesiastical offices whatsoever as benefices, according to their ancient unlawful custom, to any clerk or to any person whatsoever; or who presumed to grant and bestow with a lay hand, which was not consecrated to God – as if it was their personal property and inheritance – what originally was lawfully assigned to the Lord God as His possession and for His service and surrendered according to canon law and what belongs to the care and superintendence of the ministers of the altar and the stewards of the churches, who are consecrated to God.[532]

Sentence of excommunication was also pronounced there on anyone who presumed to despoil or to rob or by any cunning and rash device to attack the churches dedicated to God or the churchyards, cemeteries and cloisters, likewise consecrated, or the property, estates or any other appurtenances of the churches.[533] These particulars are understood

---

531 Cf. legatine council of Gerona (held by Bishop Amatus of Oloron, March/June 1078) c. 11, *Sacra Concilia* 20, col. 519.

532 The relationship of this canon (mentioned only by Berthold) to the papal prohibition of lay investiture: Schieffer (1981) pp. 168–71; Englberger (1997) pp. 102–17; Cowdrey (1998) pp. 405–6 and n. 341.

533 Cf. council of Gerona c. 13, *Sacra Concilia* 20, col. 520.

to refer both generally and specifically by name above all to the daily allowances and the various forms of administration of foodstuffs and necessary resources of canons, clergy, priests, monks, nuns and all those serving Christ according to a *Rule*.

The intention of the lord pope in making decrees of this kind had been especially that there should be peace throughout the churches[534] and, although wars and dissension predominated everywhere in the secular sphere, nevertheless among spiritual persons the worship of God and the life of prayer according to canon law should by no means cease because of the failure of material resources. The offences of subjects must sometimes be prudently overlooked but at other times, when they are widely known about, they must be borne with for the time being so that they may be corrected at a more opportune moment, because remedies only become available in the course of time.[535] The lord pope, therefore, prudently overlooked and bore with offences and very solicitously deferred judgement on the heretical wickedness, the disobedience and the many thousands of unlawful acts and scandals on the part of many bishops and priests in the German and Italian territories[536] until a suitable time, so that subsequently – after those very great divisions of the princes and nobles of the kingdom, who were fighting among themselves with such turbulence and with a partisanship worse than civil war,[537] had somehow with God's help been brought to an end and they had lawfully been reunited in the peace of Christ – he might at last no longer hesitate and with the greatest care and sagacity pursue them with correction, judgement and punishment.

The envoys of King Rudolf were sent away privately and secretly after seeking permission from [the pope] clandestinely and most circumspectly.[538] Because he had no doubt at all that [Rudolf] was most obedient towards and in agreement with himself and the apostolic see, he carefully and vigilantly sent his fatherly love, compassion and grace, together with the apostolic absolution and blessing, to him and to all

534 Cf. Gregory VII, *Register* V.15, p. 375: 'for the restoration of your peace'.

535 Cf. *Register* V.17, p. 378: 'the custom of the holy Roman church ... is to bear with some things and even to overlook some things, following the moderation of discretion rather than the rigour of canon law'.

536 Perhaps the cases of Bishops Huzman of Speyer (*Register* V.18, pp. 381–2), Henry I of Liège (*ibid.*, VI.4, pp. 396–7), Pibo of Toul (*ibid.*, VI.5, pp. 398–9) and the rebellious clergy of S. Martino of Lucca (*ibid.*, VI.11, pp. 412–13).

537 Cf. Lucan, *Bellum civile* I.1.

538 Cf. the Saxons' complaints to Gregory VII: Bruno, *Saxon War* c. 108, p. 98. See Vogel (1983) pp. 104, 116.

men, the greater and the lesser, who continued obediently to submit to the commands and decrees of the apostolic see and unanimously to support it willingly and zealously.

King Henry finally waited in Regensburg for some of his envoys, who had hastened to him more rapidly than the rest, and after he met them there, almost immediately he moved on from there in haste and in a rather sorrowful state of mind to Mainz, in order to spend Palm Sunday [1 April] there.[539] From there he proceeded to Cologne, after gathering around him such forces of knights as he could. There he celebrated Easter [8 April] with very little splendour. After his envoys,[540] together with the messengers of the apostolic see and likewise the papal legation, had now returned to him and he had taken the greatest care to find out a true account of everything that had been enacted and decided in the Roman synod, he at once with the greatest ingenuity turned to his customary senseless cunning and gathered his closest advisers around him. They advised him especially and with all their efforts and all their sagacity they contrived above all to appear to have freed him from that papal excommunication[541] without any regard for or obedience to the pope's command and decree and with all the appearance of justice to have placed the whole burden of the Roman anathema – which hung over them because of their obvious guilt – on King Rudolf and all the associates of the opposition party.

King Rudolf, however, celebrated Easter with great solemnity in Goslar, where he assembled a large number of his Saxon princes and his knights. There a certain canon, a most venerable and well-educated clerk named Wigold, who had already been tested by being appointed provost in the church of St Maurice, was first elected bishop of the church of Augsburg in truly canonical fashion by the clergy and people and by the better and greater part of the ecclesiastical dignitaries and by the election and through the consent of the Roman cardinal [Bernard] and of his metropolitan, the archbishop [Siegfried] of Mainz, and of nine other bishops who had assembled there, he was consecrated and ordained as bishop according to canon law on Easter day.[542] After everything

---

539 Cf. *DD.H.IV* 306 (Regensburg, 20 March), 307 (Würzburg, 25 March). See Meyer von Knonau (1900) pp. 121–2.

540 Benno II of Osnabrück and Theoderic of Verdun: above p. 198. The identity of the papal legates is unknown: Schumann (1912) pp. 44–5.

541 I.e. the excommunication by Cardinal deacon Bernard on 12 November 1077.

542 The election of Wigold (see above p. 187 and n. 456) was 'the classic example of a correct canonical appointment according to the Gregorians: Mirbt (1894) p. 500. See Schieffer (1981) pp. 170–1; Cowdrey (1998) pp. 542, 549.

lawfully pertaining to his ordination had been lawfully performed – that is, after he had received the ring, the pastoral staff and the episcopal throne from the archbishop of Mainz – the king for his part assiduously conferred on him what belonged to the royal jurisdiction, namely the administration of ecclesiastical property. For, as he was most obedient in all things, he took heed of what had recently been decided according to canon law in the Roman synod[543] and, after the judgement had lawfully been pronounced, had been condemned and forbidden on penalty of excommunication: that no layman should grant churches and ecclesiastical tithes and offices to any persons as their property or should presume to usurp them for themselves contrary to canon law. Moreover in the case of Siegfried, whom King Henry had placed in the bishopric of Augsburg in an uncanonical manner,[544] the archbishop of Mainz granted a truce and commanded him no longer to take possession of his bishopric so audaciously: otherwise he separated him and all his adherents entirely from the members of the Church by means of lawful excommunication. He issued the same threat to the canons of Augsburg and to the people if they did not accept their [bishop] elect, as was worthy and just. Thus the bishop of Augsburg, after receiving permission from the king, returned to his own land and prudently went with his followers to a certain castle near Füssen, because it was very strong and well fortified, there to wait for peace in the Church. There he was immediately assailed and troubled by the men of Augsburg, who inflicted very many wrongs on him. He bore it for some time, however, with considerable *forbearance and patience*[545] and most devoutly entrusted himself and his followers to God, the judge and defender.

After Easter King Henry immediately returned to Mainz and drew into his party all men, whoever they were and however he could entice them. He therefore made it known to the Saxon magnates – inveigling them to come to him by means of threatening and flattering speeches and arguments, mentioning that papal legation and papal judgement and using them as a pretext – that they should meet certain of the princes and noblemen of the kingdom in Fritzlar with the purpose of making peace and end so many divisions and conflicts throughout the

---

543 I.e. the Lenten synod of 1078: see above p. 204 and n. 532. This passage was taken as confirmation that that synod had issued an investiture decree by Schmid (1926) p. 193. The contrary argument: Schieffer (1981) pp. 170–3; Beulertz (1991) pp. 72–3; Englberger (1997) pp. 112–17.

544 See above p. 187 and n. 457.

545 Cf. Romans 2:4; Colossians 1:11; II Timothy 3:10.

kingdom.[546] The Saxon princes were delighted to hear this and were wisely spurred on by the persuasions of King Rudolf, but when they came at the agreed time to try to begin this work, King Henry sent there, apart from certain of his closest advisers, not one of the magnates of the kingdom.[547] Although they saw that they had been deceived in this way and resolved angrily to leave that place, at the urgent request of the courtiers, to whom all secrets were known,[548] they agreed to speak with them and to be led into temptation by them. There they heard nothing from them except lies about threats that the pope was supposed to have made against them because they had unjustly cast aside their lord and king, like lawless oath-breakers and traitors. They made no mention there of the truth about the aforesaid conference and the papal excommunication. Persistent and tenacious in their falsehood, they attached the whole account of the [papal] judgement to King Rudolf and his associates. When the Saxons had listened to this and at last very clearly understood why they had come there, so as not to be thought guilty of the charges that had been made against them and fearful of the coming of the lord pope and of the judgement that he had made, but rather to be proved to desire [his coming] most earnestly and to rejoice at it, they all approved the conference that he planned. They declared in public in a steadfast, most free and most emphatic manner that they awaited his arrival or that of his legates with impatience and that they would in all respects comply with his judgement and his decrees concerning this business and also those of all the magnates of the kingdom.[549] They confirmed and were certain in their judgement that all who were disobedient towards the lord pope and who opposed his judicial sentence in this matter by any device of cunning or folly should be excommunicated and actually separated from the members of the Church. In order to end the dispute between the two parties in this way, in a reasonable manner and in public, they sent their envoy with them to their lord and to the other princes of the kingdom who supported him. [The envoy] was to inform them of the place and time of the planned conference and he was to declare that they were entirely ready and prepared, if God willed it, to come there, setting aside all encumbrances and all hesitations. For

546 The Fritzlar negotiations (for which Berthold's chronicle is the only source): Meyer von Knonau (1900) pp. 123–5; Vogel (1983) p. 113; Robinson (1999) pp. 179–80.

547 Cf. Bernold, *Chronicle* 1078, below p. 262; Gregory VII, *Register* VI.1, p. 390; Saxons' letter to Gregory VII: Bruno, *Saxon War* c. 114, p. 106.

548 Cf. the Saxons' complaints about the king's 'familiars' in their letter to Gregory VII: Bruno, *Saxon War* c. 108, p. 98.

549 Cf. Saxons' letter, *ibid.*, pp. 97–9 (end of April 1078): Kost (1962) p. 106; Vogel (1983) p. 115.

some time there was a contentious discussion between the two sides, in which, however, the aforementioned unshakeable and just resolution of the Saxons concerning their obedience was newly restated in a praise-worthy manner, and afterwards peace was agreed by both sides until the forthcoming conference and they departed from one another and returned to their homes.

King Henry's advisers, however, taking with them the envoy of the Saxons, travelled towards the Rhine and to their lord. For what they had heard of the just and true language of the Saxon princes did not taste good on *the palate of their hearts.*[550] They had set out with a very different opinion and intention: namely, that of trying somehow or other to bring the Saxons over to their side. Since they could not achieve this, however, immediately on their return they spread a false rumour everywhere that [the Saxons] had certainly made a treaty of peace with their lord and had given hostages and that they undoubtedly deserved his lasting favour. They sent back [the Saxons'] envoy with this message. The king would not fix a place for any conference but for the sake of the lord pope and for love of him he was ready to do this: to receive back into his favour anyone who had rebelled against him, if only he surrendered to him in penitence and obedience.

When the Saxons and King Rudolf learned of this, however, they judged and proved that he was manifestly excommunicate, together with all his supporters, because he had so obstinately and disobediently prevented the conference that had been inviolably decreed by the pope.[551] The partisans of King Henry also showed their utter contempt for the peace that the king's advisers and the Saxons had agreed between them by attacking a certain castle[552] and storming it contrary to the promise that had been made, before the envoy [of the Saxons] had returned home to them. At the same time the bishop [Herman] of Metz[553] and very many other Lotharingians had come to King Henry under safe conduct and an attempt was made to bend them to his will. When they heard of his contempt for the papal legation, they openly declared that they would remain and be steadfast in the party of the lord pope and returned to their homes, forfeiting [Henry's] favour. He immediately

550 Cf. Augustine, *In Iohannis Evangelium* VII.2, *CC* 36, 68.

551 I.e. protocol of the Lenten synod, *Register* V.14a, c. 6, pp. 370–1. See above pp. 202–3.

552 Unidentified: Meyer von Knonau (1900) p. 131 and n. 47.

553 He was one of the recipients of the letter of the legate Abbot Bernard of St Victor (n. 428), urging him to resist Henry IV if the latter hindered the conference.

went in pursuit of them, taking with him Duke Theoderic[554] and many other bands of his knights. He unexpectedly seized the city of Metz by means of cunning, put the bishop and the rest to flight and, after he had established his garrison there, he set out for Strasbourg and entered the city. He remained there during the Rogation days [14–16 May] and enthroned Thiepald, provost of Constance,[555] who was also his chaplain, as bishop there against the will of the canons and against the command of the lord pope. For because they had been forbidden by the lord pope to receive anyone from King Henry, [the canons] decided to elect someone for themselves, according to canon law and unanimously in Christ. When, however, the canons of St Thomas[556] showed their assent and their strong approval for the appointment of [Thiepald], it was not long before they experienced God's vengeance. For fire engulfed the church, the chapter house and all their buildings and living quarters and they were burned to the ground. King Henry then planned to attack Swabia but, being unable to assemble sufficient forces to accomplish this without danger, he went in a different direction and entered Bavaria. There he celebrated Whitsun [27 May] in Regensburg and Margrave Leopold,[557] to whom he had given some offence, withdrew from there.

The papal legate,[558] who had come to King Henry at Eastertide to make arrangements for that conference that the pope had decreed, was held for some time in seclusion, above all because he very freely informed him – although he was reluctant and unwilling and paid all too little heed to the terrors with which he was threatened – of the subject of the papal legation. For this reason very many people suspected that [the legate] had been secretly killed or banished but at length he appeared in public and [Henry] treated him with reverence and conducted himself honourably towards him. Some people, however, conjectured that the reason for his being detained so long was that [Henry] might use him somehow to defend himself against the excommunication that had been imposed on him. For when everyone saw that the

554 Theoderic II (of Châtenois), duke of Upper Lotharingia (1070–1115). See Meyer von Knonau (1900) p. 131; Robinson (1999) p. 180.

555 Thiepald, bishop of Strasbourg (1078–82). See Meyer von Knonau (1900) p. 132; Schieffer (1981) p. 173 n. 310.

556 The church of St Thomas, Strasbourg: Dollinger (1991) pp. 154–6.

557 Leopold II, margrave of Austria (1075–95). The reason for his dissatisfaction is unknown: Meyer von Knonau (1900) p. 132. But cf. *D.H.IV* 305 (dated 1078), granting a property 'situated in the county of Margrave Leopold'.

558 Unknown: see above p. 206 and n. 540.

papal legate communicated with him, no one at all would believe that he was an excommunicate and no one avoided him. On the contrary, they were strongly of the opinion that whatever was said far and wide about the judgement of the Roman synod and the decision to impose the anathema[559] was a lie: because, like King Rudolf and the Roman cardinal, he could also produce a papal legate to bear witness to his obedience and his innocence publicly before all men.

King Rudolf, however, celebrated Whitsun in a magnificent manner in Goslar, where he gathered a great multitude of Saxon and Thuringian princes. Taking counsel with them there, he gave orders for an expedition against King Henry and made his preparations. Envoys from King Philip of France, from the men of Flanders, from very many Lotharingians and also from the king [Ladislaus I] of the Hungarians came to him there[560] and most eagerly promised him help in defending holy Church and the whole kingdom of the Germans for the sake of God and St Peter, although they did not at all perform what they had promised.

Subsequently throughout the whole of that summer violence boiled over in all parts of Swabia, Alsace and eastern Franconia, and in local feuds members of King Henry's faction conquered, slaughtered and put their enemies to flight, while plundering, burning and perpetrating very many acts of sacrilege even in the holy churches, which they audaciously profaned. Among them were the anti-bishops [Burchard] of Basel and [Thiepald of] Strasbourg, who barely managed to escape when their knights were valiantly encountered in battle, overcome and captured by a margrave, the son of Duke Berthold [I of Carinthia].[561] The peasants whom they had compelled to aid them everywhere throughout the counties that were their sworn adherents, were in some cases castrated. At that time Duke Berthold and Duke Welf [IV of Bavaria] laid waste to a great part of Franconia on this side of the Rhine with plunder and burning.

Meanwhile both kings planned expeditions against each other with the greatest eagerness and with extensive preparations, gathering

---

559 The excommunication by Cardinal deacon Bernard, 12 November 1077: above p. 191.

560 On Philip I: Kienast (1974) pp. 180–1. The attacks on Count Robert I of Flanders on Henry IV's supporters in Lower Lotharingia: Meyer von Knonau (1894) pp. 651, 678. Ladislaus I (n. 468) married Adelaide, Rudolf's daughter: cf. Bernold, *Chronicle* 1090, below p. 299.

561 Berthold II, margrave, duke of Swabia (1090–8), duke of Zähringen (1098–1111), son of Berthold I. His conflict with the bishops: Meyer von Knonau (1900) p. 135; Robinson (1999) p. 181.

their auxiliary troops of knights from all sides by whatever means they could. And around 1 August the aforementioned dukes with the Swabian knights decided to meet up with King Rudolf, who was marching out of Saxony. King Henry, however, came between them with a very great army and prevented this from happening. And thus they took up their position, although a very dangerous one, very near the king, hoping every day for a battle and very earnestly seeking opportunities to achieve their purpose. In addition, in their immediate neighbourhood they had to withstand the peasants of that province, who had banded together against them in all the hundreds of the regions and were equipped with the weapons of knights and who numbered nearly 12,000, very warlike and extremely hostile towards them. Thus the Saxons and Swabians were separated from each other and they were entirely prevented from being able to meet or even to consult with each other about what ought to be done, hard pressed as they were by such great dangers. King Henry, trusting in his very large army, very ingeniously decided to conquer the Saxons first and then to triumph over the Swabians and he had no doubt that this could very easily be done without any losses among his own men. After consulting with his followers about this plan, he immediately sent certain emissaries, men of noble birth, to King Rudolf and to the Saxon magnates under the pretence of concluding peace between the two sides. When this had been agreed between them and confirmed by both sides for a specific period according to the customary treaty, while [Henry's emissaries] were hastening back to their lord, that insane and treacherous man suddenly and almost without warning attacked with armed might and warlike fury those whom he had thus craftily deceived, unprepared as they were.[562]

King Rudolf, who together with his followers had difficulty in leaving his camp, made all the haste he could and wisely drew up his battle lines as best he could in such a moment and exhorted his troops to face the threat of the enemy. He fought against [his adversaries] so bravely and in such a warlike manner that immediately at the first encounter God granted that he should successfully gain the victory and in a short time overthrow the first two divisions. Without delay the king [Henry IV] was the first to flee in a shameful manner, together with his closest

562 Battle of Mellrichstadt (on the River Streu), 7 August: place-name and date in Bruno, *Saxon War* c. 96, 102, pp. 89, 92. Bruno's fuller account does not mention this surprise attack. See Meyer von Knonau (1900) pp. 135–46; Cram (1955) pp. 140–3; Robinson (1999) pp. 181–2.

supporters.[563] Then the rest of the army, seeing what was happening and being unfit for war, cowardly and remarkably frightened, also fled in various directions and, becoming more and more terrified, endeavoured only to save themselves. The Saxons, however, pursued them for more than three miles, pressing hard on the heels of the fugitives with warlike tenacity. In that place more than thirty of the more noble members of King Henry's party fell,[564] but of the lesser members it is said that almost 5,000 were killed, while of the opposite party only about eighty of the lesser men are declared to have died. In addition the bishops of this party who were present had fled with their followers in various directions after hearing from fugitives false reports of King Henry's victory. Among these the Roman cardinal [Bernard] was in great danger, together with many others. While they were looking for a hiding-place in the forest, the bishop [Werner] of Magdeburg was struck by an arrow by Slav robbers[565] and the bishop of Paderborn was captured and plundered and *fled from them* almost *naked.*[566] The bishop [Adalbert] of Worms was likewise taken prisoner and delivered up to King Henry, together with Herman, a noble count.[567] After defeating and slaying so many squadrons of their enemies, the Saxons joyfully returned to the original battlefield and to their camp. They spent the night there and on the following day they took counsel with their king and when he had acknowledged their right, according to the laws, not to proceed any further with the campaign after they had been victorious in battle, with great joy they returned to Saxony as conquerors.

King Henry, however, without delay made for Bavaria. For he greatly feared an attack by the Swabians, who for their part had fought a very hard battle with the bands of Franconians formed from the hundreds, had completely overwhelmed them, had castrated them and had won a

---

563 Bruno, *Saxon War* c. 96, p. 89: Henry was initially successful and Rudolf's position endangered by the flight of his episcopal supporters.

564 *Ibid.*, c. 102, pp. 91–2: Eberhard 'the Bearded' (son of Count Eberhard III of Nellenburg), Count Poppo of Henneberg, Margrave Dietpold of the Nordgau, Count Henry of Lechsgemünd.

565 Cf. *ibid.*, c. 96, p. 89: Werner 'was captured by the inhabitants of that country and miserably killed'.

566 Mark 14:52. No other source mentions the presence of Poppo of Paderborn at Mellrichstadt. Berthold probably confused him with Werner of Merseburg (1059–93), of whom Bruno, *Saxon War* c. 96, p. 89, reported that he 'was plundered and returned naked to his fatherland'.

567 Count Herman Billung (†1086), uncle of Duke Magnus Billung of Saxony. See Meyer von Knonau (1900) pp. 143–4.

miraculous victory.[568] When they learned of the flight of their enemies and of their king's victory and his return, they rejoiced at the success of their forces. They wrought destruction everywhere with fire and plunder and stormed very many of their enemies' fortresses before returning home joyfully and triumphantly. Finally King Henry's forgers and inventors of lies shamelessly declared throughout the lands that their lord had returned victorious from the Saxon war and they contrived that he should commit their falsehoods to writing in letters to the lord pope, the Romans and all the Lombards.[569] At this same time the abbot [Bernard] of Marseilles, the legate of the apostolic see, who was present with the Swabian commanders on the aforementioned expedition and who was fully aware of all the events of the battles, hurriedly returned to Rome to him who had sent him, because he had realised that he had not made and would never make any progress with the legation that had been imposed on him for the benefit of the Church among the enemies of the apostolic see. He was a tireless destroyer of lies and a truly suitable witness to the pure truth. He himself and subsequently very many others bore witness in detail to the actual sequence of events before the lord pope and the rest, who were in doubt and were distressed by those extraordinary lies.[570]

The following autumn King Henry once again gathered forces of knights from all directions and again planned an expedition that he pretended was bound for Saxony. When he learned that the very great army of King Rudolf was coming to meet him in a very warlike manner, he led the men whom he had assembled, who had sworn an oath to attack the Saxons, to lay waste to Swabia, as oath-breakers. There, like an utterly wild creature who despised God, he gathered together the worst and most inhuman robbers from Bohemia, Bavaria, Burgundy, Franconia and also whomsoever he could find in Swabia itself and far and wide he deplorably proceeded to plunder and burn, to destroy some castles and towns and to perpetrate unheard of acts of sacrilege against divine and sacred things. There was no difference between holy and

568 Battle on the Neckar (7 August), in which the Swabian forces of Berthold I of Carinthia and Welf IV of Bavaria defeated the Henrician army of 12,000 Franconian peasants: cf. above p. 213. See Meyer von Knonau (1900) pp. 136, 146; Höss (1950) p. 307; Robinson (1999) pp. 181–2.

569 Bruno, *Saxon War* c. 103, p. 92: Henry IV portrayed Mellrichstadt as a victory at an assembly in Regensburg, October 1078. Cf. Bonizo, *To a friend* VIII, p. 243. The contrary claims of Henrician and anti-Henrician authors: Meyer von Knonau (1900) pp. 145–6 and n. 78; Vogel (1983) pp. 123–4.

570 He next appears in Gregory VII's correspondence on 2 January 1079: *Register* VI.15, pp. 419–20.

unholy,[571] no compassion among so many miseries. For the sacrilegious and audacious men deplorably burned and plundered the churches to which the inhabitants of the land had fled for refuge and to preserve their property. They flogged priests clad in their holy vestments in a manner that would excite pity and trampled them half-naked under their feet. They took away the relics and destroyed the altars, defiling them with excrement – which is unheard-of even among pagans – and with the blood from the stolen meat that they had placed upon them and cut into pieces. They shamelessly violated in the churches the women whom they captured there, as if they were in a brothel. They set up in [the churches] stables for their horses and their animals and also latrines. Moreover they took women by force and caused the death of some of them by violating them; and they led away very many of them as captives, after cutting their hair and clothing them like men. They mutilated the wooden image of the crucified Christ at Altdorf[572] and also elsewhere, cutting off the head, the hands and the feet. What more is there to tell? They dishonoured all things that were sacred and divine and polluted them in every way with more than heathen madness.[573] All these things were done indeed with the permission of the bishops, who forced their way into the churches of God with them. This abominable trampling underfoot and laying waste of holy Church took place around the feast of All Saints [1 November].[574] A little under 100 churches were then desecrated during that expedition. Nevertheless not all these deeds went unpunished. For it is said that some of [the perpetrators] were seized by unclean spirits and were tormented to death. Some indeed were killed or captured and plundered by the Swabian princes; most of them were mutilated and had their noses cut off. When Swabia had thus been laid waste in a pitiful manner, [the perpetrators] returned home, laden with great sacks of booty and sacred objects that they had stolen, rejoicing but not entirely triumphant.

At this time Duke Berthold [I of Carinthia] ended his days – very happily, I trust – after commending his soul with hope and faith wholly into the hands of God, as was fitting, and wisely *setting* his *house in order*[575] in a successful consummation. He was a lover and zealous

---

571 Cf. Ezekiel 22:26. Cf. above p. 173.

572 The Welf family monastery of Altdorf: above p. 70 and n. 127. Cf. Bernold, *Chronicle* 1078, below p. 263: the devastation of 'the land of Welf'.

573 Cf. above p. 173.

574 Cf. Bernold, *Chronicle* 1078, below p. 263.

575 Isaiah 38:1. Berthold I † 5/6 November.

defender of the Christian religion and a remarkable cultivator of the virtuous life, of justice and peace, modesty and discipline, soberly and methodically before God and the world, always mindful of compassion and zeal for God; a most knowledgeable follower of the ancestral laws and rights, a most prudent man, very *wise in counsel*[576] and most virtuous and entirely honourable in his life.

Hildulf, that simoniac who was imposed on Cologne, who had been condemned *on earth* by the judgement of apostolic authority as an heretical *thief and a robber*, departed from the world that autumn, being also forever *bound in heaven.*[577]

A great synod was held in Rome[578] both because of the very many needs of holy Church and especially because it was necessary somehow or other to check the tyranny of King Henry. There the envoys of the two kings presented themselves on behalf of their lords and bore witness on oath that they were innocent and had not by means of any cunning or ingenious device hindered the holding of the conference that the lord pope had arranged in the last synod, commanding that no one should hinder it on pain of anathema.[579] The nobles believed King Rudolf's envoy entirely but they accused the others of perjury. The latter attempted at last to extort from the pope an anathema against Rudolf for usurping the kingdom.[580] On the contrary, however, the whole synod would not support this but, as justice required, turned [the anathema] against King Henry because of his disobedience, because of the many sacrileges mentioned above and because of his very cunning deceptions and lies. After an adjournment had been granted to him until the next synod or earlier, for his improvement and his reply, [the envoys] returned home in confusion, with dishonour and without the papal blessing. One of them, Egilbert, provost of Passau,[581] had already been lawfully excommunicated by his bishop [Altman]. When he returned thus, guilty

---

576 Ecclesiasticus 32:22; I Maccabees 2:65.

577 A conflation of John 10:1 and Matthew 16:19. Archbishop Hildulf ✝ 21 July.

578 19 November. Cf. protocol of the autumn synod, 1078: Gregory VII, *Register* VI.5b, pp. 400–6. See Meyer von Knonau (1900) pp. 163–7; Vogel (1983) pp. 126–7; Cowdrey (1998) pp. 184–5, 497–8, 507–13, 548–9, 655–6; Robinson (1999) pp. 182–4.

579 Cf. synodal protocol, preface, *Register* VI.5b, pp. 400–1: 'The envoys of Henry and Rudolf, each on behalf of his lord, swore that he would not by any artifice hinder the conference of the legates of the apostolic see to be held in the German kingdom.' See Vogel (1983) p. 127 and n. 6.

580 Cf. *Register* IX.29, p. 613.

581 Egilbert, archbishop of Trier (1079–1101), invested with the archbishopric on 6 January 1079. See Meyer von Knonau (1900) pp. 187–9.

of perjury, to King Henry, the latter set him over the church of Trier simoniacally and with his customary violence, against the will of all the clergy and people and rejecting the bishop whom they had elected according to canon law.

In that same synod these decrees and judgements were issued with the consent and the subscriptions of all. *'Every*[582] *knight and everyone, whatever his order and profession, who has received or will receive church lands from a king or secular prince or from bishops or abbots or from any rulers of churches against their will, or who has seized* or will seize *them or will hold them with* their *consent, is to be subject to excommunication, unless he restores those lands to the churches.*

'If any of the Normans invades the lands of the monastery of the blessed Benedict in Monte Cassino or unjustly takes any property whatsoever from that monastery and does not make amends after being admonished twice or three times, he is to be subject to excommunication until he comes to his senses and makes amends to the church.

'Since we have learned that in many parts of the world *investitures of churches are performed by lay persons contrary to the decrees of the holy Fathers and that from this there arise many disturbances in the Church* – nay, the ruination of holy religion – *by means of which* we have perceived that the very dignity of *Christian* authority *is trampled underfoot,* we have decreed *that no member of the clergy is to receive investiture of a bishopric or an abbey or a church* or a provostship or any clerical dignity *from the hand of an emperor or a king or any lay person, man or woman. If he presumes to do so, he is to recognise that that investiture is invalid by apostolic authority and that he is subject to excommunication until he makes appropriate reparation.*[583]

'If any bishop *sells prebends, archdeaconries or any ecclesiastical offices or appoints to them otherwise than the decrees of the holy Fathers command, he is to be suspended from his office. For it is fitting that, just as he has freely received a bishopric, so is he to distribute the members of that bishopric or* office *likewise.*

'We judge as false and *invalid those ordinations that are performed through the intervention of payment or entreaties or service given to any person with*

582/582 Protocol of the Roman synod of autumn 1078, Gregory VII, *Register* VI.5b, pp. 402–6. Berthold's version omits a number of interlinear corrections in the *Register*: see E. Caspar's variant apparatus, *Register* pp. 403–6 nn. o–y. A version also appears in Hugh, *Chronicon* II, pp. 423–4. See Hoffmann (1976) p. 115; Schieffer (1981) pp. 172–3.

583 On this papal investiture decree: Schieffer (1981) pp. 172–3 and n. 305, 180; Beulertz (1991) pp. 7–8, 57–9, 72–3.

this intention or that do not have the common consent of the clergy and people according to the ordinances of canon law or that are not approved by those who have the right of consecration, since those who are ordained in such a way do not enter through the door, that is, through Christ, but as the Truth Himself bears witness, are thieves and robbers.

'*We call those false penances that are not imposed according to the authority of the holy Fathers in respect of the nature of the offences. Therefore every knight or trader or person devoted to any employment that cannot be carried out without sin, who has become involved in more serious crimes and comes to penance,* that is, *who is unjustly holding the property of another man or who has hatred in his heart, is to recognise that he cannot achieve true penitence, through which he may be able to gain eternal life, unless* the knight *lays down his arms and bears* them *no more except on the advice of religious bishops and in defence of justice and* the trader *abandons trade and* the official *leaves his office, restores the property that* each of them *has unjustly taken and dismisses hatred from his heart. Nevertheless he is not in the meantime to despair* but *we exhort him to do whatever good he can so that Almighty God may enlighten his heart to penance.*

'*We forbid by apostolic authority the possession by laymen of tithes, which canonical authority* has ordained *to be granted for pious use. Whether they have received them* as their property *from kings or bishops or any persons whatsoever, they are to know that, unless they return them to the Church, they are committing the offence of sacrilege and* on that account *incurring the danger of eternal damnation.*

'*Because Saturday was held by the holy Fathers to be observed with abstinence, following their authority, we issue the sound admonition that whoever desires to be a sharer in the Christian religion is to abstain from meat on that day, unless one of the greater feast-days intervenes or sickness hinders it.*

'*We confirm by apostolic decree that no abbot is to withhold tithes and first fruits and the other things that belong, according to the decisions of canon law, to bishops, without the authority of the Roman pontiff or the consent of the bishop in whose diocese he lives.*

'*No bishop is to impose an exaction or unfree service on the basis of custom contrary to the Church's rules on his abbots or clergy or to restore a priestly office that is subject to interdict in return for payment. If he does so, he is in danger of losing his office.*

'*Anyone who seizes as his own property the lands of blessed Peter, prince of the apostles, wherever they are situated, or who knowingly fails to make public those that are concealed or who does not perform to St Peter the service due from them, is to recognise that he incurs the wrath of God and the holy apostles as one guilty of sacrilege. Whoever is detected in perpetrating this offence, however, is to restore that same inheritance to blessed Peter and is to pay a fourfold penalty from his own property.*

'If any bishop consents, as a result of entreaties or payment, to fornication by priests, deacons or subdeacons or to the offence of incest within his diocese or does not oppose them with the authority committed to him by virtue of his office, he is to be suspended from office.

'Every Christian is to take care during the celebration of mass to make some offering to God and to call to mind what God said through Moses: "You shall not appear before me empty." For in the commentaries on the mass *by the holy Fathers it is quite evident that all Christians are to make some offering to God according to the custom of the holy Fathers.'*[582]

In that same synod sentence of anathema was issued against all simoniac and nicholaite heretics[584] who are hardened members of their erroneous sect, knowingly disobeying the synodal decisions of the holy Fathers and the judgements of their decretals with the obstinacy and petulance of apostates and who resist earnestly and willingly. In addition many things were promulgated there *for the benefit of the Church*[585] that there is no time now to enumerate. It was enacted in the church of the Lord and Saviour in the Lateran on 9 November[586] in the year of the Lord's Incarnation 1078, in the first indiction.

Bishop Henry [I] of Chur died.[587]

1079. King Henry celebrated Christmas [25 December 1078] in Mainz with little appearance of splendour.[588] There, contrary to the usual pattern of weather in our region, great flashes of lightning were seen and dreadful thunder was heard and *a whirlwind in the storm*[589] tore off a considerable part of the roof of the episcopal church and flung it down on the ground. And that occurrence at that time caused great wonder among all men. Subsequently the king appointed a bishop in the church

584 The list of canons at the beginning of the synodal protocol (*Register* VI.5b, pp. 401–2) includes 'Concerning simoniacs' and 'Concerning the chastity of the clergy', but these canons are missing from the *Register*.

585 A quotation from the preface of the synodal protocol, p. 401.

586 19 November, according to the synodal protocol. Cf. Saxons' letter to Gregory VII: Bruno, *Saxon War* c. 102, p. 103: 15 November.

587 23 December. See above n. 165.

588 The importance of Mainz for Henry IV in 1077–80: Meyer von Knonau (1900) p. 154 and n. 91; Robinson (1999) p. 176 and n. 27.

589 Isaiah 17:13.

of Cologne, contrary to the papal decree,[590] a certain Sigewin,[591] a deacon in that place, who did not *enter by the door*,[592] according to canon law. Since he dared to receive that investiture from the hand of the king, contrary to the law, the wretched man was immediately subject to excommunication. Then the king resided, as best he could, in the area around the Rhine until the middle of Lent[593] and once more assembled all those whom he could lead and incite against the papal office and whom he privately urged to disobedience and rebellion, taking an oath from them. This he contrived to do not only privately and secretly: in a conference in Fritzlar, where his closest supporters and the Saxon magnates met together in these days, he caused it to be proclaimed openly to all men that in any activity or business that pertained to himself he would pay no attention and show no respect at all to the lord pope.[594] He provided this evidence of his attitude. Although the pope had arranged in the last synod that envoys were to be sent by [Henry] to him in Rome to the forthcoming synod to represent his cause, in his insolence he utterly refused to send them.[595]

After fighting the battle and obtaining the victory [of Mellrichstadt], King Rudolf learned that his enemy was once again about to rise up against him with a considerable army. He himself again most ardently sought by all means to encounter him with a very great force of his knights, chosen for their fighting abilities, and put [Henry], who was stunned and utterly terrified, to flight. When this was done, he considered that there was nothing else for him to do on this occasion except to send his force of knights home and therefore he himself returned exulting to his land of Saxony with his men. [Henry], however, in a savage and ferocious state of mind, unexpectedly attacked Swabia in

---

590 The investiture decree of November 1078 (n. 583). Cf. Gregory VII, *JL* 5137 (*Epistolae Vagantes* 31, p. 82, to his legates in Germany, July–October 1079): 'you are to presume to make no judgement concerning ... [the elect of] Cologne and all those who have received investiture from lay hands'. See Schieffer (1981) p. 173 n. 310.

591 Sigewin (1078/9–89). See Meyer von Knonau (1900) p. 155: Schieffer (1991) pp. 17–21.

592 John 10:1.

593 He was in Trier on 6 January (see above p. 217 and n. 581) and in Mainz on 27 January (*D.H.IV* 309). Lent 1079: 6 February–23 March.

594 See Meyer von Knonau (1900) pp. 190–1; Robinson (1999) p. 188.

595 The presence of Henry IV's envoys at the Roman synod of Lent 1079 is confirmed not only by the synodal protocol (Gregory VII, *Register* VI.17a, c. 2, pp. 427–8) and Gregory VII, *JL* 5107 (*Epistolae Vagantes* 27, p. 70) but also by Berthold himself, below p. 223 and Bernold, *Chronicle* 1079, below p. 264.

order to lay it waste (as was mentioned above)[596] but he was able even with this violence to compel almost nobody of importance to surrender or to promise fidelity, except Count Hugh.[597]

When he had sent his Saxons home, however, King Rudolf, who was totally dedicated to justice, applied himself to keeping the peace and reaching judicial decisions according to their laws *without respect of persons*,[598] as far as he could do so with their help. After a short time he was most cruelly afflicted by fever and pleurisy and for more than two months he suffered and wasted away so much that most people utterly despaired of his life and feared that he would never recover his health. Finally, however, since God was his physician amidst so many dangers, he experienced a most welcome recovery and most joyfully celebrated Christmas [25 December 1078] in ...[599] in the company of many Saxon princes in the greatest splendour. And immediately before Septuagesima [20 January 1079] he collected his squadrons of knights together again from all sides and decided to mount a rapid expedition against King Henry. As soon as the latter learned of this and saw that he could not put up any resistance in so short a time, he took counsel with his followers and hurriedly sent envoys, not on his own behalf but on that of his magnates, ostensibly to conclude a peace, albeit a very short one, between them, in order very cunningly to deceive the Saxon magnates.[600] They pretended to lament and to deplore the battles and dissensions, the destruction of churches and so many monstrous crimes and they most emphatically declared that they themselves and their lord, King Henry, were in agreement with the lord pope, with them and with each of the magnates and that they would be obedient in all respects in correcting grievances of this sort and if they would not otherwise trust their words, they would prove them by oaths and by giving hostages. When they heard this, the credulous Saxons trusted in them all too readily – for they flattered so very sweetly – and began by persuading their lord to give up the expedition that he had already begun. Then they fixed on a particular day during the forthcoming Lent to hold a conference with them in Fritzlar and when they had

---

596 See above p. 214.

597 Hugh (III), count of Tübingen.

598 Romans 2:11. See also above n. 153.

599 Place unknown but probably in Saxony: Meyer von Knonau (1900) pp. 154–5.

600 Vogel (1983) p. 151 found it difficult 'to construct a complete picture of events on the basis of this tendentious source, especially since the annalist reports the talks at the beginning of 1079 in two separate and contradictory segments'. See above p. 220.

thus secretly agreed on a treaty of peace, they joyously parted from each other.

When, however, they finally met together, as they had agreed, King Henry's magnates defended and concealed his falsehoods and his follies as best they could and made it clear that they had come for no other purpose than to help the Saxons as best they could to return to their lord's favour, if only they would come to surrender to him. Although they perceived that they had come in vain and that they had been deceived by the usual lies and tricks, [the Saxons] nevertheless with admirable patience strongly advised them that they ought to be as ready for peace, harmony and obedience to the apostolic see as they were themselves. [Henry's magnates] on the contrary declared loudly and publicly that they and their lord would pay no attention either to the peace or to the pope. After fidelity and peace had been renounced on both sides, they returned to their lands, having been summoned there to no purpose.

In these days before Lent Duke Welf [IV of Bavaria], taking his vassals with him, mounted an attack of great power against Churrätien, intending to lay it waste.[601] He proceeded to plunder and burn and defeated the son of Count Otto,[602] whom he forced to swear an oath to King Rudolf, together with certain other magnates. Then he valiantly stormed a certain fortification at a mountain pass and killed, captured and put to flight his enemies, and God so granted that he marched away as the victor with a very large force in order thereafter to conquer others.

During that Lent a great synod assembled in Rome in the year of the Lord's Incarnation 1079, in the second indiction, on 11 February.[603] The Roman cardinal [Bernard] and the bishops [Altman] of Passau and [Herman of] Metz came to it joyfully, although with difficulty, travelling secretly and by different roads to complain to the apostolic see about so many cases of injuries suffered both by themselves and by the churches, after passing safely by the grace of God through very many dangers of ambush and captivity.[604] There the bishops made their complaints in the hearing of the whole synod and were heard

601 He seized the opportunity offered by the death of Bishop Henry I of Chur (above p. 219). The province of Churrätien was equivalent to the diocese of Chur except for some territory belonging to the diocese of Constance.

602 Otto II, son of Count Otto I of Buchhorn (n. 395).

603 Cf. protocol of the Roman synod of Lent 1079: Gregory VII, *Register* VI.17a, p. 425. See Meyer von Knonau (1900) pp. 171–82; Vogel (1983) pp. 137–42; Cowdrey (1998) pp. 185–7, 498–501; Robinson (1999) pp. 185–6.

604 Cf. Gregory VII, *JL* 5108 (*Epistolae Vagantes* 26, p. 68).

with joy and well received. There the envoy of King Rudolf complained of that devastation of Swabia that has already been described, successively recounting the many calamities and miseries. He also protested emphatically against the other insane acts that King Henry had perpetrated everywhere throughout the whole kingdom with such tyrannical presumption. He, together with his fellow envoys, was heard courteously and also, as was fitting, with tears and with bitterness by the lord pope and very many sympathetic listeners.[605]

King Henry's envoy also expounded his case, as best he could, although it was truly not a very just cause, and, as was customary, it found favour with very many hearers. He, together with his followers, was proved by the pope to be guilty of falsehood but he was fully believed by some of the best people. The lord pope in fact declared publicly in the synod that King Henry's legations were false and he testified that he had judicially deposed him from the kingship and that he had not afterwards restored him.[606] He would, therefore, have excommunicated him on the spot, had not all those present of both parties preferred to delay matters and to wait until the Lord's Ascension [2 May], particularly so that the Roman synod could not be accused of having proceeded against him irregularly and over-hastily. For [Henry's] envoy openly declared that it was not through cunning but through necessity that he had omitted to send to the pope, as the latter had decreed in the last synod, such envoys as could escort the papal legates safely into the German fatherland to end so great a conflict. He swore, however, that his lord would send such men to Rome before the Lord's Ascension and that he would obey the apostolic see in all respects in the matter of the kingship. An oath was sworn on behalf of King Rudolf that he would likewise obey the pope in respect of the conference that the latter had decided on.[607] Finally the lord pope once more excommunicated anyone who by means of any ruse or intrigue prevented the conference from taking place in the previous year and similarly anyone who hindered the forthcoming conference that he had now once again decreed.[608]

605 Cf. synodal protocol c. 2 (Gregory VII, *Register* VI.17a, p. 427).

606 Cf. protocol of the Roman synod of Lent 1080 (*Register* VII.14a, p. 484). Compare Berthold's polemical account of the papal attitude towards Henry's envoys with Gregory VII, JL 5107 (*Epistolae Vagantes* 27, p. 70), March/April 1079: 'Roman gravity and apostolic gentleness compel me to proceed by the middle way of justice.'

607 The oaths: protocol of the Lenten synod of 1079, *Register* VII.17a, c. 2, 3, p. 428. See Meyer von Knonau (1900) pp. 177–8; Vogel (1983) pp. 139–42; Cowdrey (1998) pp. 186–7; Robinson (1999) pp. 185–6.

608 Cf. Gregory VII, JL 5106 (*Epistolae Vagantes* 25, p. 66).

By arranging this delay, however, he reconciled all the Romans to himself to such a degree that they requested that the anathema against King Henry should no longer be deferred if he disdained to obey [the pope]. As for the kings, the pope now decided nothing except what pleased the bishop of Passau and the bishop of Metz and their fellow legates[609] and what was appropriate to the needs of the moment. All the sounder people indeed placed themselves most firmly in the party of King Rudolf and they had testified that he was in all things most obedient to the lord pope.

Duke Theoderic [II of Upper Lotharingia] and Count Folmar[610] were excommunicated for their attack on the church of Metz. So were all persons who unjustly claimed for themselves the property of the bishop [Siegfried] of Mainz and of the other bishops who had been expelled from their sees.[611] The bishop [Tedald] of Milan and the bishop [Wibert] of Ravenna were also anathematised,[612] as were the knights of the bishop of Parma,[613] who had taken prisoner the abbot [Ekkehard II] of Reichenau, who had intended to present his own case in the synod. [The bishop] himself was suspended from his office because of that imprisonment. When at length the abbot perceived that he could not be set free by any other means, he promised money to his captors on oath and, on being released by them, he joyfully came to Rome, as he had previously planned. After his case had been brought before the pope and settled there according to his wishes, he returned, not without some danger, to his former residence of Reichenau. For King Henry had in his customary manner already at Easter [24 March] imposed as anti-abbot there that excommunicated tyrant [Udalric III] whom he had also set over the monastery of St Gallen in order to destroy it.[614]

609 Gregory VII, *JL* 5108 (*Epistolae Vagantes* 26, p. 68 and n. 6) also identified Abbot Ekkehard II of Reichenau.

610 Probably Volmar III, count of Metz. Cf. Gregory VII, *Register* VI.22, pp. 434–5. The attack on Metz: above p. 210.

611 Mainz is not mentioned in the synodal protocol. Cf. *Register* VI.19, pp. 430–1 on the case of Bamberg.

612 Synodal protocol, *Register* VI.17a, c. 5, p. 429. Archbishop Wibert of Ravenna does not appear in the synodal protocol of Lent 1079, but in that of Lent 1080 (*Register* VII.14a, p. 481).

613 Eberhard (1072/4–85). See Schwartz (1913) p. 187. On the imprisonment of Ekkehard II: *Register* VI.18, pp. 429–30. Ekkehard's 'case' was probably a conflict with the abbot of St Gallen.

614 Cf. Gregory VII, *JL* 5137 (*Epistolae Vagantes* 31, p. 82) to the papal legates, July–October 1079: 'a certain man was tyrannically thrust into [Ekkehard's] place. After expelling that intruder, cause those possessions of which he was despoiled to be restored.'

The lord pope also sent a letter to those who obeyed *St*[615] *Peter throughout the whole* German *and Italian kingdom,* containing these words. *'On behalf of Almighty God and by the authority of St Peter we forbid entry into the Church to any priests or deacons or subdeacons who are guilty of the offence of fornication, until they repent and mend their ways. If any of them prefer to continue in their sin, let none of you dare to hear their offices, because their blessing is turned into a curse and their prayer into a sin.'*[615] And so forth.

Berengar of Tours[616] abjured his heresy there and professed the catholic faith.

Henry, a clerk of Augsburg, who had already received investiture of the church of Aquileia from King Henry, testified there on the basis of credible evidence that his election was canonical. When, however, he was rejected by the pope because of the investiture that he had usurped for himself from a lay person contrary to the canonical and apostolic decree, he publicly confirmed on oath, according to the judgement of the synod, that he did not know and had never heard of the text of that decree. Then after the whole assembly had interceded for him with the pope in this matter, he firstly declared on oath his lawful and fitting obedience and subjection and support to the apostolic see and the vicar of St Peter, Pope Gregory, and received from him the ring and staff and the other insignia of the patriarchate of Aquileia according to canon law but he did not subsequently conduct himself faithfully towards him in all respects.[617]

Cardinal Bernard did not conceal from the lord pope the trouble and the dangers that he had experienced in our region and how very little use he was able to be to the Church. Among other things he reported that first and foremost with his consent King Henry had been justly excommunicated by a judicial sentence of the bishop of Mainz, together with six other bishops[618] and that he himself according to [the pope's] command separated him from the body and blood of the Lord, together

615/615 Extract from Gregory VII, *JL* 5109 (*Epistolae Vagantes* 32, pp. 84–6).

616 Berengar, archdeacon of Angers, theologian (✝1088). Cf. his oath in the protocol of the Lenten synod of 1079, Gregory VII, *Register* VI.17a, pp. 426–7; Bernold, *Chronicle* 1079, below p. 263. See Gibson (1971) pp. 67–8; Montclos (1971) pp. 228–31; Cowdrey (1998) pp. 498–502.

617 Cf. 'the oath of the archbishop of Aquileia': protocol, *Register* VI.17a, c. 4, pp. 428–9. See above p. 188 and n. 459; Schieffer (1981) pp. 145, 157–9, 173; Vogel (1983) p. 145; Beulertz (1991) p. 100.

618 The Saxons' letter in Bruno, *Saxon War* c. 112, p. 104 mentions eight bishops besides Archbishop Siegfried, on the basis of whose judgement Bernard excommunicated Henry IV on 12 November 1077: above p. 191.

with all those who supported him and drove him as one guilty of sacrilege from the threshold of the Church and forbade him, as a tyrant and
a usurper, to exercise the government of the kingdom, which he made
subject to King Rudolf, who was most obedient to the apostolic see in
all things. He also did not omit to give a systematic account of all this
to the most eminent of the Romans and to all the most prudent men.
The lord pope had known all this already for more than a year but he
had put up with it with remarkable shrewdness, virtually concealing
it. Some people wondered very much why he did this. Perhaps he felt
certain that the conference that he had now once again decreed under
the sanction of anathema, to end such very great dissension, would by
itself be sufficient to achieve what he wished. If this was not the case,
however, he had decided, as the most just and sternest of judges, that
in the case of those who would hinder the conference and who would
not obey him in establishing peace and harmony, he would unexpectedly add to the anathema that they had previously incurred so that they
might all the more suffer eternal damnation. Thus the enemies who had
held him in contempt as a mild and dissembling man would learn, once
they were utterly lost, that he was a most fearful avenger.

Presiding over that same Roman synod, Pope Gregory said: *'Following*
[619] *the footsteps of the holy Fathers, we have resolved that the ordinations of*
those who have been ordained by excommunicates are invalid.

'Again, adhering to the decrees of our holy predecessors, by apostolic authority
we absolve from their oaths those who are bound by fealty or by an oath to
excommunicated persons and we forbid them in every way to observe fealty to
them.

'Again, since we realise that, because of our sins, many men perish every day as
a result of excommunication – partly through ignorance, partly also through
excessive simplicity, partly through fear, partly also through necessity – over-
come by compassion, we are appropriately moderating the sentence of anathema
for the time being, as far as we can do so. By apostolic authority, therefore,
we remove these persons from the bond of anathema: namely, the wives, chil-
dren, servants, maidservants or dependents of excommunicates *and also the*
peasants and unfree men and all others who are not such important courtiers
that crimes are committed as a result of their advice and those who in igno-
rance communicate with excommunicates or those who communicate with those
who communicate with excommunicates. To anyone, whether ploughman *or*

619/619 Extract from the synodal protocol of Lent 1078 (n. 514), not 1079: Gregory VII,
    Register V.14a, c. 14, 15, 16, pp. 372–3. The same extract appears in Hugh, *Chronicon*
    II, p. 442.

pilgrim or traveller, who enters the land of excommunicates where he can buy nothing or who has nothing with which to buy, we give permission to buy and to receive from excommunicates. And if anyone wishes to give anything to excommunicates, not to encourage their pride but for humane reasons, we do not forbid them to do it. Enacted in the church of the Lord and Saviour on 3 March[619] in the year of the Lord's Incarnation 1079.'

The lord pope decided, therefore, that a synod should be held once more in Whitsun week [12–18 May] to settle the aforementioned case.[620] He sent the patriarch [Henry of Aquileia], the pious man Bishop Peter of Albano and Bishop Udalric of Padua,[621] together with others of his faithful followers, as his legates to King Henry and let him know properly what ruling he himself had made in the synod concerning [Henry] and he agreed that the latter should negotiate with those legates and without delay settle upon a fixed time and place for the conference according to his wishes and to his convenience. In addition he demanded of him that he should now experience in fact the true obedience that [Henry] had very often promised him and affirmed in messages sent to Rome. As proof that obedience would be shown to him, he also commanded him to conclude peace on the firmest possible basis with his enemies, to last to the end of the aforementioned conference and to grant to those bishops whom he had already expelled from their sees, without risk of injury or treachery, total freedom of possession of their churches and their property and secure and peaceful access and jurisdiction, so as to have the use and ownership of them. He was also to send seven of his more powerful and his most pious men to [the pope] in Rome at the agreed time, who were to swear an oath of security to [the pope] that they would conduct his legates to the aforementioned conference in peace and would protect them in every way while they were performing their legation there and would very carefully bring them back safely to him in Rome.[622] The patriarch, however, who was one of the closest friends of King Henry, did not attend with the utmost fidelity and zeal to the legation that had been laid upon him and sent on his own behalf

---

620 This proposal is found in no other source: Hauck (1954) p. 817 n. 4.

621 Udalric, bishop of Padua (1064–80). His legation with Cardinal bishop Peter of Albano: Meyer von Knonau (1900) pp. 182–3, 210–17, 223–5; Schumann (1912) pp. 46–52; Cowdrey (1998) pp. 188–9; Robinson (1999) pp. 186, 190–1. Berthold, like Bonizo, *To a friend* VIII, p. 245, wrongly identified Henry of Aquileia as one of the legates: Meyer von Knonau (1900) p. 182 and n. 15; Vogel (1983) p. 144.

622 Cf. protocol of the Roman synod of Lent 1079, Gregory VII, *Register* VI.17a, c. 2, p. 428: 'The oath of the envoys of King Henry. The envoys … are to conduct and bring back the legates of the Roman see in safety.'

a secret messenger, who was to hasten to the king in Regensburg and ascertain his wishes and his obedience.[623] He returned to his city of Aquileia and in this way he delayed his fellow legates, but they turned aside to Padua.

When the king learned that a legation of this kind was being sent to him by the pope, with his customary arrogance he showed no very great esteem for it, since he intended to pay no heed to it. Nevertheless, acting as if he had no knowledge of the papal legation, at the agreed time he sent as his envoy to Rome the bishop [Benno II] of Osnabrück, well provided with many falsehoods and artifices, who was on this occasion to deceive the pope again by whatever device he could and by that promise of obedience of which he had so often made a false pretence. In whatever way he could, with the greatest skill, he was to prevent the imposition of that sentence of anathema and the synod that was particularly intended to curb the king's tyranny.[624] [The king] himself finally celebrated Easter [24 March] somehow or other in Regensburg, where, as an incitement to wrongdoing, he conferred the duchy of Swabia on Count Frederick.[625] He then delivered up the abbey of Reichenau, which he had previously twice sold in acts of simony, to Ekkehard, who had been elected by his brethren according to the *Rule* and who was to be lawfully consecrated by the pope according to the privilege of that place.[626] Because [Ekkehard] did not dare to act unjustly and support his party, he was now unjustly rejected and held in captivity, as mentioned above and [the king] appointed there in an illegal manner a certain tyrant [Udalric III], the intruder and destroyer of the monastery of St Gallen whom we have already mentioned. [The king] remained in the eastern region of Bavaria and the plain of Noricum almost until Whitsun, plundering the inhabitants and compelling Margrave Leopold [II of Austria], together with certain others, to surrender to him.[627]

Ever since King Rudolf had entered Saxony, his wife Adelaide (the daughter of Margravine Adelaide and sister of Queen Bertha, the wife

---

623 Henry of Aquileia is named as intervener in *DD.H.IV* 317 (19 October 1079, Hirschaid), 318 (24 October, Regensburg) and 319 (?1079).

624 See Meyer von Knonau (1900) pp. 189, 209; Vogel (1983) pp. 148–9; Robinson (1999) p. 186.

625 Frederick I (of Büren), duke (1079–1105). See Meyer von Knonau (1900) pp. 194–6; Vogel (1983) pp. 157–60; Robinson (1999) pp. 188–90.

626 See above pp. 123 (Meginward), 126 (Rupert), 130 (Ekkehard II).

627 Henry IV's expedition against Austria before Whitsun (12 May): Meyer von Knonau (1900) p. 207; Robinson (1999) p. 190.

of Henry)[628] had lived as best she could in Twiel in the bishopric of Constance and in other castles on the Rhine. After being weakened by poverty, grief and various misfortunes and disasters, she was troubled by lengthy attacks of sickness and by lethal fevers, which finally wore her out. After she had *set* her *house in order* and, as was fitting, had made provision in every way for the salvation of her soul in Christ, dying, she most devoutly *commended* her *spirit into* His *hands*[629] in, I hope, a happy end. She was most solemnly buried in the monastery of St Blasien with all the due funeral rites.[630]

King Rudolf, however, who had now become a widower, celebrated Easter [24 March] in a magnificent manner in Goslar[631] and very wisely planned the expedition that he was very keen to launch against Henry, as soon as his magnates considered it timely to do so. Moreover the whole of Saxony was wonderfully united in the most lasting peace and he was accustomed most sagaciously to do justice to all men *without respect of persons,*[632] according to the laws and ordinances of that people, and he showed the greatest regard for equity. His son, to whom the duchy of Swabia had been committed by King Henry while he was still a boy,[633] was received by Duke Welf [IV of Bavaria], together with some of the leading men who belonged to him, and brought to Ulm. They subjected themselves to him, together with the citizens, according to legal custom, and by common consent and approval they now once more confirmed him as their lord and duke.

After they had left there and gone home, however, Count Frederick on behalf of his king gathered eastern Franconians, men from Raetia, Swabians, Bavarians and whatever forces of knights he could and he himself took possession of Ulm, not without danger, in order to cele-

---

628 Adelaide (n. 441), daughter of Adelaide of Turin (n. 347) † before 24 March. The castle of Twiel in the Hegau was later known as a Zähringen possession: cf. *Casuum sancti Galli continuatio* II.7, p. 159.

629 Psalm 30:6; Luke 23:46.

630 Rudolf was a patron of St Blasien. See Jakobs (1968) pp. 38–40, 160, 269–74; Jakobs (1973) pp. 105–6, 110–15; Robinson (1999) pp. 126–7.

631 On 25 March he was in Quedlinburg: *D Rudolf* 1 (*DD.H.IV* pp. 676–7).

632 Romans 2:11. See above n. 153. Vogel (1983) p. 160: 'in order to counteract the impression of a weakened kingship, Berthold ... emphasises Rudolf's activity as a judge'.

633 Berthold I of Rheinfelden, anti-duke of Swabia (1079–90). The initiative in Ulm of Welf IV, under whose protection Rudolf had evidently placed his son before his departure for Saxony: Meyer von Knonau (1900) p. 199; Vogel (1983) p. 159; Robinson (1999) p. 189.

brate Whitsun [12 May] there.[634] When, however, he heard that Duke Welf was making a sudden attack on him in that place, he barely spent one night there and to his shame he withdrew from there, fearful and not daring to fight but fleeing from there with his three bishops.[635] The duke, therefore, entered there and soon afterwards laid siege to a certain very strongly fortified castle in the neighbourhood. He remained there for more than two weeks as an affront to the aforementioned Frederick, very boldly and belligerently waiting for him to meet him in battle at that place, until by means of the war engines which in German are called *mangones*, he stormed the castle and burned and destroyed it utterly and forced all the castellans to surrender to him unconditionally. Frederick, however, gathered together all the men that he possibly could at such a time; but when he saw that he was far too inferior in strength to meet the duke in battle, his men ran away in all directions, to his great shame, and he returned very sorrowfully.

In these days following Easter Margrave Berthold, the son of Duke Berthold [I of Carinthia], an admirable and very generous youth, whose character was in every way honourable and who conducted himself energetically and very virtuously, took as his wife Agnes, the daughter of King Rudolf,[636] who in all that concerned her was no less virtuous than her husband.

After the aforementioned patriarch [Henry of Aquileia] and the other legates of the apostolic see had learned from the envoys whom they had sent in advance and from the bishop of Osnabrück of King Henry's replies promising obedience, although it was pretended obedience, they came to him in Regensburg around Whitsun [12 May].[637] They were not received there with appropriate ceremony but they attempted with all their might to perform the task for which they had been sent. When with all their very great skill and ingenuity they had worked upon the king and caught him unawares, at last they extorted from him with difficulty his approval and consent, although only verbal, for a peace (albeit a pretended one) and for the conference that he had sworn to uphold through his envoy publicly in the synod in Rome. And they immediately sent envoys in advance into Saxony to King Rudolf and to

---

634 The attack of Duke Frederick I of Swabia on Ulm: Meyer von Knonau (1900) pp. 207–8; Robinson (1999) p. 190.

635 Nowhere identified.

636 Marriage of Agnes of Rheinfelden (+1111) and Berthold II of Zähringen: Meyer von Knonau (1900) pp. 199–200; Jakobs (1968) pp. 160–1; Parlow (1999) pp. 66–7.

637 See Meyer von Knonau (1900) pp. 209–10; Vogel (1983) pp. 160–1; Robinson (1999) p. 190.

the other Saxon princes and also to Duke Welf [IV] and the nobler and more powerful Swabians and ordered them to meet them on the agreed day in Fritzlar to discuss this case with them.[638] After they received this message, the Saxons together with their king, being most obedient to papal commands, set off without delay, as they had been ordered to do.

Duke Welf and the others from Swabia who had been summoned there were now entirely prepared to come, but the escorts, who had been appointed by King Henry to give them safe conduct, had been withdrawn by him with his usual treachery and folly so that they would not lead them to the agreed place. With similar treachery he also set snares for the Saxons, and when they crossed the frontiers of their land on the way to meet the papal legates he dispatched behind their backs large forces of knights from Bohemia, who broke through their frontiers, bringing devastation, plundering rapaciously and inflicting every kind of harm upon them. Nevertheless, when they thus invaded the march and inflicted their injuries on it, the troops of the march joined forces and overcame them with a warlike attack, killing some of them and taking prisoner some of the defeated, except for the very few who with great difficulty had fled.

The papal legates were received most honourably in Fritzlar by the archbishop [Siegfried] of Mainz and by all the rest, the greater and the lesser men. They publicly revealed to them all the cause and purpose of their coming and to the lovers of peace, justice and obedience they pronounced greetings and apostolic blessing. After joyfully listening to them, the Saxon princes, together with their king and all his party, generally declared that they would be most obedient in all things to the lord pope, so as to preserve the peace that had been proclaimed and so that the cause of so great a division and strife should be investigated lawfully and judicially and so as to respect the decision of the conference that had been arranged, on condition, however, that the opposition party made a similar promise to agree to this, with hostages being given by both sides and supported by mutual oaths. Otherwise they declared that they would have very little faith in King Henry, whose treachery and folly they had so often experienced. The patriarch [Henry of Aquileia], however, and the other trusted followers of the king whom the papal legates had brought with them in their entourage refused to approve such an agreement, arguing against it vigorously and at great length. But when they finally realised that the legates favoured the view of the

638 I.e. a second meeting in Fritzlar (June 1079). See Meyer von Knonau (1900) pp. 210–11 and n. 64; Robinson (1999) pp. 190–1.

Saxons, as the more appropriate one, they offered little resistance and made the dissembling and foolish promise that they would compel their king to accept this agreement, even if he opposed it. For this reason the Saxons submitted to the legation of the apostolic see, declaring that they, together with their king, would be obedient in all things, if a durable peace and guarantee of security could be made. Then, after both sides had agreed on the day and the place of the conference, which was to be held in the city of Würzburg, the latter returned to Saxony, while the former hastened, together with the papal legates, to their lord in Regensburg.[639]

When they informed [Henry] of the treaty of mutual good faith that they had agreed, he, being obstinate in his heart and his speech, thought it of little value and they had great difficulty in pressing him to declare that, because of the honour in which he held the lord pope and because of his love for him, he would show himself peaceful and well disposed towards [the opposite party], but only if they were willing to come to him without delay to surrender and to humble themselves. On this condition he agreed that he would hold with the Saxons the conference, which his envoy in the synod in Rome had sworn to and which, as was decreed there under penalty of excommunication, was in no way to be hindered by any persons in either party but was to be respected in every way; otherwise he would not hold it at all. When the magnates of the Saxons and the Swabians and their other companions in war learned of this, they all wondered at the obstinate folly of King Henry and expressed their detestation of his stubborn disobedience. Although they had already shown the lord pope that they were in favour of the conference that had been agreed upon, they unanimously remained at home and confided all their cares and their difficulties to God.

[Henry], however, gathered from all sides the considerable forces of his party and his bishops and other supporters and arrived most audaciously at the aforementioned city [Würzburg] around the feast of the assumption of St Mary [15 August],[640] together with the papal legates – who, it is said, were partly corrupted by gifts, partly broken down by fear and by threats and almost brought over to his side by flattery, cunning and every kind of ingenuity[641] – as if he could by this means excuse himself to the pope and become exempt from excommunication

---

639 Henry IV was in Regensburg on 23 July: *D.H.IV* 312.

640 On 16 August he was in Nuremberg: *D.H.IV* 316. Council of Würzburg: Meyer von Knonau (1900) pp. 213–15; Vogel (1983) pp. 163–4; Robinson (1999) pp. 191–2.

641 Criticism of the papal legates: Gregory VII, *Register* VII.3, p. 463; *JL* 5137 (*Epistolae Vagantes* 31, p. 80: 'many … are beginning to murmur about your legation'); Bruno,

and the guilt of perjury. When this sham synod had been arranged there entirely as he wished through the efforts of his synod members and his advocates who were to debate according to his desire, he made a most persuasive effort to defend himself before the papal legates and complained to them about the disturbers and invaders of his kingdom and above all he repeatedly urged them to use their apostolic authority to strike down Rudolf and all his supporters with the excommunication that they deserved. Together with all his followers he produced many inventions of this kind and clamorous accusations but, it is said, not all to the purpose, speaking in a harsh, confused and hostile manner but with little sense. He also very openly asserted that he had obeyed the papal decree but that his enemies were convicted of disobedience and in this regard, being proved guilty on irrefutable evidence, were subject to excommunication. Finally the legates of the apostolic see, not strengthened, as they ought to have been, by the spirit of freedom, announced that they had been sent for the purpose of making peace and of fixing the day and the place of the conference – not a conference like this one but such a one as the lord pope had decreed in Rome – so that they might carefully test the obedience of each party and report the results to the apostolic see. They declared to those who complained to them so often that it was not they alone who were appointed to be the judges to bring a just settlement of that case and of the conflicts and battles of which they complained, but that the judgement was to be made together with others, the suitable fellow legates whom the pope would send subsequently, and was to be made not now but in the future. By means of this ingenious reply they freed themselves with difficulty from those who complained and ranted at them, knowing full well that King Henry, together with all his supporters, not only did not respect the conference that had been set up by papal authority but in fact audaciously hindered it. For this reason he had publicly fallen under the papal anathema, together with his confederates, and likewise the very site of this present sham synod and also its inhabitants had already been condemned by a just judgement on the part of its bishop [Adalbero of Würzburg][642] and they had to their great peril communicated with [these inhabitants] contrary to divine law and canon law.

Saxon War c. 116, p. 109 ('the papal legates … in the Roman manner took away with them from both parties as much money as they could collect'); Hugh, *Chronicon* II, p. 451 ('corrupted by gifts'). Udalric received *D.H.IV* 312 (23 July). See Schumann (1912) pp. 50–1; Vogel (1983) pp. 162–3; Cowdrey (1998) pp. 192–3; Robinson (1999) p. 191.

642 An excommunication perhaps pronounced in 1077 when he left the pro-Henrician city. See Meyer von Knonau (1900) p. 47; Kottje (1978) pp. 142–3.

Thus that council worthy of anathema was execrably begun with insane subterfuge and even more execrably ended. Taking the papal legates with him, King Henry in a violent and furious state of mind moved the large army that he had assembled from all sides, proposing most audaciously to attack and lay waste [the territory of] the Saxons.[643] When he learned of this hostile attack against him and his followers, however, King Rudolf, trusting in God and His compassion and strengthened by his faith, wisely set in order the large force of knights that he had carefully gathered together and advanced to meet him. After sending envoys to all the magnates of the opposing army, he entreated them by God's mercy and very humbly begged them, together with their lord, to pay heed to the conference that the pope had already decreed for the sake of the peace and the unity of the Church and of harmony throughout the kingdom and to grant a place in which to hold it faithfully and in unfeigned peace. Finally, together with all his followers, he confirmed there in the strongest terms that he would in all respects agree with and obey the lord pope and the other magnates of the kingdom in this present case. If, however, they should stubbornly refuse to do this, they should be in no doubt whatever that he would with God's grace encounter them as an armed and most zealous enemy and would avenge himself upon them, as befitted hardened despisers of peace and justice, worthy of excommunication.

When they heard this and learned beyond doubt from their scouts of the strength of the enormous army that was enraged against them, they were thoroughly terrified both by the imminence of battle and by the consciousness of their own injustice, excommunication and disobedience. They therefore forced their lord – who for a long time resisted very stubbornly with tearful lamentations – to agree to stave off the imminent danger according to their advice and by some means or other to extricate himself from an encounter with those whom he was not powerful enough to resist. For they declared unanimously that what the Saxons, together with their lord, demanded of him was just, although all his bishops distanced themselves from this opinion. The latter indeed, who were warlike only in their speech, were always tirelessly and violently urging them to try out their swords and to taste death, since they themselves were doomed to perdition and their miserable purpose was to defend and to intensify that savage devastation of holy Church and of the whole kingdom, that discord and iniquity that they

643 See Meyer von Knonau (1900) p. 215; Vogel (1983) pp. 165–7; Robinson (1999) p. 192.

had originally initiated. [The other magnates] summoned the papal legates to them without delay and most urgently negotiated with them so that they might irrevocably compel the forces of both parties on pain of anathema not to contend against each other in battle but rather to unite together in mutual peace, quickly to agree upon a conference on the current situation, like servants and fellow citizens of the kingdom, and to attempt to establish the cause of so great a division through the agency of the magnates whom they would elect for this purpose and by means of just and reasonable judgement. Moreover certain members of King Henry's party, after receiving the promise of peace from the Saxons and making them the same promise, discussed this same matter with them most strenuously, as earnest and peaceful mediators, until the decision was reached by both sides that they would all unanimously join that party that they recognised as being the just one in the course of the conference that had been enjoined on them by papal command.[644]

Those who previously had obstinately rejected a peace treaty skilfully freed themselves from the Saxons, using this argument as if it was an honourable defence. Strengthened by its most welcome assistance, they departed with their king in a retreat that looked like flight and in extreme confusion. For a large group of Bavarians was taken by surprise by the sight of the Saxons and their readiness for action and what they began was continued by the whole body of troops in the camp amidst great uproar. While they hurried away to their homes by whatever means they could, deceiving the Saxons and paying no heed to the agreement about the conference, with a great effort the king again brought back his followers, who were so easily misled, into the same state of readiness and with great exactitude he administered an oath to those men who had so often broken their oaths.[645]

The papal legates, who indeed (so they say) were unwilling participants in these proceedings, at last, laden with magnificent gifts, returned to Rome, although not together and without accomplishing all that they had been sent to do. One of them, [Bishop Udalric] of Padua, who had been corrupted by such great gifts, outstripped his fellow legate, a holy man who was only too innocent, and left him on the other side of the Alps. When he came before the lord pope, the treacherous hypocrite, wonderfully supplied with every kind of clever inventions and answers,

---

644 This truce: Meyer von Knonau (1900) p. 192; Vogel (1983) p. 167; Robinson (1999) p. 192.

645 Cf. *Annals of Augsburg* 1079, p. 129, 'the treacherous Saxons deceived the king and the legates with guile ...'

his purpose was not only incidentally to deceive the Lombards and the Romans but also to deceive the pope himself and most diligently to earn the favour of his Henry by whatever means he could.[646] The false legate conveyed to him on behalf of Henry his most humble obedience in all things, together with all the promises of service that he could devise, and he demonstrated that, as far as [Henry] was concerned, this was sufficiently proved by his conduct both in the conference and in the other concerns for which he had been sent beyond the mountains. When that shameless liar in such an audacious manner continued persistently to deceive everyone far and wide, together with his fellow liars, a certain brother,[647] who had been sent there by King Rudolf and his supporters and who had arrived before [the legate], could not contain his amazement at the impudence of such an obvious liar, who drove so many eminent men mad with his falsehoods. He was brought into the presence of the lord pope and of the other Romans and opposed [the legate] face to face, as a very self-confident witness of the truth, until with irrefutable evidence he vanquished him, together with all his fabrications, and publicly showed him to all men, exposed and confounded. For with regard to his actions and his negotiations beyond the mountains, he himself had been in his presence on many occasions or had been instructed by truthful persons who knew and investigated the whole sequence of events and who gave him a careful report of them. His refutation was the more convincing because nothing at all of what had happened was concealed from him. [The legate] was therefore most justly deprived of consecration and dismissed by the lord pope and returned to his home with much sorrow and no less shame.

The pope then sent a letter to his fellow legate Peter [cardinal bishop of Albano], ordering him to return to the apostolic see as soon as possible.[648]

---

646 Cf. characterisation of Udalric by Wido of Ferrara, *De scismate* II, p. 558 ('the dregs of all vices'); Bonizo, *To a friend* VIII, pp. 244–5 ('an extremely eloquent man and particularly loyal to King Henry'). Cf. also Gregory VII, *Register* VII.3, p. 462 (1 October 1079): 'as many Latins as they are, they all, except a very few, approve and defend the cause of Henry'. See Cowdrey (1998) pp. 192–4; Robinson (1999) p. 194.

647 According to G.H. Pertz in his edition, *MGH SS* 5, 322 n. 73, this was perhaps Berthold himself. Meyer von Knonau (1900) p. 226 n. 85, Vogel (1983) p. 170 n. 232, Cowdrey (1998) pp. 193–4: this was Giselbert, identified by Bernold, *Chronicle* 1080, below p. 266 as 'a most devout priest and monk and King Rudolf's envoy to the pope'. The complaints of Rudolf's party were known to the pope by 1 October: *Register* VII.3, pp. 462–3.

648 The sole extant papal letter to the legates, Gregory VII, *JL* 5137 (*Epistolae Vagantes* 31, pp. 80–4), rebukes them for their partisanship. Vogel (1983) p. 170: there was a dispute between the legates, whereupon Peter returned to Rome. See Cowdrey (1998) pp. 193–4; Robinson (1999) p. 194.

He obeyed the commands and, as a witness as full of faith and truth as the other [legate] was of lies, he returned with honour to his [city of] Rome, and on the subject of the tyranny of Henry he reported to the lord pope everything concerning his disobedience, his falsehoods, his deceits, his unheard-of follies and whatever else was repugnant to God and to righteousness. After he had at last learned the whole truth about the actions of his legates, [the pope] sought to discover nothing more about Henry. Nevertheless he sent a letter[649] to King Rudolf and his other supporters, informing them that he took it very ill that his legation had been ineffective and he testified, with God as his witness, that there had been in this case no *respect of persons*[650] (as certain men believed) and that he had not proceeded with levity but had hitherto favoured and acted in conformity with justice, according to the best of his understanding. He urged and exhorted them, however, with his customary fatherly declarations and persuasions to persevere in the course of justice in which they had begun.

King Rudolf returned to his [land of] Saxony.[651] He saw clearly that the conference that Henry's magnates and associates had craftily agreed with the Saxons had been both falsely promised and not observed and it was a cause of sadness to him that he had been so cunningly deceived by their folly, which he had so often experienced before. Nevertheless that high-minded and most steadfast man wisely prepared himself to encounter the expedition that was then being plotted against him. He never for one moment ceased to plan with all his strength so that if, with God's help, another such opportunity should be given to him as had occurred before, Henry and his followers should not deceive him again in the same way and make their escape.

Henry, however, spent the autumn in wandering through the whole of Bavaria.[652] He and his followers without a moment's pause gathered together, by whatever means they could, a huge and powerful body of knights in order to invade Saxony immediately after Christmas. He also incessantly through his most trusted intermediaries made approaches

649 Gregory VII, *Register* VII.3, pp. 462–3, of which Berthold gives a polemical summary.

650 Romans 2:11. See above n. 153.

651 The concept of 'his [land of] Saxony': cf. Gregory VII, *JL* 5106 (*Epistolae Vagantes* 25, p. 64): 'the German and in the Saxon kingdom'; *JL* 5108 (*ibid.*, 26, p. 66): 'the kingdom of the Saxons'. See Müller-Mertens (1970) p. 179; Vogel (1983) p. 177; Leyser (1991) pp. 237–8; Robinson (1999) p. 206.

652 He was in Hirschaid on 19 October (*D.H.IV* 317); in Regensburg on 24 October (*D.H.IV* 318).

to very many Saxons with secret promises of gifts and property on the largest scale and he hastened somehow or other to unite those whom he had bribed and who had sworn oaths to him. He thus gained the confident hope of subjecting the whole of Saxony to himself in a short time without fighting a battle.[653]

In these days he also used violence to impose Norbert, provost of the church of Augsburg and a most greedy simoniac, against the will of all men, on the church of Chur,[654] which had been bereaved of its bishop for more than a year. He could not very easily have found a man more like himself and one who sympathised with his errors. He rejected the provost of that church [of Chur], an extremely devout man whom the clergy, the nobility and the people of that same church had elected according to canon law.[655] [Norbert] immediately indulged his avarice in every possible way, as was always his custom. And because he knew well that his entry into the church was *not by the door but by some other way into the sheepfold*,[656] he attempted to bring it about that he would be subordinated to the heretical anti-bishop [Tedald] of Milan and would have to be consecrated by him as a heretic.[657] He attempted to prove somehow or other by means of certain newly fabricated privileges that the bishop of Mainz was not his metropolitan, although it is well known that the church of Chur is truly the diocesan church [of Mainz]. Nevertheless he made little progress in this.

The summer of this year passed by with excessive rainfall, although such inclement weather did not cause a great scarcity of corn.

The death occurred of Eberhard, bishop of Naumburg, who had already been condemned by the lord pope for his obstinate disobedience, but whom King Henry rashly translated, contrary to law, to the church of Würzburg, in place of the lawful bishop Adalbero, who had been expelled from there. [Eberhard], who was himself excommunicate, exerted himself to communicate with other excommunicates and breathed his last in a state of fatal obstinacy, destined to share the lot of those whom

---

653 Cf. Bruno, *Saxon War* c. 117, p. 109: 'with customary cunning he had divided the Saxons among themselves by making many promises'. See Fenske (1977) pp. 65, 76.

654 Norbert (1079–87). See Meyer von Knonau (1900) p. 233.

655 Ulrich II of Tarasp (1087–96).

656 John 10:1.

657 The diocese of Chur had belonged to the archbishopric of Milan until 843: cf. Landulf Senior, *Historia Mediolanensis* III.32, p. 126. See Clavadetscher (1968) pp. 80–1.

he freely embraced and to be most justly excluded from the kingdom of God through all eternity.[658] He was succeeded by ...,[659] canon of the church of Magdeburg, who was set in his place by canonical election.

In the same year Bishop Hezilo of Hildesheim[660] departed from this *vale of tears*[661] to the Lord – joyfully, I trust! – and his successor was Udo, a canon of his church.[662] In these days also Magdeburg, in place of the archbishop who had suffered the happy death of a martyr – at last received as its bishop, by a canonical election, Hartwig, chamberlain of the church of Mainz.[663]

The abbot of Marseilles, named Bernard, a man of great sanctity, wisdom, piety and charity, had proved steadfast while recently suffering numerous injuries through *persecution for righteousness' sake*.[664] Because of his active cultivation of such great virtues the lord pope particularly sought him out as his close associate, indeed as his most beloved friend before all others and had now, therefore, translated him as the most suitable overseer of the church of St Paul in Rome. Intending to revisit his [city of] Marseilles, he was seized by a lethal fever during his return journey and, setting his heart most eagerly on heaven, he very happily went the way of all flesh.[665] And he was buried with the funeral honours performed most devoutly in the monastery that is situated on the highway used by travellers to Rome, where *the white waters of the Nera*[666] are usually crossed, on this side of St Dionysius, and there he rests in peace.

1080. King Rudolf most solemnly celebrated Christmas [25 December 1079] with all the splendour and magnificence of a king in ...[667] There he wisely and most earnestly took counsel with his followers, as was

---

658 † 5 May 1079. See Meyer von Knonau (1900) pp. 59, 154–5 (with the inaccurate date of 1078). The expulsion of Adalbero: above p. 233 and n. 642.

659 Gunther (1079–90). See Fenske (1977) pp. 72–3, 198–9.

660 Hezilo (1054–79) † 5 August.

661 Psalm 83:7 (Septuagint version).

662 Udo (1079–1114).

663 Hartwig of Spanheim, archbishop of Magdeburg (1079–1102), successor of Werner, who died at Mellrichstadt (above p. 213 and n. 565).

664 Matthew 5:10.

665 The Sarnen MS of Berthold's *Chronicle* adds 'on 19 July'. According to Bernold, *Chronicle* 1079, below p. 265: 20 July. Bernard's relationship with the abbey of S. Paolo fuori le mura: Gregory VII, *Register* VI.15, VII.7. pp. 419–20, 468.

666 Virgil, *Aeneid* VII.517. This monastery is unknown. See Meyer von Knonau (1900) p. 236 n. 4.

667 Place unknown but presumably in Saxony.

fitting, and he very carefully discussed how he could resist Henry, who was at this very moment attempting to invade his [land of] Saxony, without loss to himself. [Henry] remained during these days in Mainz, not with the dignity of a king but living as best he could. He gathered a large body of knights from Burgundy, Franconia, Swabia, Bavaria, Bohemia and from wherever else he could and with great ferocity he continued to plan his expedition and a hostile attack on Saxony soon after the octave of the Epiphany [13 January].[668]

King Rudolf also gathered a powerful army of his knights and, greatly strengthened especially by his trust in God's mercy and His righteousness, courageously decided to meet him and most steadfastly to do battle with him. With this intention he boldly advanced to encounter him with the terror of war and he could hardly wait for the clash of arms. For he was so inflamed by the strong ardour of the zeal for God that he would by no means have refused to deliver himself up to every danger and even to death itself if he could by this means restore the standing of holy Church and his own lawful right. But Henry beguiled his knights with his customary insane cunning and falsehood and promised them, confirming it (so they say) with an oath, that the kingdom of Saxony lay open to him to take without a battle and without any resistance on the part of the enemy and that his adversary Rudolf, together with his followers, would with all the ease that could be desired be delivered into his hands as a captive by the Saxon magnates, almost all of whom he had bound to himself by oaths, and that therefore no danger or difficulty stood in their way.[669] On the contrary, the moment for which they had laboured so hard, which, like him, they had desired for so long, would soon be at hand. With such sophistries he caused those whom he had misled and who trusted in him too much to plunge into the danger of death. For without knowing it they had almost run into King Rudolf with his powerful army, which was all too ready for battle. When he learned from his scouts that they had slipped by so close to him, [Rudolf] pretended to be afraid and to flee from them, cunningly retreating with his men and giving them the opportunity to invade the province. He had dissembled with this intention: that if they met him in battle, they would be less able to flee from his pursuit

668 Henry IV in Mainz: *D.H.IV* 321 (30 December 1079). His military preparations: Meyer von Knonau (1900) pp. 235–7. In the eleventh century a military campaign in winter was unusual.

669 Bruno, *Saxon War* c. 117, p. 109: the desertion of 'Widekin', Wiprecht of Groitsch and 'Theoderic, son of Gero' (from the family of the counts of Kamburg). See Meyer von Knonau (1900) p. 236 n. 4; Fenske (1977) pp. 65–6, 73, 76–7; Robinson (1999) p. 192.

in their customary manner, because once they were inside the frontiers of that country, they could, with God's help, be attacked on all sides and surrounded by the men of that land.

They, however, believed that the flight of the Saxons was genuine and not feigned and boldly pursued them and dared – the Bohemian duke [Vratislav II] before all the rest – to plunder and burn on all sides. The archbishop [Siegfried] of Mainz, whose church lands were in that place through which they were passing and which they were laying waste, took counsel with the bishop [Gebhard] of Salzburg and other fellow bishops who supported him in this matter and imposed a just judgement on Henry, as the sacrilegious leader of this devastation, together with all his associates, and sentenced them, condemned and excommunicated as they were, to the penalty of anathema.[670] Those most insolent despisers of God's justice in their usual manner thought nothing of this and drew very near to the camp of the Saxons, rashly bent on battle and slaughter. A winter that was harsher than usual then set in and greatly hindered both sides in their proceedings.

When King Rudolf finally learned that the enemy was at hand, he advanced, warlike and terrifying, with his forces very well ordered and drawn up for battle.[671] Strengthened above all by his hope in God and in His justice, he awaited the enemies who were making this unprovoked attack on him. For he himself was not the cause and the initiator of this hostile encounter but the defender and the deliverer of himself and his followers and he was compelled to be so by supreme necessity and he considered that to be so and to be so called was the height of fame and honour. With his divisions very well prepared according to the fearful custom of warriors, Henry collided with him in the fiercest of attacks. Sometimes with a direct assault, sometimes with ambushes and with reserve troops deployed unexpectedly, he used all his energies and all his cunning to defeat those who were rebelling against him and somehow or other to bring them into subjection. But immediately at the first encounter the most warlike King Rudolf violently bore down on them with such great vigour, terror and fury that they were entirely unable to withstand his intrepid courage: on the contrary, either they were cut down and lay on the battlefield or, weak and unfit for war, they escaped from him as best they could, fleeing in confusion. The clash of

670 The excommunication: Meyer von Knonau (1900) pp. 237–8. Archbishop Gebhard was then in exile in Saxony: Kost (1962) pp. 107–12.

671 Battle of Flarchheim, 27 January 1080. See Meyer von Knonau (1900) pp. 238–41, 639–43; Vogel (1983) pp. 185–6; Robinson (1999) p. 193.

battle began after nones [3.00 p.m.] and lasted in very many different places until night. At the very beginning of the battle – and this is believed to have happened as a divine judgement[672] – an extremely violent snowstorm cast darkness over both sides in so miraculous a way that scarcely any man could recognise his own comrades until night fell and in that moment separated the combatants into fugitives and pursuers. The Bavarians and Franconians ran away in unmanly fashion from such a fearful slaughter, very swiftly and in great terror, with their king, who was the first to flee.[673] The principal victims of that defeat and that carnage were the Bohemians.[674] Trusting in their numbers, which were many thousands, they had thrown themselves most eagerly into the battle and had desired as recompense for their service only this reward: that they might be the first to attack the Saxons. They estimate the number of their [casualties] at 3,255, besides the very many Germans who fell there; of those, both [Bohemian and German] who were captured, the numbers are not fully or accurately known. Of the army of King Rudolf, however, thirty-eight are reported to have died and all these except for two were lesser men and not sword-bearers of knightly status. One of them was Meginfrid, a certain count of Magdeburg,[675] who had long ago laid down his weapons for God's sake. The apostate had, however, taken them up again for the sake of squalid gain in the shape of certain estates and therefore he perished there, pierced through by a sword, the avenger of God, the just Judge. After the enemy had been put to flight and driven in various directions by the force of war, certain members of King Rudolf's party surrounded the military post where, acting as guards, the young recruits and squires of the enemy army, far away from the fighting, kept watch over the pack-horses, the wagons and the baggage, containing provisions, money, clothing and all their household stuff, and awaited the outcome of the battle. [Rudolf's men] quickly fell upon it from all sides, captured it and, after killing and despoiling their enemies, they joyfully brought back everything with them to their camp.[676]

672 See Cram (1955) pp. 143–5, 214.

673 Cf. Bruno, *Saxon War* c. 117, p. 110: Henry 'resorted to flight soon after the battle began'. The theme of the king's cowardice in anti-Henrician works: Robinson (1999) pp. 348–51.

674 Cf. Bruno, *Saxon War* c. 117, p. 110: 'Folcmar and the burgrave of Prague and with them a great number of Bohemians and others'.

675 Meginfrid, burgrave of Magdeburg, who had undertaken a pilgrimage to Jerusalem. See Meyer von Knonau (1900) pp. 240–1 and n. 10; Fenske (1977) pp. 78–9.

676 Bernold, *Chronicle* 1080, below p. 265; Bruno, *Saxon War* c. 117, p. 110 likewise report Flarchheim as an overwhelming victory for Rudolf. Frutolf of Michelsberg, *Chronica*

Brought low, therefore, by the fierce pursuit of their adversaries, by the ravages of hunger, the bitter cold and above all by the exasperation of so shameful and wretched a flight, Henry, together with his accomplices in tyranny, somehow with great difficulty returned to his [city of] Regensburg. Of the others, no less wretched, shameful and likewise worn down by so many afflictions, each one returned ingloriously to his own land. King Rudolf, however, reassembling his forces of knights from wherever they had gone, victoriously took possession of the battlefield until midnight. But because the intensity of the cold and also the extraordinary exertions of the recent battle afflicted in many ways those who had been weakened and fatigued by it as well as the very many wounded, they abandoned the place, together with those who lay slaughtered or only half-alive there. They straightaway turned aside into a nearby village, where the frozen men warmed themselves and rested and immediately before daybreak they returned [to the battlefield] and remained there the whole day until the next morning supremely triumphant and rejoicing.

Duke Magnus [Billung of Saxony] and his uncle, Count Herman [Billung], who had been captured in a previous battle with the Saxons and handed over to Henry, were now released and given their freedom by him on condition of a promise of fidelity, which he and the duke swore to [Henry]. They most treacherously broke the fealty and the promise of aid that they had previously confirmed on oath to King Rudolf against all those who opposed him and, gathering all those whom they could, they deceitfully attempted to join forces with the aforesaid tyrant before the battle began. But certain of the Saxon magnates discovered their treachery and immediately drove them back and forced them to flee and it was with difficulty that they escaped from them unharmed and hastened to their homes. Margravine Adela[677] and her son-in-law, Margrave Ekbert,[678] were in league with that same secret and treacherous conspiracy, together with all their followers. After the outcome of the battle was known, they suddenly seized certain very strongly fortified castles with the help of their knights and openly revealing themselves to be headstrong apostates, they rebelled against their king.

1079 [=1080], p. 90; *Annals of Augsburg* 1080, p. 130 ascribe the victory to Henry IV. The Hersfeld polemic *Liber de unitate ecclesiae conservanda* II.16, p. 232 reports the battle as indecisive. See Cram (1955) pp. 144–5.

677 Adela (of Louvain), widow of Margrave Otto of Meissen, wife of Margrave Dedi of Lower Lusatia (†1083).

678 Ekbert II (of Brunswick), margrave of Meissen (1068–90). Their conspiracy: Meyer von Knonau (1900) pp. 241–2; Fenske (1977) pp. 73–7.

Thereupon through God's favour in a short time he compelled them all to surrender to him, not without a heavy cost to themselves. For he took their knights away from them and, after they had sworn oaths to him, received them himself, together with their property. He conferred their estates, benefices and marches on others who most urgently requested them and took them. He put them to flight and pursued them with royal might from one place to the next and subjected them to every misfortune, humiliating them and oppressing them with every kind of severity until they learned from experience how foolish and how very injurious it is to disobey their king and their lord without good cause and to deceive him in any way whatsoever. Thus after that very great battle that he had fought with Henry, he returned to Goslar as a glorious conqueror. From then until Lent[679] he diligently preoccupied himself with the warlike activities of those who rebelled against him and opposed him until he had vanquished and subjected them and received their surrender, as was fitting.

Henry was able to accomplish what he desired neither through warfare nor through that secret conspiracy that he plotted with the Saxon princes: on the contrary, he was aware from the evidence of his own conscience that in his stubbornness and disobedience he had openly resisted God's justice and on that account he had already been excommunicated, together with his followers, by papal judgement. Finally, pretending to be afraid of the apostolic see because of the numerous great afflictions and disasters that he, together with his followers, had inflicted on holy Church, he sent from among his anti-bishops, [Liemar] of Bremen and [Rupert of] Bamberg to Rome, taking with them, so they say, a heavy burden of gold and silver, with which they attempted to bribe the Romans in his favour.[680] He had also sent there the bishop [Udalric] of Padua, who had been sent to our land as a papal legate the previous summer, together with certain other trusted associates, weighed down with and stuffed full of very plentiful supplies of money, with the same purpose. He had already been heavily bribed by [Henry] with gifts but was now intent on bribing others. During that journey he was deliberately pierced with a lance by one of his escorts and that most corrupt man was suddenly flung into hell by the judgement of God.[681] The treasure, however, on account of which …

679 Lent began on 25 February.

680 They went to the Roman synod of 7 March 1080: Meyer von Knonau (1900) pp. 242–3; Vogel (1983) p. 187; Cowdrey (1998) p. 194; Robinson (1999) pp. 195, 197.

681 He died before 25 June, when his successor Milo participated in the synod of Brixen.

BERNOLD OF ST BLASIEN
CHRONICLE

1054. The emperor[1] appointed *his[2] cousin Adalbero[3]* to rule over *the church of Bamberg on the estate of Ötting, where he celebrated Christmas* [25 December 1053]. *At the approach of Easter* [3 April] *the lord pope[4] finally returned to Rome, a sick man. On 16 April he died a glorious death,[5] after first blessing everyone, exhorting them and bidding them farewell and after confessing his sins to St Peter and devoutly commending himself to him. He was buried in the basilica of St Peter, next to the tomb of the holy Pope Gregory and it is recorded that he was distinguished by miracles.*[2] In his place Gebhard, named Victor II, the 155th pope, reigned for three years.[6] A subdeacon gave him poison in the chalice. When after the consecration he wished to lift it and could not do so, he threw himself on the ground to pray, together with the people, in order to ask the Lord the reason for this circumstance and immediately his poisoner was seized by a demon. The reason was thus made clear and the lord pope commanded that the chalice, together with the Lord's blood, should be enclosed in a certain altar and should be preserved forever as a relic. Then, together with the people, he threw himself on the ground again to pray until the subdeacon was liberated from the demon.[7]

Baldwin[8] rebelled against the emperor.[9] Duke Godfrey[10] secretly entered

1 Henry III, king (1039–56), emperor (1046).

2/2 Abbreviated extract from the last annal of Herman's chronicle (see above p. 98).

3 Adalbero (1053–7). See above p. 98 and n. 329.

4 Pope Leo IX (1048/9–54).

5 19 April: Steindorff (1881) p. 267 n. 5. See above p. 98.

6 Gebhard I, bishop of Eichstätt (1042–57), Pope Victor II (1055–7). Bernold amended the papal number 154 ascribed by Berthold to 155, in line with the improved chronology of his own *Catalogue of the holy Roman pontiffs* (*MGH SS* 5, 399). The numbers of the following four popes are similarly amended. See Robinson (1978b) p. 82.

7 A later addition to the annal in Bernold's hand. The same passage appears in manuscripts of Lampert of Hersfeld's *Annals* as a later interpolation (O. Holder-Egger, *MGH SS rer. Germ.* [1894] p. 65 n. 1). The poisoning of popes in the mid-eleventh century: Hauck (1959b) pp. 265–74.

8/8 Abbreviated extracts from the last annal of Herman's chronicle (see above p. 98).

9 Count Baldwin V of Flanders: above p. 98 and n. 335.

10 Godfrey III ('the Bearded'), duke of Upper Lotharingia (1044–7), duke of Lower Lotharingia (1065–90), margrave of Tuscany (1054–69).

Italy and joined himself in matrimony to the lady *Beatrice*,[11] *widow of Margrave Boniface.*[8]

1055. The emperor visited Italy and brought away the aforementioned Beatrice as a captive, for it vexed him greatly that she had married Duke Godfrey. Welf, duke of the Carinthians died.[12]

1056. Pope Victor [II] sent Hildebrand, then archdeacon but afterwards pope,[13] and assembled a general synod in Tours, in which Berengar, canon of the church of Angers[14] – from whom the Berengarian heresy takes its name – was examined on the subject of that heresy by the synod, he himself being present. Since he could not defend himself, he anathematised his heresy in the presence of them all and denied it on oath according to the formula that the holy and universal synod of Ephesus prescribed.

1057. Emperor Henry commended to the princes of the kingdom his son, who had already been made king,[15] and died on 5 October.[16] In his place *his*[17] *son Henry*, who was still a boy, *began to reign with his mother,* Agnes.[18]

In Rome after Victor [II][19] *Frederick, brother of Duke Godfrey, formerly archchaplain of Pope Leo of blessed memory, who, having been a clerk, became a monk and was afterwards promoted to be abbot in Monte Cassino, took the name Stephen IX and, as the 156th pope, reigned for nine months.*[20] He separated from the communion of the Church all Roman clergy who

---

11 Beatrice of Lotharingia, margravine of Tuscany (✝1076), married (1) Boniface II (of Canossa), margrave of Tuscany (1030–52), (2) Godfrey 'the Bearded'. See above p. 98 and n. 334.

12 Welf III, duke of Carinthia (1047–55) and margrave of Verona ✝ 13 November.

13 Hildebrand, Pope Gregory VII (1073–85), probably promoted to the rank of archdeacon in 1059: Cowdrey (1998) pp. 37–9. This legatine synod in Tours took place before the death of Leo IX (19 April 1054): Montclos (1971) p. 151 n. 1; Cowdrey (1998) p. 32.

14 Berengar of Tours, archdeacon of Angers, theologian (✝1088). Cf. Bernold's polemic against Berengar's eucharistic doctrine, *De veritate corporis et sanguinis Domini* p. 380. See Gibson (1971) pp. 62–3; Montclos (1971) pp. 149–50 and above p. 44.

15 Henry IV (1050–1106), king (1056), emperor (1106), elected king November 1053 in Tribur (see above p. 96), crowned 17 July 1054 in Aachen: Robinson (1999) pp. 21–3.

16 Henry III died in 1056, not 1057: see above pp. 113–14.

17 From this point until the first sentence of the annal for 1076 (below p. 255) Bernold's chronicle closely follows the second version of Berthold's chronicle, above pp. 114–42.

18 Agnes of Poitou (?1025–77), queen (1043), empress (1046).

19 ✝ 28 July: see above p. 102 n. 39. Cf. Bernold, *Calendar* p. 511.

20 See above p. 114 and n. 64.

remained unchaste after the prohibition of the blessed Pope Leo. For thus Cardinal bishop Peter Damian[21] bears witness in his letter.[22]

1058. *In Rome after Stephen a certain Benedict was appointed contrary to canon law and through the personal favour of certain men and presided over the church without consecration for seven months.*[23] *He was expelled by Duke Godfrey, and Bishop Gerard of Florence, called Nicholas II, ruled as the* 157th *pope for almost three years.*[24] *He decreed that those who at that time had been promoted* free of charge *by simoniacs, should be permitted to exercise their office. Thereafter, however, whoever might be ordained by* simoniacs *should obtain no advantage from such a promotion.*[25] *Peter Damian, the bishop of Ostia of pious memory, also incited this pope to correct the unchastity of the clergy according to canon law.*[26]

1059. *Frederick of Gleiberg and his brothers*[27] *rebelled against King Henry.*

1060. In Rome Pope Nicholas presided over a general synod and once more examined Berengar, who appeared before the synod in person, on the subject of his heresy. At last he burned the books of his heresy in the presence of his synod, as if he had been converted, and as before he swore an oath anathematising that heresy.[28]

1061. *In Rome after the death of Pope Nicholas on 27 July,*[29] *the Romans sent a crown and other gifts to King Henry,* the fourth of that name, *and appealed to the king about the election of the supreme pontiff. He held a general council in Basel, put on the crown sent by the Romans and was called patrician of*

---

21 Peter Damian, cardinal bishop of Ostia (1057–72). Bernold's admiration of Peter Damian: annals 1058, 1066, 1072 (below pp. 250, 252); *De sacramentis excommunicatorum* p. 92 ('most renowned for his piety and scholarship and most sagacious in questions of this kind [sacramental theology]'); *De excommunicatis vitandis* p. 98 ('another Jerome in our time').

22 *Letter* 112, p. 276: 'Pope Stephen ... had commanded all the clergy of Rome who remained unchaste after the prohibition of Pope Leo to depart from the assembly of the clergy and the membership of the Church.' Allusion to the Roman synod of 1057 (*Chronicle of Monte Cassino* II.94, p. 353), *acta* not extant (*JL post* 4375) and Leo IX's *Constitutum de castitate clericorum* (*JL ante* 4215), not extant.

23 Pope Benedict X (1058–9). See above p. 102 and nn. 42, 43.

24 Gerard, bishop of Florence (1045–61), Pope Nicholas II (1058–61).

25 Cf. Nicholas II, *Decretum contra simoniacos* (*JL* 4431a, *MGH Constitutiones* 1, 549, no. 386).

26 *Letter* 61, pp. 206–18 (January–July 1059).

27 Kinsmen of Duke Frederick II of Lower Lotharingia: see above p. 115 n. 79.

28 Lateran synod of 1059: Schieffer (1981) p. 54 n. 28. The case of Berengar: Bernold, *De veritate corporis et sanguinis Domini* p. 380. See Gibson (1971) pp. 64–5; Montclos (1971) p. 163.

29 Probably 20 July: Schmidt (1977) p. 81.

the Romans. Then with the common consent of them all and according to the election of the envoys of the Romans on 26 October Bishop Cadalus of Parma was elected pope and called Honorius,[30] *but he was destined never to possess the papacy. Twenty-seven days before his appointment, however, the bishop of Lucca, named Anselm, was ordained as the* 158th *pope*[31] *by the Normans*[32] *and by certain Romans and was called Alexander. He reigned for twelve years. He destroyed simoniacal heresy with great vigour and forbade the ministers of the altar to cohabit with their wives on pain of excommunication, according to the decrees of canon law. He forbade laymen, using the sanction of anathema, to attend the services of clergy who were openly unchaste and thus he very prudently restrained the unchastity* of the clergy.[33] *The author of this regulation was principally Hildebrand, who was at that time archdeacon of the Roman church and who was extremely hostile to heretics.*

1062. In these times there was *a great famine. A great quarrel broke out between Empress* Agnes *and Bishop Gunther of Bamberg.*[34]

1063. *King Henry led an army into Hungary and restored Salomon, the son of King Andreas,*[35] *to his father's kingdom. Bishop Henry of Augsburg died and Embriko* [was appointed] *in his place.*[36] *In the church in Goslar great bloodshed* occurred *in the presence of the king.*[37]

1064. *A great conflict* arose *between Archbishop Adalbert of Hamburg*[38] *and the princes of the kingdom.*

1065. *The royal palace in Goslar was burned down.*[39] In the same year, the 1,065th of the Lord's Incarnation, when Easter was celebrated *on 27 March* – that was the day on which Christ rose from the dead[40] – on the

---

30 Cadalus, bishop of Parma (?1046–?71), antipope Honorius II (1061–4).

31 Anselm I, bishop of Lucca (1057–72), Pope Alexander II (1061–73).

32 I.e. Richard I, prince of Capua: see above p. 116 and n. 97.

33 Alexander II, *JL* 4501, c. 3, ed. Schieffer (1981) p. 219.

34 Gunther I (1057–65). The quarrel: Meyer von Knonau (1890) pp. 270–4; Black-Veldtrup (1995) pp. 365–6.

35 Salomon, king (1063–74, †1087), son of Andreas I (1046–60). The campaign: Meyer von Knonau (1890) pp. 345–8; Boshof (1986) p. 185.

36 Henry II (1047–63) † 3 September; Embriko (1063–77).

37 7 June. See above p. 118 n. 109.

38 Adalbert (1043–72). See above p. 118 n. 110.

39 An event mentioned only by Berthold and Bernold: Meyer von Knonau (1890) p. 400 n. 11.

40 The belief that 27 March was the actual date of Christ's Resurrection (and that 'the day of Judgement was at hand because Easter fell that year on 27 March'): *Vita Altmanni episcopi Pataviensis* c. 3, p. 230. See Meyer von Knonau (1890) p. 393.

third day of Easter week, 29 March, *in the third indiction,* King Henry *was girded with the sword* in the name of the Lord *in the ninth year of his reign and in the fourteenth year of his life.*[41] *The bishop of Passau died and Altman, the chaplain of the empress, succeeded him.*[42] *At this time Archbishop Siegfried of Mainz*[43] *and Bishop Gunther of Bamberg* and *Bishop Otto of Regensburg*[44] and *Bishop William of Utrecht*[45] *with a great* multitude *set out for Jerusalem. During that journey they suffered much from the pagans, for they were even compelled to do battle with them.*[46] *Gunther died on that same* journey[47] *and Ricimann succeeded him by means of simony.*[48]

1066. *Many noblemen died in a civil war.*[49] *Comets were seen on the octave of Easter, that is on 23 April, and* appeared *for thirty days.*[50]

Archbishop Eberhard of Trier[51] *departed in peace on 15 April, the Saturday before the holy day of Easter, after he had himself completed the offices of that day and while he was still clad in his priestly vestments. Conrad, the provost of Cologne,*[52] *ought to have succeeded him but he was* not elected *by the citizens. A certain count named Theoderic,*[53] *therefore, seized that same Conrad, as he travelled* to the city of *Trier. After tormenting him for a long time in prison, he entrusted him to four knights to be killed. When they had thrown him three times down a precipice and had been able to do no more than bruise his arm, one of them was led by penitence to seek pardon from him. Another, however, wishing to behead him, only cut off his jaw and thus that martyr worthy of God departed to the Lord.* His sufferings took place on 1 June in the 1,066th year of the Lord's Incarnation, the tenth year of Henry's reign and *he was buried in the abbey named Tholey. A fitting vengeance, however, afterwards pursued the three knights who were the perpetrators of the death of* this servant of God. *For one of them was unable to swallow the food that he*

41 The ceremony declared Henry to be of age: see above p. 105 n. 84.

42 Egilbert (1045–65) † 17 May; Altman (1065–91).

43 Siegfried (1060–84).

44 Otto (1060/1–89).

45 William (?1054–76).

46 This pilgrimage began November 1064 and ended summer 1065. See above p. 106 n. 89.

47 23 July.

48 Herman I, bishop of Bamberg (1065–75). See above p. 106 n. 90.

49 Perhaps the unrest in Saxony following the fall of Archbishop Adalbert of Bremen. See above p. 106 n. 91.

50 Halley's Comet. Sightings in German and Italian narrative sources: Meyer von Knonau (1890) p. 523 n. 55.

51 Eberhard (1047–66).

52 Conrad of Pfullingen. See above p. 106 and n. 94.

53 Theoderic, burgrave of Trier: see above p. 106 n. 95.

received; the other two mutilated their hands and descended to the confines of hell. *After* Conrad's *murder Udo was appointed* bishop *of Trier.*[54]

The wedding of King Henry.[55] *Again a comet was seen. At this time the venerable Peter Damian, who was originally a hermit and became a cardinal bishop, wrote many works and attacked the unchastity of priests in his writings with very many reasons. They say, however, that he treated those ordained by simoniacs with too much indulgence.*[56] *Archbishop Hugh of Besançon died. His successor, a canon of the same church, was elected by the brethren* and appointed by the king.[57]

1067. *Saxony was afflicted by civil strife.*[58] *The Normans wished to make a hostile* advance *on Rome.*[59] *Bishop Burchard of Halberstadt*[60] *courageously wrought destruction among the people of the Liutizi. Bishop Einhard of Speyer died on a journey to Rome and Henry succeeded him.*[61]

1068. King Henry, *led astray by the folly of his youth, was so forgetful of his lawful wife and was widely rumoured to be implicated in such abominable offences that his princes even attempted to deprive him of the kingship.*[62] *All that year was rainy.*

1069. *Peace and reconciliation were confirmed among the people on oath by royal edict at Christmas* [25 December 1068] *in Goslar.*[63] *King Henry brought destruction to the people of the Liutizi.*[64] *The Saxon margrave Dedi*[65] *rebelled against King* Henry *but he was subsequently forced to come to surrender.*

Abbot Udalric of Reichenau died and in his place Meginward [was appointed].[66]

54 Udo of Nellenburg, archbishop of Trier (1066–78).

55 The wedding of Henry IV and Bertha of Turin: above p. 120 and n. 126.

56 *Letter* 40 (*Liber Gratissimus*), pp. 384–509. His views on simoniacal ordinations: Dressler (1954) pp. 103–4.

57 Hugh I (1031–66); Hugh II (1066–85).

58 Probably the conflict between Adalbert of Bremen and the Saxon nobility: Meyer von Knonau (1890) pp. 513–16.

59 The attack of Richard I of Capua on the Campagna, 1066: above p. 122 n. 142.

60 The expedition of Burchard II (1059–88) took place in 1068. See above p. 68 n. 113, p. 120 n. 134.

61 Einhard II (1060–7) † 23 March; Henry I (1067–75).

62 A polemical allusion to the king's unsuccessful attempt to obtain a divorce from Queen Bertha. See above p. 122 n. 145.

63 This event as an instance of 'the peace of God' movement: Wadle (1973) p. 159. See also above p. 122 and n. 147.

64 See above p. 122 n. 148.

65 Dedi, margrave of Lower Lusatia (1046–75). See above p. 123 n. 149.

66 Udalric I (1048–69) † 7 November; Meginward (1070). See above p. 123 and n. 151.

In *Constance Bishop Rumold* died and Charles succeeded him in the bishopric by means of *simoniacal heresy.*[67] *Duke Godfrey* ['the Bearded'], *who was* most excellent *among secular men, very easily moved to tears by the memory of his sins and most generous in the distribution of alms, rested in peace* on Christmas Eve [24 December] after a most praiseworthy end.[68]

1070. *Franconia was afflicted by civil strife.*[69] *Duke Otto of Bavaria*[70] *rebelled* against King Henry and *Magnus, son of Duke Otto of northern Saxony.*[71] *When the aforesaid Otto, after being lawfully summoned to make amends for his conduct, refused to come, the king deprived him of his duchy. Meginward voluntarily* left *the office of abbot of Reichenau.* After him *a certain Rupert* was unworthily placed in *the office of abbot* and *afterwards* worthily expelled.[72] *The winter was windy and rainy.*

1071. *Welf was made duke of Bavaria.*[73] *King Henry was subjected to many plots but he manfully withstood them all.*[74] *Otto,* previously *duke of Bavaria, together with his allies,* voluntarily *came to King* Henry *to surrender at Whitsuntide* in the 1,071st year of the Lord's Incarnation, the fifteenth year of Henry's reign and the twentieth year of his life, in the ninth indiction, on Tuesday of that week, 14 June.[75]

Charles, who acquired the bishopric of Constance by simony, *scattered the treasure of* that *church for his own use, like a sacrilegious thief. At a council held in Mainz at the command of Pope Alexander* [II] that aforementioned disciple of Simon, *who was not yet consecrated,* was deposed; for when *he was accused* there *by* the clergy *of Constance, he could not deny the accusations.*[76] *Otto* succeeded him in the bishopric.[77]

---

67 Rumold (1051–69) † 4 November; Charles (Carloman) (1070–1). See above p. 123 and n. 154.

68 † 30 December: see above p. 124 n. 157.

69 Perhaps in connection with the growing unrest in Thuringia: Meyer von Knonau (1894) p. 28.

70 Otto I, count of Northeim, duke of Bavaria (1061–70, †1083). See above p. 125 and n. 163.

71 Magnus Billung, duke of Saxony (1073–1106), son of Duke Ordulf (Otto) (1059–72).

72 Rupert (1071–2). See above p. 126 n. 175.

73 Welf IV (1070–1101).

74 See above p. 125 n. 169.

75 Otto of Northeim and Magnus Billung surrendered in Halberstadt: Meyer von Knonau (1894) p. 70.

76 Synod of Mainz, 15–18 August. See above pp. 125–6.

77 Otto I (1071–86).

1072. *King* Henry *overcame those who were* resisting *him virtually without the trouble of fighting a battle.*

Cardinal bishop Peter Damian of pious memory, who had long been crucified by the world, departed to the Lord on 22 February.[78] *The lord Gerald, a true monk, who was distinguished for his knowledge of the Scriptures and whose character was similar to that of his predecessor, succeeded him in the bishopric.*[79]

Archbishop Adalbert of Hamburg and *Bremen died and Liemar succeeded him.*[80] *The king built for himself many very strongly fortified castles in the regions of Saxony and Thuringia and also unjustly seized for himself* many *fortifications and thus aroused the minds of many men against himself.*[81]

1073. *Duke Rudolf of Swabia,*[82] *Duke Berthold of* the Carinthians[83] *and Duke Welf* [IV] *of Bavaria dissociated themselves from King* Henry *because they perceived that their advice carried no weight with the king, other men having insinuated themselves into his counsels.*[84]

Count Theoderic was moved to penitence for the crime that he committed against the blessed Conrad, who had been assigned to the people of Trier as their archbishop.[85] *Although many dangers stood in his way, he nevertheless began the journey to Jerusalem with eager faith, in the company of many others. After they went on board a ship and were beset by a sudden storm and, because the day immediately darkened, they were uncertain where they were going, they were repeatedly cheered by a heavenly light. Thereafter they no longer feared death in the midst of their danger but fixed their thoughts on the eternal life that was to come. Cleansed of their filthy sins by the waves of the sea, they departed to the Lord on 17 February:* namely *Count Theoderic, Widerold, Marchwald, together with 113* others.[86]

In Rome Pope Alexander [II] *died.*[87] *It was the universal opinion that Hildebrand, archdeacon of the Roman church, should be appointed pope in his*

78 Bernold, *Calendar* p. 498: 21 February. See above p. 127 n. 177.

79 Gerald, cardinal bishop of Ostia (1072/3–7).

80 Adalbert + 16 March; Liemar (1072–1101).

81 See Meyer von Knonau (1894) pp. 857–69; Fenske (1977) pp. 28–32; Robinson (1999) pp. 82–7.

82 Rudolf of Rheinfelden, duke of Swabia (1057–79), anti-king (1077–80).

83 Berthold I ('the Bearded', of Zähringen), duke of Carinthia (1061–78).

84 See above p. 127 n. 185.

85 See above p. 249 and n. 53.

86 Cf. Bernold, *Calendar* p. 497.

87 21 April. Cf. Bernold, *Calendar* p. 503.

place. When he heard of this, the archdeacon, *regarding himself as unequal* in strength *to so great an honour, or rather so great a burden,* sought *a delay before giving his answer and then fled and remained hidden for some days in St Peter ad Vincula.* But *at length he was with difficulty discovered and brought to the apostolic see by force, ordained as the* 159th *pope on* 25 April *and called Gregory VII.*[88] *It was through his wisdom that the unchastity of priests was held in check not only in Italy but also in the German territories. That is to say, what his predecessor* forbade *in Italy, he* strove *to forbid* throughout *the* whole *catholic Church.*

The whole of Thuringia and Saxony rebelled against King Henry because of the fortifications mentioned above and because of many other things that the king did *unadvisedly in their territory against the will of that people.*[89] *Ekkehard was at length made abbot of Reichenau and was consecrated by the aforementioned pope in Rome.*[90]

1074. *King Henry, in the absence of* the princes of his *kingdom,* made peace *with the Saxons with this stipulation, that the fortifications concerning which the quarrel had arisen, should be destroyed* and they were afterwards destroyed.[91] *Duke Rudolf* [of Swabia] *and the others were reconciled to the king.*[92]

At this time *legates of the apostolic see came to the king in Swabia with the purpose of correcting the king's morals.* The king *committed himself into their hands with a promise of amendment and most firmly promised his help to the lord pope in deposing simoniacs. The advisers of the king also promised on oath in the presence of those same legates that they would restore all the church property that they had unjustly acquired. They had indeed bought that same property from simoniacs when helping those unworthy men to ecclesiastical office by their advice. After these matters had been settled, the legates of the apostolic see returned.*[93]

Margrave Herman,[94] *the son of Duke Berthold* [I of Carinthia], who most perfectly participated in the angelic way of life *in Cluny already as a young*

88 This fictitious account of Gregory VII's election, 22 April: above p. 128 n. 191. Bernold, *Calendar* p. 506 commemorates his consecration on 30 May.

89 See above p. 129 and n. 192.

90 Ekkehard II (1072–88). See above p. 130 n. 200.

91 Peace of Gerstungen, 2 February: see above p. 130 and n. 202.

92 Through the mediation of Empress Agnes: Meyer von Knonau (1894) p. 383.

93 The legation of the cardinal bishops Gerald of Ostia and Hubert of Palestrina in April: above p. 131 and n. 204. Henry IV's advisers: above p. 133 n. 215.

94 Herman I, margrave of Baden. Cf. Bernold, *Calendar* p. 503. See above p. 128 n. 189.

man, after abandoning his wife and only son[95] *and everything that he had possessed, departed to the Lord on 25 April* as a true monk.

1075. *King* Henry spent *Christmas* [25 December 1074] *in Strasbourg. He arranged an expedition* to *Saxony. Bishop Herman of Bamberg* was accused by his clergy of *simoniacal heresy and deposed by the pope. Rupert was put in his place.*[96]

In the first week of Lent [24–28 February] Pope Gregory [VII] assembled a synod in Rome,[97] in which he examined the case of Henry of Speyer, a bishop but a simoniac one.[98] On the very same day that his case was being examined in Rome, that is, on 24 February, he became ill in Speyer. Then on 26 February, when he was the subject of a definitive sentence of condemnation by Pope Gregory in the Roman synod, he died a pitiful death. *In*[99] *that synod* it was decreed by Pope Gregory *that* clergy who obtain *any rank or office of holy orders by means of money* are not thereafter to *serve in the Church;* that no one may keep a church that has been acquired by means of money *and that no one hereafter is to presume to sell or buy* a church. Then that whoever are shown to be guilty of unchastity are to cease to exercise clerical office. Furthermore, *that the people are by no means to accept the ministry* of clergy whom they know to *hold the* papal *decrees in contempt.*[99]

The king celebrated Easter [5 April] *in Worms. After Whitsun* [24 May] *he moved the army into* Saxony and during that expedition a countless multitude was slain on both sides on 9 June near the river named the Unstrut and many of the Saxons came to surrender to the king.[100]

Bishop Dietwin of Liège died and Henry succeeded him.[101] Anno, the venerable archbishop of Cologne, a man of extraordinary sanctity, rested in peace on 4 December. Hildulf, who was his equal neither in birth nor in

---

95 Judith, daughter of Count Adalbert of Calw (†1091); Herman II, margrave of Baden (†1130).

96 Rupert (1075–1102). See above pp. 137–8 and n. 232.

97 Gregory VII, *Register* II.52a, pp. 196–7. See Meyer von Knonau (1894) pp. 451–5; Schieffer (1981) pp. 118–19; Cowdrey (1998) pp. 100–8; Robinson (1999) pp. 134–8.

98 Cf. *Register* II.52a, p. 196; Bernold, *De incontinentia sacerdotum* V, p. 26.

99/99 Extracts from Gregory VII, *JL* 4933 (*Epistolae Vagantes* 8, pp. 16–18) to Bishop Otto of Constance, quoted by Berthold above pp. 132–3 and n. 214.

100 Battle of Homburg on the River Unstrut. Cf. above pp. 135–6. See Meyer von Knonau (1894) pp. 496–506, 874–84; Giese (1979) pp. 159–61; Robinson (1999) pp. 100–2. The surrender in Spier, 26/27 October: above p. 137 and n. 230.

101 Dietwin (1048–75) † 23 June; Henry (1075–91).

character, succeeded him.[102]

1076. *The king* celebrated *Christmas* [25 December 1075] *in Goslar*[103] and there he compelled certain men to swear that they would elect his son[104] to the kingship after him. At this time King Henry incessantly defiled holy Church with simoniacal heresy by conferring the investiture of bishoprics, abbacies and other such offices for money and, among other offences, also communicating with excommunicates.[105]

Cintius, a certain Roman citizen,[106] seized Pope Gregory on Christmas day as he was celebrating mass. After he had been thus taken prisoner, one of Cintius's knights resolved to kill him. But while the sword was poised over [the pope's] head, he was gripped by extreme terror and fell to the ground, unable to finish the stroke that he had begun. Cintius, however, led the pope away, captive, to his tower, which was immediately torn down by the Romans and the pope was expeditiously released. He begged for the life of his captor from the Romans and eventually, with great difficulty, succeeded.

Although the king had very frequently been admonished by the pope, he refused to amend his life and the pope accomplished nothing by his warnings. He finally informed him that he would be excommunicated in the next Roman synod if he did not come to his senses.[107] The envoys bearing this message[108] reached the king the week after Christmas. The king, therefore, held an assembly in Worms on Septuagesima Sunday

---

102 Anno II (1056–75); Hildulf (1076–8). See above pp. 138 and nn. 241–2, 216. Cf. Lampert, *Annales* 1076, p. 251: 'a man very small in stature, with a face that inspired contempt, of obscure birth and with nothing in his mental and physical attributes that could make him worthy of so great a priestly office'. See Meyer von Knonau (1894) p. 647 and n. 42.

103 See above p. 142 and n. 261. This is the final passage in the chronicle that is directly dependent on Berthold's text.

104 Conrad (1074–1101), duke of Lower Lotharingia (1076–87), king (1087–98). Cf. Lampert, *Annales* 1076, pp. 250–1. See Meyer von Knonau (1894) p. 584; Goez (1996) p. 4; Robinson (1999) pp. 103–4, 143.

105 Perhaps an allusion to the cases of bishops Poppo of Paderborn and Conrad of Utrecht reported by Berthold, *Chronicle* 1076, above p. 147. See Schieffer (1981) p. 187 n. 66.

106 Cencius Stephani (de Praefecto), son of the Roman prefect Stephen, abducted the pope during midnight mass on Christmas Eve 1075: see above p. 142 and nn. 263–4.

107 Cf. Bernold, *De damnatione scismaticorum* III, p. 49: 'King Henry ... refused to come to his senses and ... knew in advance that he would be excommunicated in the next Roman synod'; Gregory VII, *JL* 4999 (*Epistolae Vagantes* 14, p. 38).

108 Radbod, Adelpreth and Gottschalk. See above pp. 140 and n. 249, 165.

[24 January] and another in Lombardy in Piacenza[109] and caused all those whom he could to forswear the obedience that they ought to show to the aforementioned pope. He sent envoys to the Roman synod that was celebrated the following Lent[110] and insolently commanded the pope to step down from the apostolic see. But his envoys[111] were most shamefully treated in the synod and it was only with difficulty and with the help of the pope that they escaped from the Romans. According to the judgement of the synod, [the pope] deprived the king of the fidelity of his vassals, of the kingship and of communion and he absolved from their oaths all men who had sworn to accept him as king. He deprived of their office and of communion all those bishops who had voluntarily supported the king against the pope but to the others who had partici-pated unwillingly in that conspiracy he granted a respite until the feast of St Peter [29 June].[112]

Duke Godfrey, the son of Duke Godfrey ['the Bearded'], a participant in, or rather the ringleader of, the aforementioned conspiracy, was wounded in the posterior in a shameful manner by a certain cook, while he was at stool and he died before the middle of Lent.[113] Likewise Bishop William of Utrecht, who had greatly reviled the pope, was punished after Easter by sudden death while still excluded from ecclesiastical communion.[114] Conrad was put in his place.[115]

Almost all the princes of the kingdom had now separated themselves from communion with Henry. In the month of October, therefore, an assembly was held in Oppenheim by the princes of the kingdom[116] and a

---

109 Council of Worms; synod of Piacenza. See Meyer von Knonau (1894) pp. 613–30; Schneider (1972) pp. 146–53; Cowdrey (1998) pp. 135–8; Robinson (1999) pp. 143–7.

110 Roman synod of 14–20 February: Gregory VII, *Register* III.10a, pp. 268–71. See Meyer von Knonau (1894) pp. 632–45; Schneider (1972) pp. 154–7; Cowdrey (1998) pp. 140–2.

111 Roland, canon of Parma, bishop of Treviso (?1078–?89) and 'a certain servant of the king'. See above p. 144.

112 Cf. Bernold, *De damnatione scismaticorum* III, p. 52. Cf. Gregory VII, *JL* 4999 (*Epistolae Vagantes* 14, pp. 38–40).

113 Godfrey IV ('the Hunchback'), duke of Lower Lotharingia (1069–76) † 26 February. See above p. 146 and n. 281.

114 † 27 April. (Easter fell on 27 March.) See above p. 147 and n. 295.

115 Conrad (1076–99).

116 The princes met in Tribur (16 October), while the king and his advisers remained in Oppenheim, on the opposite side of the Rhine. See Meyer von Knonau (1894) pp. 729–35, 885–93; Erdmann (1940) pp. 486–95; Schneider (1972) pp. 171–87; Beumann (1973) pp. 33–44; Hlawitschka (1974) pp. 25–45; Robinson (1999) pp. 155–8.

legation of the apostolic see was present.[117] There Henry promised most faithfully that he would present himself to the lord pope in Augsburg on the feast of the Purification of St Mary next following [2 February 1077]. For he himself, together with the princes of the kingdom, invited the lord pope there.[118] Brother Kadaloh, who had left the secular career of a knight and converted to religion, brought the pope's legation to the assembly of Oppenheim, the pope having laid this duty on him while he was very sick, for the remission of all his sins. After he had completed the legation, therefore, brother Kadaloh put on the habit of a monk and rested in peace in the perfection of the Gospels.[119]

1077. The duke of the Poles crowned himself king.[120] A very great quantity of snow covered the whole kingdom from 31 October of the previous year until 26 March of the present year.[121]

Henry the so-called king despaired of his own cause and therefore avoided a public hearing. He secretly entered Italy contrary to the pope's command and the princes' advice and met the pope in Canossa[122] before the feast of the Purification of St Mary, while the latter was attempting to reach Augsburg on the day that had been agreed on. There he finally with difficulty wrung from [the pope], by pretending as best he could to humble himself to an extraordinary degree, the concession not of the kingship but only of communion.[123] Nevertheless he first took an oath that he would make amends concerning the charges brought against him, according to the judgement of the pope, and agreed that he would not inflict any injury on the pope or on anyone faithful to him as they

---

117 Sigehard of Aquileia and Altman of Passau. Berthold, above p. 174, mentions also Gebhard of Salzburg.

118 See Meyer von Knonau (1894) p. 734; Schneider (1972) pp. 176–7; Beumann (1973) pp. 42, 45; Hlawitschka (1974) p. 44.

119 † 10 November: cf. Bernold, *Calendar* p. 519. Jakobs (1968) p. 42 suggests that he became a monk of St Blasien.

120 Boleslav II, duke of Poland (1058–76), king (1076–83).

121 See above p. 155. The duration and severity of the winter: Meyer von Knonau (1894) p. 750 and n. 7.

122 The fortress of Margravine Matilda of Tuscany, south-west of Reggio. The king's absolution: Meyer von Knonau (1894) pp. 755–62, 894–903; Morrison (1962) pp. 121–48; Schneider (1972) pp. 201–13; Beumann (1973) pp. 48–55; Cowdrey (1998) pp. 156–66; Robinson (1999) pp. 160–4.

123 Cf. Gregory VII, *Register* VII.14a, p. 484: 'I restored to him communion alone, but I did not install him in the kingship, from which I had deposed him in a Roman synod.' See Morrison (1962) pp. 121–48; Miccoli (1966) pp. 203–23; Beumann (1973) pp. 49–55; Cowdrey (1998) pp. 162–4.

came or went in any direction.[124] He did not keep this oath, however, even for a fortnight, for he took prisoner the venerable bishops Gerald of Ostia and Anselm of Lucca.[125] The pope, therefore, sent legates[126] and declared to the princes of the kingdom that he had achieved little by receiving him into communion, since all the simoniacs and excommunicates were now encouraged by him just as much as before.[127]

When they heard this, therefore, the princes of the kingdom held a general assembly in Forchheim on 13 March and raised up the excellent Duke Rudolf to be their king[128] and they crowned him in Mainz on 26 March, which in that year fell in the middle of Lent.[129] The very great quantity of snow, which in that year covered the whole earth for so long, finally began to melt at the election of the new king.[130] On the day of his consecration, however, a huge riot broke out in Mainz, incited by the simoniac clergy, on such a scale that [the rioters] even wished to break into the palace and kill the most religious clergy and monks. But the right hand of God so protected the knights of the new prince, that even though they were unarmed, they lost only one of their number but they killed more than a hundred of their opponents, some by the sword, some by drowning.[131] A penance was imposed on them for these killings by the legates of the apostolic see, as follows: each of them was either to fast for forty days or to feed forty poor men on one occasion, but they were not to avoid ecclesiastical communion, as if they were murderers.[132]

After his consecration King Rudolf departed into Swabia and subjected the kingdom to himself.[133] Meanwhile Henry lingered in Lombardy.

124 'The oath of Henry, king of the Germans' (28 January): *Register* IV.12a, pp. 314–15.

125 Anselm II (1073–86), on a legation to Milan. See Meyer von Knonau (1894) pp. 768–9; Vogel (1983) pp. 12–13, 18–20. See also above p. 163 and n. 359.

126 Cardinal deacon Bernard and Bernard, abbot of St Victor in Marseilles (1064–79). See Meyer von Knonau (1894) p. 778; Schumann (1912) pp. 36–44; Hüls (1977) pp. 245–6; Cowdrey (1998) pp. 169–75.

127 Cf. Gregory VII, *JL* 5019 (*Epistolae Vagantes* 19, p. 52): 'by reason of his presence, certain very wicked men show boldness towards us and the apostolic see rather than fear at the evil they have committed'.

128 See Meyer von Knonau (1900) pp. 3–8, 627–38; Schlesinger (1973) pp. 61–85; Giese (1979) pp. 37–49; Robinson (1979) pp. 721–33; Vogel (1983) pp. 41–6; Cowdrey (1998) pp. 167–71; Robinson (1999) pp. 167–70.

129 The fourth Sunday in Lent: see above p. 167 and n. 385.

130 Cf. Berthold, *Chronicle* 1077, above p. 155 and n. 333.

131 The rising in Mainz: Meyer von Knonau (1900) pp. 10–12, 632–3.

132 Cf. Burchard, *Decretum* VI.16, col. 769B.

133 Cf. Berthold's version of his progress, above pp. 167–70.

The Roman citizen Cintius came to him in Pavia, bringing with him the venerable bishop of Como, named Rainald,[134] as his captive, wishing indeed to be rewarded by Henry because it was in his service that he had taken prisoner both this bishop and in the previous year the lord pope. But he was overtaken there by sudden death and received his due reward, which he had not been afraid to earn by his many sacrileges. When Henry heard of Rudolf's advancement, he implored the pope for help against him, although he continued to allow the aforementioned bishop [Gerald] of Ostia to be held in captivity. The pope therefore replied to him that he could not grant his request as long as St Peter, in the person of his legate, was held prisoner in his jurisdiction.[135] Since his plea was ineffectual, he directed his mind towards tyranny and he now planned to secure the kingship not through judicial process but by means of violence.

King Rudolf, however, celebrated Easter [16 April] with the greatest splendour in Augsburg with the legates of the apostolic see.[136] One of the latter, namely the most devout Abbot Bernard [of St Victor in Marseilles], was sent to Rome but was captured and plundered by Count Udalric, a supporter of Henry,[137] and spent almost a year in captivity until finally the abbot of Cluny[138] delivered him with difficulty from Henry's hands. After Easter the king held a general assembly with the princes of the kingdom in Esslingen.[139] When this was over, he went with an extremely small body of men to lay siege to a certain fortress.[140] But behold! his rival Henry unexpectedly arrived with a very great host of Bohemians and Bavarians, whose services he was suddenly able to purchase with church property. The king would most willingly have encountered them, even with the few men whom he had with him at that time, if his princes had not judged it more prudent to defer the encounter to another time. Henry, therefore, took the opportunity to lay waste all the surrounding lands with unceasing plundering and

---

134 Rainald (1061–84). His capture by Cencius Stephani (n. 106) see above p. 163. Henry IV in Pavia: above p. 163 n. 364.

135 Gerald of Ostia was imprisoned by Bishop Denis of Piacenza: above p. 163. Cf. Gregory VII, *Register* V.7, p. 357.

136 Cf. Berthold, *Chronicle* 1077, above p. 169 and n. 390, with evidence of a crown-wearing.

137 Udalric II, count of Lenzburg (Aargau). See above p. 179 and n. 431.

138 Hugh I ('the Great') (1049–1109), Henry IV's godfather.

139 Berthold, *Chronicle* 1077, above p. 169 describes Rudolf as holding court in Augsburg. See Meyer von Knonau (1900) p. 24 n. 30.

140 Sigmaringen. See above p. 173 n. 407.

with fire and sword and also to hold men captive like cattle. For his supporters from Bohemia preyed on men more willingly than on cattle so that they might inhumanly prostitute them to satisfy their lust and afterwards even more inhumanly sell them to be eaten by wild men.[141]

King Rudolf celebrated Whitsun [4 June] in the monastery of St Aurelius [of Hirsau][142] and sent a certain legate[143] to the pope and he himself hastened to Saxony.[144] At that time Henry crowned himself in Ulm and usurped the kingship that had been forbidden to him.[145] There he conferred benefices on the aforementioned Count Udalric [of Lenzburg], as one who was particularly deserving of favour, in that he had tormented the venerable Abbot Bernard, the pope's legate, whom he still held in captivity.[146]

The bishop of Vercelli, the chancellor of the deposed king,[147] together with all the latter's followers, proclaimed a general assembly in Roncaglia around 1 May, in order to depose Pope Gregory, if he could by any means do so. But he himself – alas! in a wretched manner – lost both his life and his episcopal office, while excluded from ecclesiastical communion, on the same date on which he planned with criminal presumption to depose the pope. Not long after his death the prefect of the city of Rome,[148] a tireless knight of St Peter fighting against the schismatics, was cruelly killed by a certain supporter of Henry. In a short time more than twenty miracles occurred around his body, as we have learned from the reports of trustworthy men.

Bishop Embriko of Augsburg, who had sworn fealty to King Rudolf the previous Easter, thought nothing of breaking his oath and attached

---

141 'Wild men', *cinocephali*. Cf. the usage of Augustine, *De civitate Dei* 16.8; Isidore, *Etymologiae* 11.3.15, 12.2.32. Henry IV's campaign in Swabia: Meyer von Knonau (1900) pp. 35–6 and n. 58.

142 Bruno, *Saxon War* c. 93, p. 87: Rudolf celebrated Whitsun in Erfurt. See Meyer von · Knonau (1900) p. 34 and n. 56.

143 Perhaps the monk Giselbert, identified below p. 266 as 'King Rudolf's envoy to the pope'.

144 On 29 June he was in Merseburg: Bruno, *Saxon War* c. 93, p. 87.

145 Bernold's allusion seems to be to a crown-wearing (on Whitsunday): Vogel (1983) pp. 77–81.

146 Udalric II was a beneficiary of the redistribution of property following the deposition of the south German dukes in Ulm: above pp. 173–4.

147 Gregory (1044–77) † 1 May. See Schwartz (1913) p. 138.

148 Cencius, Roman prefect (?1071–7), son of the Roman prefect John Tiniosus, killed by Stephen, brother of Cencius Stephani: Bonizo, *To a friend* VIII, p. 243. The concept 'knight of St Peter': Erdmann (1935) pp. 185–211, especially pp. 197–8.

himself to Henry on his arrival. One day, when he was celebrating mass in the latter's presence, the wretched man imposed this condition on himself: that the receiving of the sacred offering should serve as a judgement on him if his lord, Henry, had unjustly usurped the kingship. After thus rashly receiving [the eucharist], in the short time that he survived, until the moment of his death, he never again arose from his bed a healthy man. For he died around 1 July, while still excluded from ecclesiastical communion.[149] Likewise, Patriarch Sigehard of Aquileia,[150] who came to Henry's aid with an armed force against the ban of the pope, became insane in Regensburg and was overtaken during his journey by sudden death. And thus he was brought back home dead in body and soul and some of his followers were also dead.

When the month of August was already nearly over, Henry decided on an expedition into Saxony with a host of schismatics. King Rudolf, together with the Saxons, pressed forward as far as Würzburg to meet him and laid siege to that city, which was rebelling against him.[151] While his vassals were hastening there from Swabia, they ran into his rival Henry, who retreated at the sight of them. He burned more than a hundred men in a church, namely in Wiesloch,[152] when they resisted him, and thus fleeing beyond the Rhine, he was unable to turn aside the king's vassals from the expedition that they had begun.

At that time the pope, on behalf of St Peter, commanded both kings to make a truce with each other and to do nothing to hinder his coming to German territory to settle the conflict, but rather to offer him the advice and help for this journey that was due to him.[153] He commanded his legates [Cardinal deacon Bernard and Abbot Bernard of St Victor], who still remained in German territory, that they should excommunicate whichever of the two kings did not obey the aforementioned legation but on behalf of St Peter should confirm the obedient one in the kingship.[154] And not long afterwards this was done: since on the day following the feast of St Martin [12 November] in Goslar Henry was again excommunicated because of his disobedience and Rudolf

149 30 July. Cf. Berthold, *Chronicle* 1077, above p. 175 and n. 415.

150 Sigehard (1068–77) † 12 August. See above p. 174 and nn. 410–11. Only Bernold identified Regensburg.

151 Siege of Würzburg: Meyer von Knonau (1900) pp. 46–8; Höss (1950) pp. 306–7; Robinson (1999) pp. 176–7.

152 See above p. 187 and n. 455.

153 Cf. Gregory VII, *Register* IV.24, pp. 337–8. See Vogel (1983) pp. 47–51.

154 Cf. *Register* IV.23, pp. 335–6.

was raised to the kingship because of his obedience.[155] For Henry did not deign to receive the aforementioned legation from the pope and he directed his thoughts not towards the making of a truce but towards the cruelty of tyranny.

The venerable Bishop Gerald of Ostia, whom we mentioned above, who had long been alive in God and crucified in the world, was freed from the prison of this life on 6 December.[156] The most devout Empress Agnes, who had now served God most faithfully during twenty years of widowhood and who had not consented to any of her son Henry's proceedings against the apostolic see, rested in peace in Rome on 14 December.[157] She was buried in Rome in the church of St Petronilla.

1078. Henry again complained to the apostolic see about his condemnation, as if it was unjust.[158] Pope Gregory, therefore, convened a council in the month of March,* in which he again appointed suitable legates, who were to hold a general conference and settle the matter of the kingship justly. According to the judgement of the synod, he condemned all those who prevented the conference from taking place.[159] Rudolf was most willing for it to be held but Henry incessantly strove to hinder it by whatever means he could. For contrary to the pope's command, he assembled a very great host of dissolute men and prepared an expedition into Saxony. King Rudolf met him with an army on the Streu, put him to flight and held the field of victory on 7 August.[160] Nevertheless among those who were on Rudolf's side, Wezel, the venerable bishop of Magdeburg,[161] died there and the bishop of Worms[162] was taken prisoner. An infinite number of men died on both sides but on Henry's side the casualties were more numerous and more eminent.

At the same time, when the Swabians had formed an army and were hastening to their lord, King Rudolf, they were prevented from crossing

---

155 Cf. Berthold, *Chronicle* 1077, above p. 191 and n. 471. See Meyer von Knonau (1900) pp. 75–8; Schumann (1912) p. 43; Cowdrey (1998) p. 175; Robinson (1999) p. 172.

156 Cf. Bernold, *Calendar* p. 521.

157 Cf. *ibid.* Cf. Berthold, *Chronicle* 1077, above pp. 191–4 and nn. 472, 489.

158 See above p. 198 and n. 510.

159 Lenten synod, 27 February–3 March. Cf. Gregory VII, *Register* V.14a, c. 6, p. 370: 'suitable ... legates are to be sent from the side of the apostolic see to that territory'. See Meyer von Knonau (1900) pp. 103–7; Cowdrey (1998) pp. 180–1.

160 Battle of Mellrichstadt (on the River Streu). Cf. Berthold, *Chronicle* 1078, above pp. 212–13 and n. 562. See Meyer von Knonau (1900) pp. 135–46; Robinson (1999) pp. 181–2.

161 Werner (Wezilo), archbishop (1063–78). See above p. 213 and n. 565.

162 Adalbert (1070–1107).

the Neckar by sworn bands numbering almost 12,000. They killed some of them but very many of them they punished more mercifully by castration.[163] Then they attacked a certain fortress belonging to their enemies and took possession of it. When Rudolf had returned to Saxony, Henry suddenly collected his forces again and laid Swabia waste with plunder, fire and sword around the feast of All Saints [1 November].[164] He set about the complete destruction of the land of the catholic dukes Berthold [I of Carinthia] and Welf [IV of Bavaria] and of other vassals of St Peter. In that campaign a little fewer than a hundred churches also then suffered profanation. At that time also Berthold, duke of the Carinthians, of pious memory,[165] and Margrave Henry,[166] members of Rudolf's party, died peacefully.

Another council was held in Rome on 19 November, during which the envoys of both kings swore in the synod – although not equally truthfully – that their lords had not hindered the conference that was to decide the matter of the kingship. The pope, therefore, could not on that occasion judge between them, although he knew well which side justice favoured more.[167] Berengar, canon of Anjou was summoned before that synod in order that he might reject his heresy and recover his senses and a respite was granted to him until the next synod.[168]

* In this council certain persons were excepted from the Henrician excommunication, at least for the time being: namely, wives, children, servants and others who unknowingly or at any rate unwillingly associate with excommunicates.[169]

1079. In the month of February Pope Gregory assembled a synod in Rome,[170] in which Berengar was convicted for the third time and abjured

---

163 Battle of the Neckar (7 August), in which the Swabian forces of Berthold I of Carinthia and Welf IV of Bavaria defeated the Henrician army of Franconian peasants. See above pp. 213–14 and n. 568.

164 Cf. Berthold, *Chronicle* 1078, above p. 215, mentioning the destruction of Altdorf, the Welf family monastery.

165 † 5/6 November.

166 Henry, count of Hildrizhausen, deposed margrave of the Nordgau. See Meyer von Knonau (1900) pp. 41 n. 68, 153.

167 Cf. protocol of the Roman synod of autumn 1078, Gregory VII, *Register* VI.5b, pp. 400–1. Cf. Berthold, *Chronicle* 1078, above p. 216. See Meyer von Knonau (1900) pp. 163–7; Vogel (1983) pp. 126–7; Cowdrey (1998) pp. 184–5; Robinson (1999) pp. 182–4.

168 Cf. Bernold, *De veritate corporis et sanguinis Domini* p. 383. See Gibson (1971) p. 67; Montclos (1971) pp. 226, 229–30.

169 Marginal gloss in Bernold's hand. Cf. Gregory VII, *Register* V.14a, c. 16, pp. 372–3.

170 11 February: *Register* VI.17a, pp. 425–9.

and anathematised his heresy, which declares that the corporeal things placed on the altar do not truly but only figuratively change into the body and blood of the Lord.[171] In the same synod Henry, patriarch of Aquileia[172] swore to the pope that henceforward he would communicate with no one whom he knew to have been excommunicated by the pope. In this synod the pope deposed, without hope of restoration, priests who from that time forward lapsed into fornication. And he condemned the writing concerning the marriage of priests that is said to have been addressed by St Udalric to Pope Nicholas and the chapter of Paphnutius on the same subject[173] and indeed everything that was contrary to the sacred canons.

In this synod the envoys of King Rudolf accused Henry of unceasingly bringing the whole kingdom into confusion and trampling holy Church underfoot.[174] The pope, therefore, once again sent his legates to the German territory to settle the question of the kingship: namely, the venerable Peter, bishop of Albano,[175] that same Peter, in fact, who long before proved that the bishop of Florence, named Peter,[176] was a simoniac by passing through the middle of the fire without suffering any harm and hence, with the surname 'fiery', deserving to obtain the bishopric of Albano. Bishop Udalric of Padua[177] was sent with him on the legation. Before they departed, however, in the same synod Henry's envoy assured the legates of the pope on oath of the good conduct and the obedience of his lord. Rudolf's envoy likewise swore in the synod concerning his lord's obedience.[178] When the legates of the apostolic see

---

171 Cf. Bernold, *De veritate corporis et sanguinis Domini* p. 383: 'We ourselves were present at the last general synod under Pope Gregory VII in the year 1079 of the Lord's Incarnation and we saw that Berengar stood in the midst of the synod and ... renounced his heresy concerning the Lord's body with an oath' Cf. also *Register* VI.17a c. 1, pp. 426–7. See Gibson (1971) pp. 67–8; Montclos (1971) pp. 228–31; Cowdrey (1998) pp. 498–502.

172 Henry (1077–84). See above p. 225 and n. 617.

173 Ps.-Udalric, *Epistola de continentia clericorum, MGH Libelli* 1, 255–60. 'The chapter of Paphnutius' is the account of Paphnutius's defence of clerical marriage at the council of Nicea (325) in Cassiodorus, *Historia tripartita* II.14, *CSEL* 71, 107. Cf. Bernold, *De incontinentia sacerdotum* pp. 7, 12, 13, 16, 17, 20, 21. There is no reference to these texts in the synodal protocol. See Frauenknecht (1997) pp. 12–52.

174 Cf. Gregory VII, *Register* VI.17a, c. 2, p. 427; Berthold, *Chronicle* 1079, above p. 223 and n. 605.

175 Peter 'Igneus', cardinal bishop of Albano (?1072–89). See Hüls (1977) p. 90.

176 Peter Mezzabarba (?1061–8) see above p. 121 and n. 139.

177 Udalric (1064–80). See Meyer von Knonau (1900) pp. 182–3, 210–17, 223–5; Schumann (1912) pp. 46–52; Cowdrey (1998) pp. 188–9; Robinson (1999) pp. 186, 190–1.

178 Cf. Gregory VII, *Register* VI.17a, c. 2, 3, pp. 427–8.

arrived in Germany, they proved beyond doubt the obedience of Rudolf and the disobedience of Henry and when subsequently they returned, they personally bore witness to this before the pope.[179]

During this summer the venerable Abbot Bernard of Marseilles, a man full of charity, rested in peace on 20 July.[180] The teacher Adalbert, skilful in deeds and words, who had now for thirty years been crucified in the world and who was finally brought to the perfection of the Gospel, departed to the Lord on 3 December.[181]

1080. After Epiphany [6 January] Henry decided once more to come to Saxony with an army.[182] He was put to flight by Rudolf on 27 January[183] but he was not restrained from the tyranny on which he had embarked. Rudolf immediately sent an envoy[184] to the synod in Rome to report on this expedition.

Pope Gregory assembled a synod in Rome in the month of March,[185] at which the aforementioned legates of the apostolic see [Peter of Albano and Udalric of Padua], returning from German territory, reported to the lord pope the complete obedience of Rudolf and the disobedience of Henry. At the end of the synod, therefore, he deposed Henry and excommunicated him, together with all his supporters, and he confirmed Rudolf in the royal dignity by apostolic authority.[186] The latter's rival, therefore, assembled a host of all the schismatics and excommunicates in Brixen,[187] abjured the lawful pope and elected for himself, not *as a pope but as an heresiarch, Wibert, formerly bishop of Ravenna,*[188] but *deposed*

179 A different account of the legation: Berthold, *Chronicle* 1079, above pp. 232 n. 641, 236–7 n. 648.

180 Cf. Bernold, *Calendar* p. 510; but see above p. 239 n. 665.

181 Adalbert, teacher of Bernard of Hildesheim, former master of the cathedral school of Constance. Cf. Bernold, *De damnatione scismaticorum* I, II, pp. 27, 29. The same date in Bernold, *Calendar* p. 520.

182 After 13 January: Berthold, *Chronicle* 1080, above p. 240 and n. 668.

183 Battle of Flarchheim. See Meyer von Knonau (1900) pp. 238–41, 639–43; Vogel (1983) pp. 185–6; Robinson (1999) p. 193.

184 Perhaps the monk Giselbert, 'King Rudolf's envoy to the pope', below p. 266 and n. 196. Cf. Berthold, *Chronicle* 1079, above p. 236 and n. 647.

185 7 March: the synodal protocol, Gregory VII, *Register* VII.14a, p. 487.

186 Cf. synodal protocol c. 7, pp. 483–7. See Meyer von Knonau (1900) pp. 251–6; Vogel (1983) pp. 189–96; Cowdrey (1998) pp. 194–9; Robinson (1999) pp. 194–6.

187 Council of Brixen, 25 June. See Meyer von Knonau (1900) pp. 284–96; Vogel (1983) pp. 209–19; Cowdrey (1998) pp. 201–3; Robinson (1999) pp. 198–201.

188 Wibert, archbishop of Ravenna (1072–1100), antipope 'Clement III' (1084–1100). His excommunication: synodal protocol of the Roman synod of Lent 1078, *Register* V.14a, c. 1, p. 369.

without hope of restoration and excommunicated[189] three years before by Pope Gregory. Then in an assembly held in Mainz[190] he caused that election to be confirmed by whomsoever he could.

Already in the middle of October Henry again prepared an expedition into Saxony but he was put to flight by Rudolf's knights in a campaign of a single day,[191] although in that encounter King Rudolf of pious memory fell. He, I say, another Maccabeus when in the front ranks he fell upon the enemy, deserved to fall in the service of St Peter. He survived for one day after this and set all his affairs in order in a proper manner and there is no doubt that he departed to the Lord on 15 October.[192] He reigned for three-and-a-half years. All pious people of both sexes, and especially the poor, grieved for his death. The Saxons gave countless alms for the commendation of his soul. For he was beyond doubt the father of the fatherland, most attentive to justice, a tireless champion of holy Church. He was buried most gloriously in Merseburg.[193]

On the day of his death in Lombardy the knights of the most wise Duchess Matilda[194] were put to flight by an army from almost the whole of Lombardy at Volta, near Mantua.[195] Also on that day Giselbert, a most devout priest and monk and King Rudolf's envoy to the pope, rested in peace in Lombardy.[196] At this time Henry caused such disorder throughout the whole of Italy that no one could go in safety to the threshold of the apostles unless he had first promised on oath that he would not travel to Pope Gregory.[197]

1081. After the death of King Rudolf Henry came to Verona at Eastertide

189 Extracts from Gebhard of Salzburg, letter to Herman of Metz (in Hugh, *Chronicon* II, p. 459).

190 Perhaps the Whitsun assembly at Mainz (31 May) that preceded Brixen (Meyer von Knonau [1900] pp. 277–81). But Meyer von Knonau (1900) p. 326 n. 160 and Vogel (1983) p. 238 interpret this as a *second* assembly of Mainz in August.

191 Battle of Hohenmölsen ('battle on the Grune', 'on the Elster'), 15 October. See Meyer von Knonau (1900) pp. 337–41, 644–52; Cram (1955) pp. 145–8, 214; Robinson (1999) pp. 203–4.

192 Cf. Bernold, *Calendar* p. 517: '15 October. King Rudolf, vassal of St Peter, departed to the Lord.' Rudolf as a new Judas Maccabeus and vassal of St Peter: Erdmann (1935) pp. 224, 231, 253, 273; Vogel (1983) p. 241.

193 See Schramm and Mütherich (1962) p. 395; Vogel (1983) pp. 239–43.

194 Matilda, margravine of Tuscany (1046–1115).

195 Battle of Volta, south of Lake Garda, mid-October: Meyer von Knonau (1900) pp. 316–17 and n. 145; Cowdrey (1998) pp. 206, 210, 301.

196 Cf. Bernold, *Calendar* p. 517: '15 October. The priest Giselbert departed.' See above pp. 236 and n. 647, 260 and n. 143, 265 and n. 184.

197 Cf. Donizo, *Vita Mathildis* II, p. 383. See Meyer von Knonau (1900) p. 364.

[4 April] and from there he set out to attack Rome,[198] together with Wibert, who was not so much his pope as his apostate, since he had more than once broken his oath to the lord pope and had been excommunicated by him. But he returned without success.

At the same time the princes of the kingdom of the Germans – namely, the archbishops, bishops, dukes, margraves and counts – held an assembly[199] and elected the noble man Herman as their king.[200] He immediately dispatched an army from that assembly against Henry's supporters. For, wishing to hinder his election, the latter had assembled a very great host at that time. But when the new king unexpectedly attacked them, they were all either slain or irrevocably put to flight, even though they considerably outnumbered the king's knights who were pursuing them. The king felt certain of divine help in such a triumph and therefore pitched camp that night on the field of victory. Afterwards he departed to subject the kingdom to his authority. He was elected before the feast of St Laurence and it was on the day following the feast of that same saint that he triumphed over his enemies within the frontiers of Bavaria in the place that is called Höchstädt.[201] Afterwards he departed for Saxony in order to receive consecration.[202]

1082. King Herman celebrated Christmas with the greatest splendour in Goslar. There also, with the consent of the princes of the kingdom, he solemnly received from the bishops the consecration and the crown of the royal dignity on the feast of St Stephen [26 December 1081], for the latter was his patron.[203]

In Italy Henry, taking with him his apostate Wibert and joined by a host of schismatics, once again set out to attack Rome.[204] He remained there throughout that summer but laboured almost in vain, except that he stationed his knights in certain castles so that they might make war

---

198 Henry appeared before Rome on 21 May: Meyer von Knonau (1900) p. 388; Robinson (1999) pp. 211–12.

199 In Ochsenfurt, beginning of August. Bernold exaggerated the numbers of the electors, who were probably confined to the Swabian and Saxon princes. See Meyer von Knonau (1900) pp. 415–18; Robinson (1999) pp. 208–9.

200 Herman, count of Salm (Luxemburg family), anti-king (1081–8).

201 Battle of Höchstädt, 11 August: Meyer von Knonau (1900) pp. 420–1.

202 After an unsuccessful siege of Augsburg: Meyer von Knonau (1900) p. 421.

203 He was crowned by Siegfried of Mainz: cf. Bruno, *Saxon War* c. 131, p. 123. See Meyer von Knonau (1900) p. 426.

204 Probably end of February. Cf. Bonizo, *To a friend* IX, p. 249: 'he laid siege to Rome for the whole of Lent'. See Meyer von Knonau (1900) pp. 433 and n. 2, 437.

on the Romans, because they would not on this occasion permit him to enter Rome. He also wished, through the agency of a certain traitor, to set fire to the church of St Peter but, thanks to the protection of God's mercy, he was unable to do so. For he thought that if the Romans abandoned their defences and ran to extinguish the blaze, he might surprise them and burst through the gates. He therefore caused certain houses in the neighbourhood of St Peter's to be set on fire but the lord pope foiled this ruse. For when he first saw the blaze, he sent all the Roman knights to defend the ramparts, while he alone, relying on the fidelity of St Peter, made the sign of the cross against the conflagration and did not permit the fire to spread any further.[205] Henry therefore returned to Lombardy, taking prisoner the venerable bishop of Sutri[206] and some other persons and leaving his apostate Wibert in the city of Tivoli to trouble the Romans.[207]

King Herman, however, was saddened by the misfortunes of the apostolic see and, wishing to free it from the hands of Henry, he prepared an expedition into Italy. He therefore came from Saxony into Swabia.[208]

1083. King Herman celebrated Christmas [25 December 1082] in Swabia[209] in a most honourable fashion with the princes of the kingdom. From there he wished to move his army into Lombardy, when grievous news came from Saxony: namely, that Duke Otto [of Northeim], the most prudent knight whom he had left in Saxony as the chief of all his vassals, had died.[210] He had no doubt that his death would cause the greatest disunity if he did not hasten to anticipate such division. He was therefore compelled by this emergency to postpone the expedition and return in haste to Saxony.

Before Whitsun [28 May] Henry, together with a host of schismatics and excommunicates, again advanced to attack Rome and on the Saturday after Whitsun [3 June] he attacked the church of St Peter with

205 Paul, *Life of Pope Gregory VII* c. 8, pp. 265–6 reported this miracle, which he found 'in the chronicles of venerable men', i.e. in Bernold's chronicle.

206 Bonizo, bishop of Sutri (?1078–?86), Gregorian anti-bishop of Piacenza (+1089/94), canonist, theologian, polemicist. See Robinson (2004a) pp. 36–43.

207 Tivoli as Wibert's headquarters: Meyer von Knonau (1900) p. 447; Ziese (1982) pp. 75–6; Robinson (1999) p. 220.

208 *D. Hermann* 1 (*DD.H.IV* p. 677), dated 3 August, places him in Goslar. See Meyer von Knonau (1900) p. 464; Robinson (1999) pp. 220–1.

209 Place-name unknown: Meyer von Knonau (1900) p. 467 and n. 44.

210 + 11 January. See Meyer von Knonau (1900) p. 501; Fenske (1977) pp. 63–4.

an armed band.[211] He thus enthroned *the*[212] *perjured, deposed and excommunicated Wibert of Ravenna* in St Peter's,[213] not through the agency of *the bishops of Ostia and Albano and Porto*, who possess this *privilege* of consecrating the pope,[214] but by means of *the ex-bishops of Modena and Arezzo*[215] (ex-bishops because they had been deposed and excommunicated *for* many *years*).[212] He immediately fortified a certain hill near St Peter's named Palatiolus[216] and placed many knights there so that they might attack the Romans, who would in no circumstances permit him to enter those regions of the city that lay beyond the Tiber. Nevertheless many of the Romans had already come to an agreement with Henry, some induced by money, some led astray by his many promises, but all equally fatigued now by three years of attacks. What more is there to tell? Almost all the Romans, except for the prince of Salerno,[217] made this agreement with Henry: that Pope Gregory was to assemble a synod in Rome in mid-November and neither Henry nor the Romans, indeed no one at all, was permitted to oppose the decisions taken by this synod in the matter of the kingship. Henry also guaranteed on oath the security of all those going to that synod and returning from it. The pope, therefore, issued letters of summons to that synod to all devout bishops and abbots.[218] After Henry had returned to Lombardy,[219] sudden death seized almost all his knights whom he left behind in that castle near St Peter's. Among them Udalric of Godesheim,[220] who was

---

211 2 June: Frutolf, *Chronica* 1083, p. 96. See Meyer von Knonau (1900) p. 475 and n. 12.

212/212 Extracts from Gebhard of Salzburg, letter to Herman of Metz (in Hugh, *Chronicon* II, p. 459).

213 Bernold confused the mass celebrated by Wibert in St Peter's, 28 June (after the Leonine city fell into Henry's hands), with his enthronement as pope, 24 March 1084. See below p. 274 and Meyer von Knonau (1900) pp. 489 n. 22, 529–33.

214 Cf. Bernold, *Chronicon* 554, p. 413: 'this is the privilege of the church of Ostia: that its bishop … must by a perpetual law take part in the consecration of the Roman pontiff'.

215 Heribert, bishop of Modena (?1056–?92); Constantine, bishop of Arezzo (1063–?95). See Schwartz (1913) pp. 183, 201. Bonizo, *To a friend* IX, p. 250 named the bishops of Modena, Bologna and Cervia.

216 A hill east of St Peter's: Meyer von Knonau (1900) p. 479 n. 14. Frutolf, *Chronica* 1083, p. 96 identified it as the Palatine.

217 Gisulf II, prince of Salerno (1052–77, † after 1088).

218 *Register* IX.29, pp. 612–13. See Cowdrey (1998) pp. 222–3; Robinson (1999) p. 225.

219 'At the beginning of July': Frutolf, *Chronica* 1083, p. 96. See Meyer von Knonau (1900) p. 490.

220 Udalric of Godesheim (perhaps Gosheim near Donauwörth), one of the five royal advisers excommunicated in 1073 and 1075: cf. above p. 133 n. 215. See Robinson (1999) pp. 225, 359–60. The fate of the garrison: Meyer von Knonau (1900) p. 494.

the author and the instigator of the conspiracy leading to this schism, perished miserably, alas! while excluded from the communion of the Church. Of the three hundred knights who were left in that castle as a garrison, scarcely thirty, so they say, were granted their lives and escaped from the sword of St Peter. That castle, however, was pulled down by the Romans and levelled to the ground.

Meanwhile, after sending his Ravennese man to Ravenna, Henry set out for the aforementioned synod. The envoys of the German princes ought also to have gone there but they were captured and plundered by Henry on the road at Forum Cassii around the feast of St Martin [11 November],[221] even though he had guaranteed on oath the security of all those attending that synod. The Romans, therefore, began to grumble about Henry. Among those whom he caused to be afflicted by captivity were most devout monks and clergy and together with them he imprisoned the venerable Odo, bishop of Ostia,[222] who had been sent to him by the apostolic see. Nevertheless many Frenchmen, both bishops and abbots, reached that synod. The most important bishops and those most necessary to the lord pope – that is, Hugh of Lyons,[223] Anselm of Lucca and Rainald of Como – were, however, deliberately prevented by Henry from reaching the synod. The lord pope nevertheless solemnly celebrated the synod for three days.[224] He was with difficulty prevailed upon by the synod not to excommunicate Henry again specifically, but he excommunicated all those, whoever they were, who in any way hindered anyone from coming to St Peter or to the pope. But now the time had arrived at which the Romans, without the pope's knowledge, had sworn that they would cause him to be crowned either by Pope Gregory or by another whom they would elect after he had been expelled.[225] Although that oath had been taken during the previous summer, it had been kept secret from the pope's closest associates almost until that date. When the time arrived, therefore, the Romans informed the pope of the oath, saying that they had sworn to Henry not that the pope was to crown

---

221 S. Maria di Forcassi, near Sutri on the Via Cassia.

222 Odo (of Châtillon), cardinal bishop of Ostia (1080–8), Pope Urban II (1088–99). His imprisonment: Gregory VII, *Register* IX.35a, p. 628. See Becker (1964) pp. 60–1; Cowdrey (1998) p. 225; Robinson (1999) p. 226.

223 Hugh, bishop of Die (1074–82), archbishop of Lyons (1082–1106), papal legate in France.

224 20–22 November: cf. *Register* IX.35a, pp. 627–8. See Meyer von Knonau (1900) pp. 497–8; Cowdrey (1983) pp. 166–9; Cowdrey (1998) pp. 225–6.

225 'Oath of the Roman nobles', *MGH Constitutiones* 1, 651 (no. 442); Cowdrey (1983) pp. 248–9, commentary: pp. 168–9.

him solemnly with royal unction but only that the pope was simply to give him the crown. The pope, therefore, granted their wishes, in order to absolve them from their oath: that is to say, he would give Henry the crown, if he wished, with justice, if not, with a curse. The Romans then sent word to Henry that he should come to receive the crown with justice, if he wished; but if not, he should receive it from the pope by means of a rod lowered down from the Castel S. Angelo. But when Henry refused both alternatives, they sent another envoy to him who would defend them in battle if it was necessary, saying that they had paid careful attention to what they had sworn and that they were no longer bound by that oath. They therefore clung to the lord pope more steadfastly than before with their advice and help. Henry, however, laboured even more earnestly to draw them into his faction, now threatening, now promising and he remained for a long time in the vicinity of Rome, devoting all his attention to this business.[226]

At this time Stephen of pious memory, formerly king of the Hungarians, who had converted himself, together with his people, to the faith of Christ, was distinguished by miracles after the fortieth anniversary of his death.[227] Salomon, who was king of the Hungarians but was most unworthy of the royal dignity, a kinsman of the aforementioned Henry, was deprived of the kingship and imprisoned by his countryman, Ladislaus, and the latter was raised to the royal dignity in his place.[228]

Berengar, the author of a new heresy concerning the body of the Lord, became sick at this time and *went to his own place*.[229] Although he had very often abjured that same heresy in synods, he was nevertheless not afraid to return *to his vomit*, like a *dog*.[230] For he committed his heresy, in a book written by himself, to the flames, after being convicted according to canon law in a Roman synod and he abjured and anathematised his heresy but he did not afterwards give it up.[231]

---

226 Bernold alone gave these details, much disputed in the older literature (emphasising Bernold's hostility towards Henry IV): Meyer von Knonau (1900) p. 500 n. 42. Other accounts: Bonizo, *To a friend* p. 250; Frutolf, *Chronica* 1083, p. 96.

227 King Stephen I of Hungary (1000–38). Cf. *Stephani regis Ungariae vita maior* c. 20, *MGH SS* 11, 240; *Vita minor* c. 8, *ibid.*, p. 229.

228 Salomon (n. 35) married Judith, sister of Henry IV (see above p. 103 and n. 51 and below n. 243). He was deposed in 1074 by his cousin King Geisa I (see above p. 131 and n. 206), who was succeeded by his brother, King Ladislaus I (1077–95, canonised 1192).

229 Acts 1:25.

230 Proverbs 26:11; II Peter 2:22.

231 See above p. 264 and n. 171. See also Cowdrey (1990) pp. 109–38; Cowdrey (1998) pp. 501–2.

But now for seven years the whole Roman empire had been afflicted by civil war, or rather had been divided by schism, some men supporting the lord pope but others supporting Henry, and in consequence both sides laid waste the whole kingdom with plunder, sword and fire. Very few catholic bishops remained in the party of the pope and, since they had been expelled from their own sees, they were not permitted to take care of their flocks. Almost all devout men, therefore, whether clergy or laymen, avoided such evils by taking refuge in certain monasteries so that they might not look upon the devastation of holy Church and be completely unable to support it. For it seemed to them preferable to save themselves at least by going into hiding than, by labouring in vain for the sake of others, to perish with them.

At that time, however, three monasteries, together with their dependencies, excellently founded on the basis of the disciplines of the *Rule*, were held in high esteem in the kingdom of the Germans: namely, the monastery of St Blasien[232] in the Black Forest, that of St Aurelius, which is called Hirsau,[233] and that of the Holy Saviour, which is called Schaffhausen,[234] that is, 'house of ships'. At this period a wonderful host of noble and prudent men fled for refuge to these monasteries in a short time, laid down their weapons and decided to pursue the goal of the perfection of the Gospel by means of the discipline of the *Rule*. There was so great a number of them, I say, that it was necessary for them to extend the very buildings of the monasteries, because otherwise there would have been no room for them to remain there. In these monasteries, therefore, not even the external offices were performed by secular persons but by religious brethren and the more noble they were in the world, the more they desired to be employed in the more contemptible offices. Those who were formerly counts or margraves in the world now considered it the greatest delight to serve the brethren in the kitchen or the mill or to graze their pigs in the field. There indeed the swineherds and the cowherds were the same as the monks,

---

232 Bernold was a monk of St Blasien, *ca.* 1085–91: above pp. 46–7. See Meyer von Knonau (1900) pp. 614–15; Jakobs (1968) p. 42.

233 See above p. 141 and Jakobs (1968) pp. 42, 271–4, 288–90; Cowdrey (1970) pp. 196–210.

234 All Saints', Schaffhausen, where Bernold was a monk from 1091 until his death in 1100: above p. 48. Cf. *Casuum sancti Galli continuatio* II.7, p. 159: 'In addition to these evils certain monks subject to new inventions and unusual customs emerged from the monasteries of the Holy Saviour, that is Schaffhausen, and St Aurelius, that is Hirsau, and of St Blasien …'

apart from the habit.[235] They all in the same manner burned with so great an ardour of charity that each desired what was beneficial not for himself but for the others and they exerted themselves so wonderfully in showing hospitality that they regarded themselves as having lost whatever they did not spend on Christ's poor or on guests.

1084. King Herman celebrated Christmas [25 December 1083] in Saxony.[236] His rival, however, spent the winter in the territory of the Romans[237] and there he awaited the arrival of his Wibert of Ravenna in Rome in order that he might be crowned by him in St Peter's, since he could not persuade Pope Gregory to crown him, unless he was lawfully reconciled.

Bishop Rainald of Como, a man of great renown for his learning and his piety and for this reason a most zealous helper of Pope Gregory, departed to the Lord on 27 January.[238] Duke Welf [IV] of Bavaria manfully liberated the city of Augsburg – which had been seized by a certain Siegfried, who should not be given the name of bishop, together with the Bavarians – and he made it subject to its lawful pastor, whose name was Wigold.[239] Archbishop Siegfried of Mainz, the tireless helper of Pope Gregory through many tribulations, rested in peace.[240] The queen of the English died.[241] She was the wife of King William, who caused the whole land of the English to pay tribute to the Roman pontiff[242] and who permitted no one whom he discovered to be disobedient to the apostolic see to buy or sell anything within his jurisdiction.

Ladislaus, king of the Hungarians, a supporter of the party of the catholics, released his rival Salomon from prison and permitted him to go to Regensburg, to his wife,[243] although she was not grateful for this.

---

235 Cf. *Vita Willihelmi abbatis Hirsaugiensis* c. 23, p. 219: 'he ordained that the monks should use the faithful service of lay *conversi* in carrying out external functions'.

236 Place-name unknown: Meyer von Knonau (1900) p. 506.

237 Henry IV celebrated Christmas in the Leonine city in St Peter's: cf. Frutolf, *Chronica* 1084, p. 96. See Meyer von Knonau (1900) p. 501.

238 Cf. Bernold, *Calendar* p. 496.

239 Siegfried II (1077–96), appointed by Henry IV; Wigold, Gregorian anti-bishop (1077–88). See above pp. 187 and nn. 456–7, 206–7 and n. 542. The intervention of Welf IV: Meyer von Knonau (1900) pp. 574–5.

240 † 17 February.

241 Matilda (1035–83), wife of King William I ('the Conqueror', 1066–87).

242 Cf. Gregory VII, *Register* VII.23, p. 501 and n. 3; Lanfranc, *Letters* 38–9, pp. 128–33. See Cowdrey (1972) pp. 89–94.

243 Judith (?1054–92/6), known in Hungary as Sophia. See above p. 271 and n. 228 and Märtl (1986) pp. 146–7.

For neither she nor he had hitherto kept the marriage contract: on the contrary, they had not been afraid, in opposition to the apostle, to *defraud each other*.[244] She was the sister of the frequently mentioned Henry and had already for a long time been maintained by him in Regensburg, even before her husband was taken prisoner.

Henry, the ex-patriarch of Aquileia, who more than once had broken his oath to the lord pope and had been excommunicated, died in body and soul.[245]

At this time the king of Constantinople[246] sent a very large sum of money to Henry, the former king, so that he might make war on Robert Guiscard, duke of Calabria and Apulia[247] and the sworn vassal of the lord pope, to exact vengeance on behalf of that same king. For Robert had long before attacked the territory of the men of Constantinople and intended once more to lead an expedition there. But having received the money, Henry did not spend it on the military action against Robert that he had promised on oath but spent it instead on winning over the Roman mob. With their help he entered the Lateran palace, together with his Wibert of Ravenna, on the Thursday before Palm Sunday [21 March].[248] The Roman nobles, except for a very small number, held fast to the cause of the lord Pope Gregory and gave him forty hostages. The pope, however, retreated into the castle of S. Angelo and held all the bridges over the Tiber and the stronger fortifications of the Romans in his power.[249]

On the day of the Lord's Resurrection [31 March] Henry received from his Ravennese heresiarch a crown not of glory but of shame.[250] For, according to the testimony of the holy Fathers, when such a man

---

244 I Corinthians 7:5.

245 Probably in February: Meyer von Knonau (1900) p. 582 n. 72.

246 The Byzantine emperor Alexius I Comnenus (1081–1118). Cf. Anna Comnena, *Alexiad* III.10, V.3, pp. 120–3, 160–3; Frutolf, *Chronica* 1084, p. 96. See Meyer von Knonau (1900) pp. 481–5, 521–3; Cowdrey (1983) pp. 149, 152, 164; Robinson (1999) pp. 222–3, 227; Loud (2000) pp. 214–23.

247 Robert Guiscard, duke (1059–85).

248 Cf. Henry IV, *Letter* 18, p. 27. See Meyer von Knonau (1900) pp. 526–7; Robinson (1999) p. 227.

249 Cf. Henry IV, *Letter* 18, p. 28: 'all Rome is in our hands, except for that fortress in which Hildebrand has shut himself up'. See Meyer von Knonau (1900) p. 540; Cowdrey (1998) p. 229; Krautheimer (2000) p. 149.

250 Cf. Henry IV, *Letter* 18, p. 28: 'on the holy day of Easter we were, with the consent of all the Romans, ordained and consecrated emperor by Pope Clement'. See Meyer von Knonau (1900) pp. 534–5; Ziese (1982) pp. 105–7; Robinson (1999) pp. 229–31.

performed the coronation, he laid upon him whom he crowned *not*[251] *a blessing*, for that he had lost, *but a condemnation, which was what he possessed*. For he himself was at one time archbishop of Ravenna and swore complete obedience to the Roman pontiff, which he also faithfully performed for some time. But not long afterwards he rejected his oath and with extraordinary arrogance he rose up against the apostolic see. He was therefore, after the delay prescribed by canon law, *irrecoverably deposed and excommunicated by the apostolic see and by the bishops of the whole Church in a Roman synod and this not once* and not *in a single synod but in all the many synods that were celebrated in Rome* during a period of six years.[252] *This man, therefore, an inveterate oath-breaker and on that account* very often irrecoverably *deposed and excommunicated*, in the past year *seized the see of the Roman pontiff, to whom he had sworn obedience, through the agency of excommunicates, that is, men like himself, while the lawful pastor still presided over that see*. Indeed *the ex-bishops* [Heribert] *of Modena and* [Constantine of] *Arezzo*, together with the rest of *the excommunicates*, consecrated him. Even if they had been catholics and if the apostolic see had no pastor, *they would still be unable to consecrate a pope to that see. For the privilege of this consecration was granted by the holy Fathers exclusively to the cardinal bishops of Ostia, Albano and Porto* and it is not granted to any others if these are capable of performing it. But the latter would have preferred to undergo all the extremes of suffering rather than become involved in such a sacrilegious consecration of such an arrogant and presumptuous man, whom they themselves, together with the lord pope, had condemned in a synodal judgement according to canon law. *The man of Modena and the man of Arezzo, therefore*, together with the rest of the heretics, *raised that man* of Ravenna not to be *the Roman patriarch*, which was not at all in their power, *but* to be a most damnable *heresiarch*,[251] so that the more prominent he was among them, the greater the damnation that he was privileged to possess. For that reason Henry, who was crowned by him, undoubtedly inherited his damnation and likewise all those who have usurped anything that ought to be received from the lord pope under the pretence that they received it from the aforementioned heresiarch.

Henry, however, stayed in the Lateran palace with his man from Ravenna and was not allowed by the faithful supporters of the pope

---

251/251 Extracts from Gebhard of Salzburg, letter to Herman of Metz (Hugh, *Chronicon* II, p. 459).

252 Cf. Gregory VII, *Register* V.14a, c. 1; VII.14a, c. 3, pp. 369, 481; Bernold, *Apologeticae rationes* p. 96.

to pass through the city to St Peter's. But in Easter week he made war on the pope's supporters and in that attack he lost almost forty of his men, dead and wounded, for the rest fled. On the side of the lord pope, however, there was not a single casualty.[253]

King Herman celebrated Easter [31 March] in Saxony,[254] where large-scale truces were made among the faithful supporters of the lord pope. Not long afterwards these were confirmed in almost the whole of the kingdom of the Germans.[255]

After 1 May[256] Robert Guiscard, duke of the Normans invaded Rome with an armed force in the service of St Peter. Forcing Henry to flee, he completely despoiled the whole city, which was in rebellion against Pope Gregory, and destroyed the greater part of it with fire because the Romans wounded one of his knights. Then, after he had received hostages from the Romans and confined them in the Castel S. Angelo, which they call 'the house of Theoderic', he moved his army out of Rome, together with Pope Gregory, to win back the land of St Peter, intending to return again to Rome at the feast of St Peter [29 June]. In a short time he recovered very many fortresses and cities for the lord pope. Henry, however, had not the strength to resist Robert and returned in considerable haste to the territory of the Germans.[257]

At this same time the knights of the most prudent Duchess Matilda [of Tuscany] fought manfully in Lombardy against the supporters of Henry and the enemies of St Peter.[258] Of the latter they captured the bishop of Parma[259] and six of the chief vassals, together with almost a hundred good knights. After obtaining a complete victory, they came into possession of more than five hundred horses and very many coats of mail and all the tents of the enemy.

253 *Chronicle of Monte Cassino* III.53, p. 434: Henry IV besieged the Castel S. Angelo. See Meyer von Knonau (1900) p. 542 and n. 25; Cowdrey (1998) p. 229; Robinson (1999) p. 232.

254 Perhaps in Goslar: Meyer von Knonau (1900) p. 583.

255 Wadle (1973) p. 145: 'this report is very probably to be connected with the text called by Weiland *Pax Dei incerta*', i.e. *MGH Constitutiones* 1, 608–9 (no. 426).

256 24 May: Meyer von Knonau (1900) pp. 551–4 and n. 37. See also Cowdrey (1998) p. 230; Robinson (1999) pp. 232–4; Loud (2000) p. 221.

257 Cf. *DD.H.IV* 359–60 (Sutri, 23 May), 361 (Borgo S. Valentano, 24 May), 362 (Pisa, 5 June), 363–6 (Verona, 17–18 June). See Kilian (1886) pp. 101–2.

258 Battle of Sorbaria (north-east of Modena), 2 July. See Meyer von Knonau (1900) p. 565.

259 Eberhard (1072/4–85). See Schwartz (1913) p. 187.

Around 1 August, however, Henry prepared an expedition into Swabia but when the Swabians opposed him, he refused to fight, even though for many days they challenged him to battle with raised banners and either killed or captured more than a hundred of his men. For he pitched camp near the River Lech[260] and, being protected by the riverbank, he could not easily be attacked by the enemy. The Swabians, however, pitched their camp on the other side of the river, before his eyes, at quite some distance from the bank, so that they should not appear to have denied the enemy the possibility of crossing over. But it was in vain, for Henry would not cross, or rather he did not dare to do so, and even after the departure of the Swabians for almost a day he was afraid to leave the bank, fearing that they would ambush him.

Finally Henry returned to Regensburg and, crossing the Rhine, he set out for Mainz.[261] The Swabians likewise set out on an expedition across the Rhine towards Burgundy and they manfully liberated a certain castle of Duke Berthold, the son of King Rudolf,[262] which was besieged by Henry's supporters. For when they waded, or rather swam through very swiftly moving rivers, those who were besieging the castle, although they were a long way off, were so frightened that, leaving behind their tents, their horses and their coats of mail, they fled away from the siege in all directions. Afterwards they dared not offer resistance to the Swabians during that expedition, although they laid waste their land with sword, plundering and burning. After the castle had been relieved, therefore, and supplied with a year's worth of suitable provisions and after destroying certain fortresses belonging to their enemies, the Swabians returned to their homes in peace.

Meanwhile Henry assembled a host of schismatics and rewarded Wezilo,[263] a runaway clerk of the bishop [Burchard II] of Halberstadt, with the bishopric of Mainz because he had been his tireless fellow worker in all his stubborn resistance to God and St Peter. He had already long been excommunicated and he was elected by excommunicates and it was likewise by excommunicates that he was – according to Pope Pelagius – not consecrated but cursed. For according to the

260 24 July–6 August: *Annals of Augsburg* 1084, p. 131. See Meyer von Knonau (1900) p. 575 and n. 62. The Lech was the frontier between Swabia and Bavaria.

261 He was in Mainz on 4 October: *D.H.IV* 369. See Meyer von Knonau (1900) p. 576.

262 Berthold I (of Rheinfelden), anti-duke of Swabia (1079–90), son of Rudolf of Rheinfelden. See above p. 229 and n. 633. The castle was Burgdorf/Berthoud (Emmental): Parlow (1999) pp. 71–2.

263 Wezilo (Werner), archbishop of Mainz (1084–8).

most blessed Fathers Innocent, Leo and Gregory, he could receive from condemned men nothing but condemnation and malediction.[264]

The lord pope, however, assembled a synod in Salerno and once more published the sentence of excommunication against the heresiarch Wibert and against Henry and all their supporters. He had already done this long before on the previous feast of St John the Baptist [24 June 1082] in Rome, while Henry still remained there.[265] The legates of the apostolic see, namely Bishop Peter of Albano in France and Bishop Odo of Ostia in the land of the Germans, published this sentence everywhere.

While he remained in Swabia, the bishop of Ostia also consecrated a catholic pastor for the holy church of Constance, which had been widowed long before.[266] This was Gebhard, the son of Duke Berthold [I of Carinthia], who was noble by birth but more noble by virtue of the monastic way of life.[267] He was consecrated as bishop unwillingly – nay, greatly lamenting and protesting – at the request and with the approval of the clergy and laity of Constance on 22 December. [Odo] made him a priest on the previous day, that is the feast of St Thomas, together with other clerks, among whom in the same ceremony he promoted the writer of these chronicles to the priesthood and granted him by apostolic authority the power to reconcile the penitent.[268]

1085. King Herman celebrated Christmas [25 December 1084] in Goslar. After Epiphany [6 January 1085] the aforementioned bishop of Ostia came to him in Saxony and was present in the conference that the Saxons held in opposition to Henry's supporters in order to prove to the latter that according to the law they ought to avoid Henry as an excommunicate. When the conference took place,[269] a fortnight after

264 Cf. Pelagius I, *JK* 983 (*Epistola* 24 c. 7); Innocent I, *JK* 303 (*Epistola* 17 c. 3); Leo I, *JK* 532 (*Epistola* 156 c. 5); Gregory I, *Registrum* IV.20 (cited in full: Bernold, *De sacramentis excommunicatorum* pp. 89–90 and *Apologeticae rationes* p. 99). Cf. correspondence of Bernold and Adalbert, *De damnatione scismaticorum* I, p. 28.

265 See Meyer von Knonau (1900) pp. 560–3; Vogel (1982) pp. 341–9; Cowdrey (1998) pp. 231–2; Robinson (1999) pp. 234–5.

266 Bishop Otto I of Constance had been excommunicated in 1080: Bernold, *Pro Gebhardo episcopo* c. 7, p. 111.

267 Gebhard III, bishop (1084–1110), third son of Berthold I, formerly monk of Hirsau. See Meyer von Knonau (1900) pp. 605–9; Becker (1964) pp. 64–5; Maurer (1991) p. 178.

268 Cf. Bernold, *De presbyteris* c. 9, pp. 144–5: 'Bishops are accustomed to grant the right of reconciling to priests ... We ourselves indeed received this grant from our ordination.' See above p. 45.

269 Conference of Gerstungen and Berka (on opposite banks of the River Werra in

Epiphany, they proved this most effectively on the grounds that the Roman pontiff announced to them in a letter that he had excommunicated him in the Roman synod.[270] The adversaries, however, opposed them with the argument that the pope could not excommunicate him because someone who has been despoiled [of his property] cannot be summoned, judged or condemned.[271] To this the Saxons replied that they must not and could not question the judgement of the apostolic see:[272] this must be debated with him who had condemned him, not with the Saxons, who were not present at his condemnation and who must not question but obey the judgement of the apostolic see. The conference thus broke up and the two sides departed.

At that time the bishop of Hildesheim,[273] together with his followers, escaped with difficulty from the hands of the Saxons because he had joined with the Henricians against the general wish of the whole of Saxony. At the same time Count Theoderic[274] was killed by the supporters of our party for the same offence. The aforementioned legate of the apostolic see [Odo I of Ostia] also forbade the aforesaid bishop to exercise his office because he would not come to his senses.[275]

King Herman celebrated Easter [20 April] in Quedlinburg, where *in*[276] *Easter week* the lord pope's legate solemnly celebrated a general *synod*

Thuringia), 20 January. Cf. Odo of Ostia, Encyclical, *Briefsammlungen* pp. 375–80; 'Saxon report' of the conference in (a) *Annales Magdeburgenses* 1085, pp. 176–7; (b) *Annalista Saxo* 1085, pp. 721–2. See Meyer von Knonau (1903) pp. 2–12; Schumann (1912) pp. 54–5; Hauck (1954) p. 836; Becker (1964) pp. 66–70; Cowdrey (1998) pp. 235–7; Robinson (1999) pp. 242–4.

270 According to the 'Saxon report' this was the argument of Gebhard of Salzburg. Cf. Bernard, *Liber canonum* c. 13, p. 486. Bernard of Hildesheim (Bernold's teacher) is identified by Erdmann (1938) p. 204 as the author of the 'Saxon report'.

271 According to the 'Saxon report' this was the argument of Wezilo of Mainz, who 'read a chapter that no one who had been despoiled of his property could be summoned, judged, condemned'. On this argument of *exceptio spolii*: Robinson (1978a) pp. 105–9; Fuhrmann (1982) pp. 52–69.

272 Cf. the 'Saxon report', citing 'the edicts of the popes Gelasius and Nicholas and many others', an argument reflected in Bernard, *Liber canonum* c. 13, p. 486.

273 Udo (1079–1114). His followers included his brother, Count Conrad of Reinhausen. See Meyer von Knonau (1903) pp. 8–9; Becker (1964) pp. 70–1; Fenske (1977) p. 109; Robinson (1999) p. 244.

274 Theoderic II, count of Katlenburg. See Reuter (1991b) p. 305.

275 Cf. Odo I, letter to Udo of Hildesheim, *Briefsammlungen* pp. 25–7.

276/276 Extracts from the synodal protocol of Quedlinburg in Sdralek (1890) pp. 178–81; *MGH Constitutiones* 1, 652–3. Robinson (1989) pp. 183–4 argued that Bernold himself was the author of this protocol: above p. 55. The synod: Meyer von Knonau (1903) pp. 14–21 and n. 29; Schumann (1913) pp. 57–8; Hauck (1954) pp. 843–4; Becker (1964) pp. 71–4; Cowdrey (1998) pp. 238–40; Robinson (1999) pp. 244–5.

together with the archbishops, bishops and abbots who were faithful
followers of St Peter. Gebhard, the most reverend archbishop of Salzburg[277] *was present in* this *synod; also* the venerable *Archbishop Hartwig of
Magdeburg;*[278] *together with his suffragans; also the suffragans of* the see of
Mainz from Saxony. For *the bishops of Würzburg,*[279] [Adalbert of] *Worms,*
[Wigold of] *Augsburg and also* [Gebhard] *of Constance from Swabia,
who could not come because they were prevented by impediments recognised by
canon law, had themselves represented in the holy council by their envoys and
they sent word that they would consent in all respects to the decisions of that
synod. King Herman was also present in that synod, together with his princes.
When all were seated according to their rank, therefore, there were produced
before them the decrees of the holy Fathers concerning the primacy of the apostolic see, that no one is ever permitted to question its judgement or to judge its
judgement.*[280] *This was approved and confirmed by the public declaration of
the whole synod. And this was especially directed against the Henricians, who
wished to compel the faithful followers of St Peter to dare to question with
them the excommunication pronounced by the lord Pope* Gregory *on Henry. A
certain clerk of Bamberg,* named Gumpert, *however, who wished to demolish
the primacy of the Roman pontiff, appeared before the synod and declared
that the Roman pontiffs had ascribed this primacy to themselves and had not
inherited from any other person the concession that no one was to question their
judgement and that they were not to be subject to the judgement of anyone.
When he was publicly proved wrong by the whole synod, he was confuted in
particular by a certain layman with that word of the Gospel: 'The disciple is
not above his master.'* [281] *For since this* is set down *to be observed in the case
of all ecclesiastical orders in general,* that the greater is not *to be judged* by
the lesser, *who can deny this to the vicar of St Peter, whom* all *catholics revere
as their lord and master?*

In the same synod the ordination of Wezilo, the intruder in Mainz, and of
Siegfried of Augsburg and Norbert of Chur,[282] *indeed all the ordinations
and consecrations of excommunicates* were judged to be entirely invalid,
according to *the decrees of the holy Fathers Innocent, Leo* I, *Pelagius and his*

---

277 Gebhard (1060–88).

278 Hartwig (1079–1102).

279 Adalbero (1045–90).

280 Cf. Nicholas I, *JE* 2879, *MGH Epistolae* 6, 606 (= *Collection in 74 titles* 17, p. 28). Cf.
    Bernold (?), *Apologeticus super excommunicacionem Gregorii VII* p. 162; Bernard, *Liber
    canonum* c. 13, p. 486.

281 Matthew 10:24.

282 Norbert (1079–87).

successor, Gregory I.[283] *Likewise the sect* of the aforementioned Wezilo and his allies — *which claims that secular men who have been despoiled of their property cannot be subjected to ecclesiastical judgement* and cannot be excommunicated *for their transgressions and which argues that excommunicated persons can be received without reconciliation* — *was condemned and excommunicated.*[284] It *was decreed* there, however, that if anyone *was excommunicated, although unjustly,* by his bishop and the latter had not been *deprived of his office or of communion, he was by no means to be received into communion,* unless he was absolved according to the custom of the Church. Similarly *the holy synod also decreed that those who have been excommunicated for sacrilege must not be received without the customary reconciliation,* even if *they have* long ago *given back* what they *had* sacrilegiously *appropriated* to themselves. *In the same synod perpetual chastity was imposed on priests, deacons and subdeacons according to* the decrees *of the holy Fathers. Furthermore it was decreed that* laymen were not to *touch altar cloths and sacred vessels. Furthermore laymen were not to claim tithes as their property* and *also* not to claim them as a benefice, unless through a grant by the lawful possessors. *Furthermore* the spring *fast* was to be celebrated *in the first* week of Lent, the summer fast *always* at Whitsuntide.[285] Furthermore no one was to eat cheese or eggs in Lent.

Furthermore the ordination of the lord Bishop Gebhard of Constance — indeed everything that the aforesaid *legate of the apostolic* see ⌈Odo of Ostia⌉ *arranged while he was in Constance* — *was confirmed* and *approved by synodal judgement. Furthermore the question of the consanguinity* of the king and his *wife*[286] *was raised there.* The king, therefore, *stood up before the synod and declared that he would in all respects observe the judgement of the holy synod in this matter.* The holy synod, however, *judged that this case could not be tried according to canon law* at the present time *since* no *lawful accusers* were present. At the end of the synod, however, sentence of excommunication *was pronounced with burning candles upon the heresiarch Wibert, the intruder in the apostolic see,* and upon the apostates from St Peter, *Hugh*

283 See above p. 278 and n. 264.

284 See above p. 279 and n. 271. Cf. Bernard, *Liber canonum* c. 15, p. 488: 'The synod condemned the heresy of Wezilo of Mainz, which argues that anyone who has been despoiled of his property, whatever sins he may have committed in the meantime, is to go unpunished, since he cannot be summoned to a synod or judged according to canon law.'

285 Cf. Bernold's liturgical treatise *Micrologus* c. 24–5, col. 995, 997, attributing this ruling to Gregory VII. It appears (not verbatim) in Gregory VII, *JL* 5290 (*Epistolae Vagantes* 76, p. 159), which the editor considered to be probably inauthentic.

286 Sophia, wife of Herman, perhaps related to the Billungs or to the east Bavarian counts of Formbach: Twellenkamp (1991) p. 494.

the White, the ex-bishop John of Porto, the ex-chancellor Peter,[287] *also upon the ex-bishops Liemar of Bremen, Udo of Hildesheim*, Otto of Constance, Burchard of Basel,[288] Huzmann of Speyer;[289] *also upon Wezilo, the intruder in Mainz*, Siegfried of Augsburg and Norbert of Chur. *The inevitable sentence of excommunication was pronounced, I say, upon these men and upon all their accomplices.*[276]

But in the third week after the synod came to an end all these enemies of God's Church assembled not a synod but an unlawful council of Mainz.[290] There they uttered a shady sentence of excommunication against the vassals of St Peter, although they had no power at all to excommunicate them but very openly removed themselves from the communion of the catholics so that not only in the judgement of holy Church but in their own judgement they were, like all heretics, separated from the catholics. Blinded by their audacious avarice, they were also not afraid to claim for themselves the sees of catholic bishops who were still alive.[291]

Almighty God did not cease, however, to help His faithful by His intervention and He carried out His judgement on the enemies of holy Church in a miraculous way.[292] For so great a famine affected almost the whole of Italy,[293] which was the principal haunt of the excommunicates, that men ate not only all manner of unclean things but even human flesh. Such an unprecedented rate of mortality followed this famine that not even a third part of the human population remained. Because of the lack of peasants by far the greater part of the land returned to wilderness. Moreover the Po, the river of Lombardy, burst its banks and completely inundated many castles, villages and indeed the surrounding regions and rendered them uninhabitable. At that time also the chief men of the schismatics, alas! miserably *went to* their *own place*:[294] namely, the ex-bishops [Eber-

---

287 The most prominent cardinals who deserted Gregory VII, 1084: Hugh Candidus, cardinal priest of S. Clemente (?1049–85), cardinal bishop of Palestrina (?1085–99); John II, cardinal bishop of Porto (1057–?89); Peter II, cardinal priest of S. Grisogono. See Hüls (1977) pp. 111, 158–60; 118–20; 170–2.

288 Burchard (1072–1107).

289 Huzmann (1075–90).

290 Council of Mainz, in the second week after Easter (27 April–3 May): *Liber de unitate ecclesiae conservanda* II.19, p. 235; *Annals of Augsburg* 1085, p. 131. See Meyer von Knonau (1903) pp. 21–5, 547–50; Hauck (1954) pp. 844–6; Cowdrey (1998) pp. 240–1; Robinson (1999) pp. 246–52.

291 Bernard, *Liber canonum* c. 33–5, pp. 501–5, is a polemic against the 'unjust condemners' of Mainz.

292 Cf. II Chronicles 19:6.

293 Cf. *Chronicle of Monte Cassino* III.64, p. 446.

294 Acts 1:25.

hard] of Parma and Reggio,[295] Tedald, who was not the archbishop but
the antichrist of Milan,[296] the margraves Adalbert and Rainer and Count
Boso[297] and innumerable others, as a result of whose factiousness almost
the whole of Italy rose up against the lord pope and St Peter. They had
also inflicted many injuries in Italy on Matilda, the most wise duchess
and most faithful vassal of St Peter.[298] When those men were removed
from the scene by divine punishment, however, she recovered her power
and did not cease to support the holy Church of God in all things. It
was thus through her foresight that catholic pastors were ordained in
the churches of Modena, Reggio and Pistoia.[299]

But now almighty God, desiring that His servant Pope Gregory should
labour no longer, desiring indeed to give him a fitting reward for his
labours, called him away from the prison of this life. For after being
for some time weakened in body but most steadfast in the defence of
righteousness even unto death, he ended his life in Salerno. All devout
people of both sexes, and especially the poor, lamented his death. For he
was a most fervent teacher of the catholic religion and a most vigorous
defender of the freedom of the Church. He did not indeed wish the
ecclesiastical order to be under the hands of laymen but to surpass
them both in holiness of conduct and in dignity of rank. This cannot
be hidden from anyone who has read carefully the register of that same
pope.[300] After he had striven lawfully in the government of the apostolic
see, or rather of the whole Church, for twelve years and one month, he
was at last removed from this light on 25 May in the year 1085 from
the Lord's Incarnation and there is no doubt that he won the prize of a
summons from heaven.[301] He was buried in Salerno in the church of St

295 Gandulf, bishop of Reggio in Emilia (1065–85).

296 Tedald (1075–85) ✝ 25 May. See Schwartz (1913) pp. 83, 187, 198.

297 Adalbert, margrave in Italy, possibly a vassal of Matilda of Tuscany, who deserted
her in 1081: cf. *DD.H.IV* 293, 338–9, 345, 359. Rainer, margrave in Tuscany, invested
in 1081 with Spoleto and Camerino: cf. *DD.H.IV* 338–9, 345, 359 and *D.H.IV* 356
('Rainer, duke and margrave'). 'Count Boso' was perhaps the 'Count Boso of Sabbio-
neta, vassal and standard-bearer of the bishop of Parma' of *D.H.IV* 341; cf. Bonizo,
To a friend IX, p. 246. See Gawlik (1970) pp. 59–60, 66–9, 153, 155, 180.

298 On this term applied to Matilda of Tuscany: Erdmann (1935) pp. 189, 195, 201,
207–8.

299 Benedict of Modena (1085– after 1107?); Heribert of Reggio (1085–92); Petrus of
Pistoia (1085–?1104). See Schwartz (1913) pp. 184, 198, 220.

300 On Bernold's use of the term 'register' cf. his *De excommunicatis vitandis* p. 91 and n.
33. See Robinson (1978b) p. 60.

301 Cf. Bernold, *Calendar* p. 506 (red ink): 'Death of Pope Gregory VII, 159th since
blessed Peter'. See Meyer von Knonau (1903) pp. 59–60 and n. 105; Cowdrey (1998)
pp. 677–8.

Matthew, which he himself dedicated in the same year.[302] But the heresiarch Wibert rejoiced greatly at his death, although he gained little advantage from it for his party. For after the death of the lord pope all the catholics resisted that same heresiarch no less than before and forced him to retreat from Rome to Ravenna.

At that time certain of the Saxons forsook their fidelity to St Peter and, shamefully abandoning Herman, their king, they received Henry, the king whom they had so often renounced on oath.[303] They supposed that they would henceforward suffer no evil from him but that, while he reigned, they would enjoy the peace that they longed for; but the opposite of this happened. For as soon as he regained power, he did not cease to impose his former tyranny upon them. In retaliation, therefore, they put him to flight most shamefully and with much dishonour expelled him from their territory.[304] The bishops of Saxony,[305] however, and certain of the princes, together with their king Herman, adhered to their fidelity to St Peter and chose rather to abandon their honours than to communicate with excommunicates. They were, however, afterwards summoned back by the Saxons to their own sees, after the Saxons expelled Henry, as we mentioned above.

1086. King Herman celebrated Christmas [25 December 1085] in Saxony. At this time much slaughter, plundering and burning occurred between the supporters of Henry and the vassals of St Peter. Because of this dissension the apostolic see could not yet have a lawful pastor. On 27 January Henry led an army against the Saxons. But the Saxons met him with a great host and forced him to turn back with nothing accomplished.[306]

---

302 Consecration of the cathedral of San Matteo, Salerno: Meyer von Knonau (1900) p. 564 and (1903) p. 62 n. 106; Cowdrey (1983) p. 173.

303 Cf. *Liber de unitate ecclesiae* II.28, p. 250: 'since they feared ... to be attacked by the emperor, who was already present with an army around 1 July, they all, both Saxons and Thuringians, surrendered, except for a very few'. See Meyer von Knonau (1903) pp. 49–52; Fenske (1977) p. 111; Robinson (1999) pp. 254–5. Giese (1979) p. 178: the Saxons formally deposed the anti-king in an assembly that was 'a Forchheim in reverse'.

304 Under the leadership of Margrave Ekbert II of Meissen: Frutolf, *Chronica* 1085, p. 98. See Meyer von Knonau (1903) pp. 53–5; Giese (1979) pp. 178–9; Robinson (1999) pp. 256–7.

305 Hartwig of Magdeburg, Burchard of Halberstadt, Reinhard of Minden, Werner of Merseburg. See Meyer von Knonau (1903) pp. 51–5.

306 See Meyer von Knonau (1903) pp. 113–15; Robinson (1999) pp. 258–9.

At that time in Henry's party the count palatine Herman[307] and Otto, the ex-bishop of Constance died miserably[308] – alas! – without ecclesiastical communion. In the party of the catholics the most reverend Anselm, bishop of the church of Lucca, who had long been crucified by the world, departed to the Lord on 18 March.[309]

The princes of the Bavarians were reconciled with Welf [IV], their duke, at Eastertide [5 April] and deserted Henry.[310] Together with that same duke and with the other princes of the Swabians, they attacked him in Regensburg with an armed force and detained him there for a long time so that he was unable to leave.

After seizing many lands and after oppressing many poor and rich men, Robert [Guiscard], duke of the Normans throughout Calabria and Sicily, went the way of all flesh.[311] Neither Calabria nor Sicily satisfied his avarice, so that he eagerly strove to bring kingdoms overseas under his power, contrary to divine and human law.

In these days the princes of the Swabians who were faithful to St Peter held a general conference with the Saxons and Bavarians near Würzburg after the feast of the apostles [29 June].[312] Henry gathered a host of schismatics and wished to disrupt it, but when the Swabians made a sudden attack on him, he was unable to put up any resistance and abandoned the place to them for the time being. They themselves, however, advanced to Würzburg to besiege Henry's supporters and, joining forces with the Saxons, they surrounded that city with a rampart. Meanwhile Henry assembled an army of almost 20,000, including foot soldiers and knights, and sent it in battle array to free the city, which had now been under siege for five weeks.[313] When they heard of this, the vassals of St Peter abandoned the siege and advanced until they were two miles away from him, trusting not so much in their numbers

---

307 Herman II, count palatine of Lotharingia (1064–85). The year of his death: *Annals of Brauweiler* p. 725. See Meyer von Knonau (1903) p. 229.

308 'Almost one year' after the council of Mainz (May 1085): *Casus monasterii Petrishusensis* II.49, p. 648. See Hauck (1954) p. 987.

309 Cf. Bernold, *Calendar* p. 500 (red ink). His acquaintance with Anselm II of Lucca: Bernold, *De veritate corporis et sanguinis Domini* p. 91. See Robinson (1989) p. 178.

310 In Freising: *Annals of Augsburg* 1086, p. 132. Henry IV's south German enemies were present at the synod held by Bishop Gebhard in Constance, 1 April: Maurer (1991) pp. 179–80; Meyer von Knonau (1903) p. 122; Robinson (1999) pp. 259–60.

311 17 July. See Meyer von Knonau (1903) p. 69 n. 109.

312 Henry IV was already in Würzburg on 18 June: *D.H.IV* 391.

313 According to Bernold's chronology the siege lasted from 6 July to 11 August. See Meyer von Knonau (1903) p. 125.

as in the mercy of God and the justice of St Peter, not so much in their weapons as in the strength of the holy Cross. They therefore caused a very high cross, which had been set up in a wagon and decorated with a red banner,[314] to be brought with them to the battlefield. Marching with them were Duke Welf [IV of Bavaria] and his forces and the Magdeburg forces, who left their horses behind and came on foot. When they were already on the point of fighting, however, they all threw themselves on the ground and addressed themselves to heaven with a prayer, which the most reverend archbishop [Hartwig] of Magdeburg offered up there on their behalf with many tears and groans. They joined battle,[315] therefore, in the name of the Lord and wrought an incredible slaughter among the enemy so that nine extremely large piles of corpses were seen there, besides those of the fugitives who fell in the fields and the forests. In the first onset of the battle, however, Henry was the very first to flee.[316] Assuming a disguise and abandoning all his banners to our troops, with the greatest haste he made for the Rhine. But our men pursued him for a long distance and at last brought back great plunder taken from the enemy. Our men indeed obtained his treasure chests together with his royal garments and I know not how many bishops' capes and innumerable other things. We have not yet been able to discover how many thousands of enemies died. In the party of St Peter's vassals, however, we could find only fifteen dead, even though we searched with the greatest care, and of those fifteen, only three died on the battlefield, for the rest survived for some days afterwards.[317] We could find only thirty dead and wounded among our troops. This is undoubtedly to be attributed not to human but rather to divine strength since the vassals of St Peter had scarcely 10,000 men, while the numbers of the enemy are said to have exceeded even 20,000. After our men had thus obtained the victory through God's mercy, they pitched camp that night on the battlefield and, returning next day to the siege of the city, they captured it without bloodshed. The bishop [Adalbero] of Würzburg was then restored to his see amidst the great approbation and praise of the citizens, clergy and laity. After a suitable

---

314 Intended to demonstrate that the rebels ('the vassals of St Peter') were fighting a holy war: Erdmann (1935) pp. 49, 209.

315 Battle of Pleichfeld (north-east of Würzburg), 11 August. See Meyer von Knonau (1903) pp. 125–31; Cram (1955) pp. 148–9, 215; Robinson (1999) pp. 260–2.

316 Allegations of cowardice in anti-Henrician sources: Robinson (1999) pp. 348–51.

317 Cf. the pro-Henrician Sigebert, *Chronica* 1086, p. 365: '[Henry's] army was struck down by terror from heaven and gave up the fight and more than 4,000 of them were killed and only fourteen of the party of the Saxons were killed.'

garrison of knights had been stationed in the city, they each returned to their homes with great honour and joy. This battle, however, took place on the day following the feast of St Laurence [11 August], that is, on the anniversary of the day on which King Herman, together with the Swabians, defeated the Bavarians.[318] I myself, who have compiled this chronicle from the 1,054th year of the Lord's Incarnation up to this point, have contrived to proclaim to the faithful, to the praise and glory of God, not so much what others reported about the aforementioned battle, but rather what I myself saw and heard.[319]

The most reverend abbot of the monastery of St Blasien, named Giselbert, departed to the Lord on 10 October. The venerable Uto, prior of that same monastery, succeeded him in the office of abbot.[320] Count Conrad, the brother of King Herman[321] but a tireless supporter of Henry – although in the end, they say, he was reconciled to the Church – died on the journey to Jerusalem.

The blessed Anselm, formerly bishop of Lucca, began to shine forth with innumerable miracles in the very year of his burial. While he still lived in the flesh he strongly urged the vassals of St Peter to fight against Henry's tyranny after the death of the venerable Pope Gregory VII, but after his own death he encouraged them even more by the splendour of his miracles to stand firm against [Henry].[322] For this reason Henry's party began day by day to diminish but the catholics did not cease to grow in their fidelity to St Peter.

Nevertheless shortly before Christmas Henry laid siege to a certain castle in Bavaria[323] and, so they say, he wished to celebrate Christmas during that siege. When they heard of this, Duke Welf [IV of Bavaria] and Duke Berthold [of Rheinfelden][324] with a small force of Swabians and Bavarians made a sudden incursion and they did not permit him

318 I.e. the battle of Höchstädt, 1081: above p. 267 and n. 201.

319 Cf. Isidore, *Etymologiae* 1.41.1: 'Among the ancients no one wrote a history unless he had been present and seen those things which were to be recorded.'

320 Giselbert (1068–86); Uto (1086–1100). See Jakobs (1968) pp. 39, 41–2, 51, 56, 60, 63–4, 77–81.

321 Conrad I, count of Luxemburg (1056/9–86), elder brother of the anti-king Herman, † 8 August. See Twellenkamp (1991) pp. 487–93.

322 The miracle tradition of Anselm II of Lucca: Golinelli (1987) pp. 27–60.

323 Place-name unknown: Meyer von Knonau (1903) pp. 133–4.

324 Meyer von Knonau (1903) p. 133 identifies the latter as Berthold II of Zähringen but in this part of the chronicle 'Duke Berthold' means Berthold of Rheinfelden, anti-duke of Swabia (n. 262). Berthold II of Zähringen first appears in 1092: below p. 308 and n. 454.

to withdraw from the siege until they had received a guarantee from
his princes that he would allow a conference to take place in which the
long-lasting conflict in the kingdom could at last by some means or
other be brought to a suitable conclusion. When they had received the
guarantee, they granted him the opportunity of departing in peace. And
thus he was compelled on Christmas Eve to hold his celebration of the
festival elsewhere. The dukes, however, returned to their homes peacefully and joyfully and, together with the other princes of the kingdom,
they immediately made a general proclamation of the conference that
had been arranged for the third week of Lent [28 February–6 March
1087] in Oppenheim.[325]

1087. King Herman celebrated Christmas [25 December 1086] in
Saxony.

Count Berthold, a most faithful knight of St Peter,[326] died fighting most
vigorously against the schismatics.

Meanwhile Henry wished to bring it about that the aforementioned
conference would not take place, using all his cleverness and cunning,
because he could not achieve it by force; but the vassals of St Peter
arrived there at the agreed date, even though he did not wish it and
indeed threatened them with the danger of war. He himself in his usual
manner evaded justice, refused to acquiesce in the reasonable advice
of his followers and did not deign to be present. In this way he caused
nearly all his followers to murmur against him and some of them to
abandon him, while our men returned in peace to their own homes.[327]

But the apostolic see could not yet have a lawful pastor because the
oath-breaker and excommunicated heresiarch Wibert of Ravenna had
troubled that see now for eight years as a result of the machinations of
Henry. For although he himself could not possess that [see] in peace,
nevertheless he was strong enough by means of the instruments of
the devil for the apostolic see to have now been without the direction
of a shepherd for two years. Since all catholics rightly deplored this
fact, the cardinal bishops of the holy Roman church and the rest of the
catholics among the clergy and people, with the help of the Normans,
at last appointed Desiderius, cardinal of that same church and abbot of

---

325 See Meyer von Knonau (1903) p. 133; Robinson (1999) p. 262.

326 An unidentifiable Swabian or Bavarian count: Meyer von Knonau (1903) p. 159 n. 2;
     Erdmann (1935) p. 189 n. 28.

327 Cf. *Annals of Augsburg* 1087, p. 132: 'The council that had been arranged in Oppen-
     heim broke up without accomplishing anything.' See Meyer von Knonau (1903) p.
     158; Robinson (1999) p. 262.

the monastery of Monte Cassino, as the 160th pope and gave him the name Victor III.[328] Immediately after his election he sent letters everywhere, declaring that he would proceed according to the decrees of the holy Fathers.[329] He also confirmed the judgement of his predecessor of pious memory, Pope Gregory, on Henry and all his supporters.[330] He was consecrated, however, at the end of the month of May in St Peter's by the cardinal bishops Odo of Ostia and Peter of Albano together with the other cardinals.[331] But the heresiarch Wibert did not henceforward cease from the career of perversity on which he had embarked: instead he fortified himself in S. Maria *ad Martires*, which they call the Rotunda.[332] The lord pope, however, retreated to an island that was situated between two bridges.[333]

The princes of the kingdom of the Germans – I mean the vassals of St Peter – also held a general conference with Henry and his supporters on 1 August near the city of Speyer and faithfully promised him their help in obtaining the kingship if he wished to be free of his excommunication. He, however, persisted in his customary obstinacy and did not deign to admit that he was excommunicate, even though it was firmly demonstrated to him face to face by our men. For this reason our men decided to have no peace and no agreement with him. He therefore announced that he would lead an expedition against them on the octave of St Michael next following [6 October].[334] Our men, however, agreed to anticipate that expedition by eight days and to go to meet him at the assembly point with as many men as they could. In the aforementioned conference a letter of the lord pope was read out, in which he

328 Desiderius, abbot of Monte Cassino (1058–87), cardinal priest of S. Cecilia, Pope Victor III, elected 24 May 1086, consecrated 9 May 1087. See Cowdrey (1983) pp. 185–213. Bernold confused the circumstances of Victor's election with those of his consecration: Meyer von Knonau (1903) p. 154 n. 82.

329 Not extant. Cf. Peter the Deacon, *De viris illustribus* c. 18, col. 1028: 'he wrote very many letters to Philip, king of the French and to Abbot Hugh of Cluny'.

330 No renewal of the excommunication of Henry IV is extant nor is it mentioned in the report of the council of Benevento (29 August 1087) in *Chronicle of Monte Cassino* III.72–3, pp. 453–5. See Cowdrey (1983) p. 208; Robinson (1999) p. 264.

331 9 May: *Chronicle of Monte Cassino* III.68, p. 450 (he was consecrated 'by the Roman bishops, namely those of Ostia, Tusculum, Porto and Albano'). See Becker (1964) pp. 86–7; Hüls (1977) pp. 90, 102, 120, 140.

332 The Pantheon (S. Maria Rotonda), in a Wibertine quarter of Rome: Hüls (1977) pp. 262–3. But *Chronicle of Monte Cassino* III.69, p. 451 identifies S. Maria in Turri, by St Peter's.

333 Cf. *Chronicle of Monte Cassino* III.69, p. 451: 'on the island of Rome'. See below 1089, p. 295.

334 See Meyer von Knonau (1903) p. 162; Robinson (1999) pp. 263, 264.

both announced his elevation to the princes of the kingdom and most carefully confirmed the judgement of his predecessor of pious memory, Pope Gregory, on Henry and his supporters.

Ladislaus, king of the Hungarians sent envoys to that same conference and declared that he would persevere in his fidelity to St Peter and promised that he would assist the vassals of St Peter against the schismatics with 20,000 knights, if it became necessary.[335] Nevertheless the aforementioned expedition was adjourned on that date by both sides. Salomon, who was formerly king of the Hungarians but who had long before been deprived of the kingship by Ladislaus and driven into exile, died courageously after an incredible slaughter of the enemy after he bravely undertook an enterprise against the king of the Greeks.[336]

At that same time also a certain schismatic who had long ago intruded himself in the bishopric of Passau[337] while the lawful pastor was still alive, departed this life, leaving the other schismatics a most certain proof of his damnation. For while he was already lying in his last agony and was in no doubt that he would soon go to eternal damnation, the bishop of that same church [Altman] appeared to him, so that he would know more clearly the fault that he must expiate in hell. Nevertheless he asked him to pardon the fault and to absolve him from excommunication.[338] He also asked the bystanders to remove him from the bishopric and not to bury him in the bishopric. But these words seemed to the bystanders to be spoken in delirium. He, however, declared that he was of sound mind and did not cease to make the same request, but in vain; for he was overtaken by death before receiving the absolution of the Church. Nevertheless some who were present at the death of that schismatic, horrendous as it was, were filled with remorse and afterwards returned to the lawful pastor and obtained pardon and absolution.

In Rome Pope Victor, who had already been ill for very many years and who had been ordained while suffering from that infirmity, ended his life after the fourth month of his pontificate.[339] The heresiarch Wibert, together with his followers, rejoiced greatly at this.

335 See Meyer von Knonau (1903) p. 169.

336 The campaign against Emperor Alexius I Comnenus: Anna Comnena, *Alexiad* VII.1, pp. 227–8. See Meyer von Knonau (1903) p. 168 and n. 14.

337 Herman (of Eppenstein), imperial anti-bishop of Passau (1085–7), brother of Duke Liutold of Carinthia and Abbot Udalric of St Gallen.

338 Cf. *Vita Altmanni episcopi Pataviensis* c. 16, p. 234: on his deathbed Herman sent to Altman, seeking absolution from his excommunication.

339 16 September. Bernold calculated the pontificate from the date of Victor III's consecration rather than his election. Cf. his catalogue of popes, *MGH SS* 5, 400.

At that time also Henry, although ill, led an expedition into Saxony with the Bohemians.[340] But since St Peter protected his vassals, he withdrew from there ingloriously and extremely hastily. For King Herman pursued him with so great a host of Saxons that he could very easily have seized him, had he not escaped through the cunning of Count Ekbert.[341] This count indeed greatly envied the fame of his lord King Herman and preferred to free the enemies of holy Church from the latter's hands by means of his own cunning rather than to triumph over them with his lord virtually without incurring any danger to the honour of God and St Peter. This was precisely because he had already conceived the idea of depriving his lord of the kingship.

1088. King Herman celebrated Christmas [25 December 1087] in Saxony, where Count Ekbert also made public the fact that he was aiming at the kingship. But it was in vain, for the princes of the kingdom refused to give him their approval: instead they began henceforward to adhere much more steadfastly to the lord king.[342]

The excellent teacher Berthold,[343] who was extremely learned in sacred literature, departed to the Lord *in a good old age, full of years,*[344] on 12 March.

At this time the Pisans and the Genoese and very many other men from Italy made an attack on a pagan African king, plundered his land and drove him into a certain fortification and compelled him thereafter to pay tribute to the apostolic see.[345]

Duke Welf [IV of Bavaria] recovered the city of Augsburg, after Siegfried, the intruder in that bishopric, had captured it.[346] Count Hugh

---

340 See Meyer von Knonau (1903) p. 170; Robinson (1999) pp. 264–5.

341 Ekbert II (of Brunswick), margrave of Meissen (1068–90). See Meyer von Knonau (1903) pp. 171–2; Fenske (1977) pp. 115–16; Giese (1979) pp. 179–80; Robinson (1999) pp. 264–5.

342 The pro-Henrician *Liber de unitate ecclesiae* II.33, 35, pp. 260, 261 ascribes to Archbishop Hartwig of Magdeburg and Bishop Burchard II of Halberstadt the plan of raising Ekbert to the kingship. See Fenske (1977) pp. 116–17; Robinson (1999) p. 265.

343 Probably Berthold, monk of Reichenau and chronicler: above p. 23. Cf. Bernold, *Calendar* p. 499.

344 Genesis 25:8; I Chronicles 29:28.

345 Mahdia expedition of August 1087. Cf. *Carmen in victoria Pisanorum*, ed. Cowdrey (1977) pp. 24–9 (especially *Carmen* line 60, p. 28, payment of tribute to St Peter). See Erdmann (1935) pp. 272–3 and n. 100.

346 After Augsburg was captured on 12 April, Bishop Siegfried II was imprisoned for two years in Welf IV's castle of Ravensburg: Meyer von Knonau (1903) pp. 204–5.

of Egisheim[347] entered Alsace, which had long been occupied by the enemy, and attempted to recover it for himself. The people of Metz drove Bruno, the intruder in that see,[348] out of the city and confirmed on oath that henceforward they would accept no one except their lawful pastor,[349] who was at that time being held in captivity in Tuscany.

In Saxony Burchard of pious memory, the bishop of Halberstadt, most steadfast in the cause of St Peter, was alas! killed. But it makes no difference whether a fever or a sword sends us to the Lord. He departed to the Lord, however, on 6 April.[350]

The heresiarch Wibert, however, had not yet ceased his intrusion in the apostolic see and Emperor Henry would not lay aside his inveterate tyranny against the vassals of St Peter, although he could not conquer them.

In Rome the cardinal bishops and the rest of the catholics among the clergy and people appointed Bishop Odo of Ostia, who was distinguished for his piety and learning, as the 161st pope and conferred on him the name Urban II on 12 March.[351] Immediately on the following day he sent a letter to all catholics, in which he announced his appointment to all and declared that he would in all things follow in the footsteps of his predecessor of pious memory, Pope Gregory.[352]

Bishop Wigold of Augsburg ended his life[353] after recovering his city and capturing the false bishop Siegfried, who had supplanted him. Hezelo, the most faithful knight of St Peter and the advocate of the monastery of St Mary in Reichenau, built a monastery in honour of St George on his own property.[354] He himself finally became a monk there and departed to the Lord on 1 June.

---

347 Hugh VI, count of Egisheim (†1089), nephew of Pope Leo IX.

348 Bruno, imperial anti-bishop (1085–8), son of Count Adalbert II of Calw. See Meyer von Knonau (1903) pp. 40–1.

349 Herman (1073–90), deposed by the Henrician council of Mainz (1085). Cf. Hugh, *Chronicon* II, p. 471: he was 'in Lombardy, where he resided with Matilda [of Tuscany]'. See Meyer von Knonau (1903) p. 41 n. 76.

350 He was killed in Goslar in a fight between the citizens and the vassals and *ministeriales* of Halberstadt. Other sources give the date 7 April. See Meyer von Knonau (1903) pp. 209–13; Fenske (1977) pp. 116–18, 201.

351 Election of Urban II (n. 222) in Terracina: Becker (1964) pp. 91–6.

352 Urban II, *JL* 5348, col. 283–4 (13 March, to the archbishop of Salzburg, bishops of Passau, Würzburg, Worms, Augsburg, Constance, Welf IV, Berthold I of Rheinfelden and Berthold II of Zähringen): 'desiring to follow totally in [Gregory's] footsteps'.

353 11 May. See Meyer von Knonau (1903) p. 205 and n. 23.

354 Hezelo (1056–88), founder of the abbey of St Georgen in the Black Forest. See Wollasch (1964) pp. 23–8; Jakobs (1968) pp. 228–30.

At that time a certain disciple of the heresiarch Wibert, namely the false bishop of Worms[355] – who intruded in that see, receiving from the schismatics not consecration but a curse – at last came to his senses and returned to the catholic Church. He gave up the bishopric and devoted himself to penitence in the monastery of Hirsau. It was in the same way indeed that three years before another disciple of that same Wibert – I mean the false bishop of Metz[356] – had been led to give up the bishopric into which Bruno (whom we mentioned above) immediately intruded in a no less sacrilegious manner. For he entered with the support of the schismatics, in the lifetime of the lawful pastor of that see, Herman, who chose, like a catholic, rather to be kept in captivity than to be honoured as a bishop in a state of schism.

Archbishop Gebhard of Salzburg of reverend memory, who was outstanding in the cause of St Peter and who was accustomed to confute the schismatics publicly in his speeches and his writings, was taken from the light of this world on 15 June,[357] leaving the catholics in great grief. Bernard, master of the schools in Constance,[358] a most learned man, most ardent in the cause of St Peter, departed to the Lord in Saxony, where he had made his profession as a monk. The false bishops Wezilo of Mainz[359] and Meinhard of Würzburg,[360] outstanding among the schismatics for their learning and their errors, *went to* their *own place*,[361] miserably but not deserving of pity.

The Saxons fell away from their fidelity to St Peter and received Henry, whom they had very often renounced on oath.[362] The catholic King Herman, therefore, withdrew from them and went to Lotharingia and

---

355 Winither, abbot of Lorsch (since 1077), imperial anti-bishop of Worms (1085–8). See Meyer von Knonau (1903) pp. 42, 361.

356 Walo, abbot of St Arnulf in Metz, imperial anti-bishop (1085). See Meyer von Knonau (1904) p. 40.

357 Cf. Bernold, *Calendar* p. 508. His writings: *Epistola, MGH Libelli* 1, 261–79; letter to Herman of Metz (n. 251) p. 459.

358 Bernard, master of the cathedral school of Constance, then (from *ca.* 1072) of Hildesheim, monk of Corvey; polemicist, correspondent of Bernold; † 15 March: Bernold, *Calendar* p. 500 and n. 51. See above p. 43.

359 † 6 August. See Meyer von Knonau (1903) p. 220 and n. 43.

360 Meinhard, imperial anti-bishop of Würzburg (1085–8) † 20 June; formerly master of the cathedral school of Bamberg and author of an important letter collection: Erdmann (1938) pp. 16–24.

361 Acts 1:25.

362 Cf. *D.H.IV* 400 (10 August): the interveners are Archbishop Hartwig of Magdeburg, Bishop Werner of Merseburg, margraves Ekbert II of Meissen and Henry I of Lusatia. See Meyer von Knonau (1903) p. 220.

there, not long afterwards, he went the way of all flesh, in the 1,088th
year of the Lord's Incarnation, in the seventh year of his reign, in the
twelfth indiction, and he received honourable burial in his homeland of
Metz.[363]

The Saxons again rebelled against Henry through the intrigues of
Margrave Ekbert [II of Meissen]. They robbed him of the royal insignia
and drove him away from the siege of a certain fortress,[364] shamefully
forcing him to flee to a certain mountain, and there after a siege of two
days they compelled him to confess that he was excommunicate and to
beg for reconciliation. After he had made peace on these conditions, he
departed but he did not give up his customary tyranny.

Abbot Ekkehard of Reichenau, who, although he was not very devout,
nevertheless in the end (so they say) underwent a praiseworthy conversion, ended his life.[365] Udalric succeeded him.[366]

1089. On Christmas Eve [24 December 1088] Margrave Ekbert, encouraged by certain pious men, with a few knights courageously attacked
Henry and all his army, drove him away from the siege of one of his
castles [Gleichen], where he intended to celebrate Christmas, and put
him to flight with the greatest dishonour. During this attack Archbishop Liemar of Bremen[367] and Count Berthold[368] from Henry's party
were captured. He who was not so much the bishop as the antichrist
of Lausanne[369] was killed, when he bravely wished to offer resistance.
Henry, however, lost the royal insignia and was rescued with difficulty
from the hands of his pursuers. Fleeing thus from Thuringia, he finally
arrived in Bamberg and there he was compelled to celebrate the festival
in an inglorious manner. But Margrave Ekbert took possession of his
castle and the camp of his enemies almost without bloodshed. After he

---

363 † 28 September. See Meyer von Knonau (1903) pp. 221, 226 and n. 50; Robinson
(1999) pp. 268–9.

364 Ekbert's Thuringian castle of Gleichen, south-west of Erfurt. See Meyer von
Knonau (1903) pp. 222–4; Robinson (1999) pp. 270–1. Bernold repeats this report in
the annal for 1089.

365 Ekkehard II (n. 90), Gregorian anti-bishop of Augsburg (1088) † 24 November. See
Meyer von Knonau (1903) p. 205.

366 Udalric II (1088–1122).

367 He was captured by Count Lothar of Supplinburg (later Emperor Lothar III),
according to Meyer von Knonau (1903) p. 224 and n. 48. See Robinson (1999) p. 271
n. 185.

368 Identity unknown; cf. *Annalista Saxo* 1089, p. 726: 'Count Berthold, the emperor's
favourite'.

369 Burchard (1056/7–89), chancellor of the Italian kingdom.

had also captured and killed very many men, he did not cease to offer thanks to God and to St Peter and resolved that he would cling to them thereafter with a more spotless fidelity.[370]

Bishop Herman of Metz, a catholic, returned to his bishopric after a long captivity and was received with joy by many. Bruno, the rash intruder in that same bishopric, was, however, despised by all men. For because of his most disgraceful conduct he had greatly displeased even Henry himself, although the latter had formerly sold him that bishopric.[371] Under the constraints of this necessity, Bruno was forced to give up the bishopric and return to his father, Count Adalbert, in the party of the catholics.[372]

The lord Pope Urban was staying at this time in Rome on an island that lies between two bridges. He sent a decretal letter to the venerable *Bishop*[373] *Gebhard of Constance on 18 April,* in which he *granted* him *episcopal power* over *the clergy and people of the island of Reichenau, except for the monks,* giving him also the authority to install *an abbot* there *on* [the pope's] *behalf* and likewise to *take measures* to establish bishops in *Augsburg* and *Chur.* Indeed he entrusted *the office of* his *vicar* in the whole of *Swabia,* Bavaria, *Saxony* and other neighbouring *regions* to the aforementioned bishop and to the venerable Bishop Altman of Passau[374] *so that they might reject the ordinations that ought to be rejected and confirm those that ought to be confirmed.* He also *confirmed the sentence* of excommunication published by his *predecessor* Pope *Gregory,* with this difference: that in *the first place* he judged *the heresiarch* [Wibert] *of Ravenna, together with King Henry,* to be excommunicated; in *the second* place, their supporters, *who* assisted them *with arms, money, advice and obedience* and who received *ecclesiastical orders* or *honours from them or their supporters;* but *in the third place* he put those who *communicated* with them and, although *he did not excommunicate* them, he nevertheless *declared* that they were so *contaminated by communication* with outsiders *that they must not be received in* catholic *society without absolution and penance: namely, those who* had communicated *with excommunicates by means of greeting,*

370 See Meyer von Knonau (1903) pp. 246–7; Fenske (1977) p. 117.

371 Cf. *Liber de unitate ecclesiae* II.30, p. 256: 'the emperor withdrew from him the power of the episcopal office after he learned that such great scandals had been perpetrated there by him'. See above n. 348 and Meyer von Knonau (1903) pp. 248–9.

372 Adalbert II, count of Calw (✝1099).

373/373 Extracts from Urban II, *JL* 5393, col. 297B–299A [= *Briefsammlungen* pp. 254–7] (18 April, to Gebhard III). Meyer von Knonau (1903) p. 255 n. 12 suggested that Bernold himself brought this letter from Rome to Constance.

374 Papal vicars in Germany: Schumann (1912) p. 67; Becker (1964) pp. 148–9.

kiss, conversation, eating together or *through ignorance. He permitted those who had been ordained* in a state of *excommunication* but *not through simony, by bishops who had originally been ordained* in a *catholic* manner, to remain *in the orders* that they had received, without further promotion, *if* their worthiness and *the advantage* of the Church seemed to *demand* this.[375] *He conceded* also that some of them might *be promoted to higher* rank, *but this* only very *rarely and in cases of* extreme *necessity*.[373]

The heresiarch Wibert and his associates in the party of the king, however, did not cease to perform accursed ordinations and conferred them on their adherents, selling them to them at the highest price. For this reason the evil of excommunication became so widespread at that time that the catholics could scarcely keep themselves safe from its contamination. In the German territories four bishops continued stead-fastly in the catholic communion, namely those of Würzburg [Adal-bero], Passau [Altman], Worms [Adalbert], Constance [Gebhard III], but also the bishop [Herman] of Metz, and through their encour-agement the rest of the catholics resisted the schismatics from the very beginning.

Count Hugh [VI] of Egisheim, a tireless knight of St Peter,[376] who, however, trusted too much in the false bishop of Strasbourg,[377] was killed on 4 September in his bedchamber by the servants of that same bishop after he had laid down with him to sleep.

Bonizo of pious memory, the bishop of Sutri but driven out of there long ago because of his fidelity towards St Peter, after many experiences of captivity, tribulation and exile, was at length received by the catholics of Piacenza as their bishop. But his eyes were gouged out, almost all his limbs were mutilated and he was crowned with martyrdom by the schismatics of that place.[378]

In Swabia Count Otto,[379] a most shameless adulterer, who had been excommunicated by the bishop [Gebhard III] of Constance for adul-tery, was through the judgement of God most dishonourably beheaded by the knights of Count Ludwig.[380] For he had most impiously united

---

375 See Saltet (1907) pp. 221–31; Becker (1964) pp. 149–51.

376 See above n. 347 and Erdmann (1935) p. 189 with n. 28.

377 Otto (1084–1100), brother of Duke Frederick I of Swabia.

378 Bonizo (n. 206) 'survived the day of horrors in Piacenza, perhaps even for a number of years' and possibly died in 1094: Berschin (1972) pp. 13, 18.

379 Otto II, count of Buchhorn (Udalriching family). See above p. 222 and n. 602.

380 Perhaps Ludwig, count of Pfullendorf: Meyer von Knonau (1903) p. 257 n. 17.

himself with [Ludwig's] wife in a public marriage ceremony, while [Ludwig] was still alive. He was buried by his followers in the monastery that he had built on his estate[381] but he was expelled from there by the command of the bishop of Constance and, as it is written, he was condemned to *the burial of an ass.*[382] His knights also plundered his treasure and it was not his heirs but strangers who took possession both of his personal property and of his benefices, according to what is prophesied in the curses of Judah: *may strangers plunder the fruits of his toil.*[383] Thus after his death he proved most clearly both in his burial and in the pillaging of his property how effective was the sentence of excommunication that he incurred.

In Italy the most noble duchess Matilda, the daughter of Margrave Boniface [II of Tuscany], but also the widow of Duke Godfrey [IV of Lower Lotharingia], was joined in marriage to Duke Welf, the son of Duke Welf [IV of Bavaria],[384] not indeed because of unchastity but rather because of obedience towards the Roman pontiff: namely, so that she might the more effectively come to the aid of the holy Roman church against the excommunicates.[385] The latter wished immediately to attack her husband but since they could not resist him, they obtained from him through his wife's intervention a truce until Easter [21 April 1090]. Henry, the so-called king, was greatly saddened by the aforementioned marriage. He set out for Saxony once more with an expedition but was compelled to return without honour.[386]

Peter, the bishop of Albano of pious memory, most ardent in the cause of St Peter, departed to the Lord.[387] He was that Peter who proved by means of a trial by fire that Peter of Pavia, the intruder in the bishopric of Florence, was a simoniac and for this reason holy Church afterwards gave him the surname 'fiery'. For he confidently stepped on to a great pyre and passed through it without any injury, so that the flames caused

---

381 Probably Hofen near Buchhorn. Cf. necrology of Hofen, *MGH Necrologia* 1, 176: † 1 December.

382 Jeremiah 22:19.

383 Psalm 108:11.

384 Welf V, count; duke of Bavaria (1101–20). See Meyer von Knonau (1903) pp. 273–4; Becker (1964) pp. 120–1; Robinson (1999) p. 280.

385 Cf. Urban II, *JL* 5464, col. 345B: 'the most beloved Countess Matilda, daughter of St Peter, who exposed herself to the greatest dangers for the sake of the apostolic see'. See Becker (1964) p. 121 n. 406.

386 See Meyer von Knonau (1903) p. 259; Robinson (1999) pp. 271–2.

387 † 11 November. See Hüls (1977) p. 90.

his garments to move to and fro but in no way harmed them, to say nothing of himself. The aforementioned Peter of Pavia was therefore deposed by Pope Alexander, but the other Peter, who was then a monk in a very poor monastery, was elevated to the bishopric of Albano.[388] For he was a man of such great sanctity, steadfastness and faith that scarcely anyone of his time could be compared to him. When he departed this life, he left behind him great lamentation among the catholics.

The lord Pope Urban assembled a general synod of 115 bishops[389] and confirmed by apostolic authority the ecclesiastical decrees of his predecessors. The heresiarch Wibert, however, was expelled with dishonour by the Romans and forced to promise on oath not to dare to intrude in the apostolic see any more.[390] But now the longstanding conflict in the kingdom between the catholics and the schismatics began to diminish somewhat so that they judged it wiser not to make war on each other but to make peace. The dukes and counts who were vassals of St Peter, therefore, held a conference with Henry and most faithfully promised their counsel and help in securing the kingship, if he would give up the heresiarch Wibert and return to the communion of the Church through the agency of a catholic pastor.[391] He would not have objected much to this condition, if only his own princes had agreed with him in this: namely, the bishops, who had no doubt that they must be deposed with Wibert because they had received their consecration – or rather their execration – in his faction. They therefore, for their part, entirely dissuaded him from being reconciled to holy mother Church.

The lord pope absolved the emperor [Alexius I] of Constantinople from excommunication through his legates.[392] He also received a letter from Philip, king of the French promising him due submission.[393]

1090. In Bavaria the vassals of St Peter so prevailed against the schismatics that they appointed a catholic archbishop in the bishopric of

---

388 See above pp. 121 and n. 139, 264 and n. 175.

389 Synod of Melfi, 10 September, attended by 70 bishops and 12 abbots. See Meyer von Knonau (1903) pp. 271–2; Becker (1964) pp. 120, 148; Somerville and Kuttner (1996) p. 175.

390 Köhncke (1888) p. 81 regarded this report as false.

391 See Meyer von Knonau (1903) pp. 259–60; Robinson (1999) p. 274.

392 This, the only extant report of such a legation, is probably to be connected with the negotiations of Urban II and Alexius I Comnenus in 1088/9. See Holtzmann (1928) pp. 38–67; Becker (1988) pp. 113–59.

393 Philip I (1060–1108). There is no corroborative evidence of this promise: cf. below, 1091, p. 300. See Becker (1964) p. 187.

Salzburg.[394] Immediately the most devout bishop [Altman] of Passau and envoy of Pope Urban,[395] together with the bishops of Würzburg [Adalbero] and Freising,[396] solemnly consecrated him.

In the month of May Bishop Herman of Metz of pious memory[397] and Duke Berthold of Swabia, the son of King Rudolf,[398] ended their lives as faithful followers of St Peter and left behind them great lamentation among the catholics and rejoicing among the schismatics. The sister of the aforementioned duke, the queen of the Hungarians, also died in the same month.[399] In the party of the excommunicates, however, Liutold, the duke of the Carinthians was carried off by premature death,[400] after he had divorced his lawful wife and put another in her place with the permission indeed of the heresiarch Wibert. Moreover Ekbert [II of Meissen], margrave of Saxony, who was most active in the cause of St Peter, was killed in an ambush[401] through the cunning, so they say, of a certain abbess of Quedlinburg, who was in fact the sister of King Henry.[402]

At Whitsuntide the lord Pope Urban assembled by means of his legates a general synod in the city of Toulouse[403] with bishops from various provinces and there he corrected many aspects of the Church's affairs that were in need of correction. In that synod the bishop of Toulouse[404]

---

394 Thiemo, abbot of St Peter, Salzburg, archbishop of Salzburg (1090–1101), elected 25 March, consecrated 7 April. See Meyer von Knonau (1903) pp. 289–90; Becker (1964) p. 155.

395 Cf. Urban II, *JL* 5440, col. 327B.

396 Meginward (1078–98).

397 † 4 May. See Meyer von Knonau (1903) p. 286.

398 † 18 May. See above n. 262. Cf. Bernold, *Calendar* p. 505. See Meyer von Knonau (1903) p. 284.

399 Adelaide (daughter of Rudolf of Rheinfelden, wife of King Ladislaus I) † 3 May. See Meyer von Knonau (1903) p. 299. Adelaide and Berthold, like their mother Adelaide (above p. 228 and nn. 628, 630), were buried in St Blasien. See Jakobs (1968) p. 160.

400 Liutold (of Eppenstein; duke, 1077–90) † 12 May. See Meyer von Knonau (1903) p. 285.

401 † 3 July. See Meyer von Knonau (1903) pp. 292–3 with n. 36; Robinson (1999) pp. 271–2.

402 Adelaide II, abbess of Quedlinburg and Gandersheim (†1096?), daughter of Emperor Henry III. In 1088 Ekbert had besieged Quedlinburg when Henry IV's betrothed Eupraxia was there under the abbess's protection. See Meyer von Knonau (1903) p. 222.

403 Synod of Toulouse, 9 June, over which the legate Cardinal priest Rainer of S. Clemente (later Pope Paschal II) presided. See Servatius (1979) pp. 26–7.

404 Isarnus (1071–1105).

was cleared according to canon law of the accusations made against him and a legation was sent to restore Christianity in the city of Toledo at the request of the king of the Spanish.[405]

Duke Welf [V] of Italy suffered conflagrations and depredations from King Henry, who entered Lombardy in this year. But encouraged by his most dear wife, the lady Matilda, he strove courageously to resist that same Henry and to continue to be steadfast in his fidelity towards St Peter.[406]

In this year a great famine suddenly afflicted many regions, although it had not been preceded by any great failure of crops.

Bishop Adalbero of Würzburg of reverend memory, one of the most senior bishops, most active in the cause of St Peter against Wibert and his accomplices, after many dangers, persecutions and exiles, which he suffered most gladly for Christ's sake, ended his life after a good confession on his estate that is called Lambach.[407]

1091. At that time the lord pope was staying in the territory of the Campagna[408] and was treated by all the catholics with due reverence, that is, by the emperor [Alexius I] of Constantinople and by Philip [I], king of the French[409] and by both the ecclesiastical and the secular princes of the various kingdoms, except in the kingdom of the Germans, where many of the catholics, deceived by avarice, of their own free will crossed over into the party of the excommunicates. The Romans also by means of a ruse captured the tower of Crescentius,[410] which had hitherto been obedient to the lord pope, and attempted to destroy it. The lord pope, however, could easily have entered Rome with an army and vanquished the stubbornness of the rebels, had he not chosen rather to further his cause with clemency.

405 Alfonso VI, king of Castille and León (1072–1109). See Servatius (1979) p. 27: 'the distant south German chronicler must have misunderstood his informant, ... for Toledo had long been christianised and possessed in Bernard of Sahagún an active prince of the church'.

406 They were besieged in Mantua 'throughout the summer' (*Annals of Augsburg* 1090, p. 133). See Meyer von Knonau (1903) pp. 279–80.

407 ✝ 6 October. See Meyer von Knonau (1903) pp. 287–8. His monastic foundation of Lambach was consecrated 15 September 1089. See Hallinger (1950) p. 320.

408 See Meyer von Knonau (1903) p. 337; Becker (1964) p. 130; Somerville and Kuttner (1996) p. 176.

409 See above 1089, p. 298 and nn. 392–3.

410 The Castel S. Angelo became a strongpoint of the Wibertines in Rome: cf. below 1094, 1097, pp. 317, 331. See Meyer von Knonau (1903) p. 337; Becker (1964) p. 102; Hüls (1977) pp. 260–1.

At that time the people of Mantua, who had now been confined for a year by a long siege on the part of King Henry, abandoned their lord, Duke Welf [V], and surrendered themselves and their city to their destroyer.[411] The Romans also permitted the heresiarch Wibert, whom they had expelled long before, to enter Rome once again and to trouble holy Church with his blessings or rather his curses.[412]

The men of Capua expelled the Normans from Capua after having been subject to them for a long time in the reigns of very many popes and kings. The Normans, therefore, laid waste their lands on all sides as far as the city walls with plundering and burning.[413]

The lord Pope Urban assembled a general synod in Benevento and confirmed by synodal judgement the sentence of excommunication imposed on the heresiarch Wibert and all his accomplices.[414]

Frederick, count and margrave, found repose in the Lord on 29 June.[415]

Abbot William of Hirsau of pious memory, most ardent in the cause of St Peter and most zealous in monastic piety, for he was the father of many monasteries, departed to the Lord on 5 July.[416] Firstly, he exalted the monastery of Hirsau in a wonderful manner in respect both of its buildings and of its observance of the *Rule* and he freed it forever by means of a privilege of the apostolic see in the time of Pope Gregory.[417] He also built in various places very many monasteries from their foundations: namely, two in the Black Forest, one being that of St George, the other of St Gregory; another at Zwiefalten near the Danube and yet another in the bishopric of Würzburg, in the place that is called Komburg. He also established the discipline of the *Rule* in the monastery of Schaffhausen and that of Petershausen on the banks of the Rhine, which had been

---

411 In the night of 10–11 April: Donizo, *Vita Mathildis* II, p. 389. See Meyer von Knonau (1903) pp. 333–4; Robinson (1999) p. 282.

412 Cf. Malachi 2:2. Wibert in Rome: Ziese (1982) p. 191.

413 On the death of Prince Jordan I of Capua (20 November 1090) the Capuans rebelled against his son, Richard II: Meyer von Knonau (1903) p. 283; Deér (1972) p. 143.

414 Council of Benevento, 28–31 March. See Meyer von Knonau (1903) pp. 337–8; Becker (1964) pp. 120, 129.

415 Frederick, count of Montbéliard (Alsace); cf. 1092, below p. 308. See Meyer von Knonau (1903) p. 347.

416 William, abbot (1069–91). Cf. Bernold, *Calendar* p. 509. See Meyer von Knonau (1903) p. 358 and n. 43.

417 Cf. Berthold, *Chronicle* 1075, above p. 141 and n. 258.

built long before.[418] But there were also very many others in different regions that he either personally or through the agency of those subject to him built as new foundations or, where they had already been created, re-established according to the discipline of the *Rule*. He[419] also left us many memorials of his natural genius. For he invented a natural clock on the model of the celestial hemisphere; he demonstrated how to discover by precise experiments the natural solstices or equinoxes and the position of the earth and one of his confidential friends also took care to commit all of this to writing.[420] He also elucidated many questions concerning the *computus* with most excellent proofs. He was most skilled in music and explained many subtleties of that art that had been unknown to the ancient teachers and he also corrected many errors that he had detected in the chants, in a manner entirely conforming to reason and to the art.[421] In the quadrivium indeed he seemed to outdo almost all the ancients.[419] But before all these achievements what was uppermost in his mind was the zeal for monastic discipline, to which he devoted himself totally with such fervour that it was as if he had never had any other preoccupation. For he was a man of wonderful sanctity, holy simplicity, most fervent charity, living for God and truly crucified in the world, and the Lord, whom he served with tireless labour from his youth onwards during this pilgrimage, summoned him back in a good old age to the eternal fatherland.

Bernard, master of the schools of Constance, whose death we recorded above,[422] also left us many memorials of his genius and wrote many works in a most elegant style on behalf of the catholics against the schismatics of his time. The first of these was addressed to certain of his friends concerning the judgement of Pope Gregory VII on the schis-

---

418 St Georgen in the Black Forest, St Gregory in Reichenbach, abbey of Zwiefalten, the abbey of Komburg (near Schwäbisch-Hall), All Saints', Schaffhausen, abbey of Petershausen (near Constance). See Meyer von Knonau (1903) pp. 117, 349–51, 353–4, 362; Hauck (1954) p. 1021; Cowdrey (1970) pp. 207–9.

419/419 Quoted by Haimo, *Vita Willihelmi Hirsaugiensis* c. 1, *MGH SS* 12, 211; almost verbatim in 'Anonymus Mellicensis' (Wolfger?), *De scriptoribus* c. 108, p. 93 (*ca.* 1170).

420 Dr Thomas McCarthy has suggested that this is an allusion to William's *Astronomica*, of which only the preface survives, ending with a reference to the solstices and the equinoxes (*MPL* 150, col. 1642D). William's 'confidential friend' is identified in the preface as 'O.' (col. 1639B), evidently the 'Otloh' who appears in the dialogue format of the *Musica* and probably Otloh of St Emmeram: see McCarthy (2004) p. 38.

421 William of Hirsau, *Musica*, ed. D. Harbinson, *Corpus Scriptorum de Musica* 23, 1975.

422 Cf. above 1088, p. 293.

matics and concerning the sacraments that had been usurped outside the Church.[423] Afterwards he also composed in a most brilliant manner a large book on the same subject addressed to the venerable Hartwig, bishop of Magdeburg,[424] writing in the name of holy Church, in which, using the evidence of the holy Fathers, he seems sagaciously to have reduced to nothing all the deceitful sophistries of those same schismatics. But it is apparent that in these same writings he was in some passages led by excessive zeal to overstep the bounds of moderation: namely, where he deals with the sacraments of the schismatics. For he denies utterly that the sacraments can be dispensed by them or by those who communicate with them, so that he is of the opinion that those who have been ordained by [schismatics], if they come to their senses, must be ordained again.[425] But this contradicts the most holy council of Nicea, which is to be revered in the same degree as one of the Gospels,[426] which commanded that clergy who had been converted from the ranks of the Novatians were to be received with their orders and were not to be reordained.[427] We read that the African Fathers made a similar decision in the case of clergy converted from the Donatists.[428] Likewise the blessed Pope Gregory I received Maximus, the pretender of Salona, who had been excommunicated and ordained by excommunicates, together with his orders and certainly did not reordain him.[429] They would obviously not have done this, if they believed that they had received no sacrament of ordination outside the Church. Likewise the blessed Pope Anastasius, writing to Emperor Anastasius, declared that those who had been ordained by Acatius, although he was excommunicate, suffered no element of contamination as far as the integrity of their sacraments was concerned.[430] Likewise the blessed Augustine in his many writings,

---

423 Bernard, *De damnatione scismaticorum. Epistola II* (to Adalbert and Bernold), pp. 29–47.

424 Bernard, *Liber canonum* pp. 471–516, addressed to Archbishop Hartwig.

425 Bernard, *Liber canonum* c. 46, p. 515. See Saltet (1907) pp. 208–11; Autenrieth (1956) pp. 137–41.

426 Gregory I, *Registrum* I.25, *MGH Epistolae* 1, 36, frequently cited by Bernold: *MGH Libelli* 2, 7, 62, 95, 129.

427 Council of Nicea c. 8 (version of *Decretales Pseudo Isidorianae* p. 259). Cf. Bernold, *De damnatione scismaticorum* III, p. 56; Bernold, *De sacramentis excommunicatorum* p. 91.

428 Council of Carthage (419) c. 35, *CC* 149, 200. Cf. Bernold, *De sacramentis excommunicatorum* p. 91.

429 Gregory I, *Registrum* IX.176, *MGH Epistolae* 2, 171–2. Cf. Bernold, *De sacramentis excommunicatorum* p. 91.

430 Anastasius II, *JK* 744, *Epistola* I c. 8. Cf. Bernold, *De damnatione scismaticorum* III, p. 57; *De sacramentis excommunicatorum* p. 90; *De reordinatione vitanda* p. 152.

and especially in his *Book against the Donatists concerning baptism*, proved most irrefutably that the sacraments of the Church can be both received and conferred outside the Church, although they are harmful both to the giver and to the recipient.[431] We have touched on these matters in a summary fashion in order to put the reader of the aforementioned writings on his guard so that he is not over-hasty in agreeing to any opinion which he will discover to be contrary to such authentic judgements on the part of the holy Fathers. For the rest, anyone who desires to be more fully informed about these matters should carefully read through a work sent by a certain author to that same Bernard on this very question[432] and there he will be instructed most clearly by the evidence of the holy Fathers what, in the opinion of the holy Fathers, we ought to think about that question. But that same venerable Bernard did not in this matter – any more than the blessed Cyprian in his judgement concerning rebaptism[433] – proceed in a stubborn manner against the Church; but both men in their excessive zeal against the schismatics somewhat overstepped the rule of ecclesiastical doctrine.

Altman, bishop of Passau of holy memory, most zealous in the cause of St Peter and in ecclesiastical piety, after many dangers, tribulations and exiles, which he bore for Christ's sake, departed to the Lord in a good old age on 8 August.[434] He founded in his bishopric three houses of clergy living in common according to the *Rule* of St Augustine[435] and he built a third[436] through the agency of his clergy in the bishopric of Freising on a family estate of Duke Welf [IV] and established there the discipline of the *Rule*. He was a man of such great sanctity, chastity and piety that he was revered and loved by the most reverend Pope Gregory [VII] and the holy bishop [Anselm II] of Lucca and indeed by all pious men but he was hated and dreaded by the schismatics and

---

431 Augustine, *De baptismo contra Donatistas* I.3.21; III.13.20, 27; IV.17; V.27.38; VI.1.7. Cf. Bernold, *De sacramentis excommunicatorum* p. 91; *De reordinatione vitanda* p. 153.

432 Bernold's *De sacramentis excommunicatorum* is addressed 'to the most religious priest and most sagacious teacher Bernard' (p. 89).

433 Cyprian, *De catholicae ecclesiae unitate* c. 10, *CSEL* 3, 218, cited by Bernard, *Liber canonum* c. 44, p. 513.

434 In Bernold's autograph this date is written over an erasure. The Sarnen codex reads 'in the month of August', which was evidently Bernold's original version. See above p. 48. On Altman: Meyer von Knonau (1903) pp. 363–4 and n. 53; Boshof (1991) p. 140.

435 St Nicholas in Passau, St Florian and St Agapitus in Kremsmünster. See Boshof (1991) pp. 134–6

436 I.e. 'fourth': Rottenbuch. See Mois (1953) p. 28; Boshof (1991) pp. 135–6.

by wicked men. At his death, therefore, he left behind him great lamentation among good men but great rejoicing among evil men.

In the month of August Duke Welf [IV] of Bavaria came to Lombardy[437] in order to be reconciled to King Henry if he was willing to allow the apostolic see, into which the heresiarch Wibert had intruded, to be disposed of according to canon law and also if he was willing to give back to that same duke and to his son Welf [V] and to the rest of their supporters the property that had been unjustly taken from them. He was unwilling to fulfil this condition and therefore the duke did not delay in returning to Swabia. Many of the Swabians were nevertheless reconciled to King Henry and shared with Henry in the excommunication of the apostolic see. The[438] duke, however, once more incited many of his supporters against Henry, urging them to make the decision to elect a new king,[439] if the indolence and malice of certain persons did not hinder them.[438]

In these times the common life flourished in many places in the kingdom of the Germans, not only among the clergy and monks living in the greatest piety but also among laymen, who devoted themselves and their property most faithfully to that same common life. Although they did not appear to be clergy or monks in their habit, they were nevertheless believed to be in no way unequal to them in their merits.[440] They made themselves into the servants of [the clergy and monks] for the Lord's sake, imitating Him who *came not to be served but to serve*[441] and who taught His followers that they would attain greatness by performing service. For they indeed renounced the world and they most faithfully took themselves and their property into congregations both of clergy and of monks living according to the *Rule* in order to be worthy to live the common life there in obedience to them and serving them. For this reason the envy of the devil incited certain enemies to attack the

437 Verona: *Annals of Augsburg* 1091, p. 133. Cf. *D.H.IV* 424 (Verona, 2 September). See Meyer von Knonau (1903) p. 338.

438/438 This passage in Bernold's autograph is written over an erasure. The text in MS Sarnen reads: 'The excommunication therefore prevailed so much that many religious men and women chose rather to be exiled in perpetuity than perish in the company of the excommunicates.' This was evidently the original version of Bernold's text. The B codices break off here. See above p. 48.

439 W. von Giesebrecht (1890) p. 647 suggested that Welf IV envisaged himself or Berthold II of Zähringen as the new anti-king. See Meyer von Knonau (1903) pp. 368–9.

440 See Grundmann (1961) pp. 505–10; Hallinger (1956) pp. 19–27; Jakobs (1961) pp. 23–5.

441 Matthew 20:26–7.

excellent way of life of those same brethren and they gnawed away at their life with a spiteful tooth, although they saw that those men were living in common, according to the model of the early Church.[442] The lord Pope Urban, therefore, by the apostolic authority of his decree confirmed their way of life, which was established by the apostles them-selves but disseminated far and wide by their successors, and took care to announce that decision to those who were set in authority over those same brethren in these words. '*We*[443] *understand,*' he said, '*that certain men attack the custom of your monasteries, according to which you receive, to be ruled under your obedience, laymen who renounce the world and transfer themselves and their property to the common life. We, however, judge that same way of life and custom, which we have examined with our own eyes, to be laudable and to be most worthy of being preserved in perpetuity in that it is cast in the mould of the early Church and we give it our approval and call it holy and catholic and we confirm it by apostolic authority in this present letter.*'[443] An innumerable multitude not only of men but also of women entered a way of life of this kind at this time so that they might live in common under the obedience of clergy or monks and might most faithfully perform the duty of daily service like maidservants. Also in the villages innumerable peasants' daughters strove to renounce marriage and the world and to live under the obedience of some priest. But even the married people never ceased to live devoutly and to obey the religious with the greatest devotion. Such zeal blossomed with particular decorum, however, everywhere in Swabia. In that province many villages dedicated themselves wholly to religion and ceaselessly strove to surpass each other in the holiness of their morals. Thus God undoubtedly saw fit to console His holy Church miraculously in a time of the greatest danger so that she who had long been grieving over the desertion of the excommunicates, might rejoice at the conversion of many people.

In the German territories it rained flesh and blood, and toads and fish fell from heaven, as many credible witnesses state that they have seen. In Swabia at Zwiefalten on the Danube blood was seen to flow from loaves of bread. These particular events were believed by very many devout men to foretell some novelty in the kingdom.

Margravine Judith of pious memory, noble by birth but more noble in her sanctity, the wife of the most pious Herman [I], the former

---

442 See Miccoli (1966) pp. 225–99; Dereine (1946) pp. 365–406; Dereine (1951) pp. 534–65.

443/443 Urban II, *JL* 5456, col. 336. The sole extant text of this letter. See Becker (1964) p. 154 with n. 565.

margrave [of Baden], departed to the Lord on 27 September.[444] For she lived devoutly with her husband and after his death she remained for nineteen years in widowhood and in a holy way of life. Finally she came to the lord pope in Salerno and she died there under his obedience.[445]

Countess Adelaide of Turin died on 19 December.[446]

1092. The lord pope celebrated Christmas [25 December 1091] in the lands of St Peter outside Rome.[447] For the heresiarch Wibert was in so strongly fortified a place near the house of St Peter that he could not easily be expelled from there without shedding human blood.[448] Henry, his emperor, had now remained for two years in Lombardy, where he did not cease to lay waste the land of the Italian Duke Welf [V] on all sides with plunder, sword and fire in order to force that duke and his most sagacious wife [Matilda of Tuscany] to abandon their fidelity to St Peter and to join with [Henry]; but it was in vain. For the duke adhered to his own way of thinking and very courageously resisted him.[449] But the father of that duke, Duke Welf [IV] of Bavaria, confounded that same Henry in a wonderful manner before the next Christmas, when he prevented him from reaching a conference that Henry had arranged with the king [Ladislaus I] of the Hungarians and at which they almost met together.[450]

In Swabia a certain layman who dedicated himself to the common life in the manner of the apostles and who delivered himself and his property to the monastery of the Holy Saviour[451] and there for a long time showed due obedience, suddenly became an apostate and was not afraid to remove himself and his property from that monastery in a sacrilegious fashion. The lord Pope Urban, therefore, sent a letter to the venerable Bishop Gebhard of Constance, commanding him by apostolic

444 See above pp. 253–4 and nn. 94–5.

445 Urban II in southern Italy: *JL* 5450 (1 July, Capua) – *JL* 5455 (17 November, Alatri). See Meyer von Knonau (1903) pp. 338–9.

446 Adelaide of Susa, margravine of Turin (?1015–91), mother of Queen Bertha. Cf. Bernold, *Calendar* p. 522. See Meyer von Knonau (1903) pp. 347–8.

447 Cf. Urban II, *JL* 5457–66 (Anagni, January–May 1092). See Becker (1964) p. 121 n. 411.

448 See Köhncke (1888) p. 86; Ziese (1982) p. 191.

449 See Meyer von Knonau (1903) p. 380 n. 18; Robinson (1999) pp. 281–2, 284.

450 Cf. Henry IV, *Letter 23* (to the Hungarian duke Almus), p. 33: 'the treaty into which we entered with your uncle'. See Meyer von Knonau (1903) pp. 379–80.

451 Tuto of Wagenhausen (of Honstetten) in Schaffhausen. His property is identified by *Casus monasterii Petrishusensis* III.27, p. 656: 'three estates … namely Wagenhausen, where [the monks of Schaffhausen] had already made a cell, Kappel and Honstetten'. See Meyer von Knonau (1903) pp. 381–2; Jakobs (1968) pp. 179, 228–9.

authority to summon that same apostate *according to canon law* and cut
him off completely from the members of Christ with the sharp sword
of *excommunication* unless he very quickly *came to his senses* from that
apostasy and sacrilege.[452]

The princes of Swabia again met together to defend unanimously the
holy mother Church against the schismatics[453] and in order to accomplish this task, they appointed Berthold, the brother of the bishop
[Gebhard III] of Constance, as duke of the whole of Swabia.[454] He did
not yet hold any duchy, although he had for a long time been accustomed to have the title of duke.

A great famine afflicted the whole of Saxony and compelled the princes
of that province to depart temporarily for other regions that year.[455] For
that reason the general assembly that the princes of Swabia wished to
hold with the Saxons could not take place.

In Lombardy Conrad, the son of King Henry,[456] took possession of
the property of Countess Adelaide of Turin, which that countess's
grandson, the son of Count Frederick [of Montbéliard], ought to have
possessed.[457] This count, however, was a most energetic knight of Christ
in the secular sphere, according to the model of St Sebastian:[458] that is, a
most fervent lover of ecclesiastical piety and a tireless defender of catholic peace. The venerable Pope Gregory [VII] and the blessed Bishop
Anselm [II] of Lucca loved him like an only son. Clergy and monks,
indeed all pious people, loved him most fervently. He struggled most
zealously against the schismatics even unto death in his fidelity towards
St Peter and, since it was on the latter's feast-day [29 June] that he was

---

452 Urban II, *JL* 5458, col. 336–7 (28 January 1092). See Becker (1973) p. 263 n. 58.

453 2 May in Ulm, according to a charter of All Saints', Schaffhausen: Meyer von
Knonau (1903) p. 383 and n. 27. Present were Welf IV, Berthold II of Zähringen,
the counts Otto and Hartmann of Kirchberg, Hartmann of Gerhausen, Hugh of
Tübingen, Hugh of Krähenegg and Manegold of Altshausen. See Maurer (1978) pp.
160–1; Robinson (1999) p. 286.

454 Berthold II (of Zähringen), margrave, duke of Carinthia, Swabia, Zähringen
(†1111).

455 Cf. Frutolf, *Chronica* 1092, p. 104.

456 Conrad (1074–1101), duke of Lower Lotharingia (1076–87), king (1087–98), son of
Bertha of Turin, grandson of Margravine Adelaide of Turin (n. 446).

457 Peter, son of Count Frederick (n. 415), great-grandson of Adelaide of Turin. The
latter's possessions: the march of Turin and the cities of Susa, Ivrea, Saluzzo,
Pinerolo and Asti. From 1080 Margravine Adelaide shared power with Frederick,
husband of her granddaughter and designated heir of Turin. See Meyer von Knonau
(1903) pp. 347–8; Previté-Orton (1912) pp. 249–51, 255–8; Goez (1996) p. 23.

458 See Erdmann (1935) pp. 189 n. 30, 254.

snatched away from the prison house of this life, he is believed to have become his companion in the heavenly fatherland. He was, however, the son of Count Louis and of the lady Sophia,[459] who was the sister of the mother of Countess Matilda [of Tuscany], who, together with her lord, Duke Welf [V], laboured greatly in Italy against the schismatics. The aforementioned count died in the previous year, that is, the 1,091st of the Lord's Incarnation, the fourteenth indiction, on 29 June, that is, on the feast of St Peter, and he was buried on the next day, that is, on the feast of St Paul. It was his son, born to him by the granddaughter of the lady Adelaide,[460] whom King Henry, together with his son, intended to disinherit and by his hostile invasion of his land and his devastation of the surrounding country, he also inflicted many evils on the monastery of Fruttuaria.[461]

In Bavaria the venerable Bishop Thiemo of Salzburg appointed a bishop named Udalric, the provost of the holy church of Augsburg, in the church of Passau,[462] which had long been widowed, and solemnly consecrated him on that Whitsunday [16 May], together with the bishops [Gebhard III] of Constance and [Adalbert of] Worms. And this gave great encouragement to the catholics to remain steadfast in their fidelity towards St Peter and to resist the madness of the schismatics even more tirelessly.

At this time, as we have heard, many wonders happened in Hungary. For a certain mountain sank into the Danube and that river was therefore forced to change its course and laid waste the surrounding lands far and wide. Moreover elsewhere a great lake emerged on dry land and a certain mountain suddenly appeared in another lake. The river named the Theiss also flowed blood-red for three days. But an earthquake of unprecedented force happened there, so that men could not remain standing at its onset.[463] A very great thunder unheard of for centuries also terrified men there, as it passed over the earth and was felt to return the same way under the earth.

---

459 Louis, count of Montbéliard and Sophia, daughter of Duke Frederick III of Upper Lotharingia, sister of Beatrice of Tuscany, mother of Margravine Matilda. See Meyer von Knonau (1900) pp. 201–2; (1903) pp. 347 n. 27, 388.

460 Agnes, daughter of Count Peter of Savoy, margrave of Turin (✝1078), son of Margravine Adelaide.

461 See Meyer von Knonau (1903) p. 374.

462 Udalric, bishop of Passau (1092–1121). See Meyer von Knonau (1903) p. 384; Becker (1964) pp. 155–6; Boshof (1991) pp. 143–7.

463 26 June: *Annals of Augsburg* 1092, p. 134.

In Swabia Count Cuno of Wülflingen, a most energetic knight of St Peter, ended his life on 15 October[464] and was honourably buried in the monastery that he himself, together with his brother, Count Liutolf, had founded on their family estate.[465] His brother, that same Liutolf, came into possession of his property by hereditary right, although he had long given up worldly knighthood. He did this, to be sure, not with the intention of returning to the world but rather with that of improving the aforementioned monastery with that same property.

In this year four priests from Swabia, who were of no small reputation among their own people and very pious, set out for Jerusalem to pray there. After many troubles and hardships on that journey, while they were returning, they died most happily after a good confession. One of them, who was accustomed to venerate St Mary with special devotion during the daily office, died while at sea and deserved through God's ordinance to be brought by ship to a church of St Mary by that sea. There he was buried with honour by the fourth of the fellow priests, who alone among them still survived and this man who buried him departed this life not long afterwards in that same place.

Beatrice, the sister of Margrave Frederick [of Montbéliard] and the wife of the former Duke Berthold [I of Carinthia],[466] who had been mercifully chastened and tried by the Lord through a long illness, at last ended her life most happily on 26 October and was honourably buried in the city of Toul by the bishop of the place.[467]

The lord Udalric, who had obtained the abbey of St Gallen and the bishopric of Aquileia[468] not by *entering through the door*,[469] attempted to supplant Bishop Gebhard of Constance with a certain monk of his monastery[470] and obtained for him the investiture of that bishopric

---

464 Cuno of Wülflingen, count of Achalm, +16 October: necrologies of Zwiefalten and St Blasien (*MGH Necrologia* 1, 263, 324). See Meyer von Knonau (1903) pp. 387 and n. 33.

465 Zwiefalten, founded by Cuno and Liutold, count of Achalm. See Meyer von Knonau (1903) pp. 349–50, 387; Hauck (1954) p. 1021.

466 Beatrice, daughter of Louis of Montbéliard and Sophia, second wife of Berthold I. See Meyer von Knonau (1900) pp. 201–2.

467 Pibo (1069–1107).

468 Udalric (of Eppenstein), abbot of St Gallen (1077–86), patriarch of Aquileia (1086–1121), brother of Duke Liutold of Carinthia. See Schwartz (1913) p. 35.

469 John 10:1.

470 Arnold (of Heiligenberg), imperial anti-bishop of Constance (1092–1112), invested 28 March: *Casuum sancti Galli continuatio* c. 7, p. 160. See Meyer von Knonau (1903) pp. 374, 386.

from Henry. But when he wished to enthrone that same intruder before Christmas, he was not received by the people of Constance but instead he met with insults and was forced to turn back. At that time a great earthquake also occurred in the same bishopric at the monastery of the Saviour [All Saints', Schaffhausen] during the night. It was therefore noticed by few people except for certain devout men and women who had not yet been overtaken by sleep that night. The catholics were in no doubt that this earthquake signified according to the Gospel[471] God's anger at the aforementioned audacious act.

1093. The lord Pope Urban celebrated Christmas [25 December 1092] outside Rome in the lands of St Peter,[472] since he could not yet enter Rome without an armed force; for the Wibertists and the excommuni- cates were still very powerful there and would not easily allow them- selves to be driven away from there without the use of violence. At that time Wibert himself was staying with his emperor Henry in Lombardy and was plotting with him to do whatever he could against Duke Welf and his wife Matilda, the daughter of St Peter.[473]

After many struggles against the subterfuges of the schismatics the venerable Werner, bishop of the church of Merseburg at last came to the end of his life in fidelity towards St Peter. He was then the only bishop in Saxony who was in the catholic communion. When he died, therefore, he left great sadness among the catholics and great joy among the excommunicates. He died, however, very happily on 11 January.[474]

In various places in Swabia many fires were seen moving through the air together a week after Epiphany [13 January] early in the morn- ing.[475] There was no doubt that these fires signified that not long after- wards many conflagrations would rage far and wide through that land. For Duke Welf [IV of Bavaria] and Count Udalric of Bregenz[476] and very many others endeavoured in every way to destroy each other with fires.

---

471 Cf. Matthew 24:7; Mark 13:8; Luke 21:11.

472 Probably in Salerno. See Becker (1964) p. 128.

473 See Meyer von Knonau (1903) pp. 379–80, 389.

474 Werner (1059–93) † 12 January: *Vita Wernheri* c. 4, p. 248 and necrologies. See Meyer von Knonau (1903) p. 414 n. 40; Fenske (1977) p. 290.

475 Cf. Frutolf, *Chronica* 1093, p. 106.

476 Udalric X, count of Bregenz, papal partisan in Swabia. See Meyer von Knonau (1900) p. 200; (1903) p. 400; Jakobs (1968) pp. 58, 160.

Abbot Siegfried of Schaffhausen in Swabia obtained from Abbot Richard of Marseilles a monastery called *Nobiliacum*[477] and prepared there for himself and his brethren a place to which he could withdraw for a time if it chanced that he could not remain in his own monastery because of excommunication. For that old excommunication that Pope Gregory of pious memory pronounced on Wibert and his associates had now infected the greater and the lesser men in Swabia to such an extent that all the devout people despaired of continuing in their midst and preserving the catholic community uncontaminated.

The most noble Countess Sophia, the widow of Count Louis [of Mont-béliard], the mother of Duchess Beatrice of pious memory and of Margrave Frederick,[478] came to the end of her life at a good old age, after she had seen many children born of her own children.

In Lombardy the most wise vassals of St Peter, Duke Welf [V] and his wife Matilda, who had now been fighting courageously against the schismatics for three years, were greatly strengthened against them through God's help. For Conrad, the son of King Henry, abandoned his father and, together with his followers, assisted Duke Welf and the other vassals of St Peter against his father. The cities of Lombardy, Milan, Cremona, Lodi and Piacenza took an oath to band together for twenty years against Henry and they all adhered faithfully to the afore-mentioned duke.[479] Certain men took possession of the passes through the Alps so that Henry's supporters could not reach him.

The people of Augsburg drove out the bishop [Siegfried II] whom Henry had given them[480] and elected for themselves a catholic pastor[481] according to canon law. The latter imprisoned the bishop of Ivrea[482] in the castle that defends the pass through the Alps because he was

---

477 Siegfried (1082–96) received the abbey of St Leonard in the Limousin (see Meyer von Knonau [1903] p. 402 n. 20) from Richard, abbot of St Victor in Marseilles, cardinal priest (of unknown title), archbishop of Narbonne (1106–?21). See Hüls (1977) pp. 217–18.

478 See above nn. 459, 466.

479 See Meyer von Knonau (1903) pp. 391–2 and n. 4; Becker (1964) pp. 131–2; Goez (1996) pp. 29–30; Robinson (1999) pp. 287–8.

480 Since no Augsburg source mentions such an expulsion, Strelau (1889) pp. 98–9 ascribes this report to Bernold's wishful thinking.

481 Eberhard, abbot of Kempten, Gregorian anti-bishop of Augsburg (1094). See Meyer von Knonau (1903) pp. 400–1.

482 Ogerius (1074/5–?95), Italian chancellor: Schwartz (1913) pp. 118–19. G.H. Pertz, *MGH SS* 5, 456 n. 40* identifies the castle as Fort Bard and the Alpine pass as the St Bernard but the Brenner is more likely: Meyer von Knonau (1903) p. 401 n. 19.

determined to do the same to him. The churches of Metz, Toul and Verdun withdrew from the obedience of the excommunicate Egilbert of Trier[483] and they informed him quite openly that they would no longer obey him. The people of Metz rejected the bishop whom Henry wished to give them[484] and they elected for themselves a catholic pastor according to canon law and caused him to be consecrated in a catholic and canonical manner on 27 March, in the middle of Lent, by Bishop Gebhard [III] of Constance, the legate of the apostolic see.[485]

In Lent the lord Pope Urban assembled in Apulia a general synod of almost one hundred bishops from various provinces[486] and through the foresight of the synod he took pains to make suitable provision for the needs of the various churches.

In Lombardy Conrad, the son of King Henry, was intercepted through his father's cunning and taken prisoner but by God's mercy he was set free. He was crowned king by the archbishop of Milan[487] and the other vassals of St Peter with the help of Welf [V], the duke of Italy, and Matilda, his most dear wife.[488] But not long afterwards the father of that duke, Duke Welf [IV] of Bavaria, came to the newly crowned king in Lombardy and endeavoured to become his faithful adherent, together with his son. Henry, the king's father, however, went to a certain fortress and remained there for a long time without any of the dignity of a king. Afflicted by excessive grief, he wished (so they say) to give himself up to death but he was hindered by his followers and could not achieve his purpose.[489]

483 Egilbert, archbishop (1079–1101). See Meyer von Knonau (1903) p. 404; Erkens (1987) p. 103.

484 Adalbero IV, imperial anti-bishop (established himself 1097, deposed 1117/18). See Meyer von Knonau (1904) p. 7; Erkens (1987) pp. 171 n. 26, 185–91.

485 Poppo (1090–1103), consecrated by Archbishop Hugh of Lyons: Hugh, *Chronicon* II, p. 473. See Meyer von Knonau (1903) pp. 404–5 and n. 24; Schumann (1913) p. 68; Becker (1964) p. 153; Erkens (1987) pp. 172–4.

486 Council of Troia, 11–12 March, attended by 75 bishops and 12 abbots. See Meyer von Knonau (1903) p. 390; Becker (1964) pp. 120, 129; Somerville and Kuttner (1996) pp. 304–5.

487 Anselm III (of Rhò) (1086–93). See Schwartz (1913) pp. 83–4; Cowdrey (1968b) pp. 285–94.

488 See Meyer von Knonau (1903) p. 394; Becker (1964) pp. 131–2; Goez (1996) pp. 24–5; Robinson (1999) p. 287.

489 A different version in the anonymous *Life of Emperor Henry IV* c. 7, p. 27: 'although he grieved inwardly, he nevertheless outwardly maintained his gravity and he bewailed not his own, but his son's fortune'. See Meyer von Knonau (1903) p. 396. No other source mentions a suicide attempt. Robinson (1999) p. 288 suggests that Bernold's report was modelled on the fate of King Saul (I Samuel 31:4).

In Swabia Duke Berthold [II of Zähringen] built up from its foundations a new monastery in honour of St Peter on his estate in the Black
Forest[490] and endowed it with much property. But he transferred to
this monastery all the property of another monastery, which the father
of that same duke had built in another place.[491] The duke's brother,
Gebhard, bishop of Constance and legate of the apostolic see, therefore, consecrated this monastery and another Gebhard, the abbot of
Hirsau,[492] established the rule of monastic discipline there. This consecration took place on 1 August, when the divine service of St Peter in
chains is held. The venerable Abbot Siegfried of the monastery of the
Saviour [Schaffhausen] conferred a great part of these [chains] on that
place and many relics of other saints. During that same consecration
an abbot[493] was elected for that place, and the monks and the further
development of the place, together with everything that belonged to it,
were freely entrusted to his management and it was decided that the
place itself was subject specifically to the apostolic see.[494]

Likewise in Swabia Count Hartmann and his brother Otto built a new
monastery in honour of St Martin on their own family estate in the place
where the Danube and the River Iller meet.[495] Once more it was the
aforementioned bishop of Constance who consecrated it in the month
of September but the venerable Abbot Uto of St Blasien established
the discipline of the *Rule* there. At the same time that same bishop also
consecrated for the aforementioned abbot another monastery not far
from there in honour of St George. A certain nobleman Conrad and
his brothers[496] handed over this place and whatever belonged to it to
St Blasien without any condition and they asked the abbot to *establish*

---

490 St Peter in the Black Forest (near Freiburg). See Meyer von Knonau (1903) pp.
   398–9.

491 Weilheim in the Neckargau, founded by Duke Berthold I of Carinthia, suffered
   severe war damage in 1078.

492 Gebhard, abbot of Hirsau (1091–1107), bishop of Speyer and abbot of Lorsch
   (1105–7).

493 Adalbero, abbot of St Peter (1093–1100).

494 Cf. Urban II, *JL* 5545, col. 405A: 'we have received that place to be especially
   fostered under the protection of the apostolic see'.

495 Hartmann and Otto, counts of Kirchberg, papal partisans, founded the monastery
   of Wiblingen. See Meyer von Knonau (1903) pp. 383, 399; Jakobs (1968) pp. 98–9.

496 Conrad, Hawin and Adalbert of Wolfertschwerden founded St George in Ochsen-
   hausen (near Biberach). See Meyer von Knonau (1903) p. 399; Jakobs (1968) pp.
   76–7.

the service of God in that *place*[497] and the abbot did not cease to consent to their wishes.

At this time the wife of the excellent Count Adalbert [II of Calw], named Weliga, the daughter of the great Duke Godfrey ['the Bearded'], after living with her husband in the world in a most praiseworthy manner, came to the end of her life[498] and was very honourably buried in the monastery of Hirsau, which she had most especially established and loved.

A sign appeared in the sun on 23 September before noon:[499] a circle was seen in it and its light seemed to be very much darkened even though the heaven itself was bright. But certain men believed that this was an eclipse rather than a sign especially since this was the twenty-eighth day of the moon. For the excellent mathematician lord Herman also wrote that in the year 1033 of the Lord's Incarnation an eclipse occurred on the twenty-seventh day of the moon.[500]

Gebhard, bishop of Constance and legate of the apostolic see, received Duke Welf [IV] of Bavaria as a vassal by his hands,[501] just as he had done long before with his own brother, Duke Berthold of Swabia.[502] With them and with the other princes of Swabia he held a great assembly in Ulm.[503] In that assembly it was agreed in the most binding terms that they would obey the bishop of Constance in every way according to the decrees of canon law and that they would follow the commands of Duke Berthold and the counts according to the law of the Swabians. Then both the dukes and the counts, both the greater and the lesser

497 A quotation from Abbot Uto of St Blasien's foundation charter. See Jakobs (1968) pp. 76–81.

498 Weliga (Wiltrud) † 29 August. Cf. Berthold, *Chronicle* 1075, above p. 141. See Meyer von Knonau (1903) p. 428 n. 19.

499 Cf. Frutolf, *Chronica* 1093, p. 106. 24 September, according to *Annals of Augsburg* p. 134.

500 Herman, *Chronicle* 1033, above p. 68. Herman's study of eclipses: Borst (1984) pp. 440–1. Cf. Bernold, *De excommunicatis vitandis* p. 153: 'lord Herman, the excellent calculator'.

501 Henking (1880) p. 50 n. 13 identified this as a vassal oath to the bishop concerning property of the church of Constance held by Welf IV as a benefice. Strelau (1889) p. 101 suggested that Welf IV took the oath as advocate of the monastery of Zwiefalten. See also Meyer von Knonau (1903) p. 402 and n. 21; Schumann (1912) p. 70; Becker (1973) p. 268.

502 Berthold II of Zähringen (n. 454). See Maurer (1970) pp. 43–56; Parlow (1999) pp. 91–2.

503 Late autumn: Meyer von Knonau (1903) p. 403; Schumann (1912) p. 70; Parlow (1999) pp. 97–8.

men, swore that they would observe a most inviolable peace from 25 November until Easter [9 April 1094] and from Easter for two years: that is, in respect of all monks and lay brethren and clergy subject to a catholic bishop, churches and their churchyards and their endowments, of merchants and of all those who were bound by this same oath, except for Arnold, the intruder in the church of Constance, and all his supporters. This peace was sworn by the individual princes who assembled there, one by one, each in respect of the whole area of his jurisdiction.[504]

At this time King Alfonso of Spain,[505] who was catholic in faith and an obedientiary of the abbot [Hugh I] of Cluny[506] in his way of life, very often fought courageously for the Christians against the pagans and restored many churches to their original condition after they had long been laid waste. He also built the principal church in Cluny from its foundations and sent an unlimited sum of money to Cluny to build this church. He would also have become a monk there long ago, if the lord abbot had not judged it more suitable to retain him in his secular role for the time being.

In Lombardy the venerable Archbishop Anselm [III] of Milan, who was most zealous in the cause of St Peter and who had recently crowned King Conrad, ended his life[507] in a most praiseworthy manner and left the vassals of St Peter in great distress. The venerable Arnulf of Porta Argentea succeeded him in the bishopric.[508]

1094. The lord Pope Urban solemnly celebrated Christmas [25 December 1093] in Rome, although very many Wibertists were still hiding in the city and the lord pope could not easily drive them out without a military force. He preferred, therefore, for the time being to put up with their insults, rather than disturb the Roman citizens with a troop of armed men.[509] The heresiarch Wibert, however, was at that time with his emperor in Verona and he pretended that he was willing to give up the papacy if peace could not be restored in the Church by any other means.

504 On this instance of the 'peace of God': Wadle (1973) pp. 148–50; Wadle (1989) pp. 141–53; Parlow (1999) p. 98.

505 Alfonso VI of Castile and León: see above p. 300 and n. 405.

506 See Erdmann (1935) p. 61; Cowdrey (1970) pp. 146–7, 244 n. 2.

507 4 December. See Meyer von Knonau (1903) p. 395 n. 6.

508 Arnulf III (1093–7), elected 5 December. See Meyer von Knonau (1903) p. 398; Schwartz (1913) p. 84; Cowdrey (1968b) pp. 285–94.

509 See Meyer von Knonau (1903) p. 397; Becker (1964) pp. 102–3.

The wife of this emperor,[510] who had already been subjected to many injuries and had been under guard for many years lest she escape, at last fled to Duke Welf [V] of Italy. She complained that she had suffered so many, such great and such unheard-of evils among her own followers that she had no doubt that she would find compassion even among enemies and indeed she was not disappointed in this hope. For the duke and his wife Matilda received her joyfully and treated her honourably.[511]

Judith, the wife of Duke Welf [IV] of Bavaria,[512] who had been ill for a long time and who had been greatly improved by that chastisement, came to the end of her life on 4 March and was honourably buried by Bishop Gebhard of Constance in the monastery that her husband had built in honour of St Martin on his own family estate. Her husband, the duke, gave that monastery its sacred vessels, which, in gold and silver and with most precious vestments, were worth almost a thousand pounds and he added to its possessions almost one hundred hides of land. He surrendered the monastery, thus improved and freed from his jurisdiction, to St Peter under the obligation to pay tribute, so that thereafter it would be subject first and foremost to the apostolic see and under its protection and so that it might flourish by a perpetual privilege, like other free monasteries.[513]

The lord pope resided in Rome in a very strong fortification near S. Maria Nuova,[514] but the Wibertists held the tower of Crescentius [Castel S. Angelo] and were denying travellers the freedom to cross over to the pope by means of the bridge over the Tiber. For a certain abbot [Adalbero] of the monastery of St Peter in Swabia, who had been sent to the pope by Bishop Gebhard of Constance and by his brother, Duke Berthold [II of Zähringen], was taken prisoner by them when he

---

510 Eupraxia (Praxedis)-Adelaide (†1109), daughter of Prince Vsevolod of Kiev, widow of Count Henry III of Stade, margrave of the Saxon Nordmark (†1087), second wife of Henry IV (1089). See Meyer von Knonau (1903) p. 217.

511 See Meyer von Knonau (1913) p. 423; Robinson (1999) pp. 289–90.

512 Judith, half-sister of Count Baldwin V of Flanders, wife of (1) Tostig, earl of Northumbria (†1066), (2) Welf IV; † 5 March: necrologies of Weingarten and Zwiefalten (*MGH Necrologia* 1, 224, 233, 246). See Meyer von Knonau (1903) p. 427 and n. 19. She was buried in the Welf family monastery of Weingarten. See Hauck (1954) p. 1021.

513 Cf. *Germania pontificia* 2.1, 227–8, no. †2 (Urban II, *JL* †5701, inauthentic privilege for Weingarten); *ibid.*, p. 228, no. 3 (Paschal II, *JL* 6017, privilege for Weingarten). See Meyer von Knonau (1903) p. 427; Servatius (1979) p. 158 n. 41.

514 The castle of Johannes Frangipane near S. Maria Nuova: Meyer von Knonau (1903) pp. 418–20; Becker (1964) pp. 101, 103; Hüls (1977) p. 267.

wished to cross over that bridge.[515]

Duke Welf [IV] of Bavaria extended that most binding peace that he had previously initiated with the Swabian Duke Berthold [II of Zähringen] and the other princes of Swabia as far afield as Bavaria, indeed as far afield as Hungary. Franconia and Alsace also decreed on oath that they would observe this same peace in their territories.[516] Nevertheless the peace had its greatest effect in Swabia, because its princes did not cease to do justice, each one in his own jurisdiction, while the other provinces had not yet decided to do this. And above all Duke Berthold burned with such zeal to do justice in the duchy of Swabia that he surpassed almost all his predecessors in his reverence for justice and he filled the mouths of all men with pious reports of his doings.

The holy mother Church still suffered great difficulty in these territories in avoiding the excommunicates and she could not have avoided them at all if the lord pope had not long before qualified the sentence of excommunication to some extent by apostolic authority. For in the manner of his *predecessor*, the venerable Pope *Gregory* [VII], he *excluded* many persons *from excommunication* – namely, *travellers, peasants, manservants and maidservants, wives and* children – *who* had *become subject to excommunication* but not *by their own wrongdoing.*[517]

Gebhard [III], bishop of the church of Constance celebrated a great synod according to canon law in Constance in the week before Easter [2–8 April], together with innumerable abbots and clergy and with the aforementioned dukes and the other princes of Swabia and there he corrected many things that were in need of correction.[518] There he also imposed such a prohibition on the unchastity of priests and the violence of simoniacs that he even totally forbade the people, on pain of excommunication, to receive the offices of those who, being guilty of such offences, had presumed to exercise their ministry, contrary to divine and human law. There he also decreed, according to the decrees of the holy Fathers, that the fast of March was always to be celebrated

---

515 He had probably come to Rome to collect the papal privilege, Urban II, *JL* 5545 (n. 494). See Meyer von Knonau (1903) p. 422; Parlow (1999) pp. 98–9.

516 Cf. *Annals of Augsburg* 1094, p. 134. This was perhaps the occasion for the 'Bavarian Peace', 'Peace of the march of Istria' and 'Peace of Alsace' in *MGH Constitutiones* 1, 609–13. See Wadle (1973) pp. 148–50. On Berthold II: Parlow (1999) p. 99.

517 Urban II, *JL* 5393: see Märtl (1992) pp. 52–3.

518 See Meyer von Knonau (1903) pp. 428–9; Schumann (1912) p. 70; Robinson (1999) p. 278.

519 See above p. 281 and n. 285.

in the first week of Lent and that of June in Whitsun week.[519] He further decreed that both in Whitsun week and in Easter week there were to be only three days of feasting.[520] For up to that time the bishopric of Constance did not follow the custom of the rest of the province and celebrated for a whole week at Easter and only for one day at Whitsun, even though both weeks ought to be celebrated in the same way and even though almost all other bishoprics had followed the aforementioned tradition since ancient times. He was able, I say, to introduce these decrees according to canon law in his own bishopric on the basis both of episcopal authority and of the papal legation, for he was the legate of the apostolic see everywhere in the whole of Germany.[521]

The complaint of Queen Praxedis, who had left her husband a short time before and gone to Duke Welf [V] of Italy, reached the synod of Constance. She complained that she had suffered such great and such unheard-of filthy acts of fornication at the hands of so many men that she very easily excused her flight even to her enemies and reconciled herself to all catholics, who were moved to compassion by such great injuries.[522] In this synod the venerable Abbot Siegfried of the monastery of the Holy Saviour [Schaffhausen] complained of his obedientiary Tuto, who had freely delivered himself and his property to that monastery but who not long afterwards had sacrilegiously attempted to remove himself and his possessions from there completely.[523] The holy synod, therefore, judged according to the decrees of canon law that that man was to return to his abbot without offering any resistance and was to be obedient to him and that he was to remain humbly subject to him, together with his property, in perpetuity and that he must strive to perform a worthy penance, according to the abbot's command, for his past disobedience. And what the synod judged ought to be done was indeed performed.

A great pestilence spread throughout Bavaria so that in the city of Regensburg within twelve weeks 8,500 victims of that plague were counted. That same pestilence affected other provinces but not as much as Bavaria.[524] Many ominous events occurred in the German lands. For

520 Cf. *Annals of Augsburg* 1094, p. 134. A similar text in the synod of Ingelheim (948) c. 6 (*MGH Constitutiones* 1, 15). See Robinson (1989) p. 184.

521 See Becker (1973) p. 245.

522 See Meyer von Knonau (1903) p. 429; Schumann (1912) p. 70; Robinson (1999) pp. 290–1.

523 See above p. 307 and n. 451.

524 Cf. *Annals of Augsburg* 1094, p. 134; Frutolf, *Chronica* 1094, p. 106. See Curschmann (1900) pp. 123–5; Meyer von Knonau (1903) p. 433.

men hanged themselves and wolves devoured many people. And there was no doubt that this was the result of divine vengeance because they had neglected the divine law and had not been afraid to stain themselves with excommunication. Lightning from heaven also greatly terrified people. For in the monastery of Ottobeuren[525] the greater crucifix and the benches of the monks – who did not live according to the *Rule* – were destroyed by lightning. Likewise in the principal church in Basel lightning struck the beam that supported the crucifix and this was because there were many men in that place who had met with excommunicates.

At this time Master Manegold of Lautenbach[526] began to establish a monastery of clergy at Marbach[527] and he himself wished to be one of those clerks living the common life according to the *Rule*. In the Black Forest, in the place that is named after St Blasius, a monastery in honour of that saint began to be built from the foundations on 11 September.[528] For God had so exalted that place and had caused so many men to come there to be converted that of necessity more spacious buildings had to be erected. On the very day that this building work was begun, the lord Uto, the venerable abbot of that place, sent his prior, the lord Hartmann, together with other brethren, into the eastern kingdom, that is to say, into the march bordering on Hungary, to establish the new abbey in the bishopric of Passau, which is called Göttweig.[529] There was, however, in that place a monastery of clergy living according to the *Rule*, who nevertheless obtained permission from the lord pope and, through the pope, from their own bishop [Udalric], to give up their clerical way of life and to become monks. For this reason the lord abbot [Uto] of St Blasien, at the command of the lord pope,[530] and at the request of the bishop, decided to establish an abbey in that place and sent his brethren there to carry this out.

525 See Meyer von Knonau (1903) p. 433 n. 28.

526 Manegold of Lautenbach, dean of Rottenbuch, provost of Marbach; polemicist, author of *Liber contra Wolfelmum* (*MGH Quellen zur Geistesgeschichte* 8, 1972) and *Liber ad Gebehardum* (*MGH Libelli* 1, 308–430). See Mois (1953) pp. 99–106; Hartmann (1970) pp. 47–149; Fuhrmann (1975) pp. 21–42.

527 The Augustinian house of Marbach. Cf. Urban II, *JL* 5629, col. 455. See Meyer von Knonau (1903) p. 433; Mois (1953) p. 104.

528 *Annales sancti Blasii* (p. 277) place the rebuilding of St Blasien in 1092. See Meyer von Knonau (1903) pp. 431–2.

529 Hartmann, prior of St Nicholas in Passau, prior of St Blasien; abbot of Göttweig, SS Udalric and Afra, Augsburg, Kempten and St Lambrecht (†1114). See Jakobs (1968) pp. 113–20, 123–4.

530 See *Germania pontificia* 1, 235 (no. 1).

Herman, the advocate of Reichenau,[531] a young man of good character, was ambushed and alas! cruelly hacked in pieces by the servants of the church of Reichenau on 25 September, while he was going to the church to pray. He was buried with honour in the monastery of St Georgen, which his father had built on his own family estate.

The venerable priest Pericher, the most devout spiritual adviser of many nuns, departed to the Lord on 30 September, leaving behind him great lamentation among both men and women.[532] But innumerable other priests also died in German territory, leaving their parishioners in great danger from the same pestilence. For a very great pestilence raged to such an extent that in one village more than 1,050 men were counted as having died within six weeks. But elsewhere on a single day and in a single village more than forty died. The very cemeteries of the churches were so full of graves that men could not bury their dead there. In very many places, therefore, a huge trench was made outside the cemetery and they threw all their dead into it. This pestilence, however, not only troubled the Germans but was also everywhere in France, Burgundy and Italy. Nevertheless this did not seem to the wise to be so disastrous. For the greatest number of the casualties died after repentance and confession and made a praiseworthy end and those who lingered with the illness knew in advance what would happen to them after a few days. Almost all the sick indeed prepared themselves for certain death, which was something that at other times even some holy men could hardly do. Even the survivors took pains to abstain from worldly vanities, that is, from sports, taverns and other superfluous things of that kind, and to run to confession and to penance, and they did not cease to place themselves in the hands of priests. The great majority, therefore, who were victims of that pestilence died a very praiseworthy death.

In the city of the French that is commonly called Autun a general council was assembled by the venerable Hugh, archbishop of Lyons and legate of the apostolic see on 16 October, together with archbishops, bishops and abbots of various provinces.[533] In this council the excommunication was renewed against King Henry and Wibert, the intruder in the apostolic see, and against all their adherents. King Philip [I]

---

531 Herman, son of Hezelo, advocate of Reichenau (n. 354). See Wollasch (1964) pp. 10, 28.

532 See Meyer von Knonau (1903) p. 433 n. 28.

533 Synod of Autun, 15 August: letter of invitation sent by Archbishop Hugh of Lyons to Bishop Lambert of Arras, *Sacra Concilia* 20, col. 801. See Meyer von Knonau (1903) pp. 4, 425–6; Becker (1964) p. 195.

of France was likewise excommunicated because, while his wife was still alive, he had taken another woman.[534] Simoniacal heresy and the unchastity of clergy were likewise condemned. In that same council monks were forbidden to usurp for themselves the parochial functions of priests in parishes.[535] All these matters, I say, were settled there and confirmed by the apostolic legation.

Count Adalbert of Calw, a young man of good character, died on 3 December.[536]

In Alsace Master Manegold of Lautenbach through the mercy of God miraculously rekindled the religion of the Church, which had for a long time been extinguished in that region. For as that long-lasting pestilence increased among them, almost all the more eminent persons and the knights of that province flocked to him in crowds and after they had been absolved from excommunication by virtue of the power granted to him by the lord pope,[537] they did not cease to obtain from him absolution from the rest of their sins, when they had performed their penance. All these persons determined henceforward to obey the lord Pope Urban faithfully . They therefore refused utterly to receive the offices of simoniac and unchaste priests. The lord Manegold, however, was the most important cause of this obedience. For this reason he drew upon himself the deep hatred of treacherous men, which he, however, thought to be of very little account because he had no doubt that it was a most glorious thing to be held in contempt for God's sake.

1095. The lord Pope Urban, who had set out from Rome long before, celebrated Christmas [25 December 1094] with the greatest splendour in Tuscany.[538] In that province he received the most zealous service from the bishop of Pisa, named Daimbert,[539] whom he had long before exalted with the pallium and the power of an archbishop, which hitherto the bishop of the see of Pisa had not customarily possessed.[540]

---

534 Philip I married (1) Bertha of Holland, (2) Bertrada of Montfort, wife of Count Fulk IV of Anjou.

535 Cf. Bernold, *Apologeticae rationes* p. 98. See Jakobs (1961) p. 205.

536 Adalbert III, count of Calw, son of Adalbert II: cf. Berthold, *Chronicle* 1075, above p. 141 and n. 256. See Meyer von Knonau (1903) p. 428 n. 19.

537 See above p. 278 and n. 268. Cf. Bernold, *De presbyteris* pp. 144–5, written for the canons of Rottenbuch, where Manegold was dean. See Mois (1953) pp. 103–4.

538 On 19 December he was in Pistoia: cf. Urban II, *JL* 5532, col. 390. See Meyer von Knonau (1903) p. 422.

539 Daimbert, bishop of Pisa (1088–99), patriarch of Jerusalem (†1105). See Matzke (1998) pp. 21–2, 92–3.

540 Cf. Urban II, *JL* 5464, col. 345B. See *Italia pontificia* 3, 320–1 (nos. 7, 9).

At that time Henry, the so-called king, remained in Lombardy, deprived of almost all the dignity of a king. For his son Conrad, who had been crowned king long before, cut himself off from him entirely and firmly allied himself with the lady Matilda [of Tuscany] and the other vassals of St Peter and gained control of the full strength of his father's military resources in Lombardy.[541]

Welf [V], the son of Duke Welf [IV] of Bavaria, separated himself completely from his marriage with the lady Matilda, declaring that she had never been touched by him. She herself would most willingly have remained silent about the matter in perpetuity, if he had not been the first to make it public in a very heedless fashion. His father, therefore, came to Lombardy in an excessively angry frame of mind and laboured long and hard, but in vain, for a reconciliation.[542] He even accepted the help of Henry against the lady Matilda in order to force her to give her property to his son, although he had not yet had conjugal knowledge of her. His protracted labours were, therefore, useless.

Since God and St Peter favoured him, the lord pope had the upper hand almost everywhere and he announced that he would hold a general synod in the middle of Lombardy, in the city of Piacenza, in the territory of the schismatics and directed against them. He sent letters summoning to it by canonical and apostolic authority the bishops of Italy, Burgundy, France, Swabia, Bavaria and other provinces. This synod took place in Piacenza around the middle of Lent[543] and such an infinite multitude flocked to that synod that it could not by any means be held in any church in that place. The lord pope was, therefore, forced to celebrate it *in*[544] *a field* outside the city. This was not done, however, without the authority *of a* good *example*. For *Moses* himself, the first lawmaker, at God's command informed God's people of the commandments of the Law in the fields and *the Lord* himself instructed His disciples in the decrees of the Gospels not in houses but on the mountain and *in the fields*.[544] We also sometimes celebrate masses outside a church entirely appropriately when an emergency compels us to do so, although we know that the churches are especially intended for such celebrations.

541 See Meyer von Knonau (1903) p. 427.

542 See Overmann (1895) pp. 161 (no. 49b), 245–6; Meyer von Knonau (1903) pp. 447–8; Becker (1964) p. 133; Struve (1995) p. 80; Robinson (1999) pp. 291, 292, 295.

543 Council of Piacenza, 1 March (*MGH Constitutiones* 1, 561–3, no. 393). See Meyer von Knonau (1903) pp. 441–7; Becker (1964) pp. 156–9; Ziese (1982) pp. 224–6.

544/544 Extracts from the preface of the synodal protocol of the council, *MGH Constitutiones* 1, 561.

In this synod Queen Praxedis, who had long been separated from Henry, complained to the lord pope and to the holy synod about her husband and the unheard-of filthy acts of fornication that she had suffered from her husband.[545] The lord pope, together with the holy synod, received her complaint most mercifully, because he was quite certain that she herself had not committed such foul offences but had endured them unwillingly. He, therefore, mercifully, absolved her from the penance that ought to be imposed for wrongdoing of that kind, because she had not been ashamed to confess her sin freely and publicly.

Philip, king of the French sent his envoys to this synod with the information that he had begun the journey thither but that he had been hindered and had a lawful excuse for his absence.[546] Through the intercession of the synod, therefore, he obtained from the lord pope a delay until Whitsun [13 May]. The lord Hugh, archbishop of Lyons, however, who had been summoned to that synod, was suspended from his office because he neither came in person nor sent an envoy there in his place with an excuse acceptable in canon law.[547]

A legation from the emperor of Constantinople [Alexius I Comnenus] likewise arrived at this synod and humbly implored the lord pope and all Christ's faithful people to give him some help against the pagans in defence of holy Church, which the pagans had already almost destroyed in that region, having seized that territory up to the walls of the city of Constantinople.[548] The lord pope, therefore, encouraged many men to give this help, so that they even promised on oath that, with God's help, they would go there and with all their might give their most faithful help against the pagans to that emperor.

Among other things, however, these decrees were made in that synod. Those who refused to give up their concubines or to dismiss anger from their hearts or to abandon any mortal sin whatsoever, were by no means to be admitted to do penance. Likewise, no priest was to admit anyone to do penance unless his own bishop had committed this responsibility to him. Likewise, we should not deny the eucharist to those who come

545 Cf. above p. 319 and n. 522. See Meyer von Knonau (1903) p. 444; Becker (1964) pp. 132–3; Goez (1996) pp. 31–2.

546 See Becker (1964) p. 195.

547 Cf. Urban II, *JL* 5544, col. 404B (Piacenza, 9 March). See Meyer von Knonau (1903) p. 445 n. 11; Schieffer (1935) pp. 157–8.

548 Cf. Ekkehard of Aura, *Chronica* (recension I) p. 136: Alexius I 'sent many letters to Pope Urban about the barbarous brigands who had spread through the greater part of his kingdom'. Bernold alone recorded this legation. See Holtzmann (1924/5) pp. 191–2; Erdmann (1935) pp. 301–2; Becker (1988) pp. 184–5.

to confession in the correct manner and whom we know to have dwelled among the excommunicates with the body only and not with the mind and not to have participated in their sacraments. In this synod also the heresy of the simoniacs was utterly condemned, so that *whatever either of holy orders or ecclesiastical property* seemed to have been *acquired by giving or promising money* in a simoniacal manner, was to be regarded as *of no effect* and was to be judged as having possessed or as possessing *no validity.*[549] *Nevertheless mercy* was shown to those *who were ordained by simoniacs without simony* and without their knowledge and they were to keep their orders. *Those, however, who* were *knowingly* ordained by such men, were irretrievably condemned, together with those who ordained them.[550] Likewise, the heresy of the nicholaites, that is, of unchaste subdeacons, deacons and especially priests, was irrevocably condemned, so that those who were not afraid to remain in that heresy, were henceforward not to meddle in their offices and the people were in no way to receive their ministrations if those nicholaites dared to carry out their ministry against these prohibitions.[551] Likewise, the Berengarian heresy, which had very frequently been anathematised since ancient times, was condemned once more and the judgement of the catholic faith against it was confirmed: that is, that when the bread and wine are consecrated on the altar, they are changed not only figuratively but also truly and essentially into the body and blood of the Lord.[552] Likewise the sentence of excommunication against the heresiarch Wibert, the intruder in the holy see, and against all his associates was promulgated once more with burning candles according to the judgement of the synod. In this synod almost 4,000 clergy and more than 3,000 laymen are said to have been present.

In this synod it was decreed *that no payment was ever to be exacted for confirmation and baptism and burial.* Likewise *that the Ember day fasts were to be celebrated in this order,* namely *the first in* the first week of *Lent, the second in Whitsun week but the third and the fourth were to take place in September and December in the customary manner.*[553]

Present in this synod were very reverend bishops: from Bavaria, Archbishop Thiemo of Salzburg and his suffragan, Bishop Udalric of

549 Piacenza, synodal protocol c. 2, *MGH Constitutiones* 1, 561 (part paraphrased).

550 *Ibid.*, c. 3, 4, p. 561 (paraphrased).

551 See Barstow (1982) p. 84.

552 Bernold alone mentioned this canon. See Montclos (1971) p. 587.

553 Piacenza, synodal protocol c. 13, 14, p. 563.

Passau; from Swabia, Bishop Gebhard [III] of Constance.[554] At that time they also consecrated Archbishop Arnulf [III] of Milan, who had been elected long before but was not yet consecrated, in Milan with the permission of the lord pope.[555] At that time also the lord pope himself consecrated Abbot Udalric [II] of Reichenau, who was likewise present in the aforementioned synod.[556] In the presence of the bishop of Constance [the pope] denied [the abbot] all episcopal power over the clergy and people of the island of Reichenau, having previously granted this power to the bishop of Constance. Nevertheless not long afterwards that abbot possessed himself of that power. When, as a result of this, a complaint was made by the bishop, the lord pope sent [the abbot] a letter and once again restrained him from behaving with such presumption.[557]

When[558] *the lord Pope Urban came to Cremona, King Conrad*, son of Henry, went to *meet him* and performed for him *the office of a groom*[559] on 10 April. *Then he took* an oath of fidelity *to him in respect of his life, his limbs* and *the Roman papacy.*[560] The lord *pope*, however, received him *as a son of the* holy *Roman church* and *in the presence of the people* he promised him most faithfully counsel and aid *in* obtaining *the kingship* and in *acquiring the crown of the empire, reserving* indeed *the rights of* that *church and the papal* decrees, *especially* that against a layman claiming *investitures*[558] of spiritual offices.[561]

Duke Welf [IV] of Bavaria, together with his son Welf [V], at last returned from Lombardy to Swabia and worked hard among the princes

554 Bernold composed his letter *De reordinatione vitanda* for Gebhard III of Constance on the occasion of his attendance at this council. Bernold's arguments were not, however, adopted by the council: Robinson (1989) p. 188.

555 Bernold alone reported this consecration. See Meyer von Knonau (1903) p. 447; Schwartz (1913) p. 84.

556 Henking (1880) p. 57 suggested that the delay in his consecration (since 1089) was linked with the dispute about episcopal jurisdiction over the island of Reichenau. See Meyer von Knonau (1903) p. 446 and n. 14; Becker (1973) pp. 262–3.

557 Not extant. Cf. *Germania pontificia* 2.1, 157 (no. *27).

558/558 Extracts from 'The agreement of Urban II and King Conrad' (*MGH Constitutiones* 1, 564, no. 394), regarded by Becker (1964) pp. 134–5 as a 'contemporary curial record'. See Meyer von Knonau (1903) pp. 449–51 and n. 20; Goez (1996) pp. 31–2; Robinson (1999) pp. 291–2.

559 The 'office of a groom' (*stratoris officium*): *Donation of Constantine* 16, p. 92. See Becker (1964) pp. 134–5; Robinson (1990) pp. 24, 417.

560 15 April, according to 'The agreement'. This was the 'oath of security' that the German king swore to the pope before the imperial coronation.

561 See Becker (1964) pp. 135–6 and n. 481; Beulertz (1991) pp. 110–11.

of the kingdom to restore Henry to the kingship, even though he was not absolved from his excommunication; but it was in vain. For even Henry's supporters would not easily believe in his persuasions, while the catholics were afraid of incurring excommunication and the guilt of perjury if they accepted Henry after they had jointly sworn to reject him on pain of excommunication.[562]

King Conrad arrived in Pisa in Tuscany with royal magnificence and there he received as his bride the daughter of Duke Roger of Sicily,[563] who was still a very small child and who was presented to him together with an unheard-of sum of money.

After affairs in Lombardy had been put in good order, the lord pope began to turn aside into France, travelling by sea,[564] and he arrived at St Mary's church in Le Puy on the feast-day of the assumption [15 August][565] and summoned a synod by his apostolic authority to meet in Clermont on the octave of St Martin's day [18 November], sending letters to the bishops of the various provinces and inviting them with a canonical summons.[566]

Liutolf, the son of the most holy Pope Leo IX and deacon of the holy church of Toul, built a monastery of clergy, which the Romans call a house of canons, near that city, in which he gathered clergy who promised to live according to the *Rule* of St Augustine.[567] He placed over them a provost who was under the same obligation and whom the bishop of that place [Pibo] solemnly consecrated as abbot for that congregation. For it is the custom in that region that the provosts of congregations of this kind are called abbots and are consecrated as abbots but with this difference, that they do not carry staffs. The lord Pope Urban also

---

562 See Meyer von Knonau (1903) pp. 460–1; Robinson (1999) p. 295.

563 Maximilla, daughter of Roger I, count of Sicily (†1101). See Holtzmann (1963) pp. 149–67; Becker (1964) pp. 136–7; Robinson (1999) p. 292.

564 Bernold alone mentioned a sea voyage. Cf. Fulcher of Chartres, *Historia Hierosolymitana* I.3, p. 121 and n. 14: 'Crossing the mountains, he went down into France.' See Meyer von Knonau (1903) p. 456 n. 31; Becker (1964) p. 218 and n. 819; Becker (1988) pp. 435–6.

565 Cf. Urban II, *JL* 5570, col. 422BC (the dating clause should read '15 August'). See Becker (1964) p. 220; Becker (1988) p. 436.

566 Cf. Urban II, *JL* 5570, col. 422B (invitation to Bishop Lambert of Arras). See Somerville (1974) pp. 57–8.

567 Liutolf, deacon of Toul (otherwise unknown), the son of Leo IX in the sense that he was ordained by the pope when the latter was bishop of Toul (1026–51). His foundation of St Léon in Toul: Erkens (1987) pp. 9, 95, 185, 192, 199. The fraternity of prayer of St Léon with St Blasien: Jakobs (1968) pp. 151–2.

conferred a privilege on that place, in which he decreed in the strongest terms that the clergy of that place were to keep the *Rule* of St Augustine in perpetuity and henceforward should always possess the freedom to elect their abbot.[568] That monastery, however, was built especially in honour of Pope Leo and the church was solemnly dedicated in honour of that pope. This privilege was given to the venerable Liutolf by the lord pope in Lombardy in the 1,095th year of the Lord's Incarnation.

Leopold, the very wealthy margrave of Austria, who was most faithful in the cause of St Peter against the schismatics, came to the end of his life.[569] The catholics lamented at his death as much as the enemies of holy Church rejoiced at it. The count palatine Henry,[570] who was also extremely rich but who was not equally obedient to the apostolic see, went the way of all flesh and left behind great riches, which were plundered by many men and were of no use to him.

In France at Clermont on the octave of St Martin's day [18 November] the lord pope assembled a general synod, in which thirteen archbishops were present with their suffragans and 205 pastoral staffs were counted there.[571] In this synod the lord pope confirmed the same decrees as in the previous synod of Piacenza. In addition he excommunicated Philip, king of the French, because he repudiated his own wife and he contracted marriage with the wife of his vassal.[572] There also he announced that another synod was to be celebrated in Tours in the third week of the following Lent.[573]

1096. The lord pope celebrated Christmas day [25 December 1095] with the greatest splendour in Arles with the bishops of various provinces.[574] In this place the bishop of Würzburg from the party of the schismatics[575]

---

568 Not extant. See Becker (1073) pp. 263 n. 59, 272.

569 Leopold II (1075–95) † 12 October. See Meyer von Knonau (1903) p. 462.

570 Henry II, count of Laach, Lotharingian count palatine (1085–95) † 12 April. See Meyer von Knonau (1903) pp. 461–2.

571 Urban II, *JL* 5600 (col. 438B): 'the archbishops of various provinces were present to the number of twelve, together with eighty bishops, ninety abbots and more'. See Meyer von Knonau (1903) pp. 457–9; Becker (1964) pp. 187–93; Somerville (1970) pp. 56–65.

572 See above p. 322 and n. 534.

573 Council of Tours, 16–22 March 1096. See Becker (1988) p. 446.

574 Evidence that Urban II was in Limoges from 23 to 31 December 1095: Meyer von Knonau (1903) p. 460 and n. 35; Becker (1964) p. 223 n. 837; Somerville (1970) pp. 58, 60.

575 Emehard (1089–1105). See Meyer von Knonau (1903) p. 470; Becker (1964) p. 161; Robinson (1999) p. 292.

came to the pope and obtained his mercy on this basis: that this mercy should be granted to him by the pope's legates on German territory.

In the third week of Lent the lord pope celebrated a synod with the bishops of various provinces in the city of Tours, where he once more confirmed the decrees of his previous councils with the consent of the general synod and not long afterwards he received into communion the bishop [Otto] of Strasbourg, who had come to his senses after being excommunicated and who had first cleared himself of the crimes with which he had been charged.[576]

At this time a very great multitude from Italy, from all of France and from Germany began to make an expedition to Jerusalem against the pagans in order to free the Christians. The lord pope was the foremost author of this expedition.[577] For in the previous synods he had most zealously admonished everyone about this expedition and had most strongly recommended to them that it should be done for the remission of their sins.[578] He also caused all those who made a vow to go on this journey to mark their clothes with the sign of the cross and in some cases this sign also appeared on their flesh.[579] For this reason very many people believed that this journey had been undertaken through the ordinance and by the inspiration of God. An innumerable crowd of the common people, however, hurried off on this journey all too ingenuously and they neither knew how to nor were able to prepare themselves for such a dangerous enterprise.[580] A large number of them, therefore, met their deaths in Hungary when they very unwisely laid waste the land of the Hungarians. The king of Hungary[581] did not allow the rest of the crowd who were following them to enter that land and a considerable number of them also died on entering Hungary. It was no wonder that they could not complete the planned expedition to Jerusalem because they did not undertake that journey with the humility

576 See Meyer von Knonau (1903) p. 470; Becker (1964) p. 161.

577 See Meyer von Knonau (1903) pp. 482–3; Erdmann (1935) p. 375 n. 35; Becker (1988) pp. 272–4; Robinson (1990) pp. 322–3.

578 Cf. synodal protocol of Clermont c. 2: Somerville (1972) pp. 74, 143 no. 3; Urban II, *JL* 5608, ed. Hagenmeyer (1901) p. 136: 'for the remission of all sins'. See Erdmann (1935) pp. 316–17; Becker (1964) p. 222; Riley-Smith (1986) pp. 19–20, 27–31; Robinson (1990) pp. 327–9.

579 See Meyer von Knonau (1903) p. 483 and n. 35; Riley-Smith (1986) pp. 22, 24–5, 34, 41, 81–2, 113–14, 127; Robinson (1990) pp. 331–4

580 'The Peasants' Crusade': Meyer von Knonau (1903) pp. 486–512; Mayer (1972) pp. 43–5; Riley-Smith (1986) pp. 49–54.

581 Colman I (1095–1116).

and piety that they ought to have shown. For they had in their company very many apostates,[582] who had thrown aside their monastic habit and proposed to wage war alongside them. But they were not afraid to have with them innumerable women, who impiously changed their natural garments for men's clothing and with whom they committed fornication. In doing this, like the people of Israel in ancient times,[583] they offended God to an extraordinary degree. When, therefore, after many sufferings, perils and deaths, they were not permitted to enter Hungary, they began to return home without achieving their purpose and with great sadness.*

King Philip [I] of France, who had long been excommunicated because of his adultery, at last came humbly to make reparation to the lord pope, while the latter still remained in France.[584] After he had sworn to give up the adulteress [Bertrada of Montfort], he was received into favour and showed himself most ready to perform service to the lord pope.

After putting affairs in France into good order, after the reconciliation of the king of France and after many councils, the lord pope at last returned to Lombardy in great triumph and glory and he solemnly celebrated the Exaltation of the Holy Cross [14 September] in Mortara near Pavia and had many bishops and princes in his entourage.[585]

Siegfried of pious memory, the abbot of Schaffhausen, a man of great prudence and of admirable benevolence, departed to the Lord on 28 October and left great lamentation among all the faithful, both the laymen and the clergy, on his departure.[586] The venerable Gerard succeeded to his office on 2 November.[587] Count Werner died on 11 November.[588] Liutfried of holy memory, the abbot of the monastery of St Martin,[589] who for almost thirty years had been crucified in the world and lived alone in God, came to the end of his days on 31 December *in a good old age*, that is to say, *full of years*.[590]

582 Cf. Balderic of Dol, *Historia Hierosolymitana* I.8, p. 17. See Erdmann (1935) p. 310; Becker (1988) p. 391.

583 Cf. Hosea 4:12. Cf. Frutolf, *Chronica* 1096, p. 108.

584 Probably in Nîmes: Meyer von Knonau (1903) pp. 469–70 and n. 2; Becker (1964) pp. 197–8. See above p. 322 and n. 534.

585 He was in Asti on 9 September: Meyer von Knonau (1903) pp. 469, 471; Becker (1964) p. 213.

586 Cf. Bernold, *Calendar* p. 517.

587 Gerard (1096–8). See Meyer von Knonau (1904) p. 31.

588 Werner, count of Habsburg. See Jakobs (1968) pp. 50–2, 55–60, 62–4, 285–7.

589 Liutfried, abbot of Muri (1085–96). See Jakobs (1968) pp. 60, 64–5.

590 Genesis 25:8; I Chronicles 29:28.

*[In this year in certain cities the Jews were massacred with great carnage by those who were going to Jerusalem. It happened, I say, that in Speyer they fled into the palace of the king and the bishop and put up resistance, defending themselves with difficulty, and Bishop John[591] helped them. The latter was afterwards moved by his anger on this account and bribed by the Jews' money to cause certain Christians to be killed. Likewise in Worms the Jews, fleeing from their Christian pursuers, hastened to the bishop [Adalbert]. When the latter promised them safety only if they received baptism, they asked for a delay during which they might confer together. They entered the bishop's chamber and at the very hour at which our people were outside waiting for their answer, they killed themselves, at the persuasion of the devil and their own obstinacy.][592]

1097. The lord pope at last returned to the apostolic see with great glory and gladness and celebrated Christmas [25 December 1096] most splendidly in Rome with his cardinals, since almost the whole city of Rome was subjected to him, except for the tower of Crescentius, in which the Wibertists were still hiding.[593]

Margrave Azzo of Lombardy, the father of Duke Welf [IV] of Bavaria, who was, so they say, more than a hundred years old, went the way of all flesh[594] and bequeathed to his sons a great feud concerning his property. For Duke Welf wished to obtain all his father's property, on the grounds that it had been given to his mother,[595] but his brothers, who had been born of a different mother,[596] refused to be totally disinherited. They therefore denied him access to Lombardy when he went to take possession.

At that time the lady Matilda, the excellent duchess and margravine [of Tuscany], the most devoted daughter of St Peter, achieved for herself great renown everywhere. For virtually alone, she, together with her

591 John I (1090–1104).

592 This passage is an addition in the margin of Bernold's autograph, not in his own but in a contemporary hand. The pogrom in Speyer took place on 3 May, that in Worms from 18 to 25 May: Meyer von Knonau (1903) pp. 500–1 and nn. 57–8. See also Riley-Smith (1984) pp. 51–72.

593 See above p. 300 and n. 410; Meyer von Knonau (1903) p. 473; Becker (1988) p. 104; Hüls (1977) pp. 260–1.

594 Albert Azzo II (*ca.* 996–1097), margrave of Este (Otbertine family), ✝ between 13 April and 20 August. See Meyer von Knonau (1904) p. 11; Jakobs (1968) pp. 183, 193.

595 Cuniza, daughter of Welf II (see above p. 64 and n. 73).

596 Hugo and Fulco, margraves of Este, sons of Garsendis, daughter of Count Herbert I of Maine. See Meyer von Knonau (1903) p. 346 n. 26; (1904) p. 11.

followers, had now fought most skilfully against Henry and the here-siarch Wibert and their associates for seven years and at length she most courageously forced Henry to flee from Lombardy and, after recovering her property, she never ceased to give thanks to God and St Peter.[597] But Henry came with a few followers to Regensburg at Whitsun [24 May] and after he had remained there and in the neighbourhood of the castle of Nuremberg for the whole summer in a very private manner, he at last departed for Speyer, to remain there for a long time, likewise in a very private manner.[598]

Meanwhile Duke Welf [IV] of Bavaria set out for Lombardy to take possession of the inheritance of his father, Margrave Azzo, who had recently died. But the sons of that margrave by another wife resisted the aforementioned duke with all their might. That duke, therefore, was forced to accept the help of Duke Henry of Carinthia[599] and his brother, the patriarch [Udalric] of Aquileia, when he attacked his brothers and thus he laid hands on a large part of his father's inheritance.

The most celebrated Count Udalric [X of Bregenz], a most fervent defender of the cause of St Peter against the schismatics, suffered a very untimely death, alas! but ended his days after a good confession. He received an honourable burial on 27 October in Bregenz, where he himself had established the monastic life.[600]

1098. The lord pope celebrated Christmas [25 December 1097] in Rome and he most firmly established a lasting peace in the city itself and the surrounding countryside and he likewise celebrated the festival of Easter [28 March] there with great glory.[601] But his rival, Wibert, remained at that time in the territory of Ravenna and he lost a certain fortress on which his hopes principally rested, that is, the castle named Argenta, which dominated the Po and could control all those who crossed over the Po.[602]

---

597 Eulogies of Matilda in pro-papal writings: Erdmann (1935) pp. 207–8, 229, 232; Robinson (1978a) pp. 100–3; Struve (1995) p. 58.

598 Henry IV's return to Germany was the result of his reconciliation with Welf IV, which opened up the Alpine passes for him once more: Meyer von Knonau (1904) pp. 2–3 and n. 4; Robinson (1999) pp. 295–6.

599 Henry III (of Eppenstein), duke of Carinthia (1090–1122). See Meyer von Knonau (1904) p. 11.

600 Monastery of Mehrerau-Bregenz. See Meyer von Knonau (1900) p. 341 n. 174; (1904) p. 8 and n. 13; Jakobs (1968) pp. 150, 152.

601 See Meyer von Knonau (1904) pp. 15, 39; Becker (1964) p. 105.

602 Argenta, north-west of Ravenna. See Köhncke (1888) p. 91; Meyer von Knonau (1904) pp. 13–14.

The venerable Abbot Gerard of Schaffhausen was moved by humility to give up his place, with the approval of the lord pope, and he obtained from the latter permission for another abbot to be appointed to rule over that place. But a great calamity immediately fell upon that place deprived of its pastor, so that many of the brethren deserted it and secular persons sacrilegiously claimed its property for themselves. For a long time, therefore, no abbot could be appointed there, as the lord pope had ordered to be done. Even the advocate of that place, Count Adalbert,[603] fortified a certain castle nearby and sacrilegiously claimed the property of the abbey for himself. The monks, therefore, went in procession to that castle, humbly entreating with crosses and relics and prayers.[604] But all were ill treated by the knights of the count, some of them killed, some wounded, and they were forced to return or to be carried home, while the crosses and relics were smashed to pieces and alas! pitifully scattered over the field. Hence that count incurred much hatred from both clergy and laymen. But the monks themselves were judged by very many people to have deserved this judgement from God because they had not treated their abbot well and they had without adequate reason not so much released him as expelled him.

Manegold [of Lautenbach], the venerable provost of the canons dwelling in Marbach, was held in captivity for a long time by King Henry because he refused to obey the schismatics contrary to the authority of the Church.[605] The whole Church, therefore, far and wide suffered with him.

Duke Godfrey, the grandson of the great Duke Godfrey ['the Bearded'],[606] Robert, son of Count Baldwin,[607] Bohemund, son of Duke Robert of Calabria and Sicily,[608] Count Raymond of St Gilles,[609] likewise Bishop Otto of Strasbourg and Count Hartmann [I of Kirchberg] from Swabia – all these, I say, and very many others – had long since begun

---

603 Adalbert, count of Mörsburg. See Meyer von Knonau (1904) p. 31 and n. 15.

604 An example of the rite of *clamor*, 'derived from an ancient tradition of appeal to collective opinion against the abuses of the mighty': Moore (2000) pp. 22, 56.

605 He had evidently regained his freedom by 2 August 1103: cf. Paschal II, *JL* 5949, col. 117.

606 Godfrey V (of Bouillon), duke of Lower Lotharingia (1087–96), advocate of the Holy Sepulchre (✝1100), son of Ida, daughter of Godfrey 'the Bearded'.

607 Bernold perhaps confused the two crusading princes Robert II, count of Flanders (son of Robert I) and Robert II, duke of Normandy (grandson of Baldwin V of Flanders).

608 Bohemund I, prince of Tarento and Antioch (✝1111), son of Robert Guiscard.

609 Raymond IV of St Gilles, count of Toulouse, count of Tripoli (✝1105).

to march to Jerusalem with an innumerable multitude. After they had seized the city of Nicea and Antioch[610] and other cities from the power of the pagans and above all had restored the patriarch of Jerusalem to his place,[611] they came through many battles and victories to the neighbourhood of Jerusalem.[612] The lord pope, therefore, sent his legation to that multitude, namely that of the venerable Daimbert, archbishop of the church of Pisa, who was to help them in all things as papal representative and was to establish churches in the places from which the pagans had been expelled.[613] But the king of Constantinople proved a hindrance to this process, since he withdrew his help from our men in every way.[614] For he was not afraid to burn and destroy completely or to give back to the pagans those cities that our men had seized from the hands of the pagans and he utterly forbade all pilgrims to make the journey to Jerusalem through the territory under his jurisdiction.

In this year a miraculous sign appeared in the heavens on 27 September,[615] so that during almost the whole of that night part of the heavens appeared bloody. That redness did not remain only in one place but ranged through all the parts of heaven except the south and many rays, like the rays of the sun, seemed to proceed out of that redness.

1099. The lord pope celebrated Christmas [25 December 1098] in Rome in great peace.[616] For he held even the Castel S. Angelo,[617] together with other fortresses, in his power and with God's help and with great courage he had either reconciled his enemies in the city or subdued them by force. He also sent letters everywhere, announcing that his synod was to be celebrated in Rome in the third week after Easter.[618]

---

610 Nicea was taken on 19 June 1097, Antioch on 3 June 1098. See Mayer (1972) pp. 49–50, 54–6; Riley-Smith (1986) pp. 58–9.

611 A confused reference to the restoration of the patriarch of Antioch after the capture of the city: Meyer von Knonau (1904) p. 76 n. 31.

612 7 June 1099: see Mayer (1972) p. 59; Riley-Smith (1986) p. 59.

613 See above n. 539. Becker (1988) p. 429 argued that this report was false. Cf. Matzke (1998) pp. 135–7.

614 Hostility towards Emperor Alexius I Comnenus in crusading narratives: Erdmann (1935) p. 365; Becker (1988) pp. 414–16.

615 21 September: *Annals of Augsburg* 1098, p. 135. Cf. Sigebert, *Chronica* 1097, p. 367; Ekkehard, *Chronica* (recension I) p. 140.

616 See Meyer von Knonau (1904) p. 56; Becker (1964) p. 105.

617 Evidently captured 10 August 1098: Meyer von Knonau (1904) p. 46. But the accuracy of this report is doubted by Ziese (1982) p. 245.

618 24–30 April in St Peter's. See Meyer von Knonau (1904) pp. 71–3; Becker (1964) p. 112.

Rapoto, the count palatine of Bavaria, the most obstinate supporter or rather the chief of those who had hitherto opposed the apostolic see and catholic unity, came to the end of his days.[619] Likewise Conrad, who was not the bishop but the schismatic of Utrecht, died a dishonourable death, killed by a certain man whom he had ordered to be deprived of his property.[620]

In Rome the lord pope assembled a general synod of 150 bishops and abbots and innumerable clergy in the third week after Easter. In that synod, after confirming the decrees of his predecessors, he also repeated the sentence of excommunication on the heresiarch Wibert and all his associates. He also decreed there that those who kept concubines should not presume to go to communion, unless they had first completely dismissed them. As for the expedition to Jerusalem, he asked them repeatedly to go and bring help to their brothers who were labouring there.[621]

In Swabia at length after many dangers an abbot named Adalbert was appointed in the monastery of Schaffhausen.[622] He was accused of the alleged expulsion of the previous abbot and vindicated himself by the judgement of the Church in the following manner: when he was questioned by the bishop according to the obedience that he owed to the *Rule*, he declared that he was innocent of that offence. He was consecrated, however, by the venerable Gebhard, bishop of Constance and legate of the apostolic see, on the feast of the Nativity of St John the Baptist [24 June].

Count Liutold [of Achalm] of good memory, who had long suffered from an ailment of the feet but who was a tireless defender of the cause of St Peter against the wickedness of the schismatics, at last exchanged secular office for the monastic way of life and happily departed to the Lord on 18 August. He was honourably buried in the monastery that he himself had founded on his family estates, using his own fortune.[623]

In Rome the venerable Pope Urban, the second of this name, at last departed from this world on 29 July after many tribulations and after he had governed the Roman see for eleven years and five months.[624] After

---

619 Rapoto V, count of Cham and Vohburg, count palatine of Bavaria † 14 April. See Meyer von Knonau (1904) pp. 61–2.

620 Frutolf, *Chronica* 1099, p. 118: he was killed 'by his own men'.

621 See Becker (1988) p. 405.

622 Adalbert I (1099–1131). See Meyer von Knonau (1904) p. 31 and n. 15.

623 Zwiefalten: Meyer von Knonau (1904) pp. 37–8.

624 See Meyer von Knonau (1904) p. 75 and n. 30; Becker (1964) p. 112.

his death the lord Paschal, who was also called Rainer, was consecrated as the 163rd pope[625] and everywhere it was said that this had happened as the result of a divine relevation. He was solemnly enthroned, however, by the clergy and people on the sixteenth day after his predecessor's departure.[626]

Count Adalbert [II of Calw] of pious memory, who had been since olden times most zealous in his fidelity towards St Peter against the schismatics and who had finally from being a count become a monk, happily came to the end of his life on 22 September. He was honourably buried in the monastery that he himself had built, using his own property, and in which he had taken the monastic habit, namely in Hirsau, where the lord Gebhard was abbot.[627]

1100. The lord Pope Paschal celebrated Christmas [25 December 1099] in Rome in great peace and by means of a letter[628] he conferred on the venerable Bishop Gebhard [III] of Constance the papal vicariate in the German territory, which he had also received many years ago from his predecessor.

In Swabia the venerable Abbot Manegold of the monastery of St George[629] was alas! pitifully killed by one of his monks in that place, which indeed brought him to eternal salvation but the monk to the most certain damnation. He was assaulted, however, on 15 February, which in that year was Ash Wednesday. Nevertheless he survived until Saturday, accepting his martyrdom with great piety. For he came to the end of his life on 18 February.

The sentence of excommunication had now begun almost everywhere greatly to lose its efficacy so that even certain religious men, who up to this time had been most fervent in that cause, abandoned the catholics and were not afraid to accept promotion among the excommunicates.[630] But holy Church nevertheless remained steadfast in her obedience to the apostolic see on the question of the excommunicates since she knew that after the apostasy of Judas the rest of the apostles had adhered all the more steadfastly to the Lord.

625 Rainer of Bieda, cardinal priest of S. Clemente; Pope Paschal II (1099–1118). In Bernold's *Catalogue* (*MGH SS* 5, 400) he is numbered '162'.

626 14 August: Meyer von Knonau (1904) p. 79; Servatius (1979) pp. 40–1.

627 See Meyer von Knonau (1904) p. 70.

628 Not extant (but see Paschal II, *JL* 5817: *Germania pontificia* 2.1, 132, no. 32). See Meyer von Knonau (1904) p. 85; Schumann (1912) p. 71; Servatius (1979) p. 147.

629 Manegold (of Veringen), abbot of Isny. See Meyer von Knonau (1904) p. 84 n. 46.

The venerable Abbot Gerard, who had formerly laid down the abbacy of Schaffhausen for God's sake and had done so with the authority of the lord Pope Urban, set out for Jerusalem with the army of the Christians. After many labours the latter gained control of the city and they committed the guardianship of the Lord's Sepulchre to the aforementioned abbot.[631]

Otto, the schismatic of Strasbourg, who had returned from the expedition to Jerusalem but who, it is thought, had not corrected his schismatic views, came to the end of his life.[632]

630 See Servatius (1979) p. 148.

631 See Meyer von Knonau (1904) p. 31 n. 15.

632 3 August. See Meyer von Knonau (1904) pp. 100–1.

SELECT BIBLIOGRAPHY

Primary sources

Adam of Bremen, *Gesta Hammaburgensis ecclesiae pontificum, MGH SS rer. Germ.* [2] (1917) trans. F.J. Tschan, *History of the archbishops of Hamburg-Bremen* (New York, 1959)

Amatus of Monte Cassino, *Ystoire de li Normant* ed. O. Delarc (Rouen, 1892); *Storia de Normanni di Amato di Montecassino* ed. V. de Bartholomei (Fonti per la storia d'Italia 76: Rome, 1935)

Anna Comnena Porphyrogenita, *Alexiad,* ed. A. Reifferscheid 1, 2 (Leipzig, 1884)

Annales Magdeburgenses, MGH SS 16, 105–96

Annales sancti Blasii, MGH SS 17, 275-8

Annalista Saxo, MGH SS 6, 553–777

Annals of Augsburg = *Annales Augustani, MGH SS* 3, 123-36

Annals of Benevento = *Annales Beneventani, MGH SS* 3, 173–85

Annals of Brauweiler = *Annales Brunwilarenses, MGH SS* 16, 724-8

Annals of Niederaltaich = *Annales Altahenses maiores, MGH SS rer. Germ.* [4] (1891)

Anonymous of Hasenried, *De episcopis Eichstetensibus, MGH SS* 7, 253–66

'Anonymus Mellicensis' [Wolfger of Prüfening?], *De scriptoribus ecclesiasticis,* ed. E. Ettlinger, *Der sogen. Anonymus Mellicensis. Text- und quellenkritische Ausgabe* (dissertation, Strasbourg, 1896)

Anselm of Liège, *Gesta episcoporum Leodiensium, MGH SS* 7, 189–234

Arnulf of Milan, *Liber gestorum recentium, MGH SS rer. Germ.* 67 (1994)

Balderic of Dol, *Historia Hierosolymitana, Recueil des historiens des croisades, Historiens occidentaux* 4, 11–110

Benzo of Alba, *Ad Heinricum IV. imperatorem libri VII. Sieben Bücher an Kaiser Heinrich IV., MGH SS rer. Germ.* 65 (1996)

Bern of Reichenau, *Die Musiktraktate des Abtes Bern von Reichenau. Edition and Interpretation,* ed. A. Rausch (Musica Mediaevalis Europae Occidentalis 5: Tutzing, 1999)

Bern of Reichenau, *Letters: Die Briefe des Abtes Bern von Reichenau,* ed. F.-J. Schmale (Veröffentlichungen der Kommission für Geschichtliche Landeskunde in Baden-Württemberg A.6, Stuttgart, 1961)

Bernard of Hildesheim, *De damnatione scismaticorum* = Bernold, *De damnatione scismaticorum* II

Bernard of Hildesheim, *Liber canonum contra Heinricum IV, MGH Libelli* 1, 471–516

Bernold of St Blasien (of Constance), *Apologeticae rationes contra scismaticorum obiectiones, MGH Libelli* 2, 94–101

Bernold, *Apologeticus, MGH Libelli* 2, 58–88

Bernold, *Calendar*, ed. R. Kuithan and J. Wollasch, 'Der Kalender des Chronisten Bernold', *Deutsches Archiv* 40 (1984), 478–531

Bernold, *Chronicon, MGH SS* 5, 400–67; *Die Chroniken Bertholds von Reichenau und Bernolds von Konstanz* ed. I.S. Robinson, *MGH SS rer. Germ. nova series* 14 (2003)

Bernold, *De damnatione scismaticorum, MGH Libelli* 2, 26–58

Bernold, *De emptione ecclesiarum, MGH Libelli* 2, 107–8

Bernold, *De excommunicatis vitandis, de reconciliatione lapsorum et de fontibus iuris ecclesiastici, MGH Fontes iuris germanici antiqui* 15 (2000)

Bernold, *De incontinentia sacerdotum, MGH Libelli* 2, 4–26

Bernold, *De presbyteris, MGH Libelli* 2, 142–6

Bernold, *De reordinatione vitanda, MGH Libelli* 2, 150–6

Bernold, *De sacramentis excommunicatorum, MGH Libelli* 2, 89–94

Bernold, *De veritate corporis et sanguinis Domini*, ed. R.B.C. Huygens, 'Bérenger de Tours, Lanfranc et Bernold de Constance', *Sacris Eruditi* 16 (1965), 355–403

Bernold, *Micrologus de ecclesiasticis observationibus, MPL* 151, col. 977B–1022B

Bernold, *Pro Gebhardo episcopo Constantiensi epistola apologetica, MGH Libelli* 2, 108–11

Bernold of St Blasien (of Constance)(?), *Apologeticus super excommunicacionem Gregorii VII, MGH Libelli* 2, 160–8

Berthold of Reichenau, *Chronicon, MGH SS* 5, 264–326; *Die Chroniken Bertholds von Reichenau und Bernolds von Konstanz* ed. I.S. Robinson, *MGH SS rer. Germ. nova series* 14 (2003)

Bonizo of Sutri, *To a friend* trans. I.S. Robinson, *The papal reform of the eleventh century* (Manchester-New York, 2004) = Bonizo, *Liber ad amicum, MGH Libelli* 1, 568–620

Briefsammlungen der Zeit Heinrichs IV., MGH Briefe 5 (1950)

Bruno of Merseburg, *Saxon War* = *Saxonicum bellum: Brunos Buch vom Sachsenkrieg, MGH Deutsches Mittelalter* 2 (1937)

Burchard of Worms, *Decretum, MPL* 140, 337A–1058C

Carmen de bello Saxonico, MGH SS rer. Germ. [17] (1889) pp. 1–23

Casus monasterii Petrishusensis, MGH SS 20, 621–82

Casuum sancti Galli continuatio II, MGH SS 2, 148–63

Chronicle of Monte Cassino = Chronica monasterii Casinensis, MGH SS 34 (1980)

Chronicon Suevicum universale, MGH SS 13, 61–72

Codex Udalrici, ed. P. Jaffé, *Bibliotheca rerum Germanicarum* 5 (Berlin, 1869), 17–469

Collection in 74 titles = Collectio in LXXIV titulos (Diversorum patrum sententie), ed. J.T. Gilchrist (Monumenta Iuris Canonici ser. B, 1: Vatican City, 1973)

Constantine of St-Symphorian, Metz, *Vita Adalberonis II Mettensis episcopi, MGH SS* 4, 658–72

Cosmas of Prague, *Chronica Boemorum, MGH SS rer. Germ.*, n.s. 2 (Berlin, 1955)

Decretales Pseudo-Isidorianae et Capitula Angilramni, ed. P. Hinschius (Leipzig, 1863)

Deusdedit, *Collectio canonum. Die Kanonessammlung des Kardinal Deusdedit*, ed. V. von Glanvell 1 (Paderborn, 1905)

Die Ordines für die Weihe und Krönung des Kaisers und der Kaiserin, MGH Fontes iuris germanici antiqui 9 (1960)

Donation of Constantine = Constitutum Constantini, MGH Fontes iuris Germanici antiqui 10 (1968)

Donizo of Canossa, *Vita Mathildis comitissae metrica, MGH SS* 12, 348–409

Ekkehard of Aura, *Chronica* (Ausgewählte Quellen zur deutschen Geschichte des Mittelalters 15: Darmstadt, 1972) pp. 124–208, 268–376

Frutolf of Michelsberg, *Chronica* (Ausgewählte Quellen zur deutschen Geschichte des Mittelalters 15: Darmstadt, 1972) pp. 48–121

Fulcher of Chartres, *Historia Hierosolymitana 1095–1127*, ed. H. Hagenmeyer (Heidelberg, 1913)

Gebhard of Salzburg, *Epistola, MGH Libelli* 1, 261–79

Germania pontificia, ed. A. Brackmann, 1, 2.1 (Berlin, 1910, 1923)

Gregory VII, *Registrum, MGH Epistolae selectae* 2 (1920, 1923); trans. H.E.J. Cowdrey, *The Register of Pope Gregory VII 1073–1085* (Oxford, 2002)

Gregory VII, *The Epistolae Vagantes of Pope Gregory VII*, ed. H.E.J. Cowdrey (Oxford, 1972)

Hagenmeyer, H. (ed.), *Die Kreuzzugsbriefe aus den Jahren 1088–1100. Eine Quellensammlung zur Geschichte des ersten Kreuzzuges* (Innsbruck, 1901)

Henry IV, *Letters = Die Briefe Heinrichs IV., MGH Deutsches Mittelalter* 1 (1937), trans. T.E. Mommsen, K.F. Morrison, *Imperial lives and letters of the eleventh century* (Columbia, 1962)

Herman of Reichenau, *Chronicon, MGH SS* 5, 67–133; ed. R. Buchner, *Quellen des 9. und 11. Jahrhunderts zur Geschichte der Hamburgischen Kirche und des Reiches* (Ausgewählte Quellen zur Deutschen Geschichte des Mittelalters 11: Darmstadt, 1961)

Herman of Reichenau, *De octo vitiis principalibus* = E. Dümmler, 'Opusculum Herimanni diverso metro conpositum ad amiculas suas quasdam sanctimoniales feminas', *Zeitschrift für deutsches Altertum* 13 (1867), 385–434

Herman of Reichenau, *Musica*, ed. L. Ellinwood, *Musica Hermanni Contracti* (Eastman School of Music Studies 2: Rochester, 1936)

Hermannus Contractus, *Historia sanctae Afrae martyris Augustensis*, ed. D. Hiley and W. Berschin (Musicological Studies 65/10: Ottawa, 2004)

Hermannus Contractus, *Historia sancti Wolfgangi episcopi Ratisbonensis*, ed. D. Hiley (Musicological Studies 65/7: Ottawa, 2002)

Hugh of Flavigny, *Chronicon*, MGH SS 8, 280–502

Humbert of Silva Candida, *Adversus simoniacos libri III*, MGH Libelli 1, 95–253

Italia pontificia, ed. P.F. Kehr, 3 (Berlin, 1908)

Lampert of Hersfeld, *Annales* in *Lamperti monachi Hersfeldensis Opera*, MGH SS rer. Germ. [38] (1894) pp. 3–304

Landulf Junior de sancto Paulo, *Historia Mediolanensis*, MGH SS 20, 17–49

Landulf Senior, *Historia Mediolanensis*, MGH SS 8, 32–100

Lanfranc, *Letters of Archbishop Lanfranc of Canterbury*, ed. H. Clover, M. Gibson (Oxford, 1979)

Leo IX, *Epistolae et decreta pontificia*, MPL 143, col. 591–794

Lexikon des Mittelalters (11 volumes: Munich, 1980–98)

Liber de unitate ecclesiae conservanda, MGH Libelli 2, 173–284

Liber pontificalis, ed. L. Duchesne, C. Vogel 1–3 (Bibliothèque des Ecoles françaises d'Athènes et de Rome 2e série, Paris, 1886–1957)

Life of Emperor Henry IV = Vita Heinrici IV imperatoris, MGH SS rer. Germ. [58] (1899) trans. T.E. Mommsen, K.F. Morrison, *Imperial lives and letters of the eleventh century* (Columbia, 1962)

Life of Pope Leo IX trans. I.S. Robinson, *The papal reform of the eleventh century* (Manchester–New York, 2004) = *Vita Leonis IX papae*, ed. J.M. Watterich, *Pontificum Romanorum Vitae* 1 (Leipzig, 1862), 127–70

Manegold of Lautenbach, *Liber ad Gebehardum*, MGH Libelli 1, 308–430

Mansi, J.D. (ed.), *Sacrorum conciliorum nova et amplissima collectio* 1–31 (Venice–Florence, 1759–98)

Marianus Scottus, *Chronicon*, MGH SS 5, 481–562

Norbert of Iburg (?), *Vita Bennonis II episcopi Osnabrugensis*, MGH SS rer. Germ. [56] (1902)

Otto of Freising, *Chronica sive Historia de duabus civitatibus*, MGH SS rer. Germ. [45] (1912)

Paschal II, *Epistolae et Privilegia*, *MPL* 163, 31A–444A

Paul of Bernried, *Life of Pope Gregory VII* trans. I.S. Robinson, *The papal reform of the eleventh century* (Manchester–New York, 2004) pp. 262–364 = Paul of Bernried, *Vita Gregorii VII papae*, ed. J.M. Watterich, *Pontificum Romanorum vitae* 1 (Leipzig, 1862), 474–545

Peter Damian, *Letters* = *Die Briefe des Petrus Damiani*, *MGH Briefe* 1–4 (Munich, 1983–93)

Peter the Deacon, *De viris illustribus Casinensis coenobii*, *MPL* 173, col. 1003–50

Ralph Glaber, *Historiae* in Rodolfus Glaber, *Opera*, ed. J. France, N. Bulst, P. Reynolds (Oxford, 1989) pp. 2–252

Rupert of Deutz, *Vita sancti Hereberti archiepiscopi Coloniensis*, *MPL* 170, col. 389D–428A

Santifaller, L. (ed.), *Quellen und Forschungen zum Urkunden- und Kanzleiwesen Papst Gregors VII.* 1 (Studi e testi 190, Vatican City)

Sigebert of Gembloux, *Catalogus de viris illustribus*, ed. R. Witte (Bern, 1974)

Sigebert of Gembloux, *Chronica*, *MGH SS* 6, 268–374

Thietmar of Merseburg, *Chronicon*, *MGH SS rer. Germ.*, n.s. 9 (Berlin, 1935), trans. D.A. Warner, *Ottonian Germany* (Manchester–New York, 2001)

Udalric of Zell, *Consuetudines Cluniacenses*, *MPL* 149, 635–778

Urban II, *Epistolae et Privilegia*, *MPL* 151, 283A–552C

Vita Altmanni episcopi Pataviensis, *MGH SS* 12, 226–43

Vita Gebehardi archiepiscopi [Salisburgensis], *MGH SS* 11, 25–8

Vita Wernheri episcopi Merseburgensis, *MGH SS* 12, 244–8

Vita Willihelmi abbatis Hirsaugiensis, *MGH SS* 12, 209–25

Wenrich of Trier, *Epistola*, *MGH Libelli* 1, 280–99

Wido of Ferrara, *De scismate Hildebrandi*, *MGH Libelli* 1, 529–67

Wido of Osnabrück, *Liber de controversia inter Hildebrandum et Heinricum imperatorem*, *MGH Libelli* 1, 461–70

Widrich, *Vita et miracula sancti Gerardi episcopi Tullensis*, *MGH SS* 4, 485–509

Wipo, *Deeds of Conrad* = *Gesta Chuonradi imperatoris*, *MGH SS rer. Germ.* (1915), trans. T.E. Mommsen, K.F. Morrison, *Imperial lives and letters of the eleventh century* (Columbia, 1962) pp. 52–100

(Wolfger of Prüfening?), *De scriptoribus ecclesiasticis* = E. Ettlinger, *Der sog. Anonymus Mellicensis De scriptoribus ecclesiasticis. Text- und quellenkritische Ausgabe* (dissertation, Strasbourg, 1896)

Secondary works

Arnold, B. (1997), *Medieval Germany 500–1300: a political interpretation* (Toronto–Buffalo)

Autenrieth, J. (1956), *Die Domschule von Konstanz zur Zeit des Investiturstreits* (Forschungen zur Kirchen- und Geistesgeschichte, n.s. 3, Stuttgart)

Autenrieth, J. (1958), 'Bernold von Konstanz und die erweiterte 74-Titelsammlung', *Deutsches Archiv* 14, 375–94

Autenrieth, J. (1975), 'Die kanonistischen Handschriften der Dombibliothek Konstanz' in *Kirchenrechtliche Texte im Bodenseegebiet*, ed. J. Autenrieth and R. Kottje (Vorträge und Forschungen, Sonderband 18, Sigmaringen) pp. 5–21

Barstow, A.L. (1982), *Married priests and the reforming papacy: the eleventh-century debates* (Texts and Studies in Religion 12, New York–Toronto)

Becker, A. (1964, 1988), *Papst Urban II.*, 1, 2 (Schriften der MGH 19/1, Stuttgart)

Becker, A. (1973), 'Urban II. und die deutsche Kirche' in *Investiturstreit* pp. 241–75

Berges, W. (1947), 'Gregor VII. und das deutsche Designationsrecht', *Studi Gregoriani* 2, 189–209

Bergmann, W. (1988), 'Chronographie und Komputistik bei Hermann von Reichenau' in *Historiographia Mediaevalis. Festschrift für Franz-Josef Schmale zum 65. Geburtstag*, ed. D. Berg and H.-W. Goetz (Darmstadt) pp. 103–17

Berschin, W. (1972), *Bonizo von Sutri. Leben und Werk* (Beiträge zur Geschichte und Quellenkunde des Mittelalters 2, Berlin–New York)

Beulertz, S. (1991), *Das Verbot der Laieninvestitur* (MGH Studien und Texte 2: Hanover)

Beumann, H. (1973), 'Tribur, Rom und Canossa' in *Investiturstreit und Reichsverfassung* pp. 33–60

Beyerle, K. (1925a), 'Von der Gründung bis zum Ende des freiherrlichen Klosters (724–1427)' in *Die Kultur der Abtei Reichenau* 1 (Munich), 55–212

Beyerle, K. (1925b), 'Das Reichenauer Verbrüderungsbuch als Quelle der Klostergeschichte' in *Die Kultur der Abtei Reichenau* 2 (Munich), 1107–217

Black-Veldtrup, M. (1995), *Kaiserin Agnes (1043–1077). Quellenkritische Studien* (Münstersche Historische Forschungen 7, Cologne–Weimar–Vienna)

Bloch, H. (1986), *Monte Cassino in the Middle Ages* 1–3 (Rome–Cambridge, MA)

Bloch, R. (1930), 'Die Klosterpolitik Leos IX. in Deutschland, Burgund und Italien', *Archiv für Urkundenforschung* 11, 176–257

Borgolte, M. (1979), 'Über die persönlichen und familiengeschichtlichen Aufzeichnungen Hermanns des Lahmen', *Zeitschrift für Geschichte des Oberrheins* 127, 1–15

Borino, G.B. (1952), 'Cencio del prefetto Stefano l'attentatore di Gregorio VII', *Studi Gregoriani* 4, 373–440

Borst, A. (1975–6), 'Hermann der Lahme und die Geschichte', *Hegau* 32–3, 7–18

Borst, A. (1978), *Mönche am Bodensee, 610–1525* (Bodensee-Bibliothek 5: Sigmaringen)

Borst, A. (1984), 'Ein Forschungsbericht Hermanns des Lahmen', *Deutsches Archiv* 40, 379–477

Boshof, E. (1978), 'Lothringen, Frankreich und das Reich in der Regierungszeit Heinrichs III.', *Rheinische Vierteljahrsblätter* 42, 63–100

Boshof, E. (1986), 'Das Reich und Ungarn in der Zeit der Salier', *Ostbairische Grenzmarken* 28, 178–94

Boshof, E. (1991), 'Bischöfe und Bischofskirchen von Passau und Regensburg' in *Die Salier* 2, 113–54

Boye, M. (1929), 'Die Synoden Deutschlands und Reichsitaliens 922–1059', *Zeitschrift der Savigny Stiftung für Rechtsgeschichte, Kanonistische Abteilung* 18, 131–284

Brandi, K. (1890), *Quellen und Forschungen zur Geschichte der Abtei Reichenau* 1 (Heidelberg)

Bresslau, H. (1877), 'Beiträge zur Kritik deutscher Geschichtsquellen des 11. Jahrhunderts: Hermann von Reichenau und die sog. Epitome Sangallensis', *Neues Archiv* 2, 566–76

Bresslau, H. (1879, 1884), *Jahrbücher des Deutschen Reichs unter Konrad II.* 1, 2 (Leipzig)

Bresslau, H. (1902), 'Beiträge zur Kritik deutscher Geschichtsquellen des 11. Jahrhunderts. N.F. I: Hermann von Reichenau und das Chronicon Suevicum universale', *Neues Archiv* 27, 125–75

Buchner, R. (1960a), 'Der Verfasser der Schwäbischen Weltchronik', *Deutsches Archiv* 16, 389–96

Buchner, R. (1960b), 'Geschichtsbild und Reichsbegriff Hermanns von Reichenau', *Archiv für Kulturgeschichte* 42, 37–60

Bulst, N. (1973), *Untersuchungen zu den Klosterreformen Wilhelms von Dijon (962–1031)* (Pariser Historische Studien II: Bonn)

Bulst-Thiele, M.L. (1933), *Kaiserin Agnes* (dissertation, Göttingen)

Büttner, H. (1966), 'Abt Wilhelm von Hirsau und die Entwicklung der Rechtsstellung der Reformklöster im 11. Jahrhundert', *Zeitschrift für Württembergische Landesgeschichte* 25, 321–38

Büttner, H. (1973), 'Die Bischofsstädte von Basel bis Mainz in der Zeit des Investiturstreites' in *Investiturstreit* pp. 351–61

Capitani, O. (1966), *Immunità vescovili ed ecclesiologia in età 'pregregoriana' e 'gregoriana'* (Biblioteca degli Studi Medievali 3, Spoleto)

Cheney, C.R. (1961), *Handbook of dates for students of English history* (Royal Historical Society Guides and Handbooks 4, London)

Clavadetscher, O.P. (1968), 'Mainz und Chur im Mittelalter' in *Festschrift Ludwig Petry* 1 (Geschichtliche Landeskunde 5/1, Wiesbaden) pp. 78–96

Cowdrey, H.E.J. (1966), 'Archbishop Aribert II of Milan', *History* 51, 1–15

Cowdrey, H.E.J. (1968a), 'The papacy, the Patarenes and the church of Milan', *Transactions of the Royal Historical Society* fifth series 18, 25–48

Cowdrey, H.E.J. (1968b), 'The succession of the archbishops of Milan in the time of Pope Urban II', *English Historical Review* 83, 285–94

Cowdrey, H.E.J. (1970), *The Cluniacs and the Gregorian reform* (Oxford)

Cowdrey, H.E.J. (1972), 'Pope Gregory VII and the Anglo-Norman church and kingdom', *Studi Gregoriani* 9, 77–114

Cowdrey, H.E.J. (1977), 'The Mahdia campaign of 1087', *English Historical Review* 92, 1–29

Cowdrey, H.E.J. (1983), *The age of Abbot Desiderius. Montecassino, the papacy and the Normans in the eleventh and early twelfth centuries* (Oxford)

Cowdrey, H.E.J. (1990), 'The papacy and the Berengarian controversy' in *Auctoritas und ratio. Studien zu Berengar von Tours*, ed. P. Ganz, R.B.C. Huygens, F. Niewöhner (Wiesbaden) pp. 109–38

Cowdrey, H.E.J. (1998), *Pope Gregory VII (1073–1085)* (Oxford)

Cram, K.-G. (1955), *Iudicium belli. Zum Rechtscharakter des Krieges im deutschen Mittelalter* (Beihefte zum Archiv für Kulturgeschichte 5, Münster–Cologne)

Curschmann, F. (1900), *Hungersnöte im Mittelalter. Ein Beitrag zur deutschen Wirtschaftsgeschichte des 8. bis 13. Jahrhunderts* (Leipziger Studien aus dem Gebiet der Geschichte 6/1: Leipzig)

Deér, J. (1972), *Papsttum und Normannen. Untersuchungen zu ihren lehnsrechtlichen und kirchenpolitischen Beziehungen* (Studien und Quellen zur Welt Kaiser Friedrichs II., 1: Cologne–Vienna)

Dereine, C. (1946), 'Vie commune, règle de Saint Augustin et chanoines réguliers au XIe siècle', *Revue d'histoire ecclésiastique* 41, 365–406

Dereine, C. (1951), 'L'élaboration du statut canonique des chanoines réguliers spécialement sous Urbain II', *Revue d'histoire ecclésiastique* 46, 534–65

Dieterich, J. (1925), 'Die Geschichtsschreibung der Reichenau' in *Die Kultur der Abtei Reichenau. Erinnerungsschrift zur zwölfhundertsten Wiederkehr des Gründungsjahres des Inselklosters 724–1924* 2 (Munich), 773–801

Dollinger, P. (1991), 'Strassburg in salischer Zeit' in *Die Salier und das Reich* 3, 153–64

Dressler, F. (1954), *Petrus Damiani. Leben und Werke* (Studia Anselmiana 34, Rome)

Dronke, P. (1968), *The medieval lyric* (London)

Duch, A. (1961), 'Das Geschichtswerk Hermanns von Reichenau in seiner Überlieferung' in Oesch (1961) pp. 184–203

Dümmler, E. (1879–80), 'Ein Schreiben Meinzos von Constanz an Hermann den Lahmen', *Neues Archiv* 5, 202–6

Englberger, J. (1997), 'Berthold von der Reichenau und die Investiturfrage', *Deutsches Archiv* 53, 81–117

Erdmann, C. (1935), *Die Entstehung des Kreuzzugsgedankens* (Forschungen zur Kirchen- und Geistesgeschichte 6: Stuttgart)

Erdmann, C. (1936), 'Die Anfänge der staatlichen Propaganda im Investiturstreit', *Historische Zeitschrift* 154, 491–512

Erdmann, C. (1937), 'Tribur und Rom. Zur Vorgeschichte der Canossafahrt', *Deutsches Archiv* 1, 361–88

Erdmann, C. (1938), *Studien zur Briefliteratur Deutschlands im elften Jahrhundert* (Schriften der MGH 1, Leipzig)

Erdmann, C. (1940), 'Zum Fürstentag von Tribur', *Deutsches Archiv* 4, 486–95

Erdmann, C. (1951), *Forschungen zur politischen Ideenwelt des Frühmittelalters* (Berlin)

Erkens, F.-R. (1987), *Die Trierer Kirchenprovinz im Investiturstreit* (Passauer Historische Forschungen 4, Cologne–Vienna)

Fenske, L. (1977), *Adelsopposition und kirchliche Reformbewegung im östlichen Sachsen* (Veröffentlichungen des Max-Planck-Instituts für geschichte 47: Göttingen)

Fichtenau, H. (1938), 'Studien zu Gerhoh von Reichersberg', *Mitteilungen des Instituts für österreichische Geschichtsforschung* 52, 1–56

Frauenknecht, E. (1997), *Die Verteidigung der Priesterehe in der Reformzeit* (MGH Studien und Texte 16, Hanover)

Friedmann, A.U. (1994), *Die Beziehungen der Bistümer Worms und Speyer zu den ottonischen und salischen Königen* (Mainz)

Fuhrmann, H. (1975), '"Volksouveränität" und "Herrschaftsvertrag" bei Manegold von Lautenbach' in *Festschrift für Hermann Krause*, ed. S. Gagnér, H. Schlosser, W. Wiegand (Cologne–Vienna) pp. 21–42

Fuhrmann, H. (1982), 'Pseudoisidor, Otto von Ostia (Urban II.) und der Zitatenkampf von Gerstungen (1085)', *Zeitschrift der Savigny-Stiftung für Rechtsgeschichte, Kanonistische Abteilung* 68, 52–69

Gawlik, A. (1970), *Intervenienten und Zeugen in den Diplomen Kaiser Heinrichs IV. (1056–1105)* (Kallmünz)

Gericke, H. (1955), 'Die Wahl Heinrichs IV. Eine Studie zum deutschen Königswahlrecht', *Zeitschrift für Geschichtswissenschaft* 3, 735–49

Gibson, M. (1971), 'The case of Berengar of Tours' in *Studies in Church history* 7 (Cambridge) pp. 61–8

Giese, W. (1979), *Der Stamm der Sachsen und das Reich in ottonischer und salischer Zeit* (Wiesbaden)

Giesebrecht, W. von (1885, 1890), *Geschichte der deutschen Kaiserzeit 2, 3* (fifth edition, Leipzig)

Goez, E. (1995), *Beatrix von Canossa und Tuszien. Eine Untersuchung zur Geschichte des 11. Jahrhunderts* (Vorträge und Forschungen, Sonderband 41: Sigmaringen)

Goez, E. (1996), 'Der Thronerbe als Rivale: König Konrad, Kaiser Heinrichs IV. älterer Sohn', *Historisches Jahrbuch* 116, 1–49

Goez, W. (1973), 'Reformpapsttum, Adel und monastische Erneuerung in der Toscana' in *Investiturstreit* pp. 205–39

Goggin, H. (1995), *Hugh I, bishop of Die and archbishop of Lyons (1073–1106): an agent of papal reform in France* (dissertation, Dublin)

Golinelli, P. (1987), 'Dall'agiografia alla storia: le "Vitae" di Sant'Anselmo di Lucca' in *Sant' Anselmo, Mantova e la lotta per le investiture* (Atti del convegno internazionale di studi, Mantova: Bologna) pp. 27–60

Grundmann, H. (1961), *Religiöse Bewegungen im Mittelalter* (second edition, Hildesheim)

Gugumus, E. (1961), 'Dedicatio Spirensis Ecclesiae. Zur Weihe des frühsalischen Speyerer Domes im Jahre 1061' in *900 Jahre Speyerer Dom. Festschrift zum Jahrestag der Domweihe*, ed. L. Stamer (Speyer) pp. 175–87

Haider, S. (1968), *Die Wahlversprechen der römisch-deutschen Könige bis zum Ende des zwölften Jahrhunderts* (Vienna)

Hallinger, K. (1950–1), *Gorze-Kluny. Studien zu den monastischen Lebensformen und Gegensätzen im Hochmittelalter* (Studia Anselmiana 22–5: Rome)

Hallinger, K. (1956), 'Woher kommen die Laienbrüder?', *Analecta Sacri Ordinis Cisterciensis* 12, 1–104

Hartmann, W. (1970), 'Manegold von Lautenbach und die Anfänge der Frühscholastik', *Deutsches Archiv* 26, 47–149

Hauck, A. (1954), *Kirchengeschichte Deutschlands* 3 (eighth edition: Berlin–Leipzig)

Hauck, K. (1959a), 'Pontius Pilatus aus Forchheim', *Jahrbuch für fränkische Landesforschung* 19, 171–92

Hauck, K. (1959b), 'Zum Tode Papst Clemens II.', *Jahrbuch für fränkische Landesforschung* 19, 265–74

Healy, P. (2005), 'Hugh of Flavigny and canon law as polemic in the Investiture Contest', *Zeitschrift der Savigny-Stiftung für Rechtsgeschichte, Kanonistische Abteilung* 91, 17–58

Healy, P. (2006), *The Chronicle of Hugh of Flavigny: reform and the Investiture Contest in the late eleventh century* (Aldershot)

Henking, C. (1880), *Gebhard III., Bischof von Constanz 1084–1100* (dissertation, Zürich)

Herrmann, K.-J. (1973), *Das Tuskulanerpapsttum (1012–1046)* (Päpste und Papsttum 4, Stuttgart)

Hillenbrand, E. (1989), 'Die Überlieferung der Konstanzer Münsterweihe von 1052, 1065 und 1089' in *Die Konstanzer Münsterweihe von 1089 in ihrem historischen Umfeld*, ed. H. Maurer (Freiburg) pp. 85–98

Hlawitschka, E. (1974), 'Zwischen Tribur und Canossa', *Historisches Jahrbuch* 94, 25–45

Hoffmann, H. (1964), *Gottesfriede und Treuga Dei* (Schriften der MGH 20, Stuttgart)

Hoffmann, H. (1976), 'Zum Register und zu den Briefen Papst Gregors VII.', *Deutsches Archiv* 32, 86–130

Hoffmann, H. (1993), *Mönchskönig und* rex idiota. *Studien zur Kirchenpolitik Heinrichs II. und Konrads II.* (MGH Studien und Texte 8, Hanover)

Hofmeister, P. (1961), 'Die Klaustral-Oblaten', *Studien und Mitteilungen zur Geschichte des Benediktiner-Ordens und seiner Zweige* 72, 5–45

Holtzmann, R. (1941), *Geschichte der sächsischen Kaiserzeit (900–1024)* (Munich)

Holtzmann, W. (1924/5), 'Studien zur Orientpolitik des Reformpapsttums und zur Entstehung der ersten Kreuzzuges', *Historische Vierteljahrschrift* 22, 167–99

Holtzmann, W. (1928), 'Die Unionsverhandlungen zwischen Kaiser Alexios I. und Urban II. im Jahre 1089', *Byzantinische Zeitschrift* 28, 38–67

Holtzmann, W. (1963), 'Maximilla regina, soror Rogerii regis', *Deutsches Archiv* 19, 149–67

Hörberg, N. (1983), *Libri Sanctae Afrae. St Ulrich und Afra zu Augsburg im 11. und 12. Jahrhundert nach Zeugnissen der Klosterbibliothek* (Göttingen)

Höss, I. (1950), 'Die Stellung Frankens im Investiturstreit unter besonderer Berücksichtigung Würzburgs', *Mainfränkisches Jahrbuch* 2, 303–15

Hüls, R. (1977), *Kardinäle, Klerus und Kirchen Roms 1049–1130* (Tübingen)

Jakobs, H. (1961), *Die Hirsauer* (Cologne–Graz)

Jakobs, H. (1968), *Der Adel in der Klosterreform von St. Blasien* (Kölner Historische Abhandlungen 16, Cologne–Graz)

Jakobs, H. (1973), 'Rudolf von Rheinfelden und die Kirchenreform' in *Investiturstreit und Reichsverfassung* pp. 87–115

Jenal, G. (1974, 1975), *Erzbischof Anno II. von Köln (1056–75) und sein politisches Wirken* 1, 2 (Stuttgart)

Joranson, E. (1928), 'The great German pilgrimage of 1064–65' in *The Crusades and other historical essays*, ed. L.J. Paetow (New York) pp. 3–43

Jordan, K. (1938), 'Der Kaisergedanke in Ravenna zur Zeit Heinrichs IV.', *Deutsches Archiv* 2, 85–128

Kerkhoff, J. (1964), *Die Grafen von Altshausen-Veringen. Die Ausbildung der Familie zum Adelsgeschlecht und der Aufbau ihrer Herrschaft im 11. und 12. Jahrhundert* (Hohenzollerische Jahreshefte 24)

Kieft, C. van de (1955), 'Bisschop Willem en de Utrechtse synode van 1076', *Tijdschrift voor Geschiedenis* 68, 70–9

Kienast, W. (1974), *Deutschland und Frankreich in der Kaiserzeit (900–1270). Weltkaiser und Einzelkönige* 1 (Monographien zur Geschichte des Mittelalters 9/1, Stuttgart)

Kilian, E. (1886), Itinerar Kaiser Heinrichs IV. (Karlsruhe)

Klewitz, H.-W. (1939), 'Die Festkrönungen der deutschen Könige', *Zeitschrift der Savigny-Stiftung für Rechtsgeschichte, Kanonistische Abteilung* 28, 48–96

Klüppel, T. (1980), *Reichenauer Hagiographie zwischen Walahfrid und Berno* (Sigmaringen)

Köhncke, O. (1888), *Wibert von Ravenna (Papst Clemens III.)* (Leipzig)

Kost, O.-H. (1962), *Das östliche Niedersachsen im Investiturstreit* (Göttingen)

Kottje, R. (1978), 'Zur Bedeutung der Bischofsstädte für Heinrich IV.', *Historisches Jahrbuch* 97–8, 131–57

Krause, H.-J. (1960), *Das Papstwahldekret von 1059 und seine Rolle im Investiturstreit* (Studi Gregoriani 7: Rome)

Krause, H. (1965), 'Königtum und Rechtsordnung in der Zeit der sächsischen und salischen Herrscher', *Zeitschrift der Savigny-Stiftung für Rechtsgeschichte, Germanistische Abteilung* 82, 1–98

Krautheimer, R. (2000), *Rome: profile of a city, 312–1308* (revised edition, Princeton)

Krüger, K.H. (1976), *Die Universalchroniken* (Typologie des sources du moyen âge occidental 16, Turnhout)

Ladner, G. (1936), *Theologie und Politik vor dem Investiturstreit* (Veröffentlichungen des österreichischen Instituts für Geschichtsforschung 2, Baden–Brünn–Leipzig–Prague

Lange, K.-H. (1961), 'Die Stellung der Grafen von Northeim in der Reichsgeschichte des 11. und 12. Jahrhunderts', *Niedersächsisches Jahrbuch für Landesgeschichte* 33, 1–107

Leyser, K. (1991), 'Gregory VII and the Saxons', *Studi Gregoriani* 14/2, 231–8

Loud, G.A. (2000), *The age of Robert Guiscard: southern Italy and the Norman conquest* (London)

Lucchesi, G. (1972), 'Per una vita di San Pier Damiani' in *San Pier Damiani nel IX centenario della morte (1072–1972)* 1–4 (Cesena): 1, 13–179; 2, 13–160

McCarthy, T. (2004), *The study of music theory in Germany from the second half of the eleventh century to the early twelfth century* (dissertation, Oxford)

Martin, G. (1994), 'Der salische Herrscher als *Patricius Romanorum*. Zur Einflußnahme Heinrichs III. und Heinrichs IV. auf die Besetzung der *Cathedra Petri*', *Frühmittelalterliche Studien* 28, 257–95

Märtl, C. (1986), 'Regensburg in den geistigen Auseinandersetzungen des Investiturstreits', *Deutsches Archiv* 42, 145–91

Märtl, C. (1992), 'Zum Brief Papst Urbans II. an Bischof Gebhard III. von Konstanz (*JL* 5393)' in *Proceedings of the Eighth International Congress of Medieval Canon Law* (Monumenta Iuris Canonici, Series C9) pp. 47–54

Matzke, M. (1998), *Daibert von Pisa. Zwischen Pisa, Papst und erstem Kreuzzug* (Vorträge und Forschungen, Sonderband 44, Sigmaringen)

Maurer, H. (1970), 'Ein päpstliches Patrimonium auf der Baar. Zur Lehnspolitik Papst Urbans II. in Süddeutschland', *Zeitschrift für die Geschichte des Oberrheins* 118, 43–56

Maurer, H. (1978), *Der Herzog von Schwaben* (Sigmaringen)

Maurer, H. (1991), 'Die Konstanzer Bischofskirche in salischer Zeit' in *Die Salier und das Reich* 2, 155–86

Mayer, H.E. (1972), *The Crusades* (Oxford)

Meyer von Knonau, G. (1890, 1894, 1900, 1903, 1904), *Jahrbücher des Deutschen Reiches unter Heinrich IV. und Heinrich V.* 1–5 (Leipzig)

Miccoli, G. (1960), *Pietro Igneo. Studi sull' età gregoriana* (Studi storici 40–41, Rome)

Miccoli, G. (1966), *Chiesa gregoriana* (Florence)

Mirbt, C. (1894), *Die Publizistik im Zeitalter Gregors VII.* (Leipzig)

Mois, J. (1953), *Das Stift Rottenbuch in der Kirchenreform des XI.–XII. Jahrhunderts* (Munich)

Montclos, J. de (1971), *Lanfranc et Bérenger: la controverse eucharistique du XIe siècle* (Louvain)

Moore, R.I. (1977), *The origins of European dissent* (London)

Moore, R.I. (2000), *The first European revolution c. 970–1215* (Oxford)

Morrison, K. (1962), 'Canossa: a revision', *Traditio* 18, 121–48

Müller, E. (1901), *Das Itinerar Kaiser Heinrichs III. (1039–1056) mit besonderer Berücksichtigung seiner Urkunden* (Historische Studien 26, Berlin)

Müller-Mertens, E. (1970), *Regnum Teutonicum* (Vienna–Cologne–Graz)

Munier, C. (2002), *Le Pape Léon IX et la réforme de l'Eglise, 1002–1054* (Strasbourg)

Niermeyer, J.F. and van de Kieft, C. (2002), *Mediae Latinitatis Lexicon Minus* 1–2 (Leiden)

Nightingale, J. (2001), *Monasteries and patrons in the Gorze reform, Lotharingia c. 800–1000* (Oxford)

Oesch, H. (1961), *Berno und Hermann von Reichenau als Musiktheoretiker* (Publikationen der Schweizerischen Musikforschenden Gesellschaft ser. 2, 9, Bern)

Overmann, A. (1895), *Gräfin Mathilde von Tuscien. Ihre Besitzungen. Geschichte ihres Gutes von 1125–1230 und ihre Regesten* (Innsbruck)

Parlow, U. (1999), *Die Zähringer. Kommentierte Quellendokumentation zu einem südwestdeutschen Herzogsgeschlecht des hohen Mittelalters* (Veröffentlichungen der Kommission für geschichtliche Landeskunde in Baden-Württemberg ser. A, 50, Stuttgart)

Partner, P. (1972), *The lands of St Peter: the Papal State in the Middle Ages and the early Renaissance* (London)

Paulus, N. (1922), *Geschichte des Ablasses im Mittelalter* 1 (Paaderborn)

Petrucci, E. (1977), *Ecclesiologia e politica di Leone IX* (Rome)

Poole, R.L. (1934), *Studies in chronology and history* (Oxford)

Previté-Orton, C.W. (1912), *The early history of the house of Savoy (1000–1233)* (Cambridge)

Prinz, O. (1974), 'Mittelalterliches im Wortschatz der Annalen Bertholds von Reichenau', *Deutsches Archiv* 30, 488–504

Reinhardt, U. (1975), *Untersuchungen zur Stellung der Geistlichkeit bei den Königswahlen im Fränkischen und Deutschen Reich (751–1250)* (dissertation, Marburg)

Reuter, T. (1991a), *Germany in the early Middle Ages, 800–1056* (London–New York)

Reuter, T. (1991b), 'Unruhestiftung, Fehde, Rebellion, Widerstand: Gewalt und Frieden in der Politik der Salierzeit' in *Die Salier* 3, 297–325, trans. in Reuter (2006)

Reuter, T. (2006), 'Medieval Polities and Modern Mentalities', ed. J.L. Nelson (Cambridge) pp. 355–87

Riley-Smith, J. (1984), 'The First Crusade and the persecution of the Jews' in *Studies in Church History* 21, 51–72

Riley-Smith, J. (1986), *The First Crusade and the idea of crusading* (Philadelphia)

Robinson, I.S. (1973), 'Gregory VII and the soldiers of Christ', *History* 58, 169–92

Robinson, I.S. (1978a), *Authority and resistance in the Investiture Contest. The polemical literature of the eleventh century* (Manchester–New York)

Robinson, I.S. (1978b), 'Zur Arbeitsweise Bernolds von Konstanz und seines Kreises', *Deutsches Archiv* 34, 51–122

Robinson, I.S. (1979), 'Pope Gregory VII, the princes and the pactum, 1077–1080', *English Historical Review* 94, 721–56

Robinson, I.S. (1980), 'Die Chronik Hermanns von Reichenau und die Reichenauer Kaiserchronik', *Deutsches Archiv* 36, 84–136

Robinson, I.S. (1989), 'Bernold von Konstanz und der gregorianische Reformkreis um Bischof Gebhard III.' in *Die Konstanzer Münsterweihe von 1089 in ihrem historischen Umfeld*, ed. H. Maurer (Freiburg) pp. 155–88

Robinson, I.S. (1990), *The papacy, 1073–1198* (Cambridge)

Robinson, I.S. (1999), *Henry IV of Germany, 1056–1106* (Cambridge)

Robinson, I.S. (2004a), *The papal reform of the eleventh century: Lives of Pope Leo*

IX and Pope Gregory VII (Manchester–New York)

Robinson, I.S. (2004b), 'Reform and the Church, 1073–1122', *The New Cambridge Medieval History* 4/1 (Cambridge), 268–334

Saltet, L. (1907), *Les réordinations. Étude sur le sacrement de l'ordre* (Paris)

Scheibelreiter, G. (1973), 'Der Regierungsantritt des römisch-deutschen Königs (1056–1138)', *Mitteilungen des Instituts für Österreichische Geschichtsforschung* 81, 1–62

Schieffer, R. (1972), 'Spirituales latrones. Zu den Hintergründen der Simonieprozesse in Deutschland zwischen 1069 und 1075', *Historisches Jahrbuch* 92, 19–60

Schieffer, R. (1975), 'Hermann I., Bischof von Bamberg', *Fränkische Lebensbilder* 6, 55–76

Schieffer, R. (1981), *Die Entstehung des päpstlichen Investiturverbots für den deutschen König* (*Schriften der MGH* 28, Stuttgart)

Schieffer, R. (1991), 'Erzbischöfe und Bischofskirche von Köln' in *Die Salier* 2, 1–29

Schieffer, T. (1935), *Die päpstlichen Legaten in Frankreich vom Vertrage von Meersen (870) bis zum Schisma von 1130* (Historische Studien 263, Berlin)

Schlesinger, W. (1973), 'Die Wahl Rudolfs von Schwaben zum Gegenkönig 1077 in Forchheim' in *Investiturstreit* pp. 61–85

Schmale, F.-J. (1974), 'Die Reichenauer Weltchronistik' in *Die Abtei Reichenau. Neue Beiträge zur Geschichte und Kultur des Inselklosters*, ed. H. Maurer (Bodensee-Bibliothek 20, Sigmaringen) pp. 125–58

Schmale, F.-J. (1979), 'Die "Absetzung" Gregors VI. in Sutri und die synodale Tradition', *Annuarium Historiae Conciliorum* 11, 55–103

Schmale, F.-J. (1981), 'Hermann von Reichenau' in *Die deutsche Literatur des Mittelalters. Verfasserlexikon* 3, 1082–90

Schmeidler, B. (1938), 'Berthold als Verfasser der nach ihm benannten Annalen bis 1080 und das Verhältnis seiner Arbeit zur Chronik Bernolds', *Archiv für Urkundenforschung* 15, 159–234

Schmeidler, B. (1939), 'Abt Arnold von Kloster Berge und Reichskloster Nienburg (1119–1166) und die Nienburg-Magdeburgische Geschichtschreibung des 12. Jahrhunderts', *Sachsen und Anhalt* 15, 88–167

Schmid, K. (1973), 'Adel und Reform in Schwaben' in *Investiturstreit und Reichsverfassung* pp. 295–319

Schmid, K. (1975), 'Heinrich III. und Gregor VI. in Gebetsgedächtnis von Piacenza des Jahres 1046' in *Beiträge zur mediävistischen Bedeutungsforschung. Studien zu Semantil und Sinntradition im Mittelalter*, ed. H. Fromm, W. Harms, U. Ruberg (Munich) pp. 79–97

Schmid, P. (1926), *Der Begriff der kanonischen Wahl in den Anfängen des Investiturstreits* (Stuttgart)

Schmidt, T. (1977), *Alexander II. und die römische Reformgruppe seiner Zeit* (Päpste und Papsttum 11: Stuttgart)

Schneider, C. (1972), *Prophetisches Sacerdotium und heilsgeschichtliches Regnum im Dialog 1073–1077* (Munich)

Schramm, P.E. (1929), *Kaiser, Rom und Renovatio* 1 (Leipzig–Berlin)

Schramm, P.E. and Mütherich, F. (1962), *Denkmale der deutschen Kaiser und Könige* (Munich)

Schumann, O. (1912), *Die päpstlichen Legaten in Deutschland zur Zeit Heinrichs IV. und Heinrichs V. (1056–1125)* (dissertation, Marburg)

Schwartz, G. (1913), *Die Besetzung der Bistümer Reichsitaliens unter den sächsischen und salischen Kaisern mit den Listen der Bischöfe, 951–1122* (Leipzig–Berlin)

Sdralek, M. (1890), *Die Streitschriften Altmanns von Passau und Wezilos von Mainz* (Paderborn)

Seibert, H. (1991), 'Libertas und Reichsabtei: Zur Klosterpolitik der salischen Herrscher' in *Die Salier* 2, 503–69

Servatius, C. (1979), *Paschalis II. (1099–1118)* (Päpste und Papsttum 14, Stuttgart)

Somerville, R. (1970), 'The French councils of Pope Urban II: some basic considerations', *Annuarium Historiae Conciliorum* 2, 56–65

Somerville, R. (1972), *The councils of Urban II* 1: *Decreta Claromontensia* (*Annuarium Historiae Conciliorum* Supplementum 1, Amsterdam)

Somerville, R. (1974), 'The council of Clermont (1095) and Latin Christian society', *Archivum Historiae Pontificiae* 12, 55–90

Somerville, R. and Kuttner. S. (1996), *Pope Urban II, the Collectio Britannica and the Council of Melfi (1089)* (Oxford)

Southern, R.W. (1953), *The making of the Middle Ages* (London)

Southern, R.W. (1970), *Western society and the Church in the Middle Ages* (Harmondsworth)

Steinböck, W. (1972), *Erzbischof Gebhard von Salzburg (1060–1088)* (Vienna–Salzburg)

Steindorff, E. (1874, 1881), *Jahrbücher des Deutschen Reiches unter Heinrich III.* 1, 2 (Leipzig)

Strelau, E. (1889), *Leben und Werke des Mönches Bernold von St. Blasien* (dissertation, Leipzig)

Struve, T. (1969, 1970), 'Lampert von Hersfeld. Persönlichkeit und Weltbild', *Hessisches Jahrbuch für Landesgeschichte* 19, 1–123; 20, 32–143

Struve, T. (1995), 'Mathilde von Tuszien-Canossa und Heinrich IV.', *Historisches Jahrbuch* 115, 41–84

Tangl, G. (1967), 'Berthold und Bernold' in W. Wattenbach, R. Holtzmann and F.-J. Schmale *Deutschlands Geschichtsquellen* 3, 514–28

Taviani-Carozzi (1996), 'Une bataille franco-allemande en Italie: Civitate (1053)' in *Peuples du moyen âge: problèmes d'identification*, ed. C. Carozzi, H. Taviani-Carozzi (Aix-en-Provence) pp. 181–211

Taylor, D.S. (1998), 'A new inventory of manuscripts of the *Micrologus de ecclesiasticis observationibus* of Bernold of Constance', *Scriptorium* 52, 162–91

Thomas, H. (1970), 'Erzbischof Siegfried I. von Mainz und die Tradition seiner Kirche', *Deutsches Archiv* 26, 368–99

Tritz, H. (1952), 'Die hagiographischen Quellen zur Geschichte Papst Leo IX.', *Studi Gregoriani* 4, 191–364

Twellenkamp, M. (1991), 'Das Haus der Luxemburger' in *Die Salier* 1, 475–502

Vehse, O. (1930–1), 'Benevent als Territorium des Kirchenstaates bis zum Beginn des avignonesischen Epoche', *Quellen und Forschungen aus italienischen Archiven und Bibliotheken* 22, 87–160

Vogel, J. (1982), 'Gregors VII. Abzug aus Rom und sein letztes Pontifikatsjahr in Salerno' in *Tradition als historische Kraft*, ed. N. Kamp, J. Wollasch (Berlin–New York) pp. 341–9

Vogel, J. (1983), *Gregor VII. und Heinrich IV. nach Canossa* (Arbeiten zur Frühmittelalterforschung 9: Berlin–New York)

Vollrath, H. (1974), 'Kaisertum und Patriziat in den Anfängen des Investiturstreits', *Zeitschrift für Kirchengeschichte* 85, 11–44

Vollrath, H. (1991), 'Konfliktwahrnehmung und Konfliktdarstellung in erzählenden Quellen des 11. Jahrhunderts' in *Die Salier* 3, 279–96

von den Brincken, A.-D. (1957), *Studien zur lateinischen Weltchronistik bis in das Zeitalter Ottos von Freising* (Düsseldorf)

Wadle, E. (1973), 'Heinrich IV. und die deutsche Friedensbewegung' in *Investiturstreit* pp. 141–73

Wadle, E. (1989), 'Die Konstanzer Pax und Bischof Gebhard III.' in *Die Konstanzer Münsterweihe von 1089*, ed. H. Maurer (Freiburg) pp. 141–53

Wattenbach, W. (1858), *Deutschlands Geschichtsquellen im Mittelalter* 2 (Berlin)

Wattenbach, W. and Holtzmann, R. (1967–71), *Deutschlands Geschichtsquellen im Mittelalter. Deutsche Kaiserzeit. Die Zeit der Sachsen und Salier*, ed. F.-J. Schmale 2 (Darmstadt)

Weiler, B. (2000), 'The *rex renitens* and the medieval ideal of kingship, ca. 900 – ca. 1250', *Viator* 31, 1–42

Wollasch, H.-J. (1964), *Die Anfänge des Klosters St Georgen im Schwarzwald* (Forschungen zur Oberrheinische Landesgeschichte 14, Freiburg)

Wollasch, J. (1987), 'Markgraf Hermann und Bischof Gebhard III. von Konstanz. Die Zähringer und die Reform der Kirche' in *Die Zähringer in der Kirche des 11. und 12. Jahrhunderts*, ed. K.S. Frank (Munich–Zürich) pp. 27–53

Ziese, J. (1982), *Wibert von Ravenna, der Gegenpapst Clemens III. (1084–1100)* (Päpste und Papsttum 20, Stuttgart)

Zimmermann, H. (1968), *Papstabsetzungen des Mittelalters* (Graz–Vienna–Cologne)

Zimmermann, H. (1969), *Papstregesten 911–1024* (Regesta Imperii 2/5, ed. J.F. Böhmer, Vienna–Cologne–Graz)

INDEX